ENDANGERED DREAMS

AMERICANS AND THE CALIFORNIA DREAM

Americans and the California Dream, 1850–1915

Inventing the Dream
California Through the Progressive Era

Material Dreams
Southern California Through the 1920s

Endangered Dreams
The Great Depression in California

ENDANGERED DREAMS

The Great Depression in California

KEVIN STARR

OXFORD UNIVERSITY PRESS
New York   Oxford

Oxford University Press

Oxford   New York
Athens   Auckland   Bangkok   Bogotá   Bombay   Buenos Aires
Calcutta   Cape Town   Dar es Salaam   Delhi   Florence
Hong Kong   Istanbul   Karachi   Kuala Lumpur   Madras   Madrid
Melbourne   Mexico City   Nairobi   Paris   Singapore   Taipei
Tokyo   Toronto   Warsaw

and associated companies in
Berlin   Ibadan

Library of Congress Cataloging-in-Publication Data
Starr, Kevin.
Endangered dreams : the Great Depression in California
Kevin Starr.
p.   cm.
Includes bibliographical references and index.
ISBN 0-19-510080-8
ISBN 0-19-511802-2 (Pbk.)
1. Depressions—1929—California.   2. California—Economic
conditions.   3. California—Politics and government—1850–1950.
I. Title.   HB3717   1919.S73   1995
979.4'052—dc20   95-2662

1 3 5 7 9 10 8 6 4 2

Printed in the United States of America
on acid-free paper

For Alan and Arline Heimert,
remembering Eliot House

Preface

California, Wallace Stegner has noted, is like the rest of the United States, only more so. As with the rest of the nation, the 1930s were both a perilous and prodigal time for the Golden State. With agriculture at the base of their economy, augmented by such Depression-resistant enterprises as motion pictures, defense, and federally subsidized shipping, Californians did not suffer the levels of visible turmoil and dislocation of more industrialized regions. On the other hand, hardship and suffering were not in short supply, especially in the early years of the decade and the sudden slump of 1939–1940. What California lacked in industrial suffering and strife was more than compensated for in the agricultural and cannery strikes punctuating the decade. The inner landscape of California, moreover, especially in its political dimension, showed constant signs of stress as Right battled Left in a struggle that acted out on behalf of the rest of the nation a scenario of possible fascism and Communism in these United States.

While focused on the Great Depression, *Endangered Dreams*, like the previous three volumes of the *Americans and the California Dream* series, frequently moves back in time so as to establish the origins and early development of ideas and social processes emerging into significance in the 1930s. Thus, before chronicling the great strikes of the 1930s and their suppressions, the narrative begins with two chapters establishing the presence of a distinctive pre-Marxist Left and an equally assertive pre-fascist Right in nineteenth-century and early twentieth-century California. In the case of each of these strikes, moreover, the necessary pre-1930 background is provided. Just as one cannot understand the Sacramento conspiracy trials of 1935 without reference to the Criminal Syndicalism Act of 1919 and the events which led to the passage of that draconian measure, the agricultural strikes of 1933 can only be understood within the context of the distinctive structure of farm labor in California and the role of minorities in the agricultural economy. The effort to improve the life of migrant farm workers began in the Progressive period. In 1934 longshoreman Harry Bridges led an alliance of maritime unions whose militancy had been abuilding since the turn of the century. The End Poverty in California movement (EPIC) led by Upton Sinclair took strength from the earlier Socialist and Bellamyite-Nationalist traditions of Southern California. Likewise, the 1930s epic of public works construction, while energized by the Depression, rested solidly on a foundation of Progressive Era planning, which found its inspiration, in turn, in the dreams and visions of nineteenth-century pioneers.

Unlike previous volumes in the *Americans and the California Dream* series, *Endangered Dreams* is focused on the entire state, North, South, and Central. Its perspective is regionalist in the broadest sense of that term: committed, that is, to California as an important component of the American experience. *Endangered Dreams* has as its key assumption the relevance of the story of California in the 1930s to the present era, which is likewise a time of economic restructuring and recovery, dashed personal hopes, and the struggle to renew confidence, not just in California but in the entire American experiment. *Tu non poteris, quod isti, quod istae?* asked Saint Augustine of himself at a time of grave personal crisis. Are you not able to do what other men and women have done? Faced with a ruinous depression, Californians of the 1930s managed, amidst some social misbehavior, to accomplish one of the most creative decades in the history of any American state. They built bridges and hydroelectrical systems which will last for a thousand years. They wrote novels which have entered the canon of American literature. They produced films which still astonish us by their artistry. Through photography, they captured images crucial to our understanding of the beauty and environmental integrity, not just of California, but of the entire planet. They built schools, armories, libraries, and airports which remain serviceable as well as architecturally significant. They cleared paths through public parks and wilderness preserves along which hikers still tramp. And somehow—despite clashes of Left and Right, despite horrendous suspensions of civil liberties—they never completely detached themselves from the American tradition of constitutional law and fair play. Nor did they abandon the public realm; indeed, in their politics and their public works, their literature and art, they brought public values into a golden age of expression. During the Great Depression, Americans in California saw their way through the most trying ordeal possible short of invasion or civil insurrection, and they prevailed. They created a version of American culture on the Pacific Coast which, more than a half century later, continues to intrigue the rest of the nation by its resourcefulness and diversity. They endured, and so did the California Dream.

Sacramento, San Francisco, Los Angeles   K.S.
March 1995

Contents

I RADICAL TRADITIONS

Flourishing in nineteenth-century San Francisco, radicalism exercised a determining influence on organized labor; indeed, San Francisco activists brought organized labor into being in what soon became the strongest union town in the country. In and through the distinctive labor culture of San Francisco, California developed a predilection for extremes of language and behavior in labor strife that afforded the rest of the nation a representative drama of Left and Right.

The Industrial Workers of the World and California were made for each other. Each valued symbolic action. In the 1910s the IWW confronted the establishment in Fresno, San Diego, and Wheatland. The result: the sweepingly comprehensive Criminal Syndicalism Act of 1919, which set new standards for repressing dissent. In 1923 the IWW took on Los Angeles. Shortly thereafter, most of its leadership was doing hard time in San Quentin.

II A DECADE OF CONFLICT

In the first years of the Depression, thousands of Mexican, Filipino, and Dust Bowl farm workers challenged the oligarchy. In at least one important instance, the cotton strike of 1933, they prevailed. A cadre of courageous young Communist organizers from the Cannery and Agricultural Workers Industrial Union organized most of these strikes. In March 1935 the Communist Party USA, under direct

IV THE THERAPY OF PUBLIC WORKS

I

RADICAL TRADITIONS

1

The Left Side of the Continent

Radicalism in Nineteenth-Century San Francisco

*I*N order to understand the intensity of labor strife in California during the Depression of the 1930s, one must grasp a simple but elusive dynamic in the labor culture of the state, which was centered in and controlled by San Francisco. Radicalism—as a program, a style, a mode of fiery rhetoric and symbolic gesture—had deep, very deep, roots on the West Coast. It also stood in a fixed relationship to organized labor. Time and again, radical leaders, appearing from nowhere, galvanized the labor movement in San Francisco with fiery, violent language, then disappeared or were pushed aside by more centrist successors. From the start, there was something volatile about San Francisco, something that welcomed radical dissent and warred against an equally persistent bourgeois style. Perhaps this tension arose from the extremes of poverty and wealth so evident in the city by the 1870s; perhaps it possessed even deeper roots in the uncertainties of the Gold Rush, when men were transformed by wealth or went to ruin side by side in sight of one another. Whatever the nexus of causes, San Francisco functioned as the left edge of America in more than its geography. By the mid-1930s many feared that radicalism had asserted not its dialectic with mainstream labor, but its dominance. But this is to anticipate history. It is better to begin with the Gold Rush.

During the first years of the Gold Rush, labor had the advantage. The Gold Rush created an instant need for workers of every sort to build cities and towns and to service the mining economy. A washerwoman could charge $20 for laundering a dozen items of clothing. A carpenter could make a minimum of $14 a day in late 1849, and daily wages approaching $20 were not uncommon. An unskilled laborer could make $8 or more per day in San Francisco. Of equal importance to these high wages, the Gold Rush restored the dignity of labor; for every miner, no matter what his education or occupation in the Eastern states, was by definition a manual laborer. In the mines and in the cities as well, social distinctions blurred as men of various backgrounds rolled up their sleeves and performed physical work. In later years, the memory of this physical labor survived as a cherished tradition, a badge of Forty-Niner status in men who had remade themselves in the Gold Rush. A society which began as an epic of labor in the mines and prized labor so highly when instant cities had to be constructed, a society in which many of the bourgeoisie had begun their careers in shirtsleeves, however temporarily, created a subliminal affinity for labor that remained part of the local culture. For a few short years everyone had been a worker, and by and through physical work California itself had been established.

On a day-to-day basis, less subliminal realities asserted themselves. Sensing the power created by their scarcity, skilled and semi-skilled workers in frontier San Francisco organized themselves so as to control jobs and job sites. In-groups, nearly always white, excluded out-groups, frequently Hispanic or foreigners, which also meant Australians. Such exclusion, enforced by violence, did not constitute trade unionism, but neither was it mere thuggery despite its basis in force; for workers were showing the rudiments of social organization, however crudely expressed. In November 1849 the carpenters and joiners of San Francisco organized a strike demanding $16 a day. They received $13 a day for half a month, $14 a day for the second two weeks. Their strike represented a quantum leap in social organization over the job-protection groups formed earlier that year. By 1859 there were two formal unions in San Francisco, the Typographical Society, the first trade union on the Pacific Coast, and the Teamsters Union, and these organizations were in turn followed by associations (unions would be too strong a term) of longshoremen, shipwrights, plasterers, bricklayers, hodcarriers, and others. Such protective organizations were becoming increasingly necessary, for the golden age of Gold Rush labor was passing. The more San Francisco grew in population, the more workers became available. By 1853 carpenters who had been making $14 a day in 1849 were working for $8; this was still a very high wage for the United States at this period, but already the suggestion was emerging that California's protected labor market would not last forever.

The Civil War postponed the inevitable. Cut off from the East by the conflict, the San Francisco Bay Area developed its own manufacturing capacity, as in the case of the Union Iron and Brass Works of San Francisco founded in 1849 as a blacksmithery and expanded as a full-scale ironworks in the early 1860s. By 1864 some 250 ironworkers were employed there at the peak of the season, manufacturing, repairing, or refitting the intricate iron and brass fittings necessary for the mining and ship-repair industries and constructing the boilers (one hundred a year) which were the main source of industrial energy in that era. Not surprisingly, the ironmoulders and boilermakers of San Francisco organized. In April 1864 they struck, successfully, for $4 for a ten-hour day. The previous year, the San Francisco Trade Union Council, the first citywide labor organization, was formed. The Council represented fifteen labor organizations and as many as three thousand workers.

Employers were organizing as well, beginning with a restaurant owners' association formed in 1861, which defeated a citywide waiters' strike in 1863. Thus encouraged, manufacturers formed an Employers Association in 1864 whose primary target was the militant and successful Machinists and Boilermakers Union. In an effort to break the strike of April 1864, the Association recruited skilled ironworkers from the East. The union sent representatives down to Panama to meet the newcomers before they took ship to San Francisco. By the time the strikebreakers reached the city, they had joined the union. Beaten in the strike, the Association began to target union leaders for discharge. By the late 1860s the Machinists and Boilermakers Union had been shorn of its leadership, and rollbacks and takeaways had begun.

The single most contested point of struggle in the 1860s was the eight-hour day. The radical nature of this demand is difficult to grasp in our era. The bakers of San Francisco, as an example, were working seven days a week, fourteen to fifteen hours a day, in October 1863, when they struck unsuccessfully for a twelve-hour day and no Sunday work. In June 1867 Chinese workers struck the Central Pacific for a twelve-hour day and $40 a month. (They were receiving $30.) In a world where such inhumanly long hours were acceptable, the demand for an eight-hour day posed a radical threat to the established order. The fact that the eight-hour day constituted a serious demand in San Francisco in the 1860s asserted the underlying radical tradition that was already forming. Caulkers won this concession in December 1865, followed by the shipwrights and joiners in January 1866. The printer unionist Alexander M. Kenaday and carpenter unionist A. M. Winn forged the eight-hour-day movement in the mid- and late 1860s into a well-organized crusade that helped send Irish-born Eugene Casserly, a Democrat, to the United States Senate in 1869.

Starting life as a carpenter, A. M. Winn had prospered in San Francisco as a building contractor and real estate speculator. With the outbreak of the Civil War, Winn won appointment as brigadier general in the state militia. Having thus crossed class barriers so dramatically, Winn kept his working-class connections in a distinctive blend of pro-labor activism and *haute bourgeois* prosperity that said something very important about San Francisco: a carpenter had become a contractor and a militia general while remaining a union activist. On 3 June 1867 General Winn led two thousand workers on parade in San Francisco in support of the eight-hour-a-day platform. By 1868 a league of fifty eight-hour-a-day organizations had been formed throughout the state. The league succeeded in getting an eight-hour expectation passed through the legislature. Without enforcement provisions, however, and with the labor pool expanding, this law remained but a prophetic gesture on the books: a tribute to the strength of labor in San Francisco.

With the transcontinental railroad approaching completion in 1869, employers predicted the influx of thousands of skilled, semi-skilled, and unskilled workers into California, putting an end to San Francisco's protected labor market. In 1869 employers established a California Labor and Employment Exchange to encourage migration. The fact that thousands of Chinese and Irish, laid off from construction crews now that the railroad work was winding down, were pouring into San Francisco exacerbated the situation. In the late 1870s San Francisco erupted into class conflict that through mass meetings and incendiary rhetoric raised the specter—and very nearly the substance—of revolution.

San Francisco novelist Gertrude Atherton described the 1870s as terrible, and for once she was not exaggerating. When the banking house of Jay Cooke failed on 18 September 1873, the New York Stock Exchange closed for ten days, and the United States was plunged into the worst depression the country had ever experienced. A year later, the Panic reached California, putting an abrupt end to the boom ushered in by silver from the Comstock Lode. In late August 1875 the Bank of California, the premier financial institution of the Far West, closed its doors after a run on its deposits; and its secretary and presiding genius, William Chapman Ralston, who had been secretly making unauthorized loans to his many enterprises from Bank funds, swam out into the chilly waters off North Beach and died from either stroke, heart attack, or suicide. The Bank of California took a number of other San Francisco banks down with it, either permanently or for a period of time. Money dried up, and capital-scarce ventures, including Ralston's Palace Hotel, the largest hostelry in the Northern Hemisphere, went into remission.

Worse: some 154,300 immigrants had poured into California between 1873 and 1875, more than the total immigration of the 1856–1867 period. About a quarter of these newcomers were factory workers dislocated by the Panic in the East, and most of them soon found themselves milling about San Francisco looking for work, their presence ominously added to the Irish and the Chinese left unemployed by the completion of the transcontinental railroad. The eight-hour day had long since become a thing of the past as thousands of unemployed men idled around fires blazing in the empty sandlots of San Francisco, passing a bottle if one were available, muttering desperately to each other about the lack of jobs. Elsewhere in the city—in waterfront sheds, in squatters' tents in the outlying districts—an increasing number of homeless women and their ragged offspring kept shabby house as their men tramped the streets in search of work. In one short decade, a workers' paradise had become a wasteland of unemployment.

In late July 1877 the central committee of the San Francisco chapter of the Workingmen's Party of the United States called for a rally of the unemployed on the evening of the 23rd on the sandlots in front of City Hall. Eight thousand men showed up. A rally of such size in such dire times terrified the establishment. In and of itself, the Workingmen's Party—an American offshoot of the International Workingmen's Association, more commonly known as the First International, founded in London in 1864 under the leadership of Karl Marx—raised the specter of revolution through its stated goals and its identification with the uprising of the Paris Commune in 1871. That incident—the seizing of the city by radicals, the shooting of prominent citizens, including the Archbishop of Paris, the reseizure of the city by the army, followed by the mass execution of seventeen thousand *communards*, including women and children—functioned as an overture, a chillingly prophetic paradigm, to a century of revolutions that was to follow.

If this suggestion of Paris were not disconcerting enough to the oligarchy of San Francisco, the Workingmen's Party of the United States was in sympathy with the railroad strike that had broken out in the East six days before the scheduled San Francisco rally, and many of its members had participated actively in the struggle. Never before had the nation witnessed such an effective walkout, bringing the railroad system in the East and parts of the Midwest to a halt, followed by the use of federal troops to suppress the strikers. The sight of blue-coated regulars marching against civilian strikers in Martinsburg, West Virginia; Cumberland, Maryland; Baltimore, Reading, and Pittsburgh, where most of the violence occurred, including a number of deaths, offered the nation a chilling reenactment of the suppression of the Paris Commune. In St. Louis, the strikers actually seized the city, governing it in *de facto* rebellion for two weeks before federal troops gained control.

All this was occurring even as the first San Francisco Workingmen's Party rally was in the planning stages. Rumors swept the city: the workers planned to set fire to the Pacific Mail Steamship Company docks, where Chinese immigrants landed, then burn down Chinatown. On the day of the rally, a group of workers was arrested for parading the streets with a banner advertising the time and place of the meeting. The San Francisco police and the state militia went on alert.

In its early stages at least, the rally itself threatened to prove anti-climactic. Sensitive to the fears gripping the oligarchy who controlled the city government, the Workingmen's Party officials on the platform confined their remarks to expressions of support for the striking railroad workers in the East and to generic condemnations of the capitalist system. But then some young thugs on the outskirts of the crowd—hoodlums they were called, a local term which soon entered the American language—began to beat up a hapless Chinese man who chanced to be passing by. A policeman arrested one particularly violent hoodlum, but his confreres seized him back. "On to Chinatown!" they screamed, and many followed. Never in its quarter century of American existence had San Francisco witnessed such rioting as the sacking of Chinatown which followed. Although the toll was relatively minor—the destruction of twenty Chinese laundries, some damage to the Chinese Methodist Mission—the specter of similar sackings elsewhere in the city drove the already edgy oligarchy into full alert. The day following the riot, businessman William T. Coleman, leader of the Vigilance Committees of 1851 and 1856, was asked to head up a hastily organized Committee of Public Safety. Four thousand volunteers were rapidly organized into public safety brigades, each man armed with a hickory pickaxe handle attached to his wrist by a leather thong.

The next evening, 24 July 1877, a thousand men gathered for a rally before the United States Mint on Mission Street. Only the presence of armed state militia prevented them from sacking the nearby Mission Woolen Mills, an important employer of Chinese workers. On the next evening, a crowd gathered in front of the Pacific Mail docks, where Chinese workers arrived from the Far East. Blocked from the docks and depot by the police and by the Committee of Public Safety patrols, the men set fire to a nearby lumberyard, then retreated to an adjacent hill from which they harassed firefighters with stones. The police and their pickaxe-handle auxiliaries charged the hill. Gunfire broke out. When it was over, four rioters lay dead, and San Francisco had its miniaturist replay of Paris six years earlier and a parallel to the strike-struck cities of the East.

Twelve hundred militiamen, 252 policemen, and four thousand pickaxe-handle vigilantes patrolled the city. The Army in the nearby Presidio was put on alert, and three Navy gunboats took up positions offshore. Not since the Civil War itself had so much governmental and para-governmental firepower been lined up, both in San Francisco and the East, against civilians in a state of *de facto* or threatened insurrection. More rioting followed on the evening of the 26th, but by then a well-advertised instruction disseminated to the militia and the police to shoot to kill anyone destroying property or interfering with firefighters took the momentum out of the rioters, who remained quiet and disbanded on the 27th. On 28 July, Governor William Irwin felt confident enough to telegraph the Secretary of the Navy and thank him for the gunboats, now no longer necessary. Within the next few weeks, the militia went home and the Committee of Public Safety disbanded its pickaxe-handle brigade.

The events of the week 22 to 28 July 1877 blended reality and gesture. The riots were real (four deaths, property loss); but the reaction from government and the oligarchy—the police, the soldiers, the vigilantes, the offshore gunboats—while responding to a real threat, was also excessive, energized as it was by fears coming from the railroad strike in the East with its attendant suggestion of revolution. Throughout the week, San Francisco was acting out a symbolic scenario of insurrection and repression. The strikes and repressions in the East were for real: real grievances, a very real work stoppage, a real commune in St. Louis, purposeful strikers, troops advancing with rifles and bayonets. In far-off San Francisco, by contrast, this Eastern struggle engendered in the very same week a clash which in terms of organizational sophistication, violence, deaths, property loss, or effect on the nation (no railroads ceased to run, no vital traffic halted in the harbor) should have been relegated to the status of a sideshow: except for the fact that the sideshow touched even deeper fears of revolt. Had American gunboats ever before been placed in position against an American city—other than in the Civil War? Had the rioting in San Francisco grown worse, would the Secretary of the Navy, with the governor's approval, have ordered the shelling of San Francisco? Something deeper was at work here: something about the role San Francisco was destined to play in the national encounter with the rhetoric of European-style revolution and the reaction such rhetoric provoked from the right.

In terms of the protestors, the acting out had been fumbling and inept: three disorganized riots, perpetrated by apolitical hoodlums bent on some anarchistic burning of laundries and bashing of Chinese. But now, in the aftermath of the week of 22 July 1877, the radicals would escalate their symbolic response to the police, the militia, the pickaxe-handle brigade, the offshore gunboats: first on the level of fiery revolutionary rhetoric, then later as an organized political party that, for a brief moment, assumed control of California itself.

Among the pickaxe-handle men patrolling that late July 1877 was one Denis Kearney, age thirty, a native of County Cork who had settled in San Francisco in 1872 after a fourteen-year career at sea. Having risen from cabin boy to first mate on American vessels and, more important, having saved his money, Kearney sank his savings into a drayage business, which he managed meticulously. A sailor since the age of eleven, Kearney struggled manfully to make up for lost time. He spent the years 1872 to 1877 building his business and pursuing a course of self-improvement. At the public library he read Darwin and Spencer and newspapers from the great world and dreamed of a political career. On Sundays he attended discussions at the Lyceum for Self Culture, a reading and debate forum for working people bent upon self-improvement.

A small man, highly strung, with fierce blue eyes and a drooping mustache, Denis Kearney took himself very seriously, even when others considered him more than a bit of a fool. Kearney wanted desperately to lead, to play a role in the world, and he groped toward that goal with the ursine clumsiness of a sporadic autodidact, speaking over-loud in a thick brogue he never lost. At meetings of the Lyceum for Self Culture or of the Draymen and Teamsters Union, Kearney was wont to take the floor and deliver himself of harangues on innumerable subjects, rambling and pompous, which elicited catcalls and groans from the audience. His favorite topic, ironically, was the shiftlessness of working people. They smoked; they drank; they had irregular domestic arrangements; they lacked ambition. He, by contrast—and Kearney frequently referred to his own situation—neither smoked nor drank and had a respectable wife (the former Miss Mary Ann Leary), four well-cared-for children, a drayage business. Workingmen idled in saloons or at amusement parks in their off-hours. He read books at the public library. They were priest-ridden. He had seen through the sham of organized religion. No wonder employers preferred the Chinese, so orderly and diligent, so productive and self-disciplined! When the call came from the Committee of Public Safety for volunteers, Denis Kearney went on patrol with a pickaxe handle, protecting businesses which employed Chinese labor from irate white workers.

Two months later, on the evening of 16 September 1877, Denis Kearney was addressing a torchlight gathering of these selfsame workers in an empty San Francisco sandlot, telling them that the Chinese were taking their jobs. Five days later he was telling another gathering of the unemployed that they, all twenty thousand of them, should be armed and drilling so as to defy the police, the militia, the Committee of Safety. Within sixty days, the bumbling autodidact on the right had become a Jack Cade embodiment of revolution. Patrolling with his pickaxe handle in late July, Denis Kearney sensed not only the power of the oligarchy but the force of the irate workers as well. Wanting so desperately to lead, he saw in the unemployed a power which could be his as well, provided he could take proper hold. The very reason he feared and criticized the workers—because he, too, was one of them: vulnerable, clumsy, and Irish despite his sailing master's certificate, his drayage business, his teetotalism, the long hours spent deciphering closely printed books whose language he could barely comprehend—this very point of identification now became an axis on which Kearney could rotate 180 degrees and head off in the opposite direction. The Yankee capitalist Coleman might tie a pickaxe handle to his wrist with a leather thong, but Kearney would never sit down to dinner in Coleman's dining room. As far as Coleman and his class were concerned, Denis Kearney, drayman, student of Darwin and Spencer, was just another disposable Irishman. As workers, cooks, and housemen, the oligarchy preferred the Chinese.

In August 1877 Denis Kearney applied for membership in the Workingmen's Party of the United States. Flabbergasted that such a known baiter of the working class should be seeking admission to its ranks, the Party rejected his application. Kearney determined to found his own party, which he did, the short-lived Workingmen's Trade and Labor Union of San Francisco. It dissolved after two meetings. On the 21st of September Kearney made his first appearance as a sandlot orator before a crowd of two hundred. Seven hundred came to hear him two nights later. Time, place, the press of events, and inordinate ambition had transformed the fool with his rambling, bromidic monologues into the charismatic demagogue voicing the seething resentments of the unemployed with their angry cries of "The Chinese must go!"

Kearney's second attempt at forming a party met with more success. The platform adopted on 5 October 1877 by the newly organized Workingmen's Party of California seethed with high, if angry, moral purpose. The United States, it argued, must become a workers' republic—by means of the ballot box. The imperatives of religion, humanity, and patriotism demanded nothing less. The Chinese, unfortunately, had no claim on this moral commonwealth. For Kearney and his followers, "John," as the Chinese laborer was called, was strictly a dehumanized tool of the capitalist class, working longer hours for less money and making minimal demands on his employers. Brought in to do the servile work of Gold Rush California (there were fifty-four Chinese in California in 1848, more than twenty-five thousand in 1852), the Chinese were banned from the mines, frequently through violence. The construction of the transcontinental railroad, in which the Chinese achieved an epic of engineering and labor, kept them employed—and socially neutral—through the 1860s; but when the Chinese began to migrate into

San Francisco in the depressed 1870s seeking industrial employment, trouble began. They were permitted to fish and to open laundries, for white workers had no desire to become fishermen until the Italians arrived in the 1880s; nor did whites want to go into the laundry business, with the exception of the deluxe specialty operations conducted by the French. But when the Chinese sought industrial, draying, or longshoring jobs, when they edged toward the periphery of the construction trades, their willingness to work for low wages and their high productivity threatened white workers, employed and unemployed alike. The first union labels in the United States appeared on cigar boxes in San Francisco in the 1870s: white bands to differentiate work done by members of the Cigarmakers Union from cigars made in Chinese shops. Union kilns stamped their bricks with a small cross to distinguish their product from bricks baked by "the heathen Chinee."

And now the anti-Chinese violence of July, followed by the incendiary speeches of Denis Kearney and the 16 October manifesto issued by the Workingmen's Party which announced: "We have made no secret of our intentions. We make none. Before you and the world, we declare that the Chinamen must leave our shores. We declare that white men, and women, and boys, and girls, cannot live as the people of the great republic should and compete with the single Chinese coolies in the labor market. We declare that we cannot hope to drive the Chinaman away by working cheaper than he does. None but an enemy would expect it of us; none but an idiot could hope for success; none but a degraded coward and slave would make the effort. To an American, death is preferable to life on a par with the Chinese." [1]

At this point, the plot thickens—and in such a way as to reassert and reinforce the expressive, mimetic aspects of far-Left/far-Right conflict in San Francisco. First of all, Denis Kearney, firebrand revolutionist, became an ongoing media event. In an effort to sell newspapers through sensationalism, the San Francisco *Chronicle* covered Kearney's speeches at great length. The more incendiary the speech, the more extensive the coverage. There was even a suspicion, later denied by Kearney, that *Chronicle* reporter Chester Hull helped the ill-educated drayman prepare his more incendiary harangues, which always managed to appear *verbatim* and at great length in the next morning's *Chronicle* as if they had been previously transmitted to Mr. Hull in written copy or prepared by him in the first place. Or perhaps Hull merely rewrote Kearney's incoherent harangues, polishing their language, heightening their ferocity, after they were delivered?

Whatever the sequence, the language is certainly not a *verbatim* transcript. Whether Hull wrote Kearney's speeches before or after they were delivered, the fiery demagogue drew much of his power not so much from his speeches as they were delivered, but as they were reported in the next morning's *Chronicle*. Like a modern celebrity, Kearney assumed an existence halfway between event and heightened, even fabricated reportage. Denis Kearney drew his strength not merely from the realities of his massive, incoherent resentments and his semi-literate preachments, but from the celebrity's ability to be real and unreal simultaneously: to become, that is, a symbolic presence removed from ordinary reality and allowed an extraordinary latitude of behavior and statement, like a figure in a dream—or a nightmare. How else could Denis Kearney say what he said, all those violent, reckless things, unless there existed a tacit agreement in his audience, including those he baited, that Kearney was not real in the same way that other labor leaders were real? He was, rather, a collective creation of a deeply divided community, allowed to say the unsayable so that language might suffice for action and true revolution be avoided.

Take, for example, Kearney's ferocious speech of 29 October 1877. Railroad magnate Charles Crocker, the construction genius of the Big Four, was in the process of consolidating his hold on an entire city block atop Nob Hill bounded by California, Sacramento, Taylor and Jones Streets, today the site of Grace Cathedral. One householder, however, refused to be bought out, so Crocker had the home of his obstinate neighbor surrounded on three sides by a high wooden fence that blocked out the sunlight. What a perfect place, Kearney and his colleagues decided, for a sandlot rally—atop Nob Hill within shouting distance of the Crocker, Stanford, Huntington, Hopkins, and Flood mansion sites. Several thousand men crowded a sandlot on the evening of 29 October to hear Kearney, his fierce eyes and mustache Hitlerian in the torchlight, give vent, according to the next day's *Chronicle*, to the most incendiary utterances thus far recorded on the Pacific Coast.

"The Central Pacific railroad men are thieves, and will soon feel the power of the workingmen," the *Chronicle* reports Kearney as saying. "When I have thoroughly organized my party, we will march through the city and compel the thieves to give up their plunder. I will lead you to the City Hall, clean out the police force, hang the Prosecuting Attorney, burn every book that has a particle of law in it, and then enact new laws for the workingmen. I will give the Central Pacific just three months to discharge their Chinamen, and if that is not done, Stanford and his crowd will have to take the consequences. I will give Crocker until November 29th to take down the fence around Jung's house, and if he doesn't do it, I will lead the workingmen up there and tear it down, and give Crocker the worst beating with the sticks that a man ever got."[2]

If Kearney actually said all this a mere three months after San Francisco stood under *de facto* martial law, then how were such threats received by his audience? As realistic possibilities? Or as stylized rhetoric in a conflict that had already been removed to a symbolic level once the perceived threat of an actual revolution had been faced and put down the previous July? Kearney's threats evoked actions more horrible than anything attempted in the July riots. This was a call for revolution. Why, then, were not the pickaxe handles immediately issued to the bourgeois vigilantes, or the gunboats summoned once again to anchor offshore?

Recklessly, Kearney plunged ahead. "If I give an order to hang Crocker," he was reported to have told a rally at the corner of Stockton and Green a few nights later, "it will be done." Kearney's colleague, meanwhile, the marginally competent physician C. C. O'Donnell, was giving Kearney a run for his money. "When thoroughly organized," O'Donnell told a rally on 15 October, "we could plant our flag on Telegraph Hill, and our cannons, too, and blow the Mail steamers and their Chinese freight out of the waters"—a threat he repeated on the 25th. "They have got to stop this importation of Chinese," ranted the doctor on 2 November, "or you will see Jackson Street run knee deep in blood."[3]

By the evening of 3 November, after two weeks of such language, the oligarchy had had enough. The latitude tacitly granted Kearney and his followers in the matter of language collapsed. Kearney had pushed it too far. The verbal mimesis of revolution as a way of offering subliminal release had begun to sound too much like revolution itself. The militia was called out, and Kearney was arrested even as he was speaking to a mass meeting in front of Dr. O'Donnell's office. The next night three other Workingmen leaders were taken into custody. A fifth was arrested when he visited the other four in jail, where they remained under heavy bail. The militia continued to patrol.

If one considers American society inherently stable, these events hover on the edge of the comic: an *opéra bouffe* of revolution in a provincial American city. But things suddenly did not seem so stable to San Franciscans in November 1877. The leadership of the Chinese Six Companies, among others, was now taking Kearney's language as an actual threat. The Six Companies politely informed the city that should the Chinese quarter be once again invaded, the residents—despite the fact that "our countrymen are better acquainted with peaceful vocations than the scenes of strife"—were prepared to defend themselves and their property to the death.[4]

Even Kearney and his colleagues realized that they had pushed street theater beyond permissible limits. Impressed by the austerities of the city jail, they wrote to the mayor claiming they had been misreported by the press and promising, somewhat contradictorily, to hold no more outdoor meetings nor use any more incendiary language. Despite two tries, the district attorney could not gain a conviction in Superior Court, and by Thanksgiving the San Francisco Six (there had been another arrest) went free, charges dismissed. The even-handedness of the court, dismissing two separate sets of charges on constitutional grounds, suggested that however frighteningly Kearney and his colleagues had bespoken themselves, fears of actual revolution had begun to subside in the community. As many as ten thousand workers paraded with Kearney and his colleagues on Thanksgiving Day, and in the evening they voted to nominate delegates to attend the State Constitutional Convention scheduled to meet in Sacramento in April 1879.

Thus the Workingmen transformed themselves into a *bona fide* party, committed not to revolution, but to the reform of California through an adjustment of its constitution. The rank and file of the movement had seen the dead end of revolution as Kearney and O'Donnell had luridly summoned it forth from the platform, and the leadership of the Workingmen's Party realized that it now had a chance to play politics instead of talking violence. Slowly, the leadership began to squeeze

Kearney out of the picture. Kearney was owned lock, stock, and barrel by the *Chronicle*, went one rumor. He had promised the oligarchy to fade from the scene, went another report, in exchange for $5,000.

In an effort to regain his position, Kearney reverted to that which had taken him from obscurity in the first place, violent language. "When the Chinese question is settled," he said in December, "we can discuss whether it would be better to hang, shoot, or cut the capitalist to pieces." In January 1878 Kearney was reported to have said, among other things: "Are you courageous? How many of you have got muskets? Up hands, who have got muskets? How many of you have got about ten feet of rope in your pocket? Well, you must be ready and arm yourselves. This thing has got too hot. There is a white heat in this thing now, and you must be ready when I issue a call for 10,000 men." [5]

This last remark brought the Committee of Safety back into session, although patrols were not sent out. Kearney and five others were arrested and jailed. Several companies of militia were mustered, and the gunboat *Lackawanna* took up its accustomed position off the Pacific Mail docks. For Denis Kearney, the magic had worked. It was like old times. Once again, he was the imprisoned martyr, his name on everyone's lips.

Only now, he had pushed it twice too often and twice too far. The San Francisco Board of Supervisors and the California State Legislature each passed severe anti-incitement ordinances. Signed by the Governor on 19 January 1878, the state law authorized two years in prison and a $5,000 fine for use of incendiary language or any other form of incitement. The legislature also appropriated funds to expand the San Francisco police force and gave the governor a $20,000 contingency fund to deal with public disturbances.

More than ever, the growing anti-Kearney faction in the leadership of the Workingmen's Party was realizing that it could not talk revolution and run candidates for office simultaneously. Although Kearney was acquitted for the third time on 22 January 1878, he went into rapid decline. In May he was deposed from the presidency of the Party. At the Constitutional Convention which met in Sacramento from 28 September 1878 to 3 March 1879, the fifty delegates from the Workingmen's Party (out of a total of 149) allied themselves with Granger delegates from the agricultural counties and helped fashion a document which won voter approval by a mere ten thousand votes, thanks mainly to Granger support. While placing restrictions on corporate power, the railroad especially, the new constitution was not a radical document. The delegates rejected such extreme proposals as a unicameral legislature and the banishment of the Chinese from most forms of employment and trade. With eleven state senators, seventeen assemblymen, and one member of the railroad commission in its ranks, the Workingmen's Party had made the transition to respectability.

Anti-Chinese agitation flared up again in San Francisco in February 1880, with the familiar ritual of nighttime sandlot rallies by torchlight and, by day, harassment of industries employing the loathed Mongolian. Cowed employers discharged nearly a thousand Chinese workers in San Francisco and Oakland. Once again, the oligarchy formed a Committee of Safety, and there was talk of a direct appeal to President Rutherford B. Hayes to send in federal troops to quell the disturbances. Kearney leapt into the fray with an incendiary speech that earned him six months in the county jail and a $1,000 fine. He served a few months before being released on appeal. Kearney made one last sandlot speech—a cautious one—to the crowd of supporters who escorted him out of prison; but already, as the Workingmen's Party was being invaded and colonized by the Greenback Labor Party headquartered in Chicago and the renascent Democratic Party of California, Kearney's brand of politics as rhetorically violent street theater was becoming increasingly passé. Sensing this, Kearney allied himself with the Greenback Labor movement and was elected to the national executive committee in Chicago. Cut off from the sandlots, disciplined by the protocols of an earnest organization of Midwestern Protestant agrarians, Denis Kearney lost his role as rhetorical firebrand. He also lost his interest in politics.

A decade earlier, Kearney had entered public life comically, as a bumbling lyceum orator, and now he exited it in the same style, as the proprietor of a coffee and donut stand in a squatters' village, Mooneysville, at Ocean Beach. Largely organized by Kearney and Con Mooney, after whom the enterprise was named, the Mooneysville squatters attempted to occupy disputed beachfront property at the base of Sutro Heights by setting up concession stands there and claiming ownership. The fact that a subsidiary of the Southern Pacific, the Park and Ocean Railroad Company, claimed the property added to the *opéra bouffe* of it all. Once again, Denis Kearney, this time behind the counter in an apron, dispensing coffee and donuts at ten cents a round, was taking on the capitalist establishment. "The news is painful in the extreme," gloated the Town Crier column in the *California Advertiser* for 29 December 1883, "for when we look back on his glorious career from the time that he sold his horse and dray for a mess of agitation pottage up to the date he made trips to the East and posed as an Irish orator, utterly ignorant of the English grammar, we have always figured on Denis as either the next Vice-President of the United States or Poundkeeper of San Francisco." On the morning of 31 January 1884, Golden Gate Park employees assisted by the San Francisco police dismantled Mooneysville. "Let the Romans do it!" Kearney exclaimed as the park workers tore down his coffee and donut stand. He was standing on sand as he made his last public speech.[6]

Not every workingman in San Francisco approved of Denis Kearney or, for that matter, the Workingmen's Party. Formed in March 1878 at the height of the Kearney agitation, the Representative Assembly of Trades and Labor Unions, known more familiarly as the Trades Assembly, expressed the distrust of mainstream unions toward Kearney's brand of agitation. Even Workingmen's Party activists such as vice-president Frank Roney were growing disaffected. For one thing, Roney was convinced that *Chronicle* reporter Chester Hull was ventriloquizing Kearney's outrageous speeches, which were bringing such discredit on the labor movement. When Kearney named himself Lieutenant General of the Workingmen's Militia, Roney considered the man more fool than demagogue. Kearney and his cohorts, Roney believed, launched anti-Chinese attacks because they were too stupid to understand the real causes of industrial exploitation. When the Workingmen's Party took over San Francisco under Mayor Isaac Kolloch in 1879, Roney considered the city under the control of third-rate bosses.

Born in Belfast in 1841, Frank Roney personifies the trade unionist intellectual committed to militant but mainstream organizing. Only in the matter of his Irish birth and San Francisco situation did Frank Roney—literate, self-effacing, understated in his leadership style—have anything in common with Denis Kearney. Educated as an articled clerk, Roney left a fitful career as a real estate agent when he found himself unable to evict people behind on their rent. He turned instead to ironworking as a moulder's apprentice and to active membership in the fledgling moulders' union in Belfast and to the underground Fenian movement on behalf of Irish independence. Imprisoned in Dublin's Mountjoy Prison by the British government, Roney was released on the condition that he emigrate to the United States. He spent the late 1860s and early 1870s working his way westward as a moulder via St. Louis, Omaha, and Salt Lake City, sharpening his skills as a union activist and a journalist capable of strong prose on behalf of the movement.

The San Francisco to which Frank Roney arrived in April 1875 ranked ninth among the manufacturing cities in the United States. It also had an unemployment rate of 33 percent. As Roney looked for work, he kept a diary which reveals the details and texture of working-class life in the depressed 1870s. Returning to his South of Market rooms after a futile day of walking the streets in search of employment, Roney is shocked to see a furniture store owner fighting with the pregnant Mrs. Roney over a chair, which the shopkeeper wishes to repossess. Tormented by bitterness and a sense of shame and failure, he fights the temptation to drink. He envisions San Francisco engulfed by a great earthquake in retribution for the misery it has caused him. When Roney does find work as a moulder, it is intermittent: at the Pacific Iron Works, the City Iron Works, the Union Iron Works. Intermittent as well are the couple's South of Market lodgings: Clementina Street, Perry Street, Margaret Place, all within a two-month period while Roney is laid off twice. Roney ends 1875 in debt: $13.50 to the grocer, $7.75 to the butcher, $15 in personal loans, and back rent. Even when he is working, he must borrow against his salary to retire past obligations. He works the entire month of January 1876, six days a week, ten hours a day, at the Union Iron Works to clear $47.50, which is barely enough to cover his indebtedness. A man of reading and intelligence, aware of larger issues and better things, he is forced to measure his victories and defeats alike in $2 or $3 increments. On Sunday, 2 May 1875, Roney does not have the money to attend the moulders' picnic; yet he does manage a visit to Woodward's Gardens with his brother-in-law and son. Returning home from the Gardens, he notes in his diary that a man might find much mental improvement and inspiration in the many fine paintings on display at Woodward's—in the natural history museum as well, and the aquarium and deer park. When his job at the Union Iron Works proves steady, Roney manages a Saturday evening with his wife at Maguire's Opera House, where they enjoy a minstrel show.

The job at Union Iron proved steady because Frank Roney learned an important lesson about employment in an unorganized shop: the foreman hires and fires; please the foreman and you work; displease him and you are back on the street. Roney was surprised by the ever-accelerating pace of iron moulding in the United States, its constant tendency toward speed-up because of the payment of wages per piece of work, and by the status consciousness of American workers. Moulders, for example, looked down on the unskilled workers who assisted them. With no solidarity of either sentiment or organization, Roney observed of the five hundred workers at Union Iron Works, with each person vying for the foreman's favor while struggling to maintain his own uncertain status, indeed his very job, against everyone else in the foundry, life became a Darwinian nightmare of brutal competition which favored only the foreman and, beyond him, the owners the foreman served.

Having become an American citizen, Frank Roney turned to the Workingmen's Party of California in search of an answer. Joining the Party cost him his job at Union Iron Works temporarily, and he spent some months shoveling coal on the wharf before persuading the foreman to take him back. Tiring of Kearney's demagoguery and racism, Roney resigned from the Party in order to devote his best efforts to the organization of unions by trades, beginning with his own moulders. In 1879 he organized a short-lived (six months) Seamen's Protective Association, forerunner of the Coast Seamen's Union, which would emerge in six years' time. As leader of the Moulders Union, Roney played an important role in reviving the San Francisco Trades Assembly in 1881 and served two terms as president. By the end of 1883 some fifty trade unions were active in the Assembly. Two years later, Roney was elected president of an even larger umbrella organization, the Federated Trades and Labor Council.

By this time Roney was working as a stationary engineer in the basement boiler room of City Hall, which became the hub of labor activism in San Francisco as representatives of unions or would-be unionists—moulders, cigarmakers, laundry workers, cooks and waiters, seafarers, and others—sought Roney out for decisions and guidance. In his five-year emergence from newcomer to labor leader, Frank Roney resisted two temptations: German (which is to say, Marxist) Socialism and self-employment. After his break with the Workingmen's Party, Roney associated briefly with German Socialists but decided that he preferred higher wages and improved working conditions through militant trade unionism over endless talk of class struggle and revolution. He also resisted a number of opportunities to rejoin the *petit bourgeoisie* as a shopkeeper, preferring to remain a wage earner and trade unionist instead. In 1886 Roney turned down the presidency of the International

Iron Moulders Union headquartered in Chicago because he did not want to relocate his family and accepted the vice-presidency instead, which allowed him to remain in San Francisco.

Not that Frank Roney was free to pursue bread-and-butter issues unimpeded by radical ideologues. Roney's particular thorn in the side was Burnette Haskell, a Marxist lawyer with anarchist tendencies. In his peculiarly furtive, overwrought way, Burnette Haskell brought to San Francisco the international Marxist Left. Significantly, Haskell was not a workingman but a college-bred lawyer. Born in 1857 to a prominent Sierra County family of New England origins, Burnette Haskell had qualified for the California bar after intermittent study at the University of California, the University of Illinois, and Oberlin College. A diary Haskell kept in 1878, now on deposit at the Bancroft Library in Berkeley, reveals the young law clerk's emotional inner life: not just in terms of his thwarted love for Sophie, a married woman who lived with her husband in the same boarding house—their meetings at the Mechanics' Library, their stolen streetcar rides together, the evenings they managed to be seated next to each other at the theater, the poem he writes for her and publishes in the *Argonaut*—but also in terms of Haskell's general malaise with life. Confiding to his diary on a lonely Sunday, 25 August 1878, in the form of a letter to his loved one, Haskell refers to his baffled emotions, his bitterly quarreling divorced parents, his uncertain future. He contemplates suicide, or, at the least, he flirts with the desirability of death. The stylized furtiveness of Haskell's relationship to Sophie offers a clue to the later career of this erratic but brilliant figure. Haskell was drawn to the secret dumb show of a courtship impossible to fulfill, not its consummation. Something in his desperate nature thrilled to a plot keyed to unattainable goals. Enamored of conspiracy, Burnette Haskell preferred the secret longing, the furtive gesture, life in the shadows.

Haskell passed the bar in 1879 and became active in Republican politics. In 1882 he assumed the editorship of *Truth*, a small newspaper owned by his uncle, in addition to his legal practice. Almost abruptly, he became radicalized. Just exactly how this happened is uncertain. Perhaps it was revulsion resulting from his personal exposure to, and possible participation in, the standard corrupt political practices of the era. Labor leader Frank Roney, president of the Trades Assembly, later recalled the candor with which Haskell, then employed in the law office of the chairman of the Republican State Central Committee, described to labor leaders at an evening meeting the elaborate system of payoffs that characterized much of California's politics. Some of the unionists were outraged by Haskell's apparent lack of remorse.

On the other hand, the young lawyer-journalist was volunteering to place *Truth* in the service of the labor movement. Haskell had already become an ardent student of Socialist theory and had organized a clandestine organization called the Invisible Republic, a radical study group with titles and rituals borrowed from republican Rome. A successor group, the Illuminati, made direct contact with the Internationals in England and on the Continent, seeking organizational advice. Just exactly how many San Franciscans belonged to either the Invisible Republic or to the Illuminati is uncertain. We have only Haskell's word for it, together with certain membership forms and statements he drew up, which survive in his papers. Either organization, or both, might very well have been figments of Haskell's imagination. In any event, by 1882 Burnette Haskell was no longer a Republican.

Haskell's next organizational venture, the International Workingmen's Association (IWA), represented an even bolder leap into Marxist activism. Initiated by a confidential circular sent out to selected comrades on 1 June 1884, Haskell's plan called for the organization of the entire United States into revolutionary cells of nine members, each of whom belonged to another nine-member cell known only to himself. Thus each member would know no more than sixteen other members in the national network. Within the cells, members held either the red card of a student, the white card of an organizer, or the blue card of an official. Haskell named himself executive of the Pacific Coast Division. Frank Roney, who monitored the IWA with suspicion, estimated that it had no more than a hundred members in its brief existence, most of them belonging to the Coast Seamen's Union. Labor historian Ira Cross estimates that Haskell managed to establish at least nineteen cells throughout the Bay Area and Northern California.

The surviving *Minute Book* for 1884–1885 of the San Francisco cell of the IWA reveals the organization as, primarily, a study club of Socialist and anarchist theory, pursued by workingmen from the South of Market and Mission districts anxious to bring some solace into their lives through fraternal association and discussion. They were comrades, as they called each other, and their organization was a way of keeping company and dreaming of a better social and economic order ("independent of priest, capitalist, or loafer") than the one in which they were toiling out their days.

Burnette Haskell, however, a professional man, not a worker (although he did live in the working-class Mission district), wanted a more intense psychological gratification from the organization he had founded. The *Minute Book* reveals him pushing, pushing his colleagues to more radical formulations, together with suggestions of violent action. Already, Haskell had been imitating Denis Kearney, whom he professed to despise, in the pages of *Truth*. "War to the palace," he thundered on 17 November 1883, "peace to the cottage, death to luxurious idleness! We have no moment to waste. Arm, I say, to the death! for Revolution is upon you." *Truth*, Haskell later pointed out, "is five cents a copy, and dynamite forty cents a pound." An article published on 15 December 1883 was entitled "Street Fighting . . . Military Tactics for the Lower Classes." Ira Cross found the following notation in Haskell's handwriting in the membership book of the Pacific Coast Division: "Seize Mint, Armories, Sub-Treasury, Custom House, Government Steamer, Alcatraz, Presidio, newspapers."[7] According to both Roney and

Cross, Haskell went so far as to propose a scheme to dynamite the Hall of Records so as to make a shambles of property titles. Roney later claimed that some men actually showed up one night willing to go through with the plot, but Haskell was nowhere in sight.

Even as he was urging these fantastic schemes, Haskell maintained a lively law practice, with a specialty in criminal defense. Eloquent, dapper, an incessant smoker of cigarettes, he cut a colorful figure in the *demimonde* of criminal defense. He also did free legal work for the fledgling Coast Seamen's Union, helping that pioneering union through its formative stages after its organization in 1885. When he ran for the Superior Court in San Francisco in 1894, Haskell claimed to have argued successfully 284 cases on behalf of coast seamen and their embattled union.

Haskell's own organization, the International Workingmen's Association, vanished after 1886 like the dream it was. Haskell went on to devote himself to organizing work for the Federated Trades based in Denver (he later claimed to be the only lawyer ever admitted to membership in the Knights of Labor) and to the establishment of Kaweah, a Socialist colony in eastern Tulare County near Visalia. At a meeting held in San Francisco on 9 November 1884, Haskell and James Martin, recording secretary of the San Francisco chapter of the IWA, inspired sixty-eight of their fellow trade unionists to form the Co-operative Land Purchase and Colonization Association of California, dedicated to establishing a colony based on principles enunciated by the Danish-born Chicago lawyer Laurence Gronlund in his newly published *Cooperative Commonwealth* (1884), the first English-language book to set forth with any amplitude the doctrines of German Socialism. The construction of a road through the mountains, intended to link the colony to shipping points for the lumber it hoped to produce, consumed four years and most of the available capital. Not until the summer of 1890 were any permanent buildings constructed. By November 1891 Haskell was sitting alone in his cabin as a winter storm raged outside, writing an article for the San Francisco *Examiner* chronicling the collapse of the Kaweah experiment. "And is there no remedy, then, for the evils that oppress the poor?" asked Haskell as he concluded his sad tale of dreams defeated by reality. "And is there no surety that this day is coming when justice and right shall reign on earth? I do not know; but I believe, and I hope, and I trust."[8]

As bizarrely conspiratorial as Burnette Haskell could be, however, he did exercise mainstream influence, according to the time-tested San Francisco formula. The line of descent from Haskell's International Workingmen's Association to the Coast Seamen's Union is direct, and from the Coast Seamen's Union emerged an entire front of mainstream unions representing the exploited and the unorganized.

As the dominant port on the Pacific Coast, San Francisco was filled with men who made their livings on coastal vessels. Ashore, seamen were frequently victims of the crimping system. A boarding house owner secured an advance against a sailor's wages from his captain, thereby insuring that the sailor had to return to his ship to work off the money he had drawn. Middlemen, called crimps, would broker sailors' contracts to boarding houses, which overcharged, and with ships' captains, who took kickbacks. Sailors were perpetually returning to ships where they were forced to work for wages already spent. At sea, they suffered a brutal existence: long hours, miserable food, dangerous working conditions, the constant threat and frequent reality of beatings from the captain or his designated enforcer. Sailors on deep-sea vessels were treated as military deserters liable to arrest and imprisonment if they left their vessel in mid-voyage.

When on 4 March 1885 San Francisco shipowners announced major wage cuts on coastal vessels, IWA activist Sigismund Danielwicz, a close friend of Burnette Haskell, organized a rally on the Folsom Street Wharf for the night of the 6th. Between three and four hundred sailors showed up to hear Danielwicz, Haskell, Martin, and other IWA representatives urge them to form a union. By the next night, a second gathering at the Irish-American Hall was hearing Haskell read a proposed constitution and by-laws for the new union, which the sailors voted to adopt. Haskell's constitution called for a permanently established Socialist International Advisory Committee as part of the governance structure, a *politburo* intended to keep the union under IWA guidance and control. Haskell, Danielwicz, Martin, and two other IWA members were named to the Committee, and the union accepted the use of the IWA offices at 6 Eddy Street as its temporary headquarters. Miraculously, the far-left IWA, a marginal organization, now had a mainstream union under its domination. A strike was called, and the shippers backed off on their proposed wage cuts. By July thirty-five hundred coast sailors carried cards issued from 7 Spear Street near the Embarcadero waterfront, headquarters of what soon became the largest union on the Pacific Coast.

How long could such a union remain under the ideological surveillance and partial control of its radical IWA mentors? And if it did, what would be the consequences? What would happen if Haskell and his fellow agitators ever succeeded in persuading this new and powerful force to embark upon one or another of its extremist schemes?

Enter Andrew Furuseth, not only a moderating influence but as a labor leader destined to develop into one of the most impressive trade unionists of his era. In a representative San Francisco drama—radicalism provoking the mainstream into existence, then passing from power—Furuseth detached the Coast Seamen's Union from its connection with the Haskell group and helped make it (and then its successor, the Sailors Union of the Pacific), the most important union on the coast.

Born in 1854 in Norway, Andrew Furuseth was at once an intellectual and a worker, doing full justice to each vocation. As a young man he had received a solid education in preparation for an appointment to the Norwegian military academy. Failing the entrance examination, Furuseth, age nineteen, followed the accustomed Scandinavian path to the sea and spent the years 1873 to 1880 as a sailor before the mast on Norwegian, Swedish, British, French, and American windjammers in the twilight era of deep-water sailing ships. A voracious reader and natural linguist, Furuseth mastered English, German, Dutch, and French in addition to his native Norwegian. The brutality of a sailor's life prepared the failed officer candidate for a career on behalf of the rank and file. On the Indian Ocean a sadistic mate forced Furuseth to work a long shift despite the young sailor's raging fever. Collapsing in his bunk after the ordeal, Furuseth lay delirious for hours, a knife clutched in one hand, vowing to kill the mate if he tried to force him to return to work. The shocked recognition that he had been reduced by maltreatment to the brink of murder raised Furuseth's awareness to a new level, driving him to further study, in whatever hours he could squeeze from his duties, of history, biography, social philosophy, and law. Jumping ship in 1883 in Tacoma, Washington, and thereby forfeiting his wages, Furuseth worked in the coastal trade, mainly lumber and fishing off Alaska, spending his shore leave in San Francisco in a boarding house for Scandinavian sailors on Steuart Street near the Embarcadero. In June 1885 Andrew Furuseth joined the Coast Seamen's Union.

Fifteen months later, the union went on strike over a passbook system enacted by shipowners. Each passbook was in effect a report card on attitude and performance, and no sailor was hired without a satisfactory report. The strike shattered the union so bravely begun less than two years earlier, and the rank and file offered the position of secretary, or salaried executive director, to Furuseth, who had reluctantly moved into the front ranks of the organization. Not until January 1887, when the incumbent secretary died, would Furuseth accept the position. Even then, he resigned it once in 1889 to go back to sea.

Like Frank Roney, Andrew Furuseth despised Burnette Haskell and the entire IWA crowd as irresponsible provocateurs. The laconic Norwegian especially resented Haskell's readiness to take to the platform and urge radical action, such as the general strike Haskell advocated in August 1886, which helped precipitate the disastrous strike of the following month. As secretary, Furuseth chafed under the organizational hold the Socialist International Advisory Committee had on the union, thanks to the acceptance of Haskell's constitution. Himself a meticulous bookkeeper, Furuseth suspected Haskell's honesty as union treasurer and especially resented Haskell's solicitation of money from union members for the Kaweah venture. Haskell also attempted to establish an IWA-oriented radical elite within the union, which he called the Legion of Honor.

In the tense aftermath of the Haymarket riot in Chicago, Haskell proposed that the Coast Seamen's Union enter a float in the Federated Trades Council parade set for 11 May 1886 in which sailors would be shown attacking a papier-mâché Bastille with real rifles and bayonets. Roney, who had invited Governor George Stoneman to join San Francisco's first Labor Day parade, threatened to banish the Coast Seamen altogether from the event, including the contingent of uniformed sailors scheduled to lead the parade as a guard of honor, unless Haskell withdrew his float. "Your orders shall be obeyed, my Lord," Haskell replied by note. Ten thousand union members marched that evening without incident, the governor himself reviewing the procession.

Haskell's incendiary proposal for a float convinced Andrew Furuseth that Haskell and the IWA posed a clear threat to the program of mainstream militancy which he and Frank Roney were urging on the trade union movement. Within three years, Furuseth had driven Haskell and the IWA out of the union and abolished the Advisory Committee entirely. Andrew Furuseth, by contrast, grew in stature and influence after the amalgamation of the Steamship Sailors Union and the Coast Seamen's Union into the Sailors Union of the Pacific on 29 July 1891. Furuseth led this important union until 1936. Living simply on wages indexed to those of a sailor before the mast, Furuseth seemed an almost priestly figure in his dark suit, his celibate lifestyle, his simple room filled with books, the highly intellectual approach he took to his work, the prudence and caution, verging on conservativism, with which he led his union from crisis to crisis. Within the decade, Andrew Fursureth, by then a national figure, played a key role in the passage in 1895 of an act introduced by California congressman James Maguire which freed coastal seamen from imprisonment for desertion if they left their ships. It took Furuseth another twenty years to secure at the national level the full emancipation of the American merchant sailor. Signed into law by Woodrow Wilson on 4 March 1915, the Seamen's Act introduced by Senator Robert La Follette of Wisconsin removed the last vestiges of enforced servitude from life before the mast.

With the establishment of the Federated Trades Council and twenty new unions, together with the ten-thousand-strong Labor Day parade held so triumphantly in early May, Governor Stoneman attending, the year 1886 would seem to represent an *annus mirabilis* for organized labor in San Francisco. Yet even amidst these triumphs, Frank Roney found himself having to contend with the yet unvanquished Burnette Haskell and his radical element. Returning to San Francisco on 5 August 1886 from union business in the East, Roney was forced to intervene when he learned that an element of striking carmen and conductors were planning to dynamite trolleys being operated by scab motormen. Four months later, a second streetcar strike broke out on two other lines, the Geary and Sutter Street railroads, with the carmen demanding better wages, a twelve-hour day, and adequate meal breaks. This time, dynamite was used, and a convicted striker was sent to prison.

Roney barely avoided an even greater disaster in the course of this bitter eighty-six-day strike, which failed completely. Determined to exploit the stalemate, Burnette Haskell and his IWA associates, with no sanction whatever from the Federated Trades Council, organized a protest rally and parade for Sunday noon, 19 December 1886, in front of the United States Mint at Fifth and Mission streets. On Saturday evening, San Francisco police chief Patrick Crowley sent his per-

sonal secretary to Roney's home to inform him that the rally Haskell was organizing had all the makings of an event intended to provoke a bloody clash with the
police, a Haymarket riot for San Francisco. (At the Chicago melee, more than a
dozen strikers and police had lost their lives and dozens more were seriously injured.) Knowing that Haskell was behind the rally, Roney agreed with the chief
of police. The next day, single-handedly, Roney addressed the dense and nervous
crowd gathered around the Mint. Chief Crowley, meanwhile, had deployed his
men at a strategic distance, armed with riot batons. Looking out at the carmen
and their supporters, Roney knew that the rally could easily escalate into something very violent and ugly.

This was not an authorized trade union demonstration, Roney told the crowd.
It could lead to nothing but violence and disgrace for the labor movement. "As
president of the Federated Trades Council," Roney later wrote, "I advised the
carmen to return to their headquarters and requested the assembled people to
disperse. Both requests were complied with and the threatened 'revolution' was
thus postponed."[9]

Yet how long could Roney, the moderate, the centrist, prevail? Every movement has a tendency to devour its leadership, and San Francisco labor proved no
exception. Not that the pendulum swung completely back in the direction of
Haskell and company. Far from it: the threatened riot of 19 December 1886
marked the beginning of the end for Haskell as a force in San Francisco labor.
Already, Andrew Furuseth was in the process of detaching Haskell from his power
base in the Coast Seamen's Union. Yet a Haskell disciple, Alfred Fuhrman, an
early member of the IWA, now emerged as a leader of the German workers of
the city, bakers and brewers especially. Albeit distanced from the anarchic tendencies of his mentor, the militant Fuhrman would soon taint Roney with charges of
being a sellout, and this charge would finish Roney's leadership of San Francisco
labor as swiftly as it had come into being.

A German-born sailor who had attended the University of Bonn, Alfred Fuhrman joined Haskell's IWA study group and later rose in the ranks of the Coast
Seamen's Union. Like Haskell, Fuhrman also qualified for the bar, becoming
increasingly active as an attorney after 1893. The two groups Fuhrman organized,
bakers and brewers, were the industrial serfs of San Francisco. Bakers worked
fourteen hours a day, seven days a week, and were required to live in cramped
dormitories in or near their work sites. Brewers worked similar hours for $15 a
week and were also housed in sub-standard quarters. In the process of organizing
the Brewers and Maltsters Union of the Pacific Coast, Fuhrman noticed how
many of San Francisco's brewery workers, predominantly German in origin, were
in a constant state of exhaustion, being on the job since four or five in the morning until early evening, their fatigue compounded by drunkenness since so many
of them drank beer during the day to keep up their strength. Within a few
months, Fuhrman organized about a quarter of the city's eight hundred brewery
workers. In May 1887 the Brewers' and Maltsters' Union successfully struck four

San Francisco breweries for a six-day week at $15 to $17 per week, together with the right to live outside brewery dormitories, mandatory arbitration for labor disputes, and—more controversial—a closed shop, the issue that would bring on the downfall of Frank Roney.

As a Socialist, Alfred Fuhrman believed that each brewery should possess a mandatory union, enforced by both employers and employees alike. Frank Roney pleaded with Fuhrman that Socialist industrialist models were incompatible with trade unionism as it was then developing in the United States. Unions should remain voluntary and seek contracts, not governance and mandatory memberships. The Socialist model, Roney argued, would eventually deprive unions of their voluntary nature and their independence from industry. Imprudently, Roney wrote a letter to this effect for the San Francisco newspapers, which was published on 14 May 1887 as the strike and boycotts were gaining momentum. Burnette Haskell (or so at least Roney later claimed) put out the rumor that Roney was secretly on the payroll of the brewers. The Federated Trades Council of San Francisco, which Roney had so successfully led such a short time ago, passed a resolution branding Roney a traitor to the labor cause. The Iron Moulders Union, which he had helped organize and for which he served as national vice-president, passed a similar resolution. Although he held on in San Francisco for another decade, before taking a job in 1898 as a moulder at the Navy Yard on Mare Island, Frank Roney lost his credibility as a spokesman for a labor movement increasingly committed to the closed shop.

Fortunately for the written record, University of California labor historian Ira Cross made contact with Roney in 1905. Then sixty-three, Roney was working at the Mare Island Foundry and living in rented rooms in Vallejo. Cross persuaded Roney to devote his spare hours to writing his memoirs. The longtime correspondent for *Truth* and the *Moulders Journal* worked on the manuscript with Cross's help until his death in 1925. Frank Roney concluded his long life in the labor movement with the creation of a classic of American labor literature. Published by the University of California Press in 1931 as *Frank B. Roney, Irish Rebel and California Labor Leader: An Autobiography*, this excellent memoir—factual, philosophical, straightforwardly eloquent across 550 and more pages—bespeaks an era of labor intellectualism: a time when workers led their own movements and did their own thinking from within their own ranks.

As late as December 1912, Frank Roney, then in his seventies, was tramping the streets of San Francisco, looking for one last job, one last period of independence, before moving in with his son. While his age was against him, Roney had returned to what had by then become the strongest union town in America. Significantly, Roney's vision of independent non-Socialist trade unionism, as opposed to the radical vision of Burnette Haskell, had prevailed in San Francisco.

Victory had not come easily. Labor lost ground in the depression-ridden 1890s. Organized in 1891, the San Francisco Board of Manufacturers and Employers controlled forty thousand jobs in the city. Despite the organization of a citywide

San Francisco Labor Council in December 1892, organized labor lost most of its strikes in the 1890s. What Roney and Furuseth most feared, radical violence, asserted itself in 1893 when a boarding house for non-union seamen was dynamited, killing eight. Twelve-hour days remained in force throughout the decade for teamsters, conductors, motormen, cooks, waiters, laundry workers, and salesclerks. Not until 1900 did the bakers of San Francisco secure a six-day week. Not until January 1901 did women laundry workers secure a ten-hour day.

In the summer and fall of 1901 came the turning point: a citywide strike led by a new Teamsters Union, organized in August 1900 under the leadership of Michael Casey. The crisis began in late spring. Cooks and waiters, carriage makers, bakers and bakery wagon drivers, the metal trades: a total of two thousand workers struck in May with mixed results, leaving labor in a bitter mood. In mid-July the Teamsters went out when union draymen were discharged for refusing to handle baggage for the Methodist Epworth League convention, which had contracted with a non-union drayage company to handle its arrangements. Because the Teamsters belonged to a City Front Federation organized the previous February among the waterfront unions, the longshoremen, warehousemen, and the Sailors Union of the Pacific joined the strike. By late August, two hundred ships stood idle in the bay in a shutdown estimated to be costing California a net loss of $1 million a day. Mayor James Duval Phelan was forced to hire two hundred special police to escort non-striking teamsters around the city. Five men died as a result of violent clashes, and more than 250 serious assaults were reported.

And yet, the firebrand who arose on this occasion to speak for the striking classes, the Irish-born Roman Catholic priest Peter Yorke, while capable of verbal vitriol—especially against Mayor Phelan, whom he considered a traitor to the Irish—preached not Marxist revolution or dynamite, but the rights of labor as set forth by Pope Leo XIII in his 1891 encyclical *Rerum Novarum*. In a city whose labor force was predominantly Irish Roman Catholic, Yorke's fiery speeches managed to convey a message that was at once militant in its resistance yet rooted in a fundamentally conservative philosophy of social justice based on religious value. Whatever else Father Yorke wanted, it was not violence and revolution. Yorke and the other leaders appealed, in fact, directly to Governor Henry Gage to intervene, which Gage did, much to Mayor Phelan's humiliation. The settlement which the governor negotiated in secret session on 20 October 1901 did not accord a complete or even a clear victory to the unions, but it did end the strike; and the strike itself, involving so many unions willing to act in concert, asserted the unambiguous arrival of San Francisco as an organized labor town.

In the aftermath of the General Strike of 1901, labor went on to form its own political organization, the Union Labor Party, which elected Eugene Schmitz, president of the musicians' union, mayor in November 1901. The Union Labor Party was short-lived. It produced only two mayors: Schmitz, who was removed from office in 1907 for corruption (although his conviction was overturned on appeal and he later returned to government as a city supervisor), and Patrick

Henry McCarthy, president of the Building Trades Council, who served as mayor from 1910 to 1912. After leaving office, McCarthy, an immigrant from County Limerick who had worked his way up through the Carpenters' Union, Local 22, returned to the active presidency of the powerful Building Trades Council. McCarthy also served on the Board of Directors of the Panama-Pacific International Exposition of 1915, a veritable Burke's Peerage of local ascendancy. Branching out into contracting and investments, the former mayor built a home in the Ashbury Heights section of the city; in its pageantry of gleaming redwood, its Craftsman fixtures, ballroom, and grand staircase, it remains one of the splendid architectural survivals of its era.

After McCarthy's departure from City Hall, San Francisco labor opted to follow Samuel Gompers's (and Frank Roney's) advice and avoid forming British-style labor parties based on a Marxist philosophy of irreconcilable class conflict. McCarthy's successor, James Rolph, a Republican, self-made in shipping and banking, maintained excellent relations with the unions throughout his five terms as mayor. Michael Casey, founder of the Teamsters who had spearheaded the 1901 strike, registered as a Republican. Another Republican, Edward L. Nolan of Bricklayers Local 7, served on the Board of Supervisors from 1912 to 1919. Remaining in office until 1935, Casey mistrusted strikes as solutions to labor problems, preferring instead an ongoing program of active negotiations with drayage companies and employers' associations.

Yet radicalism persisted. On 22 July 1916, in the course of a Preparedness Day parade on Market Street, a bomb exploded, killing ten and injuring scores of others. A new organization, the Industrial Workers of the World, arose to keep the radical cause alive and well in the Far West. California would never sever completely its dialogue with the radical Left. Left/Center and Left/Right conflict continued down through the 1910s and 1920s with renewed intensity as Californians continued to act out a representative drama of dialectical alternatives. By the time of the Great Depression, the stage would be set for a Left/Right battle of national importance.

2

Bulls and Wobblies

The IWW and the Criminal Syndicalism Act of 1919

O N 30 April 1919 Governor William Stephens signed into law the Criminal Syndicalism Act just passed by the state legislature. The act declared it a felony, punishable by one to fourteen years in prison, to advocate or in any other way to promulgate violence as a means of "accomplishing a change in industrial ownership or control or effecting any political changes." Merely to belong to an organization advocating such doctrines constituted the full felony. Passed at the height of a nationwide anti-Red hysteria, the loosely worded, shockingly inclusive California Criminal Syndicalism Act had been lobbied through the legislature by the Chambers of Commerce of Los Angeles and San Francisco and by such employers' organizations as the Better American Federation and the Merchants and Manufacturers Association of Los Angeles. The specific target of the Act was the Industrial Workers of the World (IWW), a radical organization increasingly active in California since 1910. By 1921 forty members of the IWW had been sent to San Quentin under the Criminal Syndicalism Act. None of these men could have been convicted under contemporary legal standards.

As in the case of the 1870s and 1880s in San Francisco, the 1910s and early 1920s witnessed the surfacing of extremes of left and right in California. Once again, California was reflecting the national experience. All across the country, Americans were beginning to count the cost in lives and taxes of their recent involvement in Europe. A mood of angry, paranoid reaction began to take hold as the full price of foreign involvement dawned on the national consciousness. A shattered President, confined to his bed by a stroke and a nervous breakdown, provided one emblem of destroyed illusions. A hunt for foreign agitators offered another. Between 1919 and 1920 Justice Department agents sent out by their politically ambitious boss, Attorney General A. Mitchell Palmer, who hoped to succeed Woodrow Wilson in the White House, rounded up nearly three thousand people on suspicion of conspiracy.

Yet the Left/Right battle between the IWW and the California oligarchy so empowered by the Criminal Syndicalism Act had its specifically regional context as well. No state pursued its radicals more remorselessly than did California during this period, and in few other states did the IWW experience such success in organizing symbolic protests among working people. Unlike the sandlot rallies of the 1870s, however, the theatricality of the conflict between the IWW and the California oligarchy escalated from symbolic protest to violence to the less-than-symbolic penalties attached to the Criminal Syndicalism Act of 1919. By the mid-1920s radical, indeed any form of left-leaning, sentiment had been driven to ground with a comprehensiveness that revealed the true depth of ultra-conservative sentiment in mainstream California. As a prologue to the ensuing drama of Depression conflict, both the resistance and the suppression of the IWW revealed the paranoid underside to public life in the Golden State, a Left/Right antagonism that would resurface with Manichean intensity in the 1930s.

The clash began, symbolically enough, in 1910 with a free speech protest in Fresno in the San Joaquin Valley that cut to the core of the ambiguous nature of the IWW itself: an organization that feared power even as it tried to seize it. Founded in Chicago in 1905, the IWW was a union that distrusted organization, even its own, and espoused a vaguely romantic, quasi-pacifist philosophy that approved of violence to attain its ends. Established by labor activists of whom many, such as Eugene Debs and Daniel De Leon, were avowed Socialists, the IWW avoided the rigors of Socialist doctrine and organization and the planned industrial utopia toward which Socialists were directing their efforts. In place of Marxist theory, most IWW members espoused a vague but compelling notion of permanent class conflict and an equally hazy program for the working class to seize the state and all means of production, by force if necessary, abolish the wage system, and conduct the economy on behalf of the workers. It was this open espousal of violence, occasionally acted upon, that gave the IWW its dreaded reputation.

From the perspective of organized labor, the IWW represented a union of sorts. Unionists such as William Haywood of the Western Federation of Miners and Eugene Debs of the American Railway Union played key roles in fashioning the organization. The IWW featured dues, membership cards, locals (four in California by 1909, at San Francisco, Los Angeles, Redlands, and Holtville in the Imperial Valley) and a national publication, the *Industrial Worker*. The IWW helped pioneer the affiliation of workers, skilled and unskilled alike, on an industry-wide basis. It took the lowest, most abused and rejected sub-*lumpen* proletariat—the hobo, the alcoholic, the bindle stiff—and conferred on such outcasts the beginnings of empowerment and the rudiments of organization. Its wide net gathered moral idealists, misfits, the disturbed, and the near criminal equally into the fold. Renouncing racial prejudice at the high tide of racist feeling in America, the

IWW was perhaps the first labor movement of any kind to seek organizational contact with working minorities.

On the other hand, the IWW Preamble excoriated labor unions for fostering the illusion that workers and employers had any common interests whatsoever which could bridge the chasm created by the ongoing class conflict. As a style and an attitude, the IWW nurtured a generalized proclivity toward revolt for its own sake and a suspicion of structured power that included its own leadership. Romantically perceived, the IWW was about being free on the open road, as in the lyrics of its favorite song:

> Hallelujah, I'm a bum
> Hallelujah, a bum again
> Hallelujah, give me a handout
> To revive me again.

More than a whiff of anarchism emanated from the movement, a sense of physical threat compounded by the refusal of the IWW to renounce violence and its frequent indulgence in revolutionary rhetoric.

The IWW loved to speechify, especially in outdoor settings where one of the persistent ambitions of the organization, the raising of class consciousness among the uninitiated, could be pursued in the style of Hyde Park. In the early years of the organization, before the IWW decided that the Constitution was a bourgeois document not worth strengthening, speechifying was frequently linked to the provocation of confrontations on the constitutional issue of free speech. Between 1907 and 1916 Wobblies, as the Los Angeles *Times* first dubbed them in print (taking up a sobriquet, according to IWW lore, most likely coined by a Chinese restaurant owner in Alberta unable to pronounce properly the Ws in *Workers of the World*), provoked thirty free speech confrontations. October 1909 to June 1910 was an especially active period, with confrontations in Missoula, Montana; New Castle, Pennsylvania; and Spokane, Washington, where the IWW was especially strong in the lumber industry. The Fresno confrontation, which lasted from April 1910 to March 1911, was the most extensive and dramatic. It also served as a prologue to more serious IWW agitations in San Diego in 1912 and Wheatland in Yuba County in 1913, which further revealed the inflammatory capacities of the Left and the Right in an increasingly polarized environment.

With a population of twenty-five thousand, Fresno had emerged by 1910 as the capital city of the San Joaquin Valley and the *de facto* capital city of Central California agriculture. With many of its oligarchy of Southern origin, Fresno was a conservative sort of place, controlled by ranchers and businessmen who by prior sectional identity knew what it was to lose everything and were resolved not to have it happen again. On the other hand, Fresno also supported Local 66, the most successful IWW local in California, organized by Frank Little, a one-eyed half-Indian hard-rock miner, nearly broken by a lifetime of hard labor and a

number of particularly savage beatings. In 1910, however, Frank Little was flush
from leading the recent free speech victory in Spokane and his success in establishing Local 66.

The entry of the IWW into agriculture via its Agricultural Workers Industrial
Union represented a risky, even foolhardy crusade. What, after all, was there to
build upon? When Berkeley economist Carleton Parker studied the agricultural
work force in California a few years later, he found it the very antithesis of a
stable, motivated body of workers awaiting organization. Seventy-three per cent of
Parker's 222 interviewees had recently worked someplace other than where they
were being interviewed. Sixty-seven percent planned to be off to a new work site
in the immediate future. Seventy-six percent had abandoned wives and children.
Eighty-six percent claimed no dependents whatsoever. Seventy-seven percent admitted to alcohol abuse, and twenty-six percent had served time in prison. Nearly
half the work force was minority, hence even further removed from the mainstream. According to a Stanford study which Parker cited, the agricultural work
force also showed a high rate of feeble-mindedness, a catch-all phrase in the early
1900s for a variety of inherited or acquired difficulties. No wonder, then, that
few, if any, agricultural unions emerged in the early decades of the century.
Those which did—the Fruit and Raisin Packing House Employees, for example,
organized in Fresno in 1901 and affiliated with the American Federation of Labor
(AFL)—tended to be found in the ancillary industries of packing and shipping
where a stable, invested community of men and women with dependents and
fixed abodes constituted the work force.

Yet the very recalcitrance of the agricultural work force, its sub-proletarian status, rendered it a special challenge to IWW organizers. Was not the IWW itself
based on the premise that the stones which the builders had rejected were to
become the cornerstones of the syndicalist future once the state, private property,
and the wage system were abolished? Here in the fields, IWW organizers found,
were the true victims of the system, the very dregs of the slag heap, next to whom
two other Wobbly-favored groups, miners and lumberjacks, seemed privileged
aristocrats.

Thus IWW Local 66, Fresno, grew under the stewardship of Frank Little, to the
growing consternation of Mayor Chester Rowell, Police Chief William Shaw, and
the publishers of the Fresno *Morning Republican* and the Fresno *Evening Herald
and Democrat*. By April 1910 the mood in Fresno was becoming increasingly intense. A confrontation of major proportions began to build. The police prevented a
Mexican Marxist from addressing a meeting of his countrymen. A contractor complained to Chief Shaw that the IWW had stopped work on a dam outside the city.
On 26 May 1910 an IWW organizer, Elmer Shean, was arrested for speaking in
Chinatown, and Chief Shaw revoked all permits for street meetings of any sort. Anyone without a job, the chief ordered, was to be arrested on charges of vagrancy. In
August Frank Little was arrested and sentenced to twenty-five days for disturbing the
peace. A month later, a man with an IWW membership card on his person was shot

while trying to hold up a train depot in northwestern Fresno County. On 14 October 1910 Little was rearrested, together with twelve other Wobblies, for holding an unauthorized meeting on the corner of T and Mariposa streets. The following day, seven more Wobblies were thrown in the slammer.

At the time of Little's first arrest in August, Local 66 contacted the IWW national headquarters in Chicago for assistance. In its issue for 10 September, the *Industrial Worker* urged the membership to flock to Fresno from around the country for yet another free speech confrontation. Successive issues kept up the campaign, and over the course of the following year hundreds of Wobblies began to ride the rails toward Fresno. One contingent from Seattle, ejected by railroad police from a Southern Pacific train in Ashland, Oregon, marched 244 miles across the snow-covered Siskiyou Mountains into Northern California only to learn at Chico that the Fresno free speech fight had been won and they were no longer needed.

Naturally, the arrival of so many IWW radicals into the Fresno area fed an already vivid paranoia. (In October the Los Angeles *Times* had been bombed, with twenty people killed and seventeen injured.) In early December, the Fresno city council passed an ordinance forbidding speeches or assemblies of any sort within city limits. By then, eighty arrested Wobblies had been crowded into the Fresno city jail. On the night of 9 December 1910 anti-IWW protestors gathered outside the jail and severely beat a number of Wobblies leaving the facility after visiting hours.

IWW resistance, meanwhile, proceeded on three fronts: rallies and demonstrations; adroit legal maneuvering; and a combination of active and passive resistance, which the IWW pioneered as a confrontation technique. When Frank Little was first imprisoned in August-September 1910, he refused to rake leaves in the courthouse park as part of his punishment. Thrown into solitary confinement, Little retaliated with a concert of IWW songs promoting revolution. When he came up for trial the second time, Little skillfully defended himself on the narrow legal grounds that Fresno had never passed an ordinance forbidding street speaking—which led to the release of Little and twenty-four Wobblies and the inclusive ordinance forbidding outdoor meetings of any sort. Loathing the law and the Constitution as bulwarks of the bourgeoisie, Wobblies were nevertheless skilled in a rough-and-ready sort of way in using the law and the Constitution to their own advantage. That, after all, was what the free speech confrontations were all about: the off-balancing of the establishment by provoking it into such unconstitutional behavior as the Fresno ordinance banning outdoor meetings. Goading Fresno and the other cities into anti-constitutional misbehavior, the IWW hoped to weaken the system by provoking it to behave grotesquely. Initially, Wobblies standing trial slowed down the system through a pioneering technique of individual challenges during jury selection. Later, as matters grew more desperate, a technique of passive resistance surfaced. Accused Wobblies refused to defend themselves in trial, sitting silently like Christ before Pontius Pilate as they were processed off to prison.

The Fresno eight, by contrast, decided upon a technique of active resistance called a battleship: a continuous cacophony of IWW songs, yelling, jeering, striking of cell floors and bars. On 23 December angry jail officials called in the fire department, who pounded the incarcerated Wobblies with a 150-pound pressure hose that left many prisoners black and blue from the assault. In February 1911 the prison count reached one hundred, even as hundreds more Wobblies arrived in the city from across the United States. The Fresno court system was reduced to a shambles in the effort to process dozens of cases of Wobblies charged with speaking on the streets in violation of the December ordinance. Local and state newspapers grew more shrill in their denunciation of the invasion. Serious violence, already prefigured in the beatings outside the jail in December, appeared increasingly unavoidable.

Then suddenly, resistance from the right collapsed. For eleven months, the city of Fresno had been racked by conflict—its prisons and courts jammed, its environs filling up with stubble-faced men from nowhere and everywhere, bedrolls slung diagonally across their shoulders, congregating on streets by day, their campfires ablaze by night on the outskirts of the city, their songs and harangues heard from within the jail or on the streets, their songfests and slogan-chants wafting across the silence after dark. It was enough. It was too much, in fact. Discreetly, a committee of Fresno leaders called upon the imprisoned Wobblies. What exactly would it take, the authorities asked, to end the impasse? Freedom, they were told, and free speech. On 2 March 1911 the city of Fresno rescinded its anti-street-speaking ordinance and, more important, began to empty its jail of Wobblies. "The Free Speech Fight is over, and won," Local 66 wired Chicago on 6 March 1911, " . . . Complete victory."[1]

What exactly had been won was not that clear. Upholding the rights of free speech, the IWW bolstered the Constitution, hence the established order. Once the battle was over, the Wobblies lost interest and drifted away. A mainstream labor organization would have used the victory to strengthen Local 66 through further organization of field workers. But agricultural casuals were as migratory as the Wobblies themselves. Fresno represented a victory of sorts, but it was primarily a one-act theatrical performance, with no resolution or follow-through. The IWW had shown its ability to demonstrate, to endure imprisonment and bring the criminal justice system to a halt; but of what relevance were such feats to such bread-and-butter issues as jobs, wages, working conditions, contracts, or the creation of enduring labor unions?

And besides: the next city chosen by the IWW for a free speech confrontation, San Diego, did not prove so beatable. What surfaced so briefly in Fresno, violent vigilante resistance from the right, emerged in full force in San Diego; and the pendulum swung in its favor.

The battlefields stood in dramatic contrast. Fresno, an agricultural town of the interior, dominated by a no-nonsense grower and packing elite of Southern origins, should have offered the more fierce resistance. San Diego, by contrast, was a seaside community in the southwestern sector of Ramona Land, a pre-industrial tourist mecca, population fifty thousand, peopled by educated Easterners and dominated by a booster elite in the process of planning an enchanted Spanish city atop Balboa Park for its 1915 exposition. Such a town, as much a resort as a port city, a sun-splashed Nice on the Mediterranean shores of America, should have collapsed instantaneously before the IWW onslaught. Yet San Diego, whose elite was dreaming of castles in Spain, escalated the conflict beyond anything attempted by Fresno, the hot, dusty, workaday Central Valley town virtually devoid of amenities. The more favored the urban circumstances in terms of the California Dream, the more paranoid and violent the reaction.

As in the case of Fresno, San Diego authorities passed an ordinance in December 1911 forbidding street meetings in the downtown, effective 8 February 1912. A Free Speech League formed in protest. The League included mainstream AFL trade unionists, Socialists, single-taxers, suffragettes, anarchists, atheists, religious groups, and the IWW, who immediately dominated the League despite the fact that there were only fifty Wobblies in the San Diego local. By March an estimated five thousand Wobblies had converged on San Diego, eager for a victory similar to those of Spokane and Fresno. At first, it seemed that such a victory could be pulled off. On the evening of 26 February, the Free Speech League organized a parade of protest two miles long, with five men on the average marching abreast, an impressive demonstration of force.

The San Diego oligarchy, however, had learned from Fresno's experience not to allow its jails and courts to be filled up with defiant Wobblies. Although there were many arrests—forty-one, in fact, on the first day the ordinance took effect, with some 150 in prison by the end of the following week—and a general rounding up of hoboes and vagrants, meaning incoming IWW demonstrators, San Diego based its defense on the sealing off of the city and a covert program of establishment-encouraged vigilantism designed to run the Wobblies out of town. Armed guards were sent out to patrol the San Diego County line, and vigilantes closely monitored the one railroad route into the city. A vigilante posse of four hundred men wearing constable badges and white armbands, many of them obviously drunk, and armed with rifles, pistols, and pickaxe handles, intercepted a train carrying nearly 150 Wobblies. Pulling them off the train, the vigilantes herded them into a nearby cattle corral for a nightmarish night of harassment and beatings. "In the morning," recalled one survivor of the ordeal, "they took us out four or five at a time and marched us up the track to the county line . . . where we were forced to kiss the flag and then run a gauntlet of 106 men, every one of which was striking at us hard as they could with their pick-axe handles. They broke one man's leg, and everyone was beaten black and blue, and was bleeding from a dozen wounds."[2]

The vigilantes manning the gauntlet had behind them the solid support of a community raised to a pitch of paranoid hysteria. "Hanging is none too good for them," editorialized the San Diego *Tribune* regarding the IWW on 4 March 1912, "and they would be much better dead; for they are absolutely useless in the human economy; they are the waste matter of creation and should be drained off into the sewer of oblivion, there to rot in cold obstruction like any other ex-crement."

Not surprisingly, given such rhetoric, violence escalated. On 10 March a crowd of five thousand, protesting outside the city jail, was dispersed with high-pressure fire hoses. There was something Tsarist about it all, as if a scene from *Potemkin* were being played out in Southern California. To secure the Eisenstein compari-son, a mother with babe in arms was felled by a high-pressure hose, and another protestor faced the hydraulic assault wrapped in an American flag. A few days later, a sixty-five-year-old detainee by the name of Michael Hoy died as the result of a prison beating. A coroner's jury claimed that Hoy died from tuberculosis and heart failure.

Coverage of this small-scale civil war in the state and national press induced Governor Hiram Johnson to send Sacramento department store owner and Pro-gressive Party activist Harris Weinstock to San Diego to investigate. Weinstock held hearings from 18 to 20 April in the San Diego Court House. The very presence of the special commissioner tended to embarrass the city into a period of quiet, although realtor J. M. Porter, a major force in the vigilante movement, told an AFL investigative committee: "We are fighting for our homes. We don't care about Weinstock or Governor Johnson. Only troops can stop us." Police Chief J. Ken Wilson said of the IWW: "These people do not belong to any coun-try, no flag, no laws, no Supreme Being. I do not know what to do. I cannot punish them. Listen to them singing. They are singing all the time, and yelling and hollering, and telling the jailers to quit work and join the union. They are worse than animals."[3]

On 4 May 1912 two of Chief Wilson's officers shot and killed an IWW mem-ber, Joe Mikolash, a Hungarian immigrant, in front of IWW headquarters. The police claimed that Mikolash had attacked them with an axe. Before he died on 7 May, Mikolash claimed that he used the axe in self-defense after being gratu-itously shot in the leg by one of the officers. The city refused permission for a public funeral, which was held in Los Angeles.

At the height of the tension renewed by Mikolash's death, Emma Goldman, the Russian-born high priestess of anarchy, and her lover Ben Reitman arrived in San Diego on a lecture tour of the West Coast, and kerosene was poured on the already rekindled bonfire. No dramatist could have imagined a more inflamma-tory scenario. Arriving by train to lecture on Henrik Ibsen's *An Enemy of the People*, Goldman was already the leading spokesperson in the United States for anarchy, revolution, free love, and a half dozen other controversial causes. Gold-man had been briefly imprisoned in 1893 for inciting to riot and would twice more go to jail, in 1916 for publicly advocating birth control and in 1917 for speaking against the draft. Even in the most peaceful of times, this Lithuanian

Jewish radical from New York, a close colleague on the anarchist magazine *Mother Earth* of Alexander Berkman (who had served fourteen years in Sing Sing for trying to assassinate industrialist Henry Clay Frick), a divorced woman traveling with her lover, might not have had an easy time of it in the Anglo-Right provincial city. Given the mood of San Diego in May 1912, Goldman was fortunate to escape the city unharmed. Her lover Ben Reitman was not so lucky.

As her train pulled into San Diego, Goldman noticed an unusually large crowd. She thought that it had gathered to greet an arriving dignitary. When a group of screaming women tried to pull her off the hotel autobus, she learned differently. Only the quick response of the chauffeur, who pulled away at full speed, prevented Goldman and Reitman from falling into the hands of an angry welcoming committee. Later, a vigilante crowd formed outside the U. S. Grant Hotel, where the couple had taken separate rooms. Goldman was asked to meet Mayor James Wadham, Chief of Police J. Ken Wilson, and several other city officials in a downstairs meeting room. From the street, Goldman later remembered, came a bedlam of yells, whistles, and honking auto horns.

"You hear that mob," Goldman quoted Mayor Wadham as saying, pointing to the street. "They mean business. They want to get you and Reitman out of the hotel, even if they have to take you by force. We cannot guarantee anything. If you consent to leave, we will give you protection and get you safely out of town."

Goldman refused, asking instead to be allowed to address the crowd from an open window. Not surprisingly, the mayor refused permission. Returning upstairs, Goldman found Reitman's room empty. Terrified, she ran back to the downstairs meeting room and confronted Chief Wilson.

"Where is Reitman?" she demanded. "What have you done with him? If any harm comes to him, you will pay for it if I have to do it with my own hands."

"How should I know?" replied the chief.

Some time after midnight, the hotel detective called on Goldman with the news that Ben Reitman was safe. The vigilantes had put him on the train to Los Angeles. Goldman allowed herself to be persuaded to take the 2:45 A.M. Owl train to Los Angeles as well. A motorcade of vigilantes caught up with her at the station. As she cowered in her locked Pullman compartment, Goldman could hear shouting men rushing up and down the platform, trying to board the train. Only the crew's resistance and the train's departure prevented them from coming aboard and apprehending her, Goldman later wrote.

The next day in Los Angeles, she spent hellish hours with no word of Reitman's whereabouts. At approximately ten in the morning, she received a telephone message that Reitman would be arriving on the afternoon train from San Diego. When the train arrived at the Los Angeles station, Goldman found Reitman huddled in a rear compartment. He was wearing a pair of denim overalls. His hair was sticky with tar, and a look of terror was on his blood-drained face. Back at her apartment, Goldman helped the stricken man undress. His body, she later reported, was black and blue with bruises and covered with blotches of tar. Waking from an exhausted sleep, Reitman told his story to Goldman, some friends, and a group of Los Angles reporters.

When Goldman left the hotel office to meet with the city officials, Reitman related, he remained in the room with several men.

> As soon as the door was closed, they drew out revolvers. "If you utter a sound or make a move, we'll kill you," they threatened. Then they gathered around me. One man grabbed my right arm, another the left; a third took hold of the front of my coat, another of the back, and I was led out into the corridor, down the elevator to the ground floor of the hotel, and out into the street past a uniformed policeman, and then thrown into an automobile. When the mob saw me, they set up a howl. The auto went slowly down the main street and was joined by another one containing several persons who looked like business men. This was about half past ten in the evening. The twenty-mile ride was frightful. As soon as we got out of town, they began kicking and beating me. They took turns at pulling my long hair and they stuck their fingers into my eyes and nose. "We could tear your guts out," they said, "but we promised the Chief of Police not to kill you. We are responsible men, property-owners, and the police are on our side." When we reached the county line, the auto stopped at a deserted spot. The men formed a ring and told me to undress. They tore my clothes off. They knocked me down, and when I lay naked on the ground, they kicked and beat me until I was almost insensible. With a lighted cigar they burned the letters I.W.W. on my buttocks; then they poured a can of tar over my head and, in the absence of feathers, rubbed sage-brush on my body. One of them attempted to push a cane into my rectum. Another twisted my testicles. They forced me to kiss the flag and sing *The Star Spangled Banner*. When they tired of the fun, they gave me my underwear for fear we should meet any women. They also gave me back my vest, in order that I might carry my money, railroad ticket, and watch. The rest of my clothes they kept. I was ordered to make a speech, and then they commanded me to run the gauntlet. The Vigilantes lined up, and as I ran past them, each one gave me a blow or a kick. Then they let me go.[4]

Reitman's report of his ordeal, which seemed corroborated by his physical condition, received screaming headlines across the country. In San Francisco Mrs. Fremont Older, wife of the editor of the San Francisco *Call* and a well-known Northern California writer in her own right, told a packed rally of protest: "When the vigilantes of San Diego burned IWW into the back of a man, they burned IWW into the hearts and souls and blood of every worker in the United States."[5]

San Diego, the oligarchy realized, had pushed it too far. The IWW was bad for business, bad for the image of San Diego, harmful of its forthcoming world's fair; but equally disedifying were the howling mobs of lower-middle-class vigilantes, who were progressively earning the condemnation of even moderates and conservatives because of their violent behavior. In encouraging vigilantism, the San Diego establishment had unleashed a force which it now began itself to fear. Vigilante leader J. M. Porter soon found himself cited for contempt of court as the judiciary and criminal justice system began to take note of vigilante excesses as well as the illegal public speaking of the Free Speech League. After the Reitman affair, the San Diego vigilantes, having lost much of their support from the oligarchy, discontinued their activities, while the oligarchy began to put most of its efforts into getting the federal government to intervene. Conservative Republicans from Southern California approached President William Howard Taft, suggesting that a vigorous investigation and prosecution of the IWW in San Diego by the Justice Department would help Taft carry California in the forthcoming presidential election over Woodrow Wilson, the Democratic nominee, and former president Theodore Roosevelt and Governor Hiram Johnson of California, the Progressive candidates. Persuaded, Taft urged Attorney General George Wickersham to launch an investigation into IWW activities in San Diego that would show Californians "that we are on the job."[6] Wickersham refused to be stampeded into a full-blown prosecution, however, and the entire matter became a moot point after Taft's defeat in November.

The San Diego free speech fight, like that in Fresno, trailed off into inconclusiveness. A smallpox epidemic hit the San Diego city jail, and many of the most adamant IWW protestors, fearing the disease more than the dishonor of capitulation, rushed to plead guilty and secure release on suspended sentences. A few others received brief sentences. IWW activist Jack Whyte, an intellectual force in the movement (Whyte was later assassinated in Nevada), made a memorable speech upon the occasion of his sentencing, which became part of IWW folklore; but as in the case of Fresno, it would be difficult to cite any long-term gains from the struggle beyond the constitutional questions raised.

Perceived as social dramaturgy, however, the San Diego free speech battle revealed the depth of reaction possible in the threatened middle and lower-middle classes of California. The oligarchy, which is to say, the upper-middle and upper classes, loathed and feared the IWW; but oligarchs did not take to the streets as vigilantes. They did, however, encourage the lower-middle classes to do such work. As San Diego showed, California possessed the makings of a violent antileft reaction because there were so many newly arrived lower-middle-class people in the State who were uncertain and insecure in what they had gained or thought they had gained by coming to California. They too were seeking to beat the system—the shopkeepers, the small-scale realtors, the upper-level clerks and first-level supervisors, the ranchers and farmers in the first generation of mortgaged ownership. Because they had climbed up the social ladder by coming to California or, of equal importance, because California had helped them decelerate their social descent, they could very easily take to the streets as populist vigilantes in defense of threatened values and social structures to which they themselves were only ambiguously assimilated.

The very next year, on 13 August 1913, a deadly riot in the hop fields of Wheatland in southern Yuba County in the Sacramento Valley brought the IWW once again to the forefront of public attention. In every detail, moreover—its suddenness, the spontaneity of its organization, its escalation into violent confron-

tation, its provocation of popular hysteria, followed by kangaroo trials and a coun-
tervailing series of public investigations—the Wheatland clash stands as a prototype of the agricultural strife of the 1930s. "The riot on the Durst Ranch,"
observed University of California professor Carleton H. Parker in his official report
to the State Commission of Immigration and Housing, "is a California contribution to the literature of social unrest in America."[7] It also played a crucial role in
provoking sentiment for the Criminal Syndicalism Act of 1919.

By 1913 Yuba County hop grower Ralph Durst had become the single largest
employer of agricultural labor in California. The problem was, Durst required his
gigantic work force only during the brutally hot month of August. The rest of the
year, a small cadre of skilled and semi-skilled vineyard attendants was sufficient to
tend to the forthcoming crop. Neither as a matter of moral obligation or enlight-
ened self-interest did Durst feel any responsibility to see to the welfare of his
workers in the brief weeks they were on his ranch. They were, in fact, just another
natural resource to be exploited.

In the early summer of 1913 Durst had circulars distributed throughout California, southern Oregon, and northwestern Nevada advertising harvest work on his
Wheatland ranch. Durst promised "the going price for clean picking" and "a BO-
NUS to all pickers helping us and doing satisfactory work, to the completion of the
season—a period of three or four weeks."[8] By late July some twenty-eight hundred
men, women, and children had flooded onto the Durst Ranch in search of work.
Sociologically, they constituted a representative sample of the underprivileged sectors of California's work force. Between a third and a half were immigrant Syrians,
Mexicans, Italians, Hindus, Japanese, and Puerto Ricans, many of them speaking
no English. The American-born element ran the gamut from hoboes and bindle
stiffs, to small ranchers from the Sierra foothills looking for some extra cash, to
city workers and their families for whom a month in the hop fields constituted
their only affordable form of vacation. Significantly, between eight hundred and
a thousand of the work force were women and children; and the lack of provisions
for families—no separate toilets for women, no water for children working in the
fields since the break of day—conferred a special volatility on the situation.

Ralph Durst had attracted in excess of a thousand more workers than he actually needed, which suited him fine, for he could thus keep wages well below the
$3 to $5 a day hop pickers were earning on other ranches. Durst promised a
competitive rate, $1 for every hundred pounds of hops picked; but he trained his
checkers to compute payment on as narrow a margin as possible. Hop pickers at
the Durst Ranch averaged only $1.50 a day. Durst also retained ten cents on the
dollar to be paid out as a spurious bonus at the end of the season to workers who
had caused no trouble. Discharged workers—and there were plenty—forfeited
their withheld wages. Forbidding water trucks in the fields, where temperatures
frequently soared to 120 degrees, Durst gave a cousin a monopoly on lemonade,
which he sold from a wagon, five cents a glass, along with an unpalatable stew.
The cousin made the lemonade with citric acid to save money on real lemons,

and the stew was comparably cost-effective. Durst also banned delivery wagons from Wheatland grocers and butchers. Workers could only buy their provisions from a ranch store in which Durst secretly held a half interest.

Living conditions on the Durst Ranch were hellish. Well over two thousand men, women, and children were forced to camp indiscriminately on a treeless, unimproved hillside. Only a few had brought their own tents. Others rented tents from Durst for seventy-five cents a week, which was nearly a day's wages. In an effort at privacy, many families erected open-air enclosures of burlap sacks fastened to fences or hop stakes. (As if to emphasize the sub-human aspects of such dwellings, they were referred to as bull-pens.) Others slept blanket-less on straw pilings, men, women, children on the ground indiscriminately, with the women finding themselves especially vulnerable to sexual harassment. Since Durst had provided no garbage cans or common trash receptacles of any sort, garbage piled up throughout the encampment. Choked with garbage, two well sump-holes filled the area with stench, polluted the well water, and became the breeding ground for swarms of blue flies.

The most distress, personal and environmental, was caused by the lack of toilets. Reports vary, but there were no more than eleven, nor fewer than eight, toilet sheds for the entire work force. These consisted of two-seated stalls carelessly placed over shallow latrines. No distinctions were made for the sexes, and women, many of them with their children, were forced to wait their turn in long lines interspersed with strange men, a humiliating ordeal. Within a few days, the toilets had backed up, and human feces seeped from the shallow trenches, further polluting the environment with flies and unbearable stench. In desperation people began to use nearby irrigation ditches as latrines, and these as well became sources of stench, flies, and pollution. Durst also refused to provide portable toilets for the hop fields. Men, women, and children were forced to relieve themselves in the vineyard, finding what privacy they could amidst the hop vines. Thus the vineyards themselves, used by so many as latrines, became unpleasant and unhealthy environments. By early August the workers' encampment had become a hellhole of heat, garbage, feces, stench, flies, contaminated water, dysentery, and typhoid.

In such a situation, it did not require IWW activists, of whom there were some thirty on the Durst Ranch, to initiate a protest, although many of the IWW members, fresh from their free speech victories, had come to the Durst Ranch expressly to provoke a confrontation and played key roles in organizing the diffused anger of the exploited hop pickers. Conspicuous among the protest leadership was Richard "Blackie" Ford, a former IWW member with a gift for oratory. On the evening of Saturday, 12 August 1913, Ralph Durst agreed to meet the next morning with a delegation of workers headed by Ford. At the meeting Durst agreed to try to improve living conditions but made no concessions regarding wages. When the hop pickers' committee returned an hour later for a second confrontation, Durst struck Ford across the face with his glove and ordered him off the property. When a constable later arrived from Wheatland to enforce Durst's order, Ford demanded to see a warrant, which the deputy did not have. Pushed and jeered at by the crowd, the deputy drew his revolver. An Italian worker stepped between the deputy and a nearby girl and dramatically hollered: "Don't shoot a girl—shoot me!"[9] His pistol drawn, the deputy backed away from the angry crowd.

For the rest of the afternoon, the IWW activists went to work. A surviving photograph of the Durst Ranch, most likely taken by photographer C. C. Green on the afternoon of the 13th, depicts hop pickers gathered in groups before speakers on platforms. The photograph may very well depict the first farm labor strike in American history, for nothing less than a full-scale walkout was being urged by the IWW orators throughout the long hot Sunday afternoon, with speeches being given in seven different languages. At one point in his presentation, Blackie Ford held up a sickly child in his arms before a crowd of fifteen hundred. "It's for the life of the kids we're doing this!" Ford exclaimed.[10] Like the Italian's ploy earlier that morning, placing himself between the deputy with his drawn revolver and the little girl, Ford's gesture electrified his audience.

Ralph Durst, meanwhile, had telephoned the law in Wheatland. At approximately five-thirty that afternoon, as the migrants were singing Joe Hill's rollicking IWW song "Mr. Block," which mocks non-union labor, two cars, one of them belonging to Durst, drove onto the ranch and approached the crowd. In the open touring cars were Edward Manwell, district attorney of Yuba County, Sheriff George Voss, and a posse of sheriff's deputies (many appearing to be under the influence of alcohol) intent on arresting Blackie Ford. As the DA, the sheriff, and some of his deputies approached the platform where Ford was standing, the crowd closed in on them to block their way. A bench upon which some workers were standing collapsed, startling the crowd. Scuffling ensued, which led to fistfights. Someone began swinging a two-by-four as a club. A deputy on the fringe of the crowd fired a double-barrelled shotgun over the heads of the scufflers, intending, he later testified, to sober the crowd into cooperation. Instead, more gunfire broke out, some twenty shots in all, this time from within the melee. The deputies fought their way back to their automobiles and sped off. Separated from the group, another deputy ran to the grocery store, where he barricaded himself against his pursuers. As the crowd dispersed, five prostrate forms were revealed on the ground: Sheriff Voss, clubbed into unconsciousness but still alive, and the dead bodies of District Attorney Manwell, Sheriff's Deputy Eugene Riordan, and two unidentified workers, a young Englishman and a Puerto Rican.

Traumatized by what had happened, the workers and the IWW activists fled the Durst Ranch in all directions. Jack London encountered a group of them on the road and later observed that they seemed like panic-stricken refugees from a war or an earthquake. (The state militia, indeed, marched in the next morning to assume control of the property.) By abandoning the Durst Ranch, the workers left the impression that the deaths had been their responsibility, especially that of the

IWW agitators: an impression fanned into hysteria in the weeks that followed as sheriff's deputies and Burns detectives retained by the State of California fanned out through the migrant communities of the Pacific Coast, looking for IWW suspects. The manhunt proceeded without benefit of legal niceties. Burns men held certain suspects incommunicado for weeks at undisclosed jails, where they beat or otherwise mistreated them in an effort to secure confessions. One detective was so egregious in his beatings of a young Swedish man, Alfred Nelson, who was dragged through six separate jails before being released, that the detective was charged by his erstwhile employers, tried, convicted, and sentenced to a year in prison. Another detainee, Neils Nelson, was found dead from hanging in his cell in the Yuba County jail under very suspicious circumstances, there being no place high enough for Nelson to have committed his alleged suicide. IWW activist and prime suspect Herman Suhr was moved from jail to jail to keep him from defense attorneys: from Prescott, Arizona, where he was arrested, to Los Angeles, to Fresno, to San Francisco, to Oakland, where Suhr was kept awake for four days in a small cell by three shifts of Burns detectives until he signed a confession, which he repudiated after he awoke from two hours of exhausted sleep. It was weeks before attorney Austin Lewis, an eminent Socialist retained by a defense committee based in San Francisco, found out where his client Blackie Ford was being held.

Ford, Suhr, and two other men, Walter Bagen and William Beck, were indicted and brought to trial in Marysville in late January 1914. The prosecuting attorney, Ray Manwell, son of the murdered DA, eventually succeeded his father in office. The presiding judge, E. C. McDaniels, a lifelong friend of the murdered district attorney, ruled consistently on behalf of the prosecution. Assisted by a national IWW network which materialized a number of defense witnesses who had fled after the riot, attorney Austin Lewis provided a brilliant defense. Ford and Suhr had argued against violence. No witnesses had come forward to link either man to violent acts.

Yet the IWW chose to use the trial as yet another occasion for symbolic protest, despite the dangers such a protest posed to the Wobblies facing trial. Some sixty Wobblies rented a large house in Marysville with funds provided by the Wheatland Hop Pickers' Defense League and crowded the courtroom each day. Inflammatory statements got into the press, which compounded the hysteria with sensational reports and denunciatory editorials, and very soon it was not the Wheatland Four who were on trial, but the IWW. That Blackie Ford had been expelled from the IWW and that Herman Suhr, who suffered a slight retardation, was not an authorized organizer added some irony to the situation. In a pinch, the vaguest IWW connection would suffice. In such a confrontational atmosphere, it was surprising that the jury acquitted Bagen and Beck on the 31st of January. Ford and Suhr were found guilty of second degree murder on the dubious grounds that they had played major roles in organizing a strike committee which had created a confrontation in which two public officials had met violent deaths. (The deaths of the two hop pickers seem to have receded into secondary status.) On 5 February Judge McDaniels sentenced Ford and Suhr to life in prison.

From a number of perspectives, the Wheatland incident prefigured in content and significance the troubled patterns of agricultural labor in the fields of California during the 1930s. First of all, there was the sudden spontaneity of the strike, which a small cadre of skilled organizers proceeded to direct and focus. The prologue to a drama that would play through the 1960s, Wheatland offered proof, perhaps the first in American history, that the lowest level of the American work force, migrant agricultural labor, so much of it increasingly comprised of women, children, and non–English-speaking minorities, could sustain the self-awareness and solidarity necessary for organized protest. "Give us freedom," proclaimed a Wheatland strike poster in Spanish. "We are men. Not slaves."[11] For a brief, anticipative moment, the dispossessed had found their voice.

As in the case of the 1930s, a fierce conflict of ideologies, left and right, structured this emergence. On the left, the IWW exploited the Durst Ranch situation, which screamed to heaven for redress; but, as usual, the Wobblies did not see the matter through by staying on to organize a response to the crisis after the riot had occurred. If anything, the IWW organizers fled the ranch even more quickly than the hop pickers. Nor did the rhetoric of the IWW, together with its presence in Marysville during the trial, do anything but further harm the defendants. After the sentencing of Ford and Suhr, the IWW went into even higher gear with its threats and protests, which doomed efforts to secure the release of Ford and Suhr through a judicial reversal by the Court of Appeals. When the Court of Appeal failed to intervene, the IWW mounted an effort to secure a pardon for Ford and Suhr from Governor Hiram Johnson, a Progressive, and was joined in this effort by many prominent Californians. The ideological onslaught of the IWW, however, together with a series of specific threats—a general strike of harvest workers, a boycott of California products, talk of revolutionary struggle—backed Johnson to the wall.

The Right, on the other hand, had also done its work. Even before the murders, Ralph Durst had been conspiring with Yuba County law enforcement officials to deny what little rights of free speech and assembly the hop pickers possessed. By contemporary standards of civil rights, the very raid the sheriff and the district attorney tried to pull off against the striking workers was patently illegal; nor could the trial itself, much less the pre-trial activities of the Burns detectives, stand up to contemporary legal scrutiny. As would so often be the case during the 1930s, the courts and criminal justice system acted in collusion with the local oligarchy to prosecute dissent.

In 1925, tired of being whipsawed between right and left, Blackie Ford broke the IWW code and applied for parole from Folsom Prison, which was granted on 11 September 1925. Even then, after twelve years' imprisonment, Yuba County was not satisfied. Taken into custody as he walked through the prison gate, Ford stood trial once more, this time for the death of Deputy Sheriff Eugene Riordan, in the same Marysville courtroom in which he had been tried for the death of District Attorney Manwell, prosecuted once again by the murdered DA's son and successor. The jury of 1925, however, was not as intimidated as the jury of 1914, and Blackie Ford won the acquittal that should have been his in the first place. Herman Suhr left Folsom Prison on parole the following year.

By that time, the migrant workers of California enjoyed the services and protection of a Commission of Immigration and Housing. Here again is another pre-Depression prophetic pattern discernible in Wheatland: the effort of social reformers to bring government to the relief of migrant labor, an effort that would characterize the brilliant, compassionate work of such activists as Tom Collins, Irving Wood, Paul Taylor, Dorothea Lange, and others during the 1930s. In the spring of 1914 the California legislature, dominated by Progressives, established a State Commission of Immigration and Housing, charging it with the enforcement of the Labor Camp Sanitation Act of 1913, passed in response to the Wheatland tragedy. Seven inspectors were sent into the field. Two years later, the legislature broadened the powers of the Commission and expanded its budget. The thirty-five-year-old executive director of the Commission, Carleton H. Parker, a University of California labor economist who had taken his doctorate *summa cum laude* from Heidelberg, brought a formidable combination of academic training and field research to his task. In his determination to see for himself working conditions in the field as well as gather statistics, Parker was following in the footsteps of Princeton economist Walter Augustus Wyckoff, who had spent two years in the field as an agricultural and factory worker before writing his monumental two-volume study *The Workers—The West* and *The Workers—The East*, each of them subtitled *An Experiment in Reality*, published in 1900.

Parker's first assignment was to evaluate the Wheatland riot and to report his findings to the State Commission of Immigration and Housing as well as to the United States Commission on Industrial Relations, which was to hold hearings in San Francisco in August 1914 on California migrant labor generally and the Wheatland episode in particular. Parker's report, posthumously published in *The Casual Laborer and Other Essays* (1920) after the brilliant young economist succumbed to pneumonia and heart failure at age thirty-nine, presented the Wheatland riot as a representative enactment, compact and violently expressive, of everything that was wrong with agricultural labor in California: its cynicism born of fleeting seasonal relationships; its utter lack of regard for human resources, especially in the matter of sanitation and housing; the linkages between growers and the local legal system, leading to the *de facto* disenfranchisement, enslavement even, of agricultural workers too powerless to protest the theft of their civil liberties and too poor to move on. Wheatland, Parker argued, was the one event, the prism, through which California might glimpse the underlying injustice, the squalid horror, of its agricultural economy.

The system, Parker argued, debased ranchers and migrants alike. However kind, benevolent, or generous in his day-to-day attitudes, the California rancher put his virtues aside when it came time to employ large numbers of workers, including women and children, for a brief period. Needing workers as quickly and as cheaply as possible, the rancher wanted to be rid of them just as rapidly. There was no time for the development of an employer-employee relationship, much less the creation of a good living environment. "You can't analyze the Wheatland affair," Parker testified before the United States Commission on Industrial Relations, "and the riot that took place; you can not analyze the strike that has been in process for the last two months in the hop fields, nor can you touch the problem of the unemployed in San Francisco last winter without bringing into the analysis the seasonal character of California's demand for its labor." [12]

Parker's reference to San Francisco referred to a survey made in December 1913 which showed that some forty thousand men, seasonally out of work from lumber camps, construction projects, or ranches, were holing up in the cheap hotels and rooming houses of that city over the winter. A $30 stake was enough to see them through to the spring. In one month alone, December, the Christmas season of 1913, thirty out-of-work men committed suicide in their dingy hotel rooms. Only two bothered to leave behind any notes saying goodbye to relatives or loved ones. Seasonal labor left men physically broken, frequently alcoholic, desperately lonely. Delicately, Parker approached a *verboten* subject, homosexual activity. There was evidence, he reported, that it flourished among young male casual workers, most noticeably in the lumber camps. "Often," Parker reported, "the men sent out from the employment agencies are without blankets or even sufficient clothing, and they are forced to sleep packed together for the sake of warmth. Investigations are beginning to show that there are social dangers which a group of demoralized, women-less men may engender under such conditions of greater menace than the stereotyped ill effects of insanitation and malnutrition." [13]

When men did carry their own blankets along, moreover, slung diagonally across their shoulder, people perceived these bedrolls as badges of shame. Migrants were not workers to be treated with dignity, but hoboes, blanket stiffs, to be shunned by mainstream society. Not surprisingly, the Commission eventually demanded that ranchers provide blankets and bedding as well as bunkhouses, thus putting an end, officially at least, to the era of the blanket stiff.

All too frequently, Parker admitted, casual workers earned their reputation for shiftlessness. When they had earned a stake sufficient to carry them for a few weeks, they tended to leave the job, the single men at least, thereby forcing employers to keep a steady stream of casuals in their supply pipeline. "A big dried fruit packing firm in Fresno," Parker observed, "reported that to keep up a skilled crew of 93 men, 41 per week had to be hired throughout the season. A large ranch with a fruit season of nine weeks reported a monthly turnover of 245 percent. One power house construction job in the Sierras gave figures showing that to maintain a force of 950, over 1,500 men a month were shipped to them."[14]

As executive director of the Commission of Immigration and Housing, Carleton Parker believed that housing reform offered the most effective approach to improving social conditions in agricultural labor. The filthy migrant camps of California best expressed and perpetuated the debasement inherent to the system. Of 876 camps examined in 1914, for example, housing more than sixty thousand men, 114 had no toilets whatsoever, 364 had filthy facilities, and 179 had toilets that were seriously sub-standard. More than three hundred camps had no window screening on kitchen or dining facilities, which were frequently sited near befouled, fly-ridden toilets or near stables with their adjacent manure piles. Workers ate with one hand, cited one investigator, while brushing away flies with the other. Hindu and Japanese workers were especially repelled by these conditions and insisted on cooking and eating as far from the camps as possible.

Armed with multiple copies of an *Advisory Pamphlet on Camp Sanitation and Housing*, Parker's agents worked with cooperative ranchers in an effort to improve their facilities. The pamphlet called for proper toilets; clean kitchens and dining halls; the siting of kitchen, dining, and bunkhouse facilities away from stables or latrines; the protection of water wells; shower bath houses; screen doors; five hundred cubic feet of air per person in bunkhouses; a systematic program of garbage and waste removal, including incinerators. From the perspective of the hellhole at Durst Ranch, the Commission seemed to be calling for utopia; but Parker and his colleagues believed that if dignity were restored to the migrant living environment, then other problems—illiteracy, alcoholism, malnutrition, the neglect of children, the shaming and harassment of women, the dysfunctional sexual culture—might be more effectively addressed. And besides: during the First World War, when the respectable middle classes took to the fields in the national emergency, the Progressive dream of agrarian dignity for harvest workers came ever so briefly to be realized.

During the war, two organizations, the Woman's Land Army of America and the Boys' Working Reserve, brought thousands of middle-class harvesters into the fields of California with a level of regulation and support that underscored the class- and race-based exploitation of normal times. Under the jurisdiction of R. L. Adams, state farm labor agent, camps for young women eager to help the war effort as harvesters were established in some nineteen counties north of the Tehachapi Mountains which had developed labor shortages. Ranging in capacity from ten to one hundred young women (the majority of them from cities and towns), the camps constructed for the Woman's Land Army featured tent cabins with boarded floors and sides, shower baths, screened dining halls, and other amenities. Like sorority girls, the young women lived under the supervision of house mothers. One such worker, Susan Minor, described her experiences in a camp fifteen miles south of Chico for the *Overland Monthly*. Each morning at seven, Sundays excepted, the women—smartly attired in boots, trousers, blouses, and sun hats, and singing together as they marched from the mess hall—piled onto waiting trucks for their day's work in the peach, plum, fig, olive, and nut orchards of the fertile Sacramento Valley. After work, there was time for swimming in a nearby irrigation canal before the shower bath that ended each work day. At mid-week, the girls staged a variety show. On Saturday nights, they shampooed their hair and got dressed up for a weekly dance in Chico. Every detail of their lives, down to their mattresses and bedding, their meals and eating utensils, their uniforms and work shoes, their rest breaks, was scrupulously set forth and supervised. Amortized over a five-year period, the housing provided the Woman's Land Army cost no more than $8 per year per worker, a reasonable sum to expect from the ranchers or associations of ranchers who might be expected to continue this housing program after the war. With each girl paying a dollar per day in board, moreover, the camps were largely self-supporting.

The program for the 250,000 teenaged boys brought into the fields for the harvest of 1918 under the auspices of the Boys' Working Reserve was similarly exacting, although this program did not involve the construction of special camps. State inspectors insured, however, that only ranches which offered satisfactory needs and housing arrangements could utilize the program's services. Each boy, the requirements read, must have his own bed, and no boy could share a room with an older male worker.

For the majority of the members of the Woman's Land Army and the Boys' Working Reserve, most of them city-bred, the months they spent as harvest workers remained in memory in later years as a time of summer idyll: of hard work, to be sure, and long days in the orchards, but a time as well of camaraderie and a healthy outdoor life. Even when one grants the special nature of these programs, the paradigm they offered of inexpensive but adequate housing, board, and sanitation for farm workers—most of it capable of being put on a near self-supporting basis from modest daily fees—had much applicability to a reformed post-war era. With a minimum of investment, the growers of California might provide, if not the idyll described by Susan Minor, then at least decent living conditions for the harvest work force.

Certain growers were doing exactly that. The Limoneira Citrus Ranch in Santa Paula, Ventura County, for example, built a hundred two-bedroom cottages for its largely Mexican work force (two hundred permanent, three hundred seasonal), together with dormitory buildings for single workers. Other citrus ranches in the counties of Ventura, Los Angeles, San Bernardino, Riverside, Orange, and San Diego followed suit with cottages (average cost, $400) serviced by running water, gas, and electricity, grouped in groves of eucalyptus, sycamore, and oak trees around a central space with an open-air pavilion for recreation and religious services. Thanks to good housing, reported the *California Citrograph* for December 1929, the Mexican work force at Ranch Sespe in Ventura County had created for itself a flourishing community, proud of its heritage and employment, sending its children off to school each weekday morning in shoes and clean clothes. Wheatland, it would seem, had led to something good, after all.

Unfortunately, Wheatland also led to the Criminal Syndicalism Act of 1919. In the aftermath of Wheatland, IWW membership increased in California: forty locals by March 1914, with an estimated membership of five thousand, one hundred of whom were active as full-time organizers. The IWW responded to the conviction of Ford and Suhr with threats of organizing a general strike among all hop pickers in the state in the forthcoming harvest. There were rumors of barn, hop kiln, and haystack burnings and the destruction of fruit trees with metal spikes. When Governor Hiram Johnson received a threatening, obscene letter, the peppery former prosecutor responded that even if the Wheatland convictions were deserving of review, he would not be bullied into such an action by an organization committed to violence and class warfare.

Anti-radical sentiment was further fanned in the winter of 1913–1914 as nearly twelve hundred unemployed and homeless men took up residence in San Francisco in a building near City Hall which had been made available by a sympathetic municipal government. Dubbed Kelley's Army in honor of its leader, "General" Charles T. Kelley, a veteran of the march by Coxey's Army of unemployed on Washington, D.C., in 1894, the ragtag group began its own march on Congress in January 1914. Kelley's Army got as far as Sacramento, where eight hundred deputized citizens, armed with rifles and pickaxe handles, dispersed them from their rain-soaked camp on the outskirts of the city.

Two years later in San Francisco, on 22 July 1916, in the course of a Preparedness Day parade on Market Street, a bomb exploded, killing ten and injuring forty. Although the two men convicted of the crime on the basis of trumped-up evidence, Tom Mooney and Warren Billings, were not Wobblies but Socialists, the IWW offered the most inflammatory image of seditious anarchy to a nation made anxiety-ridden by its drift into world war.

In August 1917 Frank Little, leader of the free speech fight in Fresno, was hanged from a railroad trestle by several unidentified men in Butte, Montana. A few months later, a mob beat, tarred, and feathered seventeen Wobblies in Tulsa and drove them out of town. The Justice Department launched a series of raids on IWW headquarters across the country on 5 September 1917. In the third quarter of 1917 the New York *Times* ran more than sixty anti-IWW articles. Former president Theodore Roosevelt denounced the IWW's "frank homicidal march" in a speech given in Saratoga. The New York *Tribune* drew up a long list of acts of sabotage around the nation, blamed them on the IWW, and suggested that the IWW was a German front.

In a pattern that would become increasingly characteristic in the 1930s, California once again offered the nation yet another representative drama of Left/Right conflict. In December 1917 a bomb exploded on the back porch of the governor's mansion. A few days later, Governor William Stephens (Hiram Johnson had appointed himself to the United States Senate) received a death threat in the mail. Shortly thereafter, a wired stick of dynamite was sent to the governor by parcel post and was intercepted. All this in the midst of wartime hysteria! In the next few months hundreds of Wobblies were rounded up and interrogated. Fifty-three were held for trial in Sacramento on conspiracy charges, including Wobblies arrested in Fresno on charges of arson and sent to Sacramento to be included in the general conspiracy indictment. Five died in jail (of influenza and tuberculosis), and forty-six, including one woman, were brought to trial.

Against this wall of hostility—the conspiracy indictments; press and politicians, indeed society itself, screaming for their heads—the IWW defendants erected an equally impassable wall of silence and refused to defend themselves. Only three defendants retained attorneys, and, with the exception of spokesman Mortimer Downing's opening remarks, the undefended accused sat silently through the trial. Ironically, such organized resistance through silence reinforced the very charge upon which the IWW activists had been indicted, conspiracy. Was not their silence itself conspiratorial, the prosecution suggested?

The prosecution introduced two star witnesses, Elbert Coutts and Jack Dymond, arrested IWW activists who had agreed to turn state's evidence. Coutts and Dymond testified to numerous hay burnings throughout San Joaquin County by an IWW incendiary traveling by motorcycle. Coutts and Dymond also testified that the IWW members on trial had specifically discussed sabotaging the war effort. The prosecutors also read inflammatory passages from *Industrial Solidarity*, the IWW magazine, together with some of the more aggressive lyrics in the official IWW songbook.

Despite the raging newspapers, the lurid lyrics in praise of revolution, and the perjured evidence of Coutts and Dymond (then in the process of launching themselves into profitable careers as witnesses for the prosecution in subsequent IWW trials), Judge Frank Rudkin instructed the jury that in his opinion no conclusive case had been proven. Mere membership in the IWW did not offer proof positive of criminal conspiracy. Rudkin also reminded the jury that the guilt or innocence of each of the accused had to be decided on an individual basis, the group nature of the indictment and the trial notwithstanding. Ignoring the judge's instructions, the jury took only seventy minutes to return a verdict of guilty as charged for every defendant, with the exception of the three represented by counsel, who were found guilty of lesser charges.

While these three received light sentences—two months in jail for the men, a $100 fine for the woman—the rest of the Silent Defenders, as they came to be called, received sentences ranging from one to ten years in the penitentiary. Even before their sentencing, IWW leaders Fred Esmond and Mortimer Downing risked and most likely received stiffer sentences through fiery denunciations before Judge Rudkin of the mockery of justice their trial had put before the world. After their sentencing, the men filed out of court singing "Solidarity Forever," the most stirring of their anthems. It was pure theater, a ritual self-sacrifice by the IWW for the sake of acting out their radical opposition despite the consequences of hard prison time. Likewise, the defiance by the jury of Judge Rudkin's instructions acted out an equally confrontational response, ready and able to exercise itself as legally sanctioned vigilantism. In no way could this trial be considered a valid instance of criminal justice, either from the point of view of the accused, refusing to exercise their constitutional rights of defense, or of the prosecution and jury, refusing to adhere to even the most minimal standards of evidence. In this ritualized face-off, so prophetic of those to come in the 1930s, the IWW paid a most expensive price for its confrontational gesture. Not until December 1923 could a very reluctant President Calvin Coolidge be prevailed upon to grant amnesty to those Silent Defenders remaining in prison.

By that time, some five hundred radicals, mostly from the IWW, had been arrested under provisions of the Criminal Syndicalism Act. Half of these were tried, and 164 were sent to prison. As soon as the law was passed, the police raided IWW offices in Eureka, Stockton, San Francisco, Oakland, and Los Angeles. In Los Angeles, soldiers, sailors, and civilians trashed IWW headquarters in the Germain Building and beat four Wobblies so severely they had to be hospitalized. The raid on the meeting hall in Eureka in Humboldt County, center of the IWW effort to organize resistance in the lumber industry, yielded several arrests and convictions. In July 1923 the Supreme Court of California issued a restraining order against the IWW. This allowed for a quick hearing before a judge rather than a jury trial. Some thirty-five hundred Wobblies fled the Sacramento area for Texas to avoid prosecution. Eight of their colleagues were not so lucky; for another Eureka raid, this one on 14 October 1923, brought eight Wobbly organizers to court in a repetition of the Sacramento trial of the Silent Defenders five years earlier. This time, the men sang the "Marseillaise" as they left the courtroom to serve one to fourteen years in San Quentin.

Approximately one hundred Wobblies did time at San Quentin during the 1920s, forty-five of them in 1923, the peak year of IWW imprisonment. Hardly any of these men could have been convicted under contemporary standards of evidence. So shabby, in fact, was the process, nearly a third of the IWW convictions were reversed on appeal, despite the hysteria of the times and the catch-all nature of the Criminal Syndicalism Act. Within San Quentin and without, a prison-related IWW subculture developed. On the outside, support groups agitated for reviews and financed legal appeals. The IWW press focused attention on as many cases as possible. Within, IWW prisoners established their own organizational structure. If one of their number was unfairly punished, the rest refused to work. In one incident, dozens of Wobblies went into the San Quentin dungeon *en masse* in the course of a dispute. IWW prisoners organized two strikes in the prison jute mills. In punishment for the August 1924 strike, twelve Wobblies did thirty-seven days in solitary confinement on bread and water. Their supporters filled the cell blocs with IWW songs.

A candle can burn brightest just before it dies. So too did the IWW launch one last major offensive, the San Pedro maritime strike of April-May 1923, before disappearing as an effective force in California. The San Pedro strike ended with a vigilante action which for sheer ferocity, including violence against children, prefigured the worst that was to come in the 1930s. Driven from the fields and the lumber camps, the IWW made a temporary inroad into the maritime industry of California in the early 1920s when the Coast Seamen's Union, the American Federation of Labor affiliate headed by Andrew Furuseth, succumbed to internal dissension and a reinvigorated counter-offensive by shipowners. Furuseth, in fact, inadvertently helped recruit for the IWW-dominated Marine Transport Workers Industrial Union by driving suspected radicals from his own union, who promptly joined the IWW-led organization. Shipowners, in turn, played Furuseth off against the Marine Transport Workers Industrial Union, despite the fact that the IWW was under a restraining order from the California State Supreme Court. As might be expected in such a loosely structured leadership, the Wobbly union specialized in quick, on-the-spot work stoppages dealing with local grievances as opposed to the more systematic demands of contract negotiations backed up by the capacity to call for and sustain a strike.

In late April of 1923, however, the IWW union felt itself ready for the big time, a general waterfront strike in the San Pedro harbor of Los Angeles and in San Francisco. The official Strike Call listed fourteen demands. The first eight demands dealt with wages. Nine through Eleven called for better food, clean sheets every week, and free toilet articles. Demand Number Twelve called for union committees on every ship. Demand Number Thirteen, "a boycott of all California products in ship's stores until the Criminal Syndicalist Law has been repealed," proved the most inflammatory; for it used a strike action and the threat of an economic boycott (a technique pioneered by the IWW) to attain radical political ends, the very thing Andrew Furuseth was warning against.

Insult added to injury—the strike worked! When it was initially called, Furuseth scoffed that not one small steam schooner would be tied up. Within days, San Francisco was seriously slowed down, and San Pedro—where the longshoremen joined in—had ninety ships lying idle in the harbor: coastwise lumber ships, in the main, their cargos so necessary to sustain Los Angeles's building boom, which was why lumber magnates such as Andrew B. Hammond, whose fleet stood idle in the harbor, together with the Chamber of Commerce, and the all-powerful Merchants and Manufacturers Association, began to put such relentless pressure on City Hall and the Los Angeles Police Department to use the Criminal Syndicalism Act to break the strike. Not that Los Angeles needed much encouragement. Nearly three-fourths of the IWW men doing time under the Act in 1923 had been convicted and sentenced from the Southland. And yet, despite this repression, despite its status as an outlaw organization, here was the IWW organizing a crippling maritime strike and rubbing salt into the wounds of the oligarchy by dropping leaflets over the docks from a red airplane and running an equally red automobile through the harbor area inviting workers to open-air meetings.

More than five thousand attended a rally held on Liberty Hill near San Pedro on Sunday, 13 May 1923. When the police arrested the rally chairman and the speaker, a procession of singing and chanting protestors, three blocks long, snaked its way to the San Pedro jail. Los Angeles police chief Louis Oaks, a fervid servant of the oligarchy, sped down to the harbor to take personal command of the crisis. By Tuesday, 15 May, the Los Angeles police had arrested more than a thousand strikers and demonstrators and taken them via specially arranged streetcars to a hastily constructed stockade in Griffith Park. To a concentration camp via the Big Red Cars! The entire affair had escalated into a surreality that was simultaneously comic and chillingly prophetic of things to come, in Europe at least, in little more than a decade.

As if deliberately to heighten the representative nature of the drama, writer Upton Sinclair, appalled by the gross violations of civil rights that were taking place, had himself arrested on Liberty Hill on Tuesday, 15 May, for reading aloud from the Constitution. Another protestor, especially chosen by his IWW colleagues (perhaps because he was an epileptic), was chained to an iron lamppost at the corner of Fourth and Beacon streets in San Pedro as a *tableau vivant* entitled "Democracy in Chains." As the police hacksawed their way through the chains for nearly an hour, the epileptic fell to his knees in a violent fit, his eyes rolling, his tongue extending from his froth-flecked mouth. A crowd gathered, and IWW orators provided appropriate commentary.

As a symbol of radicalism managing to survive in the politically conservative 1920s, the Marine Transport Workers Industrial Union attracted an equal and opposite response. The Ku Klux Klan, having gone urban in the 1920s, had little trouble recruiting members throughout greater Los Angeles, where so many recently arrived citizens—insecure in their urbanism, looking for someone to blame for the feeling of incompleteness, of being cheated even, that lingered in their psyches like a bad taste in the mouth—found in the Klan the perfect outlet for their need for resentment, revenge, and community. On 1 March 1924 some three thousand Klan members paraded around the IWW hall in San Pedro. Two weeks later at the same place, a mixed group of Klan members and harbor police with drawn revolvers disrupted a meeting of the Oil Workers Industrial Union, another IWW affiliate. Lining the oil workers up against the wall, the police took three IWW activists into custody. When they left with their quarry, the hooded Klansmen remained behind to loot and trash the hall.

Intended to scare the IWW out of San Pedro, these Klan raids only intensified sympathy for the proscribed organization. Rallies on Liberty Hill were now drawing crowds approaching five thousand. During rallies such as these, the San Pedro district seemed to the Los Angeles oligarchy to be on the verge of widespread insurrection. Crowds of this magnitude seemed the very essence of Bolshevikism come to roost in the Southland. There was another raid on the IWW hall on 17 May. This time, women and children were arrested: one further increment in the acting out of a scenario of revolution and repression so intensely Californian in mood and significance. Since when, in the United States, were children to be so preemptively judged and punished for political reasons? Since when, and by what authority, were families and dependents to be caught in the dragnet of Criminal Syndicalism along with their heads of household? In Tsarist Russia perhaps, or the Russia of the Bolsheviks, but in Los Angeles? What bizarre drama was the City of the Angels acting out on behalf of the nation?

It would get even worse. In mid-June the Klan and other vigilantes declared open war on the IWW in San Pedro. The harbor police stated their neutrality, a patently illegal encouragement of the Klan and its auxiliaries to do what they did on the evening of 14 June 1924. Over three hundred men, women, and children had gathered in the IWW hall at Twelfth and Center streets for a Sunday evening benefit entertainment for the families of two union members killed in a railroad accident. As the audience settled in for an evening of comic sketches and singing, 150 men armed with guns, axes, gas pipes, brass knuckles, and blackjacks drove up to the hall in an automobile cavalcade. Sadly, the vigilante mob also included some United States Navy sailors; for IWW spokesmen had been alleged to have expressed satisfaction at the loss of forty-eight sailors when the gun turret of the USS *Mississippi* accidentally exploded. Smashing their way into the hall, the Klansmen and vigilantes flailed into the crowd. Men were beaten and clubbed, and women and children screamed in panic. Everyone, women and children included, was driven from the hall like cattle. It was later alleged that seven children, including ten-year-old Lena Milos ("the Wobbly Song Bird"), were deliberately scalded by being dipped into an urn of hot coffee. One of the children, Andrew Kulgis, age twelve, had hot grease applied to his skin. A number of newspapers, such as the San Francisco *Examiner*, claimed that the children had been scalded by accident when a coffee urn toppled; but how, others asked, could so many children have been so uniformly scalded?

Nine men were seized from the fleeing crowd and thrown into the back of a waiting truck. Escorted by carloads of vigilantes, the truck drove south for forty miles, past at least two policemen who looked the other way. When the cavalcade reached a deserted part of Santa Ana Canyon near the town of Oliver, the vigilantes disembarked their prisoners and ordered them to strip naked before a hastily lit bonfire. By its flickering light, they interrogated and abused their prisoners. One detainee, a Mexican-American named Joe Lopez, was let go because he had recently fought in a prizefight as part of a Navy benefit and was recognized. (Ten sailors were in the crowd.) Another was released because he had an AFL union card on his person. The mob tarred and feathered the remaining men, shooting pistols into the air as their ghastly victims stumbled nakedly into the night.

No free speech demonstrations followed this shocking episode. Wobblies did not, as in the past, pour into the San Pedro waterfront and bring it to a halt. An IWW demonstrator now faced up to fourteen years in the penitentiary. Upton Sinclair and other members of the newly organized Southern California chapter of the American Civil Liberties Union (ACLU) protested the vigilantism of Los Angeles and the complicity of its police department in the pages of The *Nation* and other sympathetic national publications. Sinclair won the support of such prominent Southern Californians as physician-reformer John Randolph Haynes, King C. Gillette, the razor blade magnate, and film star Charlie Chaplin.

As in the case of the outburst of anti-IWW vigilantism in San Diego twelve years earlier, the Los Angeles oligarchy grew nervous over discussions at the Jonathan and the California clubs. It was one thing for the lumber and steamship interests represented by Andrew Hammond to use the harbor police to crack down on strikes. It was another matter entirely to encourage a mob that beat women and scalded little children with hot coffee and brought bad publicity to Los Angeles. Many of the harbor police began to resent being used to do the dirty work of ownership, and at least one captain openly said so. Already, the oligarchy had brought in a reform police chief, August Vollmer of Berkeley, to replace the free-wheeling Louis Oaks. An impartial administrator and pioneering police scientist, Vollmer gave himself a year to reform the LAPD. However brief, Vollmer's reform administration signaled a backing off by the police department from the flagrant complicity with the vigilantism so evident during the San Pedro disturbances.

The Criminal Syndicalism Act, however, was to remain on the books until 1968; and for all the defiant resistance of the IWW prisoners in San Quentin, few Wobblies were eager to join them there. Deprived by the Criminal Syndicalism Act of the one organizing tool it knew best, a free speech confrontation provoking a larger demonstration, the IWW faded rapidly after San Pedro as an effective force in California labor. By 1926, as the Roaring Twenties—flamboyant in lifestyle, conservative in politics—accelerated into high gear, the Wobblies who had so frightened America in the pre- and post-war era with the specter of European-style revolution were now reduced to the image of a handful of grizzled men in shabby suits, blinking in the sunshine as they trudged through the gates of San Quentin on pardon or parole.

Among those pardoned in 1927 was Charlotte Anita Whitney, a sixty-year-old descendant on her father's side of five *Mayflower* Pilgrims and Thomas Dudley, the second governor of the Massachusetts Bay Colony and a founder of Harvard. Whitney's father had emigrated for his health from Maine to California, where she had been born in San Francisco in 1867. President Abraham Lincoln had already appointed her uncle by marriage, Stephen Field, to the United States Supreme Court. Her father later served as State Senator from Alameda County. Graduating from Wellesley College in 1889, Whitney was listed as an Episcopalian and a Republican in her class yearbook. Already an experienced Sunday school teacher, she entered settlement house work in the Lower East Side of New York following her graduation. In 1901 she returned to Oakland as secretary to the Associated Charities of Alameda County. In 1911, as the statewide president of the College Equal Suffrage League, she threw herself into the successful effort to win the vote for women in California.

By then, however, Whitney's interests had turned to politics as she became more and more convinced that social work alone could not cure the underlying causes of poverty and social stress. In 1914—radicalized, she said, by the persecution of the IWW in San Diego and by the conviction of Ford and Suhr following Wheatland—she joined the Socialist Party. In 1917, with the outbreak of the Russian Revolution, she enrolled in the pro-Bolshevik left wing of the Socialists; and in 1919, as the United States moved further to the right, she followed her wing of Socialism into the Communist Labor Party of the United States.

The atmosphere in Oakland, meanwhile, was growing poisonous. On the evening of Tuesday, 11 November 1919, American Legionnaires, with the tacit approval of the police, sacked Loring Hall, where the Communist Labor Party held its meetings. Inspector Fenton Thompson of the Oakland Police Department, meanwhile, had been compiling a dossier on the subversive activities of Charlotte Anita Whitney. Fenton's superior, Walter J. Peterson, captain of detectives in Oakland, had tried to warn Inspector Thompson off Whitney's case. "I found that she had always done an enormous amount of good in the community," Peterson later recalled. "I wasn't in sympathy with her pacifist ideas and a lot of her other notions. But I recognized that it wasn't in her nature to commit violence or to encourage it. She was one of those idealists who want to make the world better for everyone."[15] Thompson took his case directly to Police Commissioner J. F. Morse and persuaded Morse to ask for an arrest warrant against Whitney on charges of criminal syndicalism. On the evening of Friday, 28 November, the day after Thanksgiving, Whitney was speaking to a women's group, the California Civic League, at the Oakland Center. Her topic: "The Negro Problem in the United States." When she finished speaking, Oakland police officers took her into custody. She was booked and jailed, and a few weeks later the grand jury handed up an indictment for criminal syndicalism. The trial was set for 27 January 1920.

Fremont Older, the crusading editor of the San Francisco *Call*, led a chorus of protest that would swell over the next seven years until it became a major chorale of unacknowledged but subliminally powerful atonement on the part of the establishment for having allowed the Criminal Syndicalism Act to be passed in the first place. With Whitney's arrest, the Act had backfired. One of their own, albeit an errant daughter, was being devoured.

To defend Whitney, Older secured the services of Thomas H. O'Connor, a skilled San Francisco attorney who had won acquittals for two defendants in the Preparedness Day bombing trials. O'Connor's daughter, however, was ill from influenza, and he went into trial unprepared. Three days into the trial, O'Connor himself came down with influenza and died shortly thereafter. Whitney's defense collapsed. Among the evidence admitted against her was testimony that a red flag had been draped over the American flag at a Communist Party meeting in Loring Hall. It was later discovered that Inspector Fenton Thompson had personally arranged this subversive tableau through an agent. On 24 February 1920 a convicted Charlotte Anita Whitney was sentenced to one to fourteen years in prison as a criminal syndicalist.

For seven and a half years, Charlotte Anita Whitney, released on bail pending the outcome of her appeal, played a center-stage role in the subliminal life of California. With her neatly brushed hair, her rimless glasses, her print dresses and sensible shoes, her life spent in selfless service of others, Whitney neither looked nor acted the part of a criminal conspirator. Her Mayflower ancestry only intensified the irony of her conviction. Her defenders, even on the far left, frequently referred to her distinguished lineage as a talismanic assertion of innocence. People such as she, it was more than implied, were not the sort the legislature had in mind when it framed and passed the Criminal Syndicalism Act. Whitney, in turn, used the incongruity of her conviction to make an even deeper point. She refused to ask for a pardon, even when it was made clear to her that such a request would be received favorably by elected officials eager to be rid of an embarrassing situation. Why should she be pardoned, Whitney asked? She was no better than any nameless wretch without money, friends, social standing, or influence who had been railroaded into prison under the aegis of the criminal syndicalist law.

Whitney's attorney, John Francis Neylan, a former Progressive en route to prosperous and socially prominent conservativism, argued her case up to the Supreme Court, which did not overturn her conviction but went so far as to say that she would not have been convicted had a proper defense been made in the initial trial. The fact that John Francis Neylan, an attorney at the core of the San Francisco establishment (Neylan later ran the Hearst empire in Northern California), was conducting Whitney's appeal *gratis* only served to emphasize the intensity of establishment support that came Whitney's way without her even asking. In October 1925 an Anita Whitney Committee formed when Governor Friend Richardson flatly stated that he could not, or would not, pardon Whitney unless he received a personal application from her for such an action. The roster of the Committee read like a Who's Who of Northern California. It included the Roman Catholic and Episcopal bishops, a former State Supreme Court justice, a former United States senator, the president of Stanford, the dean of the law school at Berkeley, and a host of other prominent people from labor, the business community, the Republican and Democratic parties, the arts (San Francisco poet George Sterling wrote three sonnets supporting Whitney), and journalism. San Francisco district attorney Matthew Brady compared the criminal syndicalism laws of California to the laws in force in the Roman province of Judea when Jesus Christ was apprehended and crucified for sedition. In 1927 a San Franciscan, Clement Young, succeeded Southern Californian William Friend Richardson as governor of California. A longtime English teacher at Lowell High School who had turned to real estate and politics in mid-life, Governor Young pardoned Charlotte Anita Whitney on 20 July 1927, citing errors in the trial and her upstanding character. Young nevertheless defended the validity of the Criminal Syndicalism Act. Whitney, the governor argued, had been wrongly charged, but the law remained valid and necessary. Like any good politician, Governor Young was giving with one hand and taking with another. The establishment could have Whitney back, but California would keep its criminal syndicalist law on the books.

As the nation neared the execution of Nicola Sacco and Bartolomeo Vanzetti in Massachusetts on 22 August 1927, Young correctly gauged that the controversial execution of the two anarchists, believed innocent by millions, would only serve to inflame the Whitney case even further in California. The peace he bought was short-lived. The suppression of the IWW, an extremist organization, by the even more extremist Criminal Syndicalism Act displayed the deep currents of far-left and far-right sentiment that ran through more than just the fringes of California society. A special disequilibrium characterized California. Its good life, for those who had it, rested on such insubstantial foundations. At any moment, all could be lost. The constant act of redefinition which California demanded of its second-starters, indeed its second generation, made them edgy, nervous, prone to act harshly against an imagined threat. On the other end of the spectrum, the lower classes of California—migrant labor, most especially—were more firmly structured into the system than anyone cared to admit. The stress of the Depression exacerbated this disequilibrium and gave birth to even more intense Left/Right conflict.

II

A DECADE OF CONFLICT

3

Seeing Red

Strikes in the Fields and Canneries

*I*N the fields of California, the multi-ethnic, polycultural destiny of California first asserted itself. Traveling through the State in 1925, journalist Konrad Bercovici confessed his astonishment at the ethnic diversity of the agricultural regions. In the rice fields of the Sacramento Delta, turbaned Sikhs from the Punjab drove oxen-yoked wooden plows across the marshy soil in their bare feet. Outside Fresno, Armenian vineyard workers tended their vines attired in the Turkish fezzes, baggy pants, and colorful vests of their Anatolian homeland. Dalmatians grew apples and apricots in Santa Clara, while the Italians outside Santa Rosa specialized in artichokes. At intervals known only to themselves, Basque sheepherders would come in from the hills to Los Gatos in the south Bay Area or to Bakersfield in the southern tip of the San Joaquin for festivals of dancing, singing, wine drinking, and prodigious feasts of barbecued lamb.

Set squarely in the center of the Great Valley, Fresno County—with its large Armenian population, its five thousand Albanian Italians from Potenza Province, its ten thousand Volga Germans from Russia, its seventy-five thousand residents of Portuguese descent, its twenty-five hundred Swedes in and around Kingsbury, together with assorted pockets of Danes, Greeks, Norwegians, and Yugoslavs—was perhaps the most multi-cultural county in the State.

As colorful as all this might be, it obscured another reality. Despite the successful adjustment of so many immigrant groups, agricultural California could not be understood as a *tableau vivant* of picturesque peasants in native costume finding health, homes, and happiness in the Golden State. Sikh plowmen might be atmospheric, but the 1930 Census revealed only 1,873 "Hindus," as they were called, in the entire state. As of 1930 the state remained overwhelmingly white (88 percent), and that percentage was even higher among those who controlled the land.

White people owned the land, and people of color—368,000 Mexicans most noticeably—did the work.

European California had ever been so. With only four thousand whites in Alta California by 1830, Native American labor was absolutely necessary. Since Native Americans were for various reasons unable to bargain for wages or working conditions or to sell their labor elsewhere, something very much approaching slavery characterized the limited economy of the remote Mexican province. Not until 25 September 1829 was slavery officially abolished in California. Native American children were being bought and sold into the 1840s.

Chinese immigrants dominated California agriculture through the late nineteenth century. Skilled as agriculturalists in their homeland, the Chinese established the agricultural infrastructure of the state. In Northern California, especially in the Sacramento Valley and Delta regions, the Chinese reshaped and irrigated the landscape with canals and levees. In their private truck gardens they experimented with new crops, and, hiring themselves out to large landholders, they performed heroic feats of creative labor. Their numbers limited by the Exclusion Acts of 1882, 1892, and 1902, the Chinese began in the late nineteenth century to drift away from the fields of California, where chances for ownership were severely limited, and to seek new opportunities in the cities and towns.

Their successors, the Japanese, struggled their way into land ownership on long-term lease agreements, despite the weight of prejudice and envy that increasingly became their lot as they prospered. Maintaining their own bargaining associations, the Japanese rarely lost the advantage in harvest negotiations. In 1903 about a thousand Japanese joined with Mexican field workers in Oxnard in Ventura County and organized a two-month strike against beet growers, protesting "starvation wages and iniquitous conditions." Several strikers were shot, and many arrested, but the walkout, which ultimately failed, can be considered the first organized strike in the agricultural history of the state. They also had a passion for ownership, despite the fact that first-generation Japanese immigrants, the Issei, were precluded by law from owning land in California. By 1909 Japanese farmers owned 2,442 acres in California and leased another 54,830. By 1915 they controlled significant portions of the sugar beet, potato, floral, and nursery products industries. George Shima, who immigrated in 1889 and died in 1926, controlled twenty-eight thousand acres and 85 percent of the state's potato crop. By the early 1930s Issei and American-born Nisei were farming three hundred thousand acres and controlled the dairy, potato, floral, and truck garden markets in most parts of California. By the late 1930s 10 percent of the value of California's annual agricultural crop was Japanese-American in ownership or control.

No indeed: the Japanese were not likely candidates to fill the ranks of migrant agricultural labor in California. The farmers and ranchers of the state would have to look elsewhere in their search for a peasantry. During the Progressive era, an effort was made to recruit white families from the Eastern states to settle in California as small tenant farmers available for contract labor as well. Alarmed by the cohesive organization of Japanese farm labor and its drive toward ownership, the Progressives appealed to the Jeffersonian ideal of yeoman farmers living in autonomous rectitude on the land. By yeoman, the Progressives meant white people. Given the realities of agribusiness in California, however, few such yeomen would ever have the chance to become self-sufficient farmers. Should they come to California, white folk would spend their lives on the margin, working for the big growers. The effort to recruit white tenant farmers, in which Jeffersonian language masked a more sinister intention, got nowhere. What was needed was a peasantry, a permanent underclass, such as the banished Chinese were once thought to be, bound to a life of labor on the large estates by necessity.

If California was in search of peasants, it had already found its land barons. The United States Agricultural Census for 1935 revealed that 2 percent of California's farmers held 25 percent of the state's total acreage and produced 32 percent of the value of the state's annual crops. The top 10 percent of California's farms produced 55 percent of its crops. Fourteen percent of the nation's agricultural economy was centered in California—fully half of its fresh fruit, 70 percent of its canned food—and hence dominated by this top 10 percent, which employed nearly three-quarters of the state's agricultural work force. Fully 50 percent of the ranches of California were classified as medium-sized, which meant that they were still large by national standards. (As of 1930 fully a third of all large-scale farms in the county were located in California.) The top 10 percent of California's farms, and much of the middle 50 percent, were organized as industrialized plantations, heavily dependent, even by the 1930s, on mechanization (the tractor, after all, had been invented in California) and frequently specializing in one or two crops. As in the case of most corporations, an interlocking network of ownership ran through the agricultural industry. Land corporations owned processing and marketing organizations, or, in a reversal of acquisition, processing and marketing companies acquired ranches so as to insure their canneries and wholesalers a steady source of agricultural products.

The very success of these farms as mechanized operations meant that fewer permanent employees were necessary to run them. Thirty full-time workers, for example, could run a thousand-acre peach ranch. Two hundred workers, however, were needed for the pruning season; seven hundred for thinning; and nearly two thousand for the harvest. A twenty-acre hop ranch, staffed by twelve full-time employees, needed five hundred workers at harvest time. Since crops matured at different seasons, harvest workers found themselves traveling approximately a thousand miles each year throughout the state: February and March, peas in the Imperial Valley; apricots in June in Santa Clara and Contra Costa; grapes in Fresno in August. At the peak of the harvest cycle in September, California required 150,000 workers in the field. In March only 50,000 were necessary.

In the 1920s the ranchers of California, faced with a shrinking labor pool of whites at a time of prosperity, began to seek new sources of agricultural labor among people of color. Between 1920 and 1929, nearly thirty thousand Filipino men, most of them single and under the age of thirty, found their way into the harvest fields of California. Hard-working and cohesive as a social unit, Filipinos were rapidly assimilated into California agriculture. By 1930 they accounted for nearly 18 percent of the agricultural work force of the North and Central coasts and the Sacramento and San Joaquin valleys. Specializing in asparagus, they dominated that crop (90 percent of the labor pool) in Northern California by 1938.

Highly socialized, Filipino men tended to travel, hire out, and share living expenses together in groups that numbered from seven to twenty. They also went into town together in their off-hours seeking female companionship, which was frequently white, and this gave rise to a number of ugly incidents. In late 1929 in the town of Exeter in Tulare County, rioting broke out when Filipino workers brought white female entertainers to their camp. On 7 January 1930 the Chamber of Commerce of Northern Monterey County, meeting in the town of Pajaro, called for an end to the hiring of Filipino farm workers on "moral and sanitary" grounds and as a threat to white labor. On 10 January 1930 the newspaper in Watsonville in Santa Cruz County prominently quoted the racist remarks of a justice of the peace from adjacent Monterey County to the effect that Filipino workers, "little brown men attired like Solomon in all his glory, only a decade removed from the bolo and the breechcloth, were strutting like peacocks through the towns of the region to attract white and Mexican girls." Eleven days later, anti-Filipino riots broke out in Watsonville, leaving one Filipino worker, Fermin Tobera, shot dead through the heart and sixty others hospitalized. On 29 January 1930 a Filipino clubhouse was dynamited in Stockton, and anti-Filipino demonstrations followed in Salinas, San Jose, and San Francisco. University students in Manila held a counter-demonstration on 2 February, massing ten thousand people in protest.

In contrast to the predominately male Filipino immigration, so promotive of racial and sexual tension, Mexican workers, who by 1930 outnumbered the Filipinos ten to one, had come from a shorter distance and were often able to preserve their family units. Beginning in the 1880s, the Santa Fe and Southern Pacific railroads imported Mexican workers from across the border at El Paso to build and maintain their lines throughout the desert country of the Southwest. In the early 1900s Mexican construction crews built the bulk of Southern California's Pacific Electric interurban system. A labor shortage during the war years 1917–1918 brought even more Mexican workers into the Southland. By 1920 an estimated 88,771 Mexicans were residing in California, mainly in the South. By 1930 that figure had jumped fourfold to 368,013—or 6.5 percent of the state's total population.

The 1920s, then, witnessed the beginnings of the return of Mexico into its lost province California and the other provinces of the Southwest via demographic reconquest, a process which continued through the end of the twentieth century. Between 1901 and 1910 a mere 50,000 legal immigrations from Mexico into the

United States were recorded. Between 1921 and 1930 there were 459,257, nearly half a million. Like the *conquistadores* of an earlier era, the Mexicans of the 1920s pushed into El Norte, settling along the railroad lines they were building into Southern California.

When that work was done, Mexican immigrants followed the fields of cotton, which during the wartime boom years expanded through the Southwest from Texas to the Imperial Valley, then northward to the Valley of the San Joaquin. As the cotton acreage of the Imperial Valley expanded—from 61,217 acres to 126,081 acres in 1920 alone—so too did the need for thousands of seasonal workers. In the mid- to late 1920s, Imperial Valley growers turned also to lettuce, the industrial crop *par excellence*, and even more hands and bent backs were needed. By the late 1920s the entire Imperial Valley economy had become dependent upon the twenty thousand Mexicans permanently resident in the Valley (one-third the entire population) who worked through a twelve-month cycle of planting, tending, and harvest. By the early 1930s Mexicans accounted for a third of California's total agricultural labor force. In the San Joaquin Valley that figure jumped to 56 percent.

Throughout California, Mexicans lived in isolated, well-defined urban pockets, the *barrio*, or in isolated settlements, the *colonia*, which could run the gamut from a town or village serviced by its own grocery store, movie theater, pool hall, and chapel, to a collection of isolated shacks at the end of a remote canyon. Racial, religious, and cultural prejudice, together with the language barrier and class disaffinities between Anglo and Latino societies, kept the Mexican out of the mainstream of American life. The Imperial Valley sustained *de facto* Jim Crow laws through the late 1920s which excluded Mexicans from restaurants, soda fountains, beauty parlors, and barber shops and permitted them to sit only in separate parts of movie theaters. In agricultural areas such as the Imperial Valley, Mexican children, increasingly American-born, were frequently sent to separate schools. In schools requiring shoes, many Mexican children or, more correctly, many Mexican-American children, were forced to stay away. While attendance in the early grades showed promise, most children dropped out before high school.

Within their own communities, Mexican agricultural workers were not without resources. In the Imperial Valley, for example, two voluntary self-help societies, the Sociedad Mutualista Benito Juarez of El Centro and the Sociedad Mutualista Hidalgo of Brawley, provided a wide variety of benefits and services—medical care, unemployment insurance, legal aid, funeral benefits, dances and other social events on Mexican holidays—for a monthly per capita payment of $2. Nor was the concept of a union, even a strike, foreign to their experience. For back-breaking labor such as cantaloupe picking (the sack of harvested melons slung over the shoulder growing excruciatingly heavier under the 110-plus-degree sun) Mexican workers in the Imperial Valley in 1927 earned between $2.50 and $3 per nine-hour day. White workers performing the same tasks received from fifty cents to a dollar more per day strictly for being white.

Not surprisingly, the few agricultural strikes that did occur in California in the 1920s were Mexican-led. In 1927 Mexican field workers organized the pioneering Confederacion de Uniones Obreras Mexicanas, which encompassed twenty locals through Southern California. The Imperial Valley local, formed with the assistance of the Mexican consul general in Calexico, enrolled 2,746 members. It initially called itself the Imperial Valley Workers Union but backed off that designation as being too provocative in favor of the more acceptable Mexican Mutual Aid Society of Imperial Valley. In May 1928, just before the start of the cantaloupe harvest, the union submitted a written proposal asking for a rate of fifteen cents a crate or seventy-five cents per hour. The union also requested that the growers provide harvest sacks, ice blocks to cool drinking water, lumber and brush for the construction of temporary shelters, and toilet facilities. No call for a Valley-wide strike was issued, but various groups of workers in the Brawley and Westmoreland area refused to work until these conditions were met.

Very rapidly, the familiar California pattern of repression asserted itself: in this instance, the use of a Red Scare and police power to break labor's resistance. The breakup of the Mexican Mutual Aid Society of Imperial Valley can, in fact, be considered a prologue to a decade of anti-strike terrorism in California. Very rapidly Imperial County sheriff C. L. Gillett swung into action. First of all, he deputized forty men, including a number of field inspectors and foremen from local ranches. The growers were now the law. Then the arrests began, wholesale and without warrant, with bail set between $500 and $1,000, which no Mexican worker could afford. Next followed a Red Scare, promoted through local newspapers, with calls for more arrests and deportations. Communist agitators were coming up from Mexico City, it was rumored. Union members had been seen marching behind a red flag. There was a plot to burn packing sheds—even to take over the Valley. Four pool halls in Westmoreland and the union office at Brawley were closed on the pretext that they were not properly licensed. That way, the union could not hold meetings or conveniently carry on its business.

Slandered, arrested, intimidated, deprived of basic rights to organize, the union protested directly to the President of Mexico, who protested to the President of the United States, who notified the Secretary of State, who sent a State Department investigating officer into the field. Finding themselves at the center of an international incident, the sheriff and district attorney of Imperial County backed off. More than sixty Mexicans were released from jail, charges dismissed. Four or five others received suspended sentences on minor charges. Of equal importance: the workers by and large got their rates, their harvest sacks, their ice water, shelter materials, and toilets. Despite the illegal proceedings against them, they had prevailed in an agricultural strike, which had never happened before in the fields of California. Timing their demands perfectly, the Mexican workers had used seasonality and scarcity of labor to their advantage. They knew that the growers were bluffing when they threatened to bring in thousands of Mexicans from Texas and Arizona. Even if the growers could assemble such a work force, it would cost them a fortune to ship them in by train, and even then, in terms of the fields of cantaloupes ripening rapidly under the Imperial Valley sun, it would be too late. No one from the union called the results a victory; indeed, the Mexican Mutual Aid Society of Imperial Valley had not even designated its action a strike; but whatever it was called, the Mexican demands of May 1928 had shown new possibilities for organization and negotiation and, if necessary, resistance.

The Depression, however, would insure that the events occurring in Imperial Valley in May 1928 did not create a precedent, save in the matter of sheriff's deputies, jails, and law courts being used as a means of suppression. The Depression, first of all, would bring into California more than three hundred thousand new agricultural workers—not Asians or Mexicans this time, but white Americans from the Great Plains and the Southwest, the drought and Depression-stricken Dust Bowls of Texas, Arkansas, Kansas, Missouri, and, most dramatically, Oklahoma, from whence the generic pejorative epithet for all of them, Okies, was condensed. By the middle of 1934 there were 142 agricultural workers in California for every hundred jobs. The Depression drove the already low wages of agricultural California into new depths of sub-subsistence. The prevailing wage rates for agricultural labor in 1929 dropped by more than 50 percent by 1933. Increasing slowly between 1934 and 1937, they went into decline again between 1937 and 1940. In May 1928 Mexican workers in the Imperial Valley could reasonably negotiate for seventy-five cents an hour for picking cantaloupes. Between April and June 1933 pickers in the Imperial Valley were working for as little as fifteen cents. The hourly rate for pickers in the San Joaquin Valley between 1932 and the first half of 1933 also dropped to as low as fifteen cents. Apricot pickers in Contra Costa County were making twenty-five cents an hour in 1934. The rate climbed to thirty-five cents by 1937 but fell back to twenty-five cents an hour by 1939. Hourly rates such as these translated by 1935 into such average daily wages as $3 a day for hops, citrus, peaches, prunes, walnuts, apples, and apricots; $2 a day for asparagus; $1.60 a day for lettuce and melons; $1.50 a day for cotton; and $1.40 a day for peas, the lowliest and lowest-paying of California's crops. Surely, the stage was set for major strife, provided that the persistently unorganized world of migrant farm labor—over-supplied, exploited, deprived of First Amendment rights, a helotry with less status than any of its counterparts in the urban economy—could ever be given the dignity and bargaining power of organization.

Which is exactly what the Cannery and Agricultural Workers Industrial Union (CAWIU) successfully accomplished between 1930 when it was founded and 1935 when it disestablished itself in favor of the Congress of Industrial Organizations (CIO), then in the process of formation. Founded by the Trade Union Unity League, a national organization chaired by William Zebulan Foster, Communist Party candidate for president in 1924 and 1928, the CAWIU got its start in the only region in California where agricultural unionism had any standing, the Imperial Valley. In January 1930 the Mexican Mutual Aid Society, its members fed up with picking lettuce for $1.50 a day, sprang back into activity with demands for a 25 percent wage increase, the abolition of piecework and early morning shape-ups, improved housing and drinking water, and the recognition of workers' job committees. When eight thousand Mexicans went out on strike, Filipino, Chinese, Japanese, and Sikh workers joined the walkout. Sensing an opportunity, the Trade Union Unity League sent organizers into the Imperial to assist the strikers. Forming their own union, the Agricultural Workers Industrial League, the organizers recruited the Filipinos to their organization and established a strong working relationship with the Mexican union.

The most effective tools used by the new union were the mimeograph machine and the automobile. Traveling rapidly throughout the Valley, organizers from the Agricultural Workers Industrial League turned out leaflets, thousands of them, in English, Spanish, Chinese, Japanese, Tagalog, and Slavonian, together with *Vida Obrero*, a Spanish-language newspaper. Two of the original three mimeograph leafleteers were arrested, jailed, and beaten—with intensified brutality no doubt, for the embattled growers had suddenly to contend with a strike that was constantly communicating with its membership over hundreds of miles in many languages, thanks to a simple cylinder capable of turning out hundreds of leaflets every hour in different places from the back seat of an automobile.

The growers of the Imperial Valley were not without resources. They still had the Criminal Syndicalism Act. On 14 April 1930 police and sheriff's deputies raided a meeting of the Agricultural Workers Industrial League in Brawley. One hundred and fourteen people were arrested, chained together in lines and marched off to jail. The grand jury indicted sixteen on 30 April on charges of criminal syndicalism. Nine stood trial before Superior Court judge Von H. Thompson, an American Legion activist, in late May. On 13 June, after an hour's deliberation, the jury returned a verdict of guilty for all defendants. Judge Thompson sentenced J. C. Miller, Lawrence Emory, Carl Sklar, Frank Spector, and Tsuji Horiuchi to three to forty-two years in Folsom or San Quentin. Danny Roxas, a Filipino, got two to twenty-eight years. Three Mexican defendants were ordered deported. In passing these draconian sentences, Judge Thompson stated that for such as these—Communists in conspiracy to destroy the economy of the Imperial Valley—anything short of a life sentence should be considered lenient. Only one defendant, Frank Spector, a high-ranking Communist Party official, won a reversal of his conviction, on the grounds that the prosecution had not proven that he was physically present in the Imperial Valley when the conspiracy occurred. The rest served hard time until the final two were released on parole in early 1933. Upon release, Horiuchi and Sklar were deported to the Soviet Union. Organizing agricultural strikers in California was a dangerous business.

The second consolidation of the Agricultural Workers Industrial League as a major force in California agriculture under its new name, the Cannery and Agricultural Workers Industrial Union, occurred during the Santa Clara cannery strike of late July and early August 1931. (In the Santa Clara Valley, which by

1925 was producing 30 percent of America's canned fruit, August was the busiest month.) For a number of reasons—the emphasis upon repetitive piecework, the subordination of people to machines, the predominance of migrant and seasonal labor, and, more important, the harsh, grinding attitude of employers toward employees, most of whom were women—canneries epitomized the industrial nature of California agriculture. Like all agricultural work, canning was seasonal. Living in tents provided by the canneries, women workers and their menfolk—a teenaged son, a younger brother, a dependent husband—migrated from cannery to cannery according to a harvest cycle that lasted six months of the year. Canneries preferred female workers, believing them to be more adept at sorting, coring, peeling, cutting, and otherwise preparing fruits and vegetables for cooking and canning. In the case of peaches, pears, and apricots, such skills were essential if a piece of fruit were not to lose its shape in the canning process. Women were also believed to be more docile as employees, in that most of them were usually providing secondary or supplemental incomes to their family units. The sight of women working in advanced states of pregnancy was commonplace. Men were frequently hired at canneries strictly because their wives and daughters were working there as well. Cannery workers, so many of them foreign-born, thus considered their large families as sources of wealth, introducing them to the production line as soon as possible regardless of their age or the demands of the school year.

Conflict, competition, and exploitation were at the core of the canning industry. Ethnic rivalries divided the whites, who called themselves Americans, from their Portuguese (20 percent of the work force), Italian, and Mexican counterparts. Supervisors tended to favor their own ethnic group or play one off against another. In a situation in which men did all the supervising of a virtually all-female work force, or performed such essential tasks as removing and checking all completed work and delivering a new crate of fruit to be prepared, opportunities for sexual exploitation were built into the system. Even without such harassment, the work was demanding. The day began at six thirty and lasted ten to twelve hours. The women stood for most of this long day and developed cracked hands from the constant moisture or cut themselves on paring knives. Bandaged hands were a common sight, and blood poisoning a common malady. State law prohibited women from carrying heavy loads, but cannery women knew that when a lug of fruit needed moving, now, and no man was handy, she had better move it *pronto* (a box of fruit weighted forty pounds) or lose out in the piecework system. A good cannery worker was expected to prepare nearly sixty pounds of fruit per hour, and workers would frequently rock rhythmically over tasks, setting a pace against the constant flow of fruit and the eternally repeated motions, so as to hypnotize themselves into a faster and faster rate of production or merely ward off through rhythm the onslaught of boredom and fatigue.

In late July 1931 the canneries of the Santa Clara Valley south of San Francisco announced a 20 percent slash in wage rates. Nearly two thousand workers, almost spontaneously, walked off the job. Within days, organizers from the Agricultural

Workers Industrial League had seized leadership of the strike, which spread to sixteen thousand workers in sixteen Santa Clara Valley canneries.

As usual, the local sheriff swore in dozens of new deputies and began making arrests. On 31 July 1931 the League organized a rally in St. James Park in downtown San Jose, the Santa Clara County seat. A phalanx of police and sheriff's deputies stood by. Speaker after speaker was pulled from a platform and arrested. Finally, an unarmed young woman jumped to the platform and urged the crowd to march on City Hall and demand the release of all arrested strikers. The woman then leapt from the speakers' stand and took her place at the head of a quickly forming column. The police waded into the crowd with blackjacks and nightsticks. A tear gas bomb hit the young woman in the face, and she fell to the ground unconscious. The crowd continued on to City Hall, which had been hastily cordoned off by deputies and police. A pitched battle ensued, with more tear gas, blackjacks, nightsticks, flying fists, and bloodshed. Still, the crowd refused to disperse, even as more arrests were made. (All in all, twenty strikers were taken into custody.) Two hours into the confrontation, the San Jose Fire Department at last managed to disperse the crowd with water cannonades from high-pressure hoses.

By the next day, 1 August, San Jose had reached a dramatic point of Left/Right confrontation. On the left, the Communist Party of San Jose organized another rally in St. James Park to protest all wars in general and San Jose's war on strikers in particular. Newspapers, meanwhile, discussed yesterday's events in the lurid terms of a major revolution. The chief of police said that he was asking the Justice Department to step in, since so many of the strike leaders were deportable aliens. Canneries teemed with armed guards and plainclothes detectives. The Richmond Case Cannery, where fifteen hundred workers had walked out, displayed Army surplus machine guns in front of its gates. All this—the blackjacks and nightsticks, the tear gas bombs, the machine guns, the arrested strikers—provided perfect fodder for the orators in St. James Park. As a *mise-en-scène* for Bolshevik rhetoric, the situation in San Jose was perfect. Miraculously, there was no major violence that second day, as if the very theatricality of the standoff had stabilized the situation. Did the strikers really want to charge the machine-guns at the Richmond Case Cannery? Were the cannery guards really prepared to machine-gun to death hundreds of advancing strikers? How much was show, acting out, and how much was real? Neither side seemed willing to find out.

Shortly thereafter, the strike collapsed without one major demand of the strikers being met. The only winner seemed to be the League itself, which had changed its name to the Cannery and Agricultural Workers Industrial Union and moved into permanent headquarters at 81 Post Street in San Jose. For the organizers of the CAWIU, the cannery strike, like the Imperial Valley strike the previous year, had been a transforming experience of new knowledge (after all, few unionists had ever worked in this labor sector) and personal commitment. At the insistence of Samuel Adams Darcy, director of District 13 of the Communist Party USA, which included California, CAWIU organizers spent the rest of 1931 and much of 1932 tightening organizational structures and procedures. This done, CAWIU organizers fanned out from the San Jose headquarters into the fields, packing plants, and canneries of California over the next four years and spearheaded scores, even hundreds, of carefully prepared or impromptu strikes.

In the Vacaville fruit pickers' strike of November 1932, the CAWIU first showed its newfound skills and strengths. As the harvest approached, Vacaville rancher Frank Buck, who was running for Congress from this farming region between Sacramento and San Francisco Bay, initially offered $1.40 for an eight-hour day. Buck, a Democrat, was elected with farm workers' support. As a congressman-elect, Buck dropped his rates to $1.25 for a nine-hour day, and workers, prepared in advance by CAWIU organizers, walked off the job.

On 21 November 1932, led by CAWIU organizers, the strikers barricaded the main street of Vacaville to prevent scab workers being brought in by truck. When the chief of police arrested six strikers at gunpoint, a group of strikers surrounded him and forced the release of his prisoners: a reversal, albeit equally illegal, of the usual scenario. Frightened by this show of strength and by the continuation of the strike into early December, Vacaville growers rallied behind the proven technique of the Red Scare. At a rally held on 2 December there was open talk of lynch law against subversives. On the morning of 5 December masked vigilantes entered a curiously unprotected Vacaville jail and abducted six CAWIU organizers, whom they drove to a lonely spot fifteen miles outside of town. There the vigilantes gave the organizers convict haircuts, beat them, and smeared their faces with red paint. The next day the Vacaville chief of police announced that armed Communists were en route from Sacramento. The entire town mobilized. American Legionnaires joined the Vacaville police and a number of hastily created sheriff's deputies in a military-like headquarters in the fire station. "Minute Men to Fight Reds at Vacaville!" screamed a San Francisco *Examiner* headline on 7 December, in a story that described how a series of calls on the firehouse siren could mobilize up to two hundred men within twenty minutes.

On 16 June 1933 President Franklin D. Roosevelt signed the National Industrial Recovery Act (NIRA). Section 7(a) of the Act guaranteed workers the right to organize, elect officials, and engage in collective bargaining. Although the Supreme Court would within two years reduce the Act to a shell, Section 7(a) had lasting effects. Union busting, so characteristic of California agriculture, was now at least officially against the law.

Not surprisingly, 1933 proved a banner year for the CAWIU. Of thirty-seven agricultural strikes reported that year, the CAWIU played leadership roles in twenty-four of them, from a strike of pea pickers in Santa Clara and Alameda counties, which secured hourly wages of seventeen to twenty cents (up from ten to seventeen), to a beet strike in Ventura County and a peach strike in Fresno and Merced counties in August, a grape strike there as well in September, then up to the Santa Clara Valley for a cherry and pear pickers' strike. In the fall of 1933, ten thousand cotton pickers walked off the job in the San Joaquin Valley, creating the largest single agricultural strike in the history of the country up to that year.

Section 7(a) or not, strikes grew increasingly dangerous for strikers in the bleak Depression year of 1933 as the Communist-led union movement provoked extreme reactions on the right. A repeated scenario of fascist/Communist encounter—the raiding of headquarters by police, the rounding up of strikers, midnight beatings, truckloads of deputies roaring back and forth across the countryside and down the streets of farm towns like home-grown Brown Shirts—became increasingly characteristic of the agricultural counties. On 15 April 1933 at Decoto in Alameda County, for example, some five hundred pickets clashed with police and deputies in the course of a strike by pea pickers. Dispersing the demonstration with tear gas bombs, police and deputies flailed forward with clubs and blackjacks, mindless of the women and children caught in the melee. The strikers defended themselves with rocks and other improvised weapons. Some strikers threw back tear gas bombs at the police, hitting at least one officer (in the face), who was badly burned as a result. When it was over, some twenty strikers lay stricken on the asphalt highway or along the roadside, a number of them unconscious. Two days later, police dispersed a pea pickers' settlement located between Decoto and Warm Springs.

Lodi, San Joaquin County, became a lynch-mad armed camp the following October when ranch foreman Matt Beronio was shot and killed in the midst of a grape pickers' strike—even after Beronio's murderer committed suicide and the killing was proven to have nothing to do with the strike. Vigilantes led by Colonel Walter Garrison, later president of the Associated Farmers of California, rounded strikers up and brought them under guard to the center of Lodi, where, as the sheriff and local police stood by approvingly, they loaded the strikers onto trucks and shipped them from the area: a scene straight from Eastern Europe under the Nazis. The strike was broken in ten days.

In October 1933 saboteurs dynamited a Filipino bunkhouse near Gilroy. Fortunately, the building was empty. The following year, it is possible that at least one life was lost when vigilantes burned down a Filipino labor camp near Watsonville. At Ceres in Stanislaus County, two automobiles of night riders pulled an armed raid on a Filipino camp, giving the rousted workers until midnight to clear out. During the lettuce strike of 1936, the California Highway Patrol helped clear eight hundred Filipino farm workers from the Salinas Valley, which was then declared *Philippinen-frei*, or ethnically cleansed as later usage would have it.

On the other side of the equation, the Communist Party USA was sending, via the CAWIU, some of its most talented and committed organizers into the fields of California. The inner elite of organizers—Pat Chambers, Caroline Decker, Pat Callahan—were Communists working on behalf of a union with direct ties to Moscow. A former AFL organizer, William Foster, head of the American Communist Party, struggled throughout the 1920s to persuade Moscow to allow American Communists to establish their own unions rather than work within existing organizations. After byzantine negotiations, Foster prevailed. In 1929 at its convention in Cleveland, the Communist Party of the United States established the Trade Union Unity League pledged to promote revolutionary industrial unionism in conjunction with the Party. Described by Foster as the direct heir to the IWW tradition, the Trade Union Unity League reported to the Red International of Labor Unions established in the Soviet Union in 1921 to coordinate worldwide unionizing or union-related efforts.

In February 1930 the first of three long articles appeared in the magazine *The Communist* urging the Trade Union Unity League to become active in the field of migrant agricultural labor. The Cannery and Agricultural Workers Industrial Union of California represented the most successful response to this challenge. While not trumpeted, the Communist affiliation of the CAWIU was not an underground secret. In the course of the group's first foray into the field, the Imperial Valley strike of January 1930, the Land and Forest Workers Union of the USSR sent a telegram of support. On the other hand, the initial failure of the CAWIU to build any sort of permanent organization in the aftermath of the strikes of 1930, 1931, and 1932 was of grave concern to the Party. Like the IWW, the CAWIU had more success capitalizing upon a localized flare-up than it did building a permanent organization. Under the guidance of Sam Darcy, the Ukrainian-born, Moscow-trained (at the Lenin Institute), twenty-something Communist Party USA chief in California, the CAWIU lost its amateurish cast and began to build a strong rank-and-file base among field workers of color. Between 7 and 10 January 1933 the Communist Party USA–affiliated Unemployed Council sponsored a Hunger March of a thousand delegates up through Watsonville, San Jose, and Stockton en route to Sacramento, with speeches in English, Spanish, Japanese, and Chinese recruiting for the CAWIU. Yet these speakers, like the CAWIU organizers themselves, avoided overtly Communist rhetoric in favor of a program of decent wages and conditions, fair play in negotiations, equal pay for women, and racial equality.

Today, when Communism has lost its power to frighten and enrage vast sectors of the American public, it has become easier to focus upon the skills and human qualities of the CAWIU organizers, their Pauline persistence in their missionary task, without being so negatively distracted by their Communist Party affiliations. While their ideology represented a dead end, the cause they served, justice and decency in the fields, almost exempts them from the negative aspects of their Communism. You cannot have Falstaff and have him lean. There was no one else on hand to do a job crying out to be done, other than the young Communists, and they did this work with courage and high moral purpose.

Released from San Quentin, organizer Frank Spector returned to the field. On Sunday evening, 2 August 1931, we find him addressing a gathering in San Jose during the cannery strike. CAWIU organizer Patrick Chambers (his real name, John Ernest Williams) was taken into custody twenty-five times between 1929 and 1936 as a result of his participation in strikes. Arrested in Pixley in Tulare County on 12 October 1933 on charges of criminal syndicalism after rioting vigilantes had killed two during the cotton strike, Chambers languished in jail for the rest of the year until he was released on a writ of *habeas corpus*. By April we find him at CAWIU headquarters in Sacramento, directing a strike of six hundred strawberry pickers. On 16 June 1933 police arrested CAWIU organizer Patrick Callahan in the De Salvo orchard during a cherry pickers' strike. They beat him, fracturing his skull and breaking his jaw. Bailed out two days later, Callahan returned to the strike, his head swathed in bandages.

Skilled in organizing as well as being so brave and persistent in the face of a hostile criminal justice system, the CAWIU organizers used the mimeograph machine, the poster, the stump speech to communicate. At night they spoke by bonfires to circles of tired workers or met with smaller groups in sheds, shacks, tents, wherever the migrants were gathered. They pushed and pushed, and they never gave up.

One of the organizers, Caroline Decker, the twenty-one-year-old executive secretary of the union, possessed extraordinary organizational skills and charismatic leadership. An active organizer since she joined the Young Communist League at the age of sixteen, Decker was sent by the Party to California in 1931 after organizing assignments in upstate New York, Pittsburgh, Washington, D.C., Knoxville, and Youngstown. As Comrade Decker (so she is referred to in the CAWIU mimeographed newsletter), Caroline Decker traveled to the Fresno-Modesto area in the late summer of 1933 and began organizing grape pickers. She held a rally in Fresno on 11 September, and four thousand thronged the speaker's platform to hear this petite blonde, barely twenty-one, fill the space around her with impassioned words. Within the month, Comrade Decker had led six thousand off the job, the largest single agricultural strike to that point in the history of California. A month later, she replaced the imprisoned Patrick Chambers in directing the largest single agricultural strike in American history.

Across the United States the year 1933, nadir of the Great Depression, proved a year of major accomplishment for agricultural strikers. On the truck farms of southern New Jersey, the onion farms of southern Ohio, the sheep-shearing stations of west Texas and eastern New Mexico, hitherto quiescent workers staged walkouts. On the Pacific Coast alone, Berkeley labor economist Paul Taylor reported in *Survey Graphic*, there had been forty rural strikes since December 1932. Of these, the great California cotton strike of October 1933 possessed an epic sweep worthy of the Great Depression. For a few short weeks, agricultural labor, the most abused and despised sector of the economy, found strength and a voice.

Franciscan missionaries brought cotton to California in the late eighteenth century. Americans took it up as a crop in the 1850s and 1860s. By the end of the 1870s cotton was established as a major crop in the San Joaquin Valley. In the early 1900s cotton spread through the Imperial Valley and Riverside County, two other sources of the deep, rich soil, hot sun, and moisture cotton required. By

1933 cotton was the second most lucrative crop in California, the eleventh-ranked cotton-producing state in the country.

Cotton required an abundance of cheap labor through four stages—chopping, hoeing, irrigating, and picking. Even with the advent of mechanical seeders, cotton rows had to be chopped, which is to say, thinned and spaced by hoe, so as to establish proper spacing and row alignment. As the plants grew, they had to be weeded and individually irrigated via rivulets directed to each plant. All this was labor intensive and extended through much of the year. In the San Joaquin Valley, chopping and hoeing occurred from late April to June; irrigation from June through September. Because cotton bolls do not open at the same time, picking occurred in stages—a first picking in September or early October, continuing to December; a second picking beginning in December and continuing until February or early March. Picking was laborious, back-breaking work, performed under a merciless sun. As pickers moved along each row from plant to plant, filling the bags slung over their backs or across their shoulders with the cotton they had pulled from the opened bolls, they could soon find themselves dragging sixty or seventy pounds of dead weight.

The Chinese did this work in the 1870s and 1880s, but the Exclusion Acts cut down on their numbers. There were repeated efforts in the late 1880s and 1890s to recruit large numbers of African-Americans from the South, but those who came soon left the cotton fields for better opportunities. By 1933 Mexicans, Filipinos, and Dust Bowl migrants were picking California cotton.

The growers employing these workers entered each harvest season highly leveraged. Crops were frequently sold in advance to large gins or to cooperative marketing associations which advanced lines of credit. The cotton gins, not the growers, dictated wages and conditions. Fully three-fourths of the 1933 San Joaquin Valley cotton crop had been sold to Japan at seven cents a pound well before the cotton was picked, leaving no room whatsoever to pass on added labor costs to the buyer. As the first picking approached, the growers offered field workers sixty cents per hundred pounds. The CAWIU convened twenty-five locals in Tulare and the delegates demanded a dollar. Sixty cents was outrageous, the CAWIU argued. At that rate, even a strong, steadily working man could make no more than $1.20 a day. An entire family working all day would average $2. The CAWIU gave the growers a ten-day ultimatum. Having sold low to Japan, the growers believed they had no room for negotiation.

The strike began on 4 October, and by mid-October twelve thousand workers had left the cotton fields of five San Joaquin Valley counties. Ninety-five percent of the striking workers were Mexican, the rest Filipinos and whites. At the town of Corcoran in Kings County, the strikers erected a tent city for three thousand, twice the population of Corcoran itself. The massing of so many Mexican strikers kept vigilantes away, yet without proper water or sewage systems the tent city soon erupted in typhoid, dysentery, and diphtheria. At Corcoran and elsewhere, a number of small farmers, a group especially cultivated by CAWIU organizers, allowed strikers to camp on their property. Moving from place to place by automobile and motorcycle, CAWIU cadre kept their headquarters flexible and movable so as to avoid a single crippling raid by the police.

Also in the field: economics professor Paul Taylor and graduate student Clark Kerr from the University of California at Berkeley. Previously enrolled at Stanford, Clark Kerr had wanted to write his doctoral dissertation on self-help cooperatives but soon discovered that his professors preferred more theoretical research. Kerr transferred to Berkeley to study with Paul Taylor, a labor economist with a passion for field investigation. Accompanied by Kerr in the field, Taylor encouraged his graduate student to get the feel of the strike, its specifics, the very words out of the strikers' mouths. The resulting report, "Documentary History of the Strike of the Cotton Pickers in California 1933," is a masterpiece of Depression documentary art and was later appended to an even more impressive prose chronicle, the 1,707-page *Violations of Free Speech and Rights of Labor* issued in 1939 by the La Follette Committee.

Involving thousands, extending along a five-hundred-mile front, the cotton strike challenged the left, the right, and the center of the power spectrum. On the left, Communist Party official Sam Darcy, the behind-the-scenes strategist of the CAWIU, knew that the strike represented a make-or-break situation for the union. A key demand of the strikers was the recognition of the CAWIU as exclusive agent of the field workers and the establishment of union-controlled hiring halls. Without such stabilized authority, the CAWIU would remain little more than an *agent provocateur*, lurching from crisis to crisis. Skillfully, Darcy positioned the CAWIU to operate as much as possible through rank-and-file leadership, most noticeably William "Big Bill" Hammett, a patriarchal Oklahoma refugee and sometime preacher whose five sons had already proven themselves in a fistfight with growers at Woodville in Tulare County. With Darcy's encouragement, Hammett surrounded himself with a mixed Mexican, Filipino, and African-American general staff, who coordinated the strike along with Pat Chambers and Caroline Decker of the CAWIU.

In the center stood George Creel, the San Francisco–based director of the Western District of the National Recovery Administration (NRA). Although Section 7(a) of the National Industrial Recovery Act of June 1933 guaranteed labor the right to organize, neither the Act nor the National Recovery Administration it created favored strikes. Based on a premise of ongoing conflict between capital and labor, strikes emphasized labor as an autonomous sector of the industrial economy, capable of setting its own goals and acting in its own self-interest. The vision behind the National Industrial Recovery Act, by contrast, represented a revival of the Progressive vision of a planned society in which three elements—capital, labor, and government—cooperated with each other, under government's direction, to insure productive stability. A master manipulator of mass media and public awareness (as director of the Commission on Public Information during the First World War, George Creel had directed Wilson's propaganda machine),

Creel quickly realized just how threatening the cotton strike was to the crypto-Socialist vision of a government-planned society that lurked behind the NRA program. If the poorest of the poor, unlettered Mexican workers, Filipinos, and their Dust Bowl counterparts, could so effectively organize, Creel realized, how much more effectively might more advantaged sectors of American labor follow suit? Instead of an organized society marching forward toward economic recovery behind the blue eagle banner of the NRA, industrial conflict—compulsive, ritualized, murderous—would pull America down towards fascism, Communism, or anarchy. Creel set himself one clear goal: end the cotton strike through government intervention, state and federal, so as to quash the dangerous precedent being set in the cotton fields of the San Joaquin.

Liberals, as represented by Rabbi Irving Reichert of Temple Emanu-El in San Francisco, seconded George Creel's drive for government intervention. As vice president for Northern California of the NRA and a director of the NRA's Bureau of Mediation and Adjustment, Rabbi Reichert watched with increasing concern the rise of vigilantism, informal and formal, in the agricultural counties of California. As the cotton strike approached, Reichert wrote Governor James Rolph a letter on 3 October 1933 warning the former mayor of San Francisco that continuing anti-union vigilantism in agricultural California, aside from being grossly unconstitutional, could alienate large sectors of working people from the goals of the NRA, which was the cutting edge of the New Deal.

Rolph referred Reichert's letter to Frank McDonald, state labor commissioner; but events soon ran ahead of the abilities or even the authority of that well-meaning official, whose offer of mediation the cotton growers rejected. Six days later, 9 October, when Rabbi Reichert next wrote the governor, the confrontation had engendered in the fields of San Joaquin, so the San Francisco *Examiner* reported, a smoldering volcano on the verge of eruption. The Kern County sheriff deputized more than three hundred growers to confer legality on their efforts to break the strike. Madera County district attorney Sherwood Green urged a rally of growers to arm themselves and to pour castor oil down the throats of agitators coming around their ranches to organize. More than a hundred strikers had been thrown in jail. Blisteringly, Rabbi Reichert placed much of the blame for the dangerous situation squarely on the desk of the governor. "The lawlessness which I predicted has come to pass," Reichert scolded Rolph. "The high-handed and outrageous methods of the so-called Vigilantes, instead of being firmly suppressed by the civil authorities, are aided and abetted by them. Gangsterism has been substituted for law and order in the cotton area."[1]

The very next day, 10 October 1933, the gangsterism described by the rabbi erupted into murderous drama. In the small Tulare County town of Pixley, on the afternoon of Tuesday, 10 October, as CAWIU organizer Pat Chambers stood speaking to an outdoor gathering of strikers which included women and children, an automobile caravan of forty armed vigilantes drove into town. Seeing the vigilantes approaching with drawn pistols and rifles, Chambers urged his audience to adjourn to the nearby union headquarters. As the strikers retreated, a vigilante grower fired his rifle, most likely into the air. Delfino Davila, age fifty-eight, a part-time consular representative of Mexico in Visalia, approached the vigilante and pushed the barrel of his rifle to the ground. Another grower clubbed Davila to the ground and shot him to death. "Let them have it, boys!" one of the vigilantes yelled as he and the others fired into the crowd. Miraculously, only one other striker, fifty-year-old Dolores Hernandez, lost her life. Eight others lay wounded on the street or limped away in terror. Shockingly, a group of highway patrolmen and deputy sheriffs had watched the entire affair from a nearby hiding place. Halfheartedly, the officers pursued the vigilante caravan out of town. Stopping it, they confiscated a number of weapons but made no arrests.

At the same hour over at Mitchell's Corners near Arvin, a small town in Kern County, thirty armed growers faced 250 strikers on the edge of a cotton field. The face-off had started in the morning and had lasted five hours, the growers daring the strikers to take just one step onto private property, the strikers refusing to back off or disperse. Into the afternoon, under the hot sun, at approximately the same quarter hour the gunfire began in Pixley, the strikers and growers clashed. Shots rang out, and a striker, Pedro Subla, fell dead.

An estimated five thousand strikers massed outside the church of Saint Aloysius in Tulare for the funeral mass of Davila and Hernandez, and another two thousand gathered in Bakersfield for Subla's services. Never before had agricultural California witnessed such mass demonstrations. Even Governor Rolph was impressed. Receiving a delegation of strikers in Sacramento, Rolph appointed a fact-finding committee on 13 October consisting of Archbishop Edward Hanna of San Francisco, the Reverend Tully Knowles, president of the College of the Pacific in Stockton, and Professor Ira Cross of Berkeley. Rolph appointed the committee in lieu of calling out the National Guard to restore order in the San Joaquin, as many were urging. On the other hand, the arrests of strikers continued, and the growers were still arming and deputizing themselves. In Visalia Pat Chambers was arrested for criminal syndicalism. One of the growers involved in the Pixley shooting filed the complaint. Absurdly, nine strikers were arrested for the slaying of Subla in the Arvin incident—to keep in equipoise, perhaps, the eight cotton growers indicted for the murders of Davila and Hernandez in Pixley. Everyone was eventually acquitted, the innocent and guilty alike.

When the committee appointed by Governor Rolph met in Visalia on 19 October, Caroline Decker led a long line of strikers toward the courthouse where the panel was meeting. The moment called for a Sergei Eisenstein or a Bertolt Brecht or at the least a John Ford: the small fair-haired young woman at the head of a long procession of Mexican, Filipino, and Okie strikers: a secular Virgin of Guadalupe in the Gospel According to Karl Marx, Joan of Arc of the *campesinos*, seraphic in authority, confronting powers of Church and State. Acting as if she were a prosecuting attorney, with the growers on trial, Decker elicited from strikers on the witness stand the details of their impoverished existence: their low wages for a work day extending from daylight to dark, their fingers bleeding from the prickly cotton bolls, the children working beside their parents until they collapsed on the ground in exhausted sleep. At the insistence of the strikers, Patrick Chambers was brought up from the Visalia jail under guard to testify. The entire two-day hearing, observer Norman Thomas later stated—the Mexican workers on the stand, women and children as well, speaking through interpreters; the confrontations between Caroline Decker and Edson Abel, the lawyer representing the growers; Patrick Chambers, brought under armed guard to the courtroom—was a bold paradigm of the entire Depression as it affected farm labor.

NRA regional director George Creel, meanwhile, was doing his best to make sure that neither growers nor the CAWIU won too much. A victory on either side would be contrary to the NRA vision of a planned economy in which government held labor and management in balance. On behalf of the NRA, Creel had three goals: to persuade the growers, who were offering sixty cents per hundred pounds, to agree to seventy-five cents; to persuade the strikers, who were demanding a dollar, to accept seventy-five cents; and to deny National Labor Board recognition to the CAWIU as the elected bargaining agent of the farm workers because its Communist leadership and commitment to the ongoing class struggle made it unassimilable to the NRA program of reconciled differences between labor and management.

To implement his strategy, Creel brought in federal relief to the striking farm workers. Initially, the strikers refused to accept the relief since conditions were attached. In one instance, at Corcoran, it was alleged that relief supplies remained stacked and untouched outside a camp as several children died from malnutrition. (If true—how chilling, how fiercely ideological!) While Creel relented on attaching any conditions to federal relief, the assistance program still served his purposes. Now facing a federally subsidized strike force as well as a rotting cotton crop, growers had even more reason to compromise. On the other hand, Creel assured the growers that once the strike was settled, federal relief would cease, thus returning harvest workers to a direct dependence upon their labor. To establish the plausibility of the seventy-five cents per hundredweight figure, Creel contacted his New Deal counterparts in the Federal Intermediate Credit Bank of the Farm Credit Administration. The Federal Intermediate Credit Bank had financed part of the 1933 California cotton crop. The Bank agreed to back the seventy-five-cents settlement as financially sound. That, in turn, persuaded the panel appointed by Governor Rolph to recommend seventy-five cents over the objections of the growers, who found themselves even further boxed into a settlement by the federal government, which held their mortgages and was feeding the strikers.

The loyalty of the strikers—Mexicans, Filipinos, whites—to their CAWIU organizers provided George Creel with his greatest challenge. After a bumbling effort to bypass the CAWIU and deal directly with the strikers, Creel cunningly decided to let the idealism and battle fatigue of the young CAWIU organizers work on behalf of a settlement, even if such a settlement put them out of business as a union. The CAWIU leadership, Creel intuited, would not, indeed could not, refuse a settlement because of the recognition issue. Hardened Bolsheviks might sacrifice everything, including the people themselves, for the revolutionary victory of the Party; but that was Russia in 1917, and this was California in 1933. A strike, even a strike led by Communists, was not a revolution. (If a revolution was occurring in the cotton fields of California, it was a revolution from the right, a *putsch* driven by American Legionnaires and deputized vigilantes, railroading DAs and judges and their shamelessly cooperative juries.) Even Sam Darcy, a Moscow-trained hard-liner, despised bourgeois radicals who lectured workers on class theory instead of helping them to win specific benefits. Bread-and-butter issues, not doctrine, dominated discussions at the Central Strike Committee meeting on 26 October 1930. What else could realistically be hoped for? More than $1 million in additional wages had been extracted from the growers. Of equal importance, Mexican farm workers, together with their Filipino and white allies, had unambiguously signaled their refusal to become a complaisant peasantry or a benumbed proletariat. The cotton strike of 1933 introduced agricultural California to a future of organizational choice and collective bargaining that would take forty years to consolidate but was nevertheless fully present in the defiant cries of *la huelga! la huelga!* (the strike! the strike!) heard up and down the Valley of the San Joaquin throughout October 1933. And so, having accomplished so much, the CAWIU organizers had no choice but to recommend to the Central Strike Committee, comprised mainly of leaders from the rank and file, to settle and go back to work, without an officially recognized union. By the end of the month approximately 75 percent of the strikers were back in the fields of the San Joaquin, picking cotton. A year and a half later, the CAWIU was out of business.

It happened quickly—although at first, it looked as if it might not happen at all. In mid-November 1933 CAWIU organizers made contact with organizers from the Los Angeles–based Confederacion de Obreros Mexicanos regarding the organization of farm workers in the Imperial Valley before the lettuce harvest in January. The two principal CAWIU organizers, however—twenty-five-year-old Stanley Hancock from San Diego and nineteen-year-old Dorothy Ray from Los Angeles—while enthusiastic Communists, had none of the organizational skills of Caroline Decker, Patrick Chambers, Patrick Callahan, and the others connected to the cotton strike. When both the Los Angeles–based Mexican union and the locally based Union de Trabajadores del Valle Imperial withdrew from the field, Hancock and Ray welcomed what they considered the opportunity of a CAWIU-controlled strike. On 4 January 1934 a conference of leaders of lettuce workers, prompted by the CAWIU, issued its demands: thirty-five cents an hour, a guarantee of five paid hours for anyone sent into the field, free drinking water, free transportation to and from the job site, and—most brazen, given its failure to win such status after the wildly successful cotton strike—preemptive recognition of the CAWIU as exclusive bargaining agent. The Western Growers Protective Association ignored the CAWIU ultimatum. The union brought five thousand workers out on strike between 8 and 10 January 1934.

The strike was a disaster. Most of the strikers were not yet employed, first of all, and so their strike was purely symbolic. The CAWIU, second, had next to no organizational structure in the Imperial Valley. It was one thing to call a strike, Hancock and Ray soon discovered. It was an entirely different matter to make it work. Even had the CAWIU been prepared to direct what it had unleashed, the union faced a level of organized resistance among growers that set new standards for vigilante violence and oligarchical repression. Just four days into the strike, on 12 January 1934, police, deputy sheriffs, highway patrolmen, and deputized growers broke up a meeting at CAWIU headquarters in the Azteca Hall in Brawley with a ruthlessness that effectively broke the strike before it had barely begun.

Meeting in Sacramento in late April 1934 for the CAWIU's second and last annual convention, delegates took great pride in the fifty thousand agricultural workers the union had led on strike in 1933. Such self-congratulation did little, however, to shore up the delegates against the disappointments of 1934, beginning with the abortive lettuce strike in the Imperial. The CAWIU was in trouble as a union. It could galvanize and energize, but it seemed incapable of organizing farm workers into a disciplined, dues-paying membership. Realizing this, the delegates passed a number of resolutions calling for the strengthening of ties between CAWIU and its ever-elusive clientele, the migrant farm workers.

Little did they know that their time had already passed. The very next month, Caroline Decker, working alongside Julius Nathan, business agent of the AFL-affiliated Cannery Workers Union headquartered in San Francisco, did her usually brilliant job of crystallizing strike sentiment among apricot pickers in the Brentwood district of Contra Costa County. The strike began on the 4th of June. On the 7th, the apricot growers met with the strikers' negotiating team and objected to the presence of Decker, a Communist, at the negotiating table. (Julius Nathan described himself as a Trotskyite, but that did not seem to bother the growers. Nathan, after all, spoke for the AFL, a mainstream union.) Sensing an advantage for his own union, Nathan maneuvered Decker off the negotiating team. Six weeks later Decker and sixteen other CAWIU leaders were arrested at their headquarters in Sacramento on charges of criminal syndicalism. Convicted on two counts after a long and sensational trial, Decker and seven others, including Pat Chambers, went to prison.

Adding insult to injury, the Communist Party itself put the CAWIU out of business. In early 1934 Moscow reached a decision, which the Comintern communicated to the national parties. The struggle against fascism was intensifying, ran the communiqué. National Communist parties could no longer afford to go it alone. Communists should seek, rather, to align themselves with anti-fascist popular fronts. In terms of union movements in the United States, that meant the dissolution of independent unions such as the CAWIU and the scattering of its cadre into other organizations. On 17 March 1935 the Trade Union Unity League dissolved itself and its affiliated unions. Two weeks later, seventeen of its most skilled committee organizers were convicted of criminal syndicalism in Sacramento.

Simply, abruptly, not with a bang but almost with a whimper, an era of overt participation by the Communist Party USA in the union movement ended. In California agriculture, these first five years of the 1930s had been dominated by the CAWIU. The CAWIU had introduced a major idea into California agriculture: farm workers, a dispossessed helotry, the lowest of the low, could do something about their situation. This idea continued to gain new power. Between January 1933 and June 1939, more than ninety thousand harvest, packaging, and canning workers went out on some 170-odd strikes. In the mid- to late 1930s, California accounted for at least a third, and frequently all, of the agricultural strikes occurring in the United States at any given time. In 1937 the newly organized Congress of Industrial Organizations (CIO) entered the farm labor field in California with its United Cannery, Agricultural, Packing, and Allied Workers of America, which carried on the industry-wide organizing principles of the CAWIU.

By that time, the Associated Farmers of California, Inc., organized in 1934, had risen on the right to do battle with what it considered the Communist-dominated farm labor movement. The Associated Farmers were in one sense correct. Communists had played, and were continuing to play, major roles in the organization of farm labor. But was that the point? Was there not an even more basic issue? Why was farm labor such an inviting field for Communist organizers? Because, as Samuel Gompers had pointed out as early as 1911, farm labor was a condition in many ways worse than slavery itself. Farm laborers needed emancipation, now, immediately, and were willing to take it from wherever or whomever was offering it. From this perspective, the farm workers of California—Mexicans and Filipinos initially and most intensely, but later whites and African-Americans as well—were more likely to be using their Communist organizers than to be used by them, as the Associated Farmers were charging. Samuel Darcy encouraged CAWIU organizers to stay close to bread-and-butter issues because he realized that the CAWIU constituency was interested in little else. Both the Left and the Right were shadowboxing with each other: the Communists daydreaming of a Marxist-Leninist utopia as they negotiated for free drinking water and truck rides into the fields on behalf of workers more interested in tortillas, beans, and grits than revolution; the Associated Farmers, American Legionnaires, deputy sheriffs, highway patrolmen, vigilante prosecutors, intemperate judges, and complaisant grand juries using the language and psychosis of a Red Scare to protect their hegemony and investments.

Shadowboxing can escalate into conflict. Dreams of revolution can serve as preludes to revolutionary acts. Counter-revolutionary rhetoric, as Germany was even then proving, can escalate into fascist repression. In the 1930s California functioned as a testing ground for the viability of both the fascist and the Communist option. In the first half of the decade, the revolutionary impulse predominated. In 1934, astonishingly, the Socialist writer Upton Sinclair of Pasadena beat out NRA director George Creel for the Democratic nomination for governor. In the second half of the decade, a resurgent Right predominated. The turning point, when both workers and soldiers took to the streets, was the San Francisco waterfront and general strike of mid-1934.

4

Bayonets on the Embarcadero

The San Francisco Waterfront
and General Strike of 1934

DESPITE the Depression, San Francisco remained a busy port of call. Its eighty-two docks, aligned along the northern Embarcadero and the southeastern waterfront, could handle up to 250 vessels each working day. In 1933 seven thousand ships arrived and departed. One hundred and eighteen steamship lines maintained their headquarters in the city. It was a man's town, a blue-collar town—teeming, tumultuous, multi-ethnic. Of six hundred thousand residents, four hundred thousand were male. Half the population worked for wages, equally divided between white-collar and blue-collar pursuits, which meant that there were some 150,000 blue collar male workers in the city, or one in four citizens. The streets, saloons, and boarding houses of the city teemed with truckers, stevedores, merchant sailors, the majority of them single. One hundred and thirty-five brothels catered to this disproportionate population. Many of these bordellos, together with 150 gambling establishments and bookie joints, and an undisclosed number of abortion mills, were controlled by the notorious McDonough brothers, Peter and Tom, bail bondsmen who had gathered unto themselves the reins of an invisible underworld empire catering to human frailty. The McDonough brothers were Irish, as were fifty thousand other San Franciscans. There were also 58,000 Italians, 45,000 Germans, 30,000 Scandinavians, 16,000 Chinese, 13,000 Russians, and smaller groupings of Greeks, Hispanics, and African-Americans, making San Francisco as ethnically diverse as it was predominately male.

Male, volatile, close to a frontier life of men in groups, working San Francisco coalesced along the waterfront. The loading and unloading of ships by longshoremen in Frisco jeans, denim shirts, and flat white caps—their cargo hooks fastening onto rolls of hemp, burlap bags of coffee, stacks of cut lumber, guiding these cargos as they were hauled aloft by donkey engine for deposit into dark holds or onto the docks for breakdown and shipment—drove the economic engine of San Francisco. Thousands of blue-collar jobs connected with steam fitting and ship repair, drayage, railroading, and warehousing depended upon the comings and goings of the ships; but an equal number, perhaps more, of white-collar jobs in insurance, freight forwarding, and clerical administration were likewise dock-dependent, as was a major portion of the service sector—the boarding houses, restaurants and diners, the saloons, and some percentage of the transactions at the brothels doing business in the city.

Servicing this economy at its critical point of cargo entrance and departure made the Riggers and Stevedores a powerful union in turn-of-the-century San Francisco. In 1914 employers organized themselves as the Waterfront Employers Union and by 1919 were beginning to regain the initiative under the leadership of Robert Dollar, a flinty, flamboyant sea captain turned shipper and shipbuilder, who directed the successful resistance to the June-July strike called that year by the Riggers and Stevedores. It was a violent confrontation, with Dollar organizing a Law and Order Committee at the Chamber of Commerce and being quoted in the newspapers to the effect that the best way to end the strike was to send ambulance-loads of pickets to the hospital. Fortunately, no one was sent to the morgue that year, although forty-five cases of assault were reported. When the Riggers and Stevedores tried another strike in September 1919, however, one man died in the violence, and the longshoremen lost both the strike and their union. In December 1919 the Waterfront Employers' Union entered into an agreement with a union the employers themselves helped to create, the Longshoremen's Association of San Francisco and the Bay District, a company-controlled union with no ties to the AFL-affiliated International Longshoremen's Association (ILA) headquarted in New York, the most important longshoremen's union in the country. For the next fourteen years, employers dominated the San Francisco waterfront through control of the Blue Book Union, so called because of the blue membership books which each longshoreman had to carry on his person in order to get work.

The employer-controlled Blue Book union epitomized the rollback of union power experienced by labor in San Francisco in the 1920s. After defeating a building trades strike in 1920–1921, the Industrial Association of San Francisco set up a program it called the American Plan in opposition to the closed shops controlled by the Building Trades Council. The Association recruited non-union plumbers, plasterers, bricklayers, and carpenters from across the country and established schools to teach these skills to men willing to work outside the union framework. In April 1926 the United Brotherhood of Carpenters and Joiners, understandably traumatized that some $221 million in construction had taken place in San Francisco between 1921 and 1926 with American Plan labor, launched a strike that was so violent (the carpenters' union brought in professional "sluggers" from out of town) that even the pro-union Board of Supervisors voted a resolution calling for an end to the violence. In October 1926 the carpenters suffered a major blow when their vice president was arrested on murder charges. The strike collapsed, and the Industrial Association and its American Plan gained even further strength through the remaining years of the decade.

No wonder, then, that every effort in the 1920s—and there were several—to bring the AFL-affiliated ILA into San Francisco went down in defeat. Backed by the million dollar-plus war chest of the Industrial Association, the Waterfront Employers Union outmaneuvered and, when necessary, out-strongarmed any longshoremen seeking to bring an independent union into San Francisco. In these struggles the critical issue was the hiring hall. The Waterfront Employers Union did not allow the Longshoremen's Association of San Francisco and the Bay District to have its own hiring hall or even to operate a hiring hall jointly with employers. That would put a potentially dangerous weapon in the hands of labor; for in longshore work, hiring—its *what*, its *where*, and, most important, its *when*—constituted the key to success. Ships arrived and departed at irregular intervals. Scores of ships, for example, could arrive or depart on the same day or, conversely, could remain in port together. Each cargo had its own time demands. A cargo of perishable fruit required quick dispatch, and even durable cargos could come in or out of San Francisco under accelerated time pressures because of the availability of transportation and pre-contracted delivery dates. Like harvest work in the interior, longshore labor was in effect seasonal, with seasons running from a few hours to three days straight, around the clock. Whoever controlled the supply of this labor controlled the waterfront. For employers, even to think of a centralized hiring hall, much less one under union domination, was traumatizing.

And so the Waterfront Employers Union relied on the shape-up. Every morning before six, wharfside employers told a cadre of hiring agents called straw bosses how many longshoremen would be needed that day, and where, and for how long. The straw bosses, who were private contractors, went down to the Ferry Building at the foot of Market Street on the Embarcadero for a shape-up. In a movement repeated so many times it became a ritual, the longshoremen would form a horseshoe around the contractor, who would announce the jobs he was filling for that day. Looking around, the straw boss would then pick his men. A longshoreman had to hold a Blue Book to be eligible to be picked. In many, if not most, instances, a longshoreman would have to be willing to provide the hiring agent with a kickback for being selected or perhaps be known as someone willing to stand for a round of drinks when the straw bosses came through the waterfront saloons.

At best, the shape-up was a humiliating ritual, the men standing around like cattle or sheep, or (dare one say it?) like the women on parade in the city's 135 bordellos, equally humiliated, many of them, by a comparable ritual of selection. As eight o'clock approached, men who had passed unpicked through a number of shape-ups began to panic. There were approximately fifteen hundred jobs available each working day on the waterfront, and more than four thousand men were seeking them. By eight o'clock, when thousands of office workers began pouring out of the Ferry Building terminal en route to the downtown, the cops wanted the shape-ups to be finished, so as not to impede the orderly flow of pedestrian and streetcar traffic.

Those who were lucky enough to be selected might work as briefly as two hours or as long as twenty-four to thirty-six hours at a stretch, depending upon the cargo. While the going rate for 1934, eighty-five cents an hour, seems impressive in comparison to the prevailing rates in farm labor, the sum total of money taken home by individual longshoremen, few of whom ever managed a full week, reflected a less advantaged figure. The weekly take-home wage of the average San Pedro longshoreman in 1933, for example, was $10.45.

Like the shape-up, the speed-up—the pushing, pushing of the rate of work by hard-driving foremen—was also a daily fact of life. Heart attacks, many of them fatal, and the collapse of longshoremen from exhaustion were common occurrences.

Section 7(a) of the National Industrial Recovery Act of 1933 encouraged ILA organizers to return to San Francisco and other Pacific Coast ports and to try once again to establish the ILA as a bargaining agent. Many longshoremen joined the ILA quietly, while maintaining their Blue Book membership. The more militant transferred openly to the ILA, which in early September 1933 granted a charter to Local 38–79 in San Francisco and set up a Pacific Coast District. Most important, Local 38–79 won a ruling from the Board of Adjustment of the NRA stating that Section 7(a) entitled longshoremen to belong to a union of their own choosing. When, the following month, the Matson Navigation Company fired four longshoremen because they belonged to the ILA, Local 38–79 organized a strike against Matson and appealed to George Creel, the NRA regional administrator. Creel appointed a panel (a judge, a priest, a University of California professor) which on 13 October 1933 ordered the four men reinstated. Within the next few months, the Blue Book union went into permanent decline, and by 1934 the ILA had become the union of choice on the Embarcadero.

Having vanquished the Blue Book union, the ILA had now to produce further gains to hold its membership. In early December 1933, at a meeting held at the Building Trades Temple, new demands for higher wages and shorter hours surfaced, together with talk of a coastwide strike. In February 1934 ILA delegates from the major Pacific Coast ports convened in San Francisco and authorized a coast wide strike if the ILA and shippers could not reach an agreement on the newly proposed wage rates and hours. Through the mediating efforts of the ever-involved George Creel, the ILA and the Waterfront Employers Union sat down together on 5 March 1934 in the Employers Union offices at 215 Market Street for the purpose of reaching an agreement.

The meeting did not get very far. The ILA demanded that the Waterfront Employers Union negotiate for the entire Pacific Coast and that it agree to a closed shop contract. The employers denied any right or ability to negotiate for ports other than San Francisco. And as far as a closed shop agreement was concerned, the employers countered, piously using the very same argument the ILA had used to displace the Blue Book union, such an agreement would violate Section 7(a) of the NIRA, which guaranteed freedom of choice to each worker.

On 7 March 1934 the ILA voted to go out on strike on 23 March, if no agreement had been reached by that time. Several subsequent meetings arranged by Creel came to nothing. ILA demands now included a coastwide agreement and ILA control of the hiring hall, as well as a dollar-an-hour wage rate ($1.50 for overtime), a six-hour day, and a thirty-hour week. In paid newspaper advertisements which the Waterfront Employers Union issued on 19, 20, and 21 March, Thomas Plant, the Employers Union president, hammered away at the inconsistency of a closed shop and the spirit of National Recovery.

At this point, George Creel appealed directly to President Roosevelt. The President agreed to appoint a Fact Finding Commission of NRA officials from Seattle, San Francisco, and Los Angeles to investigate and mediate. Creel, in turn, persuaded W. J. Lewis, president of the Pacific Coast District of the ILA, to postpone the 23 March strike deadline and give the NRA board a chance to resolve the conflict.

Astonishingly, it looked for a brief moment as if the spirit of National Recovery, the harmonization of labor and management toward the greater good, might prevail. Throughout April 1934, Roosevelt's Fact Finding Commission hammered out points of concession and agreement. A preliminary agreement was reached as early as 3 April. (Militants later excoriated this 3 April agreement as a sellout.) The Waterfront Employers Union, for its part, agreed to recognize the ILA as the representative of the *majority* of the longshoremen of the San Francisco Bay District. The employers also agreed to a dispatch hall under joint supervision with the ILA, thus ending the hated shape-up. On 20 April employers issued a directive limiting the work week to forty-eight hours and stating that no gang could be worked for more than fifteen hours at a stretch, with time off for meals. Any discharged gang, furthermore, could not be called back to work until it had the benefit of an eight-hour rest period.

On 7 May 1934 the Waterfront Employers Union issued a lengthy proposed settlement fleshing out points under discussion since 3 April. Today, sixty years and more later, this proposal would seem to constitute a major victory for the ILA. At a time when stringent takeaways, not dramatic concessions, characterized the industrial scene, the Waterfront Employers Union, which a year previously had run the waterfront like a feudal barony, was now willing to enter into an agreement as exacting as any in effect in the United States.

Men would be hired through a dispatch hall jointly operated by the Employers Union and the ILA. Instead of the long, humiliating waits of the shape-up system, hiring would be done three times a day—7:00 and 11:30 A.M., 4:00 P.M.—and as rapidly as possible. While the straight time offered was eighty-five cents an hour, fifteen cents below what the ILA was demanding, overtime jumped to $1.25. A long list of special cargos, moreover, carried higher hourly rates. The work day was set at six hours, with an hour off for meals. If no decent restaurant existed at a work site, as was the case at Richmond in the northeast Bay, the employer was to furnish the meal. Travel to points outside San Francisco for work was to be compensated on an hourly basis, with the exception of Oakland and Alameda directly across the Bay, for which a half hour would be compensated. In case of a grievance, a three-person committee jointly appointed by the union and the employers should be selected to investigate, without a work stoppage. All these points of agreement, together with so many others contained in the document—minutiae regarding working conditions, travel and overtime, guaranteed national holidays, compensations for off-hour labor—take on even further significance when contrasted to the poor wages and debased conditions of farm workers or even, for that matter, to the situation of non-unionized white-collar workers doing the paperwork of the shipping industry in office buildings adjacent to the Embarcadero. The longshoremen of San Francisco, it would seem, were on the verge of regaining their turn-of-the-century status as a privileged caste. Even more important, the spirit of the NRA seemed to be prevailing.

What, then, was the difficulty? Why, within a few short weeks, would the ports of the Pacific Coast be shut down in a coastwide strike? The answer is twofold, power and ideology, although the two fused into one compelling motivation on either side of the battle.

The prospect of a Shipping Code drove the first fissure into the proposed agreement. The National Industrial Recovery Act of 1933 contained no code for the shipping industry. In February 1934 J. C. Bjorklund, secretary of the Pacific Coast District of the ILA, pleaded by telegram and letter with General Hugh Johnson, the choleric, hard-drinking soldier-lawyer whom Roosevelt had tapped to head the NRA, to come up with such a Shipping Code as soon as possible, lest the government seem either impotent or negligent in its dealings with the shipping industry. Meanwhile, it behooved both sides, employers and longshoremen alike, to gain or retain as much ground as possible in the way of concessions before an NRA Shipping Code was drawn up, since such a Code would tend to incorporate the structures and procedures which NRA officials, meeting in San Francisco through April 1934, had helped negotiate. Thus the Waterfront Employers Union had inevitably to resist an ILA-only closed shop, an ILA-controlled hiring hall, and a coastwide agreement with the ILA with the same fervor that the militants in the ILA were forced to demand such major concessions. An industry was up for grabs, and the clock was running for both sides of the struggle. A federally mandated Shipping Code would soon be coming which would encase each and every victory or concession in concrete.

Perceived as a bread-and-butter agreement, which was the way that ILA Local

38–79 president Lee Holman (who was soon fired) tended to perceive it, the offer from the Waterfront Employers Union, finalized in the document of 7 May 1934, represented a major success for unionism on the San Francisco waterfront. In terms of the long-range control of Pacific Coast shipping, once a Shipping Code was promulgated, a number of ILA militants, who would soon take over the union, considered the agreement a disaster. Conspiracy theories surfaced on both sides. Professor Paul Taylor, the labor economist from Berkeley, believed that the shippers were willing to take a strike, which could cost them up to $3 million, if such a strike would keep the ILA a localized power in San Francisco rather than a Pacific Coast–wide union with a closed shop agreement and control over hiring. The shippers, for their part, came increasingly to believe that Local 38–79 was a Communist-controlled organization with an agenda extending beyond issues of wages and working conditions.

Even paranoids, as Delmore Swartz pointed out, have enemies. It could not be denied that Communists were active on the Embarcadero. Ever since December 1932 the Marine Workers Industrial Union, a Trade Union Unity League affiliate headquarted in a storefront in the Civic Center area, had been producing the *Waterfront Worker*, a brilliantly effective mimeographed newsletter selling on the docks for a penny a copy. Issued under the auspices of an organization calling itself Albion Hall, the *Waterfront Worker* played a major role—*the* major role, in fact—in galvanizing sentiment for the six-hour day at a dollar an hour ($1.50 overtime), the thirty-hour week, and a union-controlled hiring hall. The *Waterfront Worker* lost no opportunity to attack the Blue Book union while it lasted or to pillory the aging Andrew Furuseth, president of the International Seamen's Union, as a reactionary. As NRA-sponsored negotiations continued through early April, with an agreement in principle coming as early as the 3rd, charges of conservativism were also leveled against Local 38–79 president Lee Holman, who was tending toward a settlement. After a hearing which he could not attend, being sick at home with pneumonia, Holman was stripped of the presidency on 19 April and proscribed from holding office for a full year.

In early May 1934 Local 38–79 of the International Longshoremen's Association held an open meeting. Fifteen hundred members attended, and a strike was voted for Wednesday the 9th. Learning of the vote in New York, Joseph Ryan, international president of the ILA, sent telegrams to the other ILA locals on the coast, asking them not to join the San Francisco strike. They ignored his request. When the longshoremen of Seattle, Tacoma, Portland, San Francisco, San Pedro, and San Diego went out on strike on the morning of 9 May 1934, their walkout had a domino effect among other maritime and waterfront unions. Despite the pleadings of an aged Michael Casey, president of the Teamsters Union, Local 85, the man who had led the General Strike of 1901, the teamsters also voted on the 13th to go on partial strike against the Embarcadero. The fact that both the longshoremen and the teamsters were each revolting against their established leadership as well as against their employers testifies to the ascendant power of militants operating in the rank and file of each union.

On the 14th the boilermakers and machinists joined the strike. The next day, the Sailors Union of the Pacific; the Pacific Coast Marine Firemen; Oilers, Watertenders, and Wipers Association; and the Marine Cooks and Stewards Association of the Pacific Coast, who had also been agitating for improved wages and working conditions and a closed shop, voted to join what was rapidly becoming a total Pacific Coast tie-up. The International Seamen's Union struck on the 16th. Within days, by the 21st, the Ship Clerks Association; the Marine Engineers Beneficial Association; and the Masters, Mates, and Pilots Association had also joined in. By mid-May a total of 34,700 maritime and waterfront workers along nineteen hundred miles of coastline had walked off the job. The gamut of strikers ran from the conservative Masters, Mates, and Pilots Association, an elite group of two hundred deck officers, to the thirteen thousand ordinary seamen claimed by the Communist-controlled Marine Workers Industrial Union. On 16 May 1934 the San Francisco *Examiner* reported that not a single freighter had left a Pacific Coast port the previous day.

Resistance to the strike showed comparable levels of organization. Such efficiency on both sides boded strongly for a protracted struggle. As negotiations began to break down in late April, the Waterfront Employers Union began openly to talk of its ability to handle a strike. As early as 22 March, executive director Thomas Plant cited the availability of twenty-five hundred strikebreakers. When the strike broke out, the Employers Union opened a recruiting office at 23 Main Street under heavy police protection. Two ships, the *Diana Dollar* followed by the *Wilhelmina*, were anchored off the Embarcadero to house strikebreakers without the necessity of their crossing picket lines to get to the docks. (The strikebreakers included three squads of University of California football players, recruited by their coach, William Ingram.) Although the teamsters were refusing to haul cargo to and from the docks, the State-operated Belt Line railroad continued to service the Embarcadero and the rest of the waterfront. The Belt Line kept cargo flowing to and from remote sites, where teamsters had agreed to load and unload. The Belt Line represented a key threat to the success of the boycott. Striking longshoremen eventually resorted to sitting down *en masse* on the tracks, in conscious imitation of demonstration techniques pioneered by Mahatma Gandhi.

The shippers and their allies were quick to welcome government intervention. The day before the strike, members of Roosevelt's Fact Finding Commission individually tried some behind-the-scenes intervention, to no avail. On the morning of the strike itself, 9 May, Senator Robert Wagner of New York, chairman of the NRA National Labor Board and the prime mover behind Section 7(a) of the NIRA, telegrammed William Lewis, district president of the ILA, begging him to postpone the strike until the NRA Fact Finding Commission could begin another round of hearings in San Francisco. On 15 May the governors of California, Oregon, and Washington jointly requested assistance from the federal government. In response, Secretary of Labor Frances Perkins, the first woman cabinet officer in American history, dispatched Assistant Secretary of Labor Edward McGrady out to San Francisco.

A trade unionist who had worked his way up from the print shop of the Boston *Traveler* to the Massachusetts legislature, McGrady had been representing the AFL in Washington prior to being tapped by Perkins. An instinctively conservative Irish Catholic from Boston, professionally oriented toward elite craft unions, the Assistant Secretary found himself in the midst of an industry-wide strike carried on by left-oriented industrial unions which he openly claimed were controlled by Communists. As a mediator, McGrady felt more comfortable with employers, whom he understood from past experience, than with the new breed of militant industrial unionists coming to the fore of the ILA.

These employers, meanwhile, were consolidating their own battle plan. On 21 May the Industrial Association of San Francisco, a citywide organization with a good budget, took over the direction of the strike from the Waterfront Employers Union, which possessed expertise and resources. Guided by its public relations counsel, McCann-Erickson, Inc., the Industrial Association devised a strategy of communicating itself to the public as the voice of reason acting on the high ground, above shippers and unions alike, on behalf of the public interest. Thus the Industrial Association sought to appear to be mediating the strike as a disinterested third party while at the same time directing its course: renting warehouses on the outskirts of the city, assembling its own fleet of trucks, recruiting strikebreakers, raising further funds. Cunningly, the McCann-Erickson strategy kept the burden of proving good faith on the striking unions while the Industrial Association, the agent of the oligarchy, counter-maneuvered on behalf of the shippers behind a smokescreen of public interest.

At the center of the anti-strike resistance stood Roger Dearborn Lapham, the fifty-one-year-old president of the American Hawaiian Steamship Company. In both his virtues and his vices, which were gargantuan, no one better epitomized the ownership class than this fleshy extrovert with sultanic appetites for wine, women, song, poker, cribbage, foreign travel, duck hunting, and golf. Born in New York City in 1883 into a New England shipping family (Yankee clippers), Lapham traveled widely in Europe between prep school and Harvard. Graduating from Harvard in 1905 with a triple major in humanities, Hasty Pudding theatricals, and golf, Lapham spent his post-college years working on the docks as a checker and at other maritime-related occupations prior to joining the executive ranks of the American Hawaiian Steamship Company, which his uncle George Dearborn founded in 1899. In 1920 Lapham settled permanently in San Francisco as president of the company.

Virile, hearty, a man's man in a man's city, Lapham soon became a fixture in the Bay Area establishment, the center of the inner circles of the Pacific Union Club atop Nob Hill, the Bohemian Grove in the redwoods of Sonoma, the golf and country clubs of Burlingame and Pebble Beach. In later years, after his one term as Mayor of San Francisco (1944–1948), Lapham's gambling got out of control, and, according to his grandson Lewis, he squandered the family fortune, frequently losing thousands at cards per day for days at a stretch. In 1934, however, Lapham's appetites were under control as he took to the field as the Henry V of West Coast shippers. Personally courageous, Lapham was capable of addressing a mass rally of striking longshoremen, as he did in 1936, bringing them to their feet in applause and admiration of his bravery, if nothing else. Like many sensual men, Lapham had a strong streak of the skeptic in his nature, which could pass for genial open-mindedness. (As mayor he appointed a number of left-wingers, including one Communist, to city commissions.) He was first and last, however, a spokesman for his class, and his geniality rapidly ran short when his personal interests or those of his class came under threat, as they did in 1934.

Soon, very soon, Roger Lapham found his nemesis, his *doppelgänger* even, in the person of longshore leader Alfred Renton (Harry) Bridges, a thirty-four-year-old Australian immigrant who reverse-reflected Roger Lapham trait for trait. Thin, sharp-featured, terse and sardonic, Harry Bridges had grown up Irish Catholic and middle class in Melbourne. A youthful reading of Jack London's *The Sea Wolf* gave him the desire to go to sea. A reading of London's *The Iron Heel* confirmed his developing bias against capitalism, a trait already in evidence in his reluctance to work for his father collecting rents from the family tenants. Going to sea in 1916, Bridges had his left-wing political vision confirmed when he contrasted the squalor he saw in India and Egypt and the slums of London with the comparative prosperity of ordinary folk in Labor Party–governed Australia. He was especially appalled by the beaten condition of the lower sectors of the British working classes, their bent bodies and bad teeth, their tendency to tug at their forelocks when their betters were around, the squalls of ineffective, self-destructive rage that suddenly swept across the seas of their resignation.

On 13 April 1920 Harry Bridges paid a $10 head tax in San Francisco and became a permanent resident of the United States. For some reason, never fully explained, he did not at the time, or subsequently, apply for citizenship. He joined the Sailors' Union of the Pacific and was briefly, in 1921, affiliated with the IWW. This brief stint as a Wobbly, together with his careless non-citizenship, would later render Harry Bridges quite naked to his enemies. In the meanwhile, he spent the 1920s and early 1930s working obscurely aship and ashore among the rank and file, among whom he preferred to be and from whom he derived his strength, style, and charisma. Lean and austere, understated and deflationary in an Australian sort of way, Bridges countered Roger Lapham's ruddy, fleshy clubman's bonhomie with the demeanor of a thin-lipped, fox-faced leader from the ranks, a look of feral distrust in his narrowed eyes. Bridges countered Roger Lapham's double-breasted suits with a comparable uniform of class identity—a flat white longshoreman's cap, a denim shirt, a cargo hook hanging from the back pocket of his heavy black canvas pants. In later life, serving as a union official (although drawing a modest salary) Bridges wore double-breasted suits and the loud ties Lapham favored and, squiring one or another attractive lady to a local nightspot, resembled his upper-class nemesis in a parallel taste for the sporting life.

Nights out were non-existent in April and May 1934, however, unless one counted the innumerable evenings Harry Bridges spent meeting and organizing as he rose to the leadership of the strike without ever seeming to leave the rank and file. In April Bridges, a member of the militant Albion Hall wing of the union, helped devise the rank-and-file strategy that ousted Lee Holman from the presidency of Local 38–79 when Holman showed signs of settling along the lines of the proposal of 3 April. Also that month, Bridges rose at a meeting and argued down district president William Lewis when that ILA official seemed in an accommodating mood. By the time the strike began on 9 May, Bridges, not Lewis, held the real power in the organization. When Assistant Secretary McGrady met with representatives of the Industrial Association and with Lewis and seven other officers from the ILA West Coast executive committee, Bridges sat quietly in the rear of the room, his chair tilted to the wall. To McGrady it was obvious that Bridges was controlling the executive committee. By the 19th Bridges held the title of chairman of the Rank and File Strike Committee, which was the *de facto* executive committee of the ILA on the West Coast. This time, Bridges did his own talking, telling McGrady that the longshoremen would not go back to work until all other striking unions had settled their disputes. Bridges also spoke to reporters that day with this condition and for the first time was quoted in the newspapers as a strike leader.

Having vanquished local president Holman and West Coast president Lewis, Bridges was ready for a third internal adversary, ILA international president Joseph Ryan. Six feet, two hundred pounds, a flashy dresser, Ryan projected the image of an ex-prizefighter who had done well. Like Assistant Secretary McGrady, Ryan was an Irish Catholic quick to attribute all dissent to Communists. When asked, he could sing a passable "Danny Boy." He had not been on the docks since 1913, and even then he had only worked for a year before being injured and elected to a cushy job by his local. International president since 1927, Ryan favored the arrangement (some would say the fix) over conflict, especially if the strife had ideological overtones. In later years he would be dumped by his union and go on trial for taking bribes.

From the beginning, Ryan was suspicious of the Pacific Coast strike, although he had gone along with it to keep up the appearance of being in charge. On 24 May 1934 Ryan arrived in San Francisco by airplane from New York and, extraordinarily, began to issue statements to the press and negotiate with shippers on his own behalf—without first seeking the approval of the local Strike Committee chaired by Harry Bridges. Four days later, Ryan announced an agreement. The newspapers ran banner headlines that the strike had been settled. There would be no closed shop, but employers could recognize the ILA as bargaining agent on a port-by-port basis. Wages and hours would likewise be settled locally by arbitration. Employers would establish hiring halls at their own expense. These hiring halls would not be under union control, but the union could negotiate on a port-by-port basis rules governing registration and dispatch. The union could also maintain a representative in each hiring hall to insure that ILA members were not discriminated against.

Harry Bridges described the proposed settlement as a sellout. In surrendering the closed shop and control of the hiring hall, Bridges argued, Ryan was allowing employers to probe the union for weaknesses from port to port. Divide and conquer. Nor should the ILA settle without the other striking maritime unions reaching agreements, for without their support the longshoremen would not have been able to mount an effective strike in the first place. On the 29th Ryan appeared in Eagles Hall at an open meeting of the membership. He was met with boos, hisses, and razzberries. Arguing against the settlement, Harry Bridges was met with cheers and applause. Ryan's proposal went down in unanimous defeat. At a secret ballot held two days later, the union rejected Ryan's settlement 2,404 votes against, 88 votes in favor. Learning of the San Francisco decision, Seattle Teamsters president Dave Beck urged longshoremen in the Northwest not to follow suit. The strike was being broken in Los Angeles, Beck stated, and Northwest ports would soon be losing seriously to Southern California. Encouraged by Beck's remarks, Ryan flew north to Portland, Oregon, where the rank and file voted him down by acclamation. He experienced the same rejection from rank and file in Tacoma.

By now, both Ryan and McGrady were openly describing the strike as Communist-controlled. Ryan was especially incensed when the *Western Worker* flooded the waterfront with four thousand copies of a special supplement arguing against settlement. The Oakland *Tribune* carried a long quote from McGrady attributing the prolongation of the strike to the Communists. As early as 19 May, McGrady had been quoted in the San Francisco *News* as saying that Communists had seized control of the strike and were preventing a settlement. Alarmed by the Assistant Secretary's accusation, the White House asked Secretary of Labor Frances Perkins to investigate. At Perkins's request, the Office of Immigration and Naturalization asked their San Francisco office to look into the case of Harry Bridges. Working with the Crime Prevention Detail of the San Francisco Police Department, an immigration inspector filed a report clearing Bridges of any Communist associations.

Even as the oligarchy railed against Communist control, Bridges threw gasoline on the flames by his willingness to accept Communist participation in the strike. The *Western Worker* reported strike news and issued strike-related extra editions, such as the one that so infuriated Ryan. Workers International Relief, a Communist Party USA affiliate, ran a strike kitchen. Another affiliate, International Labor Defense, put up bail and provided lawyers for arrested strikers. The Workers Ex-Servicemen's League and other front groups sent men over to the picket lines.

Sam Darcy, Communist Party chief on the West Coast, met frequently with the Strike Committee and was generous with his advice. Even William Z. Foster, Communist Party presidential candidate in 1924, 1928, and 1932, was in town, albeit recovering from a near-fatal heart attack and hence, to his regret, unable to throw himself into the strike effort.

The stage was set for another acting out of Left/Right–fascist/Communist mimesis, this time in urban circumstances. As if to drive home the European reference, union lawyer Leo Gallagher returned on the morning of the 19th from Berlin, where he had been defending a young Communist accused of setting fire to the Reichstag. A delegation of striking longshoremen met Gallagher when he arrived in San Francisco. With appropriate references to the situation in Germany, Gallagher exhorted the men not to trust McGrady and to hold out for complete victory, advice they proceeded to follow.

To this conflict, the Right and the Left each brought a mindset prepared for violence. Longshoremen, for their part, were by temperament and experience not averse to a punch-up as a means of settling disputes. Harry Bridges would discipline this proclivity to an impressive capacity for mass resistance at the Battle of Rincon Hill.

The Right prepared itself more systematically. In 1933, the nadir year of the Depression and the peak year of Communist-led agricultural strikes, the crusading District Attorney of Alameda County, Earl Warren, called for a coordinated state-wide assault on Communist provocateurs by the lawmen and prosecutors of California. In August 1933 San Francisco police chief William Quinn enthusiastically took Warren's call for an anti-Communist crusade to a meeting of the California Peace Officers Association. Chief James Edgar Davis of Los Angeles opened the convention with a warning that "the Reds are trying apparently to get control of labor in the State of California." Regrettably, Davis railed, most police had their hands tied. The Sheriff of San Diego County stated that the Communists were hiding out behind President Roosevelt and the National Recovery Act. The sheriff of Alameda County recommended the use of railroad brake-sticks to control riots. (A brake-stick was a four-foot wooden pole, about the circumference of a baseball bat, used to control baggage and mail sacks when they were loaded or unloaded from trains.) The sheriff of Fresno County lamented the fact that the Communists were usually too wily to place themselves in situations in which brake-sticks might be applied. Chief Davis rose to reply that his counterparts from rural areas had it easy. "In some of the larger cities," he complained to his colleagues, "it isn't possible to use the methods you can use in some of the smaller cities and counties. God knows we would like to put them all in the hospital, particularly the leaders, but we can't get away with it any more; there is too much sentiment in their behalf. . . . Too many Sentimental Alices take their side." [1]

San Francisco police chief William Quinn was determined to be nobody's Sentimental Alice. The day before the longshoremen went out on strike, Quinn organized a special anti-strike force—182 patrolmen, seventeen mounted policemen, five radio cars—and had them on alert the morning of the 9th with an unambiguous directive to bear down hard on any threats of disorder.

San Francisco's finest did not have long to wait. That very day, they were called down to the Embarcadero to break up a crowd of longshoremen trying to block a convoy of trucks bringing two hundred strikebreakers to the *Diana Dollar*. Shortly thereafter, the cops were dispatched to Pier 35 to break up a gang of longshoremen threatening strikebreakers loading a Grace Liner. That day as well, strikers pulled a man from his car on the Embarcadero and beat him severely in the mistaken belief that he was a strikebreaker.

The next day, the police were called to the recruiting office of the Waterfront Employers Union on Main between Market and Mission when demonstrators were threatening to shut down that facility, insultingly located a mere two blocks from ILA headquarters on Steuart Street. A donnybrook ensued.

Two days later, the 12th, the police were summoned to the new employers' recruiting office on Mission Street, four blocks up from the waterfront. There they clashed with five hundred longshoremen. Five policemen were injured, together with three strikers. "From now on," ran a police department communiqué after this clash, "strikers will be shown no quarter." At police request, the employers' union moved its headquarters to the waterfront, where it could be better protected.[2] On the 17th, strikers barricaded the Oakland piers and fought their way aboard the steamship *Oregon Mary*. Six strikebreakers suffered serious injuries in the melee, and several men were also hurt in another riot in San Francisco. Ambulances were kept from coming to the Embarcadero by telephoned death threats to the ambulance unit of the county hospital. Even the ILA blamed the terrorist threats on the Communists!

Chief Quinn had initially been suspicious of tear gas, but on the 13th he ordered a batch from the Lake Erie Chemical Company, represented in San Francisco by salesman Ignatius H. McCarty, a police buff whose interest in the mechanics of crowd control went beyond the call of duty, even for that era of go-getter salesmanship. "These cops here," McCarty wrote his superior in a letter later subpoenaed by the La Follette Committee, "when they hit a man over the head are not satisfied unless he goes down and a good split occurs. Our clubs are too light for this purpose. Should you contemplate making them heavier? Advise."[3]

Heads aplenty were split on 28 May. Each day of the strike since the 9th, the longshoremen had been parading a thousand strong behind an American flag along the Embarcadero. Picketing had been illegal in San Francisco since the longshoremen's strike of 1919, but only on the 28th, as ILA president Ryan was in the process of signing an agreement, did the police intervene. As the long line of longshoremen attempted to cross over to the dock side of the Embarcadero at Pier 18, a detachment of mounted and foot-patrol police officers charged into the formation, clubs swinging. The longshoremen resisted with fists, bricks, and cobblestones. A number of officers were pulled from their horses. The police withdrew, regrouped, then fired tear gas. When a cluster of longshoremen made a move in the direction of Pier 20, police lieutenant Joseph Mignola ordered his men to fire their shotguns into the crowd. Fortunately, the distances were too great for fatalities, although many longshoremen were peppered with buckshot. Captain Arthur De Guire later defended Lieutenant Mignola's action on the grounds that the parade seemed to be led by Communists. Two days later, the police charged into another parade, this time near the Ferry Building, injuring a number of longshoremen.

On Memorial Day, the 31st, Ryan's agreement, at the insistence of Assistant Secretary McGrady, was voted upon in a secret ballot after being shouted down at the Eagles Hall meeting two days earlier. Once more, Lieutenant Mignola's men went into action. This time, the police had a group of real-live Communists to charge into, members of the Young Communist League who had organized an anti-war, pro-strike Youth Day rally near ILA strike headquarters near the Embarcadero but had neglected to secure a permit or had applied for one but been refused. Because it had turned out to be too late to cancel the meeting, a crowd of some 250 young people gathered on the Embarcadero near Steuart Street, growing increasingly restless as the ill-organized event produced neither leadership nor speeches. Once again, accounts vary. Either the crowd began moving toward ILA headquarters on Steuart Street, or a young man, perched on the shoulders of another young man in the style of a college cheerleader, started to address the crowd. ("Comrades and fellow workers" was all he got to say.) In any event, the police charged, laying about with riot clubs and blackjacks. Sixty-five young men and women fell to the ground, many with serious head injuries. Twenty-four had to be hospitalized. By contemporary standards, it was a police riot, with uniformed officers and some plainclothesmen fanning out to club or beat bystanders, men and women alike.

The great maritime strike continued into June, gaining rather than losing strength. On the 8th, the tugboat engineers joined in, making it even more difficult for ships to tie up in San Francisco.

Over in Room 200, City Hall, Mayor Angelo Rossi was feeling increasing pressure from the business community to do something, anything, about the stalemate. A florist by profession, genial, outgoing, the former executive director of the Downtown Association, Rossi had succeeded the perennially popular James "Sunny Jim" Rolph in 1931 when Sunny Jim had gone to Sacramento as governor. Two years into his gubernatorial term, in the fateful year 1933, Rolph began to suffer a series of heart attacks under the pressures of office: the cotton strike, first of all, followed by a lynching in San Jose which Rolph condoned, earning himself national opprobrium and the sobriquet Governor Lynch. The maritime strike of May and June 1934, in which Rolph was under constant pressure to send the National Guard into San Francisco, finished Sunny Jim off, and he suffered a final heart attack on 2 June as the strike approached its second month. And now

Angelo Joseph Rossi, Rolph's protégé and successor, was coming under comparable stress.

Enter, or rather reenter, Joseph Ryan, the embattled international president of the ILA. Ever since the rank and file of San Francisco, Portland, and Tacoma had rejected, even hooted down, his settlement of 28 May, Ryan had been sequestered in Seattle, living at the Washington Athletic Club, with a like-minded unionist, Teamster president Dave Beck. (In later years Beck would serve the prison time Ryan narrowly escaped.) Both Beck and Ryan were by temperament and self-interest alienated from the type of left-wing industrial union, with its tedious talk of solidarity and the rank and file, being pushed by Harry Bridges and the Albion Hall clique down in San Francisco. The ILA, Ryan reminded anyone who would listen, was an AFL affiliate: an elite vertical craft union, not a horizontal industrial union cutting across scores of occupations. Bridges's talk of all unions settling simultaneously in all ports on the Pacific, or none settling at all, impressed Beck and Ryan as so much Communist-inspired nonsense—or worse, a strong step in the direction of a single coastwide union, embracing every aspect of the maritime industry, an even more dangerous Communistic notion. And as far as a union-controlled hiring hall was concerned, Ryan personally favored the shape-up. After all, union leaders as well as hiring agents could earn kickbacks from the system, as was the case on most Atlantic waterfronts.

Working together, Ryan and Beck devised a four-step strategy. First, establish a new settlement (more or less the same one rejected in late May). Second, isolate the San Francisco Strike Committee by painting it Red. Third, sign an agreement with employers in various regions. Fourth, work on ILA locals outside San Francisco to settle. When the longshoremen's united front began to break apart, the other striking maritime unions would also capitulate.

Capitalizing on Beck's local authority, Beck and Ryan presented a settlement plan to Seattle-Tacoma area employers, who accepted it. The plan called for (1) hiring halls run jointly by employers and the ILA local, (2) recognition of the ILA local as bargaining agent, but with an open shop and no provisions to equalize earnings between ILA members and other longshoremen, (3) the settlement of wages and hours by arbitration, and (4) a no-strike provision forbidding sympathy strikes with other maritime unions.

Even before the Seattle-Tacoma local could vote on the Beck-Ryan plan, the two union leaders entered into negotiations with the Industrial Association of San Francisco. Each side entered these discussions convinced that the San Francisco Strike Committee was Communist-controlled and must be isolated from the rest of the maritime industry. Each side had a stake in the outcome that went beyond the specifics of a settlement. Even to think of a coastwide maritime industrial union under Communist influence sent shudders through the spines of Beck and Ryan, old-style labor leaders whose days would soon be ended, and the Industrial Association, which would then be faced on the left by an organization equal to itself. Paul Eliel, the research director of the Industrial Association, specifically linked what was going on in San Francisco with events in the fields of California. If an industry-wide Communist-controlled maritime union were achieved, Eliel pointed out, an industry-wide Communist-controlled agricultural union and an even stronger Cannery and Agricultural Workers Industrial Union would soon follow.

Buying into Eliel's scenario, the negotiators who gathered in Mayor Rossi's office on 16 June 1934, labor and management alike, were increasingly concerned with the possibility of a Communist takeover of Pacific ports. Nothing less than the victory or defeat of Communism on the waterfront and, by implication, in agriculture—and perhaps even in all California—hung in the balance. On one side of a meeting table sat Thomas Plant, representing the combined Waterfront Employers Unions of Seattle, Portland, San Francisco, and Los Angeles. Next to Plant sat three officers of the San Francisco Industrial Association. On the other side of the table sat Joseph Ryan and three West Coast ILA officials and three Teamster officials: Dave Beck of Seattle, and Michael Casey and John McLaughlin of San Francisco. Seated at the center of the table were Mayor Rossi, representing an increasingly agitated City and County of San Francisco, and the three NRA mediators, Dean Henry Francis Grady, Dr. J. L. Leonard, and Judge Charles Reynolds, who had negotiated the almost-forgotten agreement of 3 April. Harry Bridges was not invited, nor were any other representatives of the Rank and File Strike Committee.

At one point in the four-hour meeting, Plant asked Ryan the obvious question. Would the rank and file in San Francisco accept any agreement signed at this meeting?

"I don't think so," Ryan answered unequivocally. "This local has been captured by radicals and Communists who don't want a settlement."

"Then what's the point of our reaching an agreement here," Plant asked, "if it's going to be rejected as soon as we announce it?"

"I give you my unqualified assurance," Ryan responded, "that I can make an agreement on behalf of my membership that will be effective."[4]

Casey, McLaughlin, and Beck from the teamsters chimed in. They would help Ryan and the West Coast ILA officials make the agreement stick. Solemnly, Plant signed for the employers. Ryan signed for the ILA, and J. E. Finnegan signed for the ILA's Pacific Coast District. Then the guarantors signed. Casey, McLaulgin, and Beck guaranteed on behalf of the teamsters. John Forbes guaranteed on behalf of the Industrial Association. Rossi guaranteed on behalf of San Francisco; Reynolds and Leonard on behalf of the NRA mediation board.

The men emerged from the mayor's office and smiled for the cameras. The McCann-Erickson publicity machine went into operation, and by the next day newspapers across the country were carying the story that a fair and binding agreement had been reached in San Francisco.

The next afternoon, at two, three thousand longshoremen gathered in Eagles Hall on Golden Gate Avenue. While the men waited for Joseph Ryan to arrive (he was a half hour late), speaker after speaker flailed away at the settlement. When Ryan did arrive, he was met with boos and jeers and cries of "Fink!" and "Faker!" Harry Bridges asked Ryan why the Strike Committee had never been consulted prior to the agreement signed yesterday in City Hall? Ryan made an inept answer, and the boos and jeers resumed. The contrast between the two figures at the podium—the flashily dressed Ryan, flush with good living, so obviously out of sync with his alleged constituency; the lean, hawk-featured Bridges, dressed as a longshoreman, totally in harmony with the rank and file he led— cinematically underscored the divergent styles of East Coast and West Coast unionism.

Ryan's agreement was rejected by unanimous acclamation. More important, the men voted to establish a fifty-member Joint Marine Strike Committee with five members representing each of the ten striking unions. Harry Bridges was elected chairman. Far from isolating the San Francisco longshoremen, the 16 June agreement had in one day stimulated the creation of an even stronger inter-union coastwide front and elevated Bridges to the status of labor tribune of the Pacific Coast.

Tribune Bridges, opined Joseph Ryan upon his second departure in disgrace from San Francisco, was acting for the Communists. "This immediate repudiation of an agreement made in good faith," stated Thomas Plant on the 18th on behalf of the Waterfront Employers Union of San Francisco, "is convincing evidence that the control of the Longshoremen's Association is dominated by the radical element and Communists whose purpose is not to promote industrial peace; rather their avowed purpose is to provoke class hatred and bloodshed and to undermine the government."[5]

On the same day, 18 June 1934, John Forbes telegrammed President Roosevelt on behalf of the Industrial Association: "We understand there is evidence in hands of Department of Labor that Communists have captured control of Longshoremen's Union with no intention of strike settlement. We have reached crisis threatening destruction of property and serious loss of life in various ports on Pacific Coast unless you act to compel performance on the part of Longshoremen's Unions of the agreement signed by their International President."[6]

What exactly was Forbes urging Roosevelt to do? Send in federal troops as President Hayes had done in the railroad strike of 1877? Such a suggestion lay just beneath Forbes's talk of a Communist takeover and impending death and destruction on the Pacific Coast. Roosevelt was too wily a politician to be stampeded into any such action, but the mindset revealed by Forbes, a conventional businessman addressing the President of the United States in such apocalyptic terminology, underscores how vividly the Left/Right scenario could play itself out in California during the 1930s. Forbes's talk of death and destruction, his suggestion of troops, was more than a rhetorical ploy. Like so many Californians of his class, Forbes more than half-believed what he was telling the President.

Conveniently for Roosevelt, Congress had just passed Public Resolution 44, which empowered the President to appoint special boards to mediate labor disputes affecting interstate commerce. Mayor Rossi urged Roosevelt to appoint a locally oriented board, which the President did by executive order on 26 June. The National Longshoremen's Board, as it was called, consisted of Assistant Secretary of Labor McGrady, representing the federal government, and two prominent San Franciscans, Archbishop Edward Hanna, a mediator in the 1933 cotton strike, and attorney Oscar Cushing, president of the Legal Aid Society of San Francisco. Mediator McGrady, of course, had already branded the strike as Communist-inspired.

The first meeting of the National Longshoremen's Board occurred on 27 June. The Industrial Association had already vowed to reopen the Port of San Francisco on the 28th, using the Belt Line railroad along the Embarcadero and a trucking fleet from the Atlas Trucking Company driven by non-union drivers. At the request of Hanna, Cushing, and McGrady, the Industrial Association agreed to postpone this plan (for the fourth time) while the Board attempted to mediate.

Some time during this brief cooling-off period, an ex-prizefighter who knew Harry Bridges contacted him for a private meeting. He had $50,000 in cash on his person, the former pugilist told Bridges when they met. It was his if he agreed to settle the strike. Bridges toyed momentarily with the notion of accepting the money and giving it to the strike fund, but that seemed too risky. "Hell, if I had taken that money," he later speculated, "I'd have been dead two minutes later. Then my body would have been found with the $50,000 in my pocket. I would have been dead and the union would have been dead, too." In 1964 a Matson Company executive confirmed the story, which had by then become a waterfront legend. "Oh, we tried to bribe him all right," confessed Randolph Sevier. "The money was put up by an officer of this company."[7]

By now, late June 1934, the situation in San Francisco was escalating toward increased violence, a general strike, and the arrival of troops. Each side of the confrontation, Left and Right, would soon have the opportunity to act out its deepest fears and defensive strategies. At times, there seemed to be a rehearsal, an almost choreographic quality to the conflict, as if a street-ballet entitled *Revolution* were being performed with a cast of thousands on the Embarcadero.

The Port of San Francisco had been closed to traffic since 9 May. Shippers estimated this closure was costing them $1 million a day. In its oft-delayed plans to reopen the Port, the Industrial Association had to deal with five key problems: loading and off-loading, trucks, warehousing, the Belt Line railroad, and hostile pickets. The hundreds of strikebreakers housed in the *Wilhelmina* and the *Diana Dollar* answered the first problem. The non-union trucks of the Atlas fleet and a number of privately protected warehouses away from the waterfront answered the second and third difficulties. To control the pickets so as to move their trucks and allow the Belt Line railroad to operate, the Industrial Association would need the strong support of the San Francisco police. Should the police prove unable to control the situation, the shippers would need the National Guard. Through the skilled efforts of McCann-Erickson, the Industrial Association had positioned itself on the side of law and order and the American way, with the striking unions on the side of the Red Menace. Thus the shippers received the full support of local government. In the Port of Los Angeles at San Pedro, shippers paid over $100,000 to hire private security forces. In San Francisco, by contrast, the police department confronted striking pickets at taxpayers' expense.

After a long meeting on 23 June with the Industrial Association, the Chamber of Commerce, the Police Commission, the chief of police, and members of the State Harbor Commission, Mayor Rossi announced to the press on 24 June that the Port of San Francisco would be opened, even if he had to ask Governor Frank Merriam to call in the National Guard. The governor, in turn, issued a statement that he was ready to send in the troops if the Port could not be opened through peaceful means. Despite the militancy of his rhetoric, Mayor Rossi was playing for time in the hope that the three-man National Longshoremen's Board appointed by Roosevelt could mediate a settlement. At his request, the Industrial Association postponed all plans to open the Port until 2 July. When the National Longshoremen's Board failed to mediate any sort of agreement, the Industrial Association notified Archbishop Hanna and Mayor Rossi that it would go ahead with its plans to open the Port on the 2nd, as planned.

On the morning of 2 July, fifteen hundred longshoremen gathered in front of Pier 38 and awaited the Atlas trucks. Mayor Rossi was in his office pleading with Industrial Association officials to postpone their plans for just a little while longer in hopes of a negotiated settlement. The shippers refused and demanded police protection for their trucks. Late that afternoon, after most longshoremen had drifted away, a squadron of mounted police cantered to Pier 38 and formed a protective corridor. From a side street, five trucks sped across the Embarcadero through the police ranks into Pier 38. Steel doors rang down behind them. Thanks to this furtive dash, the Port of San Francisco had been symbolically opened.

The next day, 3 July 1934, five thousand longshoremen and their sympathizers had gathered in front of Pier 38 by eleven. Seven hundred policemen stood by in various formations, a number of them wearing helmets, gas masks, and riot gear. A line of railroad boxcars sealed off the south side of the Embarcadero. On the northern end, the police had drawn up a line of patrol cars. A *mise-en-scène* as dramatic as this required an audience. On the elevation of Rincon Hill overlooking the curving sweep of the Embarcadero, a crowd gathered in anticipation of Act Two. They did not have long to wait.

Shortly after noon, the steel rolling doors of Pier 38 lifted, and five trucks escorted by eight police patrol cars made their slow exit. Police captain Thomas Hoertkorn, revolver in hand, stood on the running board of the lead patrol car. "The port is open!" Hoertkorn shouted, and the caravan began a slow progress down the Embarcadero toward a warehouse on King Street near the Southern

Pacific Depot at Third and Townsend. There the trucks were unloaded of their cargo (birdseed, coffee, automobile tires), and the convoy returned to Pier 38 for a second, then a third haul.

At approximately one-thirty, the next and inevitable stage of this stylized confrontation, violence, broke out. As usual, accounts differ. Did a group of longshoremen, as some claim, frustrated by the deliberately inflammatory unloading of trucks, begin to pelt the police with bricks? Or did Captain Hoertkorn, as others claim, cry out to his men, "Let 'em have it, boys!" when the longshoremen began to escalate the scurrility of their shouted epithets? In any event, police and pickets clashed near the warehouse. Laying down a barrage of tear gas, police wearing helmets and gas masks advanced into the crowd to disperse it into smaller sectors, which mounted patrolmen and club-wielding officers on foot then attacked. Groups of longshoremen resisted with thrown objects—bricks, cobblestones, railroad spikes—and their fists. At Second and Townsend streets, the police responded with gunfire. Two men were wounded, one of them a bank teller at work in the American Trust Company on the corner. Argonne Riley, a thirty-three-year-old strikebreaker from Los Angeles, was the day's only fatality. Riley had picked the wrong day to come ashore from the *Diana Dollar* for a few drinks. Several men had beaten him, Riley related after being found unconscious in the gutter at Clay and Embarcadero. The police had Riley treated for minor facial cuts, then booked him into the drunk tank. When Riley complained that midnight of terrible pains in his head, the cops took him over to the Harbor Emergency Hospital, where, nine minutes after his arrival, the alcoholic strikebreaker with the poignantly beautiful name died of a fractured skull.

Act Three, the Fourth of July. San Francisco observed the holiday. This itself underscored the dramaturgical nature of the confrontation. Do revolutions have holidays? (Perhaps they do.) In Sacramento, Governor Merriam, distressed by the continuing refusal of the Joint Strike Committee to allow the Belt Line to move freight (even that day, longshoremen had stopped a train headed for a Matson liner bound for the Philippines from Pier 30) announced that he had ordered Major General Seth Howard, the adjutant general of California, to mobilize units of the National Guard for deployment into San Francisco on the 5th if the Joint Strike Committee continued to block the Belt Line. San Francisco newspapers published a full-page advertisement by the Industrial Association declaring that the Port of San Francisco was open for business. At Civic Auditorium, Mayor Rossi was denouncing to a mass rally the Communists who had seized control of the strike.

Act Four, 5 July 1934, subsequently known as Bloody Thursday. The crowd which gathered on and near the Embarcadero on Thursday morning following the Fourth of July holiday, both participants and spectators alike, numbered into the thousands. As if in recognition of the staged nature of the occasion, vendors moved among the milling spectators, hawking candy bars, gum, cigarettes. All that was lacking was a program of participants. San Francisco now found itself locked into a citywide species of street theater (costly to some as it turned out) in which the fascist/Communist drama could be acted out on the great sweeping scenic northern waterfront of America's premier Pacific port, the Embarcadero. In further acknowledgment of the stylized nature of the encounter, the business of the city continued on its ordinary path. Commuters disgorged from the Ferry Building at the foot of Market Street and streamed into the downtown, which teemed with traffic as automobiles and the two competing streetcar lines of the city brought in the early morning work force.

Along the Embarcadero Chief Quinn arrayed eight hundred of San Francisco's finest, up a hundred from Tuesday's complement. The police were armed with extra-long, extra-heavy riot sticks from the Lake Erie Company (Ignatius McCarty had made his sale) and canisters of a vomiting or nausea gas, a step up from the tearing variety. Not since the eviction of the Bonus Army from Washington in 1932 had an American city fielded so many police squadrons against such a large segment of its citizenry. In the drama of Cossacks versus Bolsheviks, San Francisco was fielding an all-star cast.

The ensuing events were at once real and unreal, necessary and unnecessary. The settlement proposed on 2 July by the National Longshoremen's Board, even then meeting, was very close to what would eventually be agreed upon. In this sense, Bloody Thursday accomplished little in the way of real gains for the longshoremen. On the other hand, the police were unable to club the longshoremen into submission. Police violence, in fact, prolonged their willingness to strike. By Thursday, 5 July, each side desperately desired to act out its ideological position and to simulate, if possible, the appearance of a victory. And so the drama ensued.

At eight in the morning, on cue, just as the Governor and the Industrial Association promised, a Belt Line locomotive began nudging two refrigerator cars toward the Matson Line docks on Pier 30. A crowd of between two and three thousand strikers tensely watched. In an effort to clear the track, the police ordered the crowd to move back. Instead, pickets began barraging the police with rocks and bricks. The police drew back, and a group of pickets, rushing forward, set the boxcars afire. When fire trucks arrived, the police turned the high-pressure hoses on the crowd, then advanced into the broken ranks, clubbing the pickets, who resisted with their fists, back across the Embarcadero into the Barbary Coast district along Pacific Avenue.

Further south on the Embarcadero, meanwhile, at Piers 38 and 40, trucks from Atlas were being loaded with cargo for movement to a nearby warehouse. When a crowd of two thousand pickets failed to make way, fighting broke out. The scene quickly became a phantasmagoria of clubbing police and fistfighting longshoremen. Yells and curses filled the air. Sirens wailed. Shots rang out. Tear gas grenades hissed and smoked amongst swirling knots of longshoremen and advancing police.

Toward nine-thirty, the dispersed strikers were regrouping on Bryant Street near

Rincon Hill, a four-story knoll just off the Embarcadero bounded by Bryant, Beale, Folsom, and First. Now ensued the *sine qua non* of the unfolding scenario of urban revolution—barricades! Throwing a barricade across Bryant Street, the longshoremen resisted the advancing police until a pincer movement dispersed them from behind. Retreating to the top of Rincon Hill, the strikers assembled another barricade under the direction of longshoreman Henry Schmidt, using bricks from nearby buildings recently demolished to make way for the forthcoming San Francisco–Oakland Bay Bridge. Harry Bridges took charge of another contingent.

Slowly, behind a covering barrage of rifle and pistol fire, a line of mounted police advanced up the hillside through burning patches of dry grass ignited by tear gas bombs. At the barricade, the mounted police were driven back by a hail of bricks. A second assault on foot was also repulsed. Improvising with two-by-fours and innertubes, the longshoremen rigged an oversized slingshot capable of propelling bricks and cobblestones at a high velocity for distances up to four hundred feet. The whimsy of this weapon—boys playing with slingshots to protect their fort—added to the real/unreal nature of the day's events. When a line of police cars headed down Harrison Street bringing reinforcements, a group of longshoremen took up positions on an overpass and pelted the cars with bricks. Some vehicles veered out of action with smashed windshields. On their third and successful march up Rincon Hill, police in gas masks advanced behind a barrage of tear and vomiting gas. Fortunately, the longshoremen had already abandoned their position, and the gas fell behind an empty barricade. Bridges's and Schmidt's handling of their men that morning in the Battle of Rincon Hill would later earn them the compliments of the district commandant of the Marine Corps, who watched the siege through field glasses from his upper-story office on Harrison Street.

Noon. Lunch time. As if a work whistle had blown, each side withdrew for a mid-day break. Even a committed Communist chronicler of the day compared the lull to Hollywood extras taking a lunch break on the set. An uneasy quiet reigned along the Embarcadero. Realizing that their plans to halt the Belt Line and Atlas trucks through sheer force of pickets was now impossible, given the weight of police intervention, several thousand longshoremen regathered themselves near and around ILA headquarters on Steuart Street where downtown ran into the Embarcadero. A number of nearby union kitchens were serving lunch. Toward one o'clock Harry Bridges was eating at a union dining hall at the corner of the Embarcadero and Mission Street: a revolutionary general from the rank and file, eating unpretentiously alongside his men during a lull in the fighting.

Suddenly, shots rang out, followed by yelling and screams. Looking outside, Bridges could see the police driving back his men with clubs and gunfire. During the lull of the lunch hour, the police had regrouped themselves into two phalanxes, one north of the strikers' headquarters, the other to the south. Toward one o'clock they began to close upon Steuart Street in an effort to clear the area with a pincer movement.

A number of things were now going wrong with the stylized scenario. First of all, the longshoremen considered the area near their headquarters to be neutral territory. Pickets, punch-ups, rioting, tear gas, and the like were one thing in the accepted *mise-en-scène* of the Embarcadero, where each side had a stake in the proceedings and knew the rules; but Steuart Street was in the downtown, just across from the Ferry Building, on the edge of the commercial and shipping district. The longshoremen had not retreated here to picket or demonstrate but to tend to their wounds, rest up, and eat lunch. And besides: the pincer maneuver chosen by the police was bound to provoke dangerous violence at close quarters. A sweeping movement by the police from one direction could have cleared the area, but the pincer attack herded hundreds of longshoremen together with no avenue of retreat against advancing police.

The game had become dangerously real—and deadly, as Harry Bridges realized from his restaurant window. Assisted by tear gas salesmen Joseph Roush and Ignatius McCarty, the police opened fire on the surrounded men with tear gas bombs, then fired at them with rifles and shotguns. Roush later boasted in a letter to his home office that he had personally used a Federal Laboratories tear gas launcher to bag himself a Commie. "I might mention that during one of the riots," Roush wrote, "I shot a long-range projectile into a group, a shell hitting one man and causing a fracture of the skull, from which he has since died. As he was a Communist, I have had no feeling in the matter and I am sorry that I did not get more."[8]

Roush's alleged Communist, twenty-six-year-old longshoreman James Engle, a member of the ILA but not the Communist Party or any other radical organization, fell to the ground on the Embarcadero between Folsom and Howard, having been ambushed by Roush as he stood talking to a friend in a parked automobile. The Federal Laboratories long-range projectile created an inch-and-a-half hole in Engle's skull behind his right ear. Miraculously, the young longshoreman survived.

Concerning the fate of two men who did not survive the day, accounts vary. The police later claimed to the coroner's jury that six thousand men, congregated in and around Steuart Street, began to riot. They surrounded the car of two police inspectors rushing to the scene, pounding on the vehicle and yelling, "Kill them!" When the inspectors got out of the automobile, the police claimed, they were struck by a hail of rocks and bricks, and a number of rioters tried to overturn their vehicle. Fearing for their lives, the inspectors fired two shots from a shotgun and several shots from a revolver at the rioters.

Other witnesses before the coroner's jury disputed this version. A plainclothes policeman, claimed one witness, had jumped from the car and fired his shotgun from the hip into the crowd when he was hit on the leg by a brick. The officer in question, another witness testified, jumped from the car and taunted the crowd, "If any of you sons of bitches want to start something, come on!" He then began to fire at the crowd, dodging around his car like a man shooting birds. As Harry Bridges saw it, the officer wheeled about and fired in three directions.[9]

Three men fell to the sidewalk, one dead, one dying, one wounded. Howard Sperry, a striking sailor, died instantly a few doors from the ILA headquarters at 113 Steuart Street where he was heading to have his strike card punched after working the lunch shift at the same union kitchen where Bridges had eaten. Longshoreman Charles Olsen, shot in the arm, face and chest, lay alongside the body of Sperry. A news photographer caught Olsen as he half-raised himself from his prone position, a look of shock on his face. Nicholas Counderakis, an unemployed cook and a member of the Communist Party (where he was known as Nick Bordoise), fell to the pavement, mortally wounded, at the corner of Mission and Steuart, then staggered down Mission Street to the corner of Spear, where he died. Like Sperry, Counderakis had been working at the union kitchen through the lunch hour.

By late afternoon the San Francisco newspapers were recapping the statistics for Bloody Thursday: two dead; thirty suffering gunshot wounds; forty-three clubbed, gassed, or hit by projectiles. The emergency ward of the county hospital was overflowing. One patient: San Francisco *News* photographer Joe Rosenthal, shot through the ear by a stray bullet. A decade later, Rosenthal would win the Pulitzer Prize for his photograph of the Marines raising the flag on Iwo Jima. He was more frightened on Bloody Thursday, Rosenthal insisted. Piles of wreaths and flowers covered the spots where Sperry and Counderakis had died, placed there spontaneously in the immediate aftermath of the shootings.

By this time as well, two regiments from the 40th Infantry Division of the California National Guard, Major General David Prescott Barrows commanding, occupied the waterfront from Fisherman's Wharf to China Basin. Adjutant General Seth Howard had ordered the Guard to move into the San Francisco waterfront at approximately the same time that the shooting broke out on Steuart Street. Highly pressured to declare martial law in San Francisco, Governor Merriam refused. Declaring martial law is risky business politically, and Merriam was running for election in November. Instead, Merriam authorized the adjutant general to send in two regiments, the 159th Infantry and the 250th Coast Artillery, under the command of Colonel Richard Mittelstaedt, with precise orders to secure only state property along the Embarcadero. The 159th occupied the waterfront from Fisherman's Wharf to the Ferry Building. The 250th held the sector from the Ferry Building to the Matson dock at Pier 32. Later, the 185th Infantry was deployed inland from Pier 32 along Brannan to Third Street, then down Third to China Basin, so as to secure access routes to and from the Industrial Association warehouses. Two infantry battalions and a tank company from the 160th Infantry were held in reserve. Two battalions from the 160th occupied the Oakland water-front.

By 17 July a total of forty-six hundred National Guardsmen had been deployed along Bay Area waterfronts. Barrows established his divisional headquarters on a Sacramento River passenger steamer, the *Fort Sutter*, anchored at Pier 3 near the Ferry Building. From there, the spit-and-polish, outspokenly anti-Communist Barrows—brigadier of the line in the federal reserves, major general in the California National Guard, former president of the University of California, veteran of the American Expeditionary Force sent to assist the White Russians in their counter-revolution against the Bolsheviks—presided over a San Francisco that could no longer manage its own affairs. The next day, the Belt Line moved 203 cars. Trucks from Atlas Trucking darted back and forth between piers and ware-houses.

"No seditious force or mob," General Barrows announced to the press, "can make a dent in this force we have assembled to defend the Embarcadero."

Harry Bridges agreed. He told his men: "We can't stand up against police machine guns and National Guard bayonets."[10]

They could, however, organize a general strike in protest. In the arsenal of organized labor, a general strike is the ultimate weapon. Having been driven from the waterfront by force of arms, their strike dangerously near to being broken (even now the whistle of the Belt Line could be heard on the waterfront), Harry Bridges and the Joint Marine Strike Committee now proposed that organized labor bring San Francisco to a halt.

The leaders of organized labor, meaning the mainline AFL unions, initially wanted no part of it. General strikes were dangerous. They could easily backfire. An aggrieved public, its city shut down, could swiftly turn against the unions. The newspapers could be expected to fan the flames of an already rampaging Red Scare. The Industrial Association would call for federal troops. When Bridges brought his request for a general strike to the San Francisco Labor Council on Saturday, 7 July, union leaders balked, but they also made Bridges a counter-offer. They would form a committee of seven top leaders, headed by Edward Vandeleur, president of the Labor Council, and call on the Industrial Association and try to break the deadlock on the two most important issues, union control of hiring halls and a joint settlement among all striking unions, longshore and off-shore. The Vandeleur delegation, which called itself the Strategy Committee—heavyweights from the Butchers, the Bakery Wagon Drivers, the Molders, the State Federation of Labor, together with the editor of the *Labor Clarion*—got nowhere. With the National Guard on the waterfront, the Industrial Association felt itself dealing from a renewed position of strength.

On Monday, 9 July, Harry Bridges and the Joint Marine Strike Committee played their next hand, the funerals of Sperry and Counderakis. As political theater, as a choreographed pageant in a decade filled with highly rehearsed demonstrations on both the left and the right, the funeral was a brilliant maneuver; and it both expressed and intensified a growing sentiment for a general strike among the rank and file.

Ever since their deaths on Thursday the 5th, the bodies of Sperry and Counderakis had lain in state at ILA headquarters on Steuart Street. For three days, a steady stream of mourners had been filing past the open coffins. Sperry's casket was draped in an American flag, in recognition of his service in the World War and his membership in the Veterans of Foreign Wars. Longshoreman veterans, dressed in their military uniforms, stood by as an honor guard. A framed photograph of Franklin Delano Roosevelt was placed conspicuously on a bare wall behind the open coffins. After a tense negotiating session with Police Chief Quinn, the Strike Committee received permission for a funeral procession on the 9th, with the longshoremen acting as their own monitors. Quinn agreed to keep the police away from Steuart and Market streets on two conditions: no Communists in the parade and no strike banners or signs of any sort. The longshoremen agreed. What they were planning, the single most dramatic labor demonstration in San Francisco history, would be capable of making its own statement.

On the afternoon of the 9th, in a packed ILA headquarters, longshoreman Alex Walthers read an eloquent eulogy to Sperry and Counderakis: the Army veteran and the hard-working cook from Crete, shot in the back and dying on the street, martyrs to labor. After the service, the coffins were placed on separate open flatbed trucks, smothered in floral arrangements. Three additional flat-bed trucks laden with flowers and a car carrying Counderakis's widow and young son followed. Veterans in uniform and a color guard carrying the American flag led the procession, followed by a band playing a funeral march by Beethoven. Some fifteen thousand mourners, led off by longshoremen in their black Frisco jeans, hickory shirts, and flat white caps, marching in slow, steady step to the music, followed the cortege up Market Street to Dugan's Funeral Parlor on Seventeenth and Valencia. The procession extended the entire length of Market Street from the Ferry Building to Valencia. Thousands watched from the sidewalks. Men bared their heads as the caskets passed. With no police in sight, longshoremen performed all traffic direction and crowd control, as if the ILA, and not the National Guard, had taken over the city. In later years, people remembered how quiet everyone was, mourners and spectators alike. As the procession continued, the city fell silent, with only the music of Beethoven heard in the distance.

Each side, longshoremen and oligarchs, had mounted effective instances of street theater: the parade up Market Street, the patrolling of the helmeted, khaki-clad sentries on the Embarcadero. When the Guard had marched in, Bridges and his colleagues had been deflated. Now, with this largest and most impressive labor march in San Francisco history underway, the shippers experienced a chill. "It was one of the strangest and most dramatic spectacles that had ever moved along Market Street," admitted Paul Eliel, of the Industrial Association. "Its passage marked the high tide of united labor action in San Francisco."[11]

Throughout the week, 9 to 15 July, Monday through Sunday, Harry Bridges and the Joint Marine Strike Committee lobbied for support of a general strike to begin on Monday the 16th. On the morning of the funeral, Bridges made a brilliant appearance at the first public session of the National Longshoremen's Board. His message remained adamant: union control of hiring halls, a joint settlement with all striking maritime unions. The following evening, Tuesday the 10th, two thousand teamsters met at Dreamland, an auditorium in the Western Addition, to consider a strike vote. Teamster president Michael Casey, George Kidwell from the bakery drivers' local, and Edward Vandeleur, president of the San Francisco Labor Council, were arguing forcefully against a general strike vote and seemed to be winning the crowd when supporters from the teamsters fetched Bridges from the street where he was waiting with a thousand longshoremen and seamen for the teamster vote. Once again, Bridges pulled off a rhetorical *tour de force*, precise, idiomatic, pitched perfectly to the rank and file.

Labor stood at a crossroads, Bridges argued. The defeat of the maritime strike would threaten all labor, even the powerful teamsters. No, he was not a Communist. (This in response to a question from the floor.) "If it were true, I would have been exposed long ago." [12] Another question from the floor: what about the offer made yesterday to the National Longshoremen's Board by Thomas Plant on behalf of the Waterfront Employers Union—to submit the strike to arbitration by the Board? He was personally against it, Bridges replied; but he would abide by the vote of the membership. When it was over, Bridges secured a unanimous strike vote from the teamsters.

Yet even amidst this scene of support, there were reservations, as if in recognition of just how highly symbolic, ritualized even, the entire situation had become. An all-out general strike approaches a state of civil resistance verging on insurrection. Even as they took their strike vote, the teamsters drew back from such a position. The teamsters would stay away from the waterfront and most businesses, and pickets would turn away most trucks heading into the city; but food, dairy— and beer!—deliveries would continue. The union would also maintain an emergency dispatch line with the power to grant exceptions for humanitarian reasons to the no-delivery rule. Thus the teamsters signaled that their quarrel was with the shippers and waterfront employers, and not with San Francisco (or society) as a whole. Harry Bridges concurred. He envisioned the general strike not as a revolution but as a highly controlled demonstration against the police killings of the 5th and the use of troops to reopen the Port. In preparation for the general strike, the unions issued a leaflet (two hundred thousand copies, distributed nationally) describing its limited goals and reiterating that food and milk deliveries would continue and that there would be no effort to interfere with gas or electricity.

At a meeting of the San Francisco Labor Council held on Saturday, 14 July, representatives from 115 unions assembled to consider the general strike set for Monday the 16th. Sixty three unions voted to join the strike. Even here, however, a braking mechanism was at work as the mainline AFL leadership sought to ride out the whirlwind which the longshore and maritime strike had created. Having voted to join the strike, the unions created an expanded General Strike Committee, with Vandeleur as chairman. Nominated as vice chairman, Bridges was defeated, 262 to 203, by a representative from the ferryboatmen, who were not even on strike. Only a threatened revolt from the floor secured Bridges's appointment to the General Strike Committee of fifty. Only one other longshoreman was also appointed.

Even as the union leadership thus tempered the general strike, which rank-and-file sentiment had made inevitable, bringing it under mainline control, restricting its scope and goals, minimizing the influence of the ILA, the other side was maximizing the confrontation through the time-tested technique of a Red Scare. Their goal was to force Roosevelt to intervene, with warships in the harbor if at all possible and federal troops on the streets—in suppression of the strike, most obviously, but also in corroboration of their claim, half honestly held, half meretriciously used as a strategy of maneuver, that subversives intent on revolution had taken over the maritime unions.

Instinctively, Roosevelt was cautious. American presidents do not like to send in federal troops and have rarely done so. Democratic presidents are even more reluctant to commit troops to suppress a legitimate strike. A Democratic president struggling to reassemble a society disassembled by the Great Depression could be expected to be even more cautious. Expressing his complete confidence in Secretary of Labor Frances Perkins to handle the situation in San Francisco, Roosevelt embarked on the first of July on the Navy cruiser USS *Houston* for a vacation cruise down the Atlantic Coast through the Panama Canal to Hawaii.

Madame Perkins was not one to be bullied, even by the likes of Roger Lapham, who had been doing his best to stampede the Secretary, and thus the President, into precipitous action. An experienced social worker and government official who had risen to the post of industrial commissioner for the State of New York, where she served under Governors Alfred Smith and Franklin Roosevelt, Frances Perkins sat in the inner circle of Roosevelt's New Deal advisors. She was at once tough, pragmatic, and idealistic—and very much on the side of working people. Instinctively suspicious of Red Scares, she listened with skepticism on 14 and 15 July as Roger Lapham tried to convince her in the course of two lengthy long-distance telephone calls that Communists had seized control of the San Francisco strike.

On the 16th, the first day of the general strike, Lapham sent a telegram to the Secretary asking her to take action under federal statutes to deport aliens engaged in subversive activities (Lapham had Harry Bridges in mind) and to sue the striking unions under provisions of the Sherman and Clayton acts for conspiring to obstruct interstate commerce and foreign trade. "As I have previously told you," Lapham wired the Secretary, "and as can be verified from the Commanding General of the Ninth Corps Area or any person familiar with the situation, the present movement is largely led and directed by the Communist Party and its members, most of whom are aliens."[13] Lapham requested Perkins to ask the President to enact a Shipping Code immediately so that guidelines for negotiations could be established. Lapaham also wanted Perkins to request the National Longshoremen's Board to hold immediate elections among the rank and file on whether or not the strike should be arbitrated. Lapham's third and fourth requests, a Shipping Code and general elections on the arbitration issue, were reasonable. Even his urging of suits under the Sherman and Clayton acts, while hardball, seem understandable, given the unusual nature of a general strike. His request that the federal government deport Bridges and others as subversive aliens, however, betrayed the more fundamental strategy the oligarchy had chosen to confront the prolonged crisis: a Red Scare.

On the evening of the 14th, Mayor Rossi went on the radio with a highly charged address which ended: "Equally I am determined that as to those in this city who willfully seek to prolong strife, either for their own selfish ends or for the disturbance or overthrow of this government, and of the Government of the United States—all of the forces at my command, all others that my be required will be brought to bear to prevent their carrying out their plans." [14] Following the broadcast, the Mayor declared a state of emergency in San Francisco, which allowed him to govern with expanded powers. Following precedents set in the earthquake and fire of April 1906, to which the mayor referred frequently, Rossi named a Committee of Five Hundred, headed by attorney Florence McAuliffe, to oversee the city during the emergency.

Some took this Red Scare directly to the White House itself. On the night of 14 July James Moffett, a Department of Commerce official stationed in San Francisco, telephoned the President's personal secretary, Colonel Marvin McIntyre, with a rambling, semi-hysterical message based, Moffett told McIntyre, on information provided by Kenneth Kingsbury, president of Standard Oil. Moffett told McIntyre that the general strike was under the control of Communists, who had been planning it for months, and could be expected to spread to Seattle, Portland, and Los Angeles. Similar messages reached Secretary of State Cordell Hull and Attorney General Homer Cummings, who had to be personally calmed down by Frances Perkins. Oregon governor Julius Meier had the temerity to send Roosevelt an inflammatory telegram aboard the *Houston* itself. "We are now in a state of armed hostilities," Meier telegrammed. "The situation is complicated by communistic interference. It is now beyond the reach of state authorities." Despite the fact that he had himself not ordered out the Oregon National Guard, Meier urged Roosevelt to steam to the Pacific Coast in the *Houston* and handle the situation personally or give NRA director General Hugh Johnson the authority "to prevent insurrection which if not checked will develop into civil war." [15] Even Roosevelt's trusted secretary Louis McHenry Howe suggested by telegram that Roosevelt might direct the *Houston* to move closer to the Coast so that the President could steam into the naval base at San Diego if necessary and personally arbitrate the situation. "In the San Francisco strike," Roosevelt later observed, "a lot of people completely lost their heads and telegraphed me, 'For God's sake, turn the ship around!' . . . Everybody demanded that I sail into San Francisco Bay, all flags flying and guns double-shotted and end the strike. They went completely off the handle."[16]

And so, the Sunday silence of San Francisco on 15 July 1934—no streetcars or taxis, little if any automobile traffic, deserted streets, the downtown a canyon of empty skyscrapers—continued into Monday the 16th, Tuesday the 17th, Wednesday the 18th. For three days, San Francisco seemed a city under occupation, with various authorities—General Barrows in his headquarters on the *Fort Sutter*, Chief Quinn in his office at the Hall of Justice on Kearny Street, Mayor Rossi in Room 200 of the City Hall, Edward Vandeleur and the Strike Strategy Committee at the Labor Temple on 16th Street in the Mission district—administering their sector of the city and wondering what the other was up to. For three days, the Strike Strategy Committee functioned as a San Francisco Soviet, granting or denying permission for trucks to move, opening or closing restaurants. Across town, another Soviet had formed itself under the leadership of *Examiner* publisher John Francis Neylan and the Newspaper Publishers Council, which was in the process of seizing the initiative in the divided city.

Throughout the 1920s, 1930s, and 1940s John Francis Neylan, the San Francisco–based counsel to William Randolph Hearst, had no trouble making every short list of the most influential people on the Pacific Coast. As a recent graduate in law from Seton Hall University in New Jersey, Neylan served as a reporter on the San Francisco *Bulletin* during the graft prosecutions and caught the attention of the chief prosecutor, Hiram Johnson. When Johnson became governor in 1910, he named the twenty-four-year-old reporter director of the Board of Control, which is to say, chief financial officer of the State of California. In 1916 Neylan passed the bar and set up a flourishing practice in San Francisco. William Randolph Hearst first retained him in 1918. The next year, at Hearst's request, Neylan assumed the publisher's role at the *Call*, later the *Call-Bulletin*, in addition to his private practice. By 1934 Neylan was serving as general counsel for the Hearst organization and Hearst's personal deputy for the five Hearst newspapers on the West Coast, which included the San Francisco *Examiner* and the *Call-Bulletin*.

A Progressive en route to the right (a path he was traveling alongside his former boss Hiram Johnson, then United States Senator, and William Randolph Hearst himself), John Francis Neylan had always sustained amicable relations with mainline labor and its generally conservative leadership. Working people formed the core of the *Call-Bulletin* readership and a significant percentage of *Examiner* subscriptions. Teamster president Michael Casey was a personal friend. Neylan had even defended Charlotte Anita Whitney after her conviction on charges of criminal syndicalism in 1920. Recently, Neylan had criticized the Waterfront Employers Union for controlling its labor force through the Blue Book union. The newspapers themselves treated the typographers' union with kid gloves, which was why the typographers and pressmen did not join the general strike, allowing the news-papers to publish during the crisis. Along with the rest of the oligarchy, however, John Francis Neylan feared the young, militant leadership gathered around Harry Bridges, with its commitment to horizontally integrated industrial unionism, espe-cially now that these newcomers had demonstrated their ability to tie up the entire Pacific Coast. Cutting short his Hawaiian vacation, Neylan convened a meeting of newspaper publishers on the evening of 14 July in his suite at the Palace Hotel. (Like so many of the city's elite, Neylan maintained his major residence further down the Peninsula in San Mateo County.) That evening, after listening to Ney-lan say that subversives had taken over the strike, the publishers of the *Examiner*, the *Chronicle*, the *News*, the *Call-Bulletin*, the Oakland *Tribune*, and the Oak-land *Post-Enquirer* all agreed to form a Newspaper Publishers Council to coordi-nate an anti-strike campaign by the Bay Area press. The publishers agreed to clear all strike-related stories and editorials with each other through the Council so as to achieve a united front.

The bound volumes of the Bay Area newspapers published in mid-July 1934 reveal today just how blatantly the publishers and editors followed Neylan's sug-gestion. San Francisco is depicted as a city on the verge of armed insurrection. Photographs of soldiers, tanks, and police are everywhere. In one photograph, helmeted soldiers maneuver a wheel-mounted fifty caliber machine gun into posi-tion. Under the headline "Hatching Trouble for Possible Troublemakers," the *Call-Bulletin* ran a photograph on 17 July of a soldier peering from the hatch of a tank on the waterfront. "Ready for all comers," ran the caption, "who might wish to break the quiet that obtained throughout the city today was this tank operator of the California National Guard, who stood ready to slam down the hatches with his crew and saunter into anyone foolish enough to defy this and other heavily armored outfits." An *Examiner* photograph depicted a line of mounted police officers, wearing gas masks, prepared to sweep Cossack-like into any mob that might materialize. The *Chronicle* ran a front-page article by San Clemente developer Ole Hanson, former mayor of Seattle, describing how he had crushed a general strike in that city in 1919. When a non-striking union trashed a striking union's headquarters on Valencia Street, the *Chronicle* ran a photograph with approving captions. When on the 17th Governor Merriam, resisting the hys-teria being fanned by the San Francisco press, refused to declare martial law, the newspapers buried the story.

Such slanted, inflammatory coverage disgusted Paul Smith, the talented young financial editor of the *Chronicle*, soon to become managing editor when still in his mid-twenties and, a decade later, a Marine battalion commander during fierce fighting in the Pacific. Paul Smith was impeccably connected on both the left and the right. Lincoln Steffens of Carmel was a friend, but so was former president Herbert Hoover of Palo Alto, in whose home Smith had lived as a private secre-tary. Smith disbelieved the Communist conspiracy argument being advanced by his editors and by *Chronicle* publisher George Cameron. In the weeks prior to the general strike, Smith had walked the Embarcadero by night and talked to longshoremen as they stood around their makeshift bonfires. What the rank and file wanted, Smith became convinced, was an end to the corrupt shape-up system and a union-controlled hiring hall, not a bloody revolution.

With the help of Ray McClung, a San Joaquin Valley newspaperman trusted by the longshoremen, Smith secured an interview with Harry Bridges but was getting nowhere with the laconic strike leader. As a parodic ploy, Smith asked in mock seriousness: "Tell me, Mr. Bridges, just how serious do you think the class war is in America, and what stage is it in?" Rising to the humor, Bridges arched a thin eyebrow and, looking past Smith, said to McClung: "Kee-rist, you don't mean to tell me there's anybody on the San Francisco *Chronicle* who *knows* there's a class war in America."[17]

Dropping his initial suspicion, Bridges gave Smith his interview. Speaking on the Fourth of July, a day before the shootings on Steuart Street and the arrival of the National Guard, Bridges predicted that a general strike would bring together the left and right wings of the labor movement. By anyone's standards Bridges had given Smith a sensational story. Smith augmented the interview with the quotes from longshoremen whom he had interviewed on his nightly visits to the pickets' bonfires. Despite personal pleas to publisher George Cameron and editor Chester Rowell, Smith's interview with Harry Bridges was never run in the *Chronicle*; for it made Bridges and his men seem too sympathetic and, worse, blatantly non-subversive. Later in the year, Smith was asked to an off-the-record meeting of civic leaders, where he was horrified to hear the murder of Harry Bridges, phrased as "his disappearance from the scene," discussed as a serious option. When Smith protested, the men backed off, saying that Smith had over-interpreted the word "disappearance."[18]

An atmosphere so polarized and so poisoned led inevitably to the big Red Scare of mid-July 1934. A pattern of repression hitherto confined to rural areas now asserted itself in urban circumstances, with high-ranking government officials acting as cheerleaders. Both Mayor Rossi, on the 14th, and Governor Merriam, on the 16th, made radio addresses blaming the general strike on Communists. On the 17th General Hugh Johnson, executive director of the NRA, gave the Phi Beta Kappa address before a crowd of five thousand at the Greek Theater on the Berkeley campus. Johnson interrupted his talk to indulge in a tirade over the general strike that set new standards for this outspoken, intemperate New Deal official. In the course of his rambling invective, Johnson came close to calling for vigilante action on the part of the people of the Bay Area "to wipe out this subversive element as you clean off a chalk mark on a blackboard with a wet sponge."[19]

Even as Johnson was speaking, National Guardsmen were sealing off the Embarcadero headquarters of the Marine Workers Industrial Union with two machine guns mounted on the rear of trucks. (This is perhaps the most chilling image from the entire strike—truck-borne machine guns deployed by American soldiers on American streets for possible use against other Americans. Within the decade, thousands in Europe would be meeting horrible deaths from similar machine guns mounted atop similar truck beds.) With their quarry thus sealed off from escape, the police then moved in for a surprise raid and arrested eighty five. That evening, the *Call-Bulletin* ran a full page of photographs of billy-club–toting officers packing arrested members of the Marine Workers Industrial Union into paddy wagons. Working "with the diligence of sardine packers," the *Call-Bulletin* noted, "the police managed to cram fifty radical suspects into one wagon." All in all, some three hundred men were rounded up and packed into jail cells designed for half that number. Since few could meet the $1,000 cash bail set by the courts, they languished behind bars for weeks, with only the vaguest of charges of criminal syndicalism lodged against them.

"There is hysteria here," Lincoln Steffens wrote Secretary Perkins in an open letter on the 19th, "but the terror is white, not red. . . . Let me remind you that this widespread revolt was not caused by aliens. It takes a Chamber of Commerce mentality to believe that these unhappy thousands of American workers on strike against conditions in American shipping and industry are merely misled by foreign Communist agitators. It's the incredibly dumb captains of industry and their demonstrated mismanagement of business that started and will not end this all-American strike and may lead us to Fascism." [20]

The next day, the 18th, the Strike Strategy Committee, over the strong objections of Harry Bridges, voted 191 to 174 to end the general strike the following day and to submit the entire dispute to the National Longshoremen's Board for arbitration. Among other inconveniences, the Red Scare had reached the conservative unions. How long could they hope to remain beyond suspicion? Would the next raid be their turn? Deprived of their trade union support, the longshoremen and the other maritime unions remained on strike hoping that the teamsters, who were submitting the matter to a general vote, would remain with them. Yet even the teamsters had begun to realize that they had pushed it just about as far as it could be pushed, having tied up the Pacific Coast since the 7th of May. Anxiously, Bridges and his colleagues awaited the crucial decision of the truckers.

The teamsters voted on the 19th to return to work. Even as they were voting, John Francis Neylan was hosting a luncheon meeting for shippers and other waterfront employers at his home in Woodside south of San Francisco. Within a few short days, the Newspaper Publishers Council had become the Committee of Public Safety of the strife-torn city, the one entity superseding all others in influence. At the affair, Neylan served only ice water and coffee so as to keep the meeting focused and clear-headed. Neylan's goal was simple: to persuade the Waterfront Employers Union to agree to arbitration. Neylan read the employers the riot act. By ignoring the legitimate rights of labor, he told them, the shippers had played into the hands of the radicals. Cleverly, Neylan was now using the Red Scare as a prod in a different direction—toward settlement by arbitration. By the end of the day, Neylan had persuaded the shippers to issue a press release stating that they would not only agree to arbitration with the longshoremen but that they would bargain collectively with the seamen's unions, once those unions had elected representatives under the supervision of the National Longshoremen's Board. Rarely has ice water accomplished so much!

Encouraged by the shippers' press release of the 19th and by the return of the teamsters to work on the 21st, the National Longshoremen's Board emerged from its passivity. In a bold maneuver, the Board bypassed Harry Bridges and the Strike Committee and went directly to the ILA membership with a coastwide vote on the question: "Will the International Longshoremen's Association submit to arbitration by the National Longshoremen's Board the issues in dispute in the longshore strike and be bound by the decision of the Board?" The vote was 6,504 yes to 1,525 no. Even San Francisco, center of resistance, voted overwhelmingly for arbitration, 2,316 for, 759 against. On the morning of 31 July 1934, after eighty-three days of strike action, the longshoremen returned to work up and down the Pacific Coast. The National Longshoremen's Board began its arbitration hearings a week later, on 8 August.

Published on 12 October 1934, the Arbitrators' Award offered the longshoremen a partial but significant victory. First of all, the longshoremen won a coastwide collective bargaining agreement, thus prevailing over a major point of resistance of management that all contracts be on a port-by-port basis. Second, they won the termination of the detested shape-up in favor of hiring halls which were to be operated jointly by the union and the employers. While the union was not granted exclusive control over these halls, which represented a partial victory for management, the longshoremen did win an important provision: all dispatchers were to be elected by the men themselves, another blow to the shape-up system and its corrupt hiring agents, with their insatiable demand for kickbacks. By winning control of the dispatcher, the ILA had won *de facto* control of the hiring halls, despite the joint operating agreement. The employers, in turn, could solace themselves with the knowledge that in theory at least non-union longshoremen, once they qualified for the dispatch list, had the same right to employment as members of the ILA. The longshoremen also won a structured grievance procedure involving an outside arbitrator at each port. Their failure, finally, to win their wage demands of a dollar an hour (they were awarded ninety-five cents) was offset by their victory in securing a six-hour day, with time and a half for overtime.

In the very depths of the Depression, labor had organized, virtually overnight, a major American industry, West Coast shipping, winning agreements that in one form or another would last for the rest of the century. The 1934 strike galvanized organized labor across the United States, setting in motion an intense period of organization that resulted in the emergence of the Congress of Industrial Organizations as a powerful, militant presence in American labor. The longshoremen had done this, moreover, without benefit of protection from Section 7(a) of the National Industrial Recovery Act, which had no Shipping Code, or the further definitions of unfair labor practices set forth in the Wagner-Connery Act (also called the National Labor Relations Act) passed the following year.

Not only had the longshoremen won major concessions, they had thereby created an industrial culture balancing the rights and obligations of both labor and management in a setting in which there had previously been merely a one-sided system of exploitation, as John Francis Neylan had so outspokenly told the waterfront employers over ice water at Woodside. The longshoremen had done this, moreover, using the most problematic weapon in the arsenal of organized labor, the strike: not merely a local strike, but a coastwide, industry-wide strike lasting eighty three days, with four of these days involving a thoroughly unprecedented general strike in San Francisco.

Only in retrospect did the grave risks each side had run make themselves clear. First of all, there was the constant risk of serious violence, which both camps of the maritime strike constantly skirted: the longshoremen with their tendency to mass demonstrations and physical protest (they were, after all, physical men in a very physical milieu); the police by their seeming eagerness to be provoked and to respond with a counteractive violence far superior in firepower and deployment to anything the longshoremen could offer. Miraculously, given the intensity of the confrontations, only three men had lost their lives. Three years later, when striking steelworkers and their families marched on Memorial Day against a Republic Steel plant in South Chicago, ten fell dead and ninety were wounded when police fired into the demonstration. On numerous occasions, San Francisco had all the potential for such a disaster, or even worse.

Then there was the tenuous battle for public opinion. While San Francisco did possess a long and sustaining labor tradition and had twice previously endured serious strikes on its waterfront, the universal resort to a Red Scare by management and key government officials—shipper Roger Lapham, Mayor Angelo Rossi, General Hugh Johnson of the NRA, General David Barrows of the National Guard, Chief of Police William Quinn, the editors and editorial writers of the major newspapers, among others—put Harry Bridges and the Joint Maritime Strike Committee in constant risk of its reputation, indeed its very ability to continue functioning outside the restrictive environment of city prison, where so many of the striking rank and file were finding accommodations. Given the severity of the Criminal Syndicalism Act, a Red Scare in California was no trivial matter. At any moment, the strike of 1934 might have provoked a full-scale repression which, using the available weapon of Criminal Syndicalism, could have destroyed organized labor in the maritime industries, as the Associated Farmers would soon be doing in agriculture. Fortunately, President Roosevelt and Secretary of Labor Perkins refused to be stampeded. Had FDR, in his colorful phrase, sailed into San Francisco Bay with flags flying and ships' guns double-shotted, the fascist/Communist mimesis at the center of the strike, its acting out of an inner drama of revolution and repression, would have edged into actuality. As it was, the acting out came dangerously close to the real thing, especially in the demonstrations and shootings of early July. In the aftermath of the strike, the Right meditated its revenge. The Democratic gubernatorial nominee, meanwhile, longtime Socialist Upton Sinclair, stood on the brink of bringing the Left triumphantly into the State Capitol in Sacramento.

5

EPIC Intentions

The Gubernatorial Campaign of 1934

*B*ECAUSE California was not heavily industrialized, it took longer for the Depression to make itself fully felt. By the time of the Bank Holiday of mid-March 1933, California had caught up with the industrialized states. But then, rather rapidly, the economy of California, unburdened by a massively failed industrial infrastructure, began a spotty but discernible recovery as the nadir year 1933 edged into 1934, Year One of the New Deal. The long-shore and maritime strike took place, as such strikes frequently do, just as things were beginning to get better. By late 1934 employment in manufacturing had climbed back to 84 percent of 1923–1925 levels, although overall payrolls in this sector recovered only 64 percent. More and more people, in other words, were returning to work, but they were working for less. Such a state of partial recovery and partial impoverishment created its own special form of restlessness.

Since recovery was associated in great part with the new Democratic administration in Washington, Democrats in California began to feel a surge of hope regarding the race for governor in 1934. In April of that year, Democrats edged ahead of Republicans in registration for the first time in the century. In San Francisco, George Creel, head of the Regional Labor Board of the NRA, was preparing to parlay his impressive, if scattered credentials—newsman, propaganda chief for Woodrow Wilson, the public official most responsible for ending the great cotton strike of 1933, not to mention his personal association with FDR—into a dash for the Democratic nomination and a likely victory in November: an exhilarating prospect for a hard-drinking ex-newsman with a tenth-grade education and only a few years' residence in the state.

Down south in Pasadena, another and even more unlikely candidate, novelist Upton Sinclair, one of America's most prolific writers, was also preparing to run. A Socialist, Sinclair had left the Democratic Party a generation earlier disgusted by the corruption of the Tammany Hall machine in New York. Throughout late 1933 a group of disaffected Democrats led by Santa Monica hotelman Gilbert Stevenson had been meeting with Sinclair in an effort to persuade him to reenroll in the party of his Baltimore ancestors and challenge the Democratic establishment led by Senator William Gibbs McAdoo, the wealthy former secretary of the treasury and former son-in-law of Woodrow Wilson. It was all rather preposterous: Stevenson, the eccentric owner of a small beachside hotel, an occasional utopian tractarian, persuading Sinclair, a better-known but even more eccentric novelist and pamphleteer, a Socialist with no administrative or mainstream political experience, to seek the highest elective office in the state.

Even more preposterously, Upton Sinclair allowed himself to be persuaded that only his candidacy as a Democrat could save California from the economic slump and from the fascism he believed was coalescing behind the administration of the ailing Governor James Rolph. On the first day of September 1933, Sinclair drove to City Hall in Beverly Hills, where he and his wife Mary Craig, who passionately opposed his political plans, had recently purchased a home, and registered as a Democrat. Sinclair also completed a pamphlet cast in the form of futurist fiction, *I, Governor of California and How I Ended Poverty—A True Story of the Future*, which soon became the manifesto of one of the most improbable political campaigns in American history.

At age fifty-four, sitting outdoors in his swimming trunks in the sunshine, rail-thin from tennis and vegetables, pecking out his reformist-utopian tract on the typewriter on which he had already ground out millions of words, Upton Sinclair had many identities: novelist, playwright, pamphleteer, Socialist iconoclast who had taken on the meat industry, big oil, organized religion, the movie business, the oligarchy of the Southland. For all his quirkiness, however, indeed because of his eccentricities—his teetotalism, his diet of uncooked fruits and raw vegetables, the messianic obsession with which he pursued each and every cause, including tennis—Upton Sinclair was also the most representative Southern Californian of them all and hence, rather plausibly, the next governor of the State.

In 1906, at the age of twenty-eight, Upton Sinclair awoke like Lord Byron to find himself famous, propelled to notoriety by a best-selling muckraking novel, *The Jungle*, a story of Lithuanian immigrants working in the meat packing industry of Chicago. Aroused by Sinclair's descriptions of unsanitary conditions and practices (in one scene a worker falls into a grinder and leaves the factory as sausage links), President Theodore Roosevelt summoned Sinclair to an impromptu conference at the White House. The President found himself being lectured by a thoroughly unintimidated young writer who could talk as forcefully as Roosevelt. The furor created by *The Jungle* helped TR get a stalled Pure Food and Drug Act through the Congress.

A utopianist by temperament, Sinclair devoted his earnings from *The Jungle* to the founding of a cooperative, the Helicon Home Colony, in Englewood, New Jersey, with himself as first among equals, and a young Yale dropout, Harry Sinclair Lewis, working as a janitor. (Lewis later dropped Harry in favor of Sinclair Lewis, and the Sinclair in each writer's name frequently got them confused in the popular press.) In March 1907 Helicon burned to the ground, and Upton Sinclair's total assets went up in smoke. Homeless and broke, Sinclair and his first wife took refuge with H. Gaylord Wilshire, the former Southern California fruit rancher and Los Angeles real estate developer who had converted Upton to Socialism in 1904: a laying on of hands by the most prominent turn-of-the-century Southern California Socialist on the young champion who would carry the standard through the 1920s and 1930s. A further California connection occurred when Sinclair dedicated *The Moneychangers* (1908) to Socialist Jack London of Sonoma County.

While Helicon had vanished, the cooperative ideal behind the colony continued to burn brightly in Sinclair's breast. Indeed, it fused ever so subtly with California itself after Sinclair moved there in 1916 with his second wife, Mary Craig Kimbrough Sinclair, who went by her masculine-sounding middle name Craig, at once a family legacy and a lingering element of Greenwich Village bohemianism in a self-described Southern belle from Mississippi. Within the year, the Sinclairs became affiliated with the Socialist circle in Pasadena revolving around Chicago steel heiress Kate Crane Gartz and John Randolph Haynes, mainline Philadelphian with an M.D. degree and a doctorate in philosophy from the University of Pennsylvania who had migrated to Southern California in 1887, where he pursued Socialism of the Fabian variety, practiced medicine, and found time to make millions in real estate.

Upton and Craig moved to South Pasadena in 1916, into a rambling two-story home on Sunset Avenue, covered by a trellis of pink roses, dramatically sited on the edge of a slope overlooking the Arroyo Seco. They had moved to Southern California, Craig later claimed, above all else to be warm, which was why they were so disconcerted by their first winter there, which they spent in a leaky, drafty beach cottage on the Coronado peninsula off San Diego, battered by Pacific winds. Now Upton, an inveterate sun-worshipper, could sit all day in the garden at his typewriter, amidst the apricot, fig, peach, and guava trees which provided the fruit he enthusiastically dined on, the air scented with honeysuckle, star-jasmine, jonquils, and Chinese lilies. Dressed solely in his tennis shoes and bathing trunks, himself a replanted exotic, a semi-nude tractarian, Sinclair typed away at the endless stream of books, many of them self-published, from which he and Craig derived their income.

Like so many of his contemporaries in Southern California, Upton Sinclair was a health nut, a food faddist and a teetotaler of the most convinced sort. In 1909 he had visited the great Bernarr Macfadden, America's leading fitness guru, at Macfadden's sanitarium in Battle Creek and came away a convinced disciple and, at a generous $150 an article, a well-paid correspondent for Macfadden's magazine *Physical Culture*. Spending a few months in 1912 in the Carmel art colony amidst a like-minded group of physical culturalists, Sinclair became convinced that California offered unique opportunities for a contemplative life that was also physically active. He resolved to establish himself one day on the coast.

The prohibitionist ethos of Pasadena suited Upton Sinclair to a cup of tea; for Sinclair, the son of a drunk, was at once repelled by booze while also fearing an inherited disposition that had to be rooted out of himself and others. Booze, he pointed out, had destroyed his fellow Socialist writer Jack London, whom Upton had personally tried in vain to get off the bottle, along with London's good friend and Sinclair's Carmel host, poet George Sterling, who had disgraced himself in Upton's company one evening at the Bohemian Club in San Francisco. Sterling had rendered himself incapable of reading, later on that night, a Socialist poem he had composed for a dinner given in Sinclair's honor by the Ruskin Club of Oakland. Booze had also ruined, or would eventually ruin, Eugene O'Neill, F. Scott Fitzgerald, O. Henry, Stephen Crane, Finley Peter Dunne, Isadora Duncan, Sherwood Anderson, Horace Liveright, Edna St. Vincent Millay, Eugene Debs, and Douglas Fairbanks. In 1931 Sinclair published *The Wet Parade*, an anti-dipsomaniacal fictive tract, which Hollywood promptly made into a movie.

Abhorring alcohol, Upton Sinclair was also very particular as to what he did or did not eat. Bernarr Macfadden, the long-haired guru from Battle Creek, reconfirmed in Sinclair a proclivity toward vegetarianism. Sinclair dined mainly on boiled rice, vegetables, preferably raw, and uncooked fruit, consumed rapidly, in no more than ten minutes so as to save time for more writing; and he ceaselessly advocated that others follow his diet, if not his time schedule. (Years into adulthood, Sinclair's son David would express his resentment at being spanked as a boy by his father for eating a meat sandwich on a train when nothing else was available.) From Macfadden as well, Sinclair came to believe in the therapeutic value of fasting for ten to twelve days, followed by a milk diet for the ensuing three weeks. Naturally, Sinclair wrote a book about it, *The Fasting Cure* (1911). Throughout his life, Sinclair fell victim to dietary fetishes. He once experimented with a daily teaspoon of sand to offset constipation. Yet he fell the occasional victim to binges as well, particularly in regard to sweets (he once described himself as a sweets-drunkard) and ice cream, with which he played a cat-and-mouse game all his life: eschewing it for weeks, months, then gorging on it by the bowlful, then coming off his ice cream binge with the remorse of a lapsed alcoholic.

Tennis embodied all that Upton Sinclair wanted—sunshine, healthfulness, a suggestion of social cachet—from the good life in Southern California. He moved to South Pasadena from Coronado, in fact, because the tennis pro at the Hotel del Coronado told him that there was plenty of good tennis in that upper-middle-class enclave of high thinking and social rectitude. A crack tennis player, capable of sweating off four pounds in a ferocious afternoon match, Sinclair played regularly at the Live Oaks Tennis Club in South Pasadena and, on Sunday mornings, at the Valley Hunt Club. Tennis bridged the worlds of fitness and the social elite to which in his heart of hearts he half-aspired, believing that he belonged there by right of birth. His great-grandfather had reached the rank of commodore, after all, and his grandfather had sailed with Perry into Tokyo Bay, and his socialite cousin Wallis Warfield would eventually marry the former King of Great Britain and Emperor of India. Yet even here, frustrating barriers asserted themselves. Socialists were not socially acceptable in Pasadena. "Tennis is a leisure-class recreation," Sinclair reminisced wistfully in his *Autobiography*, "and on the courts I met some of the prominent young men of my City of Millionaires. I was amused to note that their attitude toward me on the court was cordial and sometimes even gay, but we did not meet elsewhere. Sometimes their wives would drive them to the court and call for them when the game was over; but never once was I invited to meet one of those wives. I quietly mounted my bicycle and pedaled a couple of miles, slightly uphill, to my home. On Sunday morning I had a regular date with three men: one of the town's leading bankers, one of the town's leading real-estate men, and another whose high occupation I have forgotten. We played at the ultrafashionable Valley Hunt Club, but never once was I invited to enter the doors of that club. When the game was over, I mounted my bicycle and pedaled away."[1]

Kept at arm's length by the Valley Hunt crowd, Upton Sinclair found acceptance and congenial company among the radical wing of the Pasadena elite centered around Kate Crane Gartz, the only *grande dame* in whose salon the Socialist Sinclairs found welcome. Every Sunday afternoon, at her Open Forums, held in the Cloister, her rose-covered mansion in Altadena, Mrs. Gartz served tea and serious conversation to a group of regular and irregular guests. The Gartz circle gained new intensity when Gaylord and Mary Wilshire returned to Pasadena, Mary Wilshire having studied psychoanalysis with Jung in Zurich. The circle included film star Charlie Chaplin; oil heiress Aline Barnsdale, client and lover of Frank Lloyd Wright; reform-minded newspaper publishers Bobby Scripps and Cornelius Vanderbilt Jr.; and razor blade magnate King C. Gillette. When Spanish novelist Vincente Blasco Ibañez passed through Pasadena just after the war, Sinclair gave him a dinner party to which only Socialist millionaires were invited.

Such associations partially reinforced Sinclair's ever-embattled sense of caste, positioning him at the center of a company that was at once rich, socially selective, and politically correct. Occasionally, he derived support from the circle as well. King Gillette, for example, kept Sinclair on retainer for a while ($500 a month, a princely sum at the time) in exchange for editorial services. Obsessed by vague but benevolent notions of a shared corporate economy, proposals which Gillette had already put forward in two books, *World Corporation* and *Social Redemption*, the kindly perfecter of the safety blade wanted Sinclair's help in shaping up a *magnum opus* that would introduce to the world a philosophical economy of social corporatism, which Gillette envisioned as a species of private-sector Socialism, minus the social conflict and class hatred. Growing frustrated by Gillette's endless emendations of his text, Sinclair quit his job but remained on good terms with the millionaire tractarian, visiting Gillette at his seaside retreat at Balboa Beach and his ranch in the San Fernando Valley.

When Henry Ford wintered in Pasadena in the late teens, Sinclair dropped by, finding the automotive genius in his garage, tinkering with a tin lizzie. Ford and Sinclair took to each other, two brilliant eccentrics, each with a program for world reform. Walking the foothills above the Arroyo, Ford and Sinclair discussed reincarnation and the coming social order. Twelve years later, Sinclair befriended Albert Einstein, then a visiting professor at Cal Tech, with a comparable assumption of equality. Einstein, in fact, a shy, wild-haired man in a drooping mustache and rumpled black suit, first called on Sinclair, having been in correspondence with him for some years from Europe. Sinclair arranged a dinner for Einstein at the Town House restaurant in Los Angeles, to which he invited the intelligentsia of the region to come meet the latest transplant to the receptive, eclectic Southland.

Other members of Sinclair's Pasadena circle included poet and social critic Max Eastman, just returned from the Soviet Union with his Russian bride Eliena, who kept Craig Sinclair company while the men played tennis; and Floyd Dell, another New York intellectual temporarily sojourning in the sunshine, Dell being on the coast to collaborate with Los Angeles *Times* literary critic Paul Jordan-Smith on a new edition of Robert Burton's classic *An Anatomy of Melancholy* (1621). Visitors abounded. Vachel Lindsay paced the porch of the Sinclair household one balmy evening, reciting his boom-a-lay, boom-a-lay, boom-a-lay-boom verse and telling Craig and Upton that he regretted that he had chosen poetry over acting. When Theodore Dreiser was in Hollywood on film business, he too dropped by to visit, his long-suffering wife Helen in tow. (The spectacle of so much female beauty at the studios kept Dreiser in a condition approaching priapic psychosis.) Like the Sinclairs, the Dreisers were interested in what is today called parapsychology or extra-sensory perception (ESP) and was then termed psychic research. As usual, Sinclair wrote a book, *Mental Radio* (1930), describing Craig's telepathic abilities.

All this tennis and Socialist shadowboxing and upright literary industry, with its mild touch of bohemia, nevertheless remained at a safe distance from *realpolitik*. The San Pedro dock strike and Free Speech controversy of April and May 1923 introduced Sinclair to direct political action. Appalled by the continuing arrests of IWW strikers and their sympathizers, Sinclair led a delegation of protest to the offices of Los Angeles mayor George Cryer, who courteously informed them that the situation at San Pedro was in the hands of Police Chief Louis Oaks, a surly jumped-up noncom, given to mass arrests and the liberal application of the billy club. Securing written permission to hold a rally from the owner of the Liberty Hill property where the strikers held their gatherings, Sinclair proceeded to Liberty Hill on the evening of 15 May 1923 past cordons of uniformed police and plainclothesmen, accompanied by an equally outraged group of followers: his wife, his lawyer John Packard, Mrs. Gartz, Prince Hopkins, the Santa Barbara millionaire who edited *Labor Age*, the English journalist Hugh Hardyman ("tall, pale, a Rossetti angel," Craig later remembered him), and a few others—and there, by candle-light, Sinclair proceeded to read from the First Amendment. He was promptly arrested along with three others (Chief Oaks told Sinclair to "cut out that Consti-tution stuff"), including the millionaire Hopkins, Hunter Kimbrough, another millionaire with left-radical inclinations, and the Rossetti angel Hardyman, who had tried in vain to give a speech in praise of the Southern California climate.

Packed into police cars as a nearby crowd of strikers cheered their support, Sinclair and the others were kept incommunicado for eighteen hours, shunted from jail to jail. As Chief Oaks was soon to find out, he had overplayed his hand. It was one thing to treat anonymous Wobblies this way—arrest them on trumped-up charges, no lawyers, no bail, the third degree. It was another thing entirely to take a nationally famous writer and two prominent millionaires into custody and book them on charges of suspicion of criminal syndicalism for reading the Consti-tution and praising the Southern California climate and expect to keep the situa-tion under control. Already, newspaper headlines were speculating as to the whereabouts of the arrested. Keeping law and order, or at least order, as he cor-rectly supposed the oligarchy wanted him to do, Oaks had stumbled into the no-man's-land of offending against his social superiors, no matter what their political inclinations, and doing so over an absurd issue, the reading of the Constitution. Chief Oaks had made Los Angeles look ridiculous. Dr. Haynes, Mrs. Gartz, and Sinclair's other prominent friends placed pointed telephone calls of protest to City Hall and key members of the oligarchy. A number of prominent Los Angeles clubwomen, contacted by a distraught Craig, joined the crusade; and within eigh-teen hours of their arrest, Upton and his group surfaced at the downtown city jail. Sinclair had spent the night lying serenely on his back on the hard cell floor so as to avoid the lice he knew, instinctively, to be rampant throughout his cot. Mrs. Gartz posted bail.

Sensing victory, Upton Sinclair took to the offensive, at a series of well-attended rallies in a downtown hall rented by his supporters, the nucleus of the Southern California branch of the American Civil Liberties Union which they would soon be forming. They capped their counter-offensive with a giant outdoor rally near Liberty Hill, which Chief Oaks must have found particularly galling. According to Mary Sinclair, the oligarchy soon contacted her husband via the managing editor of the Hearst-owned Los Angeles *Examiner,* who teleponed Sinclair and asked him what his conditions were for ceasing his rallies, which were giving Los Angeles a black eye, and dropping his threatened civil suit for false arrest.

"The right people have come to me," the editor told Sinclair. "They don't happen to know you and I do. I hope you will take my word." Sinclair replied that he obviously wanted the criminal syndicalism charges dropped against himself and his four compatriots. He also wanted "civic decency" in Los Angeles. The managing editor agreed. As Sinclair spoke on the telephone, his wife held up a scrap of paper on which she had written "The Chief!" Sinclair demanded the removal of Oaks. The managing editor agreed, saying it would take a month. The oligarchy had already decided that Oaks was expendable. "OK," Sinclair agreed. "I'll go back to writing a book."[2]

Shortly thereafter, Chief Oaks was arrested in his automobile at night at a remote site, a half-consumed bottle of whiskey on the floorboard and a disrobed young lady in his lap. Mayor Cryer demanded and received Oaks's resignation. The arrest had every sign of being a setup.

The importance of Sinclair's victory of 1923 to his 1934 campaign for governor cannot be over-estimated. Sinclair had tasted the pleasures of messianic mission in the service of high ideals. He—the utopianist, the eccentric vegetarian, a scribbling crackpot to his enemies and sometimes a tiresome prig to his friends—had taken on the oligarchy and prevailed. Mounting the speakers' platform in the aftermath of his release from custody, Sinclair discovered himself as an effective orator: a puritan parson in rimless glasses preaching political rectitude and, more subtly, advocating the orderly, legal, but effective overthrow of the corporate-capitalist system as it presently dominated American society.

When the San Pedro crisis passed, and Los Angeles returned to the business of business, which was the business of Los Angeles in the 1920s, Upton Sinclair receded into the private sector—albeit in a public sort of way, as the controversy surrounding his novel *Oil!* (1928) would soon demonstrate. *Oil!* remains the most ambitious Southern California novel of the 1920s. Gertrude Atherton compared it to a novel by Balzac; and there is in the sprawling canvas created by Sinclair a wealth of social observation and characters that partially redeems Atherton's comparison from charges of puffery. Chosen by the Literary Guild, *Oil!* made the best-seller list. Its sales were helped along when Sinclair, hoping to get arrested, personally hawked copies of the book on the streets of Boston, reporters in attendance, after *Oil!* was banned there for its outspoken advocacy of birth control; Sinclair had a paper fig leaf pasted across the offending passage. In his descriptions of the Beach City oil fields, derricks sown into the earth like dragon's teeth as far as the eye could see, and the strike there of ten thousand oil workers—scenes suggestive of industrial conflicts soon to happen in the Great Depression—Sinclair proved that he could once again, as in *The Jungle*, rise above the level of fictive tract and reach something very close to literature.

Throughout the early 1930s, social reform and utopianism were gaining new strength in Southern California. Two reform movements, Technocracy, Inc. (together with its spin-off, the Utopian Society of America) and the Townsend Plan, dramatically expressed the millenarianism of the era.

In 1901 William Smyth, a young English immigrant, returned to England for a visit. It was the zenith of the British *imperium*, and Smyth expected to find in the British people reflections of that power and prosperity. Instead, as he later wrote, he discovered "a stunted and disheartened people, ninety percent of whom were existing on the edge of bare subsistence in sordid, soul-shrivelling poverty, while a comparatively insignificant number were luxuriating in utmost prodigality."[3] Sojourning at this very same time among the cockneys of the East End, another young American visitor, Jack London, a Socialist from Oakland, was experiencing the same phenomenon, the squalid huddling of stunted masses within sight of the Mother of Parliaments. Back in California, London wrote *The People of the Abyss* (1903), one of his earliest and best books.

Returned to the United States, William Smyth studied law and economics and eventually settled in Berkeley, where he rose to prosperity as a patent attorney while continuing private studies in economics. During World War I he noted with approval the efficiency brought into the American economy with the establishment of a War Industries Board to supervise all aspects of production. With the war over, Smyth published in the spring of 1919 a series of three articles in the engineering magazine *Industrial Management* outlining an economic system called Technocracy. He later circulated the articles in pamphlet form and in 1926 published a book cryptically entitled *Concerning Irascible Strong*.

Simply put, Smyth was a socio-economic evolutionist with a belief in technology and the technocratic organization of society as the next item on the agenda of social progress. Free market capitalism and the price system, Smyth argued, proceeded from socio-biological traits (Smyth cited three: strength, skill, and cunning) which were destined to evolve into more cooperative characteristics as the human race solved the problem of production for consumption and use through technology. Technology, however, needed a technocracy, which is to say, a national plan (democratically and constitutionally implemented, Smyth insisted) to direct and coordinate the economy according to criteria of efficient production and just distribution. Such a scientifically engineered society, Smyth insisted, would not be Communistic or even Socialist. The Constitution and private property would remain in force. The means of production would merely be coordinated on a national level so as to insure the best possible life (education until age twenty-five, work between twenty-five and forty-five, creative leisure in the years remaining) for the greatest number of Americans. In all this, Smyth and his successors in the Technocracy movement were popularizing the more powerfully (but more obscurely) stated ideas of Thorstein Veblen as set forth in *The Engineers and the Price System* (1921) but traceable as well to Veblen's earlier *The Theory of Business Enterprise* (1904), in which Veblen argued on behalf of production for use, not for profit, a key dogma in the Technocracy creed.

It took Southern California and the Great Depression to transform this vision of an industrial utopia through social engineering into a full-blown cult, the Utopian Society of America, complete with secret cells and mystic rituals. The Depression, first of all, made the whole notion of national industrial and economic planning plausible. In New York City, Columbia University industrial engineers Walter Rautenstrauch and Howard Scott, assisted by publicist Wayne Parrish, were busily advocating a mélange of Veblenesque ideas throughout the early 1930s under the rubric Technocracy, without reference to Veblen, much less reference to the more obscure Berkeley patent attorney William Smyth. In Los Angeles, three promoters—Eugene Reed, an unemployed banker; W.G. Rousseau, an equally available promoter; and Merritt Kennedy, whose most recent position had been with the scandal-ridden Julian Petroleum Company—joined forces in July 1933 to create the Utopian Society of America, a movement which one contemporary observer described as a "goulash of Technocracy, State Socialism, Ku Klux Klan, Populism, Fascism, Evangelism, and Voodoo."[4]

Headquartered at 831 South La Brea Avenue, Utopianism did indeed in its brief flourishing justify such a colorful description. The basic ideology of the Society was the creation through Technocracy of a technologically sophisticated, centrally managed economy. To this goal, Utopianism added a communalism based loosely upon the *Utopia* (1516) of Sir Thomas More and the ideas of the nineteenth-century social reformer Robert Dale Owen: not so much Communism or collectivism in the Marxist sense of the term, more a species of communtarianism, yearning, idealistic, but angry about the way things were going: a sense of society as an extended family, a folk, the Folks of Southern California, on the march in a crusade to rescue the economy of the United States.

To express and galvanize these ideals, Reed, Rousseau, and Kennedy devised a ritual of initiation based on the medieval mystery play *Everyman*, and this, more than anything else, occasioned the Ku Klux Klan comparison. Newcomers to Utopianism, designated Hermits and assigned numbers to use instead of their names, proceeded through five cycles of initiation, which were carried out in over a thousand members' homes as the movement spread throughout Los Angeles. At the conclusion of the ritual, catechumens in the audience who had completed their home training were invited to become full-fledged Utopians amidst songs and cheers, flag waving, and other expressions of patriotic sentiment. (Utopians were extra-careful to maintain all outward signs of loyalty to the Constitution.) An estimated half million Southern Californians went through this ritual, many of them led to the movement by a series of favorable articles in October 1932 in the *Daily News*, whose publisher, Manchester Boddy, was a half-convinced fellow traveler. On the night of 23 June 1934, thirty thousand Utopians filled the Hollywood Bowl for a rally that represented the high point of their movement.

Production for use, not profit, was also the capstone of the End Poverty in California (EPIC) plan. Utopianism and EPIC were bubbling up from the same utopian Socialist soup stock: the utopia described by Sir Thomas More, and the doctrines of Charles Fourier and Karl Marx melding into the persistent utopianism of avant-garde America as expressed by Robert Dale Owen and the New Harmony colony, the New England Transcendentalists and Brook Farm, and the United States of the year 2000 as imagined and presented by Edward Bellamy in the futurist novel *Looking Backward* (1888). Only this time, a vast American state, not merely a farm in Massachusetts or a settlement in frontier Indiana, was being asked to try the experiment.

Long before the gubernatorial primary of 1934, Upton Sinclair had believed that the conceptual framework and terminology of Socialism needed to be purged of its German Marxist orientation and cast in more American terms if it were to have any chance to appeal to the American people. Such Americanization of Socialism, he believed, was the most important step taken by Bellamy in his depiction of twenty-first-century America as a cooperative paradise. In *The Industrial Republic* (1907), completed in the midst of the Helicon experiment, Sinclair made his first effort at such an American Socialist statement. Just before registering as a Democrat and declaring for office, Sinclair wrote a second manifesto, *The Way Out: What Lies Ahead for America* (1933), a plea for Socialism cast in the form of a series of letters to a young millionaire. Characteristically, Sinclair approached his gubernatorial campaign as, first and foremost, a challenge to writing. Sitting down at his typewriter, he pounded out his political platform in the form of a Bellamyesque social science fiction tract, *I, Governor of California and How I Ended Poverty—A True Story of the Future.*

I, Governor opens in the year 1938. Upton Sinclair has served one term in office. With poverty ended in California, he is preparing to leave the governorship to write a novel and to take the message of EPIC to the rest of the United States and to Europe. But first, Governor Sinclair recounts the steps he took to end poverty in California.

Taking office after a no-frills swearing-in ceremony with no inaugural ball, Governor Sinclair begins his administration by pardoning Tom Mooney, imprisoned since 1916 for the Preparedness Day bombing in San Francisco, and offering Mooney the apologies of the people of California. Openly conducting business in an office providing seating for the public (only paid lobbyists are denied access), with important administrative sessions broadcast live on the radio, Governor Sinclair proceeds to implement a twelve-point EPIC legislative and administrative program. A publicly sponsored California Authority for Land, first of all, establishes a series of agricultural colonies on idle land and land sold for taxes. Furnished with dormitories, kitchens, cafeterias, common spaces, and agricultural machinery, these colonies enable the unemployed to produce enough food for consumption and limited exchange.

Another entity, the California Authority for Production, establishes a parallel program for the unemployed in idle industrial plants, with the agricultural colonies and the factory communes providing for each other through barter and through the exchange of scrip for the drawing of goods issued by the California Authority for Money, an entity which also issues the bonds to raise money for the factories and agricultural colonies in the first place.

At the governor's request, the legislature repeals the sales tax, replacing it with a graduated income tax rising to 30 percent for incomes over $50,000. The legislature also enacts a steeply graduated inheritance tax (50 percent of all sums above

$50,000), together with an increased tax on public utility corporations. Property taxes on owner-occupied homes under $3,000 in assessed value are abolished by amendment to the state constitution. For properties assessed at more than $5,000, taxes are increased at the rate of 1 percent for each $5,000 of additional valuation. Every needy person over the age of sixty, with a minimum of three years of residence in California, is eligible for a $50 monthly pension. The same pension is available to the blind or otherwise disabled who cannot support themselves and to widowed women with dependent children, with a $25 increment for each child over two.

For all the controversy that soon engulfed EPIC, Sinclair's proposals seem relatively tame in retrospect. Even Sinclair's most controversial proposals, the self-help factories and the agricultural colonies, were cautious in comparison to the bold ambitions of the Civilian Conservation Corps (CCC), which by 1935 had more than a half million unemployed men working in twenty-five hundred camps under military supervision, and the Public Works Administration (PWA), which by 1933 employed some 140,000 workers and accounted for a third of all construction underway in the United States.

Yet just as the possibilities of national military mobilization, soon to be realized, emanated from the CCC, so too did possibilities of a more permanent Socialism lurk beneath the self-help camps proposed by Upton Sinclair through EPIC. Intended for the unemployed, these cooperatives could become successful free-standing enterprises, hence dangerous examples of state-sponsored Socialism. The emergency measure could become the accepted model, despite the fact that Sinclair advanced no broader program. There was, furthermore, just a faint suggestion of a threat in the EPIC motto "I Produce. I Defend," surmounted by a bee symbol of industry and the EPIC acronym. Defend what against whom? conservatives might very well ask. Their newly acquired cooperatives against the private sector?

And besides, as the campaign got underway, Sinclair began taking his case to a broader constituency: to the small farmers of California, for example, whom he promised in a second pamphlet, *EPIC Answers* (1934), a program of tax reduction, the payment of taxes in farm products instead of cash, the exchange of farm products for durable goods and farm machinery at state-run stores, and a lease-back system through which farmers could operate their land on behalf of the State with whom they shared profits. In a third statement, *Immediate EPIC*, issued in September 1934 after he had, to everyone's astonishment, including his own, won the primary, Sinclair began to address the needs of an even broader spectrum of voters, employed as well as unemployed, and to discuss the intricacies of state finance with the assurance of a soon-to-be governor. In one *pièce de résistance* of a proposal—a $300 million bond issue to purchase the land cooperatives and cooperative factories from their lawful owners so that they might be made permanent cooperatives, democratically managed—Sinclair, with characteristic straightforwardness, let his Socialist cat out of the bag. EPIC now stood revealed as more than an emergency measure. Upton Sinclair sought permanently to restructure the economy of California and make it, in some measure, Socialist.

Just as EPIC dovetailed with the aspirations of Utopianism, moreover, Sinclair's call for pensions of $50 per month for all those over sixty represented his attempt to deal with a rival messianic movement arising in the geriatric capital of the United States, the Los Angeles County seaside city of Long Beach. There, on 30 September 1933, at the conclusion of the same month in which Upton Sinclair had driven to the Beverly Hills City Hall and registered as a Democrat, the Long Beach *Press Telegram* published a letter by an obscure physician turned real estate salesman, Francis Everett Townsend, offering yet another solution to the Depression.

The United States, Dr. Townsend pointed out, had between fifteen and twenty million citizens over the age of sixty, who were not needed in the labor force; but neither could they be slaughtered—as Secretary of Agriculture Henry Wallace was now ordering the slaughter of six million surplus piglets and two hundred thousand brood sows in an effort to stabilize commodity prices under terms of the recently passed Agricultural Adjustment Act. If, however, these fifteen to twenty million Americans were to be granted a monthly pension of $150, raised from a national sales tax, and be required to spend the money within the month, they would become part of the solution, not the problem. Between $2 and $3 billion would be force-fed into the economy each month, and the Depression would soon be over.

Such an eccentric proposal might normally be expected to enjoy the shelf-life of one evening in the Letters to the Editor section of an obscure newspaper; but Townsend's proposal struck a nerve, in Long Beach first of all, then throughout Southern California, then throughout the United States. With Townsend's proposal, which the good doctor amplified across five more letters to the editor between 21 October and 13 December 1933, a new constituency, the elderly, entered American politics.

Between 1870 and 1930 the United States had experienced a sixfold increase in the proportion of Americans over sixty-five relative to its total population. In this growing sector, a new concept, retirement, began to evolve as an expectation. In 1890, for example, two-thirds of American males over the age of sixty-five were still employed. The figure had dropped to half by 1930. Half of the men over sixty-five in the United States, in other words, were either retired on pensions, investments, or savings of one form or another, and/or were receiving assistance from their grown children, or, in the case of many, were destitute and dependent upon local charities for support. When times were good, as they were in the 1920s, an increasingly large number of Americans were able to retire on one form or another of support in their old age. During these years, sunny Southern California became the geriatric mecca of the United States. Between 1920 and 1930 the region experienced a 100 percent increase in its population of people over sixty-five. Roughly a third of the 150,000 people in Long Beach, for example, were elderly. Never before in the history of human land use had there been so many elderly people in one place at one time *vis-à-vis* the total population.

Living on fixed incomes in simple cottages, the Long Beach elderly—the majority of them Folks from Iowa and elsewhere in the Midwest; the men in dark pants and white shirts, the women in print dresses and sturdy, sensible shoes— had come to Southern California to enjoy a simple life of churchgoing, potluck suppers, and checkers in the park, having earned, in their opinion, the right to enjoy the eleven years actuarially remaining to them in 1930. The Depression destroyed their plans as pension trusts shrank or, in some cases, as they went under entirely, and private investments yielded a decreasing income. Nor could their children continue to be of help. In 1928 65 percent of the American population over the age of sixty-five was receiving some form of assistance from children. With twelve million people out of work by 1933, voluntary assistance to parents plummeted along with the rest of the economy. To whom could the elderly now turn? Not to government. American culture had no discernible tradition of old-age pensions from government. Only six American states had any form of old-age assistance program. By 1934 a mere 180,000 elderly, out of a total population of fifteen million–plus senior citizens, were receiving any form of legally mandated assistance. Yet fully 50 percent of the elderly in America were in need of some form of outside aid if they were to make it through the slump.

Francis Everett Townsend was himself one of these dispirited, dispossessed denizens of Long Beach, searching for an escape from the Depression that was making such a horror of old age. All his life (Townsend was sixty-seven in 1933) the doctor had tried to better his condition, with mixed results. After a hardscrabble youth and young manhood—a hay farmer and cowboy in rural California; a homesteader, failed, in western Kansas; a country schoolteacher; a miner in Cripple Creek, Colorado; and an itinerant salesman of Home Comfort iron stoves— Townsend entered the Omaha Medical College at the late age of thirty-one, assisted by a $200 loan from the college dean, with whom Frank Townsend boarded. He also supported himself through a seven-mile early morning newspaper delivery route and part-time bookkeeping. After graduation, Townsend assumed a country practice in Belle Fourche, South Dakota, married his nurse, a widow, and raised three children. Despite his age, fifty, Townsend enlisted in the Army Medical Corps in 1917. Although he never saw service outside Fort Snelling, Minnesota, the war encouraged him to take a second look at his life: his frail health (tall, rail-lean, sepulchral, he lived to be ninety-three, longevity being the valetudinarian's accustomed revenge), the long South Dakota winters, the monotony of practice in a remote and declining cowtown. Not surprisingly, Townsend decided, along with a million-plus others in the post-war period, to seek a new start in Southern California. There, in Long Beach, he experienced less than success (dare one say, failure?) as a physician (with time off for ill health), an entrepreneur (he lost $5,000 for a close friend in a failed scheme to manufacture dry ice), and an intermittent salesman of real estate. The Depression destroyed Townsend's medical and real estate practice, and only an appointment to the Health Department of the City of Long Beach kept him afloat until 1933.

Townsend lost that appointment due to cutbacks in mid-1933 and was on the verge of financial disaster in September 1933 when he wrote his first letter to the *Press Telegram*. Later, he conveniently recalled the epiphanic moment, unmentioned in earlier stages of the movement, when he first decided to do something for the elderly and, in the process, end the Depression. Looking out of his window one morning, Townsend claimed, he saw three elderly women rummaging for food in a garbage can. "A torrent of invectives tore out of me," he later recalled, "the big blast of all the bitterness that had been building in me for years. I swore and I ranted, and I let my voice bellow with wild hatred I had for things as they were. My wife came a-running. 'Doctor! Doctor!' (She's always called me doctor.) 'Oh, you mustn't shout like that. All the neighbors will hear you!' 'I want all the neighbors to hear me!' I roared defiantly. 'I want God Almighty to hear me! I'm going to shout till the whole country hears.' "[5]

Most probably contrived, the incident nevertheless expresses the anger, the rage even, at the core of the Townsend movement. The Depression had disenfranchised an entire generation of elderly from the fruits of their labor. They had built the nation, so they felt, and now they had nothing. His angular features and flat nasal voice bespeaking small-town America, Dr. Francis Townsend offered a messiah from Central Casting for this mid-American resentment, so quick to attach itself to the voodoo economics of Old Age Revolving Pensions, Limited, the organization which Townsend and thirty-nine-year-old real estate colleague Robert Clements incorporated in Long Beach on 1 January 1934. Running parallel to EPIC as a panaceatic mass cult arising from the distinctive social and psychological setting of Southern California in the early 1930s, the Townsend movement outlasted EPIC by a decade (if one counts its successor, the Ham and Eggs movement) and attained greater national importance. By January 1935 a half million Americans had joined Townsend Clubs (the first was organized in Huntington Park on 23 August 1934) and were sending nearly $1 million in dues and other donations into the movement's headquarters in the Spring Arcade Building in downtown Los Angeles. By the end of 1936, some 2.2 million had joined Townsend Clubs and were paying dues to the national headquarters. The newspaper alone, the *Townsend National Weekly*, was raking in nearly a quarter of a million dollars a year in advertising fees for merchandise—trusses, foundation garments, support stockings, remedies for catarrh and constipation—which further underscored the geriatric vulnerability of Townsend's hopeful followers.

As the movement grew, economic consultants helped fine-tune it to a semblance of fiscal plausibility. The proposed monthly pension was upped from $50 to $200, to be financed by a nationally imposed "transaction sales tax" of 2 percent, which would create a revolving fund of $18 to $24 billion, which would put the pension program on a pay-as-you-go basis. With so much money being compulsorily spent each month, Townsend and his followers argued, the American economy, engorged with cash, would revive. With the election of Los Angeles *Times* editorial writer John Steven McGroarty in 1934, the Townsendites had their man in Congress: an elderly (age seventy-three), courtly lawyer-litterateur, the Poet of the Verdugo Hills, poet laureate of California since 1933, whose pageant *The Mission Play*, written in the 1920s, had won him both papal and Spanish knighthoods. The first thing Sir John did upon taking his seat in Congress in 1935 on behalf of Los Angeles was to introduce House Resolution 3977, calling for the implementation of the Townsend Plan post haste. Usurped by the passage of the Social Security Act nine months later, HR 3977 or variations thereof remained before Congress until 1940.

No matter how stiff and inept Townsend was in his testimony before Congress on behalf of HR 3977, or how outrageous his plan might seem to economists, Townsendism had struck a chord of immediate sympathy in the nation's elderly, which even the revelation that the good doctor and his partner Clements were personally pocketing some $2,000 a week from their concealed ownership of the *Townsend Weekly* (the money came from advertising revenues and kickbacks on merchandise sold through the newspaper) could not diminish. Disconcertingly Hitlerian in his stiff posture, his awkward gestures, and his gumdrop mustache, Francis Townsend of Long Beach—like the radio priest Father Charles Coughlin of Michigan, or Congressman William Lemke of North Dakota, or Senator Huey Long and the Reverend Gerald Smith of Louisiana—expressed the populist-right radicalization of lower-middle-class America: German and Irish Catholic Midwesterners, Great Plains and Southern farmers and small-town folks, retirees from Southern California, the lower-middle-class elderly from everywhere. This had implications for the rise of para-fascist politics in the United States. Urban ethnic blue-collar workers, even farm workers, might go left toward militant trade unionism, Socialism, even the Communist Party. The middle and lower-middle classes, by contrast, would move right. While industrial or agricultural workers felt permanently outside the system, excluded as a matter of enduring socio-economic structure, the middle to lower-middle classes, having once felt themselves to be on the inside, mainstream, then cynically ejected—by Wall Street, by the Ivy League patricians around Roosevelt, by international Jewry—felt betrayed and eager for retribution. Such resentment by the dutiful and the God-fearing, made to feel victims of their social superiors or, worse, the Jewish moneylenders, feeling cheated by the very system they had devoted their lives to, had all the makings of a para-fascist crusade.

Most journalists found the Townsendites slightly ridiculous. Just Folks in Utopia, one writer characterized them as they gathered at the Hotel Stevens in Chicago for the first annual convention of Townsend Clubs in November 1935, with proceedings held beneath a grand ballroom banner reading "The Three Emancipators—Washington, Lincoln, Townsend." A black delegate told the convention that his race was behind the movement. The audience responded by singing Stephen Foster's "Old Black Joe." Townsend himself hinted at further reforms once his pension plan was accomplished.

A year later, another *New Republic* writer, Bruce Bliven, was not so sure. Townsend, Bliven noted, had become not only more powerful, but more overtly political in his public presence. The Townsend organization had seven thousand clubs (or were they cells?), and its national organization was divided into ministries, like a shadow government. Townsend's followers, in turn, treated him as a Daniel come to judgment. While the Townsendites made much of the Pledge of Allegiance and the singing of hymns, one could not be so sure. (Or was it the Pledge and the hymns which the Left found so disturbing?) The Townsendites, noted Bliven in May 1936, were "economic illiterates held together chiefly by the burning conviction that our civilization could do far more for the aged—and for everybody—than it does. Mussolini in Italy, Hitler in Germany, began their rise to power by making promises strikingly similar to the fundamental concepts of the Townsend Plan; and their first followers, though their average age was doubtless lower, were much like the adherents of that plan today. That is one reason why the movement, for all the revelations regarding it in Washington, still needs watching, and will for a long time to come."[6]

What Francis Townsend accomplished on the national scene in two years, a messianic reform movement speaking to the Folks, Upton Sinclair assembled in a matter of months. Even more dramatically, Sinclair positioned his movement to gain power, legitimately, in an important American state. According to journalist Walter Davenport, who covered the campaign for *Collier's* magazine, Sinclair began his crusade with the immediate sympathy of the more than one million members of the Utopian Society in Southern California, despite the fact that most Utopians, whose proclivities were on the right, were registered Republicans. Utopians, Davenport estimated, constituted the bulk of the crowds Sinclair began attracting from the first announcement of his candidacy. Townsendites were also in view, although Sinclair's promised pension of $50 a month fell far short of the $200 advocated by Townsend. Whether Utopians or Townsendites, Henry George single-taxers, or just plain Kiwanians and Rotarians, Upton Sinclair had swiftly secured the Glory Vote: the fervid support of the evangelical Protestant mainstream, the expropriated middle class (so Carey McWilliams described them in the *New Republic*), baffled and angry at their economic betrayal.

The national press, such as the *Newsweek* reporter writing on 27 October 1934, depicted Sinclair's support as coming primarily from the marginal and the eccentric elements of the displaced lower-middle class—which represented the standard Northeastern journalistic take on Southern California, adjusted to the EPIC phenomenon. Sinclair bristled at such characterizations, even when they came from Carey McWilliams, his regional colleague on the literary left. "On the surface," McWilliams had written, "the Sinclair following would seem to be indefinably heterogeneous: various socially minded clergymen, quack astronomers, single tax-

ers, mind readers, members of the powerful Utopian Society, leaders of the unemployed cooperatives, a few Santa Barbara dowagers, the honorable Lewis Browne,
aged and infirm Democratic office-seekers, professional 'Catholic leaders,' miscel-
laneous political has-beens. Advocates of the Townsend Old-Age Pension Plan,
advocates of Synchrotax (a nostrum brewed in San Diego), followers of the Rust
Taxation Plan, theosophists from Ojai, Rosicrucians from San Jose, all support
him. There has been great unrest in California, particularly in the heavily popu-
lated southern counties; plans have been written, societies formed, banners un-
furled. Most of these groups have gravitated to Sinclair by default."[7]

He enjoyed solid support from the working class, Sinclair argued in a letter to
the *New Republic* refuting McWilliams's assertion. A grocer in a blue-collar district of Los Angeles recently reported that 230 out of 244 of his customers were
voting for him. Even middle-class academics were responding. At the conservative
University of Southern California, a meeting with graduate students was so packed
that a loudspeaker had to be placed outside the meeting hall. More than a dozen
USC professors had signed up as campaign volunteers, risking the ire of USC's
autocratic president Rufus Bernhard von KleinSmid. Even selected portions of the
elite were responding. Oil heiress Aline Barnsdale purchased radio time on the
condition that Sinclair immediately pardon Tom Mooney when he became governor. From Hollywood had come the open and courageous support of William De
Mille (Cecil's brother), Jean Harlow, James Cagney, and Dorothy Parker.

From this constituency—the Glory Vote, the Utopians, disgruntled Democrats
distrustful of the regular Party, the Hollywood Left, together with the added support of such writers as Theodore Dreiser, Oswald Garrison Villard, and Archibald
MacLeish—Sinclair and his circle assembled a grass-roots campaign prophetic of
the post-war politics pioneered in Chicago by Saul Alinsky. Nearly a thousand
EPIC clubs formed throughout the State. Autonomous entities, only nominally
supervised by EPIC headquarters on South Grand in Los Angeles, each club
raised money through picnics, barbecues, bazaars, auctions, rummage sales,
dances, sewing bees, whatever, while at the same time fanning out to register
voters favorable to the cause. Between 1 January and 19 July 1934, nearly a thousand EPIC volunteers added some 350,000 new Democratic voters to the rolls.
Approximately 255,000 copies of *I, Governor* were in circulation by March 1934,
together with a vast array of such promotional items as lapel buttons, bumper
stickers, rear tire covers, and even bars of soap, each of them bearing the EPIC
worker-bee logo. Bee-bedecked EPIC buses toured the state, organizing whistle-
stop rallies in cities, towns, and suburbs. A special march was composed, "End
Poverty in California, and Upton Sinclair Will Show the Way," and the sheet
music sent out to local clubs for performance at EPIC gatherings. Most astonishing, EPIC supporters were willing to pay an admission fee to attend these rallies, ranging from a penny to twenty-five cents for choice seats at an indoor speech
by Sinclair himself, although anyone pleading poverty was admitted free of
charge. On the advice of legal counsel, who warned that charging admission to a

political gathering might be unconstitutional, Sinclair and Richard Otto, his campaign manager, formed a separate organization, the End Poverty League, Incorporated, to receive and disperse all proceeds from club fundraisers and rallies. The League also owned the very lively, well-written tabloid *EPIC News*, which sold for a respectable nickel a copy, ran extensive advertisements, and, amazingly, had attained a circulation of two million by November 1934.

No wonder Democratic Party regulars, laughing in September 1933 when Sinclair joined their ranks and declared for governor, were panicking by the spring of 1934 as primary day, 28 August, drew near. The EPIC registration drive had brought the total of registered Democrats in Los Angeles County to 647,229, which was half the Democratic registration in the state. Sinclair's primary opponents, George Creel and Isidore Dockweiler, were Northern Californians, hence at a disadvantage regarding this Southern California vote. Observed Creel wryly: "Northern California offered no problem, for hardheaded, hard-working native sons and daughters were in a majority, but when I crossed the Tehachapi into Southern California, it was like plunging into darkest Africa without gun bearers. Epics, Utopians, and Townsendites might have their points of difference, but all turned faces of hatred to me when I attacked the validity of their creeds."[8]

Embarrassingly, Creel was revealed to have accepted $5,000 in cash from E. L. Doheny of Los Angeles during the Teapot Dome scandal as a retainer for some unspecified task. It soon became apparent that Bohemian Club member Creel, a wise-cracking, hard-living newsman and public relations executive, backed by the conservative wing of the Democratic Party controlled by Senator McAdoo, had little chance against the austere, patently sincere Upton Sinclair and his grass-roots crusade. By early August polls and pundits were predicting a Sinclair victory; but no one was prepared for its magnitude. Sinclair won 436,220 votes to Creel's 288,106. More important, Sinclair held an impressive lead over the Republican nominee, Governor Frank Merriam, who had garnered 346,000 votes. The impossible, having become improbable, now became a distinct possibility. Thanks to the newly registered Democrats of Los Angeles, Upton Sinclair had a very real chance of becoming the twenty-ninth American governor of California.

The first thing Sinclair did upon winning the primary was to head east and seek the approval of Roosevelt and his circle. If he were to win in November, Sinclair desperately needed legitimacy from FDR and the national Democratic Party establishment. Without such approval, he would remain an outsider, despite his strong showing in the primaries. A month before the primary, in July, Sinclair had been heartened when the White House announced a series of experimental programs to be administered by the Federal Emergency Relief Administration. The experiments included farm colonies in Maryland and Virginia, where the previously unemployed would grow food for the eighty thousand people on relief in Washington, D.C. Non-profit factories, similarly staffed by the unemployed, would produce clothing and other necessities for welfare recipients in the United States.

Retail outlets would distribute this merchandise, using a scrip system. Scrip would also be issued to the aged and disabled for use in the government-sponsored outlets. The State of Maine, meanwhile, announced a plan to establish construction cooperatives which would be set to work on public works. A million dollars was allocated for the first project. Then, even more dramatically close to home, Orange County announced a program of federally assisted agricultural cooperatives. Did not such programs, Upton Sinclair argued in the final days of the primary campaign, coming out of Washington itself, belie the charge that EPIC was impractical, or worse, alien or Communistic?

En route to the East, Sinclair stopped off in Chicago for a speech to the Chicago Federation of Labor, a half-hour radio address, and an interview with Mayor Fiorello La Guardia of New York, then visiting the Windy City. In each of these encounters, Sinclair sought to emphasize the mainstream American sanity, at once utopian and pragmatic, of the EPIC program. Not yet governor of California, Sinclair also began to surface with discussions of EPIC as applicable to the nation at large, even the planet. EPIC, he noted, could very well stand for End Poverty in Civilization. Not surprisingly, La Guardia listened politely but took no further action. The response of the Little Flower would soon prove prophetic of the reaction of the Democratic Party establishment, beginning with the President. What, after all, could these seasoned politicians make of the earnest amateur now thrusting himself into their midst, a schoolmaster in rimless glasses from an uncertain part of the nation, talking so majestically of destroying poverty throughout all civilization? Only California, they decided, could have brought someone so eccentric so close to important public office.

With characteristic directness, Sinclair had already sent along a copy of his EPIC proposal to Eleanor Roosevelt; and she, also characteristically, had responded warmly but non-committedly in a letter headed "Private—not for publication": "I have read your book, and I have given it to my husband to read. Some of the things which you advocate I am heartily in favor of, others I do not think are entirely practical, but then what is impractical today is sometimes practical tomorrow. I do not feel, however, that I am sufficiently in accord with your entire idea to make any public statement at present."[9]

The President, it turned out, concurred in this say nothing, do nothing policy. Faced with the rise of eccentric politicians across the country—Charles Coughlin in Michigan, Huey Long in Louisiana, Upton Sinclair in California—Roosevelt knew that either to praise or to condemn these populist insurgents with their mass followings among traditional Democrats would cost him support from outraged supporters on the fringe (and the Depression had widened the fringe to highway status) or from opponents in the regular Party organization. Sinclair, for one thing, had revitalized the Democratic Party in California, making it a force for the first time in the twentieth century. While many of Roosevelt's inner circle considered Sinclair a figure of ridicule, FDR, the more canny politician, believed that Sinclair had a good chance of winning—if Sinclair could avoid making a fool of himself. Thus Roosevelt agreed to meet with Sinclair on 5 September 1934 at Hyde Park, provided that the session be widely advertised as non-political.

Non-political? A sitting president was demanding that the duly elected nominee of his party for an important governorship eschew all talk of politics as a condition for being allowed to call a mere two months before the election. The restriction itself was an insulting forecast of snubs to come. Why else would Sinclair be calling if not to garner political support?

The insulting restriction made Sinclair somewhat manic (would any other gubernatorial candidate from a major state be treated this way?), and this in turn made him eager to hear things that were perhaps not said at all, or said exactly the way he heard and reported them, in the two-hour encounter, or to hear things that in retrospect made no sense at all. Doffing his coat, Sinclair stood in his shirtsleeves and talked to reporters on the veranda after emerging, exultantly, from his session with Roosevelt. The President, Sinclair exulted ("one of the kindest and most genial and frank and open-minded and lovable men I ever met") had kept him in conversation for an hour longer than the one hour scheduled for their meeting. "The President said he had only one grudge against me," Sinclair continued. "That was that when he was young his mother read *The Jungle* aloud to him at the breakfast table. I asked him, 'And it spoiled your lamb chops?' and he said, 'Yes.' "[10]

Roosevelt was in his mid-twenties and attending the Columbia Law School when *The Jungle* appeared and not in the habit of being read to at the breakfast table by his mother. Sinclair would have instantly understood the President's gaffe when it occurred. Had the President confused Sinclair with Rudyard Kipling or some other writer from his boyhood? So eager was Sinclair, however, to maximize the President's genial if mistaken flattery to offset the non-political restriction, he told the story to reporters (as if they did not know how old Roosevelt was in 1907!) and continued to tell it throughout the campaign.

More important, Sinclair heard, or thought he heard, the President say that he planned to give a speech endorsing the concept of production for use in a speech scheduled for the 25th of October: a statement that would cause Sinclair no end of chagrin later in the campaign when the endorsement was not forthcoming. "If you will do that," Sinclair later claimed he replied, "it will elect me."[11]

Was Upton Sinclair lying? Did Roosevelt, so eager not to alienate big business (the president of the New York, New Haven & Hartford Railroad and Joseph P. Kennedy, president of the Securities and Exchange Commission, had also visited him that day), actually make such a promise to Sinclair? Probably not. Once again, Sinclair, whether consciously or subconsciously, was pushing the interview to its limits in an effort to gain legitimacy. Had FDR said, perhaps, that he might one day talk about production for use, or that he was thinking about talking about production for use on the 25th? Or was Upton Sinclair, having launched his campaign with a novel, conflating fact and fiction as a matter of habit? Was he campaigning or writing a screenplay, an early version of *Mr. Smith Goes to*

Washington, or, more probably, doing both—attempting, that is, to impose his imagination on reality at the highest level of national politics? Was it naivete or *chutzpah* or, more subtly, the heroic will of an *auteur*, binding reality to a pre-envisioned scenario, that prompted him to call on Roosevelt, and later on Post-master General James Farley and Secretary of the Treasury Henry Morgenthau Jr., Secretary of the Interior Harold Ickes, Jesse Jones of the Reconstruction Finance Corporation, Harry Hopkins of the Federal Emergency Relief Administration, and Justice Louis Brandeis of the Supreme Court—and report their approval as well? "Just call me Jim," he reported Farley to have said, and from Morgenthau: "Whatever you need, just ask for it." [12]

In the case of Interior Secretary Ickes, Sinclair suffered another spell of delusion. Ickes, he claimed, had made promises regarding the use of EPIC programs to help construct the Central Valley Project in California, a major dam, aqueduct, hydroelectric, and irrigation scheme under the control of the United States Bureau of Reclamation, scheduled to begin construction in 1935. Ickes had been cordial when Sinclair had come calling but had made no such promises—or so he vehemently stated to the press when Sinclair reported the Secretary's support. Once again, Sinclair was chagrined. Hard-headed politicians were proving recalcitrant players in the drama Sinclair was trying to write. "I've been taken into the family," Sinclair told reporters of his imagined reception by Roosevelt and the presidential circle. He was being interviewed at the Hotel Algonquin in New York, a haven for writers, not politicians. [13] On the other hand, Harry Hopkins, the closest of Roosevelt's advisors, had come to Sinclair's defense. "Sure, I'm for him," Hopkins told the press. "He's on our side. A Socialist? Of course not! He's a Democrat. A good Democrat." [14]

Support such as this from at least some members of Roosevelt's circle, together with the passive acceptance of Sinclair by Roosevelt himself, allowed him to avoid the rout the press was predicting for EPIC and Sinclair personally at the state Democratic convention scheduled to convene on 20 September 1934 in Sacramento. Party regulars, after all, could hardly be expected to be pleased by the seizure of their organization by an outside amateur and his radical movement. On the other hand, Sinclair had inspired the registration of thousands of Democrats, putting the Party in a position of statewide competitiveness with the Republicans for the first time in the twentieth century. And so the convention compromised, voting through a platform that was compatible with EPIC, while modifying or merely finessing some of its more radical recommendations.

Others would not be so accommodating. In the course of his long, outspoken, and extensively documented career, Upton Sinclair, a writer rarely guilty of an unpublished thought, managed to offend just about everybody. In *The Money-changers* (1908), for example, he had castigated bankers and banking. In *The Profits of Religion* (1918) he had indicted the clergy and organized religion. In *The Brass Check* (1919) he gave the press forty whacks, and in *The Goose-Step*

(1923) he had excoriated university professors and higher education. Now these and his other forty-five books, so many of them hostile investigations of established interests, came back to haunt his campaign. Retained by Republican interests, two press agents, Clem Whitaker and Leone Baxter, ensconced themselves in an office in the Russ Building on Montgomery Street in San Francisco (the door read: California League Against Sinclairism) and proceeded to pore through Sinclair's writings in search of damning statements for distribution to the press. It was an easy task.

And besides: the press needed little motivation to attack Sinclair. He had already earned the enmity of the Fourth Estate. In *The Brass Check*, Sinclair had dared to say the unsayable (for a public figure at least): namely, that big city newspapers were constitutionally protected sources of money and power, the only business, in fact, explicitly mentioned in the Bill of Rights, and that the owners and publishers of newspapers ran them as businesses for their own profit and the profit of their advertisers, and that the profit motive shaped editorial content and news reporting, and that most posturing about freedom of the press was so much self-serving hypocrisy. There is a truism in politics: never get into a quarrel with someone who buys ink by the barrel—which is what Upton Sinclair had done so intrepidly. And now the press repaid him in kind. The New York *Times*, for one thing, kept a half dozen reporters on his story, the first time the *Times* was paying such attention to a California election, and their coverage set a tone of bemusement masking distaste, even fear, that other California candidates would likewise inspire in the years to come.

Locally, the nervous bemusement of the New York *Times*, *Time* magazine, and the *Saturday Evening Post* became the loathing, avid and overt, of such publishers as George Cameron of the San Francisco *Chronicle*, Joseph Knowland of the Oakland *Tribune*, C.K. McClatchy of the Sacramento *Bee*, William Randolph Hearst of the San Francisco *Examiner* and the Los Angeles *Herald-Express*, and, most virulently, Harry Chandler of the Los Angeles *Times*. Fed inflammatory passages by Whitaker and Baxter—who were in the process, whether they knew it or not, of pioneering the modern mass-media political campaign with its emphasis on thought/sound bites and damning innuendo—the major newspapers of California fed their readership a daily diet of anti-Sinclairisms from the writings, when possible, of Sinclair himself. Sinclair, as usual, responded with yet another broadside, *The Lie Factory Starts*, which appeared in July 1934 as the primary neared its finish. Press attacks gained in intensity after Sinclair won the nomination.

In one of his interviews with the press after meeting with Harry Hopkins, Sinclair stated that he had told the Federal Emergency Relief administrator that if he were elected and EPIC put into action, half the unemployed of the country would move to California so as to have a chance to get on their feet. A hostile press naturally played this gaffe on Sinclair's part as an open invitation for the unemployed to head to California with such partisan headlines as "Heavy Rush of Idle Seen by Sinclair" and "More Competition for Your Job." The Los Angeles

Herald-Express, in an act of deception despicable even for a Hearst newspaper, published stills from a Warner Brothers film, *Wild Boys of the Road*, purporting to show an army of hoboes heading for California in anticipation of Sinclair's victory. Don Belding, West Coast manager of the advertising and public relations firm of Lord and Thomas, also retained by the Republicans, hired, in his words, "the scum of the streets" to parade with pro-Sinclair placards in conspicuous public spaces. The California League Against Sinclairism wrote a special Sinclair song, to be sung to the music of Al Jolson's "California, Here I Come!"

> California, here we come!
> Every beggar—every bum
> From New York—and Jersey—
> Down to Purdue—
> By millions—we're coming
> So that we can live on you.
> We hear that Sinclair's got your State.
> That's why we can hardly wait—
> Open up that Golden Gate—
> California, here we come![15]

A hired airplane flew over major metropolitan areas, dropping a *Nuts for California* pamphlet ridiculing EPIC (other titles: *Septic Plan* and *Santa Claus for Governor of the State of California*), together with a Monopoly-like **"SincLiar Dollar"** whose seal bore the motto "Easy Pickings in California" and the rubric "Redeemable, If Ever, at the Cost of Future Generations."

When supporters of EPIC exposed the fake stills and the fake newsreels, Sinclair used the event to launch a counter-attack against his fiercest nemesis, Harry Chandler, publisher of the Los Angeles *Times*. Had not young Harry, a Dartmouth dropout, arrived penniless on the rails in Los Angeles in 1883, Sinclair waggishly asked his audience? Had he not lived down and out on the Plaza for a year before going to work for the *Times* and eventually marrying the boss's daughter? Turning on the platform so as to face the *Times* building, Sinclair would exclaim: "Come on, Harry! Give the *other* bums a chance!"[16]

Unamused, Chandler repaid Sinclair in kind, day after day. Chandler's chief henchman, Times columnist Harry Carr, attacked Sinclair as a closet real estate speculator, hypocritically pretending to be one of the Folks. The Sinclairs were vulnerable on this account, for they had made money on a property in Long Beach, and just before Sinclair had declared for governor they had moved from South Pasadena to a larger home in Beverly Hills so as to be closer to the movie studios while Sinclair worked on *Thunder over Mexico*, a disaster-stricken venture directed by the Russian *auteur* Sergei Eisenstein. They returned to their South Pasadena cottage, however, to meet with EPIC supporters, since Beverly Hills was not a preferred meeting place for Folks on the glory trail. He and Mary had picked up the foreclosed Beverly Hills property for a song, Sinclair countered, and with no down payment demanded by the distressed owners. And besides: Harry Carr was a mercenary hack who had once confessed to him that he had never, while working for the *Times*, written a word in which he sincerely believed. The *EPIC News* habitually referred to Carr as Fat Boy.

Fat Boy and his cohorts, however, had the last laugh. Over the years, Upton Sinclair had left behind a self-incriminatory paper trail of prodigious proportions, extracts from which the *Times*, among other papers, published daily under such headings as "Upton Sinclair on Sex," "Upton Sinclair on Marriage," "Upton Sinclair on Christian Science," and so forth. Among other items, Sinclair had written much criticism of middle-class marriage, which he claimed put men in power over women: this despite the fact that Sinclair bedeviled his first wife, Meta Fuller, with detailed written instructions regarding every aspect of their personal life together and the practicalities of household management. At Helicon Sinclair had preached something approaching a doctrine of free love. Sinclair and Meta practiced an open marriage. Dutifully, Sinclair would read his wife's gossipy letters when she was off with a lover. With Sinclair's approval, Meta aborted one of her pregnancies. Sinclair himself occasionally availed himself of the open relationship, despite a deep streak of prudishness which his onetime friend Frank Harris claimed kept Sinclair from becoming a first-class novelist. (Aside from this unkind remark, Harris also got Sinclair in trouble with Pasadena postal authorities by sending him a copy of his sexually venturesome autobiography *My Life and Loves* through the mail.) In any event, when Meta had an affair with a close and trusted mutual friend, a horrified Sinclair sued for divorce on grounds of adultery.

All this now became grist for the mills of a hostile press, together with Sinclair's opinions on organized religion, which he later admitted cost him more heavily in the campaign than any other source of attack. While the primary was barely underway, the third Democratic candidate, Justus Wardell, a conservative Roman Catholic from San Francisco, accused Upton Sinclair of standing on a platform in Kansas City and daring the Almighty to strike him dead if He existed—or at the least to stop his watch. No, no! Sinclair replied. That was the fictional character Elmer Gantry in the novel by another Sinclair, Sinclair Lewis, no relation. But the damage was done, and throughout the campaign the Kansas City story remained a damaging rumor.

Raised as an Episcopalian (his mother had dreamed of his becoming a bishop), Sinclair rejected organized Christianity when he converted to Socialism. In *The Profits of Religion* (1918) he launched an attack that was ecumenically offensive. The Episcopal Church, Sinclair opined, was the Social Register hypocritically at prayer. Roman Catholicism, on the other hand, was a religion for servant girls. Its hospital Sisters were slaves; and the Knights of Columbus were the secret oath-bound military arm of papal power. Mormons, Christian Scientists, and Seventh-Day Adventists belonged to quack churches. Methodists, Baptists, and Presbyterians—even Unitarians!—were likewise hypocrites; nor were the Salvation Army, the black church ("Come-to-glory-negro"), or other fundamentalist sects any better. As for the Good Book itself, the Bible was "full of polygamy, slavery, rape and wholesale murder, committed by priests and rulers under the direct orders of God."[17]

No wonder Carey McWilliams considered Sinclair to have lost the election mainly on account of the religious issue. Once having written things such as this in the ever-delicate matter of religion in the United States, most people would have had the common sense to refrain from elective politics. As it was, Sinclair faced a barrage of professionally orchestrated propaganda depicting him as a hare-brained anti-Christ. In Los Angeles Aimee Semple McPherson staged an anti-Sinclair rally in the Shrine Auditorium in October, just before the election, in which the language of Armageddon was everywhere. Once again, *The Profits of Religion* gave McPherson and the other preachers ample texts for castigation. Desperately, Sinclair countered with a religious poem entitled "Political Prayer, A Candidate's Answer to the Charge of Atheism" ("O God my Father, and God my Friend,/ And God my Guide to Poverty's End"); and the campaign organization cranked out pamphlets depicting him as "a modern prophet . . . whom God has sent to us in our affliction," with explicit comparisons to Jesus Christ driving the moneychangers from the temple, together with a special broadside aimed at Catholics citing parallels between EPIC and the economic teachings of the papal encyclicals (these were distributed in front of Catholic churches on the final Sundays before the election). But no use: the damage was irreversible.

Other attacks hurt as well. As governor, for example, Sinclair would serve as an *ex officio* member of the Board of Regents of the University of California and be responsible for presenting its budget to the legislature. As might be expected, another anti-Sinclair organization, the Los Angeles–based United for California League, distributed a pamphlet of inflammatory extracts from Sinclair's *The Goose-Step* (1923) and *The Goslings* (1924), two exposés of universities in general and the University of California in particular. Convinced that UC represented the controlling oligarchy of California (the Board of Regents consisted of "the worst plutocratic elements in the state"), Sinclair had described Cal as the University of the Black Hand, weaving a Mafia-like web of conspiracy. The fact that UC president David Prescott Barrows was a veteran of the conquest of the Philippines, an outspoken imperialist, and a major general in the California National Guard only reinforced Sinclair's assertion that the modern American university was interested, primarily, in producing new weapons systems and young candidates for military leadership. Sinclair even attacked the professorate ("rooting in the garbage heaps of man's past history, while their students go to hell with canned jazz and bootleg whiskey, and 'petting parties' "), thereby alienating yet another possible source of support among liberal faculty members.[18]

Hollywood hated Sinclair because, once again, he had launched the first attack. Like practically every other Southern Californian then or since, Sinclair had wanted to make money in the movies. As usual, his attitude was ambivalent. For the premier of *The Wet Parade* at Grauman's Chinese Theater on 17 March 1932, for example, his first well-paying film script, Sinclair showed up in a business suit, not black tie, and was ignored by Sidney Grauman, serving as master of ceremonies. Despite the fact that *The Wet Parade* barely recouped its costs ($400,000), Irving Thalberg paid Sinclair $10,000 to develop another proposal, a story of moneymen on Wall Street, which Sinclair could never give the correct slant, which is not surprising, given his Socialism.

In 1930 Sinclair backed into the business himself. The venture cost him his earnings from *Oil!*, *Boston*, and *The Wet Parade* and sent him to the hospital with nervous exhaustion. At the suggestion of Charlie Chaplin, the Russian director Sergei Eisenstein called on Sinclair in October 1930 with the sad news that Eisenstein's affiliation with Paramount had not worked out and that he had only a few days left on his visa. Among other projects, Eisenstein was supposed to have directed a film version of Theodore Dreiser's *An American Tragedy* (one can easily envision it as one of the greatest films never made), but now Moscow under Stalin, not Hollywood under Thalberg, seemed his destiny. What he really wanted to do, Eisenstein told an increasingly sympathetic Sinclair, who was a great admirer of the director's *Battleship Potemkin*, was to go to Mexico and make an epic film set in that strange and exotic land. With the quixotic rapidity that characterized everything he did, including running for governor, Sinclair began almost immediately to bombard Washington with telegrams seeking an extension of Eisenstein's visa. Within a few days, he had agreed to raise $25,000 for the Mexican project, the first $5,000 coming from Kate Gartz.

Two years, $90,000, and two hundred thousand feet of film later, Eisenstein was still in Mexico, filming, and the Sinclairs, Upton and Craig alike, were each on the verge of nervous collapse. Sinclair had to be hospitalized twice. Even Stalin, whom Sinclair had contacted by telegram, informed Sinclair—again by telegram on 21 November 1931—that he had no use for Eisenstein, a traitor to the revolution, and did not want him back. (At this point, Sinclair might perhaps have asked himself why Charlie Chaplin, a millionaire many times over, had passed Eisenstein on to Sinclair in the first place.) The film salvaged from Eisenstein's footage, *Thunder over Mexico*, an incoherent travelogue, lost money and was quickly turned over to the Museum of Modern Art in New York.

Sinclair was broke, stressed, and ambivalent to Hollywood that day in early 1932 when producer William Fox, monumentally bitter at being deposed as the head of Fox Pictures, offered him $25,000 to help him prepare his memoirs. Three times a week Fox would arrive by limousine at Sinclair's home with his lawyer, sheafs of documents, and a stenographer in tow and under Sinclair's questioning would tell his story, beginning with his boyhood in the East Side ghetto of New York. Fox was very angry, and under Sinclair's deft guidance that anger soon produced, by May, a thick manuscript, ostensibly by Fox, in which the perspectives and attitudes of Sinclair were everywhere. How else, in other words, could a Jewish producer, himself so expressive of the system, have produced such an anti-Semitic document in which Jewish villains were everywhere? Ostensibly an exposé of Hollywood and Wall Street, the Fox memoir had a strong secondary theme as well: Hollywood as the Cosa Nostra of American Jewry. Already, in *Oil!* and elsewhere, Sinclair had edged into anti-Semitism in comparing the producers of Hollywood, serving the lascivious dreams of America, to ancient Jewish traders who were purported to have sold Christian girls into concubinage.

Fox, in fact, had no intention whatsoever to publish the manuscript. He wanted to use it as leverage in his desperate effort to regain control of his studio. Learning of this, Sinclair had the *chutzpah* to publish the memoir unilaterally in 1933 as *Upton Sinclair Presents William Fox.* Causing a sensation, the exposé sold fifty thousand copies at $3 a book, enabling Sinclair to recover in part from his disastrous backing of Eisenstein. Aside from these profits, the book also earned Sinclair the undying enmity of Hollywood. According to Sinclair, notices were posted throughout the Fox studio that anyone caught with the book on the premises would be summarily dismissed.

Now, in the summer and fall of 1934, as Sinclair struggled to become governor of California, Hollywood took its revenge. Louis B. Mayer, an ardent Republican, collected a day's wages for the Merriam campaign from every employee earning more than a $100 per week. Joseph Schenck of United Artists said that if Sinclair won, the $150-million-a-year film industry would move to Florida. Sinclair retorted that Hollywood was bluffing. Under EPIC, he countered, he would get the State involved in motion picture production, with Charlie Chaplin in charge.

Working closely with the Hearst organization, no less than Irving Thalberg himself, production chief at Metro, orchestrated the filming of numerous fake newsreel shots, which were distributed free to California theaters. In them, self-respecting people—filling station attendants, business executives, the decent elderly, stenographers and exceptionally pretty office girls played by Hollywood starlets—told the camera why they were voting for Governor Frank Merriam. The disheveled and disreputable, on the other hand, many of them with thick foreign accents, stammered their support for Sinclair. Audiences soon began to look forward to the succession of bleary-eyed and shabby Sinclair spokesmen, one of whom vigorously scratched himself as he spoke, and would laugh openly when they came on screen. "Vell," said one particularly Bolshevikish gentleman, menacing in his bristling beard, "his system worked vell in Russia, vy can't it vork here?" [19]

This last suggestion, that Upton Sinclair was a Communist or at the least an active Communist sympathizer, cut to the core of the fascist/Communist battle of rhetoric and symbol California was playing out so intensely. The Depression, for one thing, was driving the Republicans of California further and further to the right. James Rolph, for example, who was in office when Upton Sinclair declared his candidacy, had spent twenty genial years as mayor of San Francisco before being elected governor in 1930. As mayor Rolph presided affably and with great success over the evolution of San Francisco into a first-class metropolis, although *Chronicle* editor Paul Smith would later characterize Rolph as "an amicable Republican knucklehead."

Smith had a point. As governor of a Depression-ridden state, Rolph was growing increasingly reactionary and peevish. The cotton strike of 1933 left him in a particularly angry mood. On the evening of 26 November 1933 a mob broke into the jail at San Jose and, dragging from their cells the two alleged kidnappers and murderers of Brooke Hart, a local department store heir, lynched them in the city square and set fire to their bodies. Four days earlier, Rolph had practically invited the event when he declared that he would not call out the National Guard to prevent plans for the lynching, which was already heavily rumored. After the lynching occurred, Rolph was quoted variously in the San Jose *Mercury Herald*, the San Francisco *Chronicle*, the New York *Times*, *Time* magazine, and elsewhere, saying (in the *Time* version): "This is the best lesson California has ever given the country. We show the country that the State is not going to tolerate kidnapping. I don't think they will arrest anyone for the lynching. If anyone is arrested for the good job, I'll pardon them all. Why should I call out troops to protect those two fellows?"[20]

Condemned by, among others, FDR, former president Herbert Hoover, Archbishop Hanna of San Francisco, Cardinal Hayes, and Episcopal bishop William Manning of New York, a score of ministers, and rabbis (led by Irving Reichert of San Francisco, a Rolph political appointee), together with assorted writers, educators, civil rights attorneys, and black leaders (Dr. Adam Clayton Powell, the NAACP), Rolph grew even more choleric and distressed, suffered a series of strokes, and died on 2 June 1934, leaving the governorship to Frank Finley Merriam.

Where Rolph had to be pushed rightwards by the force of events, Frank Merriam, age sixty-nine, was there from the start. Reactionary to the point of medievalism (so George Creel described him), Frank Merriam of Long Beach, a strait-laced Iowa émigré brought along by Harry Chandler of the *Times*, epitomized the Folks of Southern California, just as the whiskey-drinking, high-living Rolph, an Episcopalian member of the Pacific Union Club atop Nob Hill, had epitomized the more expansive mode of the city by the Golden Gate. No one seemed to like Frank Merriam (his campaign fundraiser Artie Samish called him "a bald-headed son of a bitch"), and Merriam returned the favor. Even as governor, Merriam had few friends. Rolph, at least, had been the beloved mayor of a large city. Merriam, by contrast, had served as auditor of the State of Iowa before moving to Long Beach and in his emotional life and demeanor expressed the harsher, more repressive aspects of an anti-Communist accountant sprung from the Folks. Central Casting could not have sent a more rightward adversary to place against the recent Socialist Sinclair than the exacting, humorless, Red-baiting numbers cruncher from Iowa.

Once again, Sinclair handed his enemies their weapons. In 1909 he had written a poem entitled "The Red Flag," whose fiery lines

> Tremble, oh masters—tremble all who live by other's toil—
> We come your dungeon walls to raze, your citadel to spoil!

left no doubt where its author stood, at least in 1909, on the matter of the coming revolution. Blending political and religious offense, Sinclair had in *They Call Me Carpenter* (1922) brought Jesus of Nazareth back to Los Angeles just after the World War, during a Red Scare, and had Him arrested for preaching revolutionary doctrine. In *The Profits of Religion* Sinclair had depicted the Christ as a proletarian rebel palliated into stained-glass divinity. In *Letters to Judd* (1926) Sinclair had outlined the Socialist program for the United States in a series of letters to a young worker. Among the Sinclairisms in this book: "I say if there is violence, let the capitalists start it and then you, Judd, and the rest of the workers can finish it." [21]

The California League Against Sinclairism lost no time extracting such aphorisms for inclusion in its steady stream of leaflets, together with the mention of Sinclair's membership in a half dozen or more leftist organizations. "Sinclair, Defiler of All Churches and All Christian Institutions—Active Official of Communist Organizations—Communist Writer—Communist Agitator," headlined one leaflet from the Merriam for Governor Committee of Alameda County. "I, Menace of California, And How I Ended," ran another, this one from the California League Against Sinclairism, in parody of Sinclair's *I, Governor* manifesto. "I, Menace of California," ran one section, "forgot that Californians would repudiate at the polls the man who would boast of being the teacher of Lenin and Stalin and was proud that he helped to spawn the ruthless red terror which made of working men cogs in a machine, debased womanhood, starved millions, denied the right of secret balloting which might overthrow the tyranny of Stalin, herded millions to prison camps, robbed peasants of their farms, children of a God, and tyrannized a helpless people by a red army more ruthless than any Czar. I forgot I wrote in the Moscow Daily News of Nov. 5, 1932, praising the USSR as 'the most important event in human history.' "

No wonder the New York *Times* reported that "a sense of Armageddon hangs in the bland California air." Guided by state party chairman Earl Warren, the Republicans were framing the election as the possible takeover of California by the radical left. Sinclair, in turn, gave as good as he got. As the campaign approached November, *EPIC News* pointed ominously to the pending takeover of California by fascist elements. "If Frank Merriam, the Republican nominee, is elected Governor of California," Sinclair was quoted in the New York *Times* of 3 September 1934, "a Fascist State will be created that will put even Huey Long to shame." In a radio address on the eve of the election, Sinclair explicitly cast the outcome of the campaign in terms of apocalyptic violence between Left and Right. "Our old industrial system in falling into ruins," he argued, "and a new system has to be built in the midst of the collapse. Unless democracy can find a way to do this, we shall have civil war, followed by Fascism and ultimately by Bolshevism. In an effort to avert these events we present a plan to the people of California."[22]

The *we* of "we present a plan" was the royal *we* as much as it was Sinclair speaking for the entire EPIC movement. For some months now, messianism had been seeping to the surface of Sinclair's campaign persona. He was now frequently using the royal *we* or referring to himself in the third person. More and more, he seemed to relish large rallies, with himself at the microphone before increasingly large, increasingly fervent audiences. He grew bolder in stating what he would do as governor—as governor this, as governor that—to the growing distress of Republicans and the Democratic Party establishment. What were they facing, they asked themselves, a fool, a joke, a writer on an ego trip—or a dangerous radical who might very well pull it off and capture power? If Southern California were ever to spawn a messiah, on either the left or the right, Upton Sinclair—folksy, evangelical, embattled as to status and social class—seemed the perfect candidate. He had, after all, announced his candidacy with a book. The question became: was it the *Manifesto* or *Mein Kampf?*

In this one point, Sinclair's ability to project the possibilities of dictatorship, Republicans and the Communists found themselves in agreement. *New Masses* referred frequently to Sinclair as a social fascist, doubly dangerous because he was marching beneath the banner of progressivism. Were the Communists and the Republicans totally without evidence? On his post-primary pilgrimage to the East, Sinclair had journeyed to Detroit to seek out Father Charles Coughlin, the right-wing radio preacher and political commentator. Emerging from an hour-and-a-half meeting with Coughlin, Sinclair jubilantly announced the priest's approval of his candidacy and the EPIC program. Coughlin later repudiated the endorsement (if, indeed, it were ever given), much to Sinclair's embarrassment. Too much should not be made of Sinclair's wooing of the popular radio orator. Coughlin, after all, had not yet fully surfaced as a rightist anti-Semite. Yet by the summer of 1934, when Sinclair called upon him, the direction in which Coughlin was heading was already apparent: lower-middle-class resentment, religiously reinforced, over the failure of capitalism to take care of God's own children. Such was at once Coughlin's and Sinclair's power base.

As the campaign progressed, this element of religiously reinforced resentment and economic salvationism fixed itself intensely onto Sinclair. Raised to the status of an Isaiah, Sinclair revealed an authoritarian streak and a sense of himself at center stage that verged on narcissism. He proposed, among other things, to conduct business as governor in an open hearing room, with seats provided for the public, and all proceedings broadcast live on radio, with a corps of stenographers taking down every word. "To each of these," wrote Sinclair of his proposed staff meetings in the Gold Fish Bowl, "the Governor spoke as to the commander of an army."[23] The image of the governor of California as a quasi-military figure directing a corps of equally para-military subordinates in the regeneration of the economy through a broad program of resettlement and public works, today California, tomorrow the nation, all of it live on radio, including two weekly radio addresses to the people by His Excellency, definitely possesses its unsettling para-fascist and Orwellian aspects. Like fascism, EPIC emphasized mass planning, mass conformity, mass enforcement, and, at the center of everything, a saving, self-obsessed, messianic First Consul, buoyed on a wave of lower-middle-class resentment and belief. Nor was EPIC over-much concerned with property rights or other niceties of the Constitution. As much as Sinclair defended its American-ness, there was something foreign, something foreshadowing an American *bund*, in the messianic statism of the movement. But then again: Roosevelt's critics would soon be saying the same thing about the New Deal.

Sensing the connection and wishing to dissociate his brand of statism from Sinclair's more radical proposals, Roosevelt was by the fall putting as much distance as possible between himself and the aspiring messiah of the Golden State. Party regulars such as J. F. T. O'Connor, comptroller of the currency, and George Creel spearheaded this effort to separate Sinclair from Roosevelt. Caught, in his words, "between the epilepsy of Sinclair and the catalepsy of Merriam," Creel had initially agreed to sit out the election quietly (or so he claimed) but had reentered the fray in October when Sinclair published yet another pamphlet, *Immediate EPIC*, in which Sinclair reemphasized, despite an earlier promise not to do so (or so Creel claimed), certain Socialistic aspects of the program. Under the general sponsorship of William Gibbs McAdoo, Democratic Senator from California and titular head of the Party, a group of California Democrats organized themselves as the League of Loyal Democrats, William Jennings Bryan Jr. chairman, pledged to oppose the Party nominee and his program.

Bank of America president A. P. Giannini, meanwhile, an ardent Roosevelt supporter, was trying to persuade Sinclair to withdraw in favor of Raymond Haight, a young attorney from Los Angeles, a Democrat, who was running as a third party Progressive-Commonwealth candidate. Informed through an associate that Sinclair was willing to listen, Giannini forwarded the good news to Comptroller O'Connor, a key political operative for FDR. O'Connor received permission from Roosevelt to travel out to Los Angeles to see if he could exploit Sinclair's apparent fatigue; but by the time O'Connor arrived, Sinclair had recovered his resolve—if, indeed, he had truly lost it in the first place; for Giannini, in his eagerness to save the election for the Democrats, may have forwarded an ill-founded rumor. Shortly thereafter, Giannini would have revenge for this embarrassment when Sinclair personally asked him for a $40,000 loan in the waning days of the campaign. Giannini refused. What about five thousand, Sinclair begged. No, A. P. replied, nothing.

Far from withdrawing in Haight's favor, Sinclair made an emotional appeal to O'Connor for the sort of open support by FDR that Sinclair believed he had been promised by no less than the President himself. Sinclair was especially bitter because Roosevelt had given a major radio address on the evening of 25 October without in any way mentioning production for use or Sinclair's candidacy: this after Sinclair had repeatedly referred throughout the campaign to Roosevelt's endorsement, which he predicted would be given in a radio address in the final stretch of the race.

Hearing Sinclair out, O'Connor said nothing, but the wily Irish political fox knew what he must do. Meeting with Governor Merriam on 31 October, O'Connor negotiated Merriam's agreement, in return for Roosevelt's continued boycott of Sinclair, not to claim his victory as a repudiation of the New Deal. Instead, Merrriam would describe his election as a triumph of bipartisan common sense. He would also promise to show favor to the anti-Sinclair Democrats in appointments and patronage after the election.

Sinclair now stood opposed to a *de facto* fusion ticket of Republicans and Democrats united behind Frank Merriam. If all this were not enough, two further blows struck: the *Literary Digest* published an unfavorable poll, and the attorney general of California, Ulysses Webb, a Republican, initiated legal proceedings to purge more than a hundred thousand newly registered Democrats from the voters' rolls of Los Angeles County, working-class voters, in the main, whom EPIC had brought into the political process.

Published on 27 October 1934, the *Literary Digest* poll was based, the magazine claimed, on nearly seventy thousand sample ballots sent to registered voters in California, approximately half the number of voters who had voted in the 1930 gubernatorial election. Of the 66,896 responding, Merriam claimed 42,141 or 62.70 percent of the votes; Sinclair had 17,284 or 25.72 percent; and Haight trailed with 7,471 or 11.12 percent. The American Civil Liberties Union immediately charged that the poll was rigged. No ballots, claimed ACLU executive Chester Williams, had been sent to those Los Angeles districts where Sinclair's support was strongest. Merriam supporters, moreover, had bought up blocks of ballots from scalpers, paying them twenty-four cents each, then sent them back to the *Literary Digest* with a Merriam endorsement. For the first time in American electoral history, a poll (perhaps rigged) was playing a substantive role in a major election. The *Literary Digest* poll prompted a momentary suggestion from a demoralized Sinclair that he might be willing to negotiate a withdrawal in favor of Haight.

Meanwhile, Attorney General Webb, working in cooperation with the district attorney of Los Angeles County, was sending postcards to thousands of newly registered voters, demanding that they appear in court and submit proof of legal registration. A list of thousands of other voters was published in small type in an obscure legal newspaper with a similar demand that they also appear in court and validate their registration. The Sinclair campaign appealed directly to the State Supreme Court and won a summary judgment, but the damage had been done. Thousands of Sinclair supporters, so many of them first-time voters of low-income status, were frightened off from voting for fear of becoming embroiled in the court system, despite the fact that a corps of volunteer lawyers stood ready on election day to defend any challenges to any voter by Merriam forces.

No wonder, then, as election day approached, Upton Sinclair and his wife Craig were showing signs of serious stress. In her autobiography *Southern Belle*, Craig Sinclair reveals that her husband was on the verge of a breakdown by the end of the campaign. She herself had doubts as to whether Sinclair could function as governor in the miraculous event he were elected, so distraught was his condition. A rumor that a businessman had vowed to assassinate Sinclair on the morning of that unlikely occurrence only added to their anxiety. On the evening of 6 November 1934, as results began to be broadcast over the radio, Craig wept with joy that Upton would be spared the ordeal of implementing EPIC in California.

Given the fact that even such a supportive pundit as Carey McWilliams had declared Sinclair a loser in the *New Republic* the week before the election, the actual outcome—Sinclair winning 879,537 votes to Merriam's 1,138,620 and Haight's 302,519—was astonishing. Far from being driven from the field in disgrace, Sinclair had placed a highly respectable second. Of greater importance, he had prevented Merriam from winning a majority of the votes cast. The Republican acting governor of California had been able to win a full term only with Democratic assistance and would be forced to govern accordingly. Had Haight not been in the race, most of his Progressive supporters could have been expected to have voted for Sinclair, which meant—amazingly, given the extent, resources, and unscrupulousness of the opposition—Sinclair still might have won. And even with Haight in the race, had Roosevelt come forward on Sinclair's behalf, the embattled Democratic nominee might still have won in what turned out to be a nationwide Democratic sweep.

As it was, Sinclair created something resembling a sweep of his own. Twenty-six EPIC candidates reached the State Assembly. Two of them, Sheridan Downey and Culbert Olson, soon emerged as major forces in the Democratic Party. In 1938 Downey went on to the United States Senate, and Olson was elected governor. One of Olson's first official acts was to pardon Tom Mooney, just as Sinclair had promised to do.

Sinclair, as might be expected, went back to writing. Within days of the election, he issued a manifesto in the *Nation*. "Our EPIC movement is going on," Sinclair promised. "The election was just a skirmish and we have enlisted for the war."[24] Setting up his battered Remington in the sunshine of his patio, Sinclair produced in rapid fashion *I, Candidate for Governor—and How I Got Licked* (1935) and *We, the People of America* (1935). Still smarting over the religious attacks which had done him the most damage, he also cranked out *What God Means to Me* (1936) and a novel, *Co-op* (1935), in which, as was his usual fashion, he realized in fiction that which had eluded him in reality, a program of cooperatives for California.

In *We, the People of America* Sinclair appealed directly to Franklin Delano Roosevelt not to abandon the mandate that EPIC represented for both California and the nation. EPIC, Sinclair argued, represented California's contribution to the New Deal. Rather than wait for the New Deal to be exported to California from the East, Californians had risen up to create their own version of Roosevelt's program. Generously, given Roosevelt's abandonment of Sinclair in the campaign, Sinclair urged the President to draw upon the ideas of EPIC as he shaped the New Deal. Within the year, Sinclair had the satisfaction of seeing Roosevelt send a tax message to Congress advocating such EPIC notions as increased inheritance taxes, a gift tax, and graduated corporate and individual income taxes in an effort to redistribute wealth and prime the economic pump. In *I, Governor*, Sinclair promised to increase the Supreme Court of California to seventeen to get his programs upheld, an anticipation of Roosevelt's own efforts to enlarge the Supreme Court. Sinclair also considered Roosevelt's Federal Art Project to have strong links to ideas advanced by EPIC.

Most important, Sinclair believed, the EPIC campaign had helped reverse the proclivity of California toward reactionary politics. By 1935, Sinclair exulted, Governor Frank Merriam, ("one of the oldest and stupidest reactionary politicians in America," Sinclair described him) was being forced to approve such EPIC-inspired programs as a graduated state income tax, an increase in taxes on banks and corporations, and public support for cooperatives. Indeed, by 1935, a year after Sinclair went down in defeat, seventy-five self-help agricultural cooperatives were flourishing in the state—seventy-six if we count the fictional cooperative of San Sebastian, which Sinclair created in great detail in his post-election novel *Co-op*. In a touching replay of Sinclair's pilgrimage to FDR and other national Democrats after the primary of 1934, Sinclair has the California hero of *Co-op* go back to Washington to instruct Roosevelt how to fight the Depression through cooperative production for use. In the novel, Eleanor Roosevelt provides the introduction to her husband, which she refused to do in real life. Even after Roosevelt had thrown him to the wolves, Upton Sinclair never lost a certain child-like faith in FDR: a faith reflecting that of millions of other Americans. Kept at arm's length from the President, deprived of the support that might very well have made him governor of California, Upton Sinclair began in 1939 a ten-volume series of novels centered on secret agent Lanny Budd, President Roosevelt's right arm in the war against fascism. Based in part upon Cornelius Vanderbilt Jr., the figure of Lanny Budd also represented a subliminal fulfillment for Sinclair, who had so very much wanted to become FDR's point man in California. *Dragons' Teeth* (1942), the third volume of the Lanny Budd series, earned Sinclair the Pulitzer Prize. Even as Upton Sinclair was making the most of his defeat through the churning output of his Remington, the Right was gathering its forces for an equally vigorous counter-attack.

6

The Empire Strikes Back

Testing the Fascist Alternative

*B*Y the mid-1930s, the Right had become restive. Not since the early 1920s had the Right experienced such a sense of threat. A decade earlier the Right had responded to its conviction of crisis with the passage of the Criminal Syndicalism Act and the propaganda efforts of the Better American Federation. What would be its response in the second half of the 1930s?

Centered in Los Angeles County, the Better American Federation remained a shadowy, albeit well-funded organization during its brief period of activity. Ostensibly organized to combat radicalism, the Federation also had as its goal the preservation of the open shop in Los Angeles. It was, in fact, the semi-secret political arm of the Merchants and Manufacturers Association of Los Angeles, which constituted its main source of financial support. The president of the Federation, Harry Haldiman (later indicted in connection with the Julian Petroleum Company scandal), believed that California had been going downhill since the Progressives had wrested control of the state from the Southern Pacific in 1911. The publications of the Federation—*Behind the Veil, The Red Menace, The World Endangered, America Is Calling*—spoke for themselves. The Republic, the Better American Federation argued, was being undermined by a subversive conspiracy directed from the Soviet Union. The American Civil Liberties Union was a front for the Soviet International; and the California Commission of Immigration and Housing a tool of the IWW. The Founding Fathers, the Federation argued, had created not a democracy but an oligarchical republic. Universal suffrage had subverted the intent of the framers, and the direct election of United States senators had dealt the republican ideal yet another blow.

Even during its most influential period in the early 1920s, when it maintained an office in Sacramento, the Better American Federation remained on the margin. Its efficacy, however, cannot be measured merely in terms of its enrolled members or even the direct effect of its paranoid propaganda. More influentially, the Better American Federation spoke to a latent rightism in Southern California, which itself represented a regional intensification of the American mindset in the aftermath of the First World War. The Los Angeles Police Department, for example, created what was perhaps the most aggressive Red Squad in the nation, and the open shop, a primary objective of the Better American Federation, remained in force.

Two incidents in 1933, the murders at Pixley and Arvin in Tulare County in October and the lynchings in San Jose in November, suggested another dimension—middle- and lower-middle-class vigilantism—to rightist sentiment in California.

At Pixley a group of thirty to forty Tulare County farmers, armed with rifles and shotguns, fired into a gathering of strikers near the railroad tracks who were listening to CAWIU organizer Pat Chambers. As two people in the crowd fell to the ground mortally wounded—Delfino Davila, a consular representative of the Mexican government, and Dolores Hernandez, a Tulare County striker—the farmers fired into strike headquarters, located on the highway. Thirteen men and one woman were wounded. It was a miracle no one else was killed. Meanwhile, over in Arvin in Kern County, another striker, Pedro Subla, fell to the ground, the victim of a sniper's bullet fired during a clash of armed strikers and growers. It was highly possible that the sniper was a striker and intended his fire for Deputy Sheriff T. J. Carter, who was approaching the melee with tear gas bombs. Just after the Pixley shootings, another sniper fired at Henry Behn, a black man from Madera, who was driving in his pickup truck. Behn considered himself fortunate to escape with only splinters of steel in his head and neck.

The following month, it was a largely middle-class mob which broke into the San Jose city jail and lynched the two accused kidnappers and murderers of department store heir Brooke Hart. There had not been a lynching in San Jose since 1854. The last lynching in Santa Clara County had occurred in 1883. The entire United States had witnessed only ten lynchings in 1932, down from a reported high of 145 in 1915. In the Pixley and Arvin incidents, Governor Rolph had warned the ranchers that the resort to violence on their part would not be condoned. In the case of the San Jose lynchings, by contrast, a mere month later, Rolph sanctioned the lynchings.

Just how effective vigilantism could be, especially when reinforced by legitimate government, became apparent in the abortive lettuce pickers' strike in Imperial Valley in January, February and March of 1934. Once again, as in the case of the Imperial Valley strike of 1930, the Union of Mexican Field Workers, joined by Filipinos, East Indians, Japanese, and whites, spearheaded the drive to gain wages of thirty-five cents per hour for lettuce picking in the Imperial. In preliminary meetings, the union had initially agreed to twenty-two and a half cents per hour, but the presence of organizers in their midst from the Cannery and Agricultural Workers Industrial Union strengthened their resolve to go for the higher figure. The strike began on 7 January 1934 and lasted for three months, although it barely made it through its first few weeks.

On 8 January local police and California Highway Patrol officers used tear gas bombs to disrupt a critical strikers' meeting in El Centro. Four days later, several hundred Mexican workers attempted to hold an organizational meeting in Azteca Hall in Brawley. Brawley police, Imperial County deputy sheriffs, and California Highway Patrol officers once again used tear gas to break up the meeting. The police also seized all typewriters and mimeograph machines in the building and locked the doors against further use.

With the assistance of attorney A. L. Wirin of the American Civil Liberties Union, the strikers secured an injunction from the federal district court authorizing them to hold a meeting on 23 January without police interference. Wirin drove out from Los Angeles and registered at the Barbara Worth Hotel in El Centro. There, he was kidnapped and beaten by members of the American Legion and left in the desert eleven miles outside the town of Calipatria, barefoot and stripped of his money and personal belongings. Meanwhile, back in El Centro, some two hundred vigilantes, some of them deputized Legionnaires, many of them armed and drunk, milled about the Barbara Worth Hotel. A number of them stood threateningly around the hotel dance floor. When Wirin made it back to the Barbara Worth after eleven that evening, the Congregationalist minister in Calipatria, the Reverend Harold Eyeman, went to his room and begged Wirin to get out of town lest there be further trouble. A group of deputy sheriffs came to the room, promising Wirin an escort through the armed vigilantes. By midnight, Wirin had decided that he had had enough. Escorted by the deputies, he passed through the vigilantes and was led to his automobile.

Despite the federal injunction secured by the ACLU, the strike could make little progress against the conspiracy of growers, growers' organizations, local police chiefs, the California Highway Patrol, the American Legion, and assorted other vigilantes. Arrests of suspected strike leaders continued apace. Between 9 and 22 January seventy-five men and eleven women, most of them leaders or union organizers, were arrested on such charges as vagrancy, disturbing the peace, trespassing, or resisting arrest. Few could make the inordinately high bail, and so the strike leadership languished in a half dozen jails. Justifying themselves on the basis of sanitary requirements, the police also rousted migrant camps which were known to harbor strikers.

By early March, political power in the Imperial Valley had been organized into a vertical structure which even a moderate conservative might label fascist. At the top were the growers, organized as the Imperial Valley Growers and Shippers Protective Association (a sub-organization of the Western Growers Protective Association) and the Anti-Communist Association, which served as *politburo* of the reaction. The superintendent of the Imperial County Hospital, Charles Nice, headed the Anti-Communist Association and bore the title "Commander." Hugh Osborne, a member of the Imperial County Board of Supervisors, served as secretary to the Anti-Communist Association and integrated it with the highest elected governmental body in the county. Beneath these organizations extended an intricate network of county commissioners, local police chiefs, and American Legion units. Fascism had arrived in the Imperial.

On 28 March 1934, Commander Nice of the Anti-Communist Association was involved in another instance of conspicuous violence, the beating of attorney Grover Johnson on the sidewalk outside the Imperial County Courthouse, where Johnson had just successfully petitioned for a writ of *habeas corpus* on behalf of two of the leaders of the strike, Pat Chambers and S. C. Alexander. At approximately two o'clock in the afternoon, after Judge Roy McPherrin of the Superior Court had ordered the release of the prisoners, Johnson, his wife, and the two released strike leaders left the courthouse under the escort of Sheriff Campbell and eight deputies. A group of some thirty to forty men was milling about on the courthouse lawn. At the foot of the courthouse steps, the sheriff and his deputies and the prisoners turned to the right in the direction of the jail, where the prisoners were to be processed for release. Johnson and his wife continued past the milling group toward their car. Suddenly, Chan Livingston, a county official, rushed from the crowd and struck Johnson a blow on the left side of his head, sending his glasses to the sidewalk. "You red son of a bitch," Livingston hollered, "arguing constitutional law. We'll give you a taste of our constitutional law!"

With that, Livingston resumed beating Johnson about the head and the face. At this point, Charles Nice rushed in and began punching Johnson as well. Johnson fell to the ground, stunned. Livingston and Nice continued to hit him on the face and chest. Then Hugh Osborne, a member of the Imperial County Board of Supervisors, called Johnson a Red son of a bitch and kicked him twice. At this point, Mrs. Johnson returned from her automobile, with her husband's pistol in her hand. A number of men wrestled her to the ground, while a number of others returned to beating Johnson, who was severely handicapped by the loss of his glasses. They kicked his briefcase across the lawn.

Mercifully, deputies rescued Johnson and his wife and brought him to the jail. Johnson protested to Sheriff Campbell that the sheriff had done nothing while he and his wife were being beaten. "I knew they were attacking you," Sheriff Campbell replied, "but I am satisfied it was just a ruse to get my men to leave the jail so that the mob could get the prisoners and lynch them. Therefore, I ordered all my men to stay in the jail and protect the prisoners." [1]

While Johnson and his wife remained in the jail, the mob on the courthouse lawn had grown to two hundred. Supervisor Osborne and Commissioner Nice, Johnson later claimed, were haranguing the crowd to go into the jail and "get the goddamned reds." The city siren and fire whistles were shrieking, which was the pre-arranged signal for vigilantes to gather. In between their exhortations, Nice and Osborne actually entered the jail and spoke to the deputies. Johnson demanded that Sheriff Campbell disperse the mob, which was refused. Johnson then demanded the sheriff arrest the three men who had beat him. The sheriff refused.

However, he did allow Johnson to contact Judge McPherrin by telephone. Judge McPherrin came over to the jail and conferred with Sheriff Campbell. McPherrin also conferred with Osborne and Nice, who criticized the judge for deciding in favor of "the goddamned reds." It took Judge McPherrin thirty minutes to persuade the mob to disperse.

Mrs. Johnson was arrested on charges of carrying a concealed weapon, arraigned before the justice of the peace, and jailed. Grover Johnson was escorted from the county by sheriff's deputies. On 12 April he returned to defend his wife, who was convicted. During the trial, some fifty to a hundred vigilantes milled outside the courthouse. On the night of the 13th, Johnson had to flee the California Hotel in El Centro just ahead of a group of vigilantes heading in his direction. He spent the night in a shack outside of town and was smuggled back into the courtroom the following morning.

Two other attorneys, Wilmer Breeden and Ernest Besig, another ACLU lawyer, were also beaten. Sent into the Imperial Valley by Secretary of Labor Frances Perkins, Brigadier General Pelham Glassford found himself the recipient of death threats when he came out in protest against the beating of attorneys Johnson, Breeden, and Besig. In vain, General Glassford sought to secure a grand jury investigation into the violence and the indictment of those responsible for the organized campaign of terrorism and intimidation. "After more than two months of observation and investigation in Imperial Valley," Glassford futilely argued to the Imperial County Board of Supervisors, "it is my conviction that a group of growers have exploited a 'communist' hysteria for the advancement of their own interests; that they have welcomed labor agitation, which they could brand as 'red,' as a means of sustaining supremacy by mob rule, thereby preserving what is so essential to their profits—*cheap labor*; that they have succeeded in drawing into their conspiracy certain county officials who have become the principal tools of their machine."[2] The Board of Supervisors took little notice of General Glassford's call for a grand jury investigation. By that time, the Imperial Valley had been pacified. In the one investigation that did occur, chaired by Dean Claude Hutchinson of the University of California College of Agriculture, an academic with strong agribusiness connections, blame for the disturbances was placed on the presence of Reds and other outside agitators.

Writing in *Harper's* in February 1935, California journalist Lillian Symes attempted to evaluate the psychology of California in the aftermath of the General Strike of July 1934 and the campaign to defeat EPIC. Something rather ominous, the possibility of fascism, was troubling Symes. On the one hand, she was optimistic. "We are not yet a thoroughly desperate people," Symes wrote, "and because we are not, fascism, as such, has not yet crystallized in the United States. There has been as yet no need for it chiefly because there exists, as yet, no serious and widespread threat of social upheaval."

On the other hand, the propaganda campaigns unleashed over the summer and fall of 1934 against Harry Bridges, the longshoremen of San Francisco, Upton

Sinclair, and the EPIC faithful had introduced an element of psychological distortion into the mindset of California. Because the Right had insisted and reinsisted that a threat of a Communist takeover truly existed in both the maritime strike and in EPIC, "the general public might very well start believing that such a threat was real," Symes argued.

"Should this continue to be the case in California," she continued, "we may look for the crystallization of those forces which have made so large a part of Europe what it is today." In California, "we may find the beginnings of psychological reactions not essentially different from those we have witnessed abroad." The propaganda campaigns from the right, Symes continued, were in the process of convincing the non-Communist Left that fascism was a very real possibility. During the summer of 1934, "strike sympathizers of every shade felt the pressure of sullen hostility. It was like this, I imagine, in Rome in 1922, in Berlin in 1932."[3]

Symes had hopes that the Progressive tradition of California would be sufficient to hold Left and Right in equipose. California Progressivism, after all, was a distinctive reconciliation of the two principles. Alas, Progressivism seemed to go into temporary eclipse as the Right struck back with effective fury, swamping the reform-minded, assimilative tradition in which Symes had such trust. Reaction on the right included such fringe groups as the Silver Shirts of San Diego, a revived Ku Klux Klan in the Central Valley, and the California Cavaliers, a statewide organization formed in 1935. Two mainstream organizations, however, the American Legion and the Associated Farmers of California, provided the bulk of the foot soldiers and the general staff for the continuing counter-attack.

In the January 1930 Imperial Valley strike, American Legionnaires showed their willingness to serve as strikebreaking deputies, sworn in by the local sheriff. This technique of using the local chapter of the American Legion as a *posse comitatus* to suppress strikes continued through the 1930s. Working and lower-middle-class veterans of the Great War, already organized as uniformed cadres, the American Legionnaires offered a ready, willing, and able source of personnel for vigilante action. The deputization of Legionnaires conferred on their night rides and daylight beatings, their roundups and trashings of migrant camps, the mask of legitimate police action. Legionnaires were conspicuous, as an example, in Woodville in Tulare County in the Central Valley on the night of 8 October 1933 when, many of them drunk, they tried to disrupt a meeting of eight hundred striking cotton pickers and sympathetic small farmers. The next day, in Kern County, Legionnaire vigilantes legitimized with an eviction notice dumped the belongings of two hundred families of striking cotton workers on the highway near Bakersfield. That summer, in early August 1934, enraged by the general strike in San Francisco, the state convention of the American Legion called upon the legislature to enact a law punishing radical agitation by death or one hundred years in jail. In July and August 1935, American Legionnaires from the towns of Sebastopol and Santa Rosa helped break a strike of apple pickers in Sonoma County through the ominously effective technique of parading past migrant camps each night, clubs and nightsticks held at the ready. During the Salinas lettuce strike of September 1936, some 250 Legionnaires were swiftly mobilized.

If the American Legion provided the muscle and brawn behind the clubbings, night rides, and evictions, the Associated Farmers of California, Inc., provided the statewide strategies, the staff work, and the financial support for the campaign against the alleged Communist revolution that was seeking to consolidate itself in the farm fields of California. Organized in Fresno on 28 March 1934 by members of the California State Chamber of Commerce and the California Farm Bureau, the Associated Farmers of California initially considered itself an emergency organization set up to prevent a recurrence of the strikes of 1933. At this early stage, the Industrial Association of San Francisco, which had formed the main resistance to the longshoremen's strike, provided the Associated Farmers with their sole financial support.

Through 1935 the Associated Farmers of California, Inc., remained primarily a conference group established on a statewide basis to assist local growers' organizations. By 1936, however, with the passage of the National Labor Relations Act, a more sophisticated and ambitious organization emerged. Headquartered in San Francisco, the Associated Farmers presided over chapters in forty-two counties and coordinated the efforts of such affiliate groups as the Grower-Shipper Vegetable Association of Central California headquartered in Salinas, the California Fruit Growers Exchange (Sunkist) headquartered in Los Angeles, the California Dried Fruit Organization, the Canners League of California, and the California Processors and Growers, Inc. The very concentration of agriculture in California, with 2 percent of the farmers or farm corporations owning a quarter of all farm acreage, paying 36 percent of all wages, and gathering 32 percent of total crop value, allowed the Associated Farmers rapidly to acquire a dominant influence and become the leading organizational voice for agribusiness. S. Parker Frisselle, manager of the University of California–owned Kearney Vineyard in Fresno County, served as the first president of the organization. Succeeding Frisselle as president in 1936 was another member of the board of directors, Walter Garrison, a Lodi, San Joaquin County, grower and newspaper publisher. A decorated veteran of the Spanish American War and World War I, Garrison held the rank of colonel in the United States Army Reserve and frequently appeared in uniform. After 1939, Joseph Di Giorgio, president of the Di Giorgio Fruit Corporation, assumed responsibility for organizational fundraising. By that time, the Southern Pacific Railroad, the Pacific Gas & Electric Company, Southern Californians, Inc. (a group of industrial employers paralleling the Industrial Association of San Francisco), the Holly Sugar Corporation, and the Spreckels Investment Company had joined the roster of financial supporters.

In 1939 Carey McWilliams characterized the Associated Farmers of California as Farm Fascists. Certainly, the Association had no reluctance about going after farm labor with an iron fist. Cadres of vigilantes, many of them American Legionnaires, were organized on a county-by-county basis: twelve hundred in Imperial

County, eleven hundred in Sonoma County, a thousand in Stanislaus County, nine hundred in San Joaquin County, eight hundred in Monterey County, and so forth. In the case of local strikes, Association vigilantes acted as *provocateurs* or strikebreakers and were frequently deputized by local sheriffs. Beginning with a strike of apricot pickers in Brentwood, Contra Costa County, in 1934, and continuing through an apricot strike in Yolo County in 1937, a cotton strike in Madera County in 1939, and a fruit pickers' strike in Marysville in 1939, strike after strike was broken through vigilante tactics. Targeting union leaders, the Association had them jailed or run out of the area. In Merced County, for example, in July 1934 union leader Gus Sartoris was jailed on trumped-up charges even before the harvest began. Through its affiliate, the Agricultural Labor Bureau of the San Joaquin Valley, the Associated Farmers controlled the labor supply and wages in this area from the mid-1930s.

In addition to such goon tactics, the Associated Farmers also pursued a sophisticated, well-funded lobbying effort in Sacramento with county boards of supervisors. Through the second half of the 1930s the Associated Farmers vigorously opposed any housing programs for agricultural workers in the fear that, once organized as communities, farm workers would be in a stronger position to unionize. During the Merriam administration, the Associated Farmers blocked forty pro–farm labor bills pending in the legislature. Another 140 were blocked in the Olson administration. In 1939 alone, the Associated Farmers successfully opposed, among other legislation, bills calling for a farm minimum wage and a farm payroll tax, a bill prohibiting the California Highway Patrol from making arrests in strikes, a bill mandating the inspection of labor camps by outside parties, and—rather gratuitously, even for alleged fascists—a bill that would require farmers to provide their workers with drinking cups, and not just water from canteens. Not one bill which the Associated Farmers opposed in 1939 got through the legislature.

While blocking such legislation on the state level, the Association secured the passage of anti-picketing bills in most agricultural counties. In some counties, Shasta and Mendocino for example, union organizers were required to apply for a license and pay a fee after providing written evidence of good moral character and assuring the county that they would not "resort to force, violence, threat, or intimidation or other corrupt means of solicitation."[4] In March 1939 some twenty-seven CIO organizers had themselves deliberately arrested and indicted in an effort to test the anti-picketing ordinance of Shasta County in the court system. Locally, Superior Court judge J. A. Ross upheld the ordinance. While the challenge inched its way through the Court of Appeal en route to the California Supreme Court, which would eventually find such ordinances unconstitutional, anti-picketing measures remained on the books, thus allowing for the quick suppression of agricultural strikes through the rest of the 1930s.

The propaganda campaign unleashed by the Associated Farmers during these years had one persistent theme: Communists were attempting to organize the farm workers of California. The files of the magazine *The Associated Farmer* are lurid with tales of Communist chicanery. R. H. Taylor, executive secretary of the Agricultural Council of California, told the Commonwealth Club of San Francisco on 8 June 1934, that Soviet Russia had specifically targeted California for takeover as the food supplier to the rest of the nation. On 9 May 1936 the *Associated Farmer* ominously reported the theft of fifty sticks of dynamite from a Public Works Administration project in San Mateo County and quoted the county engineer to the effect that this was enough dynamite to blow up a city and might very well have fallen into the hands of radicals. On 3 August 1940 the *Associated Farmer* ran a rogues' gallery of mug shots of farm labor organizers who had Communist affiliations.

The fact was: the organizers cited in the *Associated Farmer* were openly Communist in their sympathies and organizational affiliations. The truth or falsity of such charges by the Associated Farmers is therefore almost beside the point. The Associated Farmers were after something else: the suppression of farm labor through a Red Scare, and it worked. When Governor Merriam asked Dean Hutchinson of the University of California College of Agriculture, W.C. Jacobsen of the California Department of Agriculture, and Assemblyman John Phillips of Banning to investigate the strike by melon pickers in the Imperial Valley in April 1934, all the investigators could do was to blame Communists for fomenting the strike. Next to no mention was made whatsoever of low wages or abominable working conditions. The presence of real Reds in the field (and there were plenty) only enhanced the value of using a Red Scare as a suppressive technique.

What the Associated Farmers had in mind for farm labor in California—its vision, that is, of the good and just order in the fields—became chillingly clear in the so-called Brentwood Plan enacted in the aftermath of the strike by apricot pickers in the Brentwood district of Contra Costa County in June 1934. First of all, the Associated Farmers, led by Colonel Garrison, played a major role in suppressing the strike. Heads were busted, and the usual suspects rounded up. In this instance, 150 strikers were herded by deputies into a cattle corral–like enclosure in the center of Brentwood. This spectacle of American citizens being herded into a temporary concentration camp had prophetic import; for after the strike, the Associated Farmers leadership persuaded Sheriff John Miller to announce the so-called Brentwood Plan. The Plan integrated public and private authority (both the federal and state Employment Services agreed to the plan) with sufficient skill to lead one to suspect that Carey McWilliams's charge of Farm Fascism was not merely a matter of hooligan tactics, or even skilled lobbying in Sacramento, but a scheme based upon the vertical and horizontal integration of private power and public authority that can only be described as right-wing syndicalism.

Authority to supervise the harvest, Sheriff Miller announced, would henceforth be in the hands of a group called the Diablo Valley Public Relations Committee, comprised of five small ranchers selected by the sheriff, five large farmers selected by the farm organizations, and five merchants or workers selected by the farmers. Needless to say: members of the Associated Farmers dominated the Committee.

Every fruit picker who wished to work in the Brentwood area was required to register with the sheriff's office and receive an identity card. During the harvest, sheriff's deputies moved from site to site checking on the identification and performance of individual fruit pickers. Sheriff Miller personally gave newly registered workers a welcoming pep talk, telling them that he himself had once been a fruit worker and that, since he was their friend, he wanted them not to agitate when they had problems, but to come to him for a talk.

By 1939 some six thousand registered pickers were peacefully available to Brentwood area growers. Sheriff Miller maintained an intricate spy system to ferret out actual or possible agitators. Any union organizer attempting to make a speech was arrested. On 12 June 1936, for example, the Associated Farmers informed Sheriff Miller that labor organizer Julius B. Nathan of the newly formed Federation of Agricultural and Cannery Workers intended to organize in the Brentwood area. Seven days later, the office of Earl Warren, district attorney of Alameda County, informed Sheriff Miller that Nathan intended to create a demonstration on Saturday afternoon, 20 June, in Brentwood. Astonishingly, Sheriff Miller encouraged a local citizen to file a complaint for disturbing the peace against Nathan in advance, and Justice of the Peace Robert Wallace issued preventative John Doe warrants. Sheriff Miller also made preparations to implement the Los Angeles technique of moving Nathan from jail to jail once he was arrested, so as to avoid either bail or the granting of a writ. Thus Julius Nathan, the representative of a non-Communist affiliate of the American Federation of Labor, found himself arrested before any alleged transgression had occurred. Nathan made it as close to Brentwood as the nearby town of Byron, where he spent the night, with six sheriff's deputies surrounding the house. The next day, the deputies informed Nathan not only of his imminent arrest, but of the fact that his life would be in danger should he proceed on to Brentwood. Nathan canceled his plans to organize apricot pickers in the Brentwood area.

In fascist Europe and Soviet Russia, the drama of Right versus Left included scenarios of spies, counter-spies, forced indictments, political trials, convictions, imprisonments, and executions. Spearheaded by the Associated Farmers, the California Right employed similar techniques of counter-intelligence and legal persecution, culminating in late 1934 and early 1935 in the arrest, indictment, trial, conviction, and imprisonment of the leadership of the Cannery and Agricultural Workers Industrial Union, which effectively ended the organizing capacities of the CAWIU. Skillfully manipulating the criminal justice system, the Associated Farmers of California broke the back of the Communist-led union which had been so successfully on the offensive since early 1933.

The Criminal Syndicalism Act of 1919 offered the Right its most convenient weapon of counter-attack, provided it could find the proper venue. Already, the Right had failed in its efforts to have CAWIU organizer Pat Chambers convicted in Visalia in Tulare County, where the trial of Chambers on charges of criminal syndicalism in the aftermath of the Pixley violence had ended in a hung jury. Caroline Decker had likewise eluded conviction. The coastwide maritime strike of the summer and fall of 1934 encouraged the Right to try once again, this time in Sacramento, the sleepy Central Valley town which since 1854 had served as the capital of California. Inspired by Harry Bridges and the longshoremen of San Francisco, who had tied up the entire Pacific Coast, the CAWIU leadership and its supporters—Chambers, Decker, Harry Collentz, Mike Plesh, Martin Wilson, Nora Conklin, Lorine Norman, and others—began to centralize their activities in Sacramento, the capital of agricultural California as well as the body politic, hoping to launch a similarly effective tie-up of the entire Central Valley.

Meanwhile, the Right was seeking to spy on, even to infiltrate, the movement. Melville Harris, a timekeeper at the Libby, McNeill & Libby Cannery in Sacramento, went to work as a volunteer at Communist Party headquarters at 912½ Eighth Street. Melville was secretly reporting to Rachel Sowers in the State Bureau of Criminal Identification, who had placed Melville in the cannery as a spy. Melville was also on the payroll of the Civilian Conservation Corps, performing similar activities for federal authorities. Later, in October, the Associated Farmers purchased part of Harris's time.

Robert Hicks, an accountant from the Pacific Telephone & Telegraph Company, and an officer in the California National Guard, joined Sacramento optometrist William Harr, another National Guard officer, as a spy at the Workers Center and School at 1529 Eighth Street, where the CAWIU also maintained its headquarters. Melodramatically, Hicks and Harr dressed in shabby clothes and foreswore shaving when they attended classes at the school, hoping to resemble a Hollywood version of Bolshevik conspirators. Comically, Hicks and Harr stood out among the other neatly dressed and shaven students. These two masquerading Guardsmen had been sent to their task by the military intelligence office of the Ninth Army Corps, headquartered in the Presidio of San Francisco. Their contact there was a certain Colonel Fenner.

The deepest of Deep Throats was William Malin Hanks, whose cover was his job as a janitor at the Libby, McNeill & Libby cannery. Tall, disheveled, running to flesh, the septuagenarian Hanks posed as an old IWW anarchist, full of stories of Wobbly clashes in the old days. In reality, Hanks had joined the IWW during the First World War—as a spy on the payroll of the federal government. During the cotton strike of October 1933, Hanks functioned as an undercover agent for Tulare County officials, posing as a striker. Since November 1933, he had been on the payroll of the State Bureau of Criminal Identification, reporting to Rachel Sowers, who sent him to Sacramento with instructions to infiltrate the CAWIU and its affiliates. Hanks joined the CAWIU and courted its leadership. Quickly, Hanks began to arouse suspicion. He tried desperately, for example, to encourage union members to vandalize the Land Hotel, where strikebreakers were lodged before being shipped down to San Francisco on the Sacramento River steamers

Delta King and *Delta Queen*. Hanks also tried to organize a window-stoning attack on the Libby Cannery.

Coordinating this flow of counter-intelligence was the Sacramento County DA, Neil McAllister, and two of his deputies, Chris Johnson and Lloyd Buchler. McAllister also had the services of the Frank Parise Detective Agency, which specialized in undercover work, and Department of Justice expert William "Red" Hynes, formerly captain of the notorious Red Squad of the Los Angeles Police Department. Faced with reelection in November, McAllister hoped to ride the wave of anti-Communist sentiment being fanned by the maritime strike. The CAWIU was opposing the recruitment of strikebreakers in the Central Valley and was calling for a similar industry-wide walkout in agriculture, just as the harvest season in the Central Valley was beginning in earnest.

On 20 July 1934, at the height of the strike in San Francisco, McAllister, assisted by Sacramento chief of police William Hallanan, raided the Workers Center and School on Eighth Street, which was also the state headquarters of the CAWIU. Accompanied by a reporter and a photographer from the Sacramento *Bee*, twenty plainclothes and uniformed police entered the center armed with shotguns, blackjacks, billy clubs, and tear gas. Chief Hallinan personally supervised the raid and the arrests. All in all, twenty-four suspected radicals were booked on charges of vagrancy. The men were held for fourteen days in the Sacramento County drunk tank, a cell twenty-five by thirty feet, twelve feet high, with one toilet and one water faucet and three sleeping platforms. In the early morning hours up to seventy drunks (among them, agents sent to spy on the unionists) would be crowded into this stifling, stench-ridden cell.

The initial charges of vagrancy leveled against those arrested did not seem so serious. After two tries, however, McAllister also secured grand jury indictments against eighteen of the detainees on six counts of criminal syndicalism, a felony. Among those arraigned were Albert Hougardy, CAWIU activist Pat Chambers, unionist Nora Conklin, Caroline Decker, La Pasionaira of the 1933 cotton strike, and Norman Mini, a Trotskyite. (Shortly thereafter, the Communist Party, holding its state convention in Sacramento, nominated Hougardy as a candidate for Congress, Chambers as a candidate for the United States Senate, and Conklin for the Sacramento County Board of Supervisors.) Eleven of those charged retained attorney Leo Gallagher for their defense. Gallagher also acted as counsel to six others who were acting as their own attorneys. Mini, who had left the Communist Party before the raid and wished to distance himself from the other defendants, retained separate counsel. Only Hougardy was immediately able to make bail of $3,000 cash or $6,000 in property. With the help of the International Labor Defense Committee and donors such as Charlotte Anita Whitney, the Oakland social worker and clubwoman who had herself been convicted of criminal syndicalism in 1920, all other defendants were eventually released on bail before the trial concluded. Caroline Decker used her freedom to raise money for the defense.

At a rally held at the Dreamland Auditorium in San Francisco on 13 March, she raised nearly $1,000 to offset legal fees.

The international dimension of these trials, however local they might seem, was underscored by the fact that in 1933 Leo Gallagher had traveled to Germany to defend the Communist Party member accused by the Nazis of torching the Reichstag and had been expelled from Germany when his defense showed signs of proving effective. A graduate of Yale Law School, Gallagher had spent six years in study for the Roman Catholic priesthood, taking a doctorate in philosophy from the University of Innsbruck in 1916. After serving as an officer in Army Intelligence in the War, Gallagher had taught briefly at the Jesuit-run Creighton University in Omaha before setting up practice in Los Angeles in 1923. A brilliant debater, a Jesuit in mufti, Gallagher represented the Roman Catholic Left at a time when most of his fellow religionists, in Europe and the Americas, had chosen the Right. In January 1930 the International Labor Defense Committee of the Trade Union Unity League, which was supporting the Sacramento Defense Committee, which was supporting the Sacramento defendants, retained Gallagher to defend union organizers arrested in the Imperial Valley. In 1932 Gallagher secured a retrial for Tom Mooney, in San Quentin since late 1916. Then came the Reichstag Trial, which brought Gallagher international notoriety.

Some critics accused Leo Gallagher of losing cases due to his pugnacious counter-attack in the courtroom. But Gallagher had his defenders as well, who claimed that in politically corrupted trials only an unyielding, unflinching defense could hope to defend even a portion of the accused's rights. "More than any person I know," wrote Carey McWilliams of Gallagher in the *Nation*, "Gallagher lacks humor, detachment, tact. Blandishment is unknown to him. He is a zealot for justice."[5] In 1934 Gallagher filed for associate justice of the California Supreme Court and received an astonishing 242,313 votes, not enough to elect him but enough to signify the presence of powerful and growing left-liberal sentiment among California voters, which soon consolidated itself behind the EPIC campaign.

Despite his brilliant defense, Gallagher could win acquittal for only eight of the seventeen defendants in the first trial on vagrancy charges. Skillfully, but with desperation, he fought for the empanelment of an unbiased jury for the second trial on the six felony counts of criminal syndicalism. Judge Dal Lemmon, however, favored District Attorney McAllister's every motion. The jury selected after a month of wrangling over 350 prospective jurors, person by person, was comprised of middle-class men and women, many of them operators of small business or lower-level managers, who could be expected to be hostile to the leadership of California's most effective and openly Communist agricultural union.

In its melodrama and gross unfairness, the Sacramento Conspiracy Trial, as it came to be known, represented the most powerful courtroom counter-attack to date by the California Right. Even before the trial began, McAllister fanned the flames of an already incandescent Red Scare by claiming that CAWIU infiltrator

William Malin Hanks, one of his star witnesses, had been kidnapped and run out of Sacramento by Communists. Hanks himself seemed responsible, initially, for the story, telegraphing McAllister from Prairie Du Chien, Wisconsin, that he had been threatened with death if he testified. McAllister sent a detective to fetch Hanks back from Wisconsin, and from that time forward the labor spy turned star witness appeared in court accompanied by an armed guard. When Leo Gallagher cross-examined Hanks on the witness stand, he destroyed the story that the Communists had run Hanks out of town. But Judge Lemmon ruled that Hanks's fabrication, which was part of McAllister's Red Scare strategy, had no bearing on the trial.

McAllister also put out the story that members of the International Labor Defense Committee had threatened a prospective juror with death and had also threatened McAllister's own life if he did not drop the charges. Once again, McAllister's story collapsed under investigation, but Judge Lemmon ruled the matter irrelevant. McAllister then suggested that the three women defendants, Caroline Decker, Nora Conklin, and Lorine Norman, had approached a prospective female juror in the ladies' washroom and tried to influence her. Once again Gallagher destroyed the story under cross-examination, and once again Judge Lemmon insisted that the matter had no bearing on the trial and that it be dropped. When Gallagher protested, Lemmon threatened him with contempt of court.

By then, McAllister was continuing as prosecutor only because of the intervention of California attorney general Ulysses Simpson Webb. In November 1934 the voters of Sacramento County rejected McAllister's bid for reelection as district attorney. McAllister went into jury selection on 26 November as a lame duck. His successor, Otis Babcock, due to take office on 7 January 1935, had in the course of his campaign expressed criticism of McAllister's Red Scare tactics. When Babcock announced that he would assume responsibilities for the prosecution, Attorney General Webb used extraordinary powers recently granted him by the state legislature to name McAllister as special prosecutor, thereby voiding, in this important instance at least, the election of Babcock. Thus, an unelected special prosecutor continued the case of the people versus the alleged conspirators, despite the wishes of the majority of Sacramento County voters.

As the Right grew even bolder in its willingness to use the court system to crush the CAWIU, liberals reacted in disgust. Even as trial testimony began in early January 1935, Democratic Assemblyman Franklin Grover of Los Angeles County announced that he would soon be introducing into the legislature a bill calling for the repeal of the Criminal Syndicalism Act. On 21 January 1935 twenty-one Democrats and two Republicans joined to sponsor Grover's bill. "It is not the law itself," Assemblyman William Mosely Jones stated to a San Francisco *Examiner* reporter, "but the manner in which it has been enforced. It has led to thinly veiled fascism of a most vicious and un-American nature."[6]

As if to corroborate Jones's suggestion of fascism, the City of Sacramento put itself under a virtual state of martial law. At the request of the city manager, a military man, Colonel R. E. Mittelstaedt, recently active with the National Guard during the San Francisco waterfront strike, assumed command of the Sacramento police. Colonel Mittelstaedt swore five hundred businessmen in as deputies. A local vigilante group calling itself the Crusaders drilled with pickaxe handles in the park. The Sacramento *Bee* printed a daily dose of inflammatory stories. When the State Unemployed Convention announced its intent to meet in Sacramento in March to petition the legislature to pass an unemployment insurance bill, the *Bee* carried a report that armed Communists were expected to be marching on the state capitol.

Initially, Special Prosecutor McAllister's strategy was to associate each of the eighteen defendants with as many of the six counts as possible. He also did his best to try the case outside the courtroom. Gilbert Parker, publicity director of the Associated Farmers and an employee of the Hearst-owned International News Service, sat in with McAllister and his associates as part of the prosecutorial team. Parker also provided daily briefings for the press in which he suggested both the story of the day and its spin.

Count five of the indictment specified acts and deeds of criminal syndicalism. McAllister failed utterly to prove any such acts, and even Judge Lemmon was obliged to dismiss this count. Charges against two defendants, Luther Mincey and John Fisher, were dismissed completely. Four other defendants were freed of charges under count one. Gallagher miraculously secured a consolidation of count four, membership in the Communist Party, and count six, conspiracy to commit criminal syndicalism. By the time the case reached the jury, Gallagher had managed to whittle the indictment down to count one, the advocacy of criminal syndicalism, and count six, conspiracy to commit. Gallagher was forcing McAllister to abandon proof of actual crimes and to prove instead crimes of belief, which then had to be proven as crimes of conspiracy. Under Gallagher's skillful defense, the trial became purely political, which was where Gallagher felt he had the best chance to win his case.

While the counts alleging actual misdeeds were still being heard, witness after witness—the multi-employed Melville Harris, National Guardsmen Robert Hicks and William Harr, Rachel Sowers of the State Bureau of Criminal Identification, William Malin Hanks, who suddenly developed a hearing problem under Gallagher's relentless inquiry—collapsed under cross-examination. Nor did a string of witnesses whom McAllister hoped to use to link Pat Chambers and Caroline Decker to inflammatory statements made during the cotton strike do any better. Prosecutor McAllister was reduced to reading highly edited inflammatory statements from pamphlets, books, magazines, and leaflets seized on the premises of the Workers Center and School, together with other instances of Communist Party literature. McAllister proved himself master of the half sentence, the inflammatory phrase; and when, in his rebuttal, Gallagher attempted to re-read full passages and full sentences, Judge Lemmon ruled that Gallagher could not re-read any passages already read by McAllister.

At this point, attorney Grover Johnson, having recovered from his beating by vigilantes in the Imperial Valley, joined Leo Gallagher in the defense. Gallagher's powerful, impassioned—and very loud!—presence in the courtroom had begun to worry some of the defendants and the International Defense Committee. When a juror complained that Gallagher was shouting in the courtroom, Goldman, defense attorney for Mini the Trotskyite, openly dissociated himself, so he told the court, from Gallagher's methods.

Since the remaining counts were political and ideological in nature, Gallagher and Johnson attempted to create an impression in the jury that conditions among agricultural workers in California were so bad that one did not have to be involved in a Communist conspiracy to seek their correction. Gallagher and Johnson put fifteen cotton pickers on the stand who testified to the conditions that led to the strike of 1933. They also showcased a series of eyewitnesses to the Pixley killings who totally contradicted the testimony of McAllister's witnesses, who sought to link Chambers and Decker to statements advocating the violence that broke out. To refute McAllister's characterization of Communism as a violent conspiracy, Gallagher and Johnson put Sam Darcy, organizer of District 13 (California, Utah, Nevada, and Arizona) of the Communist Party, on the stand. Darcy testified that union organizers associated with the Communist Party were expressly urged to avoid any form of violence or illegal activity. Judge Lemmon, however, used a legal technicality to instruct the jury to ignore Darcy's testimony. Lemmon also rejected Gallagher's plea for a thirty-day continuance for further preparation of the defense.

Because six of the defendants, including Pat Chambers and Caroline Decker, were technically acting as their own attorneys, with Gallagher and Johnson serving as co-counsels, they were allowed to address the jury as the defense rested its case. Seizing the occasion, Chambers and Decker made brilliant speeches. Delegated spokesperson by many of the defendants, Decker gave a six-hour defense summary in which she vividly evoked conditions in the fields, the purposes of the union movement, and the repressive implications of the trial itself.

Harassed, reprimanded, cited once for contempt, Leo Gallagher summoned his considerable forensic force in the course of his final statement. Point by point, witness by witness, half quote by half quote, Gallagher reviewed the prosecution's shaky case. Gallagher's closely reasoned, closely argued rebuttal contrasted completely with McAllister's closing argument. In his harangue McAllister referred explicitly to the Associated Farmers of California as a bulwark against a Communist takeover. Astonishingly, McAllister also threatened the jury with increased vigilante action throughout the state, should the jury not return with a proper verdict. There will be more bloodshed, McAllister warned, another Pixley.

"Out of this primitive wilderness, ladies and gentlemen," McAllister concluded, "sprang up the greatest Democracy in the world. . . . Think of the covered wagons. Think of the Donner Party coming through the snow and getting frozen to death. . . . They propose to agitate the country and take away from you what you have and overthrow the government. From Moscow! They are paid by Moscow! . . . The eyes of the nation are on you, asking you, begging you, pleading with you, to stamp out this insurrection, this advocacy of revolution and the overthrow of your government and institutions, which you love, honor and revere, and which you hope to pass down to your children and your children's children."

Walking over to the flag, McAllister placed his hand over his heart and recited the Pledge of Allegiance. He then turned to the jury and said: "Ladies and gentlemen, I ask you to think of that flag and that jury room, and I ask you to think of what it stands for. I ask you to bring in a vote for that flag, for the good old USA, for My Country 'Tis of Thee, for the Star Spangled Banner, for the United States of America—and God will bless you."[7]

It had been the longest trial in California history, four and a half months; and the jury remained out for sixty-six hours, obviously divided as to what represented the most plausible, if not just, thing to do. At one point, the entire jury filed back into the courtroom, its path cleared by a dozen uniformed police (a ritual insisted upon by McAllister so as to sustain an element of ominous threat from the Communists against the proceedings), and asked Judge Lemmon a simple question: if any of the defendants were to be convicted on count six, the count combining membership in the Communist Party and advocacy of criminal syndicalism, would that automatically make the Communist Party illegal in California? Judge Lemmon instantly saw the paradox which could invalidate the entire case. How could the defendants be found guilty of criminal syndicalism merely because they belonged to the Communist Party, when the Communist Party was a legally recognized political party in California, with a place on the upcoming ballot? Would not the conviction of the CAWIU activists necessitate that the state, if it were to be consistent, declare the Communist Party illegal and prosecute its membership? Once again, Judge Lemmon ignored the question. The legality of the Communist Party was not an issue in this case, he told the jury, and he would offer no instruction regarding the implications of a guilty verdict on count six. The foreman then asked the judge whether or not probation would be granted any of the defendants if they were convicted. Judge Lemmon replied that the jury could recommend probation but the court was not bound by any such recommendation.

Once again, scandal broke out. Holes were found bored, from the outside, into the jury room. When Johnson and Gallagher learned of this, they demanded an investigation. Once again, Judge Lemmon ruled the matter irrelevant.

For four days, the court sat silently in session, awaiting the verdict of an obviously troubled jury regarding the guilt or innocence of the twelve defendants whose indictments had survived the trial. Pat Chambers passed the time reading a book entitled *Fascism and the Social Revolution*. Two reporters played chess. Another group of reporters got up a bridge game. Finally, on 1 April 1935, the jury filed in, its members looking worn and haggard. (The next day, the San Francisco *Examiner* reported that the jury had taken 118 ballots to reach its verdict.) First came the good news: four defendants were acquitted entirely. For the remaining eight defendants—Pat Chambers, Caroline Decker, Nora Conklin, Martin Wilson, Jack Crane, Norman Mini (the lone Trotskyite), Lorine Norman, and Albert Hougardy—the verdict was guilty on count six, conspiracy to commit criminal syndicalism. The jury recommended probation for Lorine Norman and Norman Mini. At this point, four of the jurors appeared to be weeping, and sobs could be heard in the courtroom.

Johnson and Gallagher immediately made a motion for a retrial. When Judge Lemmon heard the motion a short time later, the defense lawyers introduced a sworn affidavit by one of the jurors, Howard McIntyre, who declared that many of the jurors had been deceived into voting for a guilty verdict as a result of a compromise that was not honestly fulfilled. Judge Lemmon denied the motion for a retrial.

Judge Lemmon sentenced the convicted eight to from one to fourteen years in state prison. Decker, Norman, and Conklin went off to the state prison for women at Tehachapi, near Bakersfield; the others were sent to San Quentin. The three women served a year at Tehachapi and were released. At San Quentin, the State Board of Prison Terms and Paroles fixed the sentences of Mini and Hougardy at three and a half years. Chambers, Crane, and Wilson received five years.

On 28 September 1937, after long and tortuous arguments, the Third District Court of Appeals of the State of California reversed the Sacramento verdict and ordered the remaining defendants released from San Quentin. Even then, Attorney General Webb allowed the men to languish behind bars for another twenty-two days while he decided whether or not to file an appeal.

Although the convicted CAWIU leaders eventually regained their freedom, their convictions voided, their records cleared, the Sacramento trial had an ominously chilling effect. Even a moderate conservative might be shocked by the spectacle of perjury, subversion of legal rights, newspaper hysteria, and, most frightening, the conspiracy of Associated Farmers, federal and state police agencies, criminal justice officials, and the bench itself that characterized the indictment and trial. It would not be farfetched, in fact, to make the comparison (and many did) to political trials in fascist Italy and Nazi Germany.

The Sacramento conspiracy trial, in fact, climaxed a half-decade chorus of complaint on the part of the Left, in the *Nation* and the *New Republic* especially, lamenting what it considered the drift of California in the direction of para-fascist or outrightly fascist behavior. This indictment of California by the national Left had been growing since the strikes and repressions occurring in the Imperial Valley in 1930–1931.

"California is, industrially, a sort of seasonal slave State," Robert Whitaker wrote in the *Nation* on 1 April 1931, "and whoever touches upon this situation so as to imperil the 'institution' will be railroaded to the penitentiary by any possible means. And whoever dare say anything about it risks his living if not his life."[8]

California, claimed Ella Winter (Mrs. Lincoln Steffens) in the New Republic on 27 December 1933 in the aftermath of the San Jose lynchings, was a state where little Hitlers were seizing control. It was false to describe the San Jose lynchings (the first lynchings in years to occur in a non-Southern state) as a spontaneous outbreak by an outraged citizenry, angered by the murder of a popular young man. Far from it, Winter argued. No more than twenty people carried out the lynchings while the rest of the crowd stood back twenty to thirty yards as bystanders. One masked man, in fact, seemed to function conspicuously as leader when necessary. Here was an instance of organized, systematic vigilante violence possessed of overtly political implications. "Let's clean out the Reds while we're about it," Winter quotes an American Legionnaire as saying in the course of the incident. "What are we waiting for?"[9]

There existed, Winter argued, a major instability at the core of California society which rendered it liable to repressive aberrations. The unbelievable beauty of the state, its coastal resorts, its prosperity that did not depend upon heavy industry, did not make Californians kindlier or more generous. Far from it. The very lack of industry in California, with the exception of the industry of make-believe in Hollywood, rendered the social and psychological foundations of the state shaky. More than other Americans, Californians seemed frightened, despite the shimmering surface of their society, that it could all be taken from them: which translated into a vulnerability to Red-baiting manipulation from the right.

With the Sacramento verdicts reported and the anti-union crackdowns continuing in intensity, Los Angeles–based journalists Herbert Klein and Carey McWilliams found themselves by July 1935 even more convinced that something terrible might be coming from the right in California. "The state is full of propaganda organizations," Klein and McWilliams wrote in the Nation on 24 July 1935, "such as the reorganized Crusaders, now engaged in spying on relief workers, and the New Order of Cincinnatus. The secret militaristic bodies, such as the Berkeley Nationals and the California Cavaliers, are growing fast. The state itself is arming: the California Naval Militia has been recruited by an intensive radio campaign, and the California Marine Militia is in formation. Both of these militia organizations will be commanded by the regular adjutant general of the National Guard; they constitute, in effect, an indirect attempt to increase the strike-breaking armed forces of the state."[10]

The important thing to remember about the Associated Farmers, Klein and McWilliams continued, was that they were not exclusively an agricultural organization, but an interlocking association of farmers, packers, shippers, Pacific Gas & Electric, and affiliated industries. The Associated Farmers possessed strong ties to local sheriffs' and police departments, the California Highway Patrol, and the State Bureau of Criminal Identification. At its San Francisco headquarters, the Farmers maintained well-organized files for more than a thousand suspected subversives (read, union organizers), sharing this information with police officials throughout the state. The Sacramento trial demonstrated the control the Associated Farmers had over the legal process. Skilled in propaganda, the Association maintained four branch offices, with representatives in every county, and reached the broad population, including city dwellers, through a skilled use of radio. The Associated Farmers also offered support for local vigilante groups such as the California Cavaliers, which the Associated Farmers helped organize in Sacramento County.

Throughout agricultural California, moreover, more and more ranches were being patrolled by armed deputies. There were even reports of machine gun emplacements in several large ranches. Farm workers were being herded into company camps and kept under close scrutiny. Just outside Salinas, something shockingly resembling a concentration camp had recently been constructed. "A water tower rises in solitary grandeur in the midst of the camp," Klein and McWilliams wrote. "Surrounding the tower is a platform, splendidly adapted for observation, night illumination and marksmanship. Flood lights are located at the four corners of the stockade in such a manner that they can illuminate the interior and also encircle the stockade with a clearly illuminated zone. When local workers became curious about this menacing structure, they were referred to Mr. Sterling of the Sterling-Harding Packing Company, and to Mr. Church of the firm of Church and Knowlton, both Salinas concerns. These gentlemen informed the workers that the stockade was being built 'to hold strikers, but of course we won't put white men in it, just Filipinos.' "[11]

As late as August 1934, the New Republic was maintaining its confidence that right reason would prevail. "Recent European experience," the magazine editorialized on 1 August 1934, "has shown that a radical working class can in fact be crushed and broken, but only by out-and-out Fascism, which is prepared to go in for mass murder on a large scale and without the slightest compunction. We doubt whether the California Tories are sufficiently ruthless and cold-blooded to go through with such a program, and we question whether the rest of the country would permit such a thing even if it were tried."[12]

Even if the New Republic were correct and the Tories of California could go no further than they already had, the Right of the Golden State had played out a most vivid enactment of the fascist possibility. Nor was the Right finished acting out such a scenario. Soon, very soon, in the midst of a strike of lettuce workers, the Salinas stockade would be filled with reluctant guests; in Stockton, a cannery strike rivaling any strike of the decade would erupt; and, a year later, a prominent Associated Farmer, Philip Bancroft, would be showing a surge of political strength among mainstream voters in his campaign for the United States Senate. For the rest of the decade, the empire would continue to strike back.

In 1936 the oligarchs of Los Angeles, acting through their chief of police, made a bold preemptive gesture. They sealed off Los Angeles from the rest of California, and California from the rest of the country. By late 1935 the Los Angeles establishment—meaning the Chamber of Commerce, the Taxpayers Association, and similar civic groups—were experiencing a hardening of heart regarding the influx of transients into Los Angeles County, which was estimated to be in the range of some two to four hundred dependent boys and some one to four thousand transient men each month. While the Federal Emergency Relief Administration (FERA) was functioning, support for such transients, who were each in need of some form of relief, was available from federal sources; but in January 1935 President Roosevelt, having spent some $2 billion through FERA and fearing that such a unilateral giveaway program would soon prove a political liability, shifted the emphasis of his administration to work-for-relief programs under the auspices of the Works Progress Administration (WPA), created by executive order on 6 May 1935. FERA officially ended on 31 December 1935, but it was obviously impossible for WPA programs immediately to take up the slack in Los Angeles County. Hence the panic in the establishment as thousands of transient men and boys continued to pour in.

Not surprisingly, distress over this invasion tended to reveal the *noir* side of the establishment. The majority of transients, it began to be claimed, were either aliens or criminals or both. In early 1935 the City of Los Angeles established a Committee on Indigent Alien Transients, which reflected the bias of the city. Astonishingly, the committee openly defined an indigent alien transient "as being a transient entering the state of California without visible means of support and whose legal residence is foreign to the state of California."[13] Thus the Committee, for all practical purposes, took California out of the Union. The City of Los Angeles would soon attempt to seize control of the state.

Long skilled in the techniques of rousting transients out of town after jailing them on vagrancy charges, the Los Angeles Police Department played an important role on this committee, on which the deputy chief of police sat as chairman. On 4 November 1935 the Committee on Indigent Alien Transients issued a report calling for the establishment of checkpoints manned by police and health officials at every major point of entry into the state. Transients who could not prove California residence, the report recommended, should be put into camps, preferably operated by the State Relief Administration, where they would be fingerprinted and their backgrounds checked for a criminal record. The report also called for "Vagrancy Penal Camps" for transients arrested on vagrancy charges. These penal camps would serve as labor pools for work upon roads, parks, and other public projects. Police should monitor all common carriers, railroads especially, and all main arterial highways in an effort to apprehend indigent alien transients seeking to enter the state. State and local officials, meanwhile, should form a statewide committee to supervise these activities: an extra-parliamentary task force responsible for sealing off the borders of California from transient migration.

Not surprisingly, these recommendations, offered with a straight face—with their suggestions of checkpoints, of preemptive arrests of those whose only crime was being poor in the Great Depression, of fingerprinting in forced labor camps, and, worse, of Vagrancy Penal Camps where thousands might be concentrated— did not meet with universal acceptance throughout the state. As paranoid as main-stream California might have become, it was not yet ready for such an unconstitu-tional, police state program.

Encouraged by local oligarchs, together with the City Council and the County Board of Supervisors, Los Angeles Police Chief James Davis, a spit-and-polish officer, resplendent in shiny black riding boots and Sam Browne belt, brushed aside any constitutional scruples, of which the chief had few, and decided to go it alone. On 3 February 1936 Chief Davis dispatched 126 LAPD officers to sixteen crucial highway and railroad entry points throughout the state with orders to turn back any and all indigent transients who could not prove California residence. Within days, the Foreign Legion of Los Angeles, as it was soon called, had estab-lished checkpoints along the Oregon border in Del Norte, Siskiyou, and Modoc counties; in the central Sierra Nevada counties of Plumas, Lassen, Nevada, and Mono; in the city of Independence in Inyo County; and across the southern desert in the counties of San Bernardino, Riverside, and Imperial. To maintain a sem-blance of legality, Chief Davis requested that his officers be locally deputized, which the sheriff of Del Norte County refused to do.

While Chief Davis's blockade of California lasted little more than two and a half months before succumbing by mid-April to a combination of high costs and outrage from such differing groups as the American Civil Liberties Union and the Sheriffs Association, the Foreign Legion did manage to provide California and the nation with a chilling spectacle of unprecedented police power: in its own way a *coup d'état* on the part of the LAPD of all other forms of local and state police authority. The sheer effrontery of this program, together with the fact that it was by and large accepted as a plausible response to the transient problem, testified to the paranoid mindset of so many Californians midway through the Depression.

Affronted by the LAPD border patrol, the State Relief Administration sent agents into the field to visit the sixteen checkpoints. Their reports reveal a cumula-tive portrait of LAPD officers not only functioning as judge, jury, and law enforce-ment agency, but, more shocking, exercising extra-constitutional powers of exclu-sion, detention, and preemptive arrest. For a month at least, the entrepôts of California, north, south, and central, seemed more like the border checkpoints of fascist Europe than those of an American state.

Highways 60 and 70 on the Arizona border had the busiest checkpoints. Near Winterhaven, just across the bridge crossing the Colorado River to Yuma, the Los Angeles police also halted passenger buses to make sure that no one was at-tempting to enter California by buying a ticket for a destination a short distance across the border. Some two hundred undesirables were turned away in the first few days of the program. An official from the State Relief Administration watched as officers waved through a shiny new Packard sedan. A 1921 Ford roadster, pulling a homemade trailer, rusted, dripping water and oil, and carrying a family of nine, was not so fortunate. The father, unshaven and unwashed, a ring of tobacco juice around his lips, a sixteen-year-old son, a mother with a year-old daughter in her lap, and a three-year-old boy sat jammed in the front seat. In the baggage compartment, which had been ripped out and converted into a rumble seat, were crammed three daughters, ages five, twelve, and fourteen. An eighteen-year-old youth sat alone atop the luggage and boxes on the eight-foot-long homemade trailer. The family, from New Mexico, was heading to California, the man told the officers, where his wife had a sister. One of them said they had $30 in cash. The officers turned them back into Arizona. By night the police would search stopped trains with their powerful flashlights, taking into their dragnet men and boys and occasionally a woman illegally riding the rails. Their individual and cumulative stories expressed the desperation of the Depression: a young man en route to San Pedro in hopes of reenlisting in the Navy; an aged Mexican, who claimed to have been born in Texas (a search revealed on him a few matches, a tortilla, and a piece of string); a teenaged Mexican couple running away from El Paso, she sixteen, he nineteen, the two of them living off a pint jar of peanut butter.

Unwillingly, transient traffic also moved out of California across the border into Arizona. Transients, most of them young men and boys, were taken from the Lincoln Heights jail in Los Angeles, put into boxcars, and escorted by Los Angeles police officers across the border into Arizona. One state official witnessed a group of some 150 young men and boys being deported under LAPD auspices via the desert town of Indio in Riverside County. Charitably, peanut butter and baloney sandwiches were provided.

Understandably, the illegality of this program, if not its outright fascism, soon aroused a chorus of protest from the American Civil Liberties Union, the American Association of Social Workers, the governor of Nevada, the attorneys general of Arizona and Oregon, the city commission of Phoenix, Oregon city officials from Portland, Klamath Falls, Grants Pass, and Roseburg, even the chief of the California Highway Patrol, who resented the incursion of the LAPD into CHP jurisdiction. At Blythe in Riverside County, the LAPD stopped and questioned two members of the California senate. On 10 February LAPD police stopped and questioned John Langan, a California businessman returning home from Arizona. Outraged, Langan sued Chief Davis in the federal court for depriving him of his constitutional rights as guaranteed by the Fifth and Fourteenth amendments. Not surprisingly, the city attorney of Los Angeles, Ray Chesebro, had already declared that the border program was legal because it represented an extension of city policy used in protection of the interests of the city. Attorney General Webb, by contrast, stated in a letter dated 18 February 1936 to the Los Angeles Chamber of Commerce that in his opinion the program was illegal. But these were merely informal opinions. Langan's suit had the makings of an effective court challenge, but the federal court in Southern California declined to hear the case. The Fourteenth Amendment, the court ruled, which prohibits a state from depriving any citizen of liberty or denying equal protection of the law, could not apply in this instance because Chief Davis was not acting under the authority of the State of California. Langan's complaint, therefore, was the complaint of one Californian against another, each of them acting as private parties, and should therefore be heard by the state courts.

By this time, a mounting taxpayers' protest in Los Angeles itself, together with the crescendo of disapproval from civil rights groups and outraged government jurisdictions, had wearied Chief Davis and other supporters of the blockade. Seeking to justify the program, the chief issued a report on 11 March 1936 which claimed that 48 percent of the transients who had been turned away possessed criminal records. In LAPD terms this meant anyone who had ever been arrested for any reason whatsoever, including a minor traffic violation or simple vagrancy, which in Depression America, Southern California especially, most often translated into being unemployed and broke.

Regional lore remembers the LAPD border blockade as an aberrant, even comic, incident. But it must also be seen as yet another instance of the acting out of far-right solutions to Depression problems, however briefly. As in the case of the Sacramento conspiracy trials, moreover, the criminal justice system seemed in this instance to be aligning itself with patently illegal, unconstitutional behavior. The organizational sophistication of the blockade (whatever his faults, and they were myriad, Chief Davis ran an efficient department) made the entire incident even more ominous. This was not the misbehavior of a country sheriff's department staffed by bubbas. In this instance, one of the most efficient police departments in the United States was acting unconstitutionally, and for a while at least, the LAPD seemed to have the support of its community for its outrageous seizure of statewide authority.

By 1936, then, the California Right had perfected its ability to manipulate social and legal procedures and to enlist the support not only of Legionnaires and other vigilantes but of uniformed police. In September of that year, the quick, efficient suppression in Salinas of a strike by lettuce packers showed the Associated Farmers not just reacting, but launching a preemptive attack.

Located 150 highway miles south of San Francisco, twenty miles northeast of Monterey, the Salinas Valley runs narrowly between the Gabilan and Santa Lucia ranges, paralleling the Pacific Ocean. Watered by the Salinas River and cooled by winds and fogs from the Pacific, the Valley enjoys mild temperatures and a long growing season. Landholdings in this two-hundred-thousand-acre domain tended to remain intact from the era of the Spanish and Mexican *ranchos*, which meant that the Salinas Valley remained in the hands of a small elite who preferred to deal in one large cash crop keyed to one large market. When Claus Spreckels opened a sugar beet factory in Watsonville in 1888, with a capacity of a thousand tons of sugar a day, Salinas Valley ranchers entered the sugar beet business in a big way, deriving revenues of up to $70 an acre.

Between 1920 and 1930, as California sugar production began to lose out to Hawaii, Salinas made the transition to another industrialized crop, lettuce. Salinas shipped its first carload of iceberg lettuce to New York City in 1917. Artichokes were also introduced after World War I, but it would take time for artichokes to win acceptance in a mass market. In the meanwhile, sophisticated East Coast markets continued to import their artichokes from France. Lettuce, by contrast, made the transition from a luxury item to a household item in the 1920s.

By 1929 the Salinas Valley was producing half of all the lettuce consumed annually in the United States. Between April and November of that year, Salinas's share of the national lettuce market reached 70 to 80 percent. Forty-three thousand acres of the Salinas Valley were devoted to lettuce by 1931. Lettuce is a delicate, volatile crop; among other things, it requires three to four times more water than other vegetables. In the 1930s it involved thirteen man-days of labor through the cycle of planting to harvest. The lettuce industry was and remains a high-wire act of time and money.

Lettuce has to be harvested the day, almost the hour, it ripens: cut by hand with a knife, trimmed, then crated and iced for shipping. Left too long in the sun, mature lettuce gets tip-burned and begins to rot from within. A sudden cold spell, on the other hand, can destroy a crop within twenty-four hours, if the lettuce is not harvested immediately. In the 1930s that meant that a harvest force, Mexican and Filipino in the main, had to be available and in the fields the very day a crop ripened. Shipping schedules had to be met with exactitude, lest the iced lettuce spoil. In the 1930s lettuce had fourteen days from harvest to reach Eastern markets. Even as lettuce was heading east in refrigerated rail cars, markets could glut within hours, making expensive reroutings necessary. No California crop was worth less than a boxcar of Salinas lettuce in a New York or Chicago railroad yard on a hot summer day.

All this conspired to make lettuce a high-yield, high-risk, highly centralized, highly coordinated agricultural industry. An acre could yield up to $900 in 1935 dollars (three hundred crates an acre at $3 per crate) in gross income, provided that everything went well. By 1935 some forty-plus growers and shippers dominated the industry. Frequently, they functioned as banks to farmers, buying crops ahead of the harvest with cash advances and thereby extending their vulnerability. It cost seventy-five cents to pack, ice, and load a crate of lettuce. It cost $1.75 to ship that crate to the east. Each shipper, then, had approximately $2.50 in after-harvest costs before a crate of lettuce reached the market.

Not surprisingly, with everyone so over-extended, so dependent upon a crop that was so expensive and so perishable, the lettuce industry in the Salinas Valley tended to be a mean, hard business, even within the generally unforgiving context of California agriculture. The Depression only intensified this mean-spiritedness.

(*Above*) Nineteenth-century San Francisco was a workingman's city. By 1888, when these workers from the Whyte & De Rome Foundry posed for their portrait, organized labor was entering a decade and a half of militancy that would soon make San Francisco the city in which American labor had cut its best deal. *California State Library.* (*Right*) Dedicated to his calling with almost monastic fervor, charismatic labor leader Andrew Furuseth headed the International Seamans Union from 1908 to 1938, accepting only the wages of an ordinary seaman. *San Francisco Public Library.*

(*Above*) After the completion of the transcontinental railroad in 1869, the Chinese turned to levee-building in the Sacramento Delta, to agriculture and fishing, and in San Francisco to brick-making, cigar-rolling, laundry and restaurant work, and retail. Sometime in the early 1880s, San Francisco photographer Isaiah West Taber captured the strength and serenity of the enduring people whom Anglo-California called the Celestials. *California State Library.* (*Below*) When the city imprisoned Denis Kearney for his incendiary speeches, the Chinese had a momentary revenge, as this stereotyped but effective cartoon from the *WASP* indicates. *California State Library.*

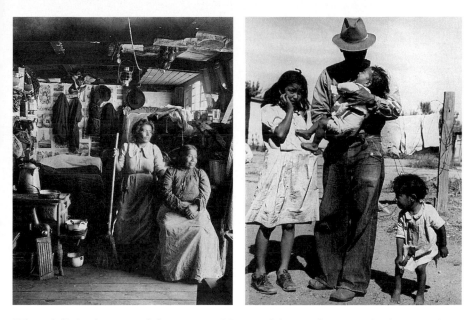

(*Above left*) At the turn of the century, Mexican labor made a comeback in Southern California. These women kept house in an unused freight car while their men laid more than a thousand miles of track that would eventually link the entire region into a single interurban network. *California State Library. (Above right)* By the late 1920s Mexican labor predominated in the fields of Imperial Valley and the southern San Joaquin Valley. Mexican workers such as this man spearheaded a series of agricultural strikes between 1929 and 1933. *Labor Archives & Research Center, San Francisco State University. (Below)* The Great Depression, after some delay, finally surfaced with full force in California. In Los Angeles, the middle classes, along with working people, took their place in line at an outdoor soup kitchen. *Security Pacific Collection, Los Angeles Public Library.*

(Above) By the mid-1930s private philanthropy in Los Angeles was joining with the public sector to offer relief programs of astonishing magnitude. Despite the evidence of this photograph from the *Herald Examiner*, it was frequently claimed by the oligarchy that there were no bread lines in the City of Angels. Herald Examiner *Collection, Los Angeles Public Library. (Below left)* Socialist, tractarian, vegetarian, teetotaler, and all-round gadfly, Pasadena writer Upton Sinclair captured the Democratic gubernatorial nomination in 1934. Sinclair and his running mate—another tractarian gadfly, lawyer Sheridan Downey—promised to End Poverty in California (EPIC). *San Francisco Public Library. (Below right)* EPIC began as a quixotic crusade, but by the eve of the election, the movement seemed on the verge of taking control of California. Accordingly, Sinclair was granted the mandatory cover on *Time. California State Library.*

(*Above*) Spring 1934. The longshoremen of San Francisco burn their blue books and walk away from the employer-controlled union. Andrew Furuseth stands by watching. *San Francisco Public Library.* (*Below*) Throughout the spring and early summer of 1934, tension grew on the Embarcadero as picketing longshoremen, marching in phalanxes in Frisco jeans and flat caps, were confronted by the San Francisco police. *San Francisco Public Library.*

(Right) From the ranks emerged the longshoremen's leader, a lean and laconic Australian by the name of Harry Bridges. As chairman of the Strike Committee, Bridges encouraged the rank and file to hang tough and stand tall. *San Francisco Public Library.* *(Below)* 5 July 1934, known as Bloody Thursday. Chief Quinn arrays some 800 policemen on the Embarcadero. All day the battle waged, and by one o'clock P.M., two strikers lay dead. *San Francisco Public Library.*

(*Above*) Following Bloody Thursday, the California National Guard occupied the Embarcadero with fixed bayonets. San Francisco seemed an occupied city, or in the throes of counter-revolution, or worse, a city seized by the Right. *San Francisco Public Library.* (*Below*) Labor Day 1939. Harry Bridges leads the triumphant longshoremen down Market Street. His men now have their own organization, the International Longshoremen's & Warehousemen's Union (ILWU). *ILWU Library, San Francisco.*

(*Above*) The Salinas lettuce strike, September 1936. Chief Raymond Cato deploys 141 California Highway Patrolmen throughout the city and all roads leading into Salinas. *San Francisco Public Library*. (*Below*) A *posse comitatus* of local American Legionnaires and their affiliates is deputized and goes on patrol throughout strike-torn Salinas, the ever-ready pick-axe handle in hand. *San Francisco Public Library*.

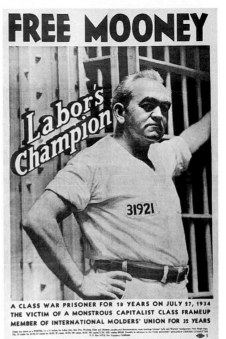

(*Above left*) The Reds, insisted Philip
Bancroft, a pistol-packing pear-grower from
Walnut Creek, were out to take control of
the state. In 1938 Bancroft, son of the well-
known pioneer California historian, ran for
the United States Senate as a conservative
Republican. *San Francisco Public Library.*
(*Above right*) If elected, promised liberal
Democratic gubernatorial candidate Culbert
Olson, he would free Tom Mooney, the labor
activist railroaded into San Quentin for the
Preparedness Day bombing in San Francisco
on 22 July 1916. Taking office in January
1939, Governor Olson kept his word and
presented Mooney with a pardon in a packed
Assembly chamber over a live nation-wide
radio hook-up. *California State Library.*
(*Left*) The next day, Mooney led a
triumphant parade down Market Street in his
home town of San Francisco. Ever defiant,
he broke ranks momentarily to carry a picket
sign in front of the Kress department store.
San Francisco Public Library.

Ham *and* **Eggs**

FOR CALIFORNIANS

(Above left) Ham and Eggs helped bring the New Deal to California. More formally known as the California Pension Plan Association, Ham and Eggs called for a constitutional amendment granting $30 in warrants every Thursday to every unemployed Californian over fifty. *California State Library. (Above right)* Narrowly defeated at the polls in November 1938, Ham and Eggs returned for a second try at the ballot the following year. On 19 May 1939, a rather weary Culbert Olson, whom Ham and Eggs had helped make governor, received the requisite petitions and pledged a special election on Ham and Eggs at the cost of a million dollars. In the rest of the nation, California was rapidly acquiring a reputation for nutty politics. *San Francisco Public Library. (Below)* Master of politics, nutty or otherwise, was the Falstaffian figure of Arthur Samish. In June 1938 Samish found himself describing to a grand jury in Sacramento just exactly how he had earned $496,138 in fees between 1935 and 1938. *San Francisco Public Library.*

(*Above left*) Undergraduates from Berkeley parade with picketing longshoremen sometime in the spring of 1934. Ironically, football players from Berkeley were also being used to help break the strike. *San Francisco State Library.* (*Above right*) Dorothea Lange, among the preeminent photographers of her generation, reached the full measure of her talent when she took to the field, camera in hand, and documented migrant labor, such as these apricot pickers, working in Gilroy during the harvest season of 1935. *Dorothea Lange Collection, The Oakland Museum.* (*Below left*) Women played pivotal roles in each and every strike. In the Salinas lettuce strike of 1936 (*left to right*) Letha Payne, Ida Mason, and Vera Necas held important posts in the central strike committee and the women's auxiliary of the Vegetable Packers Association. *San Francisco Public Library.* (*Below right*) In San Francisco, Chinese-American women struck against sweatshop conditions in the garment industry. Militancy among these women was somewhat at odds with their culture, but this was the 1930s, not to mention the fact that hours were long, holidays few, wages meager, and working conditions miserable. *Labor Archives & Research Center, San Francisco State University.*

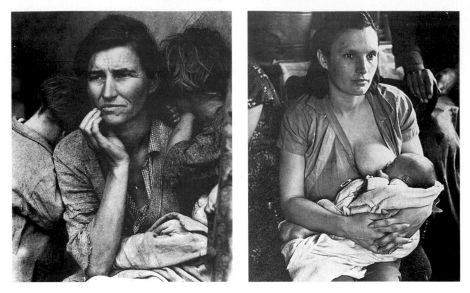

(*Above left*) In March 1936, on a cold wet miserable day in a pea-pickers camp outside Nipomo, Dorothea Lange encountered a migrant woman, Florence Thompson, and her three children. Lange exposed six negatives. One of them, subsequently entitled *Migrant Mother*, became the best-known icon of the Depression. *Dorothea Lange Collection, Oakland Public Library*. (*Above right*) Yet women were prevailing. In early 1938 photographer Horace Bristol published in *Life* this photograph of a nursing migrant mother from Oklahoma. Not surprisingly, Bristol later claimed that this image helped inspire the controversial ending of Steinbeck's *The Grapes of Wrath* (1939). *Horace Bristol Collection, 20th Century Photographs, Los Angeles*. (*Below*) Thanks to Dorothea Lange, what was known but never fully acknowledged—the presence of African Americans in both the relief programs and migrant labor—emerged in the consciousness of the State. *Dorothea Lange Collection, Oakland Museum.*

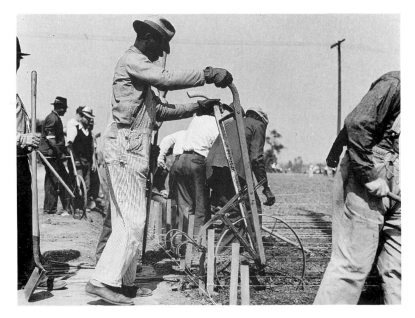

(Above left) While WHITES ONLY signs were posted in certain fields, no grower banned African Americans from picking cotton. In September or early October of 1938, cotton pickers stand in line outside a weighing station in the San Joaquin Valley. *Dorothea Lange Collection, Oakland Museum. (Above right)* The sudden arrival of more than 300,000 migrants in a few short years created a housing and health crisis of monumental proportions. Shanty and shack towns, more popularly known as Hoovervilles or Little Oklahomas, sprang up in roadside culverts up and down the Central Valley. *Labor Archives & Research Center, San Francisco State University. (Below)* In late 1935, the Resettlement Administration opened Arvin Camp outside Bakersfield in Kern County. Under the administration of Tom Collins *(right)*, a former Roman Catholic seminarian who had turned to social work, Arvin Camp became a model of what the federal government could do to help migrants. In *The Grapes of Wrath*, Collins appears as Jim Rawley, manager of Weedpatch Camp, which the Joads consider a utopia of sanitation and self-governance. *Dorothea Lange Collection, Oakland Museum.*

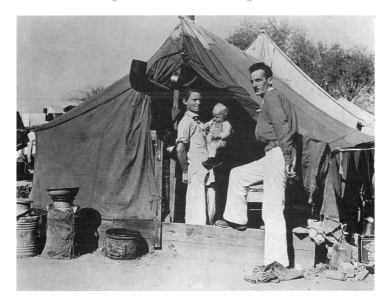

(*Above left*) The plight of migrant children broke the hearts of Collins and others. Debilitated by poverty and poor nutrition (a diet of beans, rice, and fried dough, little milk, hardly any fruits and vegetables), an estimated 27 percent of all migrant children suffered from some form of malnutrition. Collins and hundreds of others coalesced behind nutrition programs, *Labor Archives & Research, San Francisco State University*. (*Below left*) Coordinating many such relief efforts after Governor Olson appointed him Commissioner of Housing and Immigration in 1939, writer, attorney, and social activist Carey McWilliams was fired when Attorney General Earl Warren became governor in 1942. In *Factories in the Field, the Story of Migratory Farm Labor in California* (1939), McWilliams achieved one of the most influential books of the decade, *Labor Research & Archives, San Francisco State University*. (*Below right*) Working under the direction of bridge-builder Russell Cone, union men, making between $4 and $11 a day, first-rate wages for the Depression, spanned the Golden Gate with a structure later described as the most successful public work, in terms of both esthetics and engineering, since the Parthenon. *San Francisco Public Library*.

(*Above*) The 1930s represented an epic of public works, creating employment, stimulating the economy, completing the infrastructure of the Golden State. No region was more profoundly affected than the Bay Area. The Golden Gate and San Francisco–Oakland Bay bridges brought to fulfillment visions and dreams which had origins in the nineteenth century. *San Francisco Public Library.* (*Below*) In the Court of the Pacific, Timothy Pflueger's architecture and Ralph Stackpole's Pacifica looming overhead, a Cubist-Deco semi-Buddhist mother goddess, her hands positioned in prayer, sought to create a sense of impending destiny of prosperity, peace, and enlightenment for the Asia Pacific Basin. *San Francisco Public Library.*

(*Above*) In planning terms, despite its extravagant architecture, the Golden Gate International Exposition adhered to an old-fashioned grid. *San Francisco Public Library.* (*Below*) Gaining altitude over San Francisco after its take-off from Treasure Island, the *China Clipper* of Pan American Airways begins its voyage to the fabled Orient, with stopovers in Honolulu, Midway, Wake, and Guam. *San Francisco Public Library.*

Hourly wages for harvest workers fell from forty-five cents an hour in 1929 to as low as fifteen cents an hour in 1933–1934, this in an industry whose total crop had a value in 1935 in excess of $20.5 million.

Throughout 1935 Salinas lettuce packers watched with dismay the growing strength of the Fruit and Vegetable Workers Union, an American Federation of Labor affiliate. Whereas harvesters tended to be Filipino or Mexican, the shed workers, the processors, the trimmers and packers, the shippers, receivers, and truckers affiliated with the Fruit and Vegetable Workers Union tended to be native-born white Protestant Americans from Oklahoma, Arkansas, and Texas. Most of them had established a year or two of residence in Monterey County and paid taxes. Some even owned their own homes. Their union, moreover, was affiliated with the staunchly centrist and patriotic AFL, not the Communist-dominated CAWIU. In contrast to previous strikes, the Salinas lettuce strike of September-October 1936 would pit white against white, the Right against the Center.

The entire affair was more of a preemptive attack, a lockout rather than a strike, organized by the Grower-Shipper Vegetable Association and its affiliates, the Citizens Association of the Salinas Valley and the Associated Farmers of Monterey County. In May 1936, fearing a demand for exclusive representation by the Fruit and Vegetable Workers Union, the Grower-Shipper Vegetable Association recruited non-union labor from the Imperial Valley. When workers at the Ice Kist Packing Company refused to handle lettuce which these non-union workers had also handled, a brief strike broke out. Certain shippers wanted to have it out then and there—to ship the "hot" lettuce to other packing companies as well and thus provoke a general walkout by union workers, whom they were confident they could replace. More cautious shippers prevailed, arguing that further organization was necessary.

Within the next five months, the Salinas Valley oligarchy brought itself to a sophisticated stage of alert. An umbrella organization, the Citizens Association of the Salinas Valley, was formed to coordinate local interests. It included the Grower-Shipper Vegetable Association, the Pacific Gas & Electric Company, the Salinas Chamber of Commerce, local banks, ice companies and other agricultural suppliers, the Spreckels Sugar Company (a silent partner contributing 18.5 percent of the costs but preferring to remain anonymous), the leading automobile agencies, and other businesses. The Citizens Association hired Henry Strobel, a grower and ex-shipper himself, to serve as executive director, assisted by Cruse Carriel, a Los Angeles newspaperman retained as public relations consultant. Members of the Association drove to San Francisco to consult with Paul Eliel, manager of the Industrial Relations Department of the Industrial Association of San Francisco, which had directed shipping interests in the maritime strike of 1934.

Under Eliel's guidance, the Citizens Association of the Salinas Valley made every effort to make itself seem a broad community-based organization. By contrast, the Associated Farmers of Monterey County organized in mid-June expressly represented the interests of growers and shippers. Linked to the statewide Association, the Associated Farmers of Monterey County soon became the dominant force in the Salinas Valley, but like the Shippers and Growers Association, the Associated Farmers preferred to operate under the umbrella of the Citizens Association. By mid-summer the oligarchy of Salinas had organized itself into an interlocking directorate. Very soon, this directorate was to become the *de facto* government of the region.

It was a government preparing for war. Cruse Carriel drew up the battle plan, basing his strategy in part upon the molding of public opinion according to the pioneering theories of E. L. Bernays, who had evolved his theories after studying the propaganda campaigns of the First World War. It was essential, Carriel told the growers, to galvanize the entire community on behalf of the Association before conflict surfaced. The Association should also seek to have a solid file of intelligence regarding the more radical element in the union leadership. To that end, Carriel began to coordinate such a program with Major J. M. Hagens, a retired Army officer then employed by the Spreckels Sugar Company as a special investigator. About this time, the Citizens Association acquired its own intelligence operative, the enigmatic Kathryn Cree, on loan from the Industrial Association of San Francisco. Skilled in industrial intelligence (by October she would be setting up a Citizens Association in Phoenix), Cree retained the services of the Watkins Detective Service and the Glenn Bodell Industrial Detectives, Inc., of Los Angeles, who sent their operatives into the industry to gather intelligence regarding the leadership and intent of the Fruit and Vegetable Workers Union. Throughout this organizational phase, Cree kept in close contact by telephone with the Industrial Association of San Francisco, where her boss, George Barker, guided her efforts. Cruse Carriel, Major Hagens, and Cree, meanwhile, also began a systematic program of contact and negotiation with state and local law enforcement agencies.

On 27 and 28 August 1936, as contract negotiations were in progress, the Grower-Shipper Vegetable Association of Central California launched its preemptive strike, via an escalation of negotiations and a lockout. In a series of full page advertisements in several Monterey County newspapers, the Association branded the demand for exclusive representation by the Fruit and Vegetable Workers leadership as unfair and un-American. The advertisements urged rank and file to break from their leadership and settle with the shippers. A few days later, notices were posted in all shipping and packing sheds stating that wages and working conditions presently in effect would continue after 4 September. Workers who showed up on that day would be judged to have accepted this new contract.

Despite its offer to continue working through the negotiation period, the union now had no choice but to call for a strike, which is exactly what the Grower-Shipper Vegetable Association wanted to happen. Already, a large scab work force had been recruited; and three major packing sheds, belonging to the Salinas Valley Ice Company in Salinas and to the Marinovitch and Travers & Sakata companies in Watsonville, had been designated to serve as protected plants. According to the Association battle plan, all lettuce would be shipped to these barricaded sheds for processing by workers who would live on the property.

The Association designated 15 September 1936 as the D-Day on which lettuce would begin to be processed in these barricaded installations. On 4 September, the first day of the strike, officials from the Grower-Shipper Vegetable Association met with Salinas police chief George Griffin, Monterey County sheriff Carl Abbott, and Captain Earl Griffith of the California Highway Patrol to coordinate protection for Association trucks on the 15th. It was at this meeting that Chief Griffin made the suggestion (which he later repudiated) that since so many law enforcement agencies were involved—the city police, the sheriff's office, the state highway patrol—a single coordinator should be appointed.

Meanwhile, construction began on a ten-foot-high wood and barbed wire fence around the Salinas Ice Company packing shed. Searchlights were also installed. Later, a machine gun was emplaced at the entrance to one of the packing sheds in Watsonville. Contacting the Lake Erie Chemical Company of Cleveland, the sheriff's office purchased an ample supply of tear gas. The city of Salinas made similar purchases from Federal Laboratories of Pittsburgh.

As the fateful day of 15 September 1936 approached, the Salinas Valley supported a mobilization from the right unprecedented in California history. (Even the local Boy Scout troop was put into a state of readiness.) Not only were the union workers locked out of their jobs, with an unwanted strike forced on them, they also faced an unprecedented array of opposition from the interlocked public and private sectors, patiently assembled by the local oligarchy since May.

As if to round out this ultra-right scenario, Henry Sanborn, Colonel of Infantry, United States Army Reserve, slipped into town on 13 September, registered at the Hotel Jeffery under an assumed name, and assumed command of the situation. Long active in anti-union activities, Colonel Sanborn had during the San Francisco waterfront strike organized and drilled a group of vigilantes who called themselves the Nationals. He subsequently went on to promote and organize other National chapters throughout the state. During a strike by warehouse employees of the California and Hawaiian Sugar Company in Crockett, at the head of San Francisco Bay, Colonel Sanborn and his assistant, Captain Russell Tripp, trained company employees in the use of pistols, clubs, squad cars, and tear gas while also lecturing on "The Law and Tactics of Civil Commotion."

In August 1935 Sanborn launched a newspaper, the *American Citizen*, which was mainly subsidized through mass purchases by the Industrial Association of San Francisco and the Waterfront Employers' Association. The motto on the masthead of the *American Citizen* notified its readership that the newspaper was being published so that "Fascism would not be necessary to combat Communism." In July 1936 Colonel Sanborn had met briefly in Carmel with William Theile, an official of the Citizens Association of Salinas, and discussed the forthcoming confrontation. On 12 September Sanborn was contacted in Seattle by telephone by Jack Hardy, head of the Nationals in Berkeley, who was related by marriage to Theile. Hardy informed Sanborn that the sheriff of Monterey County required his presence. Twenty-four hours later, the colonel, under the assumed name of Winter, slipped into town. For approximately a week, this mysterious non-elected official, operating as "law enforcement coordinator," seems to have assumed some form of para-military power.

According to Sanborn's later testimony to the La Follette Committee, he was taken to the sheriff's office in the jail and found Sheriff Carl Abbott nervous and uncertain—"scared to death" in Sanborn's phrase.[14] Establishing his headquarters on the sixth floor of the Hotel Jeffery, the colonel organized a general staff consisting of law enforcement authorities, R. L. Hughes, vice president of the Monterey County Trust & Savings Bank, William Theile of the Citizens Association, Harry Knowland, former district attorney of Monterey County, and Lester Stirling, a grower-shipper. By that time, Captain Tripp had joined the colonel. Employing a general-staff scheme of organization, Sanborn put Stirling in charge of protection and Knowland in charge of intelligence. At Sanborn's request, Sheriff Abbott deputized Kathryn Cree and placed her on the Monterey County payroll. Expenses for this Hotel Jeffery operation, including rooms, meals, telephone calls, and $111.34 for liquor, were underwritten by the Citizens Association, the Grower-Shipper Vegetable Association, and Monterey County. Later on, everyone wanted to repudiate any association with Colonel Sanborn during this period or to deny that he held any real authority; but from 14 to 19 September, something was going on with the colonel and his general staff on the sixth floor of the Hotel Jeffery, as telephones rang and meetings convened and reconvened amidst an impressive consumption of food and drink, and as law enforcement officials and oligarchs came and went past uniformed deputies standing sentry.

At ten in the morning on the 15th, several trucks loaded with lettuce headed toward the packing shed of the Salinas Valley Ice Company and were met by pickets throwing rocks. Barricaded in the plant itself, Salinas police chief George Griffin ordered the pickets to allow the trucks through. They refused. At 10:15 Salinas police officers in the plant began launching tear gas bombs into the crowd of strikers. Some strikers threw the tear gas bombs back into the plant. Emerging from the plant, the police counterattacked and dispersed an estimated two thousand strikers with tear gas. By the end of the day, sixteen strikers had been arrested, and the California Highway Patrol, now numbering 141 officers under the command of Chief E. Raymond Cato, patrolled the city of Salinas and its environs like representatives of an occupying army. Despite this disturbance, between twenty-five and thirty refrigerator car loads of lettuce were trucked, processed, and loaded. Ten car loads were packed and shipped in Watsonville.

The next day, at the suggestion of Colonel Sanborn, Sheriff Abbott, frustrated in his efforts to have the National Guard brought in, authorized a *posse comitatus* of some two thousand local residents, who instantly became a force of deputized vigilantes, bringing the mobilization of Salinas to unprecedented intensity. On the next day, the 16th, occurred what newspapers described as the Battle of Salinas. The battle opened with police firing a salvo of tear gas into a crowd of pickets approaching the Salinas Ice Company. Shortly thereafter, some five hundred pickets stopped a convoy of trucks heading for the plant and scattered its crates of lettuce on the street. Piling out of accompanying autos, deputies and fifteen to twenty highway patrolmen flailed their clubs at the heads of strikers, men and women alike. Groups of police, sheriff's deputies, and highway patrolmen fired tear gas and nausea bombs into any groups of pickets they could locate. Some eight hundred union members took refuge in the Labor Temple on Pajaro Street. Under the direction of Sheriff Abbott, the police, deputies, and highway patrolmen bombarded the Temple at long range with tear gas, then, under protection of this barrage, moved in closer to toss tear and nausea gas and sulphur into the union headquarters. Hundreds of strikers fled the building, only to be met by police with even more tear gas bombs or deputized vigilantes wielding axe handles and clubs.

By late afternoon, Salinas had become a town under siege. The smell of tear gas was still in the air. Highway patrol squad cars, their radios squawking, crisscrossed the city. Deputized citizens, pickaxe handles at the ready, patrolled the streets. In nearby Watsonville, two sentries sat behind their machine guns at the entrance to a packing plant. Earlier in the day Chief Griffin had said: "Let's be tough. If we're not tough, we'll lose the town."[15] Sheriff Abbott agreed. Obtaining a search warrant, the sheriff led a phalanx of deputized vigilantes into the union hall on Pajaro Street, looking in vain for a cache of weapons supposedly hidden there. "We expect more outbreaks at any moment, and in any one of a number of places," Abbott told the Los Angeles *Times*. "More blood will probably have to be shed before this thing is settled, and we are ready and waiting for them."[16]

That night, a thousand members of the *posse comitatus* gathered in the National Guard Armory and were organized into patrols. Motorcades of vigilantes swept the city. Not surprisingly, the union ordered all its pickets to remain indoors.

By the 17th Salinas seemed a city in a war zone. Schools and theaters were closed, and a loudspeaker truck roamed the streets warning people not to congregate in groups. Police, sheriff's deputies, highway patrolmen, and members of the *posse comitatus* were patrolling everywhere by squad car or on foot patrol. A phalanx of deputized vigilantes lined the highway as a convoy of forty-two lettuce trucks moved toward the packing plant. The cabs of these trucks were screened in heavy metal mesh against projectiles, and deputies with shotguns sat next to each driver. Throughout the day, the atmosphere remained tense. When three automobiles filled with scab workers approached the Salinas Valley Ice Company plant, nervous deputies, mistaking them for strikers, opened with a barrage of shotgun fire. Panic-stricken, the strikebreakers leapt from their cars and ran in all directions. Highway patrol squad cars converged on the scene, adding to the confusion and the panic of the terrified workers, one of whom, Albert Blue, a thirty-four-year-old transient sawmill worker from Texas, sustained a serious wound to the head. A number of fleeing workers took refuge in a nearby field. When their mistaken identity was discovered, no amount of shouts or coaxing could persuade them to return to the packing plant. As night fell, some of the terrified workers remained in hiding, and trucks from the Salinas Fire Department, search lights blazing, were driven through the fields in an effort to find the men and assure them that they would not be fired upon if they returned to the plant.

Conspicuously effective in the disturbances of 15 and 16 September was the highly disciplined, para-military California Highway Patrol; indeed, the radio-equipped squad cars of the CHP, patrolling the streets of Salinas and adjacent roads and highways, soon became the most visible emblem of government, strongly reinforcing the image of Salinas as a city torn by insurrection. Highway Patrol Chief Cato claimed that Governor Merriam had told him on 16 September to "use gas unsparingly" and "break up the riot." If the Salinas police and the sheriff's deputies were the foot soldiers of the establishment, and the *posse comitatus* were its militia, the 140 officers of the CHP constituted an elite shock force, highly trained and disciplined, amply equipped. "My men saved the day," Chief Cato remarked on the 17th. S. Parker Frisselle, a director of the California State Chamber of Commerce and the Associated Farmers of California, agreed. "If you had not controlled this situation in the lettuce strike," Frisselle congratulated Cato, "the rest of us farmers might just as well have moved out." [17]

So as not to lose momentum in the battle for public opinion, Colonel Sanborn, who remained in a shadowy form of authority until the 20th, renewed the red baiting he had begun on 12 September in the *American Citizen*. The union leadership, the Citizens' Association vociferously claimed, was dominated by Communists. Up to twenty-four known Communist agitators had been identified. More Communist agitators were arriving by truckloads from San Francisco. Despite the fact that Timothy Reardon, state director of the Department of Industrial Relations, had personally assured Governor Merriam that Salinas was not a Communist-led strike, the governor issued a statement on 16 September saying that CHP Chief Cato had provided him with evidence that the strike leadership was Communist. Part of the evidence was a series of red flags discovered on the highway and environs which Chief Cato claimed were used by the Communist leadership to denote rallying points for strikers. Two days later, the Division of Highways revealed that it had installed the flags as reference points for checking the volume of traffic in that area. On the 24th Chief Cato claimed that a cache of Communist correspondence had been found in the home of a union leader. Colonel Sanborn, meanwhile, was claiming from his general-staff headquarters in the Hotel Jeffery that the chiefs of police of Oakland, Piedmont, and San Francisco had informed him that three thousand longshoremen from San Francisco were preparing to march on Salinas. Captain William Hynes of the intelligence bureau of the Los Angeles Police Department, better known as the Red Squad, was quoted in the San Francisco *Examiner* on 19 September as saying: "The Red agitators under the guise of tourists are slipping out of the city [Los Angeles] quietly. But our information points to a definite mobilization here for a troublesome movement to Salinas. Most of the agitators leaving here are believed to be armed, and are bent on making additional trouble in the lettuce-producing district."[18]

Among those identified by Colonel Sanborn as Communist agitators was Chester Rowell, the editor of the San Francisco *Chronicle*. There was no love lost between the colonel and the staff of this San Francisco newspaper. Under the leadership of the paper's dynamic young executive editor, Paul Smith, the *Chronicle* was serving as a rallying point for outraged reaction to the Salinas *putsch*. A brilliant shoe-leather journalist, Smith had assumed his post at the age of twenty-five. In 1933, in an effort to get the feel of the Depression, Smith had ridden the rails, pounding out reports on a portable typewriter from rolling boxcars. Piling into his private Fairchild, which he kept at Mills Field south of San Francisco, Smith flew to Sacramento to interview Governor Merriam on the 16th. Merriam told Smith that a convoy of one thousand cars was carrying longshoremen down Highway 101 from San Francisco to Salinas. Smith scoffed at this report, and Merriam dispatched Chief Cato to double-check it. Cato returned with the report that the thousand-car caravan was only a rumor but that red flags had been discovered at strikers' rallying sites in Salinas.

Revving up his Fairchild, Smith flew south to Salinas and with two other *Chronicle* reporters walked the streets of the embattled, fear-stricken city. "Tension permeated every corner of the community," he later remembered. "Some streets were blockaded by bands of self-styled vigilantes. The pool halls and bars were overflowing with rugged-looking men carrying everything from baseball bats to 45 Colt automatics."[19] Smith and his reporters also visited the packing shed and secured an interview with the thoroughly demoralized union leadership. When later on that evening he drove back to his motor court near the airport outside the city, Smith was shocked to see that barricades had been set up around the perimeter of Salinas and his staff would need passes to get back into town. Later that evening, Smith was awakened from a sound sleep by banging at his motel court door. It was his reporters, Harry Lerner and Stan Bailey. Bailey had been badly beaten near the Hotel Jeffery by men who told him that this was what was in store for Smith or any other *Chronicle* reporter butting in on the business of the town. Smith spent the rest of the night flying Bailey back to San Francisco for emergency medical attention.

The next morning, after flying back to Salinas, Paul Smith devoted himself to gathering whatever information he could regarding Colonel Sanborn's mysterious headquarters at the Hotel Jeffery. That night Smith filed the first of a series of four articles, running in the *Chronicle* from 23 to 26 September, entitled "It Did Happen in Salinas," a take-off on Sinclair Lewis' best-selling novel of fascism in America, *It Can't Happen Here* (1935). "For a full fortnight," wrote Smith, "the 'constituted authorities' of Salinas have been but the helpless pawns of sinister fascist forces which have operated from a barricaded hotel floor in the center of town."[20]

Smith's series served as a rallying point for liberals and moderates outraged by the Salinas events. From Hollywood, Gary Cooper, Humphrey Bogart, Boris Karloff, and James Cagney sent $1,000 in strike aid. Even before the Smith series, the reports by Lerner and Bailey in the *Chronicle* had undermined the authority of Colonel Sanborn. Chief Griffin, Sheriff Abbott, and CHP Chief Cato found themselves personally and professionally embarrassed by reports that they were being supervised by a non-elected, self-appointed public safety coordinator. They began to disassociate themselves from the sixth floor of the Hotel Jeffery. The American Civil Liberties Union, meanwhile, was pressing the Attorney General to look into the entire question of Sanborn's assumption of authority. Sensing the erosion of his power, Sanborn slipped quietly out of Salinas early on the morning of 21 September.

The colonel might have decamped, but others carried on the fight, empowered by a strong anti-picketing ordinance passed by the City Council on 5 October. Urged on by the Citizens Association, which was in turn controlled by the Associated Farmers of Monterey County, Salinas authorities filed a total of 167 complaints in the month of October alone, turning the town into a virtual police state. "The activities of the police in town," reported a mediator from the National Labor Relations Board, "do not inspire one with a sense of respect. Innumerable false arrests were made, many without a shadow of evidence. Large numbers of persons were kept in jail for four or five days without having any charges brought against them."[21] As part of this pattern of suppression, squad cars from the CHP cruised in sight of Filipino lettuce pickers, lest they be tempted to join the packing shed workers. Two Filipino labor activists especially troublesome to the growers, C. D. Mensalvas and Manuel Luz, were conveniently arrested on charges of vagrancy.

The Salinas strike ended on 3 November 1936 with the complete victory of the Grower-Shipper Vegetable Association and the intricate network of organizations behind it, led by the Associated Farmers of Monterey County. Workers drifted back on an individual basis, without any negotiated recognition of their union.

Having perfected its plan—organize ahead of time, provoke a strike preemptively, crush it through police and deputized power—the Associated Farmers took their show on the road to Stockton, the next big trouble spot. Point by point, the Stockton cannery strike of April 1937 demonstrated how efficiently the Associated Farmers had polished their strategy.

Located one hundred miles east of San Francisco, the city of Stockton holds a strategic position at the northern head of the San Joaquin Valley. Linked to the San Francisco Bay Area via the San Joaquin River, which flows into San Francisco Bay, Stockton represents a meeting point of the populous Bay Area and the agricultural empire of the interior. Thus it became a natural site for the canning industry. In May 1936 the local oligarchy of growers, canners, and shippers went into red alert when the American Federation of Labor chartered the Agricultural Workers Union, Local 20221, and authorized the organization of cannery workers in the Stockton area.

Under the direction of Colonel Garrison, statewide president of the Associated Farmers of California, the Salinas scenario was repeated in Stockton. First of all, the local chapter of the Associated Farmers, the Associated Farmers of San Joaquin County, remaining in the background as they did in Salinas, stimulated the creation of a broad Citizens Committee, which served as an umbrella organization for such participating members as the Chamber of Commerce of Salinas, the local sheriff's office (Colonel Garrison and San Joaquin County Sheriff Harvey Odell were close personal friends), the Canners League, a statewide trade association, and other civic and regional groups. One organization, the California Processors and Growers, was organized to speak and act for all Stockton canneries. Its spokesman and negotiator, Oakland attorney J. Paul St. Sure, had, like Colonel Garrison, an excellent reputation as a hard-line, anti-union activist.

As in the case of Salinas, one plant, that of the Stockton Food Products Company, suitably barricaded, was designated to handle business, the canning of spinach, during the forthcoming strike. The usual Red Scare was initiated. "You are in real danger of not being able to harvest your crops or get them to market if you do harvest them in the year 1937," the California Processors and Growers, Inc., warned Stockton area farmers in April. "So is every other grower in the state. It is planned that ILA Warehousemen and Communist pickets will, by force, prevent you. The question is, Shall there be anarchy on the farms and in the towns or will the public authorities of the State, the counties, and the towns prevent our farmers and workers from being beaten up? Will they keep the peace or won't they?"[22]

In preparation for keeping the peace, Sheriff Odell contacted Ignatius McCarty of San Francisco, the redoubtable sometime labor spy and tear gas salesman for the Lake Erie Chemical Company who had provided such expertise to the San Francisco Police Department during the longshoremen's strike. Enthusiastically, McCarty began filling orders for state-of-the-art tear gas equipment. Labor spy George Gorman, meanwhile, also in the employ of Sheriff Odell, penetrated the inner circle of Local 20221.

Next, according to scenario, the California Processors and Growers stonewalled all demands by Local 20221 that wages, working conditions, and representation be negotiated. As predicted, the union announced a strike for 15 April. The night before the strike was scheduled to go into effect, the Citizens Committee met in the City Council Chambers of the Stockton City Hall for a pre-strike rally and warm-up. Everything was in readiness. The Highway Patrol was on alert. The deputy sheriffs had their tear gas. The Stockton Food Products Company cannery was suitably armed and barricaded.

The next morning, like clockwork, the strike began. Nearly three hundred striking cannery workers, men and women, set up their pickets outside the high wire fence surrounding the Stockton Food Products Company cannery on Waterloo Road just outside the city. When a melee broke out between pickets and a group of non-strikers trying to cross the picket line, Deputy Sheriff E. G. Hill brought in his men and the tear gas. An even larger melee ensued, with Hill receiving a severe head wound.

The oligarchy now had its *casus belli*. Ralph Hill, the local representative of the statewide California Processors and Growers, contacted Sheriff Odell and told him that people wanted to go to work, and asked, "was he going to do [his] duty?"[23] Colonel Garrison of the Associated Farmers reinforced Hill's demand. There was, of course, no pressing demand to open the plant; but the scenario worked out in Salinas dictated that such a forced opening was the best means to provoke the union into further violence.

Again, according to script, Sheriff Odell called for a *posse comitatus* and within the next six days organized twelve hundred men into an armed force under the *de facto* control of Colonel Garrison. In Salinas, Colonel Sanborn had remained a shadowy presence on the sixth floor of the Hotel Jeffery. Colonel Garrison, by contrast, was very much in evidence as civilian commander of the citizens' army raised by Sheriff Odell. Garrison appointed Fred Hogue, president of the Associated Farmers of Stanislaus County, and S. E. Losher, president of the Merchants Bureau of the Chamber of Commerce of Modesto, to serve with the rank of major in the citizens' brigade, which soon numbered two thousand men. In lieu of rifles, pickaxe handles were issued, although many of the men—each of them officially deputized—carried private weapons as well.

So successful was Colonel Garrison in raising and organizing this para-military force on such quick notice, a force responsible to him and him alone, even some Stockton businessmen and District Attorney Clowdsley grew fearful and requested Governor Merriam to send in the National Guard. As in the case of Salinas, Merriam refused; and Colonel Garrison and his army remained the preeminent force in the area.

Governor Merriam did, however, make every effort to mediate the strike, bringing together representatives from both sides to his office in the capitol. Reasonably, Governor Merriam proposed that three agencies mediate the dispute: the National Labor Relations Board, a mediation commission to be appointed by the governor, and a committee of five—two from labor, two from the California Processors and Growers, and one appointed by the governor. Union representatives immediately accepted the governor's offer. Speaking for the canners, St. Sure rejected it out of hand. Caucusing in a corridor of the capitol, union leaders agreed that they would call off the strike and send their membership back to work on one condition and one condition only: that the California Processors and Growers would resume negotiations with Local 20221 on the 1st of May. Sensing the weakness of the union, the canners ignored this offer and prepared to open the Stockton Food Products Plant by force: to provoke a confrontation, to crush the union once and for all with an overwhelming show of force.

The opening of the Stockton Food Products Cannery was set for Friday, 23 April. Highway Patrol captain Ben Torres, a veteran of Salinas, assisted by tear gas salesman George Cake of the Federal Laboratories of Pittsburgh, another Salinas veteran, gave his men a crash course in the handling of crowds and tear gas. Colonel Garrison put his citizens' army on alert. Garrison and Sheriff Odell also secured the services of Ivan Hitt, superintendent of the San Joaquin County Bureau of Identification, who set up a hidden moving picture camera at the entrance to the cannery, with specific orders to photograph strikers in the act of violence.

In the early morning hours, just before the orchestrated encounter, union president Vance Ambrose and his assistants continued desperately to try to get Ralph Hill, representing the California Processors and Growers, not to open the plant that morning since negotiations were scheduled to start at noon between the union and Paul St. Sure. Ambrose was confident that some kind of agreement could be worked out within the next twenty-four hours. Over the telephone, Hill told Ambrose that whatever the strikers had decided, the cannery would open that day. "Yes, I understand how you intend to open the cannery," the weary union official told Hill, "—with machine guns, tear gas, and vigilantes."[24]

Ambrose was correct. At six o'clock Friday morning, even as the union leadership was preparing for a peaceful return to work, Colonel Garrison, a .45 caliber pistol strapped to his side, marched 150 deputies, armed with pickaxe handles and arm shields (many of them carrying pistols and shotguns as well), into the Stockton Food Products Cannery. At six-thirty tear gas expert Ignatius McCarty, now a deputy sheriff, arrived at the plant with a supply of tear gas candles and a long-range tear gas gun, which he emplaced advantageously on the roof of the Plant Packing Shed. Photographer Ivan Hitt stood ready at his camera.

Even as these preparations were underway, a delegation of union leaders was meeting in the office of District Attorney Clowdsley, trying desperately to head off the confrontation. Sheriff Odell, who had done nothing to prevent Colonel Garrison from occupying the plant, also attended the meeting. After some discussion, a member of the labor delegation began to type up the conditions under which the workers would return to the canneries. At this point, Sheriff Odell left the room to take a telephone call. Returning, he announced: "The war is on."[25]

At approximately 8:45 A.M. a truck loaded with spinach, driven by Ed Devine of the Associate Farmers, accompanied by Sheriff's Deputy Ralph Post and one other man, each of them armed with shotguns, reached the Stockton Food Products cannery under an escort of CHP squad cars. At the entrance to the plant, the convoy was blocked by a crowd of three thousand pickets. When the truck stopped at the cannery gate, the pickets attacked it, and a melee ensued. From within the cannery, McCarty and Cake, assisted by CHP officers, began to fire tear gas bombs into the crowd. Skillfully judging the wind, McCarty laid down a barrage in back and in front of the pickets, catching the strikers between two

cloudbanks of gas. At this point, truckloads of citizen deputies reached the scene
from their bivouac at the County Fair Grounds. A battle of fists, pickaxe handles,
and baseball bats broke out, as the citizen deputies tried to clear a way for the
truck. Shotgun fire erupted from the cannery into the pickets. The citizen deputies succeeded in getting the truck into the plant. Union leaders, meanwhile,
rushed to the scene and were making every effort to calm the crowd. By ten
o'clock the situation had quieted down. Fifty-eight people were taken to the hospital, twenty-seven of them for gunshot wounds. Within the next few weeks, a
demoralized union leadership abandoned efforts to secure a contract. Once again,
the Associated Farmers had won the day.

The period between the Sacramento conspiracy trials of 1935, the Salinas strike
of 1936, and the Stockton strike of 1937 constituted a high-water mark of influence by the Associated Farmers. The success of the Farmers stimulated a drive
toward consolidation—the term *syndicalism* might even be used—on the part of
oligarchs up and down the state. In February 1936 corporate officials from
throughout the Pacific Coast met at the Del Monte Hotel in Monterey for a
Pacific Coast Economic Conference. In the course of these proceedings, John
Forbes, president of the Industrial Association of San Francisco and *éminence
grise* of the Associated Farmers (the Industrial Association advised and coordinated
the Associated Farmers in their organizing activities), warned the industrialists
present that a Moscow-directed effort was underway to organize the maritime industries of the Pacific Coast. S. Parker Frisselle of Fresno, president of the Associated Farmers, described how his organization had kept agricultural strikes at bay
throughout 1934. Most important, L. P. St. Clair, president of the Union Oil
Company, urged the companies present to sponsor sophisticated public relations
programs aimed at galvanizing public opinion against unions. The effective work
of public relations consultant Cruse Carriel in Salinas reinforced St. Clair's point
that the corporate sector should wage its battles over radio and in the press as well
as in the fields and on the job site.

For the oligarchs of Southern California, the need for a propaganda counter-
attack became pressingly evident in late March 1937 when the Teamsters won a
strike against Pacific Freight Lines, a rare event in the militantly anti-union open
shop Southland. At the urging of Harry Chandler, editor and publisher of the Los
Angeles *Times*, two organizations, one producer-oriented, the other consumer-
oriented, were created by the Merchants and Manufacturers Association of Los
Angeles. Founded in 1937, Southern Californians, Inc., an umbrella trade organization advised by the advertising firm of Batten, Barton, Durstine and Osborn,
launched a mass media campaign (newspaper and radio ads, billboards, work-
shops, press agentry) aimed at persuading Californians that unions were vicious,
un-American, foreign-dominated. Under the direction of veteran public relations
executive Paul Shoup, Southern Californians, Inc., embarked upon a nitty-gritty,
down-and-dirty program of union busting for its dues-paying companies. Through

its Employees Advisory Service, Southern Californians, Inc. advised companies on the organization and enforcement of company unions. It also assisted trade associations in their union-fighting activities. When restaurant workers struck at the Brown Derby in August 1937, for example, the Southern California Restaurant and Hotelmen's Association, advised by Southern Californians, Inc., circulated the names and Social Security numbers of all striking workers so that they could be blacklisted at other restaurants in the region. Financed in large part by secret donations ($362,649 in 1938 alone), Southern Californians, Inc. also engaged in statewide lobbying on behalf of anti-picket ordinances.

At the instigation of Chandler and his cronies at the Los Angeles Chamber of Commerce (Chandler also controlled the statewide Chamber), a sister organization, initially calling itself The Women of California, then The Women Consumers, and finally, The Neutral Thousands, TNT for short, was established to work in tandem with Southern Californians, Inc. Directed by Bessie Ochs, peroxide blonde, fiftyish, tough as nails, TNT enlisted over a hundred thousand women "to fight labor racketeers, self-seeking labor organizers, and trouble-making radicals."[26] TNT's radio program, the "California Caravan," mixed entertainment and right-wing propaganda in a manner prophetic of Southern Californian politics to come.

When the La Follette Committee investigated working conditions in Southern California in late 1939 and 1940, it found the entire region under the control of an interlocking network of employers' associations, with the Merchants and Manufacturers Association of Los Angeles acting as the urban counterpart to the Associated Farmers. Southern Californians, Inc. the La Follette Committee found, was basically a dummy organization for a few corporate interests. Barely two hundred of the 109,000 names listed in the organization were honest members. Worse, Southern Californians, Inc., engaged in mail fraud, forgery, threat and intimidation, and the transportation of strikebreakers across state lines. Claiming to be an educational organization, Southern Californians, Inc., spent a mere $9,000 of the $500,000 it collected for educational purposes. The rest had been spent lobbying on behalf of state and local anti-picketing ordinances, assisting employees in breaking unions, and radio publicity. Following the revelations of the La Follette Committee, the Justice Department brought charges against officials of both Southern Californians, Inc., and The Neutral Thousands, and the organizations were dissolved. But for two years, 1937 and 1938, the Right held the initiative in the Southland.

Sometime in 1938 the tide began to turn; but from 1933 to 1938 the empire was striking back in a manner chillingly suggestive, in certain instances, of consolidations and arrangements between the public and private sectors which can arguably be compared to the fascist consolidations of Italy, Germany, and Spain. Such suggestions of fascism must, of course, be carefully qualified. In parts of Europe, fascism represented the established order; in California, it was a tendency among some interests. Were Sacramento Berlin, the CAWIU leaders convicted on charges of conspiring to commit criminal conspiracy would have been arrested and murdered before they came to trial. Were Salinas and Stockton in Italy, Germany, or Spain, corpses would have littered the street after the clashes. As it was, not one person was killed in either city despite heroic onslaughts of tear gas, shotgun pellets, pickaxe handles, and fists.

Californians such as Robert Hale Merriman, commander of the Abraham Lincoln Brigade in Spain, would consider Salinas and Stockton a species of theatrical performance. The brightest and most respected UC Berkeley graduate student of his generation (so classmate John Kenneth Galbraith later described him), Merriman forsook the comforts and security of academic life to fight for the Spanish Republic against the fascist revolt led by Franco. Tall, handsome, trained as an infantry officer in the United States Army Reserve, Merriman rose to the command of the American-sponsored Abraham Lincoln Brigade. Ernest Hemingway was so impressed by Merriman that he transformed him into Robert Jordan, the tragic hero of *For Whom the Bell Tolls* (1940). Like his fictional counterpart, Robert Hale Merriman lost his life to fascism on the field of battle. Because he was so talented, and because he died so young, and because Hemingway immortalized him, Merriman must be given the first position in any roll call of Californians in battle against the ultra-Right.

But Merriman fell in a real war, fighting real fascists. His counterparts in California, where the lanky Nevadan had journeyed to pursue a Ph.D. in economics, faced a more shadowy opponent—a tendency, rather than a reality—which only occasionally demonstrated its power. And yet, when this tendency surfaced, as it did in Sacramento, Los Angeles, Salinas, and Stockton, it proved itself capable of making a considerable transition from subliminal gesture to effective action in the body politic. A present-day observer might very well dismiss Colonel Henry Sanborn as a posturing fanatic, a figment of his own imagination; but as the *Christian Century* pointed out, so was Adolf Hitler.

In Stockton there was no doubt whatsoever that Colonel Walter Garrison of the Associated Farmers was in charge. Hitler's Brown Shirts began as a lightly armed para-military citizen army similar to the two-thousand-strong force Garrison assembled. Despite the kangaroo trial in Sacramento, the Los Angeles police cars sealing off the borders, the tear gas and compromised police officials in Salinas and Stockton, the complacent district attorneys, the hysterical Red-baiting press, the machinery for propaganda and intimidation, California was in no real danger of a fascist *putsch* during these years. But it was supportive of an acting out of the fascist alternative. That was the role played by California during this troublesome time, the testing of the far-Right alternative just as Upton Sinclair and EPIC had explored the possibilities of the far Left. But then again: as the history of both Communism and fascism showed in Europe and Russia, dumb shows and shadow gestures can, in the proper circumstances, become the realities of revolution, counter-revolution, and power. In comparison to Europe, fascism in California remained embryonic. Like any embryo, however, it possessed a capacity for gestation—and birth.

III

EFFORTS AT RECOVERY

7

Ham and Eggs

The New Deal (Almost) Comes to California

*E*VEN as a militant Right preened in the aftermath of so many tactical victories, California was preparing to go Democratic in the gubernatorial election of 8 November 1938. Such a victory by the Democrats represented a break with nearly forty years of tradition. Not since 1899 had the state had a Democratic governor, Stockton attorney James Herbert Budd. In the United States Senate, Democrats had done slightly better. In 1914 James Duval Phelan, former mayor of San Francisco, won popular election to the Senate; and in 1932 William Gibbs McAdoo, a Los Angeles attorney who had served his father-in-law Woodrow Wilson as Secretary of the Treasury from 1913 until 1918, was swept into the Senate in the Roosevelt landslide, the first time since 1916 that California had gone Democratic in a presidential election. Throughout the 1920s, however, there were no Democratic senators and only two Democratic representatives. In terms of registration, Republicans outnumbered Democrats three to one in the decade prior to EPIC.

For all its distinctiveness and its reputation, frequently deserved, for eccentricity, California was in the main a suburbanized Anglo-American, even Protestant, sort of a place, lacking, with the exception of San Francisco, the big city political cultures and machines beloved by Democrats. Even ethnically diverse, labor-dominated San Francisco elected more Republicans than Democrats to such important political offices as mayor, congressman, state senator, and assemblyman through the 1930s.

The Republican ascendancy in California was a matter of culture, sociology, and political structures. Without heavy industry (not until the Second World War did California get its first important steel mill); without ethnically fortified big city machines (outside of San Francisco); without major immigration from the South (another source of Democrats), political ascendancy in California belonged to

Anglo-American suburbanized elites and their affiliates, whose paragon and political champion was the brilliant mining engineer from suburban Palo Alto, Herbert Hoover, the first Californian to reach the presidency. Hoover's Progressivism—his suspicion of big government, big business, and big labor, his faith in engineering and the gospel of efficiency, his rags-to-riches advocacy of individual initiative and self-reliance—struck the deepest possible chord in California's inner political self; for as California entered the twentieth century, it spoke most directly to middle- and upper-middle-class whites wishing to migrate westward to the sun to a more improved, which is to say, more Progressive, commonwealth. Literally and figuratively, Progressivism stole the thunder of the Democratic Party of California in the early twentieth century. Speaking to both reform and the value system of middle-class America, Progressivism, which was basically Republican in its political sponsorship, made the Democratic Party seem too urban and corrupt in a state of reforming suburbanites, too Catholic in a commonwealth dominated by Protestants, too ethnic amidst a larger mid-American whiteness, and too wet in a state where an entire region, Southern California, was strongly prohibitionist.

There were also structural difficulties. In 1913 the legislature, dominated by Progressives, initiated cross-filing, which lasted until 1959. This meant that a candidate could file for nomination in either party or both. In 1918, for example, San Francisco mayor James Rolph, a Republican, filed for governor in both the Democratic and Republican primaries. Rolph won the Democratic nomination but lost the Republican nomination to William Stevens, who had succeeded Hiram Johnson when Johnson appointed himself to the Senate. Under the rules, Rolph, a Republican, could not run for governor on the Democratic ticket if he did not win the Republican nomination as well; and so, in the election of 1918, the Democrats suffered the humiliation of not having any candidate for governor, a fitting symbol of the difficulties of being a California Democrat in the first four decades of the twentieth century. Using cross-filing, liberal or reform Republicans could easily win enough support among like-minded Democrats to prevent Democratic candidates from building a base for election in their own party, much less amassing the strength themselves to cross-file and counter-attack in Republican territory.

In the 1930s the Republican ascendancy began to lose its dominance. First of all, when Hiram Johnson went to Washington, he returned the Progressive Party to the Republican fold. In the conservative 1920s old-fashioned Republicans began to replace Progressive Republicans in influential party circles. The Republican Party entered the 1930s dominated by such Bourbons as Los Angeles *Times* publisher Harry Chandler, railroad heir and banker William Henry Crocker, industrialist Herbert Fleishhacker, San Francisco *Chronicle* publisher Michael De Young, and Oakland *Tribune* publisher Joseph Knowland (Chandler, Knowland, and De Young being as much interested in real estate as newsprint): hardly the sort of elite that would encourage Republicans to look to innovative solutions for the Depression.

When Roosevelt swept William Gibbs McAdoo into the Senate in 1932 after McAdoo helped swing the Democratic Convention to FDR, McAdoo was able rapidly to enlarge the Democratic Party apparatus in California through federal patronage handed out by a grateful Roosevelt. In the meanwhile, California was filling up with new voters from the South, the border states, and the Old Southwest, all of them accustomed to vote Democratic. Between 1932 and 1934, Democratic Party registrations doubled, although Republicans still outnumbered Democrats by four hundred thousand registrants. Between 1930 and 1940, Democratic Party registration in California increased by 431 percent. As the election of 1938 approached, California had 2,144,360 registered Democrats and 1,293,929 registered Republicans.

This is why Democratic Party regulars were so infuriated by Upton Sinclair's end-run in 1934. Sinclair had dissipated a growing Democratic strength. In the general election of 1937, a recovered Democratic Party took forty-seven out of forty-eight seats in the state assembly. One of these seats belonged to Culbert Olson, state senator from Los Angeles County and a supporter of EPIC in 1934. Born in Utah in 1876 of Danish parentage, Olson, while not a Mormon, had been touched early in his development by cooperative Mormon ideals. Qualifying for the bar while working as an aide to his congressman cousin, Olson returned to Utah in 1916 and won election to the state senate. As a gentile in a Mormon state, however, especially a gentile with left-of-center orientation, Olson realized that his political future in Utah was limited. In 1920, he moved to Los Angeles, where he rose steadily in Democratic Party circles. In 1934, as president of the Los Angeles County Democratic Club, Olson staunchly backed Upton Sinclair and served as the closest thing Sinclair would allow to a campaign manager, while at the same time running successfully for the state senate. A defeated Sinclair, in fact, saw Olson's victory as a partial vindication of his own candidacy, and for the next few years Olson led the EPIC-liberal wing of the Democratic Party, the ideological opponent and arch-enemy of Senator McAdoo, a strongly conservative Democrat, despite his backing of FDR. Respected for his intelligence and fair-mindedness, Olson succeeded to the chairmanship of the Democratic State Central Committee, a powerful position which enabled him to build a victory coalition in the gubernatorial primary of 1938.

There could be no greater political and personal contrast than that between Governor Frank Merriam, running for reelection, and Olson, the Democratic nominee. For the previous four years, Merriam had done his best to justify George Creel's description of him as "reactionary to the point of medievalism." Time and again, during the San Francisco strike, the Sacramento conspiracy trials, the Salinas and Stockton *putsche*, Governor Merriam had shown himself a solid, stolid, accommodating servant of the boyars. Given Olson's platform, it is remarkable that Merriam did not level his favorite charge of Communism at his Democratic opponent; for in Olson's advocacy of such ultra-New Deal measures as the public ownership of utilities, self-help and production for use (a toned-down version of the EPIC platform of 1934), slum clearance and housing subsidies, aid for the elderly, a public program of medical insurance, an extension of veterans' benefits, prison reform, small business and consumer advocacy, and a California Wagner Act to protect labor, the silver-haired Dane was testing the outer limits of permissible California politics. Even more shocking, Olson campaigned directly against the Associated Farmers of California. The New Deal might be late in coming to California, but in the figure of Culbert Olson, who was not so far removed politically from his mentor Upton Sinclair, it promised to come with a vengeance.

Republican candidate for the Senate, Philip Bancroft, president of the Associated Farmers of Contra Costa County, went ballistic at the very mention of the New Deal. Only Central Casting could have provided the voters two more contrasting candidates for the Senate than Sheridan Downey, a Social Democrat (although there was no such party in America) if not a crypto-Socialist, and Philip Bancroft, a pistol-packing pear grower from Walnut Creek. A Sacramento attorney lately moved to Atherton, a small suburban town on the San Francisco Peninsula, Sheridan Downey was even further to the left than Culbert Olson. Downey was a shabby, shadowy ne'er-do-well, defeated in three tries for public office, who inherited the Glory Vote from Upton Sinclair, on whose ticket he had run for lieutenant governor. In just about every possible way—his rural origins, his removal to California in hopes of better days, his bitter disappointment in the Golden State, his shabby genteel poverty, his passion for utopian solutions—Sheridan Downey epitomized, even better than Sinclair (Downey, after all, was no writer, but a man of the people, one of the Folks) the mindset and obsessions of the displaced senior citizens who were infusing such volatile millenarianism into California politics.

Born in Laramie, Wyoming, in 1884, the sixth of ten children, Sheridan Downey grew up in an atmosphere of politics and eccentric utopianism verging on American Gothic crankiness. His father, Stephen Wheeler Downey, a Maryland-born attorney and aspiring man of letters, represented the Wyoming Territory in Congress. While there, Downey introduced a bill to spend half a million dollars decorating the interior walls of the national Capitol with frescos depicting the life of Christ. Downey introduced his bill with the Apostle's Creed as a preamble. In support of this measure, he also had printed in the Congressional Record the complete text of his blank verse epic *The Immortals*, which told of a tour taken of the afterlife by Phantasmagoria, daughter of the West. Raised in such a ramshackle, Dickensian environment (Downey's mother was the daughter of English immigrants) in which the siblings were encouraged to write poetry and memorize Latin orations, Sheridan Downey grew into a dreamy eccentric, hoping one day, so he later informed Mary Craig Sinclair, to deliver the greatest oration ever given in the history of the United States. To prepare for such a possibility, Downey attended the University of Wyoming, took his law degree at Michigan, then settled in Laramie.

In 1913, skeptical regarding his prospects in a small Wyoming town, Downey moved to Sacramento to join his brother in the practice of law. For a while, he prospered, gaining election to the Sutter Club, hangout of the Sacramento establishment. Dreaming of one day giving America's greatest speech, Downey also dreamed of getting rich quick. Throughout the late 1910s and 1920s, as most of the nation prospered, Sheridan Downey was busy going broke. Noticing how expensive brook trout was in a railway dining car, Sheridan Downey lost money on a trout ranch in Wyoming. Getting interested in the circus business and the populating of zoological gardens, he lost $10,000 in a scheme to import elephants and monkeys to the United States. He even lost money in real estate, which was almost an impossible thing to do in the 1920s. By 1928 Sheridan Downey was $250,000 in debt. Negotiating this down to approximately fifty cents on the dollar, he paid it off with a $40,000 loan from his brother and most of his wife's $75,000 inheritance. The 1930s found Sheridan Downey a marginally employed Sacramento attorney, struggling to support his wife and five children, his house lost to the bank, his membership in the Sutter Club canceled. Downey fled his failure, moving to the small suburban town of Atherton. Bitterly, he cast about for someone or something to blame for his condition, now so massively reflected in a nationwide Depression. He became an indefatigable pamphleteer and letter writer and voluble orator on matters economic. His politics shifted from Progressive Republican to Social Democratic, even Socialist perhaps, masquerading as liberal Democratic.

All this was of minor interest: a shabby pamphleteer self-publishing his nostrums, a common story in the Depression. In 1932 Sheridan Downey had run for Congress and lost and had generally been regarded around Sacramento as a crank. In 1933, an obscure lawyer on the edges of bankruptcy, he declared himself a candidate for governor in the Democratic primary and seemed crankier than ever. Crankiness, however, was not something that bothered Upton Sinclair. Sensing in Downey the paradigm of wounded and rejected righteousness which was the foundation of his own candidacy, Sinclair invited Downey to Pasadena for, as it was later described, a conversation lasting, like the creation of the world, seven days and seven nights. When it was over, Downey withdrew his name from the gubernatorial race and became the EPIC nominee for lieutenant governor. He also made contact with Dr. Townsend of Long Beach and tried, unsuccessfully, to get Townsend and Sinclair to agree on a jointly sponsored pension proposal. At age fifty, after a lifetime of failure, Sheridan Downey caught the wave that he would ride into the United States Senate. All around him, in the EPIC campaign and in the Townsend Movement, which hired him as chief counsel, Downey beheld the cumulative power of thousands and thousands of elderly also-rans focused on a single issue, the redemption of their frustrated lives through old-age pensions. Suddenly, miraculously, Downey's personal failure, indeed his very physical appearance, graying and nondescript, became the unexpected measure of political success.

The political dimension of the Townsend Movement became especially impressive at the mass picnic rallies favored by the doctor. At one of these, held in Long Beach, nearly thirty thousand Townsendites attended, and Downey received an especially exhilarating opportunity to exercise his oratory when a false report reached the speakers' platform that Townsend had been killed in a plane crash. Fearing mass hysteria, Downey took to the podium and asked a clergyman to offer prayer. He then launched into an *ex tempore* eulogy of Townsend which seemed to release in him decades of oratorical ambition. By the time it was announced that Townsend was alive and well, Downey was in tears, and so were hundreds in the audience. At long last, Downey had given the speech he had always wanted to give. It was one thing to grind out economic pamphlets in obscurity. It was quite another thing altogether to face ten thousand upturned faces and experience their collective assent. Even then, however, nothing came easily to Sheridan Downey. In 1936 he ran for Congress as a Townsendite and for the third time went down in political defeat. By 1937 and early 1938, he was still a small-time lawyer, barely getting by, currently being sued for $43,328 in back debt.

Meanwhile, in downtown Los Angeles, a group of pension zealots, many of whose life stories resembled that of Sheridan Downey, was holding a series of meetings through September and October 1937 in the Clifton Cafeteria on Seventh Street. Some of the meetings were attended by as many as forty men and women, most of them past fifty, the sort for whom the Clifton Cafeteria served not only as an economical place to eat, but as a club, a hangout, a forum for debate and discussion. The Clifton Cafeteria forum had a rather ambitious topic before the house: pensions of $30 every Monday (later changed to Thursday), for every unemployed Californian past the age of fifty.

In 1931 Yale University economist Irving Fisher had advanced yet another solution for the economic slump: stamped scrip to promote consumption. The restoration of the economy, Fisher argued, should begin with the consumer. The federal government could stimulate consumption, hence the economy, by issuing to needy citizens specified amounts of scrip. The scrip would have a dollar value and had to be spent within the week. Irving's proposal struck a chord with Robert Noble, a onetime candidate for the ministry who had also been attracted by the anti–Wall Street diatribes of Father Coughlin and the Share the Wealth program proposed by Huey Long of Louisiana. Impressive in appearance and eloquence, Noble had all the makings of what would later be termed a media evangelist. Unfortunately, a spell of religious delusion had necessitated his hospitalization and subsequent withdrawal from a clerical career. Since leaving the seminary, Nobel had turned to selling real estate in Los Angeles (the second career, it seems, of every other person in the city), shifting his emphasis from religion to economic salvationism. Active on behalf of EPIC and the Utopian Society of America, Noble also discovered an alternative pulpit, the radio. As a commentator on station KMTR, Noble blasted the corrupt and inept administration of Mayor Frank

Shaw. He also began to advocate a pension plan based on a fusion of Irving Fisher's scrip system, Huey Long's Share the Wealth program, Utopianism, EPIC, and the Townsend Movement. Every Monday, Noble urged, the State of California should issue $25 in warrants to every unemployed Californian over the age of fifty. Response from Noble's radio audience was widespread and enthusiastic.

Now ensued a melodrama of skullduggery, greed, mass manipulation, and politics, all of it carried on by characters straight from the pages of Horace McCoy, Raymond Chandler, and Nathanael West, which yet awaits its deserved movie, starring Jack Nicholson, with script by Robert Towne. To put the scenario briefly, two Hollywood publicists, the brothers Willis and Lawrence Allen, highjacked Noble's proposal and transformed it into the dominant single political force in California for the rest of the decade.

Like his father, who had done time for fraud, Lawrence Allen was an attorney. Brother Willis, a former USC cheerleader, sold real estate and organized radio promotions. The Allens' client list included Grey Gone, a hair rinse and nutrient for graying, balding men. Grey Gone actually caused hair to fall out and attracted a number of lawsuits. By the time the Grey Gone scandal had subsided, Willis Allen was serving two years' probation for mail fraud. Like father, like son. Noble contacted the Allen brothers, who operated out of Hollywood as the Cinema Advertising Agency, to represent him in negotiations with radio station KMTR. Ever mindful of the main chance, the Allen brothers soon realized that Noble's pension proposal represented a venture too electric with possibilities to be left in the exclusive control of an emotionally unstable minister manqué.

City Hall, meanwhile, sensing the power of the growing reform movement, was looking for ways to quiet its most vociferous critic, radio commentator Robert Noble. Commissioned by the mayor, the chief of police, and other interests to find a way to neutralize Noble, Captain Earl Kynette of the LAPD made contact with the Allen brothers. Noble's real power over the airwaves, Kynette had decided, came as much from his pension plan as it did from his attacks on the administration of Mayor Shaw. At the same time, even Kynette, dissatisfied with his captain's salary, saw the economic potential of the pension proposal if it became an organized mass movement. Deftly, he suggested to the Allen brothers that they hustle the pension idea from Noble and organize their own campaign. Kynette went so far as to provide the Allen brothers with the funds, so he later alleged, with which to launch their own pension campaign, and received from them an IOU.

Hence the orchestrated meetings in September and October 1937 in the Clifton Cafeteria in downtown Los Angeles, as the Allen brothers sought to launch their own grass-roots campaign. To replace Noble as a radio personality, the Allens invited Sherman Bainbridge, a commentator whose angular presence, an Ichabod Crane in tortoise-shell glasses, belied the power of a mellifluous baritone which had won him the sobriquet "the Voice." Also on hand in these Clifton

Cafeteria meetings: Roy Owens ("the Brain"), age fifty-two, a self-taught, self-described "engineer economist," whose formal education had ended in the ninth grade, a salesman by profession and a longtime admirer of the black evangelist Father Divine. Arriving broke in California in 1929, Owens had spent time, so he later told the *Saturday Evening Post*, "walking on my uppers and thinking." Owens emerged from this enforced sabbatical on the streets a convinced pension advocate. The Clinton coterie later expanded to include in its inner circle Lenn Reynolds, whose most recent occupation was driving a cab in Santa Monica; Raymond Fritz, a sometime IRS auditor reputed to have Nazi sympathies; and Will Kindig, who, thanks to EPIC, had spent one term on the Los Angeles City Council. By October the Clifton cabal was ready to go public as the California Pension Plan Association, a non-profit organization sharing office space with the Cinema Advertising Agency.

Sheridan Downey, meanwhile, was, with mixed success, trying to revive his legal practice in Atherton: a bitter exile for an ambitious man who in his run for lieutenant governor had received more votes than any Democrat in the history of California and still lost. Throughout the mid-1930s, Downey managed to keep contact with the Townsendites and other pension plan activists, mooching rides to Southern California to attend rallies. In late 1937 Downey declared as a candidate for the Democratic nomination to the Senate.

In the Southland, a plot was underway that would within the year transform Downey from a marginalized has-been into a United States Senator, whom his supporters among the senior citizens of America wished to see in the White House. The plot concerned the Democratic incumbent, William Gibbs McAdoo. Polished, assured, the former son-in-law of an American president, the close personal friend of FDR, a wealthy attorney for corporate oil, the social arbiter of Southern California, McAdoo had his enemies. One of them was John Elliott, the shrewd, self-made, tough-talking, number-one independent oil man in Southern California. Elliott did not like McAdoo nor his big oil clients, who now had their man in the Senate; neither did Manchester Boddy, the equally independent owner-publisher of the *Daily News*, an illustrated tabloid, which Boddy, a quirky patrician-populist, had brought out in favor of EPIC, Townsendism, and the Utopian Society of America. Joined by Delwin Smith, a former salesman of fraternity pins now serving as Sergeant-at-Arms of the California Legislature, Elliott and Boddy plotted to replace McAdoo with Peirson Hall, a popular Southern Californian politician. Impressed by the votes that Downey had won in his race for lieutenant governor, the group initially offered to sponsor him for attorney general if he would leave the Senate race in favor of Hall.

Sheridan Downey was sorely tempted. How long, after all, could he maintain the masquerade that he had a political destiny? What was he anyway but a marginal candidate for the Senate, supported only by a few pension advocates? Interestingly enough, it was these very pension advocates—Townsendites, followers of Robert Noble, members of the Clifton Cafeteria group—who in the course of a two-day marathon meeting in a Southern California hotel convinced Downey to stay in the race: Downey, emotionally distraught much of the time, occasionally in tears, was on the verge of abandoning the Senate race in favor of a more certain shot at the attorney generalship.

State Sergeant-at-Arms Delwin Smith, meanwhile, was conducting a secret poll (another contribution by California to American political culture) which showed that McAdoo would win if both Hall and Downey stayed in the race. The swing vote in the primary, the poll revealed, would be EPIC and pension advocates. Should Hall challenge McAdoo, McAdoo had a chance of getting what the plotters called "the goofiness vote." On the other hand, "no one on earth could take the goofiness vote from Downey." Peirson Hall withdrew from the Senate race and became Downey's campaign manager on the promise that Downey would have him appointed a federal judge when he reached the Senate. At this point, Sheridan Downey, who only a few months earlier was a self-proclaimed candidate with marginal support, had become a highly credible challenger, backed by the Elliot-Boddy group and the pension movement.

By then, the California Pension Plan Association, now popularly known as Ham and Eggs, had become a statewide phenomenon. First of all, the Allen brothers incorporated a board of directors which eliminated Robert Noble from the movement. Noble fought back, trying to organize his own rallies, but Captain Kynette of the LAPD had them dispersed with stink bombs and tear gas. Noble next went to the secretary of state of California, Frank Jordan, to register his program of $25 every Monday. The Allens counter-registered a more elaborate program, drafted by Roy Owens and Sherman Bainbridge, calling for a constitutional amendment granting $30 in warrants every Thursday to every unemployed Californian over fifty. Owens and Bainbridge also threw together a campaign booklet, *Ham and Eggs for Californians*, complete with an ambitious bibliography of writings by technocrats and economists.

Under the guidance of the Allen brothers, the California Pension Plan Association soon mushroomed into a statewide campaign to get a constitutional amendment implementing the pension program on the ballot in the November 1938 election. Two thousand dollars a day came in via the mail in small contributions. By the end of the campaign, a statewide staff of more than a thousand had become necessary to handle the volume of mail and to help coordinate thousands of precinct workers. The Allens took no salary from the movement. Instead, hundreds of thousands of dollars in radio and newspaper advertisements and associated printing costs were handled by their Cinema Advertising Agency at a healthy commission of 15 percent. The brothers took over an entire floor in their Hollywood office buidling. Willis bought a big home on the Westside. Lawrence secured the services of a Jean Harlow look-alike as his stenographer: a drop-dead peroxide blonde who dressed like a million and accompanied her boss around the state.

Three weeks before the California primary, the Pension Plan presented Secretary of State Frank Jordan with a petition to place the pension plan on the November ballot signed by 789,000 voters, a quarter of all registered voters in California. Faced with the largest petition in the political history of the state, the secretary of state had no choice but to comply. Suddenly, overnight, California had a powerful third party, ostensibly Democratic but outside the traditional party apparatus, allied in fact with the rump group headed by Elliott and Boddy seeking to dislodge McAdoo.

Initially, the phrase "ham and eggs" had been derisively employed by critics of the pension plan, in much the same manner as "pie in the sky," mocking the image of Ma and Pa California eating ham and eggs for breakfast every Thursday morning when their warrants arrived in the mail. Radio commentator Sherman Bainbridge seized the epithet and made of it a positive designation: a Folksy suggestion for the well-fed prosperity the Pension Plan would bring. The movement, Bainbridge told his radio audience, wanted ham and eggs not only for California but for all of America as well.

Soon, banners proclaiming HAM AND EGGS FOR CALIFORNIA festooned pension rallies. Speakers were expected to holler, "Ham and Eggs, everybody!" before beginning their address. "Ham and Eggs!" the crowd would holler back, or "Ham and Eggs and glory glory Hallelujah!" If a speaker attempted to speak without the expected proclamation, the audience would cry out, "Ham and Eggs! Ham and Eggs!" until the speaker complied and hollered "Ham and Eggs, everybody!" before beginning his speech. Carey McWilliams noted that this incantatory ritual of hollering "Ham and Eggs!" disconcertingly resembled the *Sieg Heil!* of Nazi rallies. Jews were conspicuously absent from the Ham and Eggs movement, and much of its anti–Wall Street rhetoric was touched with more than a suggestion of anti-Semitism.

The movement even had its own Horst Wessel, a counterpart to the famous Nazi martyr. His name was Archie Price, an unemployed sixty-two-year-old who had committed suicide on 24 July 1938 in San Diego. Financially destroyed when his life savings, $15,000 in building and loan society stock, were lost in the crash of 1929, Price had drifted out to San Diego, which for a while in the 1930s had the highest suicide rate in the nation. (The Jumping Off Place, Edmund Wilson called it.) By the late 1930s Price was in dire straits. He was twice treated for malnutrition. When he tried to secure a job with the WPA, he was told that the age limit was sixty. When he applied for an emergency Social Security pension, he was told that he would not be eligible until he was sixty-five. The day before his death, Price walked into a local San Diego newspaper to discuss his dilemma with an editor. Price suggested that his only recourse was suicide. Leaving a note in his pocket, "Too young to receive an old-age pension, and too old to find work," Price took poison the next day in a San Diego park and was buried in a potter's grave, just one of the hundreds of suicides by the lonely and impoverished who had been drifting into San Diego since 1929.

When Sherman Bainbridge heard of the incident via his newspaper contacts, he began in his broadcasts over KMTR to build Archie Price into a martyr for the pension movement. On 13 August 1938 Bainbridge led a caravan estimated to contain a thousand automobiles from Los Angeles to San Diego for reinternment ceremonies. Exhumed from his pauper's grave, Price now lay in state in Merkley's Mortuary in a luxuriant metallic casket. After ceremonies at the Little Church of the Roses, the cortege proceeded to the Glenn Abbey Memorial Park, where seven thousand Ham and Egg believers thronged the grave site. The featured eulogist was Sheridan Downey, and by every report he made a second, and rather impressive, attempt at that great speech which had haunted him for a lifetime.

As primary day approached, William Gibbs McAdoo sensed that he was in trouble. As was his wont, McAdoo turned to FDR for help. A few days before the primary election, Roosevelt criticized Ham and Eggs in one of his Fireside Chats. In political terms, McAdoo's opposition to Ham and Eggs was suicidal. Not even Franklin Delano Roosevelt could turn the tide. When the primary vote had been counted, Sheridan Downey had sent McAdoo into early retirement.

Downey's opponent in the general election, Walnut Creek rancher Philip Bancroft, a regional president in the Associated Farmers, could not have offered a more dramatic contrast. Once again, in the juxtapositioning of a far-left social democrat and a Red-baiting right-winger, California was showing its accustomed proclivity for extremes.

No one could better embody the agricultural Right than Philip Bancroft, "the Fighting Farmer from Walnut Creek." Born in 1881 in San Francisco, Bancroft was raised in upper-middle-class comfort. His father, Hubert Howe Bancroft, had prospered as a stationer, bookseller, publisher, and, most important, as the impresario (and putative author) of a multi-volume *History of the Pacific States*, which Bancroft salesmen took to the road and sold throughout the Far West as a later generation of salesmen would sell the Encyclopedia Britannica. After graduating from Harvard College, Class of 1904, where he also served as president of the undergraduate California Club of Harvard, fifty strong, Bancroft took a master's degree in law from the Harvard Law School and finished his legal training at Hastings College of the Law in San Francisco. Financially secure and socially well-connected, Bancroft prospered as a San Francisco–based attorney until he enlisted in the Army at age thirty-seven in 1917 for duty as a transportation officer in France.

Upon his return, Bancroft abandoned the law and went into walnut and pear growing on Walnut Creek properties which he had inherited from his father and where he had spent happy summers in his youth. Pears from Bancroft's Mount Diablo Fruit Farm—Mount Diablo the premium brand, Aloha the standard—took top prizes; and Bancroft prospered as the sort of gentleman farmer Jack London always dreamed of becoming: a manly figure in boots, jodhpurs, a military-style khaki shirt, and Baden-Powell hat, walking his properties with a German shepherd at his side, scientifically cultivating the soil, living the good life; a California patriarch, on the ranch with wife, three children and, later seven grandchildren and assorted in-laws.

This patriarchal contentment masked a seething political resentment. As a young man, Bancroft had been a devoted Teddy Roosevelt Progressive, a member of the Lincoln-Roosevelt League, an ardent backer of Roosevelt and Hiram Johnson in the Bull Moose campaign of 1912. The First World War, however, set many such California Progressives on a rightward course. Bancroft's friend John Francis Neylan, for example, who had served Hiram Johnson in Sacramento as director of the budget and finance, seeing the mass graves of American soldiers killed in France, became profoundly isolationist, as did Hiram Johnson himself. As a veteran of the fighting, albeit only in a quartermaster and transportation unit, Bancroft had become similarly affected. The War took him from San Francisco and the law in search of a more isolationist lifestyle as a rancher. Like so many former Progressives, Bancroft blamed the carnage of France on the unwise involvement of the United States in European disputes. He also became rabidly anti-Communist, seeing in Communism the essence of the internationalist quagmire which the United States should avoid. Bancroft loathed Teddy's cousin Franklin. He became active in such anti-interventionist groups as Pro-America and America First. When the Associated Farmers organized in 1934 and reorganized in 1936, he became a state vice-president, president of the Contra Costa County chapter, and a key spokesman.

On 26 April 1935, for example, Bancroft appeared before the Commonwealth Club of California, meeting in San Francisco, and lambasted the agricultural union movement as a Communist plot spearheaded by Pat Chambers and Caroline Decker of the CAWIU. Bancroft went so far as to smear his fellow Harvardian, the Sacramento philanthropist Simon Julius Lubin, a defender of strikers' rights, as someone who was Communistically inclined. For good measure, he praised the American Legion and San Francisco police chief William Quinn for the strong stance Quinn had taken against Harry Bridges and the other Communists during the maritime strike of the previous summer. Bancroft concluded his address with the recommendation that the deportation of alien Communist agitators be resuscitated.

Although one of his barns had been burned down in the course of a labor dispute, Bancroft himself had never been the object of a strike action. Nevertheless, he kept shotguns mounted in his office, carried a revolver, for which he had a permit, and conspicuously performed target practice on Sunday mornings. That such a Darth Vader figure could win the senatorial nomination in the Republican primary only testified to the strength of the Right by 1938. Regular Republicans were aghast at Bancroft's primary victory, while he saw himself repeating the Lincoln-Roosevelt coup of 1910. Senator Hiram Johnson, in fact, who had become governor in that remarkable 1910 offensive, openly endorsed Bancroft for the Senate, saying that he was running a bully campaign and that it was like old times being with him once again on the campaign trail.

Throughout the primary and the general election, Philip Bancroft made masterful use of the radio. Since he had no official Republican backing and hence little by way of campaign staff, Bancroft turned to the radio, buying prime time every Monday night at six o'clock over NBC, and conducted a hard-hitting campaign against the New Deal in general, Roosevelt in particular, and such assorted Communist sympathizers as Secretary of Labor Frances Perkins, her Russian-born radical protégé, David Joseph Sapos, Harry Hopkins, Rexford Tugwell, Jerome Frank, and the others surrounding the President who, Bancroft charged, were "giving the Communists aid and comfort and playing into their hands at every turn." [1]

Thus a left-wing upstart, Sheridan Downey, and a right-wing upstart, Philip Bancroft, faced each other in the general election. Downey had Ham and Eggs, Proposition 25. Bancroft had Proposition 1, a serious anti-picketing ordinance.

Galvanized by the call to unity issued at the conference of corporate leaders held at the Del Monte Hotel in 1936, a consortium of business organizations and interests that included the usual suspects—the Associated Farmers, the Industrial Association of San Francisco, the Merchants and Manufacturers Association of Los Angeles, the Los Angeles Chamber of Commerce, Southern Californians, Inc.—joined in the spring of 1938 and retained the law firm of Gibson, Dunn & Crutcher in Los Angeles to draft a statewide initiative, Proposition 1, severely curtailing the burgeoning union movement. Proposition 1 placed strong statewide restrictions on picketing, forbade secondary boycotts, and made unions responsible for all damages caused by picketing members. Throughout the summer and fall of 1938, Californians were treated to a highly financed propaganda blitzkrieg in newspaper and radio advertisements, billboards, subsidized public meetings, and varieties of brochures, leaflets, and pamphlets all extolling the dangers of unionism and the benefits of Proposition 1. In terms of licit political actions, the Proposition 1 campaign, linked closely with Philip Bancroft's candidacy, constituted the high-water mark of the Associated Farmers as a political force in California. Should Proposition 1 pass and Philip Bancroft go to the Senate, the Associated Farmers had every chance of becoming the dominant force in the state.

By November 1938 the general election had crystallized not around the personalities of Olson, Downey, and Bancroft, but around Propositions 1 and 25. Californians were either for or against severe restrictions on picketing and for or against Ham and Eggs. Seeing how Ham and Eggs had plucked William Gibbs McAdoo from the Senate after one term and yet not wishing to alienate mainstream voters, Culbert Olson remained mute on the issue, which polls showed was running fifty-fifty or dead even in voter approval. Olson saw no percentage in alienating a swing vote in either camp.

Throughout the final days of the campaign continued the American Gothic melodrama of Ham and Eggs. Returning from Archie Price's second funeral, Sherman Bainbridge drove his automobile off Highway 1 and nearly died in the resulting crash. Ham and Eggs had to do without "the Voice" for six crucial weeks as Bainbridge lay in a full body cast in Los Angeles County Hospital. Then Captain Earl Kynette, ever scheming, ever enamored of dramatic solutions, got himself arrested for planting bombs in the vicinity of an opponent. Languishing in the Los Angeles city jail, Kynette began to demand through his lawyer that the brothers Allen start sharing the profits from Ham and Eggs as had been initially promised in the fall of the previous year. Kynette also suggested that he held an IOU from the brothers proving his claim. Los Angeles newspapers had the proverbial field day with the scandal, which qualified the reputation of Ham and Eggs as a Hallelujah-Come-to-Glory crusade.

Never at a loss in a crisis, the brothers Allen imported a ringer from Chicago: Miss Gertrude Coogan, a comely young economist and security analyst for Northern Trust who had been responsible for most of Father Coughlin's economic statements, only breaking with the priest when Coughlin began to go morbidly right. Dressed dramatically in black, her black hair parted severely and drawn behind her head in a Grecian knot, Gertrude Coogan not only knew her economics and history, she was also a mesmerizing platform speaker, as a capacity audience gathered in the Shrine Auditorium in Los Angeles ecstatically discovered one night just before the election when Coogan gave the first speech of a statewide eight-day tour arranged by the Allen brothers. On the Saturday before election day, Coogan spoke to an audience of fourteen thousand gathered in the Civic Auditorium of San Francisco. In Los Angeles, Fresno, Stockton, San Jose, Sacramento, San Francisco, and elsewhere, Coogan preached the same message, which she shored with a blizzard of facts and statistics. Money was not wealth. Money was only a medium of exchange intended to stimulate the production, distribution, and consumption of goods. The federal government was refusing to put enough money into circulation; hence the Depression was continuing. By passing Proposition 25, Californians were reasserting their sovereign power to authorize and issue a medium of exchange so as to stimulate consumption, and hence production and distribution, and end the slump.

Coogan enlivened her disquisition with appeals to the Founding Fathers and the Constitution and with references to the history of banking and finance which might have seemed arcane to her audience, were it not for the fact that her scholarship belied the most hurtful charge of all, namely, that Ham and Eggs was something irresponsible, something goofy. Making Ham and Eggs seem respectable, making it seem the logical solution to the Depression, Coogan comforted her audience with the notion that they were not elderly eccentrics but a mighty phalanx that, having redeemed California, would move on to save the rest of the nation.

As someone who wanted to give America's greatest speech, Sheridan Downey watched Coogan's progress with fascination and envy. Although his strength had come primarily from Ham and Eggers and Townsendites, "the goofiness vote" as Elliott and Boddy called it, Downey was doing everything possible to appear mainstream and respectable in the waning days of the campaign. Jack Elliott and Peirson Hall, Downey's campaign manager, kept him from openly endorsing Ham and Eggs, lest he alienate moderate Democratic voters. Yet without the pension movement, Sheridan Downey would still be back in Atherton, struggling to practice law.

On the Sunday night before the November 1938 election, more than twenty-five thousand true believers filled the Hollywood Bowl for the mother of all Ham and Egg rallies. Downey's controllers did not want him to attend the rally, fearing that last impressions were the most powerful. Downey rebelled and wheedled from his handlers a compromise. He would sit silently on the stage during the rally and give only a few words of greeting. To place Sheridan Downey at the speakers' rostrum in the Hollywood Bowl packed with twenty-five thousand cheering, singing, Hallelujah-Come-to-Glory Ham and Eggers and ask Downey not to give an oration—he who had sent Archie Price to glory—was the equivalent of asking Casanova to remain celibate in the Grand Harem of Istanbul. Rising to the microphone, Downey began to give his brokered greeting, but when it was all over he had given an enthusiastic endorsement of Ham and Eggs, and the crowd had leapt to its feet and filled the Hollywood Bowl with singing and cheering.

That Tuesday, Ham and Eggs went down in defeat—1,143,670 to 1,398,999. But so did Proposition 1, which lost by an even narrower margin. Culbert Olson, who had remained neutral on Ham and Eggs, barely unseated Governor Merriam. Sheridan Downey, militant Ham and Egger, trounced Philip Bancroft. With Proposition 1 defeated and Democrats elected to Sacramento and the Senate, California was showing signs of joining the New Deal, however belatedly. Yet the movement which had energized this Democratic revival, Ham and Eggs, was also its albatross; for in a few short weeks the Allen brothers and their cohorts were regrouping for another try at the ballot. This second intrusion of eccentric millenarian fervor into the politics of California would help substantially to hamper, then thwart, the one-term Democratic administration of Culbert Olson, through whom the New Deal almost came to California.

In December 1938, Governor-elect Olson traveled to Washington for a personal interview with FDR. The most important item on Olson's agenda was an appeal for more federal assistance for migrants in California, but Olson was also seeking to identify himself with the Rooseveltian magic. After all, Olson had campaigned on the explicit promise to bring the New Deal to the Golden State.

On the other hand, the long-range reforms which Olson did achieve in the next few years—in prisons and health care especially—constituted more a resumption of the Progressive agenda than any California version of the New Deal. With the help of the Right Reverend E. J. Flanagan, the founder of Boys' Town in Nebraska, Olson reformed the Whittier State School for Youthful Offenders and established a Youth Authority to handle convicted Californians under the age of twenty-one in a separately structured criminal justice system. Working with another national expert, penologist Kate Richards O'Hare, and his lieutenant governor, Ellis Patterson, Olson also reformed parole procedures and brought California's ancient central prison at San Quentin, established in 1852, into the mid-twentieth century. Prior to these reforms, the massive, gloomy fortress on a small peninsula jutting into San Francisco Bay retained many of the procedures and much of the cruelty of a nineteenth-century penitentiary. Olson's most brilliant move was the replacement of Warden Court Smith, the brother-in-law of a former governor, with the youngish (under forty) Clinton Duffy, assistant secretary of the Board of Prison Terms and Paroles. Born in 1898 at San Quentin, where his father was a guard, Duffy entered prison work at San Quentin, becoming secretary to the warden in 1929. Throughout his lifetime, Duffy had lived closely with the day-by-day grimness of San Quentin where underground dungeons, beatings, prolonged confinement in solitary, the conspicuous numbering of prisoners' shirts, poor food, minimal work or educational opportunities and, most horrible, the exploitation, sexual and otherwise, of younger prisoners had filled the mind of the young penologist with numerous ideas for reform. Taking office in 1940, Clinton Duffy went on to become one of the great reforming wardens of the twentieth century.

Equally influential, thanks to the intervention of Governor Olson, were the efforts on behalf of the reform of mental institutions inaugurated by Aaron Rosanoff, a Los Angeles psychiatrist and expert in the hospitalization of the mentally ill whom Olson appointed to reform California's neglected state mental institution system. Within two years, Rosanoff had added 1,284 beds to the vastly over-crowded system and had raised the paroling of manageable patients to their families by 67 percent. Rosanoff also established the Langley Porter Clinic in San Francisco, named for the recently retired dean of the School of Medicine of the University of California. The Langley Porter Clinic pioneered the delivery of state-supported mental health programs on an out-patient basis.

As important as all this might be, it did not represent the sort of massive government reform front which a California New Deal might be expected to take. After all, the reform of prisons, mental hospitals, and juvenile detention centers had been high priorities on the agenda of the Progressives a quarter of a century earlier and had indeed been implemented in the decade 1910–1920, only to be lost sight of in the general hardening of heart that characterized the 1920s. Olson's promise to transfer Pacific Gas & Electric and the other privately owned utilities to state ownership, by contrast, went nowhere; and the Sacramento lobby of PG&E, the other utilities, the Associated Farmers, and other large corporate interests made mincemeat of the host of reform bills Olson sent to the legislature in 1939.

Indeed, were one to seek the most representative figure in Sacramento in this era, 1938–1942, one might look not to Olson or even to his brilliant young commissioner of Housing and Immigration, Carey McWilliams of Los Angeles, but to the Falstaffian figure of Arthur Samish, Artie or Mr. Big for short, the six-foot-two, three-hundred-pound legislative lobbyist who during these years was fully earning his accustomed sobriquet, the Secret Boss of California. If the New Deal never fully got to California, it was in part because Artie Samish did not want it to. Samish, after all—as Earl Warren was later to admit—had a power over legislation akin to that of the governor himself.

Born in Los Angeles but raised in San Francisco, where his abandoned mother ran a boarding house, Artie Samish served his apprenticeship as a young functionary in the San Francisco machine before being sent, when barely in his twenties, to the Motor Vehicle Department in Sacramento. From there, in 1921, at age twenty-three, he wrangled himself into the crucial position of enrolling clerk for the legislature, responsible for the tracking of legislation and, more important, the tracking of legislators. Not only did Samish learn the intricacies of the legislature in these years, he also mastered the preferences and foibles of assemblymen and state senators. "Select and Elect" became his model in the 1930s when he went out on his own as a lobbyist for the California State Brewers Association, liquor distributors, racetracks, tobacco interests, film studios, and (to add a note of wholesomeness perhaps) orange growers, all of whom he represented under the euphemistic title of public relations counsel. Samish maintained elaborate dossiers on the financial, sexual, and other peccadillos and preferences of every state senator and assemblyman. Those whom he favored, he helped elect. Those who opposed interests represented by Samish soon found themselves faced with a well-financed challenger from their own or another party.

Between 1935 and 1938 Samish earned a reported $496,138 in fees. His offices in the Kohl Building in San Francisco spread out to include two floors and the penthouse. There, or over lunch at Jack's on Sacramento Street, or in his offices in the Biltmore Hotel in Los Angeles, or in some Sacramento watering hole, Samish worked the legislature on behalf of his clients. When the legislature was in session, Samish maintained an around-the-clock hospitality suite in room 428 of the Senator Hotel, with food, booze, and companionship in abundance. To his credit, Samish seemed to love notoriety more than hard cash. Sensitive to the fact that he had not finished grammar school, that he was large, loud, and florid, and frequently scented by cigars and liquor, that he wore over-assertive suits and ties, Samish performed a significant amount of *pro bono* lobbying on behalf of the University of California in an effort to win some measure of respectability. To his hurt, Samish discovered himself socially unacceptable to the men whose bills he could get through the legislature but who never seemed to invite him to their clubs. Not surprisingly, Samish identified, in his own way, with the underdog. In his pocket was ever an ample cabbage head of rolled bills, which he dispensed freely to his many friends in the *demimonde* or used to place a bet in a discreet off-track site. Each Christmas, he gave an elaborate party for the prisoners of San Quentin. For all the suggestions and possibilities of his métier—hotel rooms blue with cigarette and cigar smoke, where conversations ran in tandem to the tintinnabulation of tinkling ice and splashing liquor—Samish remained touchingly devoted to his mother, wife, and family, whom he supported in middle-class propriety in a heavily Catholic neighborhood in San Francisco.

The power of Artie Samish was not comparable to the power of the political bosses of the East and Midwest, men who had come up through the machinery of ward politics and exercised their influence at the apex of an intricate political network. In the new, distinctively Californian style, Artie Samish made an end-run around the intermediate machinery of politics, ever weak in the Golden State, and achieved a direct connection between big-moneyed corporate interests and individual legislators. This money was not proffered as bribes (try as it might, no grand jury would ever indict Artie for something so lacking in finesse as bribery) but was marshalled on behalf of election campaigns. Samish employed corporate money to elect his friends and defeat his enemies. Long before another Falstaffian figure in the legislature, Assembly Speaker Jess Unruh, coined the phrase, Artie Samish knew that in California money had become the mother's milk of politics.

In the early 1930s Clem Whitaker and his partner (later his wife) Leone Baxter virtually invented the systematic mass media–oriented political campaign in its modern form. As a reporter and editor in Sacramento in the 1920s, Clem Whitaker had organized a press service, which he sold to UPI in 1929, designed to feed state capital coverage—articles, cartoons, political commentary—into newspapers too small to maintain their own Capitol bureau. Leone Baxter, meanwhile, was learning promotional techniques as manager of the Chamber of Commerce of Redding. The couple met in 1933 and formed a press agency and campaign service. In their first big election, they defeated the efforts of Pacific Gas & Electric to sink the Central Valley Water Project. (Shortly thereafter, PG&E put them on retainer for life.) The next year, the pair was retained by a temporary alliance of Republicans and conservative Democrats to defeat the candidacy of Socialist turned Democrat Upton Sinclair for governor. Whitaker and Baxter destroyed Sinclair in a mass media blitz which has become a founding classic of the genre.

Clem Whitaker and Leone Baxter grasped a simple but essential truth—true initially for California, later for the nation at large. Californians, later Americans in general, could be reached individually—by the millions!—through the mass media: which in the 1930s meant pamphlets, leaflets, newspaper and magazine advertising, planted stories, commentary and cartoons, billboards, spot announcements on radio, slides and trailers in motion picture theaters, and direct mail. To this program of managed media, Whitaker and Baxter added the values of contest, image, and timing. Americans, they realized, could relate best to political questions if there were a clear-cut argument. Such an argument was best advanced through precise, tightly controlled imagery. It also had to be released most intensely in the final weeks of a campaign. Do not lay out to the voters a complex program, Whitaker and Baxter advised their clients. Pick one dominant issue and run with it. Characterize the opposition in a single negative slogan and your own position in a single positive image. Unleash the full force of your campaign just weeks before election day, when voters tended to make up their minds. Today, sixty years later, the Whitaker and Baxter revolution seems commonplace, so prevalent has it become in our national political life. In the 1930s and 1940s, however, Whitaker and Baxter evolved their system, a forecast of things to come, in the special context of politics in California. Artie Samish instantly understood the implications of the media techniques of Whitaker and Baxter. Given enough money for mass media campaigning, Samish could in effect function as a one-man political party, or if not a party, then a center of influence equal to Democrat and Republican alike.

As if Artie Samish were not trouble enough for Olson, within a week of his election, Ham and Eggers were once again rallying, eight thousand strong, in the Shrine Auditorium in Los Angeles, demanding that Governor Olson allow the voters of California to vote once again on the pension plan in a special election. Olson was appalled. He considered Ham and Eggs ill-conceived, eccentric, the brainchild of the goofiness vote which threatened to derail his long-delayed Democratic administration. The unkindest cut of all, Olson's lieutenant governor, Ellis Patterson, openly backed this idea. Intending to challenge Hiram Johnson for the United States Senate, Patterson hoped to be struck by the same Ham and Egg lightening that had struck Sheridan Downey. In May, Ham and Eggs enthusiasts presented Olson with a petition signed by 737,000 voters demanding a second referendum. Protesting that he did not endorse the idea, Olson called for a special election to be held on 7 November 1939.

In an effort to win more voters, the second Ham and Eggs proposal exempted pension warrants from the 3 percent sales tax. It also called for the appointment of a statewide pension plan administrator, whom the governor could appoint from a very short list of two, Roy Owens or Will Kindig, both of them directors of the movement since its foundation in the Clifton Cafeteria. Either Owens or Kindig would serve until January 1945, at which time he would be succeeded by a popularly elected State Retirement Life Payments Administrator. Owens, the self-described engineer-economist, was the preferred favorite of Ham and Eggers for the post. Such a position, were it ever established, would relegate the governor's chair to obscurity. The proposed post of administrator, moreover, struck many— and not just those on the left—as a post more appropriate to Mussolini's Italy or even Germany under Hitler than to California under the Constitution.

Mercifully, Ham and Eggs lost in every county in the state, 993,204 to 1,933,557. The Allen brothers and Roy Owens, however, blamed Olson for their defeat and began to circulate petitions for his recall. In the course of his single term, Olson would face three such recall efforts, each of them animated by Ham and Egg vitriol: significant distractions to the governor's concentration and even more dangerous erosions of his power base. Nor could Culbert Olson recover from the disastrous fact that he had fainted in full view of 130,000 spectators at the Sacramento State Fairgrounds, had to be helped to his feet, and was hospitalized for a month of recuperation: and this in his first month in office!

Ironically, the fatigue which felled Olson and provided a fixed public image of his administration came directly from the stress of Culbert Olson's most dramatic political success, the pardoning of Tom Mooney. The conviction and death sentence handed down by a San Francisco court to two Socialist activists, Thomas Joseph Mooney and Warren Knox Billings, for the bombing of a Preparedness Day parade held in San Francisco on 22 July 1916 in which ten people were killed and forty injured represents the Dreyfus case of mid-twentieth-century California. Only the conviction and execution of Sacco and Vanzetti reached comparable intensity as a symbol of oligarchical vengeance on a radicalized working class. Subsequent scholarship has convincingly revealed the extent to which a politically ambitious district attorney, Charles Marron Fickert, collaborated with members of the grand jury to convict Mooney and Billings on the basis of fabricated and altered evidence and perjured testimony. The most knowledgeable authority on the Mooney case, Curt Gentry, aside from establishing Mooney's and Billings's innocence and Fickert's guilt, convincingly suggests that an underground German espionage network operating out of the German consulate in San Francisco initiated and orchestrated the bombing. No matter: Mooney, a well-known Socialist activist, and Billings, who had already been convicted for transporting dynamite, were set up and convicted.

Billings went quietly to Folsom Prison. Since he had been convicted of a prior felony, his case, both legally and in terms of public relations, was more difficult. Billings busted rocks at Folsom for a number of years (his crew won the highest ratings for productivity) before turning to watch repair. After the execution of Sacco and Vanzetti in 1927, by contrast, Tom Mooney became the leading international symbol of the oppressed Left. Although the Irish have no monopoly on this type, there is in the Irish character and temperament a capacity for fierce resistance. In Mooney's case, such resistance glowed white-hot from his four-by-eight-by-seven-foot cell in San Quentin for more than twenty years. His life had been ruined by this terrible and unjust conviction; but paradoxically, the incalculable injustice which had been done to him also transformed a minor Socialist agitator into a figure of worldwide importance.

As early as 1918, the railroading of Tom Mooney stood apparent to major portions of the American public, including President Wilson and many members of the Supreme Court; but Governor William Stephens, prodded by Wilson himself, had only the courage for a commutation of Billings's and Mooney's death sentence to life imprisonment, not the pardon they deserved. It would take another twenty-one years of ceaseless agitation to see justice done. Despite a steady onslaught of lobbying from labor and the Left, Governors Stephens, Richardson,

Young, Rolph, and Merriam each refused to grant Mooney the pardon demanded by justice. For his part, Mooney resisted the advice of such supporters as H. L. Mencken and San Francisco newspaper editors Fremont Older and Chester Rowell and refused to accept parole, a possibility which surfaced as a political solution in the late 1920s. The acceptance of parole would have implied an acceptance of guilt. As a paroled felon, Mooney would be barred from participation in politics or organized labor. Mooney chose instead to remain behind bars, the most revered martyr of the labor movement.

Even had any governors after 1930 been inclined toward a pardon, such an inclination would run contrary to the recommendation of the Supreme Court of California in July 1930 that Mooney was not eligible for a pardon. Republican governor Clement Young, in fact, lost renomination because he had even dallied with the idea. His successor Rolph was determined to make no such mistake. The entire Mooney pardon crusade, Rolph snorted, was a Communist conspiracy. While less outspoken, Rolph's successor, Frank Merriam, harbored a similar attitude.

Meanwhile, Tom Mooney, San Quentin convict 31921, became, after Mary Pickford and Douglas Fairbanks, the best-known Californian in the world. The warden and staff at San Quentin appreciated the fact that Tom Mooney was a special case. Many of them believed him to be innocent. While Mooney was not coddled, he was allowed, after the commutation of his death sentence, a cell of his own, lit by a solitary bulb of low wattage (kept low so as to preclude self-electrocution), where he read and stacked the New York *Times*, the Portland *Oregonian*, the Baltimore *Sun*, the *Nation*, the *New Republic*, and other periodicals. Seated with his back to the wall, his typewriter resting on his bunk, Tom Mooney pecked out thousands of letters to his worldwide correspondents, making and saving the carbons in the knowledge that he had become a historically important figure. Preserved now in the Bancroft Library in Berkeley, these letters reveal a bitter, self-centered, strangely great man, quarreling constantly with those who sought to help him. Racked by ulcers, Mooney won a major concession from Warden Frank Smith, who believed in his innocence: the assignment, for eleven years, as a trustee kitchen attendant in the officers' and guards' mess, where he could secure the bland diet he required. Symbolically, this trustee position allowed Tom Mooney to wear white, instead of the usual blue denim, as if to mark him even further, a wronged innocent in white, from the rest of the convicts.

Having been taken from the world, Tom Mooney made the world come to him. A widely circulated newspaper and a magazine were devoted specifically to his case. In the early 1930s, as the Left regained its intensity, agitation on behalf of Mooney came to the forefront. At the 1932 Olympics in Los Angeles, six young protestors raced around the track in the Coliseum wearing "Free Tom Mooney" signs and were given the harsh sentence of nine months in jail for disturbing the peace. In 1933 the Socialists of Los Angeles sent a hearse with the sign "California Justice is Dead" on its side, a rented skeleton in its glass-pane casket space, on a tour of cities of the United States to publicize the Mooney case. Thousands rallied around the hearse at streetcorner demonstrations and in more organized efforts. Building on support already established by Socialist leaders Eugene Debs and Norman Thomas, writers such as Lincoln Steffens, Upton Sinclair, Theodore Dreiser, and Sinclair Lewis made what soon became pilgrimages to San Quentin to be received by Mooney. Sinclair Lewis organized an authors' league in Mooney's support which included, along with Theodore Dreiser, such well-known figures as Sherwood Anderson, Mary Austin, Stephen Vincent Benet, Edna Ferber, Robinson Jeffers, and Carl Sandburg. Mayor Jimmy Walker of New York also visited Mooney in San Quentin and later called on Mooney's aged mother Mary Mooney (Mother Mooney to the movement) at her home in the Mission district of San Francisco. Standing in Mother Mooney's house, Walker made a personal plea to Governor Rolph for a pardon.

In February 1932 Mother Mooney, age eighty-four, made a national tour. In October she visited Russia and called on President-elect Roosevelt on her return. Mother Mooney kept active on her son's behalf until her death in the autumn of 1934. Mooney's wife Rena, by contrast, exhausted by her own indictment and trial for the alleged conspiracy (she was acquitted) and by efforts throughout the 1920s to free her husband, began to lose her hold on things around 1925. A gentle, non-political person, drawn to Socialism merely to keep her husband company, Rena turned to her violin and piano pupils and, increasingly, to alcohol for consolation.

Meanwhile, a host of state and national activists—Mary Gallagher, Clarence Darrow, Fremont Older, Austin Lewis, the Bay Area labor attorney who had also been such a good friend to Jack London, the Quakers, faculty from the University of California and Stanford—united behind a continuing effort to free Mooney through the courts. Between 1933 and 1938 Mooney's legal campaign revolved around the attempt to secure a writ of *habeas corpus* from the federal courts. Spearheaded by a brilliant young defense attorney, George Davis, the effort began in the federal district court for Northern California and progressed toward the Supreme Court of the United States. In June 1935 the Supreme Court of California granted a hearing on the writ of *habeas corpus*. While a referee of the Supreme Court of California was hearing arguments in late 1935 and 1936, Mooney was moved from San Quentin and housed in the City and County Jail of San Francisco. While there, he was treated as a celebrity. As was the case of San Quentin, most of his jailers believed him innocent. Granted special privileges in his home town, Mooney enjoyed a number of supervised outside excursions for lunch at local restaurants.

When the California Supreme Court rejected his case and he was sent back to San Quentin in June 1937, he fell into deep depression. His ulcers resumed bleeding, and he nearly died. On 10 October 1937 the United States Supreme Court refused to hear Mooney's petition for a writ of *certiorari*, which is to say, permission to appeal to the Court. "My only immediate hope," Mooney now wrote his supporters, "lies in the election of State Senator Culbert L. Olson as the next Democratic Governor of California."[2]

Certainly, something approaching divine intervention had become necessary, for the state legislature twice rejected motions to pardon, thereby cutting off this political path. In March 1937 the California Assembly voted Mooney a pardon, 45 to 28, but the state senate tabled the motion without a roll call vote. In March 1938 the assembly voted 36 to 30 to subpoena Mooney and hear new evidence. Mooney himself was brought to Sacramento from San Quentin and presented his case on 10 March 1938 to the assembly, which was meeting as a committee of the whole. On the next day, the assembly once again passed a resolution of pardon, 41 to 29, which the senate, once again, tabled without a roll call vote. With some interesting cross-overs, it was mainly a case of Republicans versus Democrats, the rural against the urban. Tom Mooney stood at the center of the political imagination of California, a figure of judgment and contradiction.

As a candidate for the state senate in 1934, Olson had joined Upton Sinclair in a promise to pardon Tom Mooney if they ever got the chance. When Olson declared for governor in the late summer of 1937, he wrote a secret memorandum to George Davis saying that he would free Tom Mooney if and when he became governor. By doing this, Olson was signaling Mooney supporters not to make Mooney a major issue in the campaign and thereby cost Olson his centrist support. During the campaign itself, Olson avoided the Mooney issue as much as possible, which he was able to do because the Mooneyites knew his intentions.

On 7 January 1939 Culbert Olson made good on his word. Mooney awoke that morning, his last day as a prisoner, and was chauffeured to Sacramento, where Culbert Olson awaited him in the governor's office for a meeting at ten o'clock. By ten-thirty Olson, Mooney, and Davis were standing before a packed assembly chamber. There, over a live nationwide radio hook-up, Olson gave Tom Mooney a full and unconditional pardon and restored to him all civil rights and privileges. Olson also promised to take up the more legally complicated case of Warren Billings. "Tom Mooney," announced Olson, "you are now a free man."

Stepping to the microphones, an unyielding Mooney described his case as a symbol of a repressive economic system and challenged the governor to free Warren Billings as well. And then, as was so typical of the 1930s, Mooney made the fascist comparison. "You hear much today about the liquidation of the Jews in Germany and Italy," Mooney told the Assembly and his vast radio audience, "but we must not forget that that was not the beginning of liquidation in fascist Germany or Italy. The first liquidation was the trade union movement and then the Socialists and the Communists. Now the Jews, then it will be the Catholics and the Protestants and all of us in a common purpose must fight that reaction that intends to blight our life and the life of all civilized people, and we must establish a real social order wherein people will live for the benefit of one another and not for the profit of themselves at the expense of one another. . . . I thank you, Governor Olson."[3]

The next day, accompanied by his wife Rena, George Davis, the actor Melvyn Douglas and his wife Helen Gahagan Douglas, Tom Mooney motored south from Sacramento to Berkeley, then took the ferry across the bay to San Francisco. A triumphant parade ensued up Market Street, Tom Mooney out ahead of the crowd, followed by a phalanx of supporters which included his wife, Davis, San Francisco congressman John Shelley, and Harry Bridges. Ever defiant, Mooney broke ranks momentarily to carry a picket sign in front of the Kress Department Store, where AFL clerks were on strike. He gave the captain of the pickets one of the two $5 bills he had been issued that morning when he left San Quentin. He was sending the other $5, Mooney told reporters, to the newspaper people on strike against Hearst in Chicago. A rally attracting twenty-five thousand followed in the Civic Center. A week later, fifty thousand showed up to hear Mooney speak in the Los Angeles Coliseum.

Once he was no longer a martyr, Tom Mooney's life began to disintegrate. He shocked his supporters when he announced his intention to divorce Rena and marry another woman. Racked by bleeding ulcers, he spent the remaining three years of his life in hospitals, enduring four major operations before his death in San Francisco on 6 March 1942 at age fifty-eight. Once again, there was a public gathering in the Civic Auditorium of San Francisco, but by then America had other things on its mind.

As Harry Bridges marched up Market Street in January 1939, he had every reason to believe that he might be soon replacing Tom Mooney as the leading martyr in the pantheon of the American left. After all, Bridges already had been suffering from ulcers since the mid-1930s. Part of his stomach had to be removed in 1936. Ever since the great maritime strike of 1934, it had been Get Harry Bridges Time in San Francisco. Spearheaded by Thomas Plant, chairman of the Shipowners Association, with special assistance from shipping magnate Roger Lapham, the Get Bridges effort had two possible avenues of action, aside from the option of assassination, which Paul Smith purports to have heard being seriously considered. Bridges could be gotten on criminal grounds—kickbacks, bribery, racketeering, income tax evasion, and other such foibles of longshoremen leaders in the East—or he could be deported as a Communist. In 1921 Bridges had filed a preliminary application for citizenship but had never bothered to complete the process.

Getting Harry Bridges on criminal charges was impossible. Austere in his personal lifestyle, Bridges lived off his salary from the ILWU. As late as 1941, he was making as little as seventy-five dollars a week, despite the fact that he was the most powerful labor leader on the Pacific Coast. His federal and state income tax filings were equally exemplary.

Soon convinced of Bridges's invulnerability to criminal charges, the shipping oligarchy turned to the deportation strategy. After all, deportation had proven an effective means of sending agricultural strike leaders back to Mexico. Paul Smith later estimated that the shippers spent nearly $6 million in a decade-plus effort to get Harry Bridges deported as a Communist. Their motivation doubled in intensity between 29 October 1936 and 4 February 1937 as, once again, Harry Bridges took his longshoremen out on strike, this time a week and more longer than in 1934. Harry Bridges entered the strike as western director of the newly formed Congress of Industrial Organizations (CIO), an appointment he received personally from John L. Lewis. At the conclusion of the strike, Bridges also became president of the Pacific Coast Division of the International Longshoremen's Association. These two offices, together with his presidency of the San Francisco–based ILWU, rendered Harry Bridges the labor czar of the West Coast.

During the 1936–1937 strike, Bridges was once again reviled by shippers, public officials, and the press as a Communist. These charges were given new life when a rival labor leader, Harry Lundeberg, president of the Sailors Union of the Pacific, broke with Bridges on the issue of Communist influence in the maritime unions and signed a separate agreement with shippers fifty-two days into the strike. Born in Oslo, Norway, and a veteran of the British and Australian merchant service, Lundeberg had arrived, like Bridges, in San Francisco in the early 1920s and had risen in the labor movement. Like Bridges, Lundeberg was devoid of personal corruption. The bolting of the Sailors Union of the Pacific broke the united front, and Bridges and his allies in the Maritime Federation of the Pacific Coast ended the strike in *de facto* defeat.

Like pit bull terriers, the Associated Farmers joined the Get Bridges crusade. Throughout 1936, 1937, and 1938, hardly an issue of the *Associated Farmer* magazine lacked an attack on Bridges as the evil avatar of Communism in the labor movement. Once again, local law enforcement officials and prosecuting attorneys joined the oligarchy and the Associated Farmers in pressing the Communist case. By 1939 Harry Bridges was facing a deportation hearing.

Deportation hearings against Bridges began in the Department of Immigration offices on Angel Island in San Francisco Bay in August 1939 and lasted for nine and a half weeks, for a total of 7,724 pages of transcribed testimony. At the request of Secretary of Labor Frances Perkins, James Landis, dean of the Harvard Law School, sat as special hearing officer. The government brought thirty-two witnesses forward; the defense brought twenty-nine, including president David Barrows of the University of California, who lectured the hearing on Marx, Lenin, and the theory and practice of Communism. Under cross-examination, however, Barrows, who as major general in the Reserve had commanded all troops in San Francisco in the summer of 1934, admitted that the General Strike of 1934 was, from the perspective of accepted Communist tactics, a poor stratagem. Under cross-examination, no government witness could offer any convincing testimony that Harry Bridges was or had ever been a member of the Communist Party.

On the afternoon of 30 December 1939 Harry Bridges learned that Dean Landis had filed a finding acquitting Bridges of any provable charges that he was a member of the Communist Party. While Bridges accepted support from all quarters,

Landis wrote, and employed certain strike strategies also employed by Communists, there was no proof that he was himself a member of the Communist Party. Bridges celebrated with his labor friends in a bar and restaurant on Broadway in North Beach, blissfully unaware that both the oligarchy and its allies among ambitious federal prosecutors had some fifteen years of fight left within them.

The year 1939 opened with the freeing and pardoning of Tom Mooney and closed with the temporary acquittal of Harry Bridges. But it also opened with the collapse from exhaustion of Governor Olson on 7 January at the Sacramento Fair Grounds, another symbol entirely. Rushed to Sutter Hospital, Olson was forced to govern the state through a regency of cabinet officers as he recovered his strength. From the perspective of Olson's ability to quicken in California a local version of the New Deal, the freeing of Mooney and the acquittal of Bridges represented pyrrhic victories. Throughout most of 1939, Ham and Eggs remained an enervating embarrassment and distraction. Even now the Republican attorney general of California, Earl Warren, no friend of either Tom Mooney or the New Deal, was preparing to displace Olson in 1942. The first Democratic governor in California in the twentieth century was destined to last only one term. Not until 1958, with the election of Edmund G. Brown, would there be a Democratic successor. For the time being, and for some time to come, California—despite the vitality of its left-liberal sector—would remain a right-of-center Republican state, governed by a white, middle-class, and largely Protestant majority. It would take another twenty years and more for Democratic liberalism to emerge as an equal force in California politics, and even then victories would be hard fought, closely won, and tenuous.

Only the federal government could successfully bring the New Deal to California. While accepting the national will and largesse in this regard—the bridges, dams, tunnels, and canals of the PWA; the plethora of WPA projects; the various forms of housing and agricultural subsidy and emergency relief—Californians remained resistant to the spirit and intelligence behind the New Deal. This effort at national recovery, after all, exuded the presence and the privilege of the East. Few Californians could be found in the inner circle of President Roosevelt or at the helm of New Deal agencies. While eager for a myth of individualism and self-improvement, Californians seemed incapable, the majority of them, of moving to an expression of such ambitions beyond the instant solution of an old-age pension plan. The affluence and altered attitudes of the 1950s and 1960s would reverse this orientation and make of California, briefly, the very model of the social democratic experiment. But by that time, the population of the state had burgeoned from nine million to twenty-plus million; and most Californians were from somewhere else, where they had absorbed other political traditions.

8

Give Me Shelter

Soup Kitchens, Migrant Camps, and Other Relief Efforts

*A*MONG Culbert Olson's most fervent supporters in the 1938 election was
a new type of Californian: migrants from the South Central states of
Oklahoma, Texas, Missouri, and Arkansas. From the start of his campaign, Olson wooed this constituency, considered by so many Californians to be
the lowest of the low, riffraff, social degenerates, Okies. These migrants wanted
more of the New Deal; for the New Deal, specifically the Farm Security Administration, had already championed their cause. Thanks to the migrant vote, Olson
swept Kern, Madera, and Fresno counties in the San Joaquin Valley; indeed,
Olson was more successful in the upper San Joaquin than he was in his home
constituency of Los Angeles. While Olson would have won the governorship without the migrants, they nevertheless provided him with half of his two-hundred-
thousand plurality over Merriam. Eight years earlier, this constituency of migrants
from the South Central states hardly existed in California. Now it had become
half of the swing vote that aligned California, at least ostensibly, with the New
Deal. In political terms, caring for the migrants had paid off. In moral terms, it
had provided Depression California with some of its best moments.

The Gold Rush, the Boom of the 1880s, the Boom of the 1920s: the population
of California had always grown in spurts. Most recently, the population of the
state had grown by 60 percent between 1920 and 1930, from 3,426,861 to
5,677,251. Approximately 1.8 million of this 2,250,390 increase had come from
migration from other states. Throughout the 1920s "flivvers," or open-air touring
cars, packed with people and piled high with goods, arrived in a steady stream on
Highway 66. A new institution, the auto camp, prototype of the motel, evolved
to serve their needs. By the late 1930s, an estimated 683,000 migrants had arrived
in California, most of them by automobile. In 1931 alone a total of 876,194
automobiles entered the state. Along Highway 66, which led into Southern Cali-

fornia via the American Southwest, a sub-culture of gas stations, diners, auto courts, and roadhouses offering a variety of legal and illegal services was thoroughly in place by the mid-1930s.

Although there were some protests by residents that California was growing too fast, the flivver migrants of the 1920s, however gypsy-like in their mode of arrival, brought their working skills and in many cases their nest eggs to the Golden State. Within a year, they generally found their place in the booming economy of the 1920s. The migration of the 1930s—more than three hundred thousand arriving between 1930 and 1934 alone—was another matter entirely. This human river, as Paul Taylor described it, consisted of the displaced and dispossessed. Later reports would refer to these new Californians as Dust Bowl migrants, perpetuating a phrase first used by Robert Geiger of the Associated Press to describe the catastrophic blizzard of black dust that struck Cimarron County, Oklahoma, on the afternoon of Sunday, 14 April 1935. Long before the dust storms of the mid-1930s, however, forces were in motion that would displace vast portions of the farm population of America, with special displacements caused to the farm folk of Arkansas, Missouri, Texas, and Oklahoma.

Agronomists and economic historians have long since explicated the macroeconomic forces behind the displacement. Agronomists cite a great variance of soils and climate throughout the region, demanding a level of scientific farming beyond the capacity of the population. Too many farmers, they point out, had been settled by the homestead system and by high-pressure land companies on marginal properties. Throughout the boom years of 1916 to 1921, moreover, farmers of the South Central plains tended to over-capitalize their properties. With their lands heavily mortgaged to build homes and purchase modern equipment, too many farmers of the region were living on the margin. Public debt, hence taxes, was also over developed in the region as new states (Oklahoma only came into the Union in 1907) sought to create overnight the necessary public infrastructure. Thus the farmers of the region tended to owe heavy taxes as well as large bank payments. As long as the oil boom held, both the public sector and the mortgaged farmer could be sustained by an economy fueled by gushing wells of Texas and Oklahoma crude. The economy of the 1930s was another matter.

More immediately, the displaced farmers of the South Central region, fleeing west in the 1930s, might use two shorthand terms—tractors and the Dust Bowl—to account for their displacement. Between 1930 and 1937 the sale of tractors in the cotton states—Oklahoma, Texas, and Arkansas especially—increased by 90 percent. In southwestern Texas during this period, the use of tractors increased by 165 percent. Tractors displaced tenant farmers by the tens of thousands as landowners hired one man to operate one tractor at a wage of $1.25 per day to plough and cultivate acreage, whether in wheat or cotton, previously tended by hundreds of tenants and sharecroppers. "Tractored out" was how tenant farmers described their displacement.

Then, beginning in 1934, came the most apparent and fearsome cause of the hegira, drought and the Dust Bowl. Between 1929 and 1933 dry and wet years alternated, but with an increasing factor of dryness. In 1934 disaster struck: widespread drought, which lasted through the decade. In many sections of the region, even weeds were unable to grow for an eight-year period. In the high and level southern portion of the Great Plains, a region which included parts of Colorado, New Mexico, Nebraska, Kansas, Oklahoma, and Texas, the burning sun baked ninety-seven million acres of parched topsoil into finely grained dust. Poor farming practices—the one-way plough, which barely turned over the surface and left behind a layer of unstable, unirrigated soil; the irresponsible destruction of grasslands in a headlong rush to plant vast acreages in wheat and cotton (five million acres plowed and planted between 1925 and 1930 alone)—had prepared the way for the disaster which drought and winds would finish.

Starting in 1932, the winds of the region began to lift the dry dust into the atmosphere. Hundreds of localized dust storms ensued over the next two years. Then, on Black Sunday, 14 April 1935, in Cimarron County, Oklahoma, the big storm struck, blackening out the sun, covering a five-state area with millions of tons of dust. Day became night. Cattle and humans, children especially, were lost in the dust banks. Automobile ignitions went dead. Dust banked up against farm houses and was blown within. In the morning, only the spot on one's pillow where one had laid his or her head the night before remained unsmudged. Dust banks which were in one place on one day were blown away the next, then recreated in another place by capricious winds. Cattle died, and calves succumbed within a day of being dropped. Wheat seeds refused to sprout, and nothing, not even weeds, grew.

Many sections of the Dust Bowl lost up to 40 percent of their population after 1935. Those who headed west to California in their overloaded jalopies came to find work in the crop which, ironically, had helped turn the soil of their region into dust, cotton. Between 1926 and 1937 the cotton acreage of Central California grew from 170,000 to 600,000 acres, making cotton the fourth largest crop in the state. At the same time, the Mexican work force of California, whether voluntarily or involuntarily, was being repatriated to Mexico, and further Mexican migration was severely curtailed. By 1937 nearly 150,000 Mexican field workers had returned to their homeland. Federal and state policy favored this exodus, for Mexican farm workers had comprised the core cadre of resistance in the strikes of 1930–1934. While federal officials might want to reclaim jobs for Americans, California growers breathed a sigh of relief at the departure of the militant Mexican work force. The actors in the drama of farm labor in California in the first half of the 1930s had been Spanish-speaking and brown-skinned. In the second half of the decade, they became white, English-speaking, of the oldest Anglo-American stock. Yet the sufferings they endured in their first years in the Golden State recapitulated, and frequently surpassed, the hardships of their Mexican predecessors. A new racial epithet, Okie, was coined to express the contempt with which many Californians viewed this second wave of agricultural helotry.

In addition to the migrants, who came with their families and had every hope of finding work and residence in California, a large number of males, unemployed and unattached, commonly known as transients, was also arriving. An estimated ten thousand transient men and boys were arriving in Los Angeles County each month by 1931. In one month of 1932 alone, the Southern Pacific evicted an estimated eighty thousand transients from its boxcars.

In the first two and a half years of the Depression, the Hoover years through 1932, communities in Southern California sought to cope with the problem of unemployment and relief as being, primarily, a local matter; indeed, many communities were reluctant to admit that there was a problem at all, seeing in such imagery as public soup kitchens and long lines of unemployed men awaiting a meal or a bed for the night images of social disgrace.

At first, many communities tried to organize relief on a private basis. Santa Barbara, for example, a wealthy resort city, quickly organized a voluntary private program in 1930 under the direction of a Citizens Employment Committee created by the Chamber of Commerce. Funds were solicited from wealthy Santa Barbara and Montecito residents to create employment through public works and park improvement. The Citizens Committee aimed its efforts at Santa Barbara residents, many of them hotel and estate workers laid off when the Depression began to take effect. By October 1931, however, the Salvation Army Men's Center was reporting a year-end total of 2,750 transient men, non–Santa Barbarans, applying for shelter. By April 1932 the Salvation Army had provided a total of 28,594 meals and 9,625 beds to transients. Significantly, the previous optimism regarding the ability of Santa Barbara to cope with the crisis locally and privately began to wane. Fear of the transients also surfaced as reports circulated of radical talk in the shelter. "No Political Argument Permitted" and "No Religious Argument Permitted" warned two prominent signs in the Center. This time, another and more hostile citizens' committee was formed, an Emergency Police Force, which assisted Police Chief G. G. Sloan in sweeping the streets, pool halls, and hobo camps free of undesirables, meaning unemployed single men. By May of 1932 the Emergency Unemployment Relief Committee of Santa Barbara, then in the process of disbanding, openly admitted that adequate relief could only come from government.

The City of Los Angeles showed a similarly defensive belief in private solutions. Soup kitchens and other signs of social stress, after all, ran headlong into Los Angeles's booster conception of itself. Although the private sector—downtown missions, the Salvation Army, the Volunteers of America, the YMCA, the YWCA, the Foursquare Gospel Church, and other Christian and Jewish service agencies—did its best to respond to the crisis, municipal government remained reluctant to enter into any wholesale relief effort. "The situation is remarkably good," reported Mayor John Porter in 1931. "I feel sure that the recent rains will bring us out of the slump. The situation is not at all alarming. We do not find it necessary to feed our unemployed men here. In San Francisco I saw free soup kitchens. There are none here. All we have to do is to give our men jobs and the problem is solved."[1]

Brave words, but also futile and self-deceiving. In 1933 the Depression arrived in California in earnest. By June of 1934 some 1,225,000 Californians, out of a population approaching six million, were dependent upon some form of public assistance. More than 465,000 of these were in Los Angeles County alone. These welfare recipients were by and large residents of the state. The more that residents of California were found on the welfare rolls, the more intense grew resentment against transients. It was one thing to help your own. It was quite another thing to turn California into a mecca for people seeking relief.

In May 1933 Congress created the Federal Emergency Relief Administration (FERA), which empowered Roosevelt to spend $500 million in matching funds ($1 federal to every $3 local) in direct community relief. A department of FERA was the Federal Transient Service, keyed to the relief of the transient homeless. The Federal Transient Service soon became one of the busiest federal agencies in California. By April 1935 the agency was handling a peak load of seventy-seven thousand cases a month. By that year, the State of California, with 4.7 percent of the nation's population, had 14 percent of the country's dependent transients.

Not surprisingly, on 17 May 1935, a bill was introduced in the legislature calling for the banning of indigents from California. In September 1935 FERA ordered the liquidation of the Federal Transient Service, which by this point had expended some $9 million in federal money. Now, the Los Angeles Chamber of Commerce made its chilling recommendation that a hard-labor concentration camp for vagrants be established to cope with unemployed transients already in the county and discourage others from coming. Shortly thereafter, in February 1936, LAPD Chief Davis dispatched his men to seal off the borders of the state against Los Angeles–bound transients.

In Los Angeles and other California cities, police departments had long since become reluctant relief agencies. In Fresno the police department opened a thirty-bed shelter for male transients in 1935 on the outskirts of town, partly intended to keep transients out of the city. The Fresno police demanded two hours of work for every meal and restricted stays to one night. The Los Angeles Police Department, meanwhile, found itself overwhelmed by transients during this same period. Since the LAPD was, after all, a police department and not a welfare agency, it chose to process adult male transients through the usual police procedures, which is to say, they were booked, fingerprinted, and routinely given thirty days for vagrancy, with the expectation that they would be released and encouraged to move out of the area within the first week of their sentence. Female transients, however—up to fifty to seventy-five a week between December 1935 and January 1936—were lodged in the Lincoln Heights jail without being fingerprinted or booked. The majority of such female transients had personally requested lodging at the jail. Approximately 8 percent of the unattached transients thus processed in fiscal year 1934–1935 were under the age of sixteen and were sent to the juvenile detention center, where some effort was made to link them with relief agencies. Sadly, thirty-three unattached transient girls under the age of sixteen filtered through the system that year as well.

For three months in 1936, Herbert McCanlies, a social worker for the California State Relief Administration, went underground as a transient, keeping a minute and precise journal that chronicled what it was like to be down and out in California in the Depression. The State Relief Administration released a typescript version of McCanlies's "Journal of a Transient" as part of a larger typewritten report entitled "Transients in California." Gripping in its evocation of transient life—with its prime directive "No work, no relief, keep moving!"—McCanlies's journal is especially evocative of life as a guest of the Los Angeles police.

Apprehended in the railroad yard by two plainclothes men, McCanlies was arrested and taken to the Lincoln Heights jail, where eighteen men and a boy of thirteen awaited processing. The boy was sent off to the juvenile center while McCanlies was fingerprinted and booked. During the fingerprinting, the hands of an elderly man in the group began to shake uncontrollably. "The officer swore and raged at him," McCanlies noted, "and by the time he got through the old man was almost in tears. He made a pitiful picture, small, stooped, and gray, standing there in his dirty, ragged clothes beside the big, robust officer in his uniform. As he tried to obey the cop's sharp orders, he became more and more confused and nervous; his ragged knees shook, and there was panic and stark fear in his old blue eyes. I found myself gritting my teeth before the ordeal was over, and several of the other men mumbled subdued oaths at the cop. When we were taken into the mess room for our lunch of brown beans, dry bread and coffee, the old man ate as if he were starving and stuffed five slices of bread after the beans and coffee were all gone."[2]

Following lunch, McCanlies was held with seventeen others in tank number twelve, directly across another tank holding between fifteen and twenty other vagrants. Eleven of the men were black. One was Mexican. No one had been arrested for any crime other than being broke and hungry. Informing an officer of his true identity, McCanlies persuaded him to call the Relief Administration to corroborate. Released from the Lincoln Heights jail, he headed north to gather information on a large hobo jungle outside Oakland.

En route, McCanlies might very well have passed through one of the many migrant camps which now dotted the San Joaquin and Sacramento valleys. While unattached male transients might be briefly jailed, then run out of cities, migrants from the Dust Bowl had come as families, in many cases as clans, and were determined to stay. City police forces such as the LAPD might be capable of sweeping the streets free of undesirable transients; but out in the countryside where the migrants were camped, no single authority—with the exception of mass-mobilized and deputized vigilantes—was available to clear the countryside. And besides: the migrants were necessary, now that the Mexican work force had departed.

The sudden arrival of more than three hundred thousand migrants within a few years, most of them settling in the Central Valley, created a disaster in housing and health. Established in 1921, the State Commission of Immigration and Housing was intended to enforce housing and health care standards among migrant workers. Suspicious of the Commission staff, whom they believed to be troublesomely pro-labor, Governors Rolph and Merriam had severely axed the Commission budget. By 1933, in the midst of the first phase of mass migration, the Commission of Immigration and Housing for the entire State of California had a total staff of eleven, with only four employees in the field as camp inspectors. No wonder, then, that scenes of incredible squalor and suffering soon pervaded the California countryside.

Migrants tended to concentrate in four types of clusters: private labor camps, auto and trailer camps, shacktowns, ditch-bank or roadside squatter camps. Unregulated, uninspected, private labor camps consisted in the main of one-room frame cabins in various stages of dilapidation or tents with or without wooden floors or chicken sheds, pump houses, barns, or other service buildings reconverted to dormitory use. Located on roadsides, auto and trailer camps initially offered better accommodations but were soon rendered equally unsanitary by overcrowding. In the case of the shacktowns, popularly known as Hoovervilles or Little Oklahomas, the migrants themselves erected cabins, tents, or other forms of housing on land which had been subdivided by local farmers. The Little Oklahoma outside Modesto, for example, was first subdivided in 1935, with lots selling at an average of $125, with terms set at $10 down and $5 a month. By the summer of 1938 more than two hundred families, approximately one thousand people, lived in this Little Oklahoma. Many of these shacktowns, such as the Little Oklahoma outside Modesto, eventually made the transition from a haphazard collection of tents, trailers, packing boxes, cardboard, tar paper, and gunny sacks to rows of whitewashed frame houses; but such transitions took years, and in the meanwhile most of these shacktowns, like squatters' settlements everywhere, were strewn with garbage piles and polluted by human waste. The stench was terrible, and flies were everywhere. In terms of health and sanitation, the camps hastily thrown up on roadsides or in ditch banks were the filthiest. Periodically, local health officials, assisted by sheriff's deputies, would order migrants to move on and would then burn such camps to the ground.

The plight of migrant children made the strongest impression on local educators and health officials. Debilitated by poverty and poor nutrition (a steady diet of beans, rice, and fried dough, with next to no milk and rarely fruits or vegetables), an estimated 27 percent of all migrant children suffered from some form of malnutrition. During the cotton strike of 1933, nine migrant children died from malnutrition or related diseases. Other children never made it as far as California. Etta Pitchford, for example, aged thirty-nine and suffering from tuberculosis left Antlers, Oklahoma, with her three children and got as far as New Mexico. Broke, denied relief, too proud to beg, Pitchford gathered some weeds and boiled them to feed her children. She, her ten-year-old son Hanley, and her eight-year-old daughter Eliza suffered food poisoning and died. Only her daughter Ova Belle, aged twelve, survived.

While many children thus died from accidents or sickness, others were rescued through the intervention of local public health officials. Public health nurse Eva Barnes visited a migrant camp in Kern County in 1932. In one cabin she found a small girl lying on an old quilt in one corner of the room. Removing a soiled white blanket, she saw that the child's entire right hip was covered with a third-degree burn. Four days earlier, the child's clothing had caught fire while she was putting wood into a stove. Her infected and festering hip had been smeared in salve and covered with a sheet of paper. Trudging out to the cotton fields, Barnes found the little girl's father, who told her that he had eight other children and could not afford a doctor. Barnes arranged for the child to be brought into town and treated. In another cabin, she found a boy of ten wrapped in blankets and an overcoat, suffering from acute tonsillitis. Barnes returned later that evening with the county health officer. The physician reexamined the boy and told the parents he would not live unless he were rushed to the hospital. Laying the boy out in the back seat of his Ford, the public health doctor drove him fifty miles to the county hospital and saved his life.

Yet how could even the well-intentioned ever hope to manage to cope with the crisis among migrant children? Despite so many efforts, it got worse—and worse. Between July 1936 and June 1937, the State Bureau of Child Hygiene surveyed a thousand migratory children in the San Joaquin Valley counties of Fresno, Kern, Tulare, Madera, and Kings. Eight hundred and thirty-one migrant children, the Bureau discovered, were suffering a total of 1,369 ailments, most of them due to malnutrition and bad hygiene. Rickets, poor muscle tone, apathy, abnormal tonsils and adenoids, respiratory infections, carious and decalcified teeth, diarrhea: the Bureau found a pediatric nightmare.

Principals and teachers in the counties of the San Joaquin Valley made a significant effort to persuade migrant children to attend local public schools. In Bakersfield, Kern County, in 1935, public school teachers pooled their own private donations to provide migrant children food at lunch time. While generally anxious to have their children educated, migrant parents frequently needed them in the fields as workers. Tired, hungry, chronically malnourished, ill-clothed, barefoot, and unwashed, migrant children made difficult pupils. Nearly all of them felt ashamed of their appearance in contrast to the other children, who were frequently cruel to their unkempt classmates. Rarely could migrant children finish a year or even a semester. Records from public schools in the Bakersfield area show that 48.6 percent of all schoolchildren transferred schools one or more times in 1935.

As a direct result of all this—their poverty, their squalid living conditions, their gaunt and unkempt appearance, their listlessness borne of malnutrition and chronic fatigue, their sheer presence as an alien, threatening migration, even their drawls and their religious practices (snake handling, rolling on the ground, speaking in tongues)—Dust Bowl migrants experienced a process of social debasement. Although they were white Anglo-Americans, they were regarded as a despised racial minority, Okies, Arkies, Texies, by much of white California. The same denigrating charges leveled against blacks, Mexicans, and Filipinos—laziness, shiftlessness, promiscuity, including incest, a predilection for squalor—were now lodged against the white migrants. In open testimony before a government agency, Dr. Lee Stone, public health officer of Madera County, attacked the migrants as lazy social degenerates. "If you came down to me," Dr. Stone opined, "I would say, sterilize the whole bunch of them."[3]

Fortunately, the migrants had their defenders, including Simon Julius Lubin, one of the most active reformers of the Progressive Era, then in his late fifties. As an employer in the private sector, Lubin pioneered such amenities as a medical plan, a pension program, and a credit union. Serving on a federal committee investigating the 1934 Imperial Valley cotton strike, Lubin returned from the field an outspoken champion of migrant rights. On 23 March 1934 he took his advocacy to the Commonwealth Club of California, a prestigious town hall forum in San Francisco whose proceedings were broadcast live over radio station KPO. In his speech Lubin made the most stirring defense of farm labor prior to the published efforts of Carey McWilliams and John Steinbeck in 1939. Entitling his address "Can the Radicals Capture the Farms of California?" Lubin sarcastically suggested that the radicals would have no use for the farms of California since they were in such a mess.

No photographs and no words could do justice to the squalor of the camps. In its treatment of migrants, California was in the process of dismantling Progressive regulations and programs put into effect in the aftermath of Wheatland. Desperately, in the very same year in which the Associated Farmers was being organized, Lubin was arguing for a reaffirmation and revitalization of the Progressive agenda: a renewed Commission of Immigration and Housing, a judicial commission to insure fair courts on the local level, a commission to help small family farmers obtain land, a commission charged with promoting the exportation of California produce to undeveloped markets in Asia and the rest of the Americas. Speaking for himself, Lubin concluded, he had little to fear from radicals or agitators. "But there is genuine ground for fear—great fear—in the greed and selfishness, the intellectual sterility, the social injustice, the economic blindness, the lack of political sagacity and leadership and the mock heroics and hooliganism we observe within our State today."[4]

Lubin's wife later claimed that the ordeal of seeing all that he had worked for, his entire Progressive agenda, collapse, drove Lubin to an early death. By 1936, in any event, at age sixty, the first great champion of the migrants was gone. After his death, a group of social activists—Hollywood actor Chester Conklin, Los Angeles writer Carey McWilliams, Los Angeles politician Samuel Yorty, San Francisco *News* columnist John Barry, Father Charles Phillips of Oakland, philanthropist Helen Hosmer—joined to found the Simon J. Lubin Society of California to carry on his work. Headquartered in the Phelan Building in San Francisco, the Lubin Society functioned as the watchdog and antidote to the propaganda efforts of the Associated Farmers. Its magazine, the *Rural Observer*, countered the *California Farmer* of the Associated Farmers. The Society also issued a series of pamphlets on agriculture and migrant labor, including two very powerful publications: *Their Blood Is Strong* (1938), a collection of reports from the field by novelist John Steinbeck, initially appearing in the San Francisco *News*; and Edith Lowry's *Migrants of the Crops, They Starve That We May Eat* (1938). During the election of 1938, the Lubin Society issued a pamphlet attack on the Associated Farmers which was distributed in a hundred thousand copies. Carey McWilliams believed this pamphlet played a critical role in electing Olson.

While the Lubin Society was capable of focusing attention on the plight of the migrants, no private organization could be expected to cope with the thousands of displaced families in the fields. Only government possessed such resources. Throughout the 1930s, as the New Deal expanded its scope, government, state and federal, progressively entered the field of migrant housing and health. In mid-1933 the California State Relief Administration was established as a state agency under provisions of the Federal Emergency Relief Administration. The California State Relief Administration, in turn, established a Rural Rehabilitation Division, the counterpart of the federal Rural Rehabilitation Division operating under FERA, to deal with the housing and health crisis in the fields. In 1935 Roosevelt consolidated the agricultural and farm labor programs of FERA, the Agricultural Adjustment Administration, and the Department of the Interior into one new super-agency, the Resettlement Administration, under the leadership of Rexford Guy Tugwell, an economics professor from Columbia University, who had previously been serving as assistant secretary of agriculture under Henry Wallace. In July 1935 the Resettlement Administration assumed control of the Rural Rehabilitation Division of the California State Emergency Relief Administration.

For two years, between 1935 and 1937, Tugwell and the Resettlement Administration pursued an aggressive agenda that included not just measures of emergency relief but an ambitious program of flood control, reforestation, loans for land and equipment, and, most controversial, resettlement efforts aimed at placing more tenant farmers on their own properties. In 1937 Tugwell resigned under fire, and Roosevelt transferred the programs of the Resettlement Administration to the newly created Farm Security Administration (FSA), headed by Will Winton Alexander, a Missouri-born Methodist minister, educator, and tenants' rights activist who had served as Tugwell's deputy. If anything, the Farm Security Administration under Alexander was even more radical in its ambitions. Under Alexander, the Farm Security Administration sought nothing less than the establishment of a new rural social order based on individual farm ownership and the elimination of farm tenancy, sharecropping, and migratory labor. Not surprisingly, vested interests cried Communist, and the Farm Security Administration was disbanded in 1942.

To recapitulate: the Rural Rehabilitation Division of the California State Emergency Relief Administration held jurisdiction from 1933 to 1935. The Resettlement Administration held jurisdiction from 1935 to 1937. The Farm Security Administration held jurisdiction from 1937 to 1942. The first two years of state control, however, saw few results. Only the growing involvement of the federal government resulted in any discernible breakthroughs in migrant housing and health care, and even the federal response, given the enormity of the situation, was inadequate. In the long run, it would take the Second World War to end the migrant crisis.

In the meanwhile, much of what was accomplished came directly through the efforts of Paul Taylor, a professor of labor economics at the University of California. Taylor played a key role in alerting state and federal officials regarding the dimensions of the crisis, and he helped establish the first of the migrant camps. Throughout the 1930s, in fact, the energetic, inexhaustible Taylor functioned as a churning documentary engine producing facts and statistics regarding the catastrophe and, more important, along with his wife the photographer Dorothea Lange, helping state and federal officials personally experience what Taylor described as the human erosion, the cracked and sunbaked lives, which the Dust Bowl had wrought.

Like Simon Julius Lubin, Paul Taylor was a Progressive turned New Dealer. Born in 1895 in Sioux City, Iowa, into prosperous middle-class circumstances— his mother a schoolteacher, his father an attorney prominent in Republican circles—Taylor absorbed a strong dose of Progressivism at the family hearth. Later, at the University of Wisconsin, another Progressive enclave, Taylor studied law and economics under the reform social scientist E. A. Ross, whom Mrs. Stanford had previously fired from her university for advocating the municipal ownership of urban railways. In 1917 Taylor won a commission in the Marine Corps, saw combat in France, and was gassed at Belleau Wood. Leaving the Marines in 1919 as a captain, Taylor traveled to the University of California at Berkeley to do graduate work in economics after his physician recommended against Columbia, where the harsh New York climate would be too much for his recuperating lungs. Taylor was supposed to stay at Berkeley for a year. He remained there for the rest of his career and an equally busy twenty-year retirement.

As a combat Marine in the trenches, Taylor kept notes of his experiences, which he later expanded into a detailed narrative. This practice of turning direct observation into rapid field notes for later expansion remained with Taylor for a lifetime. Like his predecessors Walter Wyckoff of Princeton and Carleton Parker of Berkeley, and like the contemporary writers Robert Coles and Studs Terkel, Paul Taylor had to get out on the ground, see the places, hear the voices, get the story, and, most important, let the people speak before he drew conclusions. To prepare himself for his Ph.D. thesis, a history of the Sailors Union of the Pacific, Taylor went to work on the San Francisco docks. He also developed the technique of gathering as much on-site material as possible—handbills, posters, clips from local newspapers, and any and all other sorts of printed ephemera—for later use as sources and corroborating quotations. By 1970 Taylor's office at 380 Barrows Hall on the Berkeley campus would be lined with fifty-two volumes of his collected books, papers, articles, and reports. Taylor's graduate student and field assistant Clark Kerr, later president of UC, described his mentor as an economic anthropologist with an interest in labor problems. "Paul was always out there," Kerr remembered, "finding out what was really happening while others played around with their theoretical models and ran their regression analyses."[5]

Aided by grants from the Social Science Research Council, Taylor spent the years 1927, 1928, and 1929 on leave from Berkeley, crisscrossing the United States in his beat-up Dodge, studying the society and culture of Mexican migration. To prepare for this project, Taylor took a crash course in Spanish and studied Mexican history and culture under the guidance of Berkeley historians Herbert Bolton and Herbert Priestley. *Mexican Labor in the United States*, the resulting three-volume study published in 1931 by the University of California, is a panoramic study of life among Mexican migrants in California, Colorado, Texas, Illinois, Michigan, and Pennsylvania. Compassionate, humanistic, filled with facts, statistics, descriptions, and quotations; blending social scientific and statistical description with on-the-ground observations giving the taste, touch, and feel of everyday experience, *Mexican Labor in the United States* equals the best of Wyckoff or Parker as social science and has, indeed, more than a passing resemblence to the novels of Taylor's contemporary John Dos Passos. University of Southern California historian Manuel Servin later claimed that Taylor's report was the first and best place to begin Mexican-American studies.

In 1933, with the outbreak of the cotton strike, Taylor returned to the field in the company of Clark Kerr. Once again, Taylor omnivorously assembled the documentary materials of this largest and most successful agricultural strike in the history of the United States. The resulting "Documentary History of the Strike of the Cotton Pickers" for which Taylor assigned Clark Kerr equal credit, remained in manuscript until 1984. It served, however, as an arsenal for the innumerable essays and reports Taylor was publishing at this time in the *Monthly Labor Review* and *Survey Graphic*, an illustrated monthly intended to supplement the journal *Survey* as a venue for social research. The "Documentary History of the Strike of the Cotton Pickers" also served as an arsenal of reference for the La Follette Committee in 1939. When a mob in Santa Rosa tarred and feathered two migrants as suspected Communists, Taylor put news clippings of the event into a report he sent on to Washington to give federal regulators a better feel for the tension and violence in rural California.

By the mid-thirties Paul Taylor had emerged as the leading expert on the economic and social crisis created by the Dust Bowl migration. Many of Taylor's colleagues at Berkeley resented his productivity and notoriety. They criticized him for his prolonged absences from the classroom while on research grants, and they chided him for his reluctance to involve himself in what they believed to be the theoretical center of labor economics, workmen's compensation. Others criticized the use of the UC publication budget to publish extensive interviews with obscure Mexican workers. While granted tenure, Taylor nevertheless spent nine years as an associate professor, a record he held for years in his department.

In 1934 the Division of Rural Rehabilitation of the California State Emergency Relief Administration retained Taylor to research and write an official assessment of the distress among migrants in the field. Taylor held the title of field director and had the assistance of two Berkeley graduate students, Ed Rowell and Tom Vasey, and Bay Area photographer Dorothea Lange, whom he would shortly marry. Lange was officially listed as the team's typist. Taylor later transferred his team to the Resettlement Administration, where he held the title of labor advisor. In June 1936 he made yet another shift, this time to the Research Division of the Social Security Board, where he served as a consultant from 1935 to 1941.

The collaboration between Paul Taylor and Dorothea Lange resulted in a Depression classic, *American Exodus* (1939). For the time being, Taylor and Lange, in addition to their growing personal relationship, had more immediate goals in mind: the establishment of a network of federally supported migrant labor camps. While in Nipomo in San Luis Obispo County in 1935, Lange took photographs of several hundred families stranded there when rain ruined the pea harvest. Shortly thereafter, Taylor displayed Lange's photos when he spoke before the Commonwealth Club in San Francisco on 13 September 1935, describing to his audience the squalor and suffering at Nipomo and elsewhere in the field. Taylor also included Lange's photographs in the extensive report he filed with Rexford Tugwell in Washington. Tugwell circulated the Taylor-Lange report through top circles in Washington in an effort to justify his efforts for an expanded role for the Resettlement Administration.

Already, Taylor had set in motion a process that would result in the first federal camps at Marysville in Yuba County and at Arvin in Kern. In May of 1935 Taylor and Lange took Lowry Nelson and his wife for a tour of migrant camps, with special attention paid to entrance points to the Imperial Valley at Yuma, Arizona. A professor of rural sociology at Brigham Young University, Nelson was serving as regional representative for the Rural Rehabilitation Division of FERA for Utah, California, Nevada, and Arizona. Lowry returned from the trip convinced that the federal government had to get into the business of migrant camps. Finding a disallocated $20,000 in his budget for a canceled project, Nelson wired Washington for permission to use the money to build two camps. He received approval.

Only in such a highly personal, even haphazard way could such a significant federal program as this be initiated. Had Washington announced such a program in advance, the Associated Farmers and their allies would have easily been able to out-maneuver the proposal when it came through the California legislature for matching funds. In a manner locally suggestive of the larger New Deal, two college professors, Taylor and Nelson, were performing end-runs around the opposition.

In July 1935 construction began on the Marysville camp. Designed by Resettlement architects Garrett Eckbo and Vernon de Mars, the Marysville camp provided facilities for 230 families: one-room frame cabins or tent platforms, a communal cooking shed, a sanitary building containing toilets, showers, and laundry tubs, a sewing room, a first aid dispensary, and a children's nursery. Rexford Tugwell himself came out from Washington for the dedication on 12 October 1935. "Well, it works," Tugwell told Taylor at the Marysville train station.[6] Work was already underway on a second camp at Arvin.

Paul Taylor envisioned a network of twenty-five camps across the Western United States. By 1939 the Farm Security Administration was running ten migrant camps in California alone. By this time, cement floors for cabins and tents had appeared, together with running water. Each camp enjoyed a clinic staffed by a resident nurse, a recreation hall, a camp school (or else busing was provided to local public schools), a library, an amphitheater for meetings and movies, and in many cases a baseball diamond. The Farm Security Administration also developed mobile camps in which portable tent platforms were moved by truck, which also pulled along a mobile shower bath trailer and laundry unit. Beginning in 1937 at Arvin, the Farm Security Administration also got into the home-building business, constructing twenty-three homes with plumbing and electric lights, which it rented to migrants at $8.20 per month, including utilities. By 1940 more than five hundred such homes were available. All in all, approximately 45,000 migrants were living in the federal camps or renting federal housing. By the close of fiscal year 1941 the Farm Security Administration was maintaining thirteen permanent and six mobile camps in California.

Even then, the crisis continued. As ambitious as the federal program was, it reached little more than a fifth of the migrants. But the quality of life in these camps made a powerful statement. The sight of orderly, clean, self-respecting migrants, their children washed and scrubbed and fed and going to school, offered a necessary counter-image against the charge that the Dust Bowlers were of degenerate stock. In John Steinbeck's *The Grapes of Wrath*, the Joad family arrives at one such camp, Weedpatch Camp, run by the federal government. Steinbeck devotes a lengthy chapter (chapter 22, fifty-four pages long), to a description of Weedpatch as a utopia of sanitation, dignity, and self-governance through elected committees amidst the distopian squalors of migrant life. Here the Joads discover not only toilets, showers, tent cabins laid out in neat rows, Saturday night dances, but their self-respect as well. Under the benevolent encouragement of Jim Rawley, the camp manager, the migrants conduct their own affairs, including the decision to accept or reject work, free from the intimidations of an association run by growers.

Steinbeck's account was based upon his field investigations of one of the two federally sponsored camps which Paul Taylor helped to initiate in late 1935. Initially called the Kern Camp, later the Arvin Camp, this Resettlement Administration facility (later transferred to the jurisdiction of the Farm Security Administration) was located outside the city of Bakersfield in Kern County in the southern San Joaquin Valley. Arvin Camp was run with compassionate exactitude by its manager, Thomas Collins, who reported to Paul Taylor's University of Wisconsin classmate, Irving Wood, at the headquarters of the Rural Division of the Resettlement Administration in Berkeley. Collins had studied for the Roman Catholic priesthood before turning to social work. Under Collins's administration, Arvin Camp became a model of what the federal government could do to help the migrants in their transition to employment and self-dignity. Visitors such as Steinbeck, Carey McWilliams, Dorothea Lange, and no less than the Secretary of Agriculture himself, Henry Wallace, visited Arvin Camp during Collins's administration, from December 1935 to February 1937, and came away convinced that for a mere pittance (after all, Arvin Camp cost little more than $20,000 to construct and put into operation) the federal government could make gratifying inroads into the migrant problem.

During this period, Thomas Collins filed weekly reports to Irving Wood, and Wood in turn kept in contact with Collins and his other camp managers through frequent memos. These letters, memos, and reports emanate a New Deal idealism, a social democratic decency, in glaring contrast to the paranoid, accusatory publications and correspondence of the Associated Farmers and allied groups. Reading them, one can almost hear Woody Guthrie, Pete Seeger, or Ramblin' Jack Elliott singing in the background. "Many of the campers had their own musical instruments," Collins reported. "With these, we developed a camp orchestra of eleven stringed instruments. This made possible evening concerts, bi-weekly dances, and community sings. We also made available horse shoes, cribbage, chess and checker boards, volleyball and soft baseball. There was something interesting every evening and every Sunday." The dances, Collins reported, were immensely popular, and by April 1936 they were attracting up to 250 visitors from outside the Arvin camp. No violent incidents were reported. Fortunately, the ultra-religious did not oppose the dances nor the other entertainment programs. "In fact," Collins noted of the Full Gospelers (Holy Rollers) and Free Methodists, "they were the best dancers in the camp."

On Sunday afternoons, the community gathered for amateur entertainment: skits by the children, tap dancing, humorous monologues and dialogues, the singing of duets, quartets, folk songs, and religious music. On weeknights, Collins would tell or read stories to the children around a campfire or organize an impromptu songfest. Wonderfully, the migrants taught Collins their songs, some of which, he reported, went back to the Elizabethan era. In his weekly reports to Wood, Collins would occasionally toss in the lyrics of old ballads and folk songs he had heard, together with new lyrics the migrants were composing regarding their current experiences in California (such as the rousing hymn written for the Pentecostal Gospel Mission Old Time Revival held at nearby Shafter, "There Is No Depression in Heaven"). In later years Bakersfield would emerge as one of the country-and-western music capitals of the nation, a secondary Nashville.

Collins also organized baseball games for the children late in the day after work or on weekends. Like the Saturday night dances, these weekend baseball games soon became popular attractions. "A big crowd was on hand for the game," Collins reported on 28 March 1935. "Spectators were most farmers and their families and farm laborers. A touch of the old west was added to the gathering when cow hands and farm laborers from the mountain ranges and isolated ranches arrived at camp via horse." He also established a library, which soon grew to two hundred volumes, and a recreation room, where cards and checkers were available.

With Collins's advice, a mothers' committee organized a day care center where parents could leave their children when working in the fields. Calling itself the Good Neighbors or the Women's Club, this committee also sponsored an ambitious outreach program which included health education and instruction in proper cooking and diet and gave individual counseling for families experiencing domestic difficulties. The photographs which Collins sent along with his reports show an increasingly clean and prosperous-appearing clientele: the men in work clothes, the women in washed print dresses, the children neat and clean in their bib overalls. Obviously, the health and sanitation program of the camp was beginning to take effect. One boy needed three showers, Collins reported, to remove totally a long accumulation of dirt. A better diet was also showing its effects. Economic necessity, Collins reported approvingly on 7 March 1936, was turning the migrants away from sow belly and fat-fried dough to the fresh fruits and vegetables available in the area.

Migrants had initially stayed away from the camp because they feared mandatory vaccinations. Fortunately, representatives of the State Department of Public Health were able to persuade them otherwise. Between July 1936 and the end of 1939, the Department of Public Health provided a total of 19,991 smallpox vaccinations, 61,546 injections of typhoid serum, and 3,058 injections of diphtheria serum. The Bureau of Child Hygiene of the Public Health Department also launched a program of child-care demonstrations for migratory mothers and their children. The Department fielded three (by 1939) station wagons equipped as dental clinics which moved from camp to camp. The Planned Parenthood Federation sent a nurse, Mildred Delp, into the field charged with the heroic task of dispensing birth control advice out of a mobile van to migratory mothers accustomed to marrying between fourteen and seventeen and having a child a year into their thirties. Migrant women even had a term, "all frailed out," to describe the debilitating effects of these multiple pregnancies.

Irving Wood directed camp managers to encourage self-governance through committees. During the tenure of Tom Collins at Arvin Camp, committees and sub-committees presided over such matters as fire and safety, recreation, the children's playground, and child welfare. Committee and sub-committee minutes on file include the discussion of such questions as: Who is responsible for the music for this Saturday night's dance? Are the toilets being cleaned with disinfectant twice a day? Are the fire hoses being used for any other purpose? The minutes give further insight into camp life: No cigarette butts should be thrown on the floor of the sanitary units, nor should children swing on the shower nozzles. All wood should be piled neatly behind the tents. All tools should be returned to the camp manager the same day that they are borrowed. Certain books are missing from the library. New jerseys are available for the camp softball team and will be distributed by the camp manager. The Woman's Club has agreed to prepare candy baskets for Easter.[7]

The self-governing aspects of the federal camps, and the refusal of camp managers to function as labor contractors provoked the ire of the Associated Farmers and allied groups, who saw the federal camps as a dangerous source of independence for the migrant workers fortunate enough to find room in these facilities. Some growers advanced a compromise: private labor camps built with federal assistance; but the idea was resisted by Farm Security Administration officials.

By this time, in any event, from 1937 onwards, the matter had become moot; for migration had increased its tempo and continued unabated for the rest of the decade. Only a negligible percentage of migrants would ever find haven in a federal camp.

Between July 1935 and January 1940 another 352,000 migrants entered California, adding their number to the estimated 300,000-plus migrants already in the state. Fifty-two percent of the migrants entering between 1935 and 1939 came from Oklahoma, Texas, Arkansas, Missouri, and Kansas, with Oklahoma in the lead. Seventeen percent settled in six adjacent San Joaquin and Sacramento Valley counties. Fifteen percent settled in Los Angeles County, still the leading agricultural county in the state. The remaining migrants settled throughout the rest of California. The southern San Joaquin counties, Kern County especially, absorbed 37 percent of this in-migration. Some districts in this region doubled in population between 1935 and 1940.

Against such a renewed onslaught of migrants, the programs of the federal camps, however animated by the idealism of young New Dealers, could offer only a statistically negligible response. Soon, very soon, the five counties of the southern San Joaquin Valley found themselves overwhelmed by the situation. Between 1937 and 1939 the number of people receiving state unemployment relief in this region nearly quintupled from 8,975 to 45,391. During the period between 1935 and 1940 in the same area, local taxes increased by 100 percent, as county health, education, and relief officials struggled to cope with the crisis. Between 1935 and

1940, for example, school districts in Kern County reeled under a 300 percent increase in enrollment. During the same period, the adjacent Los Angeles County experienced an 80 percent increase in relief and a local tax increase of 55 percent.

To read descriptions of health and sanitation conditions among migrants by 1937 is to conclude that the example offered by the federal camps had been totally forgotten. The Oakland *Tribune*, in fact, called the migrants "the forgotten men of 1937." "One comes little more than one hundred miles from Los Angeles," wrote a *Tribune* reporter on 23 July 1937, "and feels as if he might be in China living among the coolies."

By 1938 California was finding itself gripped by anti-Okie hysteria. Over the next two years, this hysteria proclaimed an increasingly vitriolic list of grievances and canards. A statewide California Citizens Association, drawing its membership from members and supporters of the Associated Farmers, orchestrated the anti-Okie attack. In this effort, without a doubt the most lurid propaganda campaign of the decade, the California Citizens Association was joined by the State Chamber of Commerce, the Associated Farmers, and other similar groups.

Ironically, the California Citizens Association turned, like the New Deal activists, to the federal government for relief: only in this instance, the Association called upon the federal government to return Dust Bowlers to their home communities. The Association also enjoined federal authorities to spread the word throughout the Dust Bowl that there was no more relief in California. Most important, the Association demanded that the federally sponsored Farm Security Administration stop giving immediate relief in California to migrant families. When federal officials rejected these demands as cruel and unconstitutional, the California Citizens Association stepped up its anti-Okie campaign: a propaganda smear which advanced against these white Anglo-Saxon Protestants long-standing stereotypes previously restricted to despised minorities of color.

The Okies, it was charged, were coming to California strictly to get on relief. The vast majority of them were lazy, shiftless failures in their home state. In California, they were lending their support to such crazy schemes as Ham and Eggs and the Olson for Governor campaign. (The fact that Olson opposed Ham and Eggs seems to have been lost on the Association.) While too uneducated to be actual Communists, the Okies, so the Association claimed, lacked education and were hence vulnerable to manipulation by Communists and other radicals.

Obviously, members of the Association had not been present at the Arvin Camp in February 1936 when, after presenting three one-act plays, the children of the camp lined up on the stage and, facing the flag which flew every day on the premises, repeated the Pledge of Allegiance and sang the National Anthem. The relief charge was also patently false. While some Dust Bowlers were perhaps attracted to the possibilities of getting on federal relief rolls in California, they could do that as well in their home states. In California itself, only those who had been in the state for a year were eligible for even the most minimal levels of local relief. The Dust Bowlers came to California not for relief but for work. The average farm wage in Oklahoma in 1938 was $1.35 a day without housing. In California it was $2.95 a day, with some form of housing included. And besides: by 1938 there was precious little work to be had in the Dust Bowl, and so the decision to migrate west to California in search of employment, not relief, was logical, despite the pain of leaving home behind.

True, California had a golden reputation—but for work, not relief. The prospect of spending long days bent under the scorching California sun picking cotton, vegetables, or fruit—which the Dust Bowlers realistically faced—hardly constituted a self-deluding or self-seeking fantasy. It merely offered a slightly better chance at survival. Once they arrived in California, moreover, Dust Bowlers faced an over-supplied labor market. By 1939 California had a total of 470,000 more unemployed than it had in 1930. Wages were falling to disastrous levels, below the nadir year of 1933, and families, epitomized by the fictional Joads of John Steinbeck's *The Grapes of Wrath* (1939), were forced to travel as much as three thousand miles a year up and down the state in search of work.

In and behind the relief charge lurked something even more vicious: the Tobacco Road canard one might call it, in reference to Erskine Caldwell's novel and play. *Tobacco Road* (1932) and its sequel, *God's Little Acre* (1933), reinforced a stereotype that one can find operative as early as William Byrd's early eighteenth-century *History of the Dividing Line* and as recently as James Dickey's *Deliverance* (1970): that of the vacant-eyed, slack-jawed, sexually degenerate, sub-human white trash. Even efforts to sympathize with the migrants frequently fell prey to the *Tobacco Road* stereotype. The *Saturday Evening Post* for 12 November 1938, for example, ran a sympathetic series of colored photographs of California migrants, including one of a mother and her three children, clean and dignified and self-respecting beneath their canvas tent, and a migrant woman tending a bed of flowers outside her newly acquired cottage in a Little Oklahoma. The text, however, makes reference to the photographer's visit, not to the spic-and-span sights illustrated in the photographs, but to another scene entirely: a brush-covered lean-to surrounded by several broken chairs, a kitchen table covered with dirty plates and flies, an open truck parked nearby, and, lying on a mattress on the ground, a young man in faded blue overalls. "A hat is pulled down over his eyes, a cigarette hangs from his lips. He is languidly strumming a guitar. Around him are grouped four children, ranging in age from five to fifteen. They are slovenly, truculent, suspicious of everyone. In the vacant eyes, the slack jaws of the youngsters, you sense the sinister heritage they are bringing from their mountain home."[8]

The implications of the scene are obvious, and they were made even more explicit in an article published around the same time in *California*, the journal of the State Chamber of Commerce, an article which historian Walter Stein justifiably considers the low point of the anti-Okie campaign. "'Tobacco Road has come to California,' a dozen different men said to me up and down the Valley," runs the report. "I thought the play, with all its poverty and filth, was a gross exaggeration—until the same kind of folks landed here on. . . . There is so much unmorality among them—not immorality; they just don't know any better. There was a father who was arrested for outraging his daughter. His whole family appeared in court to defend him, and when he was sent to jail his wife said, 'They oughtn't to send Paw to jail for that. She's his own property and he can do what he pleases with her.' "[9]

Such selective depictions mocked the efforts of Paul Taylor, Irving Wood, Thomas Collins, and the others. Unfortunately, because such lurid scenes spoke to the all-pervasive Tobacco Road canard, they succeeded in degrading an entire people. Thus the power of John Steinbeck's *The Grapes of Wrath*, with its depiction of the Joads as archetypal Americans, loyal, dignified, enduring; but, it must be admitted, thus as well the furor caused by Steinbeck's final scene in which the young nursing mother Rose of Sharon offers her breast to a starving old man in a railroad boxcar. Was this not, some argued, proof positive of sexual degeneracy among the Okies?

The campaign against migrant relief, meanwhile, continued unabated. In the spring of 1940 the legislature passed an Unemployment Relief Appropriation Act which increased eligibility requirements from one year to three. As an even more draconian coda, migrants entering California after 1 June 1940 would have to live in the state five years before they were eligible. In addition to these restrictions, the total amount of individual relief payments was trimmed by 40 percent. An outraged Governor Olson vetoed the bill, but both the assembly and state senate overrode his veto, and the Emergency Relief Appropriation Act became effective on 23 February 1940.

An even more outraged Carey McWilliams, state commissioner of housing and immigration, traveled east to Washington in a vain effort to get the federal government to assist those migrants being purged from the relief rolls of the State Relief Administration, now that the new eligibility requirements were in effect. McWilliams got nowhere in a Washington whose attention was shifting rapidly from the Depression to international questions of war and peace. Bitterly, McWilliams blasted the Associated Farmers upon his return, charging them with being the organization behind the new law. Unwisely, he also threatened that "hell is going to start popping before long in California unless solutions of the relief and migratory labor problems are found."[10] Even such pro-migrant newspapers as the San Francisco *News* and the *Chronicle* upbraided McWilliams for the implied threat of civil disorder.

On the other hand, awareness was increasing, even among conservatives, that the migrants were not shiftless degenerates, but new Californians, in the state to make their homes, to work and prosper. Even *Westways*, the voice of the Southern California establishment, edited by arch-conservative Phil Townsend Hanna, was capable in June 1939 of running an essay and picture story which praised the migrants for their strength, dignity, and courage and exculpated them from the most heinous charges of the anti-migrant lobby. "These refugees are not downtrodden coolies or peons accustomed to serfdom," ran the text accompanying photographs by Paul Dorsey: text most likely written by Hanna himself. "They are native Americans. Most of them are destitute through no fault of their own. . . . Californians should know the truth of their plight, for only with full knowledge can we strive intelligently to solve this heart-breaking and alarming human problem." [11]

When the State Chamber of Commerce convened a specially appointed Migrant Committee in early 1940, the panel bore no resemblance to the stridently right-wing hanging committees which had characterized the State Chamber through the mid-and late 1930s. While the Committee did include such well-known figures from the right as S. Parker Frisselle, and Dr. George Clements, a virulently anti-migrant economist on the staff of the Los Angeles Chamber of Commerce, it also included such liberal personalities as Paul Smith of the *Chronicle* and Florence Kahn, former congresswoman from San Francisco, together with the presidents of UC, Stanford, the College of the Pacific, and the University of Southern California.

Largely researched and written by Paul Eliel, the Stanford Business School industrial relations expert who had been the chief intelligence officer of the shippers' resistance to the longshoremen in 1934, the Chamber of Commerce report, issued in May 1940, struggled to achieve a balanced position. With the dramatic influence of *The Grapes of Wrath*, the novel and the motion picture, on everyone's mind, the report went out of its way to praise the industry and integrity of the migrant community, implicitly exempting them from the ugly charges being leveled over the previous two years by the California Citizens Association. On the other hand, the report also underscored the crushing burden, on both the state and county level, which the migration of 1.2 million people over the previous decade, 75 percent of them arriving between 1935 and 1940, had placed on Californians.

Without mentioning *The Grapes of Wrath*, the report repudiated the implication of the novel and the film that Californians had met the migrants with closed hands and hard hearts. A barrage of statistics was offered in proof of how the taxpayers of California had come to the support of the migrants, especially in the fields of welfare, public health, and education. Steinbeck's most stinging charge—that California farmers advertised for more migrants than were actually needed so as to drive down labor costs—was refuted. The blame for such advertisements was laid at the door of Arizona cotton growers who had advertised in the Dust Bowl states for more help than they needed. Unable to find work in Arizona, the migrants continued on to California in force.

The report advocated a six-point program, equally divided between liberal and conservative solutions. On the conservative side, the Chamber recommended that federal relief should be increased in the Dust Bowl states so as to stabilize potential migrants. The federal government should help California farmers develop permanent housing for migrants on their properties. Third, the State Employment Service should be reorganized so as to be able better to match the work force with growers' requirements. On the liberal or New Deal side of the spectrum, the report advocated an expansion of Farm Security labor camps and the curtailment of unsound employment and labor practices in Arizona. The report also advocated the support of House Resolution 63, sponsored by Congressmen Alfred Elliott of Tulare and John Tolan of Alameda, calling for a federal investigation into the migrant problem at the national level.

Significantly, both Tolan and Elliott were motivated by exactly that mixture of sympathy and reluctance which now characterized the mainstream attitude of Californians towards the migrants. Congressman Elliott hailed from ground zero of *The Grapes of Wrath*, and Congressman Tolan possessed all the sympathies of a highly developed Roman Catholic social activist. Yet each of them believed that the Farm Security Administration camps in California, however humane and successful, only served to stabilize large populations of migrants in certain parts of California. The FSA camps, they argued, served only the need for housing. It was still up to local government to deal with such issues as health, sanitation, education, crime, and relief; and this was not fair for California in general and for the five southern counties of the San Joaquin Valley in particular. Further more, by their very success, the FSA camps tended to attract more migrants. The federal government should be putting its efforts, Elliott and Tolan argued, into programs aimed at the Dust Bowl states. In March 1940 Tolan and Elliott took their argument to Will Alexander, head of the Farm Security Administration, and the heated encounter almost ended in a fistfight.

Finally, however, the FSA chief agreed to back Tolan and Elliott's resolution calling for a national survey of the migrant problem. As the meeting broke up, Alexander made one last point: the migrants were now permanent Californians. Any proposal to use the federal government to repatriate them to their home states was ridiculous. The hot-headed Alexander had made his most telling point. The Okies were now Californians. Migrant but not migratory, they had come to California like every wave of migration: to seek and find a better life. Displaced, dispossessed, despised, they had nevertheless prevailed. Already by 1940, in Little Oklahomas throughout the southern San Joaquin, a new people, a new type of Californian, had its version of the California Dream. The controversy that surrounded these people arose from the larger controversy of the Depression itself. During the next five years, the war years, twice as many Oklahomans came to California as arrived between 1935 and 1940, but no one took special notice, for willing workers were needed desperately in the shipyards and the airplane and munitions factories of the wartime state.

By this time, Californians had recovered an older antagonist, the Japanese, to replace the Okies as objects of hate and a new people (or rather, a re-recruited people), Mexicans and Mexican-Americans, to do the work of the fields: people such as the Chavez family, most recently from the north Gila Valley in Arizona, father and mother Librado and Juana, daughter Rita, sons Cesar and Ricardo. Losing his Arizona farm because of unpaid taxes, Librado Chavez packed his family into a battered Studebaker in June 1939 and headed toward coastal Southern and Central California in search of harvest work. Mexicans and Mexican-Americans had constituted but a small percentage of Depression-era migrants, but now, with the war, with the soon-to-be-enacted *bracero* program, the complexion of the agricultural work force of California would change rapidly from white to brown; and it would be they, the people of color, led by Librado Chavez's son Cesar and Larry Itilong of the Filipino-dominated Agricultural Workers Organizing Committee, who after long struggle would achieve some measure of justice for the farm workers.By that time, the migrants of the Depression, the Okies, had long since assimilated themselves, or been assimilated, into the complex mosaic called California.

9

Documenting the Crisis

Annus Mirabilis 1939

*I*N addition to its gift of moral uplift, the crusade on behalf of the migrants also produced some stunning documentation and art. The Depression was an era of great documentary art, and nowhere was this more true than in California. In photographs, field reports, government hearings, and documentary fiction, the migrant crisis was put on record and, simultaneously, raised to the level of imaginative expression. The year 1939 alone witnessed the publication of John Steinbeck's *The Grapes of Wrath* in April, Carey McWilliams's *Factories in the Field* in June, and *An American Exodus* by Paul Taylor and Dorothea Lange in October. Throughout 1939 as well, the La Follette Committee held hearings in California, and its proceedings, *Violations of Free Speech and Rights of Labor*, issued the following year, brought the genre of government report to new levels of moral and imaginative intensity. And then in 1941, six volumes strong, appeared the *Hearings Before the Select Committee to Investigate the Interstate Migration of Destitute Citizens, House of Representatives, Seventy-Sixth Congress*, more briefly known as the Tolan Report, which approached the document issued by the La Follette Committee in comprehensive detail, psychological intensity, and moral imagination.

In terms of California, Paul Taylor and Clark Kerr initiated this outpouring of documentary art with their report on the cotton strike of 1933; but it took a photographer, Dorothea Lange—petite, dark-haired, intense, her right leg withered below the knee by childhood polio, fighting a feeling of fatigue for most of her life—to give the era its most enduring icon, *Migrant Mother*, one of the best known photographs in history.

Born of German ancestry in Hoboken, New Jersey, in 1895, Dorothea Nutzhorn suffered two childhood traumas: polio and her father's abandonment of her and her mother, this occurring when she was twelve. Even as an adult, she could never bring herself to talk about it, and in her late teenage years she dropped her father's name in favor of her mother's maiden name Lange. Two former San Franciscans, dancer Isadora Duncan and photographer Arnold Genthe, helped direct her troubled young life. At age thirteen, recently abandoned by her father, Dorothea went alone to the Metropolitan Opera House to see Isadora Duncan dance. She returned again and again, for as long as Duncan was dancing: transformed, enraptured, as she later recalled, the whole thing resembling a religious experience.

After high school, having fixed upon photography as her calling, Lange went to work for the famed Arnold Genthe at Genthe's studios at 562 Fifth Avenue in New York City. Prussian-born, a doctor in classics from the University of Jena, Genthe had spent the years 1895–1911 in San Francisco, where his pre-earthquake photographs of Chinatown and his post-earthquake documentation of San Francisco in ruins had won him an assured place in the history of American photography. From Genthe, Lange absorbed two impulses: pictorialism, with its emphasis upon luminosity and the composed portrait—the photograph as painting, as art; and, in the case of Genthe's San Francisco work, the ability of the camera to document history. In Lange's case, the first aspect of Genthe's influence, his luminous pictorialism, predominated. Lange arrived in San Francisco in May 1918 in the course of what she hoped would be an around-the-world trip. A pickpocket divested Lange of her tickets and cash and changed her plans. Stranded in San Francisco, she secured employment as a photo-developer and within a few years had established her own portrait studio on Sutter Street.

Eclipsed by her later work, Lange's portraits from this period—like novels from the pen of Edith Wharton or Willa Cather—continued to emanate the serenity and well-being of genteel affluence in a privileged American city. Resplendent in her kimono, a young matron, married into a prominent German-Jewish clan, bends lovingly over her child in a curtained nursery, as if the world would ever remain this safe and serene. The Haas brothers, boys in starched white sailor collars, stare serenely into the future assured for them two generations earlier by Levi Strauss. Young women, the next matronly generation of the German-Jewish elite, arrayed serenely in chiaroscuro light, are caught in the exquisite transition between privileged young adulthood and an ensuing forty years of family life, summers in Lake Tahoe, the opera, the symphony, temple charities.

In March 1920 Dorothea Lange, aged twenty-four, married the San Francisco–based painter Maynard Dixon, aged forty-five. Then at a low point in his career, Dixon was supporting himself as an illustrator for the billboard company Foster and Kleiser. Ironically, this billboard experience, together with the covers he was designing for *Sunset* magazine, would prove the making of Dixon as a painter and muralist, introducing into his work a powerful simplicity of line and color; but for the time being, the work seemed a dead end. The couple moved into a one-room emergency earthquake cottage at 1080 Broadway atop Russian Hill.

Lange had doubts about the marriage from the start. There was something cold and detached about Dixon, and when he resumed his painting career he was wont to disappear for long stretches of time into the Southwest. The couple had two sons, who when they were four and seven were placed in a boarding school in San Anselmo so their parents could devote more time to their careers. (Thirty years later, talking to an interviewer at the Bancroft Library, Lange still felt pangs of guilt over doing this: the abandoned daughter abandoning her own offspring.) She and Dixon eventually lived in separate studios, three buildings apart, on the 700 block of Montgomery: and even before this there were other involvements on both their parts.

By 1932 Lange was finding herself overwhelmed by the incongruity between the world of wealth and privilege parading through her studio and the tension she could feel on the streets. Developing a proof at the south window of her studio, she saw an unemployed young man walk forlornly up the street. Coming to the corner, he stopped and stood for the longest time, obviously not knowing what next to do. That image of the young man, transformed by the Depression into a pillar of salt, galvanized Lange's growing determination to get out on the street and in the field and document the calamity. Within months, she had tapped deeply into the other dimension of her talent. Within the year, she had captured two of the most powerful images of economic and social disturbance in Depression San Francisco. Passing a breadline at the White Angel mission, walking haphazardly, without premeditation but with her camera in hand, she caught a lone grizzled man, his tin cup hugged against his threadbare coat, staring blankly away from his fellows, alone, despairing, his eyes fixed indeterminately on a past and identity which the Depression had stolen.

Hearing of a May Day demonstration in the Civic Center, she walked there as well and caught an image of San Francisco police chief William Quinn standing against a background of placards and pickets. Assured, resplendent in blue and gold, almost Napoleonic in his posture, the chief embodied the power of established authority as it struggled to contain the increasing restiveness of the populace. When in the next year violence broke out on the docks of San Francisco, Lange, vacationing at Fallen Leaf Lake near Lake Tahoe, asked herself what in God's name she was doing there amidst the comforts of her previous life and rushed back to photograph the general strike. The result, Workers, Unite!, a young intellectual in rimless glasses addressing an unseen crowd via a microphone, a rolled newspaper in his coat pocket, embodies the tensions of this period, with its intense suggestions of radical incitment to mass action.

In the summer of 1934, at the Group f/64 gallery in Oakland, Paul Taylor first saw Dorothea Lange's photographs of poverty and civil unrest in San Francisco and determined, immediately, that here was the photographer he needed to verify his reports. In February 1935 Lange, carried on the books as a typist for the State Emergency Relief Administration with the salary of $1,560 per year, joined Taylor in the field for the first time, traveling to Nipomo in San Luis Obispo County to document conditions among migrant pea pickers. Maynard Dixon accompanied his wife on this first trip. Dixon was not on hand, however, when Lange and Taylor traveled to the Imperial Valley on their second investigative expedition.

There, in the desert, Taylor and Lange found themselves increasingly attracted to each other. Sensing the obvious, Maynard Dixon remained friendly. He went so far as to help Lange and Taylor prepare their joint report, contributing colored maps and migration routes in his own hand. Still a couple, Dixon and Lange hosted Taylor in San Francisco for a dinner at which their Nipomo report was presented to George West, an associate editor at the San Francisco *News* and a boyhood friend of Taylor's. West ran a prominent article in the *News* on 18 August 1935 based on Taylor's report, using two of Lange's photographs, one of them of a migrant mother and her children that foreshadowed the memorable photograph she would be taking of another migrant mother and her children in the same place, Nipomo, the following year. Both the Nipomo and Imperial Valley reports were forwarded to Rexford Guy Tugwell at the Resettlement Administration in Washington, where they caught the attention of Roy Emerson Stryker, director of the Photograph Division of the Resettlement Administration, which became the Farm Security Administration in 1937.

In August 1935 Stryker hired Lange as a photographer-investigator for the Resettlement Administration, assigned to the San Francisco office at a salary of $2,300 a year. Lange was joining the most distinguished photographic team ever assembled in American history. The group included Ben Shahn, Walker Evans, Russell Lee, Gordon Parks, Paul Carter, John Colier Jr., Jack Delano, Theo Jung, and others, each of them assigned to document the Depression in the various regions of the country in an effort to record the effects of the Depression and thereby bolster Resettlement and other New Deal programs. All in all, some 270,000 negatives were created, now on deposit in the Library of Congress.

Lange and Taylor divorced their respective spouses in the fall of 1935 and were married on 6 December 1935 in Albuquerque. Supported by Lange's Resettlement/Farm Security Administration salary and by Taylor's retainer from the Social Security Board, the couple spent the next five years traveling the Far West, the Middle West, and the South from Texas to Florida in Taylor's battered sedan in search of the facts, statistics, voices, and images of the Depression among agricultural migrants. The reports they compiled (to borrow a later term) were mixed-media presentations. They included photographs, essays, quotes from migrants in the field, newspaper articles clipped and pasted at appropriate intervals, and drawings by Dixon and others: all of it gathered into bound spiral notebooks, which were intended to give state and federal officials the feel, the texture of what was happening in the field.

Among the photographs Lange forwarded to Washington was one which soon achieved the stature of an American masterpiece. Subsequently entitled *Migrant Mother*, Lange's photograph has become not only the best-known image of the

270,000 plus negatives assembled by her Resettlement/Farm Security Administration team, but one of the most universally recognized and appreciated photographs of all time.

She almost missed taking it. Returning in March 1936 after a month in the field, Lange was heading north to San Francisco past Nipomo. On the side of the road, on a cold wet miserable day, she saw a sign that said "Pea Pickers Camp." She passed it. After all, at her side on the car seat rested a box containing rolls and packs of exposed film. Accompanied by the rhythmic hum of the windshield wipers, she debated over the next twenty miles the pros and cons of returning. In a sudden instinctive decision, she made a U-turn on the empty highway and returned to the pea pickers' camp. "I saw and approached the hungry and desperate mother, as if drawn by a magnet," she later recalled. "I do not remember how I explained my presence or my camera to her, but I do remember she asked me no questions. I made five exposures, working closer and closer from the same direction. I did not ask her name or her history. She told me her age, that she was thirty-two. She said that they had been living on frozen vegetables from the surrounding fields, and birds that the children killed. She had just sold the tires from her car to buy food. There she sat in that lean-to tent with her children huddled around her, and seemed to know that my pictures might help her, and so she helped me. There was a sort of equality about it."[1]

Some critics have made much of the fact that Lange did not learn the woman's name, which was Florence Thompson, taking this as proof of Lange's photographic detachment. In the woman and her three children, stranded in a roadside canvas lean-to, such critics suggest, Lange found a subject for her photographic art: a subject removed in time and circumstances from her prosperous clients in her previous practice; but she approached her nevertheless from a similarly detached perspective. The primary subject of *Migrant Mother*, from this perspective, is photography itself. Such a criticism ignores the fact that as soon as Lange returned to San Francisco and developed these Nipomo negatives (there were actually six, not five as she remembered), she rushed with them to George West at the San Francisco *News*, telling him that thousands of pea pickers in Nipomo were starving because of the frozen harvest. West got the story out in both the *News*, using two of Lange's photographs (but not *Migrant Mother*), and over the wires of the United Press. The federal government, meanwhile, rushed in twenty thousand pounds of food to feed the starving pea pickers.

On the other hand, while Lange's compassionate response is evident, the fact remains: she did withhold the most astonishing of her six images from West, recognizing, most likely, that in the split second of this final exposure, she had achieved something astonishing, something that was not only about starving pea pickers, but beyond that, something about motherhood itself. Here was an image of every mother's anguish, in all times and places, whether coming from drought, flood, famine or war.

Migrant Mother first appeared in the *Survey Graphic* for September 1936.

Lange forwarded the negative to Stryker in Washington, and it became the property of the federal government, which it remains; but almost immediately, *Migrant Mother* also entered the visual consciousness of the twentieth century. Like the Madonna which stood as its archetype, *Migrant Mother* became an archetype for others: Spanish Loyalists; Latin American reformers; the Black Panthers, who made Florence Thompson and her children African-American, just as the images of the Madonna shift in setting and ethnic identity from time to time and place to place. Made possible by Lange's instant, intuitive decision to return to the pea pickers' camp, *Migrant Mother* fused document and art. Here was the Depression in its most universal terms, caught in an instant of time for all time to come.

Commissioned by George West of the San Francisco *News*, Steinbeck spent the late summer and fall of 1936 in Central California, investigating conditions among migrants. Seven reports by Steinbeck were published in the *News* between 5 and 12 October 1936 under the title "Harvest Gypsies." These reports, in turn, became the basis for *Their Blood Is Strong*, a booklet published by the Simon J. Lubin Society in April 1938. A photograph by Dorothea Lange adorned the cover. Taken in 1936, the photograph depicted a young migrant mother breast-feeding her child. Despite the hardship of their surroundings, both the mother and the child are exceptionally attractive. The young mother possesses clear and appealing features; and the baby, despite its dirty feet and face, is blond and cherubic. Properly scrubbed, the child—entered under the category white Anglo-Saxon Protestant—might easily win one of the baby contests which were so popular in the 1930s. In contrast to the physically compelling mother and child depicted by Dorothea Lange in the photograph, the beautifully formed maternal breast emanating primal nurture, the mothers and children depicted by Steinbeck are more often than not encountered in a state of physical deterioration, their eyes glazed, their breasts shrunken against their chests.

Just about the same time Lange's nursing mother appeared on the cover of Steinbeck's report, photographer Horace Bristol, whom Steinbeck accompanied into the field in early 1938, depicted an even more robust nursing Oklahoma woman in the pages of *Life*. In the case of Bristol's photograph, the distant discretion of Lange's perspective has become intimate, full-blown, intense. The viewer is almost overwhelmed by the handsomeness of the woman, who could be the twin of Lange's subject; by the unveiled luxuriance of her nursing breast; by the well-nourished contentment of her child, who is as well-formed as his mother. Not surprisingly, Bristol later claimed that this photograph helped inspire the famed ending of Steinbeck's *The Grapes of Wrath* in which Rose of Sharon, her own child stillborn, nurses a starving man in a railroad boxcar.

Through the 1930s at least, maternal nursing was not a common subject of either American art or photography. Like sexuality and childbirth, nursing remained hidden behind a veil of discretion, even taboo. Yet Lange, Bristol, and, most dramatically, Steinbeck, each focused upon an Oklahoma woman nursing in an effort to say something important about the migrants. What was it? Why this fascination with nursing migrant mothers? They were white, first of all—white Anglo-Saxon Protestants, the matrix stock of America—and their bloodlines were strong, as Steinbeck suggested; and they would survive and prevail, despite their depressed California circumstances. Steinbeck's reportage might depict a physically eroded people, but his ultimate judgment, ringingly suggested in the title of his booklet and repeated throughout the reports, directly or by indirection, and so strongly corroborated in the Lange photograph on the cover, was that the Dust Bowlers, coming from the core stock of Anglo-America, possessed the sheer biological strength to make it through their ordeal.

Such a notion, embodied in the image of a strong, clear-featured woman breast-feeding, is at odds with our contemporary values and insights. Were not Mexican, Filipino, African-American, and Asian migrants similarly capable of biological resilience? Why should white migrants have any advantage over their counterparts of color?

The 1930s were not the 1990s. The documentarians of migrant stress—Taylor, Lange, Steinbeck, Horace Bristol, Arvin Camp manager Tom Collins—were forced, each in his or her own way, to deal not with the color, but with the whiteness, of their subjects. For those who did not accept the Tobacco Road canard—the assumption, that is, that the poor white trash Dust Bowlers emanated overtones of animalism and perverse sexuality—redemptive imagery had to be found within the distressing sights of migrant camp life. Hence, the nursing mothers. Even one of Lange's six photographs from Nipomo shows Florence Thompson with an infant at her partially exposed breast, which is the exact opposite message of maternal distance borne of powerlessness Lange chose for *Migrant Mother*.

Throughout the 1930s Steinbeck anchored his fiction in a biological-environmental vision. The short stories collected in *The Long Valley* (1938) are especially dependent upon biological symbolism and imagery, climaxing in the three-part *The Red Pony* sequence, which represents Steinbeck's highest achievement as a short story writer. While Steinbeck was disposed to avoid teleology or historical process in his fiction, he required, like most of us, some conviction of progress in human affairs. Once again, a biological metaphor, that of group man, came to the fore. Just as cells formed colonies and organisms within the tide pool, so too did men and women, linked biologically to each other through family, clan, or other intense form of association, form group man, which was something beyond the individual.

So then: Steinbeck went into the field in 1936, 1937, and 1938 and encountered the migrants as human waves of migration leaving behind teeming tide pools of human vitality. This last migration was only the most recent in the larger westering movement which had created California. ("We carried life out here," says Jody's grandfather in *The Red Pony*, "and set it down the way those ants carry eggs. And I was the leader. The westering was as big as God, and the slow steps that made the movement piled up and up until the continent was crossed. Then we came down to the sea, and it was done.")[2] Despite their physical and social afflictions, the Okies impressed Steinbeck with a powerful capacity for physical survival, for the transmission of life expressed in the figure of a nursing mother that spoke to his conviction as to what California was all about and, simultaneously, rescued these white people from social stigma. These migrants, Steinbeck asserted in his reports for the San Francisco *News*, were a new race being reborn in California—the nursing mother, the child—and they were here to stay.

Steinbeck's biologism also had its prophetic social dimension, its New Deal. In 1936 Steinbeck had spent time with Tom Collins at the Arvin Camp near Visalia and had been impressed by the reformist dimensions of the camp culture Collins was fostering. In Collins, Steinbeck beheld the best possibilities of the New Deal pragmatically at work. Steinbeck encouraged the publication of Collins's camp reports in the San Francisco *News* and offered to edit them as a book. When it came time to write *The Grapes of Wrath* between May and October 1938, Steinbeck used a stack of Collins's reports as a ready source of Okie folkways, folklore, and speech patterns. He dedicated *The Grapes of Wrath* "to Tom who lived it" as well as to his wife Carol "who willed this book."

It took four tries before Steinbeck knew exactly the sort of book he wanted to write. A skilled reporter, he briefly thought of expanding "The Harvest Gypsies" series into an ambitious non-fiction report. By late 1937, after a month-long field trip with Tom Collins, Steinbeck had turned to fiction as the best way to present the migrant crisis. Tentatively, he got to work on a novel which he called "The Oklahomans." Steinbeck envisioned "The Oklahomans" as a sweeping documentary, extending in fictional form the "Harvest Gypsies" reports. But he had trouble with its tone and point of view. The detached perspective of a documentary novel, he found, kept him at a distance from his protagonists, with whom he ardently identified.

By January 1938 Steinbeck had abandoned "The Oklahomans" in favor of a diametrically opposed format, tentatively entitled "L'Affaire Lettuceberg." Set in the Salinas lettuce strike of September 1936, "L'Affaire Lettuceberg" suffered from a syndrome diametrically opposite that of "The Oklahomans." If Steinbeck found that the attempt to remain impersonal, detached, and all-knowing in "The Oklahomans" blocked his creative energies, the effort to return in fiction via "L'Affaire Lettuceberg" to his home town of Salinas, pitting the Okies against the very same oligarchy toward which he bore such a complex response, also brought his creative energies to a grinding halt. Steinbeck's first wife, Carol Henning Steinbeck, one of the few people to get a glimpse of "L'Affaire Lettuceberg," criticized it as an unwieldy tract, tedious in its preachments and almost vulgar in its excessive emotion.

Plainly, John Steinbeck had to learn to split the difference: to balance, as Dorothea Lange had learned to do, emotion, imagination, and documentary vision. Tom Collins had expanded the genre of government report with novelistic inclusions of quotations and folkways. Lange and her colleagues at the Farm Security Administration were sending powerful emotional messages back to Washington while remaining within the formal limits of field notes and photography. Steinbeck was already exploring the possibilities of a cooperative venture with Collins. The Lange photograph on the cover of *Their Blood Is Strong* suggested another possibility. Margaret Bourke-White and Erskine Caldwell, after all, had already cooperated in the production of the documentary book *You Have Seen Their Faces*, an exploration of the sharecropper South which had appeared in November 1937. Four years later, James Agee and Walker Evans would bring this genre to an idiosyncratic conclusion with the publication of *Let Us Now Praise Famous Men* (1941).

Yet Caldwell, Bourke-White, and Agee, and to a lesser extent Evans, had all used their subjects shamelessly. Caldwell was the very *fons et origio* of Tobacco Road imagery, and even in the overtly sympathetic *You Have Seen Their Faces* seemed to be obsessed by what he took to be the animalism of his subjects. Bourke-White was an expert at catching people at their most eccentric or inconvenienced: a jaw dropped slightly agape; a black preacher's face distended by oratory, eyes ablaze in a religious frenzy bordering on the grotesque. These moments of oddity were given documentary value for the *Life* audience by the stealthful appropriation of her invasive camera: just another form of mass entertainment. Another Luce protégé, James Agee, would also egregiously offend against his subjects, in *Let Us Now Praise Famous Men*, shamelessly using a family of Georgia sharecroppers as a blank screen onto which he might project a variety of narcissistic obsessions, primarily sexual in inspiration. Even Walker Evans, who had the most integrity of all of them, would leave hidden and unused a photograph of the Gudger family scrubbed clean and combed and coping in their Sunday best in favor of images of the Gudgers as exploited whites who were, by implication, poor white trash.

Steinbeck wanted none of this, neither the exploitative pseudo-documentation of Margaret Bourke-White, or Erskine Caldwell's subtly masked contempt, or (as it would later turn out) Agee's preppy lubricity. Steinbeck wanted something approaching the balanced power of a Lange photograph or the photographs Lange's FSA colleague Arthur Rothstein would later, in March 1940, take of the men and women of the Visalia Camp: photographs depicting the Oklahomans as full human beings, embattled but coping, each face with a separate story to tell.

It was a documentary filmmaker, Pare Lorentz, who helped Steinbeck find the necessary balance. A film critic who had turned to filmmaking under the stimulus of the New Deal, Lorentz had recently completed two federally financed documentaries, *The Plow That Broke the Plains* (1936), dealing with the Dust Bowl, and *The River* (1937), dealing with flood problems on the Mississippi and its tributaries and the beginnings of the Tennessee Valley Authority. Like Dorothea Lange, who advised Lorentz on *The Plow That Broke the Plains*, Lorentz worked for the Resettlement Administration. Enhanced by a brilliant score by Virgil Thomson, based in part on Protestant hymns and classic American folk songs, *The Plow That Broke the Plains* remains a high point of Depression era documentary art.

When President Roosevelt saw Lorentz's *The River* at a private screening, he resolved to create a United States Film Service, with Lorentz in charge, responsible for creating documentaries dealing with American social, economic, and environmental problems. While Pare Lorentz produced one film under federal auspices, *The Fight for Life*, an evocation of childbirth and child mortality in the slums of Chicago, the notion of government-sponsored films, especially in the hands of such an effective filmmaker, ran counter to both an innate American resistance to government propaganda and the competitive interests of a justifiably threatened Hollywood film industry. A third documentary epic, dealing with the displacement of men by machines (Lorentz gave it the rather obscurantist title *Ecce Homo!*, "behold the man," the Latin Vulgate version of Pontius Pilate's remark as he displayed a beaten Jesus, crowned with thorns, to the howling multitude) never progressed beyond the state of a radio script.

John Steinbeck admired Pare Lorentz, and Pare Lorentz admired John Steinbeck. Lorentz found in Steinbeck's published work—especially the lengthy strike novel *In Dubious Battle* (1936) and the novella *Of Mice and Men* (1937)—compelling film scenarios. He invited Steinbeck to Hollywood in February 1938 to discuss a possible collaboration among Steinbeck, Lorentz, and the producers King Vidor and Lewis Milestone. Although nothing much came of this visit, aside from a conversation with James Cagney, who wanted to play Mac the labor organizer in *In Dubious Battle*, Steinbeck did get the opportunity to review Lorentz's great Dust Bowl documentary and to discuss with him documentary technique. From *The Plough That Broke the Plains*, *The River*, and a radio broadcast of *Ecce Homo!*, Steinbeck swiftly absorbed Lorentz's synesthetic approach, mixing images, words, and music, and, of equal importance, Steinbeck connected with Lorentz's narrative technique and pace. Under Lorentz's influence, Steinbeck decided to combine the best aspects of the documentary approach of "The Oklahomans" and the emotional content, now controlled, of "L'Affaire Lettuceberg."

By 31 May 1938 Steinbeck was at his desk in the small (five rooms, eight hundred square feet) cottage he and Carol had built in mid-1936 on Greenwood Lane (Arroyo del Ajo, Steinbeck called it, Garlic Gulch) in the hillside San Jose suburb of Los Gatos, fifty-plus miles south of San Francisco.

Just before Steinbeck seriously got down to writing, Pare Lorentz visited him in Los Gatos in late May and played for him a transcription of the radio play *Ecce Homo!*. Nor was Lorentz the only visitor to drop by during the five months it took Steinbeck to write his epic novel. The journal Steinbeck kept during this period reveals how even in the midst of an ostensible seclusion, producing nearly a thousand typewritten pages in five months, Steinbeck maintained an active social life, including a half dozen or more monumental drinking sessions and hangovers, together with numerous visits from friends and such Hollywood celebrities as Broderick Crawford, then starring as Lennie in the stage version of *Of Mice and*

Men, and Charles Chaplin. In addition to his daily stint of writing, Steinbeck's journal records numerous dinner parties, trips to the vineyards of Martin Ray on a nearby hillside and to the rodeo in Salinas, the bothersome banging of hammers from a nearby construction site, the blaring of a radio from an adjacent cottage, and the bankruptcy of his publisher Pascal Covici, who went over to Viking as an editor, taking Steinbeck with him. As if all this were not enough, the Steinbecks found time to purchase a spectacular house site on the Biddle Ranch near Los Gatos, with a dazzling view of the Santa Cruz mountains and the Pacific, and to initiate plans to build a new home there, complete with swimming pool.

John Steinbeck, in other words, wrote *The Grapes of Wrath* (his wife Carol selected the title, pulling the phrase from Julia Ward Howe's "Battle Hymn of the Republic") as, to all outward appearances, a prosperous literary celebrity ensconced in suburban comfort. Just over the mountains, as he wrote his agent Elizabeth Otis in February, "there are about five thousand families starving to death over there, not just hungry but actually starving."[3] Steinbeck was destined to make an awful lot of money from dramatizing their misery, one of the enduring paradoxes in American literary history. Appearing in April 1939, *The Grapes of Wrath* sold 429,000 copies in hardcover in its first year of publication. By 1941, when The Sun Dial Press issued an inexpensive reprint, more than 543,000 copies of the Viking hardback edition had been sold, the demand driven to a frenzy by John Ford's equally powerful 1940 film starring Henry Fonda. John Steinbeck spent the rest of his life a wealthy man for having told the story of impoverished Oklahomans.

Which does not imply that *The Grapes of Wrath* was not in its own terms, as an instance of documentary fiction, an effective, even great, statement. Learning from Lorentz, Steinbeck alternates sixteen narrative chapters dealing with the Dust Bowl and the migration of Dust Bowl migrants to California along Highway 66 with fourteen chapters dealing with the specific experiences on the road and in Central California of the Joad family of Oklahoma. Steinbeck's documentary evocations of the coming of the Dust Bowl, the tractoring out of sharecroppers, the migrations of the tin lizzies, the plowing under of an orange crop in California, all of it laced with snatches of religious and folk music, quotations from the people, documentary close-ups and wide-angle vision, constitute a mixed-media technique flourishing at the center of Depression art.

The Joad story which weaves itself through these general chapters is not heavily plotted; rather it possesses the loose-jointed, segmental development of natural experience, or as Steinbeck would put it of non-teleological experience. The Joads' journey puts the action into the context of basic myth—departure, hardships, river crossing, desert crossing, mountain crossing, descent into a valley—a mythic dimension that structures the seemingly random progression of the action. Strictly by having the Joads leave Oklahoma and arrive in California, Steinbeck has available to him a primal narrative, epic in its associations, yet natural, totally appropriate for his humble protagonists. Steinbeck's biological viewpoint, moreover, together with his tide pool technique of depicting his characters at a middle distance, is totally in harmony with the documentarian impulses of American writing in the 1930s.

Under the influence of Pare Lorentz, Steinbeck wrote *The Grapes of Wrath* in great part as a documentary film. Edmund Wilson suggested that *The Grapes of Wrath* was perhaps the first important American novel to be written with its next stage, a film script, and its third stage, a film, vividly in the author's mind. Producer Darryl Zanuck treated *The Grapes of Wrath* as reportage. Before he embarked upon filming the novel, Zanuck sent investigators into the field to cross-check Steinbeck's descriptions. Zanuck's agents reported that Steinbeck hadn't told the half of it. It was all true. So Zanuck went ahead. Whether or not John Ford actually read the novel—and there are those who claim that he did not—might be considered beside the point, given the power of *The Grapes of Wrath* as reportage. Its very story line, in other words, could speak directly to Ford with an imaginative power that came, not from literary subtleties, but from daily headlines. Being told the plot, Ford energized himself through newspaper accounts and photographs appearing in the popular press, including Lange's *Migrant Mother*, and these facts and images, in turn, were instantly integrated by Ford into a sure knowledge of the film he wished to make. Let the screenwriters read the novel: John Ford already had his story from a documentary novel that had begun in part as reportage and a film treatment.

But was *The Grapes of Wrath* true? Was it valid as a documentary? In general, such a question—is a novel factual?—shows the naiveté of the questioner. While based in fact and experience, the novel, being imaginative art, is not judged primarily as reportage. But since *The Grapes of Wrath* made its powerful impact in 1939, 1940, and 1941 equally as documentary tract and imaginative literature, the question of its validity is itself valid. To this day, the reputation of *The Grapes of Wrath*, especially among Californians, depends in significant measure on its value as a true account of migrant life and character and and the repression and exploitation of the migrants by California growers.

Not surprisingly, the growers of California howled in protest. But so did Oklahomans, who resented Steinbeck's depiction of the Joads as typical of the people of their state. Although he admitted he had not read the book, Oklahoma congressman Lyle Boren, himself the son of a tenant farmer, rose in the House to denounce *The Grapes of Wrath* as "a lie, a damnable lie, a black, infernal creation of a twisted, distorted mind."[4] The Chamber of Commerce of Oklahoma tried to dissuade Darryl Zanuck from filming the novel, fearing that it would give Oklahoma a bad name. In testimony before the Tolan Committee in the House of Representatives, Wheeler Mayo, editor of the *Sequoyah County Times* of Salislaw, Oklahoma, where the Joad family came from, disputed Steinbeck's depiction of conditions in Salislaw point by point, as if the Joads actually existed. In 1938, when the novel was written, Mayo argued, there were no more than ten tractors in all of Sequoyah County. Perhaps, he ironically observed, Steinbeck had alerted local farmers to new ideas, for there were now approximately sixty tractors in the county. Between 1930 and 1940, Mayo huffed, Sequoyah County, far from losing its families, had actually increased its population by four thousand.

The wet-nursing by Rose of Sharon of the starving old man in the boxcar caused special affront to Boren and other Oklahomans as well as to Archbishop Francis Spellman and Clifton Fadiman in New York. Spellman denounced the novel from the pulpit, and in his review of *The Grapes of Wrath* for the *New Yorker* Fadiman described the ending as "the tawdriest kind of fake symbolism."[5]

Even if one disagrees with such objections, one cannot dismiss Congressman Lyle Boren, as so many commentators have been wont to do, as an ignorant redneck. For many reasons, including, no doubt, the desire to sell books, Steinbeck did inject an element of *Tobacco Road* into *The Grapes of Wrath*. While tame, even puritanical by contemporary standards, there was a suggestion or two in the novel of dishevelment, profanity, and sex. Oklahomans such as Boren and Mayo and the members of the Oklahoma Chamber of Commerce were legitimately on the alert against the Tobacco Road canard. For many, Steinbeck was seen as a writer defaming the very people he was purporting to defend.

The truth, as usual, was complicated. Both *Life* magazine and the New York *Times* ran stories supporting the veracity of the novel, with *Life* providing photographs of squalid, makeshift shacks and debilitated, disheveled migrants. A year after the publication of *The Grapes of Wrath*, on the other hand, FSA photographer Arthur Rothstein did a series of photographs of migrants living in the Arvin camp which depict a healthy, self-respecting, orderly, and very clean camp population going about its daily tasks. Far from seeming poor white trash, the men and women depicted in Rothstein's images seem more like the beginnings of a new California people, direct descendants of one of North America's most venerable European stocks. This, of course, was the very point Steinbeck sought to make in *Their Blood Is Strong*; but his Rose of Sharon ending, following more than six hundred printed pages of vernacular life, including rough language and sexuality, offended Oklahomans, hurt the feelings of many migrants, and handed his enemies a cudgel. Among other places, Kansas City banned the novel from its public libraries for being obscene.

On the other hand, the fact that Wheeler Mayo, testifying before Congress, treated the Joad family as real residents of Salislaw emphasized the power the Joads possessed as documentary protagonists. Of the million-plus migrants to come into California between 1930 and 1940, the Joads, creations of John Steinbeck and John Ford, quickly became the few migrants to be known by name, then and subsequently. Shortly after the publication of *The Grapes of Wrath*, in fact, journalists and politicians were discussing the Joads as if they were real people and using the designation "the Joads" to refer to migrants as a class. In the course of a Fireside Chat, FDR mentioned reading *The Grapes of Wrath* and, in discussing certain federal housing proposals, referred to the Joads as if they were real people.

Given the reality ascribed to the Joads, it is not difficult to understand the affront felt by many Californians in Steinbeck's description of the hard-hearted reception the Joads experienced in California, with the exception of the federal camp, and their cruel exploitation. Defeated senatorial candidate Philip Bancroft jumped most noticeably into the fray, together with growers Joseph DiGiorgio and Holmes Bishop, the then-president of the Associated Farmers, novelist Ruth Comfort Mitchell, publicist Frank Taylor, and a number of other oligarchs, including ex-governor Frank Merriam. These oligarchs had their own agenda, but this does not automatically negate all of the criticisms and corrections they leveled against the *Uncle Tom's Cabin* of California.

In March of 1940 Philip Bancroft took his attack to New York, appearing in a radio debate on the Town Meeting of the Air with Rexford Tugwell, Carey McWilliams, and Hugh Bennett, with the topic set as "What Should We Do for the Joads?" Bancroft more than held his own against his liberal opponents, quoting Congressman Boren at length as to the slanderous effect of Steinbeck's novel. Later that month, Bancroft took his critique to a meeting of the Commonwealth Club of San Francisco, where on Friday, 29 March 1940, he spoke on the subject "Does *Grapes of Wrath* Present a Fair Picture of California Farm-Labor Conditions?"

Some of Bancroft's remarks represented the usual rhetoric of the Associated Farmers. *The Grapes of Wrath*, Bancroft claimed, was "straight revolutionary propaganda, from beginning to end, and strictly conforms to what the Communists call the 'party line.' In page after page it tries to build up class hatred, contempt for officers of the law, and for religion, even going to the extent of attacking the Salvation Army."[6]

Other criticisms by Bancroft had more credibility. They ranged from trivial errors of fact to more profound affronts against the generosity of the people of California. Take, for example, Steinbeck's depiction of handbills being distributed by California growers in the Dust Bowl encouraging migrants to head to California, inflate the labor force, and drive down wages. This never happened. On the contrary, the Associated Farmers placed advertisements in Dust Bowl newspapers to the opposite effect, warning migrants to stay away. When Arizona cotton growers advertised in 1937, the California Chamber of Commerce protested, knowing that a majority of the migrants answering these handbills would continue on to California. Try as hard as they might, the investigators of the La Follette Committee could not unearth a single handbill of this sort issued by California farmers. While the existence of such handbills from California growers survives today as received truth (similar to the charge that General Motors conspired against the streetcar system of Los Angeles), no handbill ever surfaced in the ensuing half-century-plus, which defies the laws of bibliography. And besides: why would the farmers of the five southern San Joaquin counties want hundreds of thousands of migrants flocking in on them, swelling local relief rolls, burdening local schools and hospitals, so that they could create a labor pool far in excess of anything they would ever need in even the most bountiful years, while at the same time over-burdening the local public infrastructure which they themselves had created and were continuing to support through their taxes?

This last issue, of charity and public relief, especially vexed Bancroft. "Our farmers," he told the Commonwealth Club, "are in very much the same position as any of your city people would be if you should wake up some morning and find ten or a dozen families camped on your lawn or on the sidewalk in front of your home, all asking for jobs you didn't have, or for relief you couldn't afford to give. Just what would you do? Well, I'll tell you what the California farmers and farm communities did. The people of Kern, Kings, Madera, Fresno, and Tulare Counties, who had been bearing the brunt of this migration, found that their fine local schools and county hospitals, which they had built up at heavy cost, were suddenly swamped by these uninvited guests who appeared on their doorsteps, hungry, homeless, and destitute. These farming communities built additions to their schools and hospitals; they hired additional teachers, nurses and doctors. In Kern County, the local taxes for health, sanitation, charities and corrections have more than doubled, and the school taxes have almost trebled in the last five years. While in Kings County and Tulare County, they have almost quadrupled."[7]

Statistics bear out Bancroft's assertion. The Irving Wood Collection in the Bancroft Library and other archival deposits contain ample evidence, not only of increased tax revenues spent on relief and public services in the southern San Joaquin, but dozens and dozens of compassionate, hard-working social workers, teachers, public health nurses, and other officials in these counties who worked long hard hours against great odds on behalf of the migrants. With the exception of camp manager Jim Rawley, based on Tom Collins, no such Californians appear in *The Grapes of Wrath*. It can be argued, in fact, that California maintained the most generous local and state relief program in the United States between 1935 and 1941. Certainly, its farm wages were the highest, which was the reason the migrants came to California in the first place. The fundamental implication, in popular terms, of *The Grapes of Wrath*—that Californians had met the crisis with hardness of heart—affronted Californians in the center as well as on the right.

The event in the novel most expressive of this hard-heartedness—the nighttime burning of a Hooverville encampment, intended to drive the migrants, including the Joads, from Kern County or to force them into growers' camps, where they could be better managed—earned Philip Bancroft's special scorn. Both he and Frank Taylor, writing in the November 1939 issue of *Forum* magazine, took special pains to dispute this inflammatory incident. The Hooverville in question, Bancroft and Taylor pointed out, had been festering since 1931 (it began as a hobo camp) near a river bottom just north of Bakersfield on property owned by the Kern County Land Company. Public health officials had become progressively concerned over the settlement from 1933 onwards as it filled with migrants. Children from the camp, afflicted with flu, chicken pox, skin diseases, and other ailments, brought these infections to nearby public schools, earning the ire of non-migrant parents. By 1937 the Bakersfield Hooverville had become a full-blown disaster, a crowded, filthy source of contagion. By this time, Bancroft and Taylor argued, Kern County public health officials had identified a number of families in the Hooverville who had been living there four years and more. Something had to be done. For six months, public health officials worked patiently with each identifiable family unit, persuading it to move to a county-run campsite, with graded streets, running water, and toilet facilities. All but twenty-six families (another count has twenty-eight) moved from the Hooverville, despite the fact that a number of these families who stayed were working and could afford better facilities. It took well into the fall of 1937 to persuade these final families to vacate their cardboard, gunny sack, and scrap wood lean-tos.

"Not a single family was forcibly evicted," Bancroft argued. "No deputy or other police official took any part in the proceedings. No armed person ever issued an order regarding the evacuation of the camp. No farmer group, organized or unorganized, ever made any demonstration against any member of the camp. As the cardboard and packing box shacks were vacated, they were torn down and burned, in order to prevent their being later occupied by new arrivals. In no case was any cabin, shack or shelter demolished until the occupants had left and had taken with them every single personal possession they wanted."[8]

As a novelist shaping his materials according to an imaginative pattern, Steinbeck had every right to depict, as he did, the nighttime burning of the Hooverville by para-fascist vigilantes and Legionnaires. Such a scene, as parable, as imagined event, was true to the notion of the empire striking back. Ask the strikers from Salinas or Stockton. Ask the convicted organizers from the CAWIU. But because *The Grapes of Wrath* was presented and received as a documentary, activists among growers such as Bancroft and Taylor had every right to dispute the factual content of *The Grapes of Wrath* point by point and to prove that no such Hooverville in Kern County was ever raided and burned, as Steinbeck was claiming in a novel passing as history.

And besides, Steinbeck's critics argued, *The Grapes of Wrath*, even in its truthful moments, told only part of the story. Just outside Salinas, for example, Steinbeck's home town, an enterprising wheat farmer had subdivided a section of his ranch into half-acre lots selling for $250 per lot, $5 down, $5 a month. Dust Bowl migrants had snapped up the properties and created Little Oklahoma City, where trailers and tents were rapidly yielding to frame cottages peopled by three thousand migrants turned lettuce packers, earning fifty to sixty cents an hour. Ruth Comfort Mitchell, another novelist from Los Gatos, countered Steinbeck's exposé with a novel entitled *Of Human Kindness* (1940) in which a young migrant named Lute finds work on a ranch and marries the owner's daughter, having resisted the blandishments of the Black Widow, a sexy Communist organizer who seduces and otherwise misleads the rancher's son.

Whatever the truth or falsity of specific events in *The Grapes of Wrath*, in any event, Steinbeck had created a wave of emotion in favor of the migrants. Okie Chic swept the nation. *Life, Time, Newsweek, Fortune*, the New York *Times* ran Okie stories. Secretary of Labor Frances Perkins and First Lady Eleanor Roosevelt toured migrant camps. A select committee from the House of Representatives began hearings on interstate migration. Suddenly, Tobacco Road had become Main Street USA. Even at his angriest, Philip Bancroft waxed lyrical when it came his turn to praise the migrants as yeoman American stock, paradigms of Jeffersonian rectitude, shamelessly exploited by a money-hungry writer named Steinbeck and by Hollywood, where a spate of Okie movies was following the success of John Ford's film. Even the Dead End Kids took to the migrant trail in *You're Not So Tough* (1941), falling prey to pinko unionists and grower thugs before themselves striking a blow for Okie integrity and the family-sized farm.

Two months after the publication of *The Grapes of Wrath*, Little Brown issued the second controversial California documentary of 1939, *Factories in the Field: the Story of Migratory Farm Labor in California*. Its author, Carey McWilliams, sat precariously in Sacramento as Commissioner of Housing and Immigration in the Olson administration. *Factories in the Field* had its essential power not as academic history, but as an impassioned polemic from the left. If John Steinbeck was a novelist seeking documentation, Carey McWilliams was a documentary journalist seeking the moral and imaginative intensity of art. As in the case of *The Grapes of Wrath*, to quibble with one or another point in *Factories in the Field* was to make minor dents on the surface of a masterpiece.

Factories in the Field possessed such persuasion because, like Steinbeck, Carey McWilliams was a skilled writer possessed of style, rhetorical force, moral vision, and socio-historical imagination. At the University of Southern California in Los Angeles, McWilliams had graduated in law, joined a blue-chip firm in Pasadena, and married into a prominent academic family. As a student at USC, McWilliams had maintained a passionate interest in literature. While in law school, he researched and wrote a biography of Ambrose Bierce, published by Albert and Charles Boni in 1929, which remains today not only the best biography of its subject, but one of the founding texts of the literary history of California.

As in the case of Dorothea Lange, the Depression and the desire for a divorce turned Carey McWilliams, slowly, from the establishment to a more radical posture. The literary radicals of the 1920s, he later argued, became the political radicals of the 1930s. Tiring of his blue-chip legal practice and the increasing constraints of his marriage into the Pasadena establishment (by 1941 he would be divorced and remarried), Carey McWilliams began to hang out in the early 1930s with the circle of artists, journalists, assorted intellectuals, and a Hollywood actress or two, most of them on the left, revolving around Los Angeles bookseller Jake

Zeitlin. McWilliams's closest friend in the Zeitlin circle was another aspiring literary journalist, Yugoslavian immigrant Louis Adamic, who like McWilliams had made the transition from H. L. Menckenism to the left under the influence of the Depression. At this time, McWilliams began to shift his legal practice from oil rights and securities to labor law and to expand his activities as a literary critic and journalist. No practicing journalist or academic in California at the time knew the literature of California better. The book review column which McWilliams conducted in the mid- to late 1930s in *Westways*, the magazine of the Automobile Association of Southern California, remains to this day a lavish cornucopia of bibliography, biography, and criticism of California life and letters. While McWilliams was producing this outpouring of erudite book reviews and literary essays, he was also sending a series of hard-hitting reports to the *New Republic* and the *Nation* dealing with politics and labor strife in California which gave evidence to his growing involvement with the Left. McWilliams was also spending his spare hours in Los Angeles area libraries, researching the history of farm labor in the Golden State.

In early 1939 McWilliams joined the Olson administration as commissioner of Housing and Immigration, the top state official responsible for the welfare of migrants. Established a generation earlier by Governor Hiram Johnson at the height of the Progressive era, the Commission of Immigration and Housing had been directed in the 1920s by no one less than Simon J. Lubin himself, prophet and patron saint of reform. Appointing McWilliams, Governor Culbert Olson had done a daring thing: placing an articulate, frequently published left-wing intellectual in an important state office. The governor did not have to wait long for the inevitable controversy. Touring the camps and work sites of the Central Valley, McWilliams, who was modeling himself on the independent role pursued by Lubin in the 1920s, erupted in a fusillade of press statements and written reports condemning the treatment of migrants by California growers, with special emphasis on the violation of civil rights and the perpetuation of unsanitary camp conditions. When it came time for Governor Olson to appear before the La Follette Committee, McWilliams wrote his statement, in which the governor came squarely out against the growers for violating the civil rights of farm workers.

As if all this were not enough, *Factories in the Field* appeared just as *The Grapes of Wrath* was beginning to cause a furor. Not only had Carey McWilliams placed the previously dormant Commission of Immigration and Housing on the offensive, he had written a book that backed the general thesis of *The Grapes of Wrath* with documentation and impassioned prose. McWilliams reviewed *The Grapes of Wrath* in *Westways*, calling it "the finest novel that has come out of California since *The Octopus*." Now it was McWilliams's turn to step into the ring as defending champion. For Ella Winter, writing in the *New Republic*, *Factories in the Field* confirmed "the cold, horrible, statistical reality" in the background of *Grapes of Wrath*. "Here is the data," wrote Robert A. Brady in *Books*, "that gives the terrible migration of the Joad family historical and economic meaning not only for the immediate present, but also for the larger canvas of American rural life at the end of a long, rich cycle."[9] Certainly the growers saw it that way. By 1940 Carey McWilliams had become Public Enemy Number One on the Most Wanted List of the Associated Farmers. To no one's surprise, Philip Bancroft branded him a Communist sympathizer. Running against Olson, Attorney General Earl Warren, who had refused to cooperate with the La Follette Committee, promised to fire McWilliams upon taking office. Neither Bancroft nor Warren can be faulted in this regard, for McWilliams concluded *Factories in the Field* with a ringing call for the collectivization of California agriculture. Like the final scene of *The Grapes of Wrath*, McWilliams's shocking conclusion, a call for the transfer of California agriculture to collective public ownership, infuriated both the Center and the Right—and perhaps obscured the validity of his larger argument.

Like Lange, like Steinbeck, Carey McWilliams could not help exulting in the special role played by the white Anglo-Saxon Protestant migrants of the 1930s: this despite McWilliams's equally strong sympathies for migrants of color. A few months after the near-simultaneous appearence of *The Grapes of Wrath* and *Factories in the Field*, a third book, *An American Exodus*, with photographs by Dorothea Lange and text by Paul Taylor, further reinforced this notion of Anglo-Saxon specialness. Alongside Lange's photograph of a preternaturally handsome female farm worker, her classic WASP beauty resplendent beneath a Mother Hubbard cap worn as protection against the sun, Paul Taylor wrote:

> Young girl,
> cotton picker,
> she
> migrates with her family
> from
> crop to crop,
> and
> lives under conditions of deprivation.
> Anglo-Saxon type.
> This persistent line
> reaches back
> from the western cotton fields of California and
> Arizona
> through the little settlements in the Ozarks,
> through the Appalachians, with Nancy Hanks—
> and
> across the Atlantic Ocean
> to Elizabethan England.

Not for nothing had Dorothea Lange spent fifteen years as a society photographer! The young cotton picker of the photograph would seem equally at home in a

Radcliffe or Wellesley yearbook as she did in a book documenting the migrant crisis across America. In another, *Ruby from Arkansas, 1935,* Lange gives us a perfect Rose of Sharon look-alike. Again, in the young woman's elegantly crossed legs, the flair of the raised collar of her flannel shirt, her beautiful Anglo-Saxon face framed by well-brushed hair waved to current fashion, one encounters a young woman immediately transferable, as far as appearance is concerned, to the company of her sisters and blood kin in the privileged Northeast. No college girl could wear her denims with more elegant nonchalance.

Working together in a rented room in Berkeley near the Pacific School of Religion through the summer and fall of 1938, the same weeks that Steinbeck was writing *The Grapes of Wrath* in Los Gatos, Taylor and Lange compiled a book of text and photographs documenting—one is tempted to say, celebrating—the exodus of white Anglo-Saxon America from the Dust Bowl, the black sharecropper South, and Mexican farm labor in the Southwest. As documentary art, *An American Exodus* is an exquisitely realized evocation, showcasing the best images gathered by Lange across four years in the field. Its cross-referencing to *The Grapes of Wrath* was thoroughly evident. Like Steinbeck, Lange and Taylor employed the Biblical metaphor of the wandering of the Israelites in the desert in search of the promised land to organize their story. In one photograph, *Ditched, Stalled, and Stranded, San Joaquin Valley, California,* 1935, a Henry Fonda look-alike stares from behind the wheel of his stalled jalopy in what could be taken as an illustration for *The Grapes of Wrath* or a still from the John Ford film. In another photograph, *Jobless,* five men stare into the camera, all but one of them in denim coveralls, ready for work that is not available. Their strong Anglo-Saxon faces are touched with a resignation that carries with it the faintest suggestion of hostility. In another, *Jobless on Edge of Pea Field, Imperial Valley, California,* 1937, a solitary male worker stands against a vast backdrop of tilled fields. The work is done, and he is no longer needed. In another photograph, a small girl, not more than six or seven, drags her heavy sack across a cotton field in Kern County early in the morning. Her coat is tattered, and there is a sleep-starved look on her small face. In still another, two men bend over in a field of pea vines near Niland, California, in February 1939, picking peas at a cent a pound, twenty-eight pounds to a hamper. We feel the pain in their backs.

As effective as *An American Exodus* remains as documentary art, the book had already passed its peak in the market of 1940–1941. Random House and Covici Fried, in fact, each turned the book down before Reynal and Hitchcock accepted it. After publication, *An American Exodus* sat stacked on the remainder shelf: a triumph of art and documentation, a bust in terms of sales. Rapidly, as the United States turned its attention to questions of war and peace in the foreign arena, the migrant crisis, while still statistically present, receded as a national priority. The two final documentary masterpieces to come in part from California in the 1930s, the reports of the La Follette and Tolan committees, while possessed of great force as documentary art, were published at a time when America had other matters on its mind.

Considered as historical literature, the La Follette and Tolan reports climaxed on a note of intellectual and moral triumph all efforts to document the Depression. The reports built upon the interactive tradition of documentary art that had been achieved since 1933. Paul Taylor went into the field at about the same time that Carey McWilliams went into the archives. Taylor, in turn, recruited Dorothea Lange as a photo-reporter. Lange's photographs, in turn, stimulated Steinbeck's investigations and helped him frame his perspective. Carey McWilliams, meanwhile, was having his perspective shaped by Steinbeck's strike novel *In Dubious Battle* (1936) and Steinbeck's reportage as well as by Lange's photographs. John Ford, in turn, obtained the black and white look of his film version of *The Grapes of Wrath* from the Farm Security Administration photographs taken by Lange and others. In 1940 the Public Affairs Committee of New York issued Paul Taylor's collected reports under the title *Adrift on the Land*, illustrating it with stills from John Ford's film. In *Adrift on the Land*, Taylor refers to both Steinbeck and McWilliams as parallel commentaries and partial sources. It was now time for government reports to participate in this synergy—to rise to the level of documentary art.

On 19 May 1936 the United States Senate passed Resolution 266, which empowered the Senate Committee on Education and Labor, chaired by Senator Elbert Thomas of Utah, to seek out violations of labor law and civil liberty guaranteed by Section 7(a) of the National Industrial Recovery Act of 1933 and the expanded successor to Section 7(a), the National Labor Relations Act of 1935 (more popularly known as the Wagner Act after its sponsor, Senator Robert Wagner of New York). Sweeping in its implications (William Green of the AFL called it the Magna Carta of Labor in the United States), the National Labor Relations Act of 1935 overwhelmingly established the rights of labor to organize into unions and to bargain collectively with management. Based on a vision of collective bargaining as the best model for labor-management relations in an industrial democracy, the National Labor Relations Act established a reviewing agency, the National Labor Relations Board, to function as arbiter and, if necessary, enforcer in union-management disputes. Senator Thomas appointed Senator Robert Marion La Follette Jr., the Wisconsin Republican, to chair the subcommittee on Senate Resolution 266, the hearing and investigative arm of the Committee.

As senator, La Follette had surrounded himself with left-liberal staff members and advisors, including his college and Marine Corps friend Paul Taylor. As chairman of the Subcommittee of the Senate Committee on Education and Labor, popularly known as the La Follette Committee, the senator gathered a team of like-minded attorneys, investigators, researchers, and writer-editors which soon emerged as one of the most dedicated and effective governmental teams in New Deal Washington. In 1936 and 1938 staff members of the Committee made preliminary investigations in California on behalf of the National Labor Relations Board. These investigations fully confirmed the suspicions of the senator and his staff that civil and labor rights were being suppressed in California to an unprecedented degree.

For some time, Paul Taylor had been urging La Follette to launch a full-scale investigation in California, which Taylor described as an industrial battlefield: America's most dramatic arena of labor conflict and class antagonism. La Follette, however, did not have the necessary budget. In 1939 the newly elected senator from California, Sheridan Downey, helped secure an additional appropriation of $50,000 to bring the La Follette Committee to California. Downey's fellow Democrat, Governor Culbert Olson, welcomed La Follette to the state. Then came *The Grapes of Wrath* and *Factories in the Field,* exposing the underside of California to the rest of the nation and giving the La Follette Committee further impetus to set up a West Coast investigation. In late 1939 the La Follette Committee opened offices in Los Angeles and San Francisco, with its thirty-five-person staff headed by Henry Fowler, a brilliant young lawyer whom La Follette had recruited from the Tennessee Valley Authority.

The La Follette Committee held hearings in San Francisco and Los Angeles over twenty-eight days extending from December 1939 to January 1940. The Committee issued more than 500 subpoenas, heard 395 witnesses, compiled 2,451 pages of printed testimony, and assembled 1,747 exhibits for entry at the time of testimony, followed by 5,875 supplementary exhibits. Paul Taylor, who appeared as the lead witness in the San Francisco hearings, served as an active consultant throughout this period, as did Carey McWilliams, who wrote Governor Olson's searing testimony.

Growers, industrial officials, district attorneys, and county sheriffs, for their part, remained unintimidated, even brazen, in appearances before the Committee. Earl Warren, the Republican attorney general of California, refused to cooperate with the La Follette Committee and backed local county sheriffs resisting subpoenas. Most arrogant in appearances before the Committee were officials of the Industrial Association of San Francisco, the organization that had provided bankrolling and intelligence for dozens of grower and other anti-union groups. When the Committee sought to examine the conduct of the Association during the waterfront strikes of 1934 and 1936, an Association spokesman blandly asserted that all its files prior to 1937 had been destroyed. Appearing before the La Follette Committee on 18 December 1939, Philip Bancroft, outspoken as usual, pointedly told Senator La Follette that he was a great admirer of the senator's father and approved the senator's efforts to keep the United States out of war but could not understand his giving aid and comfort to the Communists by his deliberate effort to smear the farmers and law enforcement officers of California.

The investigations of the La Follette Committee in California should be considered from two perspectives: as a congressional inquiry—a quasi-judicial review, that is, strongly affected by political ideology and practical politics—and as a re-

port moving toward documentary art. As a Senate committee with no prosecutorial power, the La Follette Committee brought no indictments. The chief prosecutor of California, Earl Warren, refused to cooperate. In 1942 Warren defeated
Olson for the governorship and fired Carey McWilliams on his first day in office
with the same symbolic intensity with which Olson had pardoned Tom Mooney
four years previously. By the time the report of the La Follette Committee was
being published in nine installments by the Government Printing Office between
1942 and 1944, the hearings seemed, for the time being at least, something from
a previous era. Yet the report issued by La Follette's sub-committee, *Violations of
Free Speech and Rights of Labor*, 1,707 pages in nine parts continuously numbered, sat on library shelves latent with the power of documentary art that would,
a half century later, win for it ranking alongside the reports of Paul Taylor, the
history of Carey McWilliams, the fiction of John Steinbeck, the photographs of
Dorothea Lange.

Only an era and an entity exquisitely keyed to collective effort, the federal
government at the height of the New Deal, would be capable of taking the gross,
incoherent materials, the raw documentation, of a federal investigation and transforming them into documentary art. Like the *American Guide Series* and the local
histories and bibliographies being concurrently produced by the writers of the
Works Progress Administration, *Violations of Free Speech and Rights of Labor*
possesses the power of anonymous statement. It is as if the nation itself, in its
collective consciousness, were writing and editing the document. Dozens, perhaps
a hundred, hands went into the assembling of *Violations of Free Speech and
Rights of Labor*, and subsequent scholarship might reveal the controlling presence
and editorial vision of one editor or two; but in its essential dynamics the La
Follette Report is an assemblage of narrative, testimony, excerpted statement, and
documentary evidence (newspaper stories and headlines, handbills, letters and
memoranda), that speaks with one vast collective voice, as if America were unifying itself through the assembly of its fragments. *Violations of Free Speech and
Rights of Labor* represents history as the search for fact, for experiential and veri-
fiable truth; but it also represents history as the search for moral meaning. From
this perspective, the report constitutes one of the great documents of California
history; indeed, the compilers of *Violations* took their responsibility to the specifics
of California quite seriously. Before they ventured to present the results of their
hearings, the writers and editors of *Violations* assembled a history of agriculture
and farm labor in California, with its long and sorry tale of disenfranchisement,
exploitation, and repression, which further corroborated *Factories in the Field* in
much the same way that *Factories in the Field* corroborated *The Grapes of Wrath*.
While the writing was undoubtedly produced by many hands, it possesses the
clean, swift assertiveness of a Streamline or Modern post office from the PWA.
Part 3 presents a comparably effective book-length history of industrial relations
in California. Then there are the assemblies of testimony, narrative redaction,
and documentary evidence through which specific case studies of suppression are

presented. The material relating to the cotton strike of 1933, the Brentwood Plan of 1934, the Sacramento conspiracy trials of 1935, the Salinas lettuce packers' strike of 1936, and the Stockton cannery strike of 1937 are especially vivid; for in these instances is asserted and proven the essential thesis of *Violations of Free Speech and Rights of Labor*, which is nothing less than the existence in California in the 1930s of a conspiracy to suppress constitutional rights that, in a comparison made frequently in the report, made California seem more a fascist European dictatorship than part of the United States.

Making this fascist comparison, the La Follette Committee brought to a climax (or was the real climax even now occurring on the battlefields of North Africa and Europe?) an entire decade of fascist/Communist mimesis in California. La Follette and his staff were pro-worker, pro-union, to be sure; but La Follette instructed his investigators to focus not on the political affiliations of any of its targets for investigation, but on the question of whether or not their civil rights were violated. It was the growers and industrialists, on the other hand, who unleashed the Communist comparison in their testimony. In counter-action, one suspects, the writers and editors of the report unleashed the fascist metaphor.

What was true of the La Follette Report—brilliance, comprehensiveness, and, alas, a temporary irrelevance—was even more true of the report issued in 1941 in ten parts of documents and testimony and one part of summary analysis by the Select Committee to Investigate the Migration of Destitute Citizens authorized in 1940 by Resolutions 63 and 491 of the House of Representatives. Popularly known as the Tolan Committee in honor of its chairman, Representative John Tolan, an Alameda County Democrat, the Select House Committee, like the La Follette Committee, employed a gifted, dedicated staff, which included Dr. Robert Lamb as chief investigator, James Owens as chief field investigator, and Richard Blaisdell and Harold Cullen as editor and associate editor of the final report. Throughout 1940 the Tolan Committee held hearings in New York, Montgomery, Chicago, Lincoln, Oklahoma City, San Francisco, Los Angeles, and Washington, D.C. *Interstate Migration*, its final report, remains alongside *Violations of Free Speech and Rights of Labor* as a documentary masterpiece of the Depression that was ending even as it went to press.

National in its scope, sweeping and comprehensive in its detail, profoundly humanistic in its respect for testimony from the humble, with its details of day-to-day migrant life, *Interstate Migration* approached its subject with a scrutiny extending far beyond the confines of California—although, once again, Professor Paul Taylor played an important role in persuading his fellow Berkeleyite, Congressman John Tolan, to call for the Select Committee and the hearings. Filed in 1941, the Tolan Report suffered the same wartime eclipse as its counterpart from the La Follette Committee. (Epics have a way of appearing in the twilight time of the eras which inspire them.) Already, in fact, in parts 9 and 10 of the Tolan Report, attention was turning to the problems of workers migrating not to the fields of California or other agricultural states, but to military construction sites under rapid expansion in the South.

Today, a half century and more later, *Interstate Migration*, no longer a government report calling for immediate action, represents itself to us as documentary art of the highest order. The war, after all, solved the migrant crisis by creating an even more intense dislocation accompanied by massive government spending. The thousands of defense construction workers living in tents depicted in the final sequences of the Tolan Report soon swelled into the millions and, miraculously, were properly housed. But that is another story. In terms of the Depression era, the Tolan Report presents a rich choral symphony of migrant voices. It is a Pare Lorentz documentary realized through transcribed testimony and clean and direct prose refreshingly free from jargon. Encouraged to testify alongside the luminaries—including Eleanor Roosevelt (who showed herself an astute and compassionate observer); Carter Goodrich, professor of economics at Columbia; Ernesto Galarza, chief of the Division of Labor and Social Information of the Pan American Union; Katherine Lenroot, chief of the Children's Bureau of the United States Department of Labor; Edward Kelly, the mayor of Chicago; and scores of other expert witnesses—the ordinary migrant also had his or her say. Among others we hear from Antonia Arana, a migrant from Puerto Rico; Rebecca Cole, a black migrant from Memphis; Joe Frank Holloman, a migrant oyster shucker from Port Norris, New Jersey; John Heard, a migrant apple picker from Georgia; Silas Lowden, a young man on the road from Chicago; Katherine Odgers, a migrant mother, also from Chicago; Guy Gulden, a one-time Nebraska farmer and sometime plasterer currently earning $400 a year as a farm worker in Watsonville, California.

Mothers talk of their difficulties in feeding their family and getting their children to a school. Fathers talk of a feeling of uselessness when work is not available. Men and women alike give the excruciating details of harvest work in the field and camp life. Descriptions of jalopies, contractor kickbacks, the absence of privacy, and fear of what the future might bring—all of it told by individual migrant Americans in their own language—proceeds side by side with graphs, charts, narrative summaries, and other instances of statistical and social science.

By background, John Tolan was a social worker, and, reading the Tolan Report fifty years later, one cannot help but believe that something of a social worker's concern for the specifics of suffering entered into the hearings of the Committee he headed. From this perspective, *Interstate Migration* constitutes a 5,032-page elaboration and corroboration of *Migrant Mother*, the Arvin reports of Tom Collins, *The Grapes of Wrath*, *Factories in the Field*, *An American Exodus*, and all the other instances of documentary art to emerge from California and the nation during the Depression. Significantly enough, the Tolan Report also included a comprehensive selection of photographs from the Farm Security Administration, vivid with visual corroboration of the life that was being described through migrant testimony.

Interstate Migration concluded with Congressman Tolan speaking to Philip Ryan, a national official of the American Red Cross. Laconically, after five thousand pages of testimony, Congressman Tolan summarized the proceedings with one final query: "Well, it all comes down to the question again as to whether the Federal Government owes a duty to people who are hungry or naked or on account of circumstances over which they have no control, are in need. Do we owe that duty or do we not?"[10] Tolan's question became moot almost as he uttered it or at least almost as soon as it saw print. In late 1941 Dorothea Lange, now working for the Office of War Information, photographed a blue-collar couple employed at the Kaiser Shipyards in Richmond, California. Their faces are those of migrants, but they are dressed in denim and hard hats. Standing outside a local market, they are holding full bags of groceries. The Depression is over.

IV

THE THERAPY OF PUBLIC WORKS

10

Valley of Decision

San Francisco and the Hetch Hetchy Project

ALONG with the rest of the nation, California experienced the therapeutic presence of the federal government operating through public works during the Great Depression. While two of the most important works completed in this period, the Hetch Hetchy Aqueduct and the Golden Gate Bridge, were built without significant federal involvement, the federal government, operating through its established agencies and emergency programs, initiated in California during the 1930s an epic of construction without precedent in the history of the state. Spending untold millions of dollars, the federal government countered unemployment with the therapy of public works. These public works, in turn—the Hetch Hetchy Aqueduct, the Colorado River Project, the Central Valley Project, the San Francisco–Oakland Bay Bridge, the Golden Gate Bridge, together with innumerable projects of flood control, urban improvement, wilderness management, and military construction—met practical needs of long standing.

While they were made possible through the federal government and hence expressed the national will, each of these public works had in its background an equally long-standing history of California planning and debate. On a grand scale, they materialized time-honored dreams: water and electricity for cities and farms; access across great bodies of water; amenities for city, town, and countryside. From the spinning generators of Hoover Dam, dispatching their currents to an emergent Southern California, to the Pythagorean purity of the Golden Gate Bridge, uniting the cityscape of San Francisco with the wild headlands of Marin, each of these successfully achieved public works functioned on the most powerful level of social and cultural symbol as well as doing its day-to-day work.

As texts, as symbols in a social landscape, moreover, public works challenged Californians to consider and reconsider elemental questions of social goals and identity. Growth or no growth? California as city and suburb, or California as wilderness? The public or the private sector? Progress for whom? And was such progress necessary? Could the outcome of so much intervention in the existing arrangements of the planet be accurately predicted? Such questions adhered most powerfully to the large-scale public works of the period: the great dams and hydro-electric plants; the aqueducts, tunnels, and bridges; the Arroyo Seco Parkway, the first freeway in the state. To the smaller-scale accomplishments of the era—the countless schools and post offices, the libraries and National Guard armories, the parks, playgrounds, zoos, and swimming pools, the improved campgrounds and other recreational amenities, the regional airports, the public hospitals and other institutions of public care—were attached equally important, if somewhat quieter, questions about social democracy and shared quality of life in a state called California, in a country called the United States.

In their localized, more minor modes as well as in their heroic dimensions, the public works of the Depression continue to haunt American California with their expressions of shared value and public life, achieved after a great controversy. As much as they disagreed with each other, and as much as powerful interests fought for their own goals, the Californians of the 1930s, if one is to judge them by their major and minor public works, were capable in the long run of shared identity and unified public action. Crossing the Golden Gate Bridge, visiting an improved campground, Californians of the 1930s, torn from each other by so much social controversy and economic tension, were re-reminded that they still possessed something in common: California improved, California as a public place.

For those who wished to define and develop California in terms of its metropolitan identity, one necessity above all others—the need for water and electricity—asserted itself. Two heroic projects, the Hetch Hetchy Aquaduct and the Colorado River Project, were pushed to completion in the 1930s. Once completed, these public works assured California its urban future.

Even as the stock market was crashing, workers were tunneling and constructing and pushing forward a 150-mile-long aqueduct intended to bring the waters of the Tuolumne River in the Sierra Nevada to San Francisco and its adjacent communities on the western edge of the Bay. California as city, California as wilderness? The fundamental question involved in the Hetch Hetchy project—so named after the magnificent Valley of the Hetch Hetchy where the waters of the Tuolumne were impounded by O'Shaughnessy Dam in 1923—went to the core of the struggle for the identity of California itself. Point by point, personality by personality, the search of San Francisco for water paralleled that of Los Angeles, which completed its Owens River Aqueduct in 1913. In each case a city engineer, William Mulholland of Los Angeles and Michael O'Shaughnessy of San Francisco, joined a former mayor, Fred Eaton and James Duval Phelan, to put the water project in motion.

Taking office in 1897, James Duval Phelan, a Democrat of the Progressive persuasion, was determined to solve the problem of the long-range water needs of San Francisco. Phelan embarked upon this project under the influence of two previous reports. In 1882 consulting engineer J. P. Dart had recommended that San Francisco build a canal from the Tuolumne River in the Sierra Nevada to the Crystal Springs Reservoir immediately south of the city. Such a canal, Dart noted, would operate along its entire length by gravity fall. In 1891 engineer John Henry Quinton had recommended that the Hetch Hetchy Valley in the northeast sector of the Yosemite National Park provided the best site for a dam and reservoir on the Tuolumne River. Quietly, in 1900, Mayor Phelan, after obtaining the approval of city engineer Carl Grunsky and Marsden Manson, commissioner of the Board of Public Works, retained the services of J. P. Lippincott, an engineer on the staff of the United States Geological Survey. Phelan asked Lippincott to conduct a discreet survey of the Hetch Hetchy area so as to corroborate or reject the recommendations of Dart and Quinton. As an engineer on the federal payroll, working secretly on behalf of a municipality seeking federally controlled water, Lippincott was crossing the flexible boundaries of conflict of interest, even for that more accommodating era. Two years later, Lippincott, by now on the payroll of the newly established Bureau of Reclamation, would provide the same discreet service for water-thirsty Los Angeles in the Owens Valley.

In July 1901 Lippincott reported favorably to Phelan regarding the recommendations of Dart and Quinton. Yes, the Tuolumne River was the best source of water for San Francisco; and yes, the Hetch Hetchy Valley was the most suitable site for a dam and reservoir. On 29 July 1901 Lippincott made a filing with the Department of the Interior on behalf of James Duval Phelan, who was in turn acting on behalf of the City and County of San Francisco, for permission to siphon water from the Tuolumne for San Francisco and to build two reservoir sites, one at Hetch Hetchy, the other at Lake Eleanor to the northwest.

Phelan's filing sat for two years on the desk of Secretary of the Interior E. A. Hitchcock. Finally, on 20 January 1903, Hitchcock rejected Phelan's request on the grounds that the Secretary of the Interior, in Hitchcock's opinion, did not possess the authority to dispose of properties within the boundaries of the federally protected Yosemite National Park. By this time, Phelan was no longer mayor, having been defeated for reelection in the aftermath of a bitter waterfront strike. Phelan and Marsden Manson, also out of office, sustained their hopes regarding the Tuolumne–Hetch Hetchy project, as did Phelan's friend Franklin Lane, another Progressive Democrat, who had won election to the office of city attorney of San Francisco when Phelan had become mayor and had managed to remain in office.

Franklin Lane had close connections to President Theodore Roosevelt, who would soon name him to the Interstate Commerce Commission. In the summer of 1905 Lane and Manson secured an interview with Roosevelt in Washington and asked the President to review the refusal of Secretary Hitchcock to grant Phelan's request on behalf of San Francisco for Tuolumne water and the two reservoir sites. Temperamentally disposed toward engineering projects sponsored by patrician Progressives, Roosevelt, who also played an important interventionist role in implementing the water ambitions of Los Angeles, promised Manson and Lane that he would seek a second opinion. A few weeks later, United States Attorney General M. D. Purdy reported confidentially back to Roosevelt that in his opinion the Secretary of the Interior did indeed possess such discretionary powers. For some reason, Purdy's opinion remained confidential until former mayor James Duval Phelan learned of it in April 1906.

In the meanwhile, the San Francisco Board of Supervisors, under pressure from landowners dependent upon the natural flow of the Tuolumne for irrigation, had all but abandoned the Hetch Hetchy claim on the grounds that Phelan's 1901 filing, given the difficulties it had encountered with the federal government, was little more than a symbolic gesture. Matters might have languished indefinitely had not the earthquake and fire of April 1906 brought the water-seeking elite of San Francisco even more closely in touch with President Roosevelt. Warned against the administration of Mayor Eugene Schmitz, which was dominated by political boss Abraham Ruef, Roosevelt channeled federal emergency relief to San Francisco through a Committee of One Hundred, led by former Mayor Phelan. In the months that followed, Roosevelt received favorable reports regarding Phelan and the reforming Progressive wing of the San Francisco oligarchy, both Republicans and Democrats, which Phelan led. This same group soon went on the offensive against municipal corruption, assisted by none other than the President himself, who lent the Phelan group the services of William Burns, head of the Secret Service, and Francis Heney, the best-known and most effective special prosecutor in federal service. By 1908 Schmitz was out of office, replaced by the scholarly educator Edward Robeson Taylor, dean of the Hastings College of Law, and Boss Ruef was en route to San Quentin. President Roosevelt took great satisfaction in having helped usher San Francisco into the Progressive era.

Not surprisingly, the Phelan group also renewed its dialogue with the President regarding the disposition of the Tuolumne River and the Hetch Hetchy and Lake Eleanor dam sites. Already advised by Attorney General Purdy that such a transfer was legal, Roosevelt authorized his new Secretary of the Interior, James Garfield, to reopen the matter. On the evening of 27 July 1907 Garfield met with mayor Taylor, former mayor Phelan, Marsden Manson, whom Taylor would soon appoint city engineer, and a number of other selected San Franciscans for the purpose of reviewing his predecessor's negative declaration.

After hearing Manson's presentation on behalf of San Francisco, Garfield returned to Washington, where he consulted with Roosevelt's other key advisor on environmental matters, Chief Forester of the United States Gifford Pinchot, who had done so much to help Los Angeles obtain development rights to the Owens Valley. The Secretary also conferred with the President. Both the President and his chief forester were favorable to the ambitions of San Francisco toward the Hetch Hetchy. On 11 May 1908 Garfield granted San Francisco permission to develop Lake Eleanor. He also assigned to San Francisco secondary rights to the

Hetch Hetchy, to be used after the Lake Eleanor reservoir no longer met the city's water needs.

When the Garfield decision became public, Taylor, Phelan, Manson, and other members of the pro–Hetch Hetchy block swung into action. Their first challenge was to align the legislators of San Francisco behind the project. In August 1908 the entire Board of Supervisors, accompanied by the city engineer and representatives of the Mayor's office and the press, embarked by train, stage-coach, and horseback for a two-week tour of Lake Eleanor and the Hetch Hetchy. The sojourn of the San Francisco officials into the High Sierra back country had its idyllic aspects: trout dinners on the shores of Lake Eleanor, the camaraderie of good whiskey by the campfire, the learned lectures on water management given by former state engineer William Hammond Hall, who unbeknownst to the Supervisors was busy buying up critical property in the vicinity against the day that San Francisco would be forced to meet his price. Convinced as they were intended to be, the Supervisors placed a measure on the ballot for 12 November 1908 asking approval of the project and authorizing $600,000 in bonded debt to purchase needed private properties outside Yosemite Park. The measure passed seven to one.

Not everyone approved of San Francisco's plans. If one side of the Progressive imagination favored well-ordered cities, organized and governed in the public interest and served by grand public works, there was another side of Progressivism enamored of the fact and symbol of wilderness. Founded in June 1892 in San Francisco, the Sierra Club gave organizational expression to a conservationist sentiment that had been building throughout the post-frontier era. The charter and early membership of the Sierra Club included the academic elite of the Bay Area and other urban professionals for whom the outdoor life, focused mainly upon mountaineering, constituted a cherished ritual of California identity. The first president of the Sierra Club, the naturalist John Muir, epitomized to his own and succeeding generations the way in which the highest form of self-expression was to be found in the relationship to wilderness.

The members of the Sierra Club were by definition Progressives, wedded to a philosophy and practice of public interest. So too were the backers of the Hetch Hetchy venture. As much as Phelan appreciated the outdoors (preferably as a formal Italian garden), the millionaire former mayor—well traveled, urbane, a lover of opera and the good life—envisioned California primarily in terms of its cities or, at its most rustic, as a suburban villa in the Italian style, such as his own neo-Mediterranean estate, Montalvo, south of San Francisco. For Phelan, California was the splash of baroque fountains in a sun-drenched plaza. For John Muir and his fellow Sierra Club members (Phelan never joined), California was a trek through the High Country. If one probes the attitudes of the Sierra Clubbers closely, so many of them Berkeley and Stanford faculty and their suburbanized fellow travelers, an anti-urban bias, especially an anti–San Francisco bias, can quickly be discerned; for there, across the Bay from Berkeley, in San Francisco, among immigrants, Catholics, Jews, workingmen and women, ward heelers and political bosses, seethed a sensibility that had concerns other than the High Country on its mind. For Phelan and the others sharing his opinion, the loss of the Hetch Hetchy Valley (the Little Yosemite, it was called) to a dam and reservoir was tragic but worth the price; for from the water resources of the Tuolumne a great urban civilization could be achieved. For the activists of the Sierra Club, the proposal to dam the Tuolumne at Hetch Hetchy constituted an act of desecration of what California was most fundamentally about.

In April 1909 attorney William Colby, a Berkeley resident, organized the Society for the Preservation of National Parks to oppose awarding the Hetch Hetchy to San Francisco. Sharing headquarters with the Sierra Club in the Mills Building in San Francisco, the Society, with John Muir as president, enlisted supporters from around the United States, including a number of politically skilled activists from the Appalachian Mountain Club. Before Colby could bring the resources of the Sierra Club to bear on the struggle, he had to face significant dissension in the membership. Sierra Clubbers such as Mayor Edward Robeson Taylor of San Francisco and William Hammond Hall, both of them charter members, and city engineer Marsden Manson, also a member, could be expected to be on the side of San Francisco. But support for San Francisco was coming from other members as well, from such influential figures as University of California president Benjamin Ide Wheeler, who had played a key role in getting Manson to Gifford Pinchot and Theodore Roosevelt in 1905, and Professor Charles Marx of Stanford, a charter member of the Sierra Club who was an engineering consultant and chief spokesman for the Hetch Hetchy project.

The support of the San Francisco proposal by such respected conservationists underscored that the Progressive mind, Bay Area version, was significantly divided on the Hetch Hetchy question. Unkindest cut of all, Warren Olney, the San Francisco attorney in whose offices the Sierra Club had been incorporated in June 1892 and still a director of the organization, emerged as defender of the Hetch Hetchy option. The Sierra Club, Olney argued in an open letter dated 22 December 1909, was acting as a selfish elite. As beautiful as the remote valley of the Hetch Hetchy might be, only the affluent few could afford to get to a place unserved by roads. Even John Muir, until recently at least, had seemed indifferent to the charms of the remote valley. Under the Progressive principle of the greatest good for the greatest number, Olney argued, the Hetch Hetchy would have to be sacrificed so that the San Francisco Bay Area could attain its proper growth and thereby extend the benefits of prosperity and health to one million residents and to future generations who might choose to live in this favored urban setting.

At a special election held in January 1910, the Sierra Club voted 589 to 161 in favor of fighting the Hetch Hetchy proposal. For the next four years, the Club, acting as the Society for the Preservation of National Parks, waged a brilliant campaign of delay against the City and County of San Francisco. Lake Eleanor and the nearby Cherry Creek watershed sufficed for San Francisco's needs, the Sierra Club argued. Even proponents of the Hetch Hetchy site admitted that there were other possibilities: the South Eel River and the Putah Creek watersheds in Humboldt County, for example. Others argued on behalf of the Stanislaus, the Mokelumne, the Feather, the American, the Yuba, the Sacramento, and the San Joaquin rivers. Clear Lake and Lake Tahoe had their advocates. However late his appreciation of Hetch Hetchy might have been, John Muir was quick to throw the full force of his personality and the full power of his eloquence behind the defense of the endangered Valley. It became the last great battle of his life.

In a bold opening attack, the Nature Lovers, as their opponents derisively called them, bombarded the House of Representatives Committee on Public Lands hearing the Hetch Hetchy proposal in December 1908 and January 1909 with enough telegrams of protest to fill more than one hundred densely printed pages in the *Congressional Record*. Convened to review an exchange of properties between San Francisco and the federal government as advocated in a bill submitted by Senator Frank Flint, the Southern California attorney who had played a major role in securing the Owens Valley for Los Angeles and was sent to the Senate as a reward, the House Committee buckled under the deluge of telegrammed protest, reinforced by the articulate opposition of the preservationists and a brilliant brief submitted by the Appalachian Mountain Club. Dispiritedly, the San Francisco delegation—Supervisor A. H. Giannini and city engineer Manson, reinforced by Olney, Phelan, city attorney Percy Long, and others who rallied to their side when the efficient opposition surfaced—asked Flint to withdraw his bill while it returned to San Francisco and regrouped.

John Muir thereupon carried off the bold stroke of bringing no less than the newly elected President himself, William Howard Taft, to the Yosemite in September 1909. Sweating profusely, the three-hundred-pound President followed Muir down the four mile trail from Glacier Point to the Valley floor. After allowing the exhausted President time to rest, Muir broke out his maps and charts and argued against the damming of the Hetch Hetchy. On the contrary, Muir argued, the Hetch Hetchy should be connected to the Yosemite by roads and trails so as to make it accessible to tourists. Mesmerized by Muir (and perhaps fearing another four-mile hike!), Taft promised to have his Secretary of the Interior look into the matter. As a result of Muir's advocacy, San Francisco's water project languished throughout the Taft administration, despite the fact that on 10 January 1910 the voters of San Francisco authorized $45 million in construction bonds, nearly twice the cost of the Los Angeles Aqueduct.

As early as February 1910 Taft's Secretary of the Interior, R. A. Ballinger of Seattle, notified San Francisco that since he was satisfied that Lake Eleanor alone was sufficient, he was giving serious thought to eliminating the promise of Hetch Hetchy from his predecessor's decision. It was up to San Francisco to show cause why the Hetch Hetchy Valley and reservoir should not be eliminated from such a permit. At Ballinger's request President Taft appointed the Army Corps of Engineers to sit as a board of review. At the hearing, held on 25 May 1910, the San Francisco delegation—the new mayor of San Francisco, P. H. McCarthy, a building trades union official lacking the erudite smoothness of either Phelan or Edward Robeson Taylor, together with city engineer Manson and Professor Marx of Stanford—soon discovered that it did not possess sufficient information to make its case against the preservationists and the Spring Valley Water Company, the private company which had been supplying San Francisco with its water since 1858. Spring Valley was also waging an effective campaign against the Hetch Hetchy project so as to prevent the municipalization of water in San Francisco, a measure Spring Valley had lobbied against and defeated in the bond issue of January 1910. Unable to prove conclusively that it required the Hetch Hetchy in addition to Lake Eleanor, San Francisco asked for and received a year's postponement.

San Francisco also received some crucial advice from President Taft himself: if San Francisco wanted to make its case effectively before the Board of Army Engineers and eventually to Secretary Ballinger and the White House, it would need a comprehensive report prepared by an engineer of the stature of John Freeman of Providence, Rhode Island, the consultant who had helped Los Angeles formulate its aqueduct plan in late 1906. Freeman had already been active as a consultant to the San Francisco delegation as it prepared to face the Army engineers. San Francisco took Taft's advice and retained Freeman to prepare an extensive report. The Army itself, meanwhile, acting in its capacity as administrator of the Yosemite and as public works advisor to the President through its Corps of Engineers, sent two platoons of cavalry into the Yosemite to make its own independent survey of the watershed.

Most reports are filed and forgotten. Some have a partial effect on the decision-making process. A few reports, the very few, envision and help materialize the future. Issued in 1912 in 401 closely printed pages, the Freeman Report evoked for San Francisco and Washington, D.C. the urban culture Tuolumne water from Hetch Hetchy might bring about. Working with former city engineer C. E. Grunsky and the incumbent city engineer Marsden Manson, Freeman expanded the scope of Manson's 1908 proposal, which had itself expanded Grunsky's plan of 1902. Manson had called for the delivery of sixty million gallons daily, intended for San Francisco. Freeman increased the system's capacity to 160 million gallons daily, to be increased over time to 400 million, intended for the entire San Francisco Bay Area. With an adequate water supply, projected over a hundred years, the communities circling the Bay would develop into a great metropolis, which Freeman's allies in the Greater San Francisco Movement, established in 1907, envisioned as an integrated borough system on the model of New York City. To serve further this impending metropolis, Freeman added a strong program of hydro-electrical generation. Cheap and abundant electricity, he argued, was just as necessary as water for the urban future.

Where Manson considered Lake Eleanor and the Hetch Hetchy as separate storage sites, Freeman linked the lake, the nearby Cherry Valley catchment area, and the Hetch Hetchy into one integrated system. The waters of Cherry Valley and Lake Eleanor would be stored in a main reservoir created by the dammed Hetch Hetchy. From there it would be fed by tunnel to an outlet point above Moccasin Creek, where, falling 1,250 feet, it would drive the generators of the principal power plant. Passing by tunnel through the Sierra foothills, the water would cross the San Joaquin Valley by pipeline, move through the Diablo Range by another tunnel system, then proceed via pipeline to the San Mateo County reservoirs of the Spring Valley Water Company, which Freeman integrated into his program rather than replace them with a competing distribution system.

With elegant precision Freeman set forth in the language and imagery of water engineering the great city that would one day be materialized around San Francisco Bay after the City of San Francisco had seized its opportunity and constructed the Hetch Hetchy project. In this regard, the Freeman Report resembled the city plan submitted to San Francisco by Daniel Hudson Burnham in April 1906—an unembarrassed, unequivocal election of urbanism as the destined future and dominant imagery for California. Freeman illustrated his report with photographs of great cities, together with their reservoirs and water distribution systems: Boston, New York, London, Oslo, each of them a suggestion of San Francisco's own future as an important city. Nor did Freeman avoid addressing objections to the loss of Hetch Hetchy. Should the city of San Francisco be compelled to spend some $10 or $20 million extra for another less desirable source of domestic water, he asked, simply in order that ten or twenty lovers of solitude might have this beautiful valley mostly to themselves? The lake created by the damming of Hetch Hetchy, Freeman argued, could itself become a popular tourist destination, once a road system was established. Freeman illustrated this argument with photographs of Boston's Middlesex Fells Reservoir in Winchester surrounded by Sunday strollers, Croton Lake in upstate New York, Lake Oifjord in Norway, Loch Katrine in Scotland, the Graig Goch dam and reservoir on the Elan River in Wales. Hetch Hetchy advocates would soon be employing with telling effect before elected officials in Washington Freeman's argument that the proposed Hetch Hetchy reservoir could be transformed into a landscaped, accessible lake, to be enjoyed by the general public.

Once the Hetch Hetchy advocates had their proposal in the professional format demanded by Washington, they began to search for an engineer capable of translating Freeman's recommendations into reality. City engineer Marsden Manson, unfortunately, had so overworked himself on behalf of the Hetch Hetchy project, which he personally had done so much to keep alive between 1900 and 1912, that his health had weakened. If this were not enough, Manson's professional reputation had plummeted when leaks developed in the Twin Peaks reservoir he had hastily designed while distracted by the Hetch Hetchy negotiations.

Dispirited, Manson resigned under pressure. Elected on 8 January 1912, the new Mayor of San Francisco, James Rolph, a Progressive Republican shipper and banker, turned to the well-known engineer Michael Maurice O'Shaughnessy. Then forty-eight, O'Shaughnessy had arrived in San Francisco from his native Ireland in the mid-1880s and prospered as a consulting engineer. By 1892, however, the Board of Supervisors was refusing to pay O'Shaughnessy $10,000 in fees he felt was owed him, and so he shook the dust of San Francisco from his feet and moved to Hawaii, where he built thirty-two miles of tunnels and aqueducts in four years. In 1907 O'Shaughnessy became chief engineer of the Southern California Mountain Water Company of San Diego, which he proceeded to expand and modernize.

Determined to build the Hetch Hetchy while he was mayor and otherwise to expand the public works infrastructure of post-earthquake San Francisco, Rolph wanted the best possible city engineer he could find. When all recommendations pointed to O'Shaughnessy, Rolph set about to woo the one-time San Franciscan back to the Bay Area. At a Sunday morning meeting on 31 August 1912 in the Whitcomb Hotel on Market Street, where San Francisco maintained its temporary city hall after the earthquake and fire, the persuasive mayor—resplendent as ever in pin-striped pants, cutaway coat, cravat, and Hamilton collar, a fresh boutonniere in his lapel, and on his feet the cowboy boots that were his trademark—outlined to the hesitating but tempted O'Shaughnessy what he had in mind.

First of all, Rolph argued, there was the Hetch Hetchy project itself, a public work on a scale even more impressive than the Los Angeles Aqueduct currently under construction. Then there was the Spring Valley Water Company for O'Shaughnessy to run once San Francisco purchased it, and a great city hall for O'Shaughnessy to build from the designs of John Bakewell and Arthur Brown, architects trained at the Ecole des Beaux Arts, who had submitted to Rolph plans for what remains one of the finest public buildings in the United States. San Francisco also needed an expanded streetcar and tunnel system through Stockton Street and Twin Peaks so as to open new areas to settlement, along with a new high-pressure water system so as to prevent a reoccurrence of the great fire following the earthquake of April 1906. Then there was the Ocean Beach highway as called for in the Burnham Plan, and the Panama-Pacific International Exposition planned for 1915, which necessitated the draining of the marshy Harbor View area at the northern edge of the city.

Dazzled by the prospect of being personally responsible for the creation *a novo* of the public works infrastructure of an emergent American city, O'Shaughnessy also believed Rolph when the mayor promised that as city engineer O'Shaughnessy would have no unnecessary political interference. Encouraged by his wife, a native San Franciscan with a bad case of homesickness, O'Shaughnessy accepted Sunny Jim's offer. Over the next twenty years, this Irish engineer, like his counterpart William Mulholland in Los Angeles, lived and worked on the cutting edge of civic construction, a living avatar of urban renewal and expansion.

O'Shaughnessy spent his first month in the field, the Freeman Report in hand, reviewing its recommendations. Returning to San Francisco from the High Sierra, the city engineer of San Francisco held a press conference on 20 September 1912 and endorsed Freeman's recommendation of the Hetch Hetchy dam site. Over the next year, O'Shaughnessy adapted the Freeman plan so as to place certain portions of the pipeline in better conformity with the terrain. He also adjusted the aqueduct route so that the total fall of water from Hetch Hetchy to the Crystal Springs reservoir south of San Francisco would be, elegantly, by gravity alone, with no mechanical pumping. In most instances, however, O'Shaughnessy accepted the Freeman Report as his marching orders. Generously, he praised Freeman for his vision in expanding a one-city, sixty-million-gallon system into a regional resource with an eventual capacity of four hundred million gallons a day, capable of serving a metropolitan region of four million residents.

Once again, the debate shifted to Washington, this time for its denouement. Two developments stood in San Francisco's favor. In February 1913 the advisory Board of Army Engineers appointed by President Taft issued a decision more or less in favor of the Tuolumne (and by implication the Hetch Hetchy) on the basis of comparative cost; and in March the ambivalent Taft himself and his skeptical Secretary of the Interior, R. A. Ballinger, were replaced by President Woodrow Wilson and his new Secretary of the Interior, Franklin Lane, formerly the city attorney of San Francisco. As city attorney in the Phelan administration, Lane had prepared San Francisco's first filings on the Tuolumne. A mere month into the Wilson administration, John Raker, in whose congressional district was the Hetch Hetchy, introduced a series of five affiliated bills into the House that would empower the complex exchange of properties, grants of right of way, and construction permits necessary for San Francisco to build its water system.

Hearings began in late June amidst conditions of torrid heat. Now was played out for the last time—in committee, in hotel lobbies and corridors, on the floor of the House and Senate—the drama of Hetch Hetchy preservationists versus Hetch Hetchy constructionists that so remarkably distilled and expressed two radically opposing views of what California was or should become. Supporting the preservation of the Hetch Hetchy, the National Committee for the Preservation of the Yosemite National Park, chaired by Robert Underwood Johnson of New York, editor of *Century* magazine, aligned such prestigious figures as John Muir (then weakening and no longer in control of the movement); Charles Eliot, the former president of Harvard; Lord James Bryce, British ambassador to the United States and author of *The American Commonwealth* (1888); and a host of prominent naturalists and conservationists, who either testified personally or filed briefs opposing Baker's resolutions.

San Francisco, its opponents argued, was exaggerating its need for water and was unfairly making the Hetch Hetchy seem the most cost-efficient means of meeting that fabricated need. San Francisco was being especially dishonest, they charged, when it argued that the Hetch Hetchy would be aesthetically improved by its transformation into a lake surrounded by landscaping and architecture. To counter this notion that a lake would be just as beautiful as a valley—upon which the San Francisco forces were repeatedly insistent—the preservationists circulated a portfolio of photographs of the Hetch Hetchy Valley taken by J. N. LeConte which unambiguously, so they thought, verified the beauty for what they were then referring to as the Grand Canyon on the Tuolumne.

O'Shaughnessy and Phelan, two very different types of Irish-Americans, played conspicuous roles as lobbyists in San Francisco's final offensive. Bluff, direct, inspiring confidence in himself as an engineer and man of action, O'Shaughnessy roamed the corridors of Capitol Hill lobbying on behalf of the Freeman Report. The Nature Lovers, as O'Shaughnessy insisted on calling his opponents, cared more about trees than about people. When Underwood Johnson of *Century* suggested that San Francisco turn to condensed sea water as a water source, O'Shaughnessy gleefully derided this impractical solution (it would cost, he claimed, $2.25 a gallon to distill sea water) as conclusive evidence that the Nature Lovers were incapable of making valid recommendations for alternative sources of supply.

It was James Duval Phelan, however, the originator of the Hetch Hetchy project in 1901, who gave the most effective testimony during House and Senate hearings. Polished, erudite, assured, a Progressive patrician Democrat who would himself be returning to Washington the next year as United States Senator, Phelan epitomized the very urbanity he was pleading for on behalf of San Francisco. A lack of civic spirit and a neglect of public duty, Phelan argued, had for too long delayed not only the necessary water development, but the entire civic maturity of San Francisco. San Francisco was now asking the Congress and the nation for assistance in struggling toward its long-delayed coming of age as a metropolitan region. The waters of the Tuolumne would make possible a progressive urban civilization on the shores of San Francisco Bay.

Converted to a program of public water and power by the example of Los Angeles, publisher William Randolph Hearst lent his formidable assistance to the lobbying efforts of his native city. On the morning of 2 December 1913, the day the Senate was to take up debate on the Raker Act, each senator received a special Washington edition of the editorial page of the San Francisco *Examiner* depicting the Hetch Hetchy as a lake ringed by landscaped boulevards and Doric observation temples. "Does this beautiful lake ruin this beautiful Valley?" the *Examiner* asked. The answer was obviously no. Seventeen days later, after prolonged and acrimonious debate, the Senate passed the Raker Act 43 to 25 and sent the measure to Woodrow Wilson, who signed it into law on 19 December 1913. After thirteen years of maneuvering, the Federal government was responding to San Francisco's water needs as the *Examiner* flyer had urged it to do—"in an open-handed, open-hearted American manner."

In 1916 bond revenues became available, and the Hetch Hetchy project commenced with the construction of the necessary camps and a sixty-eight-mile standard-gauge railroad linking the valley to the outside world. In late 1919 the Utah Construction Company of San Francisco began work on the Hetch Hetchy dam itself. Unlike Los Angeles, San Francisco preferred to put its project out to bid rather than build it directly through its Board of Public Works.

In the first phase of this $5 million project, the Tuolumne River was temporarily dammed and diverted by tunnel around the permanent dam site at a narrow gorge where the river left the valley. Then ensued the heroic task of excavating the gorge down to the bedrock on which the iron and steel framework could be emplaced preparatory to the pouring of concrete. Unlike Mulholland, O'Shaughnessy left the design of his dam to others, specifically to his longtime associate R. P. McIntosh, who devised an expandable scheme that would allow the Hetch Hetchy dam to be thickened at its base and heightened by eighty-five feet when an increased capacity became necessary. Even in its first phase, however, the Hetch Hetchy dam—226.5 feet high, 298 feet thick at its base, 605 feet across— was at the time the second highest dam in the United States after Arrowrock Dam in Idaho.

It took five hundred men a year and a half, working from the fall of 1921 to the spring of 1923, to pour the 398,000 cubic yards of concrete that went into the gargantuan structure, the single most ambitious public work ever to be undertaken in California to that date. At night they worked under floodlights, and the resulting spectacle—the hoists and conveyors flying against the glare of searchlights, the dinky trains bringing construction materials to the pouring sites, the rivers of concrete descending in torrents through directed chutes; men everywhere, clambering over the steel and molds, directing their machines like figures in a High Sierran *Peer Gynt*—asserted unequivocally and with eerie beauty (one report compared the illumined scene to a fairyland) that after its eons of timeless solitude the Hetch Hetchy was being transformed through engineering on behalf of San Francisco. On 7 July 1923 Mayor Rolph dedicated the completed dam: O'Shaughnessy Dam (not even Mulholland of Los Angeles had been so honored), with its holding capacity at sixty-seven billion gallons, three times that of the San Mateo reservoirs of the Spring Valley Water Company. O'Shaughnessy Dam, the mayor orated, was the masterwork of the great engineer whose name it bore, a dam destined to stand throughout the centuries as one of the mightiest structures built by man.

It took O'Shaughnessy another eleven years of construction to get the waters stored by O'Shaughnessy Dam down to San Francisco. All in all, the project cost $100 million. Former state engineer William Hammond Hall and his associates alone demanded and received $1 million for property they had acquired for about $100,000 in the Cherry Creek watershed in anticipation of the Hetch Hetchy project. (At long last, after a lifetime of trying, Hall had made his big score and could settle comfortably into his leather chair at the Pacific Union Club atop Nob

Hill, a wealthy man among his kind.) By 1924 the original bond issue of $45 million had been used up. The voters of San Francisco authorized an additional $33 million on 7 October 1924.

Two men played key roles in keeping the Hetch Hetchy project financially feasible: O'Shaughnessy himself and A. P. Giannini, founder and president of the San Francisco–based Bank of Italy, later the Bank of America. By keeping the project on schedule, O'Shaughnessy was able to bring on line the revenue-producing hydro-electric Moccasin Power Plant by 14 August 1925. San Francisco was thus able to defray costs through collecting $2 million yearly from the sale of public power. As a key organizer of a banking syndicate calling itself the Construction Company of North America, Giannini led the sale of the first $45 million bond issue. In December 1928, when sluggish bond sales threatened to bring construction on a tunnel through the Diablo Range to a halt, Giannini's Bank of Italy bought up $41 million in unsold bonds. Giannini himself presented Mayor Rolph with a check for $4 million on the steps of City Hall, a timely payment which enabled San Francisco to continue construction. Thanks to Giannini, San Francisco was capable of financing its future from a local lending institution. In 1932, despite the Depression, another $6.5 million bond issue was passed to complete the last five miles of the aqueduct.

Thirty-four years after Mayor Phelan made his first filing on the Tuolumne, twenty-two years after O'Shaughnessy arrived in San Francisco to take charge, the Hetch Hetchy project—four dams, five major reservoirs, a hydro-electric power plant, nearly a hundred miles of pipeline, sixty-six miles of tunnel—reached completion. The system incorporated major dams at Hetch Hetchy and Lake Eleanor, together with an Early Intake Dam twelve miles downstream that put the released waters into the aqueduct. Even further downstream, the Moccasin Power House was generating five hundred million kilowatt-hours annually, an amount capable of meeting over 80 percent of San Francisco's needs in the mid-1930s. This hydro-electricity was not sold directly to consumers, as was the case in Los Angeles, but was sold wholesale to a private utility, Pacific Gas & Electric. While publicly generated electricity was used to power the streetcars of San Francisco's municipally owned streetcar system, San Francisco voters had rejected the municipalized model of the Department of Water and Power of Los Angeles, preferring instead to leave the distribution of hydroelectricity to the privately held Pacific Gas & Electric. San Francisco did, however, take its water public, acquiring the Spring Valley Water Company in 1929 and in 1932 establishing a Public Utilities Commission to supervise the water delivery.

From the Moccasin Power House in the Sierra foothills, the San Francisco aqueduct crossed the San Joaquin Valley via pipeline in a route parallel to the Tuolumne riverbed, entered the Diablo Range tunnel, traversed the southern edge of San Francisco Bay via a trestle bridge, and flowed through one last tunnel, the Pulgas, before roaring beneath a serene Greek temple in the style of an *erectheum* for storage in the upper and lower reservoirs of Crystal Springs Lake. The entire system operated by gravity fall, as O'Shaughnessy had insisted. As much as possible, the engineering upon which San Francisco envisioned and materialized its future functioned as a natural event.

Eighty-nine men lost their lives in the course of the twenty-year, $100 million project; so did one woman, Ethel Earl Moyer, a nurse who died in a hospital fire in 1922. Sixteen days before the waters of the Tuolumne arrived at the Pulgas Water Temple on 28 October 1934 for storage in the Crystal Springs reservoirs, Michael O'Shaughnessy died of a heart attack at the age of seventy. He never heard the roar of the water god as it rushed beneath the *erectheum* toward the city whose future was now being so dramatically assured.

11

Angels, Dams, and Dynamos

Metropolitan Los Angeles and the Colorado River Project

*T*O achieve its urban destiny, San Francisco appropriated the water and hydro-electricity of the Tuolomne. To become the center of an emergent American region, Los Angeles required the sixth largest river in the United States, the mighty Colorado, the Mississippi of the Far West, the dependable supply of water for 244,000 square miles touching upon seven Western states. The Colorado River Basin includes parts of southwestern Wyoming, eastern Utah, western Colorado, eastern Nevada, western New Mexico, the entire state of Arizona (the only state whose entire land mass is within the Basin), and a fragment of southeastern California, the Salton Sink.

The moment planning seriously began in the 1920s to impound the waters of the Colorado at Boulder Canyon on the Arizona-Nevada border, it was recognized—by Arizona especially, which fought the project to the Supreme Court—that Southern California would be its prime and most immediate beneficiary. Wyoming, Utah, Colorado, New Mexico, Nevada, and Arizona, after all, were but in the infancy of their population and land-resource development. Southern California, by contrast—Los Angeles, especially, the largest city in the state since 1920—was entering into its second great boom of subdivision and population growth. A phalanx of prominent Southern Californians and their allies in the North played the determinant role in getting the Colorado River Project envisioned, approved, funded, and constructed, in the full knowledge that in doing so they were establishing the foundations of a mighty region, dominated by an all-powerful Los Angeles.

As early as 1859 Dr. Oliver Wozencraft was calling for the construction of a gravity canal from the Colorado to southeastern California. Irrigation engineer George Chaffey of Los Angeles completed such a project in May 1901. Chaffey brought the waters of the Colorado into the Salton Sink, which he renamed Imperial Valley, via a superficially dug gravity canal which followed the course of a long-vanished river westward across the northern edge of Baja California before recrossing the border. Hardly a scratch on the surface of the desert, the Imperial Canal soon filled with silt, and its levee collapsed in a catastrophic flood in 1905. Nevertheless, Chaffey's canal proved that the waters of the Colorado River could be successfully brought into Southern California.

In 1918 Secretary of the Interior Franklin Lane, who as city attorney of San Francisco had done so much to make the Hetch Hetchy project a reality, commissioned engineer C. E. Grunsky of San Francisco, another Hetch Hetchy activist, and Dr. Elwood Mead, a professor of irrigation engineering at UC Berkeley and chairman of the California Land Settlement Board, to report on the possibilities of an All-American Canal to replace the largely Mexican channel built by George Chaffey. Mead, Grunsky, and other experts on the duly established All-American Canal Board reported favorably back to Lane in June 1919 with specific recommendations for a Colorado River irrigation canal into southeastern California on American territory. Two years later, the Bureau of Reclamation began geological surveys and exploratory drillings on the Colorado River as it flowed through a series of canyons on the border between Nevada and Arizona to determine the best site for a dam. By April 1923 Reclamation geologists and engineers were recommending Black Canyon, a site some thirty miles southeast of Las Vegas, as the best place to impound the waters of the Colorado.

Three other Californians, meanwhile—Herbert Hoover, Secretary of Commerce in the Harding administration, United States Senator Hiram Johnson, a former governor of California; and Phil Swing, congressman from the district that included Imperial Valley—were also playing important roles in advancing the project. Convening representatives in November 1922 from the seven Colorado River Basin states at Bishop's Lodge, a resort outside Santa Fe, Herbert Hoover hammered out over fifteen days of intense negotiation an agreement, the Colorado River Compact, which established formulas for the sharing and distribution of Colorado River waters and hydro-electricity once a dam and aqueduct system were constructed. With a site chosen and a compact tentatively complete (Arizona would soon bolt the agreement), Senator Hiram Johnson and Congressman Phil Swing introduced the Boulder Canyon Project Act into Congress in 1923. The Act called for the Bureau of Reclamation to build a dam at Boulder/Black Canyon as the centerpiece of a seven-state water project. (Although Boulder Canyon had placed second to the nearby Black Canyon in the recommendations of the Bureau of Reclamation, the name Boulder Canyon, hence Boulder Dam, had by then attached itself to the entire project.)

As soon as the Bureau of Reclamation made its proposal for Boulder Dam, William Mulholland, chief engineer of the Municipal Water Bureau of Los Angeles, began to position his city as the prime participant in the project. First, Mulholland sought and obtained a bond issue to finance a feasibility study as to how Los Angeles could obtain water and hydro-electricity from the Colorado. In

October and November of 1923, Mulholland and a small party of engineers surveyed the Boulder Canyon site and searched for possible routes for an aqueduct from Boulder Canyon into Southern California. Over the next four years, Mulholland sent sixteen survey parties into the rugged desert and mountainous back country between Boulder Canyon and Southern California. Now past seventy years of age, Mulholland was planning a project that would bring into Los Angeles four times the water that he had brought in from the Owens River in 1913.

In 1924 Dr. Elwood Mead of the University of California, an ardent backer of the Boulder project, became commissioner of the Bureau of Reclamation. Mead, Mulholland, Hoover, Swing, Johnson, and the other backers of the great dam were Progressives in the grand manner: advocates, that is, of large-scale public works as substance and symbol of modern American civilization. For each of these men and for so many others who put themselves behind the Boulder Canyon Project Act, public works administered by appointed officials acting in the public interest constituted a mode of public service psychologically and morally higher than the elective politics which authorized and financed construction. Politicians lived for the victories and exhilarations of the moment. Engineers and dam builders, and the appointed public officials who directed their efforts, built for the ages, functioning in a higher realm, in terms of struggle and results, than the day-to-day compromises, the naked greed and self-interest, of elective politics.

Not surprisingly, elected politicians, especially those from Utah, Nevada, and Arizona, states which felt they had the least to gain from the Project, delayed it for five years in the Congress. Only reluctantly did President Calvin Coolidge, arch-advocate of minimalism in government, sign the fourth version of the Swing-Johnson bill in December 1928, authorizing the construction of Boulder Dam, as it was then called, and its supporting systems. Arizona proceeded to take its case to the courts.

Very soon, Herbert Hoover—Californian, Progressive, the greatest engineer of them all—succeeded Coolidge in the Oval Office. While sharing some of his predecessor's caution regarding the scope of the federal government, Hoover believed ardently in public works, and with equal ardor he assented to the importance to the southern regions of his home state of what was shaping up to be the most ambitious public work in human history: the Great Dam first called Boulder, then called Hoover, then called Boulder again, then renamed Hoover Dam for the ages.

In the *Atlantic Monthly* for February 1929, Arthur Powell Davis, the nephew of Major John Wesley Powell, who had first explored the Colorado in 1867–1869, made what became the controlling case, the establishment rationale, for the construction of Boulder Dam. Davis's essay carried great weight, for he had served as an engineer for the Reclamation Service since it was founded in 1902, had become chief of the Bureau, resigning in 1923, and had been the first to advocate a dam at the Black Canyon site, doing this as early as 1902. Arthur

Powell Davis, in fact, deserves as much credit as anyone for envisioning the Boulder Dam project.

The Dam, Davis wrote, had four major benefits: flood control, water conservation, domestic water supply, and power. Boulder Dam, he argued, would be good for each of the seven states in the Colorado River Basin, especially Arizona, which was fighting the Project in the courts. For all of Davis's interstate Basin-wide arguments regarding irrigation, flood control, evaporation, and silt control, however, it was his arguments on behalf of municipal water supply and hydro-electrical power that were of most relevance to Southern California; and even Davis, the most disinterested of federal civil servants, could not help but zero in on the benefits of water and power that the Boulder Dam would bring to the Southland. Enthusiastically, Davis linked Boulder Dam and the proposed Los Angeles Aqueduct, part of the newly organized Metropolitan Water District of Southern California, as part and parcel of the same bold plan.

From the first, Southern California could not help but dominate the planning process. Writing in *The Annals of the American Academy of Political and Social Science* for January 1928, Dr. E. F. Scattergood, chief electrical engineer and general manager of the Bureau of Power and Light of the City of Los Angeles, while paying attention to the benefits of flood control and irrigation, together with the patriotic necessity of having a canal on American soil, waxed especially rhapsodic when it came to the question of using Boulder Dam to bring water and power into Southern California. The City of Los Angeles, Scattergood pointed out, had more than doubled its population in the decade of the 1920s. It now stood at 1.2 million. The Owens Valley Aqueduct had made this growth possible. Soon, not only Los Angeles, but the entire south coastal region would be able to experience similar growth with the arrival of water and electricity from the Colorado.

The primacy of Los Angeles and Southern California in the Boulder Dam scheme became even more apparent in October 1929 (an otherwise fateful month!) when Secretary of the Interior Ray Lyman Wilbur received twenty-seven applications for Boulder Canyon Project water and power. Under the formula authorized by Congress, the users of water and power would finance the Project through the rates they paid the Bureau of Reclamation. A lifelong friend of Herbert Hoover, Wilbur had graduated from Stanford with the Chief, as Hoover was known to his friends, had worked with him on the Committee for the Relief of Belgium during the War, shared Cave Man Camp with him in the Bohemian Grove, and had been serving as president of Stanford University, on whose campus Hoover had maintained his home, until both the Chief and Wilbur went to Washington. Secretary Wilbur, in other words, a physician by training, came from the very same science- and engineering-oriented, Stanford-and California-based Progressive ethos which had produced Hoover. It was Wilbur who, unilaterally, named the Dam in honor of Hoover, even before it was completed, seeing in it the fulfillment of everything that the Chief stood for as a Progressive public servant. Rather mean-spiritedly, Roosevelt's Secretary of the Interior, Harold Ickes, later stripped the defeated Hoover of this honor, and the Dam reverted to Boulder. Not until 1947 did the Eightieth Congress officially designate the structure Hoover Dam for all time to come.

When all applications were in, Secretary Wilbur found himself with bids for more than three times the 3.6 billion kilowatt-hours Boulder Dam, as it was then named, would generate. Had Wilbur come from Wyoming, Utah, Nevada, Colorado, or Arizona, he might have been influenced toward a different decision. As it was, he allocated 36 percent of the water and power to the Metropolitan Water District of Southern California. To the City of Los Angeles, which owned and operated its own Department of Water and Power, Wilbur allocated 13 percent of the hydro-electrical power. He allocated another 15 percent of the hydro-electricity to the Southern California Edison Company and a handful of other Southern California cities. Although Wilbur allotted Nevada and Arizona 18 percent of the output, he allowed these two states to transfer some of these allocations to the City of Los Angeles and Southern California Edison until the population of Nevada and Arizona created a larger demand. In both its intent and financing, the Boulder Canyon Project had become a Southern California enterprise.

Appropriately, a California-based consortium, the Six Companies, Incorporated, of San Francisco, won the construction contract in March 1931 with a low bid of $48.9 million and an unprecedented performance bond of $5 million as a pledge that they could fulfill the terms of the contract. Thus a President and a Secretary of the Interior from California set in motion a project which a California senator and a California congressman had pushed through Congress, to be supervised in its construction by a government agency headed by a former California professor, with financing from revenues paid by Southern California water and power organizations, with construction being performed by a consortium dominated by California-based companies, with the eventual recipients of the water and power made available by the Dam, once completed, being millions of Southern Californians. Boulder/Hoover Dam stood on the border between Nevada and Arizona. It was, however, for all practical purposes, a California enterprise in conjunction with the federal government, with the minor—and very reluctant—participation of the other Colorado River Basin states.

Built between 1931 and 1935, Hoover Dam and its appurtenant works constituted the engineering epic of America to that date. Three and a quarter million cubic yards of concrete, rising 726.4 feet above bedrock, the arch gravity dam was the greatest dam in human history. Only the Great Pyramid of ancient Egypt possessed comparable volume. Behind the Dam, Lake Mead (named in honor of Reclamation commissioner Elwood Mead, who died in office in 1936) extended 110 miles upriver at an average depth of five hundred feet when at full capacity, storing 28.5 million acre-feet. At the power plant at the base of the Dam churned an eventual (by 1961) total of seventeen gigantic generators fed by four thirty-four-story-high intake towers. By 1940 the twelve generators in operation were producing a total of three billion kilowatt-hours, which is to say, one-eighth of the electricity being generated in the United States.

There are many ways to evaluate Hoover Dam. The most obvious is as an epic feat of construction, the most ambitious American venture of its sort since the Panama Canal, heroic in even the most impressionistic *impasto* sketch of what was accomplished: the diversion of the Colorado River through two tunnels which themselves set new records of granite drilled; the construction of two temporary coffer dams, themselves astonishing achievements of the dam-builders' art; the preparation of the dam site, necessitating the removal of gargantuan amounts of earth and sediment until bedrock was reached; the smoothing of the walls of Black Canyon by hundreds of high scalers hanging by ropes on the edge of the abyss, chipping away at the flaky and uneven Canyon walls with pneumatic jackhammers so that the Dam might be fitted into place with mathematical precision. Then the construction of molds and the weaving together of steel rods and the pouring of concrete from a great crane bridging the Canyon—more concrete than had ever been poured in a single place in human history, enough to pave a six-lane highway from Seattle to the Atlantic Coast.

Had the concrete been poured as one unified mass, it would have taken more than one hundred years for it to settle and dry, and the internal heat created by the drying would have cracked the structure. Instead, the concrete was poured block by block, each block separately framed and steel-rodded and laced with copper piping through which refrigerated water was pumped to assist in the cooling; the pipes themselves were force-fed with concrete once the cooling was complete so as to create a totally solid structure. Photographs of construction, taken day by day, week by week, month by month, during the pouring reveal the concrete sections rising from the Canyon floor from the day of the first pouring, 6 June 1933: rising one upon the other, interlocked like replicating crystals, like a Bach fugue materialized in concrete, the melodic structure repeated and repeated in counterpoint until each repetition coalesced into a completeness that bode to fill the very universe with the music of some primal stuff seeking form and meaning against the void.

Among its many dimensions of significance—as construction epic, as a counterattack against the Depression, as collectivist social drama, as a New Deal expansion of the role of the federal government as provider of water and power, as matrix for Southern California growth and development, as a quasi-transcendental symbol of technology and futurity—the construction of Hoover Dam unequivocally announced the untapped industrial capacity of California and the West. Engineers from the Bureau of Reclamation designed the Dam as a system and oversaw its construction, but the building of the Dam itself was in the hands of the Six Companies, whose component entities and personalities fully represented the history and style of construction engineering as it had grown up in the West.

Headquartered in Ogden, the Utah Construction Company, founded by the brothers W. H. and E. O. Wattis in 1900, brought with itself the Mormon West, with its dominating urge to make the desert bloom through engineering for purposes of profit and religious witness. In 1917 the Wattis brothers had met their greatest challenge to date in the construction of O'Shaughnessy Dam on the Tuolumne River in Hetch Hetchy. And now there was to be built a dam even higher (by three hundred feet), at an even more remote location, for the purposes of bringing into being an even more extensive metropolis than San Francisco. Another member of the Six Companies, the Morrison-Knudsen Company of Boise, founded in 1912 by Morris Knudsen, an ex–construction superintendent with the Reclamation Service, had also proved itself on dozens of construction projects in the Far West.

Perhaps the most important contribution Morrison-Knudsen brought to the construction site was the services of Frank Crowe, the greatest dam builder in the United States. A graduate in civil engineering from the University of Maine, Crowe had spent the first twenty years of his professional life building dams for the Bureau of Reclamation in Idaho, Wyoming, Montana, and Washington. Appointed its superintendent for construction in 1924, Crowe left Reclamation the following year to join a partnership being formed by Utah Construction and Morrison-Knudsen to specialize in the construction of government dams. For the next five years, Crowe supervised the construction of dams on the North Platte River in Wyoming, the Bear River in California, and the Deadwood River in Idaho. He was, in short, the damndest dam builder of them all, as signified by the outstanding salary of $25,000 a year offered him by the Six Companies to superintend the Colorado project, which was four times the salary paid Crowe's supervisor, Reclamation chief engineer Walker Young. To use a comparison that anticipates history by a decade, Frank Crowe was the George Patton of dam construction: the one powerful figure, omnipresent, encouraging, sometimes harsh and brutal, capable of motivating thousands of men through a mixture of admiration and fear to heroic, very dangerous effort.

Frank Crowe knew dams. Forty-seven-year-old Charles Shea, president of the J. F. Shea Company of Portland, Oregon, knew tunnels and sewers. Harddrinking, profane, a cigar ever projecting from his Irish mug, Shea, like Crowe, hated offices and paperwork, preferring to run his company from hotel rooms near the construction site. In the course of building sewers for San Francisco, for example, and assisting in the construction of the aqueduct from Hetch Hetchy, Shea had based himself out of a room in the Palace Hotel and in a short while, given his proclivities for boozy good times and the track, had become a wellknown figure around town, especially in the Damon Runyon *demimonde*. Two other San Franciscans—Felix Kahn, a rabbinical engineer, aged forty-eight and the son of a Detroit rabbi, and Kahn's partner, Alan MacDonald, a choleric Scotsman with an engineering degree from Cornell—knew their steel. Founded in 1911, the MacDonald & Kahn Company had done the steel work for $75 million worth of construction throughout the Far West, most recently for the Mark Hopkins Hotel atop Nob Hill in the partners' home city of San Francisco.

Rounding out the Six Companies were two other Bay Area firms on the verge of a take-off that would transform them into industrial giants in the postwar period: the W. A. Bechtel Company, founded in 1898 by W. A. "Dad" Bechtel, an Illinois-born cattleman and railroad builder *sans* degree in engineering; and the Henry J. Kaiser Company, founded in 1913 as a road-paving outfit by an idiosyncratic figure, Henry J. Kaiser, equally self-taught, a photographer turned contractor, destined to develop under the challenge of the Depression and the Second World War into one of the most important industrialists in the history of American business. Having just completed a $19 million highway building contract in Cuba, Kaiser, then approaching fifty, was joining the truly big time at the Hoover, along with Dad Bechtel, by finding a place at the table in the Six Companies. Like Bechtel, who ran his company through sons Warren, Stephen, and Kenneth, Kaiser tended to put his trust in his son Edgar and a handful of son-substitutes, such as the youthful Clay Bedford, Edgar's fraternity brother at Berkeley.

Taken together, the Six Companies represented a dramatic new assertion of Far Western industrial capacity headquartered in California. The experience of building Hoover Dam made money for MacDonald & Kahn, the J. T. Shea Company, and the Pacific Bridge Company of Portland, Oregon. But it propelled the Kaiser and Bechtel companies, and to a lesser extent Utah Construction (later Utah International), into a condition approaching, by the end of the Second World War, that of corporate nation-states. This was especially true of the Bechtel Company after the Kaiser Companies had passed from the scene in the 1980s, with Bechtel remaining an entity so powerful, so international in its scope, that its officers— among them John McCone, Casper Weinberger, and George Shultz—could move to the CIA, the Department of Defense, and the Department of State respectively as if they were merely shifting assignments at Bechtel.

But that was thirty or more years into the future. For the time being, Bechtel, Kaiser, and the others in the Six Companies, operating through construction superintendent Frank Crowe, had to drive their work force to heroic efforts so as to stay in compliance with their contract or, even better, to finish the project early, which they did by more than two years, winning millions of dollars in savings and bonuses.

In its merciless schedule, its driving of men to the outer limits of endurance and safety, the Six Companies operations revealed the iron fist of industrialism. In so many ways, especially before it came under the supervision of Harold Ickes and the New Deal, but even after that, right up to the very moment of completion, the Boulder Canyon Project revealed the iron fist, the rightward-leaning thrust, of laissez-faire industrialism. This tendency to the right linked the project, for all its later New Deal rhetoric, to industrial philosophies comparable, in direction if not degree, to the industrial cultures of Germany and Japan.

Acting on behalf of the Six Companies, Frank Crowe pushed the Project ahead ruthlessly—three shifts, twenty-four hours a day, seven days a week—finishing two years ahead of schedule. By even the more flexible standards of the early 1930s, health and safety violations were scandalous. Men worked in heat that hovered frequently between 110 and 120 degrees. In the tunnels it could get as high as 140. While the heat of the Nevada and Arizona desert was not the fault of the Six Companies, the initial absence of potable drinking water, the failure to schedule adequate rest periods, the running of gasoline engines in the tunnels while the men were working, indeed the entire work culture that drove men to exert themselves until they dropped from heat prostration, many of them fatally, proceeded directly, via Crowe and his George Patton philosophy of push, push, push, from the ethos established by the Six Companies. All in all, ninety-six men lost their lives: from heat prostration, from heart attack or other forms of exhaustion, and from industrial accidents. The loss of life was most intense in the first two years of the Project before the Roosevelt administration, operating through Secretary Ickes, made an effort to mitigate the work environment.

Indeed, it was as if American industrialism, operating through the Six Companies, was consciously feeling itself under assault by the Depression, and was girding for counter-attack. The fanatical schedule maintained at Hoover asserted to the nation the idea that private companies, faced with the greatest public works project since the Great Pyramid, could push flesh and blood against earth and stone, steel and concrete, and demonstrate to Depression America the driving, regenerative capabilities of American industrialism. While the federal government had authorized and sponsored the project, the private sector was building it—on time and on budget—and in the process providing the nation with a prophetic paradigm of industrial renewal.

No unions ever established themselves at Boulder Canyon, and wages remained lower there than on other federally sponsored projects, even after 1933. To add to the representative nature of the scenario, in which industrialism confronted its opponents, members of the IWW attempted a strike early on, in August 1931, complaining about the unsafe conditions, the fetid drinking water, the low wages, the hellish housing—and were adeptly suppressed by company bulls and federal marshals. A decade earlier, the IWW had struck fear in the hearts of Western industrialists as a conspiracy that could cause significant damage. Correctly, the leaders of the 1931 strike saw that if they could bring the largest public works project in the country to its knees, they would strike a telling blow to the system, then reeling in confusion from the Depression. Within a few days, the IWW leadership found itself being rounded up and put on trucks and shipped back to Las Vegas, its strike over almost before it had begun.

Although it failed to halt the project, or unionize the workers, the 1931 IWW strike did alert the Six Companies management to the notion that it would have to provide better conditions for its work force. Working closely with the Hoover administration, the Six Companies evolved patterns of employment, compensation, and housing that constituted a demanding, if vaguely benevolent, dictatorship. Thousands of men lived communally in military-style barracks, which after the strike were air-conditioned. At the mess hall 1,150 men were served at a sitting by waiters and busboys. The food was good and wholesome—meat, fresh fruits and vegetables, dairy products, home-baked bread and pastries, far beyond the diet of an increasingly hungry America—and the men could eat as much as they wanted. Approximately $1.50 a day was deducted from the workers' wages for room and board, and the catering company which ran the commissary made a profit: another sign of capitalism at work.

At Boulder City, the planned community on federal property where married employees lived, the appointed city manager, Sims R. Ely, functioned as de facto dictator, capable of going so far as to reprimand wives whom he thought were too flimsily attired in the desert heat. Deputy United States Marshal Glenn "Bud" Bodell—an archetypal union-busting bull, given to boots and jodhpurs, a pistol conspicuously on his belt—presided over a phalanx of deputy marshals, company bulls, and a network of spies in the ranks, reporting on any suspicious activities. Between city manager Sims and federal marshal Bodell, virtually every detail of the lives of workers and their dependents was regulated. The key point of coercion in this system, obviously, remained threat of dismissal without recourse: a possibility rendered rather vivid by the swarms of unemployed men on the streets of nearby Las Vegas or milling around outside Boulder City, asking for work. Discharged employees were blacklisted for the duration of the project and, most likely, for any future employment by the Six Companies, who very soon sustained a considerable monopoly on big construction projects in the Far West.

Asian workers could not even think of gaining employment at Boulder, for Six Companies contracts with the federal government explicitly precluded the employment of anyone of the "Mongolian" race. Although not explicitly excluded along with the Asians, African-Americans also found themselves blacklisted. When African-American veterans living in Las Vegas protested, and the National Association for the Advancement of Colored People came to their assistance, eleven—eleven!—black workers eventually secured jobs by July 1934, out of a work force that peaked at 5,251.

When Harold Ickes stripped the dam of its name Hoover, he was at once exacting political vengeance and signaling to the Bureau of Reclamation and to the Six Companies that the New Deal was now in charge. While Ickes did secure a number of improvements in working conditions and safety, ended the exploitative practice of paying wages partially in company scrip, and pressed the Six Companies for overbilling on overtime, it was too late for the New Deal, which had itself not yet stabilized, to affect the essentially rightist-industrialist culture of the Boulder Dam project. Far from it: at Boulder the Bechtel and Kaiser Companies had not only defied the Depression through public works, they had glimpsed the possibilities of corporate-industrial empire, dazzling in its vistas. The remaining six years of the Depression would witness each of these companies grow geometrically through a dozen dam and bridge projects, among them Grand Coulee Dam in

Washington State and the San Francisco–Oakland Bay Bridge. And then the Second World War, with its bonanza contracts for ports and ships and airfields and training centers and innumerable other necessities of civil and military engineering. From this perspective, Hoover Dam first demonstrated the industrial capacity of the United States that would, more than any other factor, lead to its victory in the Second World War and its preeminence in world affairs in the decade that followed.

The corporate-industrial transformation actualized and symbolized by Hoover Dam created corporate giants and industrialist heros, the Bechtel brothers and Henry J. Kaiser most notably; yet most intellectuals of the period, leaning leftwards, saw the Dam in terms of its workers, whom they exulted as a perfected species of group or common man. Virtually no commentators, even the Communists, seem to have grasped the point that the Hoover Dam represented a subtle triumph of the industrial Right; instead, with much justification, they exulted in the bravery, skill, competitive motivation, and, in many instances, cultural superiority of the young white men who were building the Dam. Journalists covering the project exulted in its Social Darwinism, its survival of the fittest. Unfit men, they reported, were fired from the job or not hired in the first place. Thus even the exultation of the common man, the worker, had its right-leaning aspects. Photographers covering the project seemed obsessed by the image of shirtless workers, younger men in the peak of physical condition, their denim pants slung low around their hips, their hardened muscles rippling in the sunlight. The workers are caught in demeanors approaching beefcake as they lean against their shovels or drink from a waterbag. The contemporary German filmmaker Leni Riefenstahl could not have come up with more appropriate examples of Nordic masculinity than these Hoover hunks, their photographs so suggestive of strength and erotic presence: their chests bared despite the blazing sun, the low-slung Levis, the studied poses so refractive of Donatello's and Michelangelo's David. Was there a gay sub-culture at Hoover, one speculates? There must have been, although its authentication must now rest upon fragile documentary evidence and the testimony of men in their eighth or ninth decade.

As in the case of the corporate consolidations and transformations the Hoover project was effecting, the Nordic Darwinism of Hoover Dam remained only obliquely stated. More common were the effusions of such journalist observers as Theodore White, a recent Harvard graduate, writing in *Harper's*, and the New York *Times* correspondents Duncan Aikman and Mildred Adams. White, Aikman, and Adams depicted the Hoover project as a renewed Western frontier in which, once again, the common man was triumphant. The history of the West, they wrote, most noticeably in mining, was characterized by great groups of single men converging on a site. From this perspective, Hoover Dam was another gold, silver, copper, or land rush, or another railroad construction site—although, in this instance, the camp was controlled from the start by the Six Companies and the federal government and the entire quality of the experience had been up-graded. The Far Western worker had never lived so well, Theodore White observed, as he had at Boulder, nor had he ever represented a higher social type. "Two-thirds of the four thousand and more men employed on the dam and its appurtenant works," White wrote, "have at varying times and in different degrees been subjected to a college education. . . . The number of educated men on the project is confirmed by the lending library. The woman who runs it is a person accustomed to working men, keen in her estimate of them, and intellectually interested in them as individuals and a group. I noticed that the library was some seventy-five percent non-fiction, the books being largely biography and history."[1]

In Las Vegas, the men temporarily put aside their taste for good books while pursuing whiskey, cards, and women in an oasis whose overnight growth forecast its post-war future. If Boulder City represented order and stability brought to the Wild West, Las Vegas testified to the fact that the more robust appetites of single men on the frontier were alive and well. Eastern journalists such as Theodore White, and Edmund Wilson and Bruce Bliven of the *New Republic*, were mesmerized by the casinos and bordellos of Las Vegas. "It is a bit startling, at first," noted Bruce Bliven, "to walk down the main street [of Las Vegas] at eleven am and see in almost every block one or more gambling houses, doors open to every passerby, crowded with men and women, old and young, playing Keno, roulette, poker, shooting craps, or betting on horse races described by a raucous-voiced gentleman who gets his facts by direct wire from the track. Las Vegas' Painted Ladies go in for raspberry-colored sailor pants, coral-tinted blouses, and high-heeled slippers; their faces, beneath the metallic-looking orange rouge which is universal in the Southwest, are haggard and burned like the faces of all desert people. Every second or third man you meet has had about three drinks too many, and is glad of it. The ladies, as always, drink less or hold it better, and obligingly help keep their gen'l'men friends from rolling into the gutters."[2]

On his visit to Las Vegas, Theodore White encountered a scene worthy of Bret Harte. Entering the Nevada Bar in that city, White heard above the raucous talk and laughter the sound of classical music. "In the toughest place in town," he noted, "a young girl was playing Beethoven. A couple of maudlin drunks hung on the piano, weeping gin tears. Gently removing them, I asked the only female 'professor' what she would drink. An orange blossom was made for her—without gin—and we talked. She had run away from home in Oklahoma, and had banged out her keep on a piano as far as Nevada. The ultimate goal was a conservatory in Los Angeles. The Beethoven was a lapse, she explained. 'When they get drunk enough, I play it. They don't know it, and I get my practicing done.' "[3]

Culture on the frontier: a familiar theme in both Bret Harte and Josiah Royce. As usual, the argument cut both ways. Eastern men recovered themselves on the frontier, and in the Nevada Bar at least, Beethoven was being played in the Wild West. "The chords of cultivated Easternism dropped quickly," noted Theodore White of the Boulder experience. "Inhibitions are not apt to be very deep. I saw men whose cultivated accents and college jargon were unmistakable take it side by side with the laboring 'stiff' and like it. Boulder Dam is a common denominator."[4]

The frontier metaphor, so much a part of American folklore, allowed East Coast journalists from conservative publications to deal with the common-man aspect of the project without references to anything even vaguely collectivist. The frontier comparison also allowed an explanation of why ordinary workers were participating so deeply on a personal, emotional level in a project which, while it gave them wages and a living, demanded a level of labor and personal risk far in excess of any stake they could possibly have in the outcome. As on the frontier, it was suggested, Americans were reexperiencing at Boulder the thrill of being part of something vast and great, a frontier, while remaining ordinary men among their kind.

Even Frank Crowe later acknowledged the construction of Hoover Dam as, in part, an epic of anonymous heroes. The workers themselves, he admitted, made most of the crucial on-the-job decisions. In the first years, fierce competitions arose between work crews drilling the gigantic diversionary tunnels through the solid rock walls of Black Canyon. Some of this competition came from the way tunnel drillers always tended to see themselves: as subterranean intruders drilling against time and rock in environments where human beings had no business being in the first place, hence by its very nature rushed and dangerous works. Some of this competition came from a fear of being fired, which happened to drilling crews who proved too slow. Yet, as even Crowe admitted, collective identities were forged and collective creativities tapped, even in such Darwinian circumstances. The Dam itself had a way of enforcing a collective identity that went beyond politics. "From designing engineer to lowest laborer," Theodore White wrote, "they are acutely aware of the immensity and importance of the Dam. To them it assumes a personality and they are devoted to it. When they have surveyed the result, the pride of the man who designed it will be no greater than that of anyone who has driven a single nail in its making."[5]

For the English playwright and novelist J. B. Priestley, wintering in Arizona in 1936–1937, Boulder Dam embodied the very image of the technocratic future forecast by H. G. Wells. "It is like the beginning of a new world," Priestley noted of the Dam, "that world we catch a glimpse of in one of the later sequences of Wells' film, 'Things to Come,' a world of giant machines and titanic communal enterprises. Here in this Western American wilderness, the new man, the man of the future, has done something, and what he has done takes your breath away." The skyscrapers of New York, Priestley argued, were but the prologue to what the new man had achieved in Boulder Dam. "This a first glimpse," Priestly rhapsodized, "of what chemistry and mathematics and engineering and large-scale organization can accomplish when collective planning unites and inspires them. Here is the soul of America under socialism."[6]

Priestley's paean to Hoover Dam as the prophetic image of Machine Age futurity had been inspired by Hoover Dam as a triumph of engineering in the desert—and by its architectural stylization. Designed as an engineering system by Bureau of Reclamation engineers, Hoover Dam could have been stylized in any number of architectural idioms. Fortunately, the architect granted the commission, Gordon Kaufmann of Los Angeles, proved himself a master of Machine Age futurity.

How Gordon Kaufmann received the commission in the first place remains a mystery. His patron, publisher Harry Chandler, for whom Kaufmann later designed the new headquarters of the Los Angeles *Times* (1935), had vehemently opposed the Boulder Dam project because the All-American Canal would replace the canal running through Chandler's extensive holdings in Baja California. Although Kaufmann would soon achieve masterpieces of Art Deco futurism in the Hoover Dam and the *Times* headquarters, the work of this English-born architect through the 1920s had been largely residential and in the mode of Spanish-Californian or Jacobean Revival. While Kaufmann was well connected in Los Angeles, which in so many ways was calling the shots for the project by the late 1920s, architects such as John Parkinson, Albert Martin, and Robert Farquhar were even better connected than Kaufmann, who was Jewish, bookish, and slightly bohemian. In any event, with no previous record of industrial design (he would not start work on the design of the Los Angeles *Times* building until 1931), Kaufmann was chosen by the Bureau of Reclamation, without open competition, to design the single greatest industrial project in the history of the United States.

Perhaps the engineers of the Bureau, knowing that it would be politically expedient to choose a Los Angeles architect, consciously or subconsciously rejected the possibility of working with such established figures as Parkinson, Martin, or Farquhar—or such radical modernists as Rudolph Schindler and Richard Neutra, then the leading exponents of the International Style in the Southland. Chameleon-like, Kaufmann had been in the habit of providing Pasadenans with Jacobean and San Marinans with Spanish Revival. With similar empathy, he turned to the task of providing the engineers of Reclamation with the appropriate stylization of their great enterprise. For inspiration, Kaufmann turned to the futurist renderings of Tony Garnier, Antonio Sant'Elia, Hugh Ferris, and (after all, this was Hollywood!) the expressionist sets from Fritz Lang's film *Metropolis* (1927). The French futurist Garnier and the Italian futurist Sant'Elia had each sketched great dams into drawings, rendered in the early 1900s, through which they had attempted, with great success, to envision the future. The American architectural illustrator Hugh Ferris had also provided numerous suggestions in his book *The Metropolis of Tomorrow* (1929) of gigantic building forms, awesome in their vertical and horizontal setbacks. (Interestingly enough, Ferris would later do a series of renderings of Boulder Dam, capturing in charcoal and pen the awesome structure which his own earlier imaginings had helped inspire.) In Fritz Lang's *Metropolis*, Kaufmann, a film buff who maintained part of his practice in Hollywood, also glimpsed the way in which the future might be envisioned as gigantic architectural structures refracted in a chiaroscuro of light and shadow.

Between December 1930 and November 1932, Kaufmann worked on designs for the dam and the powerhouse, and the four intake towers. First of all, he allowed the curved massivity of the great gravity arch dam to speak for itself. Even the artists of Reclamation, who had provisionally surmounted the dam with two gigantic eagles, had allowed its surface to remain powerfully unaltered. Across the top of the dam, Kaufmann emplaced four vertical piers interspersed by smaller vertical outcroppings in a series of four. At the base of the dam, he continued this verticalism in bold fenestration panels that swept uninterruptedly up the entire facade of the powerhouse, restating the verticalism of the dam crest. Behind the dam, the four intake towers rose as great sculptural forms, Art Deco skyscrapers that would pass their existence largely submerged beneath the impounded waters of the Colorado.

Kaufmann also colored the dam and powerhouse with a deep warm red at the base, giving way to a lighter red at the middle and upper levels—as if the dam and powerhouse were themselves geological formations in the Arizona-Nevada desert. Within the powerhouse itself, as well as in the lobby leading to the elevator that descended through the interior of the Dam and the small lobbies which surmounted the four intake towers, artist Allen True of Denver, retained as a color consultant, selected stones and concrete tints of dark green and black terrazzo, broken by patterns inspired by the baskets, bowls, and sand paintings of the Native American Southwest. True also colored the turbines, railings, piping, and overhead cranes with an intricate scheme of ten dazzling Southwestern colors, among them jade green, vermillion, yellow, blue, and gray. Kaufmann's Machine Age exterior played off against True's Art Deco reinterpretations of the Native American Southwest, as if to suggest how technology and the Machine Age future were hovering over interior spaces that were also suggestive of temples and palaces left behind by pre-Columbian inhabitants.

This blend of history and the future in and through technology, so powerfully conveyed in Kaufmann's stylizations and True's interior schemes, possessed an even deeper dimension—something cosmic, something akin to the deepest implications of myth, even religion—which pervaded the principal monument at the Dam site, designed by the Norwegian-born artist Oskar Hansen. Located on the Nevada side of the river, the monument featured a base of polished black diorite surmounted by a 142-foot flagpole. At the entrance to the monument sat two thirty-foot-tall winged bronze figures whose unity of arms and wings, raised in salute to the universe, reflected the verticalism with which Kaufmann had unified the crest, intake towers, dam face, and powerhouse.

Who were these winged creatures, with their Nordic features, their militant stance? Angelic guardians from the Hebrew and Christian scriptures? Eagle-people from Native American mythology? Phantoms from a Nordic daydream, suggestive in their Aryan regularity of feature, their muscled arms and biceps, their stunning capacity for flight, of neo-Wagnerian myths in the desert? Were they higher beings from another planet, alighted for the ages in watch upon a structure which itself seemed built, as in science fiction, by an alien race?

As if to answer this enigma, Hansen inlaid in stone on the ground at the base of the monument the Great Seal of the United States and the signs of the Zodiac, together with a large galactic map indicating the position of the stars at such important historical dates as the construction of the Great Pyramid and the birth of Christ. Dominating this map was a star chart of constellations, stars and planets joined by intersecting lines indicating the precise day and time—30 September 1935, at eight hours and fifty-six minutes and 2.25 seconds in the evening—that Franklin Delano Roosevelt had dedicated the structure. The universe, Hansen suggested, had fixed itself on Hoover Dam at this moment, and the structure now belonged to the cosmos. Indeed, the universe was now working in and through the dam and falling waters and spinning turbines of the project. Through technology, human beings had approached the creative work of the cosmos itself.

To bring the impounded waters of the Colorado River to Southern California, the Metropolitan Water District commenced construction of Parker Dam and the Colorado River Aqueduct in 1932. In September 1931 the voters of the eleven member cities of the District, led by Los Angeles, had authorized by a five-to-one majority $220 million in bonds for the project. During the campaign, arguments for and against the measure were each motivated by a knowledge of the growth which water and hydro-electricity from the Colorado River, four times the volume of what was currently available from the Owens Valley, would mean to Southern California. As it was, Los Angeles voters had already authorized the previous May a $38.8 million bond issue for the improvement of the Los Angeles Aqueduct–Owens Valley system.

Each side advanced environmental arguments. Opponents claimed, for one thing, that water from the Colorado River contained too much silt ever to be acceptable as drinking water. Proponents of the Colorado Aqueduct pointed to the fact that Southern California had virtually exhausted its watershed. Each day, they argued, Southern California was consuming approximately 170 million gallons of water above the amount that could be replaced by either man or nature. Southern California was dangerously close to exhausting underground basins which had taken thousands of years to form. Not only would the depletion of water resources destroy the environment, it would put an end to future growth. The election served, then, as a final referendum regarding the nature of life and society in Southern California. Overwhelmingly, the people voted for growth.

In Northern California, a generation earlier, a similar debate had pitted the Sierra Club and its allies against the San Francisco oligarchy. In the Los Angeles election of 1931, environmentalists and growth advocates aligned themselves on the same side. There was, for one thing, no Hetch Hetchy to lose, or even an Owens Valley; and Black Canyon, in a hellish place between Nevada and Arizona, had few champions.

And so, even as Hoover Dam progressed to completion, work commenced on an equally ambitious aqueduct system. It came in four parts: Parker Dam, a diversion dam downstream from Hoover Dam, behind which formed Lake Havasu on the Arizona-California border; a 242–mile aqueduct to transfer the water from Lake Havasu to three storage reservoirs in the District; the three reservoirs themselves; and more than 150 miles of distribution lines connecting the reservoirs with the member cities. Also authorized in the 1931 bond issue were power transition lines to bring hydro-electricity to District cities and to furnish the energy necessary to run the gigantic electrical pumps of the aqueduct.

The pumps, five major pumping stations in all, capable of lifting ninety thousand gallons of water per minute, were necessary because, unlike its counterpart connecting Hetch Hetchy and San Francisco, the Los Angeles Aqueduct was not gravity-operated. Far from it: water from the aqueduct had to be lifted by pumps a total of 1,617 feet in elevation during its journey from Lake Havasu to the District. It took a near decade for an army of eight thousand men to complete this extraordinarily intricate system of ninety-two miles of tunnels, pumping stations, sixty-three miles of lined canals, covered conduits, twenty-nine miles of inverted siphons, dams and reservoirs, and local distribution systems.

Payrolls and other benefits totaled $17.4 million between November 1932 and June 1935: welcomed relief from the Depression. A total of $46 million was spent for labor and materials through fiscal year 1935–1936. Eighteen million of this money went directly into the pockets of aqueduct workers.

Employees of the privately held Southern California Edison Company also had their livelihoods preserved in dire times by this project, for there would be no other hydro-electrical construction of this magnitude in Southern California during the 1930s. In Northern California, construction at Pacific Gas & Electric also came to a virtual halt. PG&E had completed Pit 3, its second great hydro-electrical powerhouse on the Pit River in Shasta County, in July 1925. Not until July 1941, however, with war in sight, would PG&E be able to muster the financial resources to begin work on Pit 5, which took two thousand men nearly three years to complete. It would take until 1955 to complete Pit 4 and Pit 6, giving the system an aggregate capacity of 440,000 kilowatts.

At the urging of Henry J. Kaiser, Dr. Sidney Garfield, a physician from the University of Southern California surgical unit at Los Angeles County Hospital, organized a system of pre-paid comprehensive medical care for dam and aqueduct workers, the precursor of a similar but much expanded program Kaiser would sponsor during the construction of Grand Coulee Dam in eastern Washington State in the late 1930s and in the Kaiser Shipyards in Richmond on San Francisco Bay during the Second World War. These programs, in turn, engendered the

Kaiser-Permanente health maintenance organization that would recast the economics of medicine in the United States by the 1990s.

In January 1935 a subcontractor went broke attempting to drill the San Jacinto tunnel, and the work had to be taken over by the Metropolitan Water District itself. Private contractors, including Bechtel and Kaiser, constructed Parker Dam under the general supervision of the Bureau of Reclamation and the immediate supervision of Frank Crowe, who barely caught his breath after Boulder Dam was turned over to the Bureau of Reclamation in 1936. The Colorado River Aqueduct was constructed in the main by District employees, working under the supervision of Frank Weymouth, a University of Maine–trained civil engineer in his mid-fifties, recruited from Reclamation after a thirty-year career which included projects in Nicaragua, Ecuador, Montana, Idaho, Oregon, Wyoming, and Boulder Canyon.

"Flung out in a thin line across the desert," noted *Los Angeles Saturday Night* on 19 October 1935, "all the way from the Colorado River to Los Angeles and its twelve sister cities of the Water District, this army of workers in engaged in man's latest and greatest battle against his age-old enemy—thirst. It is a battle which has been fought countless times in years gone by—in Babylon, in Carthaginia, in Egypt—in all the great empires which have risen from a semi-desert soil."[7]

The comparison to the empires of the ancient world represented more than a rhetorical flourish, for by the time the aqueduct was approaching its delivery date, the region served by the Metropolitan Water District of Southern California had increased by a third, to approximately three million or 45 percent of the population of the state, despite the decade-long slowdown of the economy. By 1939 Los Angeles County alone led the nation in agriculture, the manufacture of aircraft, and motion picture production. It ranked second in automobile assembly and the manufacture of tires; third in the nation in oil refining; fourth in the manufacture of women's clothing and furniture. Not only had they been growing steadily despite the Depression, the thirteen cities of the District—Los Angeles, Burbank, Glendale, Pasadena, San Marino, Beverly Hills, Santa Monica, Torrance, Compton, Long Beach, together with Fullerton, Anaheim, and Santa Ana in Orange County— were poised on the brink of a half century of growth that would see their population increase itself sevenfold, pushing its economy to the eleventh largest GNP on the planet. In 1931 the voters of this region had consciously willed such a future into being through public works.

They had likewise enabled, through the All-American Canal, the continuing vitality of the Imperial Valley as the agricultural hinterland for coastal Southern California. Authorized by the Boulder Canyon Act of December 1928, the All-American Canal came under construction by the Bureau of Reclamation in 1934 and was put into its initial operation in September 1940, with full service reached early in 1942. A third dam on the Colorado, the Imperial, some eighteen miles upstream from Yuma on the Arizona-Colorado border, provided the intake point through which fifteen thousand cubic feet per second of water entered the system for delivery to the Imperial and Coachella valleys. It is astonishing that the second phase of the Boulder Canyon project—the Colorado River Aqueduct and the All-American Canal—and the first phase of the Central Valley project—Shasta Dam—should have been under construction simultaneously. But then again: also under construction at the same time were the San Francisco–Oakland and Golden Gate bridges, the Golden Gate International Exposition on Treasure Island, and hundreds of other PWA and WPA projects. In terms of its public works, such was the prodigality of California through the late 1930s.

12

Completing California

The Therapy of Public Works

P UBLIC works created jobs, thousands of them; yet these vast projects were far from mere make-work programs. Most of them brought to fulfillment decades, even half centuries, of planning. From the nineteenth century, Americans in California had realized that if California were to reach its full potential as a regional civilization, it would have to be physically adjusted. It would have to be rendered complete. Completing itself as a physical place, then, became the central public challenge California presented to itself in the 1930s through public works programs. The Central Valley Project, Shasta Dam, the transformation of the inland city of Stockton into a deep-water port, the Arroyo Seco Parkway, the San Francisco–Oakland Bay Bridge, the Golden Gate Bridge: these and innumerable other public works projects brought to completion California as a modern region, setting in place a public works infrastructure that remains to this day, and will remain for hundreds of years to come, the engineering foundation of California in terms of its water, electricity, and transportation. Public works projects on a lesser scale, meanwhile—schools, libraries, post offices, hospitals, airports, armories, recreational parks, and other facilities—improved the quality of life, first of all; but of equal importance, they enlarged shared public identities. Thanks in great measure to federally assisted public works projects which were based on longtime local planning, Californians had more in common with each other by 1941 than they did in 1929. To the employment-oriented therapy of public works was added the therapy of an enlarged, and shared, California.

As in the case of the Boulder Canyon Project, the Central Valley Project culminated more than a half century of dreams and plans. Bounded on the west by the Coastal Range and on the east by the Sierra Nevada, the Central Valley runs five hundred miles north to south, averaging 120 miles in width. Comprising a third of the land mass of California, the Central Valley consists of two parts, the Sacramento Valley in the north and the San Joaquin Valley in the south. Each valley slopes toward a convergence point in the Delta Country northeast of San Francisco Bay.

Flooded by the mighty Sacramento River, the Sacramento Valley is water-rich. Beginning its journey near Mount Shasta in southeastern Siskiyou County near the Oregon border, the Sacramento River runs southward through the Sacramento Valley, engorged by the tributary waters of the Pit, the Feather, the Yuba, the Bear, and the American rivers, as well as by three major creeks—the Stony, the Cache, and the Putah—and innumerable rivulets and runoffs from melting mountain snows. Fully two-thirds of the water resources of the Central Valley are found in this top tier drained by the Sacramento River.

The San Joaquin Valley, by contrast, is, in its southern reaches, a near desert. Only the San Joaquin River and its tributaries alleviate the aridity—and this only in the northern half of the San Joaquin Valley. Flowing from the Sierra Nevada onto the valley floor at the latitude of the city of Fresno in the center of the Valley, the San Joaquin River flows northwards, joined by the Fresno, the Chowchilla, the Merced, the Tuolumne, and the Stanislaus as it wends its way to the Delta to mingle its waters with the Sacramento River and flow into San Francisco Bay. Taken together, this San Joaquin River system and the rivers of the southern San Joaquin Valley—the Kings, the Kaweah, the Tule, and the Kern—comprise one-third the water resources of the Central Valley and cover two-thirds the land mass. Were the bottom two-thirds of the Central Valley ever to achieve its potential as an agricultural region served by flourishing market and service cities and towns, it would need the waters of the Sacramento River and its tributaries.

Then there was the question of flood control. Were the Sacramento River less volatile, it might be called the Mississippi of Northern California. Since the Gold Rush, the Sacramento River had been navigated by paddle wheel steamers plying between San Francisco and the riverside city of Sacramento. But the Sacramento River, especially from the city of Sacramento northwards, was far from serene. Engorged by rainfall or melting snows, it could expand into a powerful and dangerous inland sea up to one hundred miles in length. Time and again, this inland sea broke its levees and flooded the the plain. In 1937 and 1938 alone, flooding from the Sacramento caused $150 million in damages, which was significantly close to the $170 million projected cost of the Central Valley Project designed in part to contain its waters.

The effort to contain the raging waters of this inland sea provoked the longest continuous public policy debate in California history. Who should do it? California or the federal government? The Sacramento was, after all, a navigable river, hence a national resource under federal jurisdiction. Not until 1917 did the Congress, with the passage of the Flood Control Act, provide any measure of funds for flood control programs on the Mississippi and Sacramento Rivers.

In 1873 Colonel Barton Alexander of the Army Corps of Engineers submitted a detailed plan of a system of dams and canals for flood control and irrigation throughout the Central Valley which prophetically anticipated the eventual solution. Alexander's report exudes the confidence of an Army engineer who had been constructing important public works since his graduation from West Point in the mid-1840s. This bold and imaginative military officer must be given credit for first envisioning what would be constructed sixty-plus years into the future. As the senior Army engineer on the Pacific Coast, Alexander embodied not only the technical expertise of the federal establishment but its imagination and will as well. A quarter of a century before the establishment of the Reclamation Service, Alexander—the engineer who had rebuilt Minot's Ledge Lighthouse on the Massachusetts coast, one of the brilliant construction feats of its era—laid down a simple premise: through public works, California might reorder its water resources to a level unprecedented in the American experience, and through such reordering through public works California could rescue nearly a third of its land mass for agriculture and human settlement.

In time, such rescuing approached the intensity of salvation itself. For Progressives, after all, public works inspired an assent and commitment approaching religious intensity. In 1910 A. De Wint Foote, a civil engineer active in the Inland Waterways Association of California, in the course of a report to the American Society of Civil Engineers, expanded the proposals of Colonel Alexander, charging them with the energies of history, destiny, and religion. Entitled "The Redemption of the Great Valley of California," Foote's discussion moves beyond Colonel Alexander's belief that it *could* be done to a passionate commitment that it *must* be done. In his report, Foote outlined a comprehensive $75 million program of damming, dredging, drainage, flood control, irrigation, and deep-water navigation for both the Sacramento and the San Joaquin valleys. Dramatically, Foote called for the canalization of both the San Joaquin and the Sacramento rivers, so that Sacramento and Stockton might each be transformed into an inland deep-water port—which is exactly what the city of Stockton did for itself in the early 1930s.

In cross-cultural reference, Foote made extensive comparisons between the Great Valley, as he called Central California, and Egypt, ancient and modern, together with the canal and drainage systems of northern Italy and Islamic Spain. He bolstered his report with citations from classics of irrigation literature dealing with these regions. The very title of his report, "The Redemption of the Great Valley of California," with its profound religious metaphor of redemption, suggests the powerful social and cultural argument which permeated Foote's technical discussions of dams, canals, and water flow. As an agency of American civilization, as a moral and cultural force, the State of California could not allow one-third of its land mass to remain either flooded or arid—and still consider itself a worthy steward of its environment. Flood control, irrigation, and water management, after all, had brought civilization into being some five thousand years ago.

Upon the redemption of the Central Valley through public works rested the moral and imaginative reputation of California as a commonwealth in dialogue with the great irrigation societies of the past.

In 1919 came another equally powerful report, *Irrigation of Twelve Million Acres*, filed by Colonel Robert Bradford Marshall, chief hydrographer of the United States Geological Survey, acting on his own initiative as a citizen of California. Reaching back to the reports of Colonel Alexander, state engineer William Hammond Hall, A. De Wint Foote, and others, Marshall made a passionate plea in which he chided the people of California "indifferent to the bountiful gifts that Nature has given them, sit[ting] idly by, waiting for rain, indefinitely postponing irrigation, and allowing every year millions and millions of dollars in water to pour unused into the sea."[1]

By this time, the general outline of the work to be done stood clear. A dam would be built across the Sacramento River in the mountains fronting the northernmost tier of the Central Valley. Two canals, one on either side of the Sacramento Valley, would transport this water by gravity to a transfer point where the Sacramento Valley and the San Joaquin Valley met. At this point, the water would be pumped into another canal system, which would take it south. The American River would also be dammed at Folsom east of the city of Sacramento and its waters fed into the system. The San Joaquin River, meanwhile, would be dammed in the Sierra Foothills northeast of Fresno. Two other canals would move this water northward through the upper San Joaquin Valley and southward through the lower San Joaquin Valley as far as Bakersfield in lower Kern County. Another canal, the Contra Costa Conduit, would carry fresh water through the Delta for use in the farms and industries of Contra Costa County in the northeastern sector of the San Francisco Bay Area.

Published by the California State Irrigation Association, Marshall's report stimulated a decade of planning and research. In 1921 the legislature appropriated $200,000 for a study to be undertaken by the state engineer. This plan went through four revisions and cost taxpayers approximately $1 million in research costs before state engineer Edward Hyatt issued it in 1930 as the State Water Plan. In 1931 the legislature adopted the State Water Plan, and Governor James Rolph Jr. appointed a California Water Resources Commission to refine further its proposals in conjunction with the federal government. In 1933 the legislature passed, and Governor Rolph signed, the Central Valley Project Act, which called for the construction of three dams, reservoirs, and hydro-electric stations, four canals, and all necessary pumping stations, hydro-electrical transmission lines, and other necessary works. The act also placed on the ballot a $170 million bond proposition to finance the initial phase of the project, which the voters passed.

At the depth of the Depression, the people of California authorized the most ambitious public works project in the history of the state: a project that would take more than thirty years to complete. The social disruptions of the Depression, especially the great cotton strike of 1933, had thoroughly befuddled Governor

Rolph; but in the case of the Central Valley Project Act, which he actively sponsored, Rolph tapped into his lingeringly Progressive faith in public works, which had made him such a brilliant success twenty years earlier during his first term as mayor of San Francisco.

As it emerged from the legislature and was authorized by the bond issue of December 1933, the Central Valley Project Act represented the highest possible public vision in the history of the state. Never before had the politicians and voters of California committed themselves to a public works project of such magnitude. Only the highway and road system of the state could even be said to compete in range and magnitude.

No wonder the privately held utilities, led by Pacific Gas & Electric, fought the project so intensely, going so far as to sponsor a referendum rejecting the Central Valley Project Act in December 1933, which PG&E lost by a mere 33,603 votes. At stake was not only the right of private utilities to generate and transmit electricity in this vast region; as in the case of the Boulder Canyon Project, an entire philosophy of public ownership and governance of water and power had surfaced through the Central Valley proposal. When it came to opposing strikers, Governor Rolph could Red-bait with the best of them; but even he saw nothing Communistic or even leftist in the Progressive notion of having the State of California publicly own and organize its water resources. Governor Rolph, indeed most of California, still nurtured Progressive attitudes and traditions toward public works as embodiments of the *res publica*, the shared public thing. PG&E and the other utilities were, after all, only companies and could eventually be included as clients and subcontractors (despite the fact that they continued, bitterly and sometimes illegally, to oppose the Project through the 1930s); but the Central Valley Project was not a company. The Central Valley Project was the people of California.

Unfortunately, the people of California happened to be broke. No one bought the bonds, which remained unsold through 1935. Enter the federal government, in the form of the War Department, which in 1935 recommended the construction of the first phase of the Central Valley Project, Shasta Dam, on the basis that by controlling flood waters, Shasta Dam would restore the all-year navigability of the Sacramento River as far north as Red Bluff and was hence of importance to the national defense. Building Shasta Dam would also create desperately needed employment. In August 1935 Congress passed the Rivers and Harbors Act, which allocated $12 million toward the construction of Shasta. That September, President Roosevelt took an even bolder step, approving a $20 million subvention from the Emergency Relief Appropriation funds under his jurisdiction. Roosevelt was soon forced to reduce the grant to $4.2 million; but the nature of the Project had been redefined.

The Central Valley Project was now a state project under federal auspices. In December 1935 the State of California yielded responsibility for building the Central Valley Project to the United States Bureau of Reclamation. Reviewing the Project, the Bureau of Reclamation upped its estimate from $170 million to $228 million. In 1936 Congress authorized another $6.9 million toward the Project on the condition that all irrigated lands be brought under Reclamation law. Budgeted at $36 million, Shasta Dam ranked second in expense only to Boulder Dam as a federal irrigation project.

Bidding for the Shasta contract opened at ten in the morning on 1 June 1938 at the district office of the Bureau of Reclamation in Sacramento. Two companies, Pacific Constructors and the Shasta Construction Company, posted certified checks for $2 million, the first installment on a total of $9.5 million in bonding which the government required, and made their bids. Before the bidding, odds favored the Shasta Construction Company, which represented a reconfiguration of the Six Companies, which had built Boulder, Bonneville, and Grand Coulee. But Pacific Constructors, which had been organized in Los Angeles in December 1937, won the contract with a bid of $35,939,450 to Shasta Construction's bid of $36,202,357.

Having lost the project by such a small margin, Shasta Construction Company, in the person of Henry J. Kaiser, sought to have the contracts reawarded on technicalities; but Secretary of the Interior Harold Ickes, having been forced to deal with the Kaiser Group through three major dams, welcomed the opportunity to deal with a new cast of characters. And besides: Pacific Constructors had secured the services of Frank Crowe to serve as general superintendent. The man who built Boulder Dam and Parker Dam and seventeen other dams in his forty-year career now moved north to Redding, seat of Shasta County, on the upper Sacramento River, this time bringing his wife and daughters along and buying a home and a cattle ranch. Once again, on 21 August 1938, Frank Crowe was on hand to supervise the bulldozers as they began preparing the site for the construction of the 602-foot-high arched gravity dam designed under the supervision of J. L. Savage, chief designing engineer for the Bureau of Reclamation.

Comparisons and contrasts between Hoover Dam and Shasta Dam involve questions of engineering as well as metaphor. Located in a remote and towering desert gorge, Hoover Dam was more obviously an act of assertion, even defiance, against nature. Hoover Dam rose 726 feet in comparison to the 602 feet of Shasta. With a narrow crest length of a mere 1,282 feet, Hoover seemed inserted into its site by all-powerful extraterrestrials, a gigantic version of the monolith in the film 2001. Shasta Dam, by contrast, ran serenely across a low-lying canyon with a crest length of 3,500 feet. With 6,246,000 cubic yards of concrete contained in its structure, Shasta Dam contained almost twice the volume of Hoover. If Hoover was a monolith, an obelisk, a towering temple, Shasta moved horizontally across its site with the power and serenity of Mount Shasta itself. Stylized by Gordon Kaufmann into an Art Deco monument to Machine Age futurism, Hoover Dam was consciously linked to architecture and fine art. In Shasta Dam, by contrast, engineering spoke for itself with direct minimalism. Shasta Dam swept serenely across its expansive site like a granite wall shaped in its place by an ancient glacier.

If Hoover Dam bespoke the eclectic complexity of Art Deco, Shasta Dam, completed in 1944, bespoke the austerities of wartime America.

As in the case of Hoover Dam, Shasta Dam had its fundamental meaning as part of a system. Even before work started on Shasta, construction began on the Contra Costa Canal in October 1937. In November 1939 construction began on Friant Dam on the San Joaquin River, which was also completed in 1944. Three hundred feet in height and 3,430 in length along its crest, Friant Dam ranked, when completed, as the fifth largest dam in the world after Grand Coulee on the Columbia River in Washington State, Shasta Dam on the Sacramento, Fontana Dam on the Little Tennessee River in North Carolina, and Boulder Dam on the Colorado. Thus by 1944 three of the five largest dams in the world were serving California. Unlike Hoover and Shasta, Friant was a straight gravity-type dam, not curved. As such, it swept at a relatively low level across its site in the Sierra foothills of Fresno County like a graceful water bird which, having alighted on the San Joaquin River en route to the south, raised its white wings in the sunlight in preparation for further flight. Then came more dams: Keswick, Folsom, Auburn, Red Bluff Diversion; and their reservoirs: Shasta Lake, Clair Engle Lake, Lewiston Lake, Whiskeytown Lake, Folsom Lake, San Luis Reservoir, Millerton Lake; and the canals: Corning, Stony, Tehama-Colusa, Delta Cross Channel, Folsom South, Contra Costa, Delta-Mendota, Madera, San Luis, Friant-Kern; and the pumping plants at Tracy and Dos Amigos, which accomplished the heroic task of moving millions of acre-feet of water up the gentle incline of the Valley of the San Joaquin.

But all this was for the future. It would take thirty years to complete the Central Valley Project. Yet Californians had willed the Project into being in the depths of the Great Depression and, with the help of the Bureau of Reclamation, continued to build dams and canals through the war years when such enterprises were being destroyed in Asia and Europe. By 1944 millions of acre-feet of fresh mountain water no longer flowed needlessly into the Pacific. Nor were lives and hundreds of millions of dollars of property lost in recurrent floods. By the 1950s the Central Valley, thanks in significant measure to the Project, had been transformed into a vast invented garden: a third and co-equal partner to Northern and Southern California.

As in everything human, there was controversy. Reclamation law, for one thing, restricted the ownership of federally irrigated land to 160 acres per person, 320 for a married couple. So many of the prophets of irrigation—most notably Elwood Mead, a former Californian at the helm of Reclamation when both the Boulder Canyon Project and the Central Valley Project were being planned—envisioned federally sponsored irrigation as a way of getting families on to the land. By the late 1940s, however, it had become apparent that large-scale agribusiness, more than the small farmer, was profiting from these Reclamation projects. When the Bureau made gestures in the direction of enforcing the 160–acre limit, a fierce battle broke out, comparable to that waged by PG&E against public power in the previous two decades. This battle pitted two worthies from the Depression era against each other in mortal combat: Professor Paul Taylor of UC Berkeley, who wished to see the acreage limitation enforced, and United States Senator Sheridan Downey, who championed the right of large-scale farmers to continue to avail themselves of the federal waters. The ferocity of that battle, which has continued for a half century, is part of a later story. For the time being, as the late 1930s rushed precipitously toward the war years, the Central Valley Project, then being materialized in great dams and canals which would soon rank among the civil engineering marvels of the world, testified to the power of public works as technology, as engineering, as therapy for a battered economy—and symbol of shared identity and purpose.

Completed in 1933, the Stockton Channel traced itself to the 1870s report of Colonel Barton Stone Alexander which had also originated the Central Valley Project. Located on the San Joaquin River on the northwest edge of the San Joaquin Valley, the city of Stockton stood tantalizingly close to the Bay of San Francisco. Only a hundred miles of waterways including the San Joaquin River, the channels and sloughs of the Delta, Suisun Bay, and Carquinez Strait separated Stockton from the deep-water possibilities of San Francisco Bay. In 1870, when Colonel Alexander first broached the idea of linking Stockton with the Pacific via this waterway, Stockton was the third largest city in the state. Colonel Alexander's recommendations revived, at least on the level of imagination, that passion for canals which was so characteristic of Americans in the early nineteenth century. President John Quincy Adams, for example, dreamt of an America unified beyond sectional rivalry through a network of canals and turnpikes. In 1825 the Erie Canal linked the Great Lakes with New York City via the Hudson River, and this prototype no doubt informed the suggestion of the Colonel that Stockton be linked to the Bay of San Francisco via the San Joaquin. While railroads began to replace the older canals in the 1850s, water transport still maintained its efficiency. A canal linking Stockton with one of the great harbors of the world, the Bay of San Francisco, could transform an inland agricultural town into an urban shipment and reception center of great economic importance.

By the early 1900s, Stockton had become the dominant shipping and receiving center for San Joaquin County, served by the Southern Pacific, the Santa Fe, and the Western Pacific railroads. Not surprisingly, the citizens of Stockton began to revive Colonel Alexander's suggestion of a direct connection with the Pacific. Why, they asked themselves, should Stockton allow the railroads to control the shipping of the rich produce of the San Joaquin Valley? Why should not the Valley have its own maritime connection with the Atlantic states and Europe, without the burdensome added cost of hauling by transcontinental railroad, or the expensive transference of cargo from rail to ship? For more than a half century, the domination and exorbitant rates of the railroad had been galling San Joaquin

Valley ranchers. In 1900 novelist Frank Norris had used one violent clash between ranchers and railroad men, the shootout at Mussel Slough in May 1880, as the basis of his novel *The Octopus* (1901), among the most notable novels to be set in the Golden State.

Throughout the first two decades of the 1900s, San Joaquin Valley ranchers and their allies in the Stockton Chamber of Commerce lobbied ceaselessly with state and federal authorities on behalf of a deep-water channel connecting Stockton with the Bay of San Francisco. In 1919 the Stockton Chamber of Commerce commissioned engineer S. A. Jubb, who had laid out the Port of Los Angeles, to devise plans for a deep-water port on the Stockton riverfront. The Army Corps of Engineers, meanwhile, under the command of Major Ulysses Simpson Grant III, surveyed a channel route, which the Corps of Engineers continued to plan and improve through the 1920s. Herbert Hoover, then serving as Secretary of Commerce, placed himself solidly behind the project. Thanks in part to Hoover's intervention and continuing sponsorship, President Calvin Coolidge signed a Rivers and Harbors bill into law on 21 January 1927, which contained a provision authorizing a port and channel project for Stockton. In May 1927 the state legislature authorized the State Board of Control to make all property purchases necessary for the project from a fund of $419,000 which the legislature made available. The City of Stockton had already voted $3 million toward the cost of the project in 1925 and set in motion the legal processes necessary to create a Port District.

Dredging began in April 1930, with the Corps of Engineers supervising a fleet of privately owned hydraulic pipeline dredges, hopper dredges, clamshell bucket and dragline dredges, steam shovels, and pile drivers. This ungainly fleet dredge-drudged at its task for three years, sucking or scooping the sometimes nearly fluid mud at the bottom of the channel route, then depositing it behind pile-driven levees, where it blended its primeval richness with the already fertile farmlands of the Delta, rescued some sixty years earlier by the heroic labor of the Chinese.

Finally, early on Thursday morning, 2 February 1933, the *Daisy Gray*, an oceangoing lumber-carrier, sailed triumphantly into the Port of Stockton with its cargo of seven hundred thousand board feet. Church bells pealed, factory whistles blew, and hundreds of automobile horns honked as the *Daisy Gray* slid into its berth alongside a newly constructed warehouse wharf. For the next seven years, further construction and dredging continued with the assistance of PWA and WPA funds and a $900,000 bond issue passed by a newly created Stockton Port District in February 1934. Tonnage more than doubled between 1933 and 1940. Thanks to civil engineering, the City of Stockton was now a deep-water port. For the rest of the century, oceangoing ships glided past farms and ranches like great sea creatures that had learned to love the land.

In other instances, the land proved less friendly. One month after the *Daisy Gray* sailed into the port of Stockton, the earth shook with great ferocity in the area in and around the city of Long Beach for ten terrible seconds at 5:54 in the early evening of 10 March 1933, followed by thirty-four additional aftershocks within the next five days. At 6.3 on the Richter Scale, the Long Beach earthquake was not the most intense in recorded history, but then again, Long Beach was not the best-built city either. Fifty-two people lost their lives, many of them in the collapse of buildings whose flimsiness of construction, much of it unreinforced brick, reflected the boom-town way Long Beach had developed through the Oil Rush of the 1920s and the rapid expansion of the port during the same period. Fortunately, the Pacific Fleet was at anchor in the outer Long Beach Harbor, and at the request of city officials Admiral Richard Leigh sent two thousand sailors and marines ashore to insure good order and assist in rescue operations.

As if the Depression were not enough, Long Beach now faced the necessity of rebuilding much of its civic fabric. As luck would have it, the most important buildings in Long Beach, each of them constructed after the boom era of the 1920s—the seaside Municipal Auditorium, among others, and the Villa Riviera Apartment Hotel, two of the most distinctive buildings in Southern California— survived the temblor. Nearly every school building in the city, however, some thirty-eight buildings in all, suffered significant damage. As a godsend, the earthquake had struck outside regular school hours, or else hundreds of schoolchildren most likely would have been killed or injured.

The reconstruction of the Long Beach school system with a mixture of almost $5 million in local bonds and another $4 million in PWA loans and grants serves as a cutting-edge example of Public Works Administration and Works Projects Administration activities in California during the Depression. The entire school system of Los Angeles County, for one thing, primary and secondary, was scheduled for renovation or new construction with a combination of state and PWA funds. Under the supervision of a board of forty-eight architects, engineers, and construction experts appointed by the Board of Education, a total of 536 school buildings were either rehabilitated or constructed over a three-year period for a total cost of $34,144,000, with PWA loans and grants providing more than half the necessary funds. Between August 1934 when the project began and April 1938 when it was officially completed, the Los Angeles School Project provided nearly twenty-seven million man-hours of employment, for a total of $10.5 million in wages paid.

Not only were these 536 schools soundly and seismically constructed of steel and concrete, they were designed by such distinguished architects as Richard Neutra, Norman Marsh, David Smith, Herbert Powell, O. W. Morgan, J. A. Walls, and William Henry Harrison. Today, more than a half century later, the schools constructed by the PWA in Los Angeles County—among them, the Thomas Jefferson High School and the Emerson School in Los Angeles, Pasadena City College, South Pasadena High School, the Lou Henry Hoover School in Whittier, and the triumphant Hollywood High School—remain serviceable survivors of Streamline Moderne and its affiliated styles, which will always bespeak what many consider the golden age of Southern California architecture. Young Californians attending these and other PWA schools, in the 1930s and subsequently—with their distinguished architecture, so vibrant with futurity, their sculptured facades, invoking the pageant of the ages, their instructive murals centered on high points of science and the arts—absorbed at an impressionable age an all-important message: they counted, learning counted, and the society in which they were preparing to play a part counted as well.

All in all, the PWA financed the construction of more than 221 government buildings and more than 140 new schools in California between 1933 and 1939. Alameda County, for example, received a stunning new county courthouse on the shores of Lake Merritt in downtown Oakland. Artists employed by the WPA Federal Art Project used more than fifty different colors of marble to execute a mural in the foyer depicting the history of Alameda County in the Spanish and Mexican era and the Gold Rush. Santa Barbara received a National Guard armory and a new central post office, designed by the architect Reginald Johnson in a style blending Spanish Revival and Moderne. New central post offices, equally distinctive in architecture and murals, were constructed in San Francisco, Hollywood, and Santa Monica. With the help of PWA funds, the Federal Reserve Bank opened a bold new Los Angeles branch, the General Services Administration built a new federal building, and the City of Los Angeles completed its long-delayed Union Station, the last great railroad terminal constructed in the United States. With WPA funds, the City of Long Beach constructed an airport terminal adjacent to Douglas Aircraft, finishing it just in time for the Second World War.

Not every major public work under construction in California in the 1930s, it must be admitted, was a PWA- or WPA-assisted project. Two of the triumphs of this period, the twenty-five-hundred-bed Los Angeles County General Hospital, completed in 1933, and the Golden Gate Bridge, completed in 1937, were financed at the county level. Another enterprise, the memorial on Santa Catalina Island honoring the recently deceased William Wrigley Jr., which remains to this day the most imposing funerary monument in the state, was financed from private resources. The Department of the Navy, meanwhile, unilaterally constructed a gigantic airship hangar at Moffett Field south of San Francisco. Completed in 1933, the hangar soon became an impressive anachronism, intended to service an era of Zeppelin-sized lighter-than-air craft, which sadly ended with the loss of the *Shenandoah*, the *Akron*, the *Macon*, and the *Hindenberg*.

Nor were recreational facilities neglected. In San Francisco, the WPA helped construct a bath house at Aquatic Park, a spacious gymnasium and playground atop Potrero Hill, and monkey, lion, and elephant habitats at Fleishhacker Zoo. Across the Bay in Alameda County, workers hired by the WPA and young men enrolled in the Civilian Conservation Corps relandscaped and improved Tilden Park for the East Bay Regional Park District.

As in the case of smaller PWA and WPA projects—police and fire stations, jails, small-town schools (the town of Sebastopol in Sonoma County achieved an architectural classic in its PWA high school)—it would prove futile to attempt to

inventory the numerous park and public forest rehabilitation projects completed
in California by the young men of the Civilian Conservation Corps during the
middle to late 1930s: the soil erosion projects, the rivers cleared of debris, the
hiking trails established, the roadside picnic shelters and rest stops constructed,
the millions of trees planted (two billion trees in all, across the United States), all
of it done by young men between the ages of seventeen and twenty-four, including
nineteen-year-old Owen Lee Starr of San Francisco, who later described his days
in the CCC as the happiest time of his life. This experience of living in remote
camps under the supervision of Army officers, gathered in companies of two hundred, spending the work week on worthwhile projects, answered the personal question for thousands of young men of what to do while they were young and unemployed in the Depression, at the same time suggesting the possibilities of
cooperative action, of social democracy, in their and the American future. Retro-
spectively, the CCC can be evaluated as a dress rehearsal for military life, for war,
or as a youth movement paralleling comparable mobilizations of youth in Germany and Italy. There is some truth to this. But it is also true to say that the
CCC, by putting young men to work on public works of such obvious benefit to
society, also communicated to them that whatever the temporary difficulties in
the economy, they were known and cherished, each of them, name by name, as
in their early morning roll calls and evening flag retreats, and that the American
people whose sons they were would one day need them returned to productive
work in a recovered economy.

In its administration of the Civilian Conservation Corps, the Army, fearful of
being charged with unwarranted control over civilians, exercised a light, diplo-
matic touch. The Army Corps of Engineers, by contrast, had long since become
assured of its prerogatives in river and flood control and hence showed no reluctance to exercise a heavy hand in Los Angeles County, where flooding had proven
such a perennial problem.

Three basic stream systems—the Los Angeles River, the San Gabriel River and
Rio Hondo, and Ballona Creek—drain the Los Angeles Basin. Having their origins in the San Gabriel Mountains, these rivers drop precipitously to the plain
below in their progress to the Pacific. The Los Angeles River, for instance, is only
fifty miles long, yet its source is a thousand feet above sea level. The Los Angeles
River, in other words, drops as much in fifty miles as the Mississippi does along
its entire 2,348-mile length. When these stream patterns, the Los Angeles River
especially, became engorged by storms during the rainy season, they flooded thun-
derously onto the plain below and the hapless communities in their path, most
notably the City of Angels. Between 1815 and 1876 eight major floods devastated
the area. Between 1884 and 1938 there were nine more. In 1915 the cities of the
region formed the Los Angeles County Flood Control District, passed a bond
issue, and began construction on fourteen dam and channel projects.

None of this seemed of much value in 1934 and 1938 when massive floods swept through Los Angeles and adjacent cities. The flood of New Year's Day 1934 in the La Crescenta–Montrose area caused $6 million in damage and the loss of forty-one lives. At this point, with $31 million in unsold bonds in its empty portfolio, the Flood Control District turned to the federal government. In 1936 Congress authorized $70 million for flood control projects on the Los Angeles and San Gabriel rivers, Ballona Creek, and tributaries, together with $13 million for flood control projects on the Santa Ana in Orange County. The Army Corps of Engineers assumed responsibility from the Flood Control District for construction of these public works. Then came the flood of 2 March 1938, which caused $40 million in damage and killed forty-nine people. For two days, the city of Los Angeles lay sunk like Atlantis beneath an inland sea.

At this point, the Corps of Engineers declared war on the Los Angeles River. By 1939 flood control projects approaching the cost of the Panama Canal were on the books for Los Angeles County. If every authorized project were to have been enacted, the aggregate cost would have exceeded $501 million. Rolling up its sleeves, the Corps of Engineers got to work on Hansen Dam in the San Fernando Valley, 71 debris basins, 290 miles of concrete-lined channels, 187 miles of channels with bank revetment, and numerous other flood control works. Widening the Los Angeles River at strategic intervals into a rectangular channel, the Army Engineers buried the sections of the river which ran through the metropolitan region under hundreds of thousands of cubic yards of concrete. A public works project thus did its best to destroy a river possessed of its own special sort of greatness, depriving Los Angeles in the process of its central landmark. A half century later, many in Los Angeles would look disappointedly at the concrete channel that ran through the downtown en route to the Pacific, through which trickled a vestige of the River, and wonder if the Corps of Engineers had made the right decision. So many great cities, after all, are organized around their rivers. Can Los Angeles ever be most completely its best urban self after destroying its river, needlessly, many believe, in the effort to achieve flood control? Public works—or at least public works exercised in a vengeance of poured concrete—are not always the answer.

To the question of automobile traffic in the 1930s and beyond, public works provided a glorious answer of parkways, tunnels, and bridges. Completed in November 1932, for example, the Bixby Creek Bridge, also known as Rainbow Bridge, soars 714 feet, 285 feet above Bixby Creek as it flows into the Pacific at Big Sur on Pacific Coast Highway 1. One of the highest single-span concrete arch bridges in the world, the majestic Bixby Creek/Rainbow Bridge belies its massivity of construction—sixty-six hundred cubic yards of concrete and six hundred thousand pounds of reinforced steel—through the sheer rainbow-gracefulness with which it spans Bixby Canyon and Creek (to which the sea otters returned, after long absence, in March 1938). Other places and times might celebrate Rainbow Bridge as a preeminent masterpiece, which it was; but for California in the 1930s this exceptionally graceful public work, so perfect in its setting, almost slipped by as just another federally assisted project. In any event, the Bridge helped knit coastal California into further unity. Thanks in part to this elegant public work, the Pacific Coast Highway eventually swept uninterruptedly up the coast from San Diego to the Oregon border, ever in sight of the Pacific and the changing land forms of the coast.

The Arroyo Seco Parkway, for its part, opening on 30 December 1940, brought Pasadena and Los Angeles within seven and a half minutes of each other. As the first freeway in California, it also prophesied the freeway system of the post-war era. Before the Arroyo Seco Parkway opened, it could take as long as an hour to drive between Pasadena and Los Angeles on Figueroa Street through the commercial district of Highland Park. Pasadena and Los Angeles remained in many respects competing rivals as cities and contrasting lifestyles: Pasadena, aloof, genteel, upper-middle-class; Los Angeles, brassy, sprawling, polyglot. Between the two cities runs the Arroyo Seco, a steep declivity, extending from the San Gabriel Mountains to the Los Angeles River, on whose upper edges artists, writers, and artisans gathered at the turn of the century to create the Arroyo Culture, which was the Southern California version of the Arts and Crafts movement.

Beginning in 1922, Los Angeles and South Pasadena began to acquire Arroyo properties in the hopes of linking the two cities via a park belt. Others, meanwhile, were seeing transportation-related uses for the Arroyo. In 1895 Pasadenan T. D. Allen had proposed a bicycle speedway through the Arroyo between the two cities. By the late 1920s the idea for a roadway through the Arroyo had gained wide acceptance. Highland Park business interests, however, fearful of losing the traffic on Figueroa, delayed events, as did the City of South Pasadena, which would be bisected by the proposed roadway.

By the time planning for the roadway had passed these obstacles, it was the late 1930s and, not surprisingly, the PWA and the WPA were on hand to assist local efforts. Construction began on 21 March 1938 after Rose Queen Cheryl Walker pulled the lever on a steam shovel to move the first earth. Her successor by two Rose Queens, Sally Stanton, was on hand to assist Governor Olson and other dignitaries in cutting a chain of roses on the completed Parkway on 30 December 1940, just two days before the annual Tournament of Roses parade. A few days earlier, a delegation of Native Americans had met with Highway Patrol Chief E. Raymond Cato and declared the Arroyo Seco free of evil spirits.

Considered in its time as well as from the perspective of the future, the Arroyo Seco Parkway, renamed the Pasadena Freeway (State Highway 110) in 1955, was a remarkable public work. Only the Pennsylvania Turnpike, dedicated two months earlier, could compete with it in its uninterrupted flow of automotive traffic. Although they later wanted to forget this, the engineers responsible for the Parkway had made a thorough study of the *autobahns* under construction at the time in Nazi Germany. Following Germany's example, the engineers from the California Highway Department paid special attention to the siting of the Parkway on the Arroyo and to the landscaping on either side of the roadway. Tunnels and overpasses were designed in monumental Moderne, with Art Deco and WPA Moderne bas-reliefs electric with triumphant national symbolism. On opening day, an Army motorcade from Fort McArthur rumbled down the Parkway to demonstrate its *autobahn*-like military value for troop movement, should Southern California ever be invaded.

Some mistakes were made. Entrances and exits were abrupt and severely curved, making it necessary to enter flowing traffic from a virtual stop. But the seven-mile roadway, built at the cost of $1 million per mile, foretold the future. Riding on this uninterrupted roadway, two lanes in each direction, set perfectly in its Arroyo Seco site, passing in and out of monumental Moderne tunnels and overpasses, motorists of 1941 could experience the Southern California of the future: the continuous sub/urban metropolis which the successors to the Arroyo Seco Parkway—the Golden State (5), the San Diego (405), the Foothill (210), the San Bernardino (10), and the Pomona (60), six hundred miles in all—would soon be effecting in the Southland.

Fifty years after its dedication, the Pasadena Freeway remained a major carrier. By this time, a portion of the Los Angeles oligarchy had conveniently relocated itself to the suburb of San Marino, adjacent to Pasadena (the remainder settled in Hancock Park in central Los Angeles); and for a number of decades this San Marino establishment, conservative, Republican, commuting each business day on the Pasadena Freeway between splendid Mediterranean Revival homes in San Marino and office buildings in downtown Los Angeles, wielded predominate financial and political influence in the region.

A linking between the suburbs and the central city, such as the Arroyo Seco Parkway made possible between Los Angeles and the towns of the San Gabriel Valley, was also the goal in Northern California of the Alameda–Contra Costa Tunnel, later called the Caldecott Tunnel, another PWA project. By the late 1930s it had become apparent that metropolitan San Francisco possessed all the elements of an important urban region: the fourth largest metropolitan region in the nation, in fact, by the 1970s. For this to happen, however, Contra Costa County in the East Bay would have to be knit more closely into the urban fabric of Oakland and San Francisco. The vast plains of Contra Costa stood in a comparable relationship to urban settlements around the Bay as, at first, the San Fernando Valley and, later, Orange County stood in relation to Los Angeles. For there to be any form of meaningful connection, Contra Costa would have to have automotive access to San Francisco Bay settlements and vice versa. This meant tunneling through the Contra Costa Range, which sealed off the spacious plains of Contra Costa County from the cities and suburbs surrounding San Francisco Bay.

The Caldecott Tunnel made no sense whatsoever without a direct surface access to San Francisco. It was no easy task. Fresh from its Hoover Dam triumph, the Six Companies won the contract in May 1936 from the joint Highway District formed by Alameda and Contra Costa counties to build the twin-bore tunnel. No sooner had work begun under the supervision of Stephen Bechtel, the serious nature of the project asserted itself. The rock was fractured shale, for one thing, running at a ninety-degree angle over an earthquake fault. Slippage and cave-ins were common. One cave-in killed three workers. When the Six Companies found itself well ahead of its $3,683,931 bid in costs, it called in the lawyers, together with Frank Crowe, the construction boss of Hoover. Crowe told them that the worst was past. "Stop lawin' and start diggin'," as he put it; but lawyers dig deeper than hard hats, and with their advice, the Six Companies exited the job, which was completed by a consortium of smaller companies.[2] The Highway District took the Six Companies to federal court and won. All in all, the *wunderkind* of Hoover lost $2.4 million on the Thomas E. Caldecott Tunnel, named in honor of the chairman of the board of the District. Aside from the money and the loss of face, the Six Companies also learned a valuable lesson: do extensive geological surveys before you come in with a low-ball bid, especially when the project is a tunnel. Fortunately, by the time the Caldecott Tunnel opened to traffic on 5 December 1937, a stunning highway and interurban railway ran directly from Oakland to San Francisco via the San Francisco–Oakland Bay Bridge. At long last, San Francisco enjoyed a direct surface link to the East Bay and its transmontane hinterlands.

No American city is more fortunately, or more unfortunately, sited than San Francisco. Surrounded by water on three sides, San Francisco stands in splendid isolation, a virtual island off the coast. Since the early 1860s, a rail line had linked San Francisco with the city of San Jose at the southern end of the Bay; but only its ferry boats linked San Francisco with the rest of the nation. With the exception of traveling south on the east side of the Bay to San Jose, then proceeding north on the west side to San Francisco, a journey of one hundred miles, there was no other direct way to get into San Francisco, except by ferry boat. Transcontinental trains completed their journey at the Oakland terminal, then brought passengers across the Bay by ferry boat to the Ferry Building at the foot of Market Street. In 1925 alone, a peak year, there were some forty-one million passenger crossings by ferry to and from San Francisco. The Depression dropped this figure to thirty-five million in 1930, but the fall-off was temporary. By 1933 some fifty thousand commuters were coming into and out of San Francisco each weekday via a fleet of ferry boats, some of them capable of handling up to two, even three thousand passengers. In addition to this passenger traffic, ferries were carrying an average of 4.5 million vehicles back and forth across the Bay by 1930, a figure which doubled by 1937. Ferry boats which averaged thirty miles per hour in 1925 were revved to average forty-five miles per hour by 1930 to serve the increased traffic.

Commuting by ferry boat was efficient and pleasant. Railroad companies—the Northwestern Pacific, the Southern Pacific, the Santa Fe, Western Pacific, and the Key System—scrupulously maintained their giant ships. The larger ferry boats operated on-board restaurants (the corned beef hash on Key System boats was to die for), together with newsstands, candy stores, and, before and after Prohibition, small bars, where, especially on homeward trips, commuters might ease the transition from office to home-front, watching the sun set over the Pacific, adult beverage in hand. With this many people commuting each day, a good-sized-town's worth, a ferry boat sub-culture arose around card games, birthday parties, holiday celebrations or just plain kibitzing among passengers accustomed to meet each other each day across ten, twenty, thirty years of a working life. An informal, yet adhered to, system of seat assignment was common on most boats, it being considered vulgar to appropriate the accustomed seat of a regular commuter. Commuters to the East Bay enjoyed the added benefit of the efficient interurban electric Key System, which combed the area between Hayward and Berkeley with its swift trolleys.

Miraculously, no commuter had ever lost his or her life on these ferry boats, with the exception of the odd suicide. On 24 April 1927, in the midst of a deep fog, the steamer *Newport* rammed the ferry boat *Golden City*, cutting it into two sections, which floated out through the Golden Gate and sank. Fortunately, there were only six unaccompanied automobiles on the ferry at the time, and the crew escaped. On the evening of 17 February 1928 the ferry boat *Peralta*, its water ballast improperly handled, plunged into a swell off Yerba Buena Island, sweeping more than thirty passengers into the chilly waters of the Bay. Five of them drowned. Five years later a fire in the terminal on the Key System Pier off Oakland destroyed the terminal, gutted the *Peralta*, and ruined fourteen interurban electrics. Proponents of a bridge between San Francisco and Oakland maximized these two disasters in their public relations campaign.

Credit for originating the idea of bridging San Francisco and Oakland most likely belongs to William Walker, editor of the San Francisco *Herald*, who first proposed the idea in 1851. In August 1853 Tom Maguire, an impresario in Gold Rush San Francisco, featured at San Francisco Hall on Washington Street near Montgomery a pageant entitled "The Past, Present, and Future of San Francisco." One scenic backdrop, designed by a certain Dr. D. G. Robinson, depicted a spectacular suspension bridge soaring across San Francisco Bay between Telegraph Hill and Mount Diablo. In 1856 Lieutenant George Horatio Derby, a Massachusetts-born Army engineer who wrote humorous sketches under the name of John Phoenix or Squibob, published a comic poem entitled "O'er the Bay, or The Song of the Oakland Bridge," in which he decried the perils and discomforts of crossing the Bay by barge. That same year, a bill calling for such a bridge was introduced into the state senate by State Senator William McCoun, but languished for lack of interest.

As the transcontinental railroad reached completion in 1869, interest in the proposal flared briefly among railroad men, intrigued by the possibility of bringing trains directly into San Francisco. One of the Big Four, Leland Stanford, had already raised the idea twice, in 1859 and again in 1867. In 1869 Joshua Norton, the self-proclaimed Emperor of the United States and Protector of Mexico, who lived as a revered street character in San Francisco, resplendent in a military frock coat and other regalia, called for his subjects to construct a bridge between the two cities. Thanks to an anonymous pamphlet entitled *The Railroad System of California* (1871), most likely written at the behest of the Central Pacific, plans surfaced briefly in the early 1870s for the construction of a causeway linking Oakland and Yerba Buena Island, which anticipated the eastern half of the eventual solution. In 1906 the Southern Pacific, successor to the Central Pacific, constructed a low-level trestle across the shoals and mud flats of the south Bay between Dumbarton Point and Palo Alto. In 1927 a parallel span for automobiles was added. Also completed in 1927: Carquinez Bridge across the Carquinez Strait in the north Bay, followed in 1929 by a low-level trestle between San Mateo and Hayward which, like the Dumbarton Bridge, had a drawspan in its center, just in case vessels of any size were ever foolhardy enough to enter the shallow shoals of San Francisco Bay south of Hunters Point.

The Bay between San Francisco and Oakland, by contrast, was deep and foreboding. No mere trestle could negotiate these waters. A major bridge, some four and a half miles in length, would be necessary. In 1914 San Francisco engineer F. E. Fowler submitted plans for a cantilevered bridge across the Bay, which the War Department immediately rejected as a barrier to naval traffic.

As in the case of so many important public works in California during this period, Herbert Hoover, engineer and Californian, came to the rescue. As Secretary of Commerce in the Harding and Coolidge administrations, Hoover made the cause of a San Francisco–Oakland Bay Bridge a continuing priority. Since the most formidable barrier was the military, Hoover persuaded President Harding in 1922 to appoint a new Army-Navy commission to investigate the feasibility of a crossing. While the military held fast to its objections, it did agree, finally, at least to the idea of a crossing no further north than Hunters Point, provided that naval traffic remained unobstructed.

In late March of 1928, Mayor Rolph of San Francisco, United States Senator Hiram Johnson, and other interested parties testified before the Senate Committee on Commerce regarding the necessity of a bridge from Rincon Point in San Francisco to Oakland via Yerba Buena Island. Johnson took strong issue with the objections of the Navy Department and the Hunters Point site. The San Mateo Bridge causeway, Johnson argued, made the Hunters Point site redundant. What was needed was a direct connection linking San Francisco, Oakland, and the emergent suburban regions in the East Bay. Pointing to the growth that would come once the Hetch Hetchy project was complete, Mayor Rolph argued that only a bridge between San Francisco and Oakland could handle the expected growth. San Francisco city engineer Michael O'Shaughnessy and harbor pilot Captain George Harrison described the growing congestion on the Bay and predicted that the recent drowning of five passengers from the *Peralta* was only the first of many predictable disasters.

In a stump speech characteristic of his political style, James McSheehy, a member of the Board of Supervisors of the City and County of San Francisco, lamented the fact that there had been little if any advance in the technology of crossing the Bay since he was a small boy sixty years ago. Famous for his solecisms and malapropisms, McSheehy, a semi-self-educated Irish contractor, brought the Senate Committee to bemused silence as, in one long run-on sentence, he extolled the Army and the Navy, San Francisco, again the Army and the Navy, all this laced with reminiscences of how, sixty years earlier, he had taken the *Piedmont* across San Francisco Bay, and the *Piedmont* was still in service. More shrewdly, Supervisor McSheehy also entered into evidence a scrapbook containing forty-seven thousand column inches of newspaper clippings proving interest and support for the project among Bay Area voters.

When many of those very same voters sent Herbert Hoover to the White House later that year, prospects for a San Francisco–Oakland Bay Bridge improved dramatically. In August 1929 Hoover joined Governor Young to create the high-level Hoover-Young Commission to make a final recommendation. To the Commission, Hoover appointed two close friends, Professor Charles Marx of Stanford, the Hetch Hetchy activist who had taught Hoover engineering as an undergraduate, and Mark Requa, a mining engineer who had remained a close friend and confidant of Hoover throughout the President's public career. On 12 August 1930 the Hoover-Young Commission, after extensive hearings, recommended that a bridge be built from Emeryville on the flats north of Oakland to Yerba Buena Island in the middle of the Bay, then on to Rincon Point in San Francisco.

Concurrently, the California State Legislature created the California Toll Bridge Authority, authorizing it to own and operate a bridge across San Francisco Bay, to be constructed by the California Department of Public Works. Thus the San Francisco–Oakland Bay Bridge came into existence as a state project, authorized by the California legislature and facilitated by the federal government.

Federal as well was its financing. Again through the intervention of Hoover, the Reconstruction Finance Corporation purchased $62 million in state bonds from the California Toll Bridge Authority. (Hoover also used RFC funds to initiate the Boulder Canyon Project.) Another $15.2 million in loans and grants was authorized by the PWA, bringing the entire cost of the bridge to $77.2 million, which made this structure, arguably, the most expensive single public works project to that point in American history. Many claimed it to be, all things considered, the most expensive public work in the history of the human race.

The San Francisco–Oakland Bay Bridge proceeded directly from the highway-building impulse. At four and one half miles in length, the Bridge was planned as a gigantic roadway over water, completed in three parts: a suspension bridge between Yerba Buena Island and Rincon Point in San Francisco, and a hybrid fourteen-hundred-foot cantilevered span (the third largest structure of this type in the world) linked to a 291–foot truss span ending in Emeryville. A no-nonsense, battleship-gray structure such as this, combining suspension, cantilever, and truss systems, with two decks—the top for automobile traffic, the bottom for trucks and Key System trains—has never overwhelmed its viewers as an aesthetic statement. As engineer in charge of design, Glenn Woodruff tackled the problem of devising this over-long bridge with efficient practicality. San Francisco architect Timothy Pflueger was invited to chair a committee of consulting architects, but one strains to see any element of Pflueger's styling genius in even the suspension half of the structure, which he did work on as a designer. As straightforward civil servants, responsible to the Department of Public Works in Sacramento, neither design engineer Woodruff nor chief engineer Charles Henry Purcell had either the budget or the inclination to commission Pflueger or any other of the fine architects practicing in the Bay Area to stylize the four 518-feet-high suspension towers as Gordon Kaufmann was asked to stylize Hoover Dam. In terms of design and style, the San Francisco–Oakland Bay Bridge bespoke the engineering aesthetic of public works and the Toll Bridge Authority rather than the aesthetic proclivities of San Francisco. Only when the towers and suspension cables of the bridge were permanently strung with lights, fifty years after its opening, did the San Francisco–Oakland Bay Bridge achieve any suggestion of what could have been an even more compelling aesthetic power.

In any event, the Bridge was built between July 1933 and November 1936, with former president Herbert Hoover on hand for both the initiating and dedicatory ceremonies. Twelve men lost their lives in constructing the colossus, an extraordinary safety record, given the difficulties of sinking forty-four underwater piers. The single greatest engineering challenge posed by the San Francisco–Oakland Bay Bridge was, as is usual with bridges of this sort, the supporting piers. Engineer Daniel Moran resolved the difficulty with a series of floating caissons, which allowed foundation structures to be constructed above water, then sunk slowly to bedrock as more steel and concrete was put in place. The cantilevers on the eastern section were also fast-tracked, built out, piece by piece, over the water, instead of being lifted by cranes and jacks from below.

In his dedicatory remarks, Hoover referred to the San Francisco–Oakland Bay Bridge as "the greatest bridge yet constructed in the world."[3] Hoover was correct. In the midst of the Great Depression—as if Hoover Dam, Parker Dam, the second Los Angeles Aqueduct, the All-American Canal, the Hetch Hetchy Aqueduct, the beginnings of construction on Shasta Dam and the Central Valley Project, the Arroyo Seco Parkway, the Rainbow Bridge were not sufficient—the State of California, with a minimum of political controversy, almost casually, without popular vote, completed the single largest bridge in human history and the world's most expensive public work, which gave the City of San Francisco its long-delayed direct connection to inland California.

If the San Francisco-Oakland Bay Bridge was the largest bridge in the world, the Golden Gate Bridge was the most beautiful—and the most intelligent. It is tempting, in fact, to think of the Golden Gate Bridge as a living entity, so vital is it with an intelligence that can be described as Pythagorean, reflecting the teaching of that ancient Greek philosopher who saw the basis of being in materialized Number. Even the vast literature associated with the Golden Gate Bridge—the innumerable technical reports, the newspaper and magazine stories, at least four histories, including John Van Der Zee's magisterial *The Gate* (1986)—fails to account fully for the Golden Gate Bridge in terms of its cumulative power as a work of engineering art. Like any masterpiece, in other words, the Golden Gate Bridge transcends the story of its genesis, design, and construction. It has become something more than the sum total of its parts.

In the case of the San Francisco–Oakland Bay Bridge, two cities needed to be joined, and, more important, the City of San Francisco required a connection to the mainland. The Golden Gate Bridge was not brought into being by such self-evident necessitiy. It seemed, rather, to gather its strength from ever deeper levels of motivation. The Golden Gate Bridge began with a reference to Antiquity, a classical metaphor.

The regions north of the Golden Gate, it must be remembered, were only sparsely settled when the idea of the Golden Gate Bridge first surfaced in August 1916 in an editorial in the San Francisco *Bulletin*. In contrast to the talkative ruminations associated with the San Francisco–Oakland Bay Bridge, one searches in vain for nineteenth-century discussions of a bridge across the Golden Gate, with the exception of some passing remarks in 1872 by Charles Crocker, the man who built the transcontinental railroad. The author of the 1916 *Bulletin* article, James Wilkins, was a UC-trained engineer who had turned to journalism. In his proposal, Wilkins made the expected references to the eventual settlement of the northern counties as one of the reasons a bridge should be built across the Golden Gate, but even he could not push the population of Marin beyond a few thousand residents, and the north coast above Marin, as Wilkins well knew, would remain sparsely settled for the rest of the century.

More powerfully on Wilkins's agenda was another motivation: building the bridge almost as an end in itself, as an expression of a powerful need in the human species, as an effort to match the classical past. "Even in the remotest times, long preceding the Christian era," Wilkins wrote, "the ancients understood the value of dignifying their harbors with impressive works. The Colossus of Rhodes and the Pharaohs of Alexandria were counted among the seven wonders of the world. The same tendency appears in our own times. Witness the cyclopean statue at the entrance of New York Harbor. But the bridge across the Golden Gate would dwarf and overshadow them all."[4]

If this is the founding text of the Golden Gate Bridge (and few competitors have surfaced), the immediate appeal to classical metaphor reveals the underlying *raison d'être* of the structure. Prior to any discussion of future growth in the counties of the North Bay, or delays in the waiting ferry slips of Marin, was the desire to grace the harbor with a monumental work of art equal to the wonders of the ancient world. The justification for the Golden Gate Bridge went beyond statistics.

It was nurtured in an American imagination for which Antiquity provided the only worthy measure of comparison.

The notion of the Bridge, or more correctly, the notion of the Bridge as a compelling symbol beyond all practical need, caught fire in the breasts of two other engineer-visionaries as well: Michael O'Shaughnessy, city engineer of San Francisco, then preparing to build the Hetch Hetchy, and Joseph Strauss, a bridge builder from Chicago. O'Shaughnessy took Wilkins's visionary suggestion and helped make it politically acceptable. After all, O'Shaughnessy was then in the process of creating the entire public works infrastructure of post-earthquake San Francisco, and the very fact that the city engineer would publicly entertain the idea of a bridge made it plausible in the minds of others. Then O'Shaughnessy mentioned the idea to Strauss, president and chief engineer of the Strauss Bascule Bridge Company of Chicago, when Strauss was in San Francisco supervising the installation of a small bridge across Fourth Street in the China Basin district of San Francisco. Very soon, a bridge across the Golden Gate became for Strauss the *idée fixe* of his life, the one great task worth living and dying for.

Born in Cincinnati in 1870, Joseph Baermann Strauss was one of those quirky, obsessive, self-promoting dreamers one encounters so frequently in nineteenth-century America. In later life, he was fond of telling the story of how he got into the bridge-building business. It may or may not have been true, but it does not matter, for the truth is in the parable, not the fact. As a freshman at the University of Cincinnati, Strauss related, he had tried out for the football team despite his five feet and 120 pounds. The first scrimmage landed him in the infirmary. From his infirmary window he could see the Cincinnati-Covington Bridge spanning the Ohio River into Kentucky. Designed by John August Roebling, who later designed the Brooklyn Bridge, this pioneering suspension bridge, more than a thousand feet in length, had taken more than twenty years to build before it was completed in 1866. Gazing at this soaring structure from his infirmary bed, Strauss would later claim, he decided to devote his life to the construction of a comparable structure. For his senior thesis at Cincinnati, Strauss designed a bridge to connect Alaska and Russia across the Bering Strait: a proposal beyond any existing technology, but poetically alive with the symbolism of bridging two continents.

Joseph Strauss was a dreamer, a crank, a mystic, an occasional poet. By the time he first discussed a bridge across the Golden Gate with O'Shaughnessy, Strauss was nearing fifty without having accomplished the great bridge which he believed to be his destiny. True, he had built up a successful company and had built hundreds of bridges in the United States and abroad, but the majority of those four hundred bridges were of one type, the Bascule or counter-balanced drawbridge, which, while useful in a work-a-day way, could never be great in the way that Roebling's soaring suspensions across the Ohio and the East rivers were great: great for all ages to come.

And besides: Joseph Strauss did not have the talent to design such a bridge. His initial proposal for the Golden Gate, a hideous hybrid of cantilever and suspension, proved this incontrovertibly. But no matter: a designer could be found (and later banished to obscurity!). Strauss's genius lay in the promotion of the cause. Since the Golden Gate Bridge was primarily a dream in these early years, not fully backed by necessity, Strauss's promotional talents, his ability to inspire others with the dream of spanning the Gate, were directly relevant to the continuing existence of the project. From this perspective, he deserves a portion of the credit which he later claimed in its entirety.

Very soon, O'Shaughnessy, sensing the egomaniacal power of Strauss, began to distance himself from the project, ostensibly on the grounds of its disputed cost. Did O'Shaughnessy find Strauss's cantilevered behemoth as hideous as it strikes a contemporary observer, or did he sense in Strauss a messianic purpose he could not control? In any event, by 1930 O'Shaughnessy had become a bitter opponent of the entire idea. Strauss had edged out the city engineer whose imprint was otherwise on every major public work in San Francisco between 1912 and 1934, including the noble Hetch Hetchy. The Golden Gate Bridge had need of only one messiah.

The absence of a compelling need for the Bridge is evident in the almost off-handed manner in which the project inched toward actuality. Had the Board of Supervisors not shown any interest in January 1920, the matter would have languished. Had the newspapers not published Strauss's drawings in December 1922, there would have been no groundswell of public support. As it was, only 125 people gathered in mid-January of 1923 in the council chambers of the city of Santa Rosa, a small market town fifty miles north of San Francisco, to hear testimony from Mayor Rolph, O'Shaughnessy, three San Francisco supervisors, and the president of the San Francisco Chamber of Commerce. (Strauss was delayed in Chicago.) The meeting ended with the formation of a volunteer citizens' committee calling itself the Bridging the Gate Association.

Within a few months the California legislature upgraded the association into a governmental entity, the Golden Gate Bridge and Highway District, legally authorized to raise taxes, borrow money, issue bonds, and exercise right of eminent domain, toward the construction of a bridge across the Golden Gate. The counties of San Francisco, Marin, Sonoma, Napa, and, inexplicably, Del Norte on the Oregon border, joined the District.

A decade of legal maneuvering, public debate, surveys, and engineering proposals followed. The Bridge had many opponents: shipping companies, who claimed that the Bridge would impede navigation; the Southern Pacific–Golden Gate Ferries, Ltd., anxious not to lose its monopoly on the sole means of getting across the North Bay; the War Department, which claimed that the Bridge could be destroyed by naval gunfire in time of war and its collapsed structure would block the port; Sierra Club activists, who resented what they considered a needless intrusion of engineering onto a spectacular natural site. (Sierra Club activist Warren Olney, an attorney, challenged the legality of the District through the court system, casting a pall on the entire project.) Despite this opposition, however, in

November 1930 voters in the District, anxious in part to stimulate the economy, authorized the District to issue $35 million in bonds toward the construction of the Bridge. After some controversy regarding interest rates, the Bank of America, at the urging of its founder and chairman A. P. Giannini, purchased $6 million in bonds in the fall of 1932. Strauss had personally intervened with Giannini on behalf of this purchase. How long would the bridge last, Giannini asked Strauss? "Forever," Strauss replied.[5]

Strauss spoke with such confidence because he never doubted the importance of anything he was doing. He also had in hand the stunning suspension designs of Charles Alton Ellis, professor of engineering at the University of Illinois. In August 1929 the Golden Gate Bridge and Highway District had appointed Strauss Chief Engineer with overall responsibilities for design and construction. The District also appointed O. H. Ammann and Leon Solomon Moisseiff of New York City and Charles Derleth Jr. of the University of California to serve on an Advisory Engineering Board under the chairmanship of Strauss. Of the three consultants, Moisseiff had the reputation of an engineering genius. Born in Latvia in 1872, Moisseiff had studied civil engineering at Columbia after emigrating to the United States. Going to work with the Department of Bridges of New York City, Moisseiff embarked upon a career of bridge design which, step by step—the Philadelphia-Camden Bridge, the George Washington Bridge, Bayonne Bridge, the Ambassador Bridge at Detroit, and the Maumee River Bridge at Toledo— advanced the state of the art of bridge building incrementally. Employing metallurgy, calculus, and intricacies of vertical dead load, horizontal wind load, truss and cable deflection, Moisseiff and his collaborator, Frederick Lienhard, an engineer with the Port Authority of New York, brought the theory and practice of suspension bridges to a high art.

In this select company also belonged Charles Alton Ellis, a Maine-born Wesleyan University graduate in mathematics and classical Greek. For the three decades following his graduation in 1900, Ellis had devoted himself to two pursuits, bridge building and the translation of Greek classics. Going to work for the American Bridge Company, Ellis made the transition from higher mathematician to structural engineer. Among other accomplishments, he used his mathematical skills to analyze stresses in the subway tubes under the Hudson River. Turning to the academic life, Ellis wrote a standard textbook on the theory of framed structures, taught at Michigan and Illinois, and continued his translations of Greek classics.

Joseph Strauss recruited Charles Alton Ellis to the Strauss Engineering Corporation in 1922, appointing him design engineer. The tall, lanky, reserved Downeaster, a quintessential Yankee, left the academic world and returned to active practice for the exhilaration of working for Strauss, the diminutive engineer-promoter and flamboyant German-Jewish romantic, on such long-spanned structures as the Quincy Memorial Bridge over the Mississippi and the Longview

Bridge over the Columbia. In these and other projects, Strauss did the promoting. Ellis did the design.

On 27 August 1929 the Advisory Engineering Board convened for an all-day meeting at the Alta Mira Hotel in Sausalito, from whose terrace they could enjoy a spectacular view of the Golden Gate. Already, Strauss had jettisoned his hybrid cantilevered-suspension design, despite the fact that it had been incorporated into the logo of the Golden Gate Bridge and Highway District. Ammann, Derleth, and Moisseiff had convinced Strauss that only an all-suspension bridge was suitable for the channel. It can be said that Moisseiff and Ammann theorized the Golden Gate Bridge—envisioned it, that is, as an engineering possibility, an engineering idea—and Charles Alton Ellis realized these theories as design. But even here, the resulting bridge, so perfect as engineering and art, seems superior in result to its design history. During these crucial months of 1929, the Golden Gate Bridge seems almost to have descended like a Platonic archetype from a higher plane of being, an idea possessed of existence descending into the realm of matter.

Given the specific fact that Charles Alton Ellis went to work on designs for the bridge, these classical comparisons are not farfetched. Ellis knew the stories of how Xerxes and Alexander the Great had bridged the Dardanelles with a line of boats and how the name John Charles Frémont had chosen for the Golden Gate had been meant to suggest the Golden Horn of Byzantium. Ellis was also aware of the harbor monuments at Rhodes and Alexandria. But more important, Ellis the classicist had absorbed something of the imagination of ancient Greece in his practice of engineering design. For the pre-Socratic philosopher Pythagoras, harmonies of Number, which is to say, co-existences of number and material event, were at the ontological core of creation itself. Numbers were not only the code, but the source of being, of the material universe. In applying higher mathematics to engineering questions of load and stress, trusses, cable, wind, weather, and tide, Ellis was reexperiencing that sense of intelligible unity at the heart of the universe which so exhilarated the ancient Greeks. Working at his calculations and drawings, Ellis, in the Greek-influenced side of his imagination at least, must have sensed, albeit subliminally, that the Golden Gate Bridge was not so much to be designed as it was to be discovered; for in a very real way, as the ancient Greeks would understand it, the bridge was already there as number and idea, and it was Ellis's task to discern the pattern of this pre-existence. Thus, Michelangelo had once stated that he did not carve his statues from marble. He rescued them from the marble. They were already there.

Throughout 1930 and 1931, Ellis labored at his desk in Chicago, simultaneously making new bridge theory while designing the greatest bridge in the world, and all this, a seeming infinitude of calculations, done without benefit of a computer. Fortunately, Ellis had Moisseiff in New York with whom to check his calculations; otherwise he might have been frighteningly alone as he ventured into the unknown. With Strauss growing increasingly impatient at his slowness, Ellis designed—and tested mathematically to his own exacting *standards*—the greatest bridge thus far envisioned in human history.

As engineering, the Golden Gate Bridge would accomplish the impossible: it would span through suspension a length of 8,981 feet, abutment to abutment, with the intervention of only two 746–feet towers. Like a living being, the bridge designed by Ellis balanced and harmonized every possibility of steel, weight, stress, concrete, tide, and wind action. Its eighty thousand miles of cable, spun and respun into sixty-one cable strands, which were then compacted into suspension cables thirty-six inches in diameter, seem possessed of a tensile intelligence that went beyond engineering. The very height of the bridge roadway could vary by as much as sixteen feet as the bridge sensed, then reacted to, fluctuations in temperature and tide.

Even as Ellis worked at his calculations, San Francisco architect Irving Morrow proceeded to stylize Ellis's astonishing creation and thereby, like the work of Gordon Kaufmann on Hoover Dam, coax a great work of engineering into its fullest expression as art. As in the case of Gordon Kaufmann, there was no prior indication that Morrow, like Kaufmann a local architect, could rise so successfully to the challenge. Born in Oakland in 1884, Morrow had studied architecture at Berkeley and at the Ecole des Beaux Arts in Paris, then settled into a moderately successful San Francisco–based practice as a residential architect. In the summer of 1930, Strauss asked Charles Duncan, his public relations counsel, to recommend an architect for the bridge. Duncan consulted his brother-in-law, the artist Maynard Dixon, who recommended Irving Morrow. Once again, as in the case of so much connected with the building of the Golden Gate Bridge, the selection of its architect was that simple, that local, almost that haphazard.

Morrow's obscurity, combined with his evident talent, no doubt helped make him acceptable to Strauss. Had funds been available, an international competition, which would have been appropriate, would have brought a more eminent architect to the project, someone of the stature of Frank Lloyd Wright, or even a noteworthy local, such as Timothy Pflueger, George Kelham, or John Galen Howard. But could such an architect have worked with Strauss? Or could Strauss have controlled such an architect, or apportioned the proper measure of credit? Would not the bridge have become Wright's or Kelham's or Pflueger's bridge rather than Strauss's? The question answers itself. Strauss picked Morrow, and because Morrow did not threaten Strauss, Strauss gave Morrow infinitely more leeway and a greater measure of public recognition than he would have granted a competing personality.

· Morrow already had in hand Maynard Dixon's promotional rendering of Ellis's preliminary designs. In its stylization, then, the Golden Gate Bridge begins its life, not as engineering, but as a painting by Maynard Dixon. The importance of Dixon's early rendering, which depicted the Golden Gate Bridge as something grand and romantic, cannot be over-estimated. From Dixon's rendering, Morrow caught a certain vision of the bridge, which he proceeded to translate into architectural terms. Morrow sought to embellish, even increase, the bridge's message of soaring height through patterns of vertical fluting stamped into steel-plate housings covering the bracing struts of the two towers. Morrow simplified the rails and created special lighting. The result, when further intensified by the red-lead color of the actual bridge, represented Art Deco Moderne refined to universality, refined to Greek classicism, as was appropriate to an architect trained at the Beaux Arts. Critics have assailed Art Deco for not being a serious style. Perhaps. Irving Morrow, however, put just enough Art Deco into the Golden Gate Bridge to make it a creation of its time and place, America in the 1930s; but he likewise avoided the compacted eclecticism, the festive theatricality, which many critics feel keeps Art Deco from greatness. In its own way, the Golden Gate Bridge is as restrained as a Greek temple, as if Art Deco were in the process of alligning itself with classicism.

In the case of the color of the Golden Gate Bridge, which is essential to its total effect, one encounters that same haphazardness, of accident even, which lends force to the suggestion that the Golden Gate Bridge was coming into being from a prior inevitability. Once the towers were constructed, they were kept coated in a red lead primer, which was extended to the rest of the bridge as work continued. The question of final color was kept in abeyance. Almost accidentally, the bridge was completed in red lead primer, while Strauss and his consultants continued to debate the final color. By this time, Strauss, Morrow, Moisseiff, and the others found themselves converts to the red lead primer, variously described as orange vermillion and, later, International Orange, as the color that displayed the bridge to its best advantage through the cycle of weather and atmospheric effects that was so gloriously characteristic of the mountain-guarded Golden Gate strait.

But that was in the future. For the time being, the District was running a nip-and-tuck race toward a scheduled construction date of January 1933. Continuing court battles, launched by Bridge opponents, spurred on by the Sierra Club, together with an unexpected dispute regarding bond interest rates, made it sometimes seem probable that the Bridge would have to be postponed, another casualty of the Great Depression. Frustrated by Ellis's slow pace of design, Strauss discharged him in December 1931, terming it "an indefinite vacation without pay."[6] Ellis spent the following three years in a desperate search for employment, before securing a professorship at Purdue. Not until the publication of John Van Der Zee's book in 1986 would the full story of Ellis's contribution be known. Joseph Strauss was given the credit for designing the Golden Gate Bridge, a credit Strauss willingly assumed in his lifetime.

In the case of the construction of the Golden Gate Bridge, however, which commenced on 5 January 1933, even Strauss's egomania could not obscure the bravery and brilliance of the construction team headed by Russell Cone, a thirty-six-year-old bridge builder who had studied under Charles Alton Ellis at the University of Illinois. What the master envisioned and tested through mathematics, the pupil now built; and the construction challenge posed by the Golden Gate Bridge put the pupil in the worthy company of his abused teacher.

There could be no greater contrast, in fact, than that between the reserved, scholarly Ellis and Russell Cone, a brilliant construction engineer and a natural leader of the fiercely independent, hard-drinking men who built great bridges. Outgoing, physically courageous, Cone had already inspired a film directed by Frank Borzage, in which Cone was played by Spencer Tracy. The casting was perfect; for Russell Cone possessed the hard-charging charisma, the essential masculinity, necessary for leadership among bridge construction workers. Like his men, Cone was tough, physical, given to roistering good times. As a young man he had fought with the Rainbow Division in France, where he became the boon companion of Charles McArthur of *Front Page* fame. Like McArthur, Cone cultivated a devil-may-care insouciance befitting the top construction figure in the most glamorous aspect of the construction business, high steel suspension bridges.

It took four years and three months for Cone and his men to complete their task. Employed by various subcontractors and working under Cone's overall supervision, the men were union and earned from $4 a day for unskilled labor to $11 a day for skilled—first-rate wages for the Depression. On weekends, many of them crowded the bars of Sausalito or waterfront San Francisco. Cone provided free sauerkraut juice on Monday mornings to help settle hangovers before the men ascended the high steel.

Built near the shore, where the channel was no deeper than thirty-two feet, the Marin pier was finished sixty-four days ahead of schedule. Good thing, too, for the San Francisco pier proved a horror. Sited eleven hundred feet offshore, in the swiftest waters of the channel, the San Francisco pier was first intended to be built from a wooden trestle built out to the site. Unfortunately, the *Sydney M. Hauptmann*, a McCormick Line freighter, rammed the trestle on the night of 14 August 1933 and did extensive damage. On 14 December, a storm destroyed eight hundred feet of the rebuilt trestle, pounding it into useless scraps.

Deep-sea divers such as Bob Patching, meanwhile, were working, an hour and fifteen minutes at a time, in the treacherous channel floor, clearing and smoothing the sea bed with hoses capable of exerting up to five hundred pounds of hydraulic pressure. The divers worked almost blind in the darkness, having themselves become antediluvian sea creatures devoid of sight.

The surface cleared, the divers emplaced steel I-beams on the channel floor as guides for the metal fenders which would provide the forms for the concrete. When the traditional technique of using a floating caisson proved impossible because of violent swells, Joseph Strauss rose to the occasion and authorized a fast-tracking technique that closed the fender without the stabilization of a floating caisson, pumping the hollow fender walls with concrete so that they anchored firmly to the bedrock, then pumping the interior space dry, so that carpenters could move in and build wooden forms to receive the concrete. After the foundation rock was inspected one last time by geologists, who reconfirmed that it could support the weight of the bridge (there had been a last minute challenge), the elliptical hollow created by the steel fenders was filled with concrete, section by section, until on 3 January 1934 the San Francisco pier stood solidly on the channel floor, rising forty-four feet above the water, ready to receive the steel of the San Francisco tower.

Prefabricated, forged and tested in the foundries of Bethlehem Steel at Potts-town and Steelton, Pennsylvania, the steel sections of the tower were shipped by barge through the Panama Canal, stored at Alameda in the East Bay, then brought by barge to the site in interlocking units which averaged sixty-five tons apiece. Iron-workers like Harold McClain and Peanuts Coble, working higher and higher above the channel, would guide these sixty-five-ton sections into place like building blocks. Workers marveled at the precision of the cuts. Sometimes, the final six or eight inches of fitting proved the most difficult. "Sixty-five ton of steel," Peanuts Coble later reminisced, "and it wouldn't budge an inch, it fit that tight. So we would take a twenty-five-ton—or maybe it was a twelve and a half, I don't recall—airhammer and piledrive that sonofabitch into place."[7]

Then came the riveting of the steel sections, the men working in groups of two, heater and riveter, the heaters pulling the rivets from open coal-fed fires in black iron tubs, bringing them to perfection like a barbecued steak, then feeding the glowing rivet via a tube to the riveter, who pounded it into place with an airjack.

Slowly, into early 1934, Irving Morrow's elegantly stylized towers rose from their piers. For a month or two the twin towers stood alone, oddly complete as sculptural forms, covered in their red lead primer as protection against the abrasive salt air.

Symbolically, the firm of John A. Roebling & Sons, builders of the Brooklyn Bridge, received the contract for spinning the two main cables, each of them an amalgam of twenty-seven thousand rows of wire—eighty thousand miles of wire in all—spun on site, then stretched from shore to tower to tower to shore by hauling trams, which moved back and forth via strung cable across the void like spiders bridging space with a metallic web.

Miraculously, no worker lost his life through the first forty-six months of the project. A bridge this beautiful, embodying such Platonic perfection, might appro-priately move from ideal to reality with a safety record appropriate to its beauty. On the other hand, the comparison could cut the other way. A bridge this beauti-ful could be seen to demand, inevitably, some terrible sacrifice. Already, by early 1937, eleven men had fallen into the safety net strung beneath the developing structure. Proudly, they called themselves the Halfway to Hell Club, even though in one instance, that of Albert Zamp's fall, on 17 October 1936, the trip halfway to hell had resulted in a broken back and eight months of invalidism. Four days later, Kermit Moore, aged twenty-three, became the bridge's first fatality when a crane collapsed on the Marin side of the bridge, crushing Moore against a girder.

On the morning of 17 February 1937 came an even more exacting toll. Due to inadequate bolting, a five-ton platform structure, sixty feet in length, snapped loose from the bridge, then descended into the safety net, which it ripped from the base of the bridge like so much gossamer fabric. Twelve men rode this one-way elevator 220 feet, twenty-two stories, into the strait, their cries seeming to those who watched in horror from above to be the cries of babies in the roaring wind. Some men clutched girders of steel as they fell, as if seeking anchorage. Others seemed to be struggling to climb the safety net, which was descending into the water as fast as they were. Two men survived the fall; one other survived but was killed by falling debris. The others died on impact or died from their injuries in the water before help arrived. "Ten of my friends," stated survivor Slim Lambert from his hospital bed. "I saw them die all around me, and there wasn't a damn thing I could do about it."[8]

By mid-April 1937, the paving of the Bridge, the last of the structural chores, was complete. A succession of protagonists—James Wilkins, the engineer-journalist who proposed it; Michael O'Shaughnessy, the city engineer who advanced it; Charles Alton Ellis, the engineering professor who designed it; the politicians who framed its enabling legislation; A. P. Giannini, who financed it; Russ Cone and his men, who built it; and in and among them all, Joseph Strauss, who promoted the idea in season and out—had brought into being a bridge whose $35 million price tag made it the public works bargain of a decade. On 27 May 1937, at six o'clock on a foggy morning, the Bridge opened to pedestrian traffic and some two hundred thousand pedestrians crossed and recrossed the structure throughout the day. The next morning, beginning at nine-thirty, a series of elaborate ceremonies opened the Bridge to automobile traffic. At noon, President Roosevelt pressed a telegraph key in the White House announcing that the Golden Gate Bridge was now in public use. At that moment, some five hundred Navy and Army aircraft flew in formation over the triumphant new public work. As in the case of Hoover Dam, the United States was now possessed of a planetary-level public work through which it might further express and probe its national identity.

Bridge historian John Van Der Zee has compared the Golden Gate Bridge to the Parthenon. In the entire history of man-built structures, Van Der Zee asserts, the Parthenon and the Golden Gate Bridge stand in a class by themselves as harmonizations of site and structure, nature and public work. In American terms, the Golden Gate Bridge, like the Brooklyn Bridge joining Brooklyn and Manhattan, ranks with our most cherished symbols of social identity. For the urbanist, the Golden Gate Bridge represents a near-perfect expression of city and nature in balance: the gleaming white and pastel city of San Francisco joined by a skyway of International Orange to the wild headlands of Marin, lion-colored for most of the year, and the cypress and pine-green hillsides of Sausalito and craggy slopes of Mount Tamalpais in the near distance.

Three years remained to the 1930s, yet the opening of the Golden Gate Bridge offered a triumphant climax to a decade of construction which represented a powerful act of anti-Depression therapy. Hundreds of thousands found work. Of equal importance, millions experienced the healing symbolism of collective action in a time of grave social crisis. Its public works infrastructure in operation or under construction by the end of the decade, California had realized the visions and dreams of its pioneers. With the exception of the excessive canalization of the Los Angeles River and the more ambiguous loss of Hetch Hetchy Valley, nature had been altered and amended with respect. In the case of the Golden Gate Bridge, nature had been brought to new levels of meaning through the challenge of engineering as architecture and social symbol. By 1940 California—as an engineered place, as a unity achieved through public works—had reached a long-lasting plateau of completion.

13

Atlantis on the Pacific

The Golden Gate International Exposition of 1939

*T*HE completion of the San Francisco–Oakland and Golden Gate bridges provoked the organization and construction of a third momentous public work, the Golden Gate International Exposition on Treasure Island in San Francisco Bay. In so many ways—its artificially created site; its City Beautiful arrangements; its festive architecture, color scheme, and landscaping; its evocation of San Francisco as a Pacific Basin city—the Golden Gate International Exposition of 1939 and 1940 reprised, point for point, the Panama Pacific International Exposition of 1915. The oligarchy had used that earlier fair to boost San Francisco into full recovery from the earthquake and fire of April 1906. By 1937, when planning for an exposition began in earnest among a circle of boosters connected with the San Francisco Chamber of Commerce, an even more ambitious agenda was asserting itself. First, and most obvious, the completion of the two bridges required a celebration. Second, the construction and operation of an exposition would create jobs and stimulate the economy through the influx of millions of tourist dollars. Then there was the question of development. In 1915 the Panama Pacific International Exposition had served as a vehicle for the transformation of the northern edge of San Francisco from marshy shoals into the reclaimed Marina District. In the case of the Golden Gate International Exposition, a similar cluster of shoals adjacent to Yerba Buena Island in San Francisco Bay midway between San Francisco and Oakland could be filled and engineered into a permanent island which could serve, after the fair, as a regional airport for both land-based and sea-based aircraft.

The proposed exposition offered San Francisco—the Bay Area in general, and the City and County of San Francisco in particular—a means of boosting itself into an identity which had haunted it ever since Commodore Perry had steamed into Tokyo Bay: San Francisco as the financial, trading, travel, and cultural capital of the Pacific Basin. To suggest how deeply this Pacific ambition was lodged in the psyche of San Francisco (despite its frequent anti-Asian outbursts) would require a monograph. No city could sit so superbly on the edge of this vast ocean and not dream such dreams. San Francisco businessman Anson Burlingame, Minister to China from 1861 to 1867, had dreamt such dreams in the 1850s and 1860s, as did his successor as Minister to the Celestial Empire, San Francisco journalist Benjamin Parke Avery. Since that era, San Francisco had sustained a bi-weekly steamship connection with Japan, which by the 1880s had been extended to include China, Southeast Asia, and the South Pacific. The employment of San Francisco as port of embarkation for the invasion of the Philippines stimulated countless columns of commentary connecting San Francisco with its Pacific Basin future. The completion of the Panama Canal in 1914 unleashed a further flood of trans-Pacific boosterism. The San Francisco–Honolulu connection, meanwhile, symbolized by the Hawaiian investments of the San Francisco–based Spreckels family, reached a point of intensity in the pre–World War I era which virtually made of Honolulu a San Francisco suburb.

The taste of proper San Francisco ran strongly in the direction of an aesthetic that blended Europe and the Far East. No vendor served this preference more completely than Gump's department store and art gallery on Post Street. Founded in 1865, Gump's was as much a museum as it was a retail establishment. It was also an intense locus of regional and social identity, a Polo before its time, serving for seventy-five years as a vital point of connection, on the level of taste, between San Francisco and the Far East. Abraham Livingston Gump confessed himself delighted by the Pacific Basin theme of the forthcoming Exposition, feeling that it even further materialized what he had been pursuing his entire life: the vision of San Francisco as an Asia Pacific entrepôt. Even as the Exposition was being planned, agents of Gump's were ranging, as usual, throughout the Far East—through China, India, Burma, Cambodia, Thailand—acquiring beautiful objects for shipment back to San Francisco. Among other things, Gump's was by then the finest dealer in carved jade in the world, a subject in which Abraham Livingston Gump held a connoisseur's and a scholar's preeminence, despite his failing eyesight. Since there was no important museum of Asian art on the West Coast (although Chicago collector Avery Brundage did use the services of Gump's to establish the collection that would eventually find a home in San Francisco), Gump's served as a powerful channel of Asian art into the United States. Through art and furniture, Gump's fostered a consciousness of Asia as a high civilization, fully equal to Europe in aesthetic achievement. In doing this, Gump's ranked with the Japan Society of New York as a key point of connection between East and West in elite circles. What Ralph Lauren would later do as a contrivance, Abraham Gump did as a matter of spontaneous taste: establish a style that reinforced an identity.

No one better embodied the aspirations of San Francisco to become an important Pacific shipping center than Captain Robert Stanley Dollar, the self-styled grand

342 THE THERAPY OF PUBLIC WORKS

old man of Pacific shipping and an avid patron of Gump and Company. Ever since World War I, the Dollar Steamship Company had been operating scores of ships between San Francisco and the Far East. In this enterprise, Dollar was carrying on a connection first established in 1867 by the Pacific Mail Steamship Company of San Francisco with its service to Yokohama and Hong Kong. In 1882 the Oceanic Steamship Company entered the Pacific trade, inaugurating regular service to Australia and New Zealand in 1885. Matson Navigation entered the Pacific in 1882 as well and eventually bought out Oceanic. Then in the 1890s came the Dollar Lines, followed in the early 1900s by the American Hawaiian Steamship Company. In 1923 Dollar purchased (for the proverbial song) a fleet of surplus ships from the United States Shipping Board which had been built during the war as troop transports. Two of these, the *President McKinley* and the *President Hoover*, became the largest passenger steamers to sail the Pacific through the 1930s.

Robert Dollar's trans-Pacific fleet of passenger liners and steamers, each of them named in honor of an American president, had been bankrolled by the taxpayer, sold at minimal cost, and had its profitability enhanced through generous mail subsidies. Captain Dollar might very well wear a white beard and play the part of the lovable old China hand, and San Francisco novelist Peter B. Kyne might supplement Dollar's act with a series of stories based on reputed incidents from the captain's life; but Dollar was not so much the colorful (albeit pious) old salt he pretended to be as he was a shrewd capitalist, specially skilled at turning to his advantage persistent American fears that the United States was declining as a maritime power. Interestingly enough, when it suited his purposes, which was frequently, Dollar sailed his ships under foreign registry.

When Dollar passed on in May 1932 at the age of eighty-eight, his death warranted front-page treatment in all four San Francisco newspapers. When the heavily subsidized Dollar Lines, hit by cutbacks in federal mail subsidies, reverted to federal ownership in 1938, a chill went through the business establishment. Had a fatal blow, it asked itself, been dealt to the trans-Pacific ambitions of the city?

The failure of Dollar Lines—occurring at the same time as the Golden Gate International Exposition was rising like Atlantis from the sea between San Francisco and the East Bay—made the oligarchy even more convinced than ever that the Pacific Basin destiny of San Francisco could not be taken for granted. It had to be boosted, boosted, boosted, if it were to remain a credible possibility, especially now that Japan was in the process of establishing its Greater East Asia Co-Prosperity Sphere. By the late 1930s, in fact, part of San Francisco's essential formula for well-being, its deepest image of itself, was that of a polyglot Pacific capital, combining the charms of Europe, California, and the Far East.

The rapid construction of the Golden Gate International Exposition, following so soon upon the completion of two great bridges, recapitulated the creation of San Francisco itself over the previous ninety years. From this perspective, the Golden

Gate International Exposition represented an idealized theme park of urban planning and design, a fast-forwarded utopian metaphor for all that San Francisco had been and wished to be—as place, as culture and society, as a built environment. As in the case of all major expositions, the Golden Gate International Exposition offered San Francisco the opportunity to compress and idealize its history.

The very siting of the Exposition on a four-hundred-acre man-made island expressed this retro-constructivist dynamic, which began with a Genesis-like creation of the very Earth itself. It took eleven Army Corps of Engineers dredges eighteen months, from 11 February 1936 to 24 August 1937, to create Treasure Island atop the shallows north of Yerba Buena Island. Financing came from a $3.8 million grant from the WPA and $776,780 raised in the private sector by the Exposition Committee. First, sucking dredges removed twenty-five million cubic yards of soft fill, the muck of the ages, including fossilized ferns and the skeletal traces of extinct animals which roamed the plain in the eons before the Pacific had rushed in to form San Francisco Bay. Next, 287,000 tons of boulders were dumped on the site to create the bed and rim of the Island. Next came millions of cubic yards of sand from around the Bay, towed in by barge, dumped onto the site, day in and day out, until the surface of the Island began to take shape. Millions more cubic yards of topsoil were then spread smoothly by bulldozers, then steamrolled into an even surface. Finally, three hundred wells were dug into the Island, and millions of gallons of brine were pumped back into the Bay, which allowed the Island to dry into solidity.

Like the San Francisco Peninsula in ages past, Treasure Island was treeless and uninhabited; and so the second and third phases of construction—the building of the dream city and its landscaping—swiftly redacted what the Spanish and the Yankees had already accomplished in San Francisco, the landscaping of a primeval emptiness into an urban garden. No less than John McLaren himself, the gardener who had created Golden Gate Park on acres of shifting sand dunes over the past forty years, was called in as a consultant by his protégé, Julius Girod, like McLaren a San Francisco park superintendent. Girod directed a corps of twelve hundred landscapists, gardeners, and workers whom he paid from a $1.8 million WPA fund. Four thousand trees were transported to the Island for replanting, including an entire olive grove. Acres of shrubs and flowering plants were established.

Two San Francisco architects, George Kelham and Timothy Pflueger, played key roles in determining the distinctive architecture of the Golden Gate International Exposition: an architecture that somehow managed to combine Mayan, Cambodian, Cubist, Art Deco, and Moderne motifs within a relatively traditional City Beautiful site plan. In terms of his social connections and important public buildings, George Kelham, who died three years before the Exposition which he planned opened, led the conservative wing of the San Francisco architectural establishment, despite the fact that he was also a master of Art Deco. An architect who had already proven his skilled classicism in the Post Office and Court of

Appeals Building (1905), the Customs House (1911), the Public Library at Civic Center (1917), and the Federal Reserve Bank (1924), Kelham had switched to Gothic for his thirty-one-story Russ Building (1927), a skyscraper which asserted (and perhaps brought to conclusion) the preeminence of San Francisco as the business and financial capital of the Far West. Next came the Shell Building (1929), a second neo-Gothic masterpiece, inspired by Eliel Saarinen's proposal for the Chicago *Tribune* tower. Variously described as Art Deco or Moderne, the Shell Building contained elements of Gothic verticality with an Art Deco treatment (including Egyptian motifs) that anchored its corner of downtown San Francisco with élan and urbanity. In later years, the Art Deco Society of California would vote the Shell Building the single most distinguished Art Deco building in San Francisco.

There could be no greater contrast than that between the reserved and patrician George Kelham, a graduate of the Ecole des Beaux Arts, nearing sixty, who had practiced in New York with the firm of Trowbridge and Livingston before being sent to San Francisco in 1908 to supervise the construction of the new Palace Hotel, and Timothy Pflueger, a self-taught, raffish bohemian bachelor in his mid-forties. Yet each of these men, point architects for San Francisco in the 1920s and 1930s, had been learning from, and even pacing, the other, in the effort to re-present downtown San Francisco in Art Deco terms.

If George Kelham was the Edward MacDowell of San Francisco architecture, the college-educated classicist with a capacity for innovation, Timothy Pflueger was its George Gershwin: the self-taught celebrator of urbanism, a designer whose creativity, like Gershwin's music, blended the rhythms and syncopations of jazz Art Deco with a sense of civic culture, of the romance and excitement of urban life, which Pflueger's buildings both symbolized and reinforced. Born in San Francisco in 1892 into the flourishing German community of the city, Pflueger graduated from Mission High School, then headed downtown to work in an architectural office. In those years, when an entire city was being rebuilt, such practical experience, combined with ready talent, more than compensated for the lack of formal training. Soon, Pflueger was showing his gift for festive urbanity in designs for the Castro Theater (1921), an Ibero-Moorish fantasy worthy of the best picture palaces of the period, and Roosevelt Junior High School (1924), a rare instance of Knickerbocker brick on the West Coast. In 1924, inspired like Kelham by Saarinen's second-place entry in the the Chicago *Tribune* competition, Pflueger presented San Francisco with its first modern skyscraper, the twenty-six-story Pacific Telephone and Telegraph Company headquarters (1925), a building that soared with the strength and vertical configuration of the Sierra granite with which it was faced and the festive modernism of the new American downtown it so exuberantly celebrated.

As Art Deco swept the nation, Pflueger again and again proved his mastery of this essentially urban populist idiom. In 1929 he designed a stunning Stock Exchange Building, completed in 1930, despite the crash of the previous October.

Completed that year as well: the twenty-five-story Medical-Dental Building, which lightened the massivity of the neo-Mayan with undulating verticals running from sidewalk to roof and window lines that wrapped around corners and setbacks. In 1931 Pflueger designed the Paramount Theater in Oakland, a thirty-five-hundred-seat auditorium that, transcending the purposes and limitations of a movie picture palace, created the single most joyous gathering place in the entire Bay Area.

A lifelong bachelor, living like Rolph in the family home in the Mission, kept company by a steady lady friend, Timothy Pflueger was so capable of catching the mood and feel of San Francisco as destination, as pleasure resort, because he was himself such a consummate man about town. He belonged to three clubs—the Family, the Olympic, and the Bohemian. For the Family retreat in Portola Valley near Stanford, Pflueger created a number of elegantly rustic camps.

For his locker room suite at the Olympic Club, where he swam daily, he designed an orchestration of lockers, mirrors, bar, and lounge in the Moderne idiom which testified to his extraordinary skills as an interior designer. For the Lunch Club associated with the Stock Exchange, Pflueger created an Art Deco *mise-en-scène* that made even stockbrokering in the Depression seem fun. Above its central staircase, Diego Rivera created perhaps the most ambitious mural in the city, with tennis star Helen Wills posing as California, earth mother of industry and plenty. For the general public, Pflueger designed three of the most successful cocktail lounges in the city: the Circus Lounge in the Fairmont (1934), the Patent Leather Lounge at the Saint Francis (1939), and the Top of the Mark at the Mark Hopkins (1939). In these lounges Pflueger blended every detail of glass and fabric, including a brilliant use of leather as decorative skein, to create environments that practically jump-started their own convivial chic. Rarely have the martini and the scotch and soda found more dashing surroundings! For the Top of the Mark, Pflueger ran bold and oversized windows around the 360 degrees of the penthouse lounge, making of San Francisco, perceived in every direction, a real-time diorama.

To design the Golden Gate International Exposition, George Kelham assembled a team of established San Francisco architects which included Pflueger; Lewis Hobart, creator of Grace Cathedral atop Nob Hill; William Wurster, along with Pflueger one of the most brilliant architects of the forty-something generation; and Arthur Brown Jr., one of San Francisco's preeminent classicists, responsible for the City Hall, Civic Auditorium, the Federal Building, the Opera House, and the Veterans Building. With the exception of Pflueger and Wurster, it was a conservative Beaux Arts–oriented team, representing the formalism characteristic of San Francisco after 1906.

Critics have frequently seen in San Francisco's remorseless grid the fundamental source of anti-aesthetics in the city. First set down around the central plaza of the sleepy Mexican village of Yerba Buena in 1839 by Swiss surveyor Jean Vioget, the San Francisco grid was extended to the entire tip of the peninsula in 1847 by Jasper O'Farrell, surveyor general of Alta California during the administration of the conquered Mexican territory by the Army and Navy of the United States. Running a line from Twin Peaks to San Francisco Bay, which eventually became Market Street, O'Farrell extended two grid systems away from this bold diagonal, one heading north and west toward the northern edge of the peninsula and the Pacific Ocean, the other proceeding eastward toward the Bay. O'Farrell's grid conferred upon the developing city of San Francisco a fundamental and constant power of clarity and purpose.

From 1870 onwards, in and through the O'Farrell plan, San Francisco remained affixed to and controlled by a survey that would allow it to become nothing less than a classic city, unified and coherent, resisting the temptation to evolve, not as one city, but as linkages of private lanes and enclosed spaces, such as those that managed to establish themselves on Telegraph and Russian hills: picturesque perhaps, but not fundamentally urban. Because of O'Farrell, San Francisco would be a place of streets, boulevards, park squares, and accessible open spaces, such as Golden Gate Park: a city, that is, in which each street and place was linked to a coherent whole. Running straight up and over the city's many high hills, O'Farrell's grid also endowed the future city with a plenteous array of views.

A significant percentage of the streets of San Francisco were either ascending or descending or peaking between ascent and descent—and looking across to a vista of bay, ocean, or other ascending or descending streets. With its grid streets thus rising and falling on nearly every block, San Francisco became, once its built environment was fully materialized, a reflecting complexity of views and counterviews: a three-dimensional labyrinth of sight lines and perspectives.

In 1877 photographer Eadweard J. Muybridge set up his camera atop Nob Hill and photographed a multi-plate panorama of the city below. The intrinsic urbanism of the city was immediately apparent in the array of orderly streetscapes which descended down Nob Hill over Russian Hill toward North Beach, Telegraph Hill, and the Bay. Since the late 1880s a dream of a grand ensemble of buildings, courts, colonnades, gardens, and boulevards had remained an active idea in the minds and imaginations of the Bay Area establishment. Leland and Jane Stanford initiated the quest in 1888 when they commissioned H. H. Richardson to draw up a comprehensive scheme for the university they were planning on their farm south of San Francisco. Completed by the successor firm of Shepley, Rutan & Coolidge after Richardson's death, with landscaping by F. L. and J. C. Olmsted, the Stanford Quadrangle brought both the reality of systematic planning and a grand example of integrated structures and landscaping to the Bay Area.

No sooner was Stanford's City of Learning rising in the wheat fields of Palo Alto than Phoebe Apperson Hearst was setting in motion a similar process for the state-controlled University of California at Berkeley. By 1898 eleven architects and civic planners of international rank had submitted to the jury established by Mrs. Hearst plans for the Berkeley campus. When the architects came to San Francisco that December, James Duval Phelan feted them at a dinner. In his after-dinner remarks, Phelan suggested that a similar competition be held for the city of San Francisco. Both Phelan's speech and the newspaper reports in the following days ran riot with comparisons to Florence, Rome, Constantinople, and Jerusalem.

Phelan served one term as mayor and, upon his defeat for re-election, threw himself into the cause of developing San Francisco along grand lines. Organizing the Committee for the Adornment and Beautification of San Francisco, Phelan gathered and galvanized other oligarchs who had also been influenced by the construction of the Stanford and Berkeley campuses and the Midwinter Exposition of 1894, a reprise of the Chicago World's Fair of 1893, which had launched the City Beautiful movement. In 1895 the Committee brought to San Francisco no less than Daniel Hudson Burnham, architect and planner of the Chicago Fair, commissioning him to do a City Beautiful plan for San Francisco. After the fire and earthquake, Burnham rushed back to San Francisco from Paris, believing that his plan would be put instantly into effect. Rather than implement a virtually impossible spatial reorganization of the city along the lines advocated by Burnham, however, San Franciscans chose to rebuild as soon as possible on the grid set down by Jasper O'Farrell in 1847. Yet the Burnham Plan was realized on an ideal basis as the Panama Pacific International Exposition and, with some adjustment, in the permanent buildings of the new Civic Center.

Not long after the ashes had cooled, a circle of artists and writers, led by Arthur and Lucia Mathews, gathered to form the Philopolis Society, dedicated to the propagation of ideas and imagery intended to stimulate the rebuilding of San Francisco. From October 1906 to September 1916 the Society issued *Philopolis, A Monthly Magazine Published for Those Who Care*, and under the imprint the Philopolis Press issued a number of books of poetry and *belle lettres*, much of it concerning the needs and aspirations of the new, rebuilt San Francisco. The murals which Mathews created in the aftermath of the earthquake and fire—most noticeably in the lobby of the Mechanics Building in San Francisco and the State Capitol in Sacramento—are powerful in their depictions of some great new city, a shimmering new Byzantium on the shores of the Bosphorus, rising in a splendor of dome and colonnade on the shores of San Francisco Bay. Which was exactly what the Panama Pacific International Exposition achieved two years later, on its splendid site by the Bay. While only Bernard Maybeck's Palace of Fine Arts, a romantic Piranesean dome, colonnade, and lagoon, survived the fair, San Franciscans and hundreds of thousands of visitors nevertheless were able to enjoy— and be instructed by!—the largest and most dramatic urban ensemble ever materialized in the West: a titanic, multi-colored daydream of the City Beautiful, constructed along classical lines, an urban image which had been increasingly possessing the imagination of San Francisco ever since H. H. Richardson had unveiled his proposal for the Stanford campus in 1888.

Not surprisingly, then, the Kelham group employed the ever-persistent City Beautiful format for the Golden Gate International Exposition which Kelham and his colleagues envisioned from the start as a rectilinear orchestration of courts, exhibitions halls, open spaces, and promenades. Such an urban ensemble, after all, however *retardaire* it might be in planning terms, expressed San Francisco's image of itself as a stately, orderly city by the sea. For perhaps the final time in its history, then, San Francisco proceeded to act out the City Beautiful option.

As was usual with such schemes, the Exposition had a focal point, a center, the four-hundred-foot high Tower of the Sun, designed by Arthur Brown Jr., with obvious reference to to the Tower of Jewels at the Panama Pacific Exposition of 1915 and the Hoover Tower, also designed by Brown, then under construction on the Stanford campus. Running on the north-south axis anchored by the Tower of the Sun was a series of courts and exhibition halls: Kelham's Court of the Moon and the Stars and Court of the Seven Seas (finished by J. H. Clark after Kelham's death); Pflueger's triumphant Court of Pacifica, dominated by Ralph Stackpole's towering sculpture. Crossing this axis at a right angle ran the Portals of the Pacific, the Court of Reflections, the Court of Flowers, and the Court of the Nation, all by Lewis Hobart. Flanking these two series of courts, again at right angles to each other, were six exhibition halls. Pflueger's semi-circular Administration Building stood at the southwest corner of the Island and anchored a second east-west axis continuing through the Enchanted Garden, Wurster's stunningly successful Yerba Buena Clubhouse, a masterpiece of Streamline Moderne (the Navy would soon make use of it as the finest officers' club on the Pacific Coast), the Hall of Air Transportation, and the Palace of Fine and Decorative Arts. The West Ferry Terminal on the northwest corner of the Island described a third east-west axis that continued through the Court of Pacifica and was flanked by seven pavilions. An Esplanade culminating in Pflueger's ultra-Moderne Administration Building ran along the eastern edge of the Island. The entire ensemble represented a perfect presentation of City Beautiful ideals. Nothing could have been more safe or conservative.

The architecture, however, was another matter entirely. A phantasmagoric amalgam of Pacific Basin themes (from Mayan to Cambodian, all of it channeled through a Cubist–Art Deco filter), the festival architecture of the Exposition brought to extravagant conclusion the Art Deco era which had seen so many festive buildings rise in San Francisco and had inspired the stylization of Hoover Dam and the Golden Gate Bridge. If there was any rationale to the architectural scheme on Treasure Island, it was in its very eclecticism, its headlong effort to suggest that all architectural styles of the planet—Asian, pre-Columbian, classical, Gothic, Renaissance, and all the variations of modernism coalescing in Art Deco—could be harmonized provided that site design remained rigidly Beaux Arts, and that landscaping and color were used for unifying effect. After all, this was the very process of rationalized eclecticism that had created San Francisco in the first place, and had not San Francisco earned a reputation as one of the most beautiful cities of the world? Visitors entered the Exposition through the Mayan-Cubist Portals of the Pacific under an arch of rearing elephants suggestive of Southeast Asia, then abruptly beheld the Gothic-Deco monumentalism of the

Tower of the Sun, so suggestive of a medieval cathedral. The Court of Honor recalled classical Greece. The Court of Pacifica evoked Italian futurism. Only the Art Deco sensibility of the late 1930s could hold together such centripetal eclecticism, whose unity came from a spectacular color scheme and nighttime lighting effects, from landscaping, and from the underlying rigidity of the site plan.

The Golden Gate International Exposition presented, albeit in temporary form, the greatest California garden of them all, with the possible exception of Balboa Park in San Diego and Golden Gate Park in San Francisco, whose superintendent, John McLaren, master gardener of California, served as a supervising consultant. As in the case of Golden Gate Park, McLaren anchored the western shore, buffeted by prevailing winds, with carpets of multi-colored flowering ice plant—light and dark pink, yellow, orange, red, scarlet—more formally known as mesembryanthemum. Officials dubbed this lavish display the Magic Carpet, and critics praised it as a horticultural *tour de force*. Because Treasure Island had been wrested from the sea, and because its earth was saline and resistant, the Exposition gardens represented an especial triumph over nature and, more important, a perfect example of how California—arid, semi-arid, or waterless in so many of its settled regions—was so much a product of a very deliberate program of landscape architecture, park design, and garden practice. The very trees which dominated landscaping—palm, olive, poplar, eucalyptus, and madrone—made explicitly Californian statements. Palm, olive, and poplar spoke to California as a neo-Mediterranean shore, rich with associations of Spain, Greece, and Italy. The red-flowering eucalpytus trees (some of them already fifty feet tall when they were barged over to Treasure Island) were originally migrants from Australia. Now as prevalent and flourishing as the native pine and redwood, the eucalyptus bespoke California as a transplanted creation, an overnight society, the product of will and choice and deliberate plantation. The madrone, the most exquisite of native trees next to the sequoia and the redwood—orange and cinnamon colored, with dark glossy foliage, clinging to places on hillsides where the sun warmed—bespoke California as indigenous place. No landscapist had ever used madrone before in such public groupings as McLaren was now doing. In its native habitat—which in the case of the trees planted on Treasure Island meant the mountain forests of southern San Mateo County—the madrone prefers solitude as it gathers unto itself shafts of forest-filtering sun, hearing only its own subeval music, kept company by the darting blue jay. By being thus boldly displayed, the madrones on Treasure Island suggested a California that would always linger in the imagination, always thrive on the outer edge of development (unless destroyed): the California of unspoiled mountain and forest.

As brilliant as it was, floral color was but one component of the overall color scheme of the Exposition. In 1915, under the direction of color scenarist Jules Guerin, San Francisco had made a bold departure from the Great White City of Chicago of 1893, which it now repeated with the redoubled intensity of the color-friendly Art Deco palette. To outdo the four color tones of 1915 (warm red edging into orange, cool red edging into pink, cold blue edging into purple, and warm blue incorporating an element of green), the Golden Gate International Exposition added congeries of colors expressive at once of Art Deco exuberance across the United States, and, locally, of California as land of color and the sun. To express California as Mediterranean garden of the south, there was Old Mission Fawn (a neutral yellow), Pebble Beach (a light coral), Santa Clara Apricot, Del Monte Blue, and Santa Barbara Rose. Asia Pacific colors included Sun-of-Dawn and Pagoda Yellow, Imperial Dragon Red, Hawaiian Emerald Green, Polynesian Brown, and three blues, Pacific, China Clipper, and Southern Cross. By day, these colors blazed in the sunlight or defied the fog. By night, an intricate and theatrical scheme of direct and indirect lighting transformed the Exposition into an Art Deco Atlantis reborn from the sea.

As in the case of all Depression-era public works, the Golden Gate International Exposition was intended to create jobs and stimulate the economy. Not only did it do this, it also ushered San Francisco into its post-war identity as a tourist city. The war would postpone this identity, and the city would remain a center of insurance, banking, and finance through the 1960s; but the Exposition, a tourist strategy *par excellence*, anticipated the transformation of San Francisco from manufacturing and shipping to a hotel, restaurant, convention, and tourist economy. Through the 1930s, having so much real work to do—shipping, manufacturing, canning and packaging, import and export—San Francisco only incidentally thought of itself as a pretty place. Within a few years, however, its scenic beauty and urban charm would be at the forefront of its self-image and its economy as Cleveland by the Bay transformed itself into Monte Carlo or Nice.

The promotional program launched by publicist Clyde Vandeberg on behalf of the Exposition promoted San Francisco and its surroundings as the Europe one might visit were there not a war in progress and could one afford it in the first place. To carry the message of the fair and San Francisco to the rest of the country, Vandeberg sent theme girl Zoe Dell Lantis, a dancer from the San Francisco Opera Ballet, on a nationwide publicity tour. Lantis made her public appearances attired in a pirate's costume as befitting the Treasure Island theme. It was a typically 1930s starlet strategy—Lantis dressed in a floppy pirate's hat, eighteenth-century man's blouse, tattered shorts, buckler, sword, and high-heeled boots—and it got the desired result in hundreds of publicity photographs in newspapers around the country. In 1939 tourist revenues in California increased between 22 and 33 percent over 1938, for a gain of $38.3 million. In the Bay Area alone, a million tourists spent $43.5 million in 1939 for an increase of 146 percent over the previous year. Tourism fell off in the second year, but altogether a million and a half visitors to the Bay Area had spent $64.7 million in the local economy by the time the Exposition closed its doors.

Beginning with the Century of Progress Exposition in Chicago in 1933, the expositions of the 1930s focused on Progress with a capital *P*; and the Golden

Gate International Exposition was no exception. Exhibit after exhibit trumpeted the impending triumph of the post-Depression era: a world of Lucite, chrome, plastic dinnerware, prefabricated steel, and, in the Electricity and Communications Building, a working television set from RCA. In the Palace of Foods and Beverages, Lucky Stores suggested the impending world of the supermarket. As chief architect of the buildings sponsored by the California Commission, Timothy Pflueger supervised the design of a series of Streamline-Moderne pavilions, including the San Francisco Building, which presented California in all its glorious futurity. After seeing such Pflueger-supervised structures as the Los Angeles and San Diego Counties Building, the San Joaquin Valley Building, the Shasta Cascade Building, the California Auditorium, the California State Building, the Alameda–Contra Costa County Building, the San Francisco Building, and the Hall of Flowers, one had a clear image of what the built environment in California would look like—strong, assertive, modern, encompassing, and democratic—ten to twenty, even to thirty, years hence. Sadly, these pavilions also suggested buildings which Pflueger himself might have designed for more permanent construction, had he not died in his early fifties of a heart attack. The San Francisco Building featured an exhibit displaying a model of San Francisco in 1999. It was as if Timothy Pflueger had designed the entire city.

All world's fairs are alike—yet different. In the case of the Golden Gate International Exposition, two components, the Palace of Fine Arts and the Court of the Pacific, held special meaning for a city aspiring to international status. Under the chairmanship of Richard Montgomery Tobin, formerly Ambassador to the Hague, and the vice-chairmanship of Pflueger, who also served as general director of the entire program, the Fine Arts Committee assembled exhibitions of paintings, sculpture, photography, and other fine art from Europe, the United States, and Latin America that was without precedent on the Pacific Coast.

Walter Heil, director of the de Young Museum in Golden Gate Park, assembled a collection of Old Masters and Impressionists of such density and stature that it seemed as if Europe itself were sending its art to California in anticipation of the conflict soon to break out. Thomas Carr Howe Jr., director of the Palace of the Legion of Honor in Lincoln Park, assembled an exhibition of contemporary Mexican paintings, watercolors, and prints that represented the first important display in the United States of the impressive but largely unknown world of Mexican art. Diego Rivera traveled to San Francisco to work with a group of WPA-sponsored artists in full public view on a mural scheduled for the new building of the City College of San Francisco, which Pflueger was designing. Hermon More of the Whitney Museum of American Art in New York assembled an exhibition of American masters from John Singleton Copley to Georgia O'Keeffe.

In terms of quality and comprehensiveness, there had never been brought together in one exhibition so much fine American work, including ninety-five paintings by nineteenth-century artists in California and another four hundred contemporary paintings, testifying to a vitality of American art in California that would only begin to be recognized in the 1960s. In the exhibitions of the Palace of Fine Arts, San Francisco managed to position itself, however briefly, as a museum capital city. The experience was exhilarating. San Francisco, after all, had tended in the frontier side of its being to prefer style over quality; and now, for a year at least, it had both.

While the art assembled in the Palace of Fine Arts looked to Europe, the United States, Mexico, and Latin America, Pflueger's Court of the Pacific, dominated by Ralph Stackpole's eighty-foot-high statue of Pacifica, suggested the ambition of San Francisco to become more than a collector and connoisseur of past achievement. In the Court of the Pacific and the gigantic Pacifica, which was scheduled for permanent installation on the Bay after the Exposition closed, Pflueger and Stackpole spoke to the deep desire of the oligarchy to position San Francisco as a hub of that Pacific Basin matrix which so many, if only on the level of dream-wish and rhetoric, seemed convinced was on the verge of coalescence.

Ten years earlier, for example, in a speech before the Chamber of Commerce of the United States, San Francisco *Chronicle* editor and columnist Chester Rowell had put forward a bold plan for the wholesale entry of American banking, business, import-export, and cultural activity into the Pacific Basin. If anyone could speak for the Bay Area establishment, Chester Rowell could. A leading member of the Progressive generation, possessor of a German Ph.D., a University of California regent, a respected and strategically placed editor and columnist, a Berkeley resident whose hilltop Shingle Style aerie, filled with books, enjoyed a commanding view of the Golden Gate and was filled so often with academics, diplomats, journalists, business people passing to and from the Pacific, Rowell stood at the very center of Bay Area intellectual life, with its Pacific orientation. With great force, Rowell sketched the hitherto hesitant involvement of the United States in this region, destined now, so he argued, to become increasingly important to the American economy. The very Golden Gate itself, Rowell rhapsodized, beckoned to the American future: "Facing Eastward on the Western sea, dwells half the human race. Until now it has been to us a world apart, as if on another planet. Henceforward, forever, it is to be the other half of our world and a participant in our life. This is the great fact which distinguishes our generation and its successors from all that went before." [1]

The Golden Gate International Exposition mounted a pioneering presentation of what Chester Rowell had postulated: the unity of the Pacific region and its importance to the United States. Buildings, exhibits, murals, maps, sculptures, fountains, landscaping: everything was integrated to suggest that this unity—so analogous to the Mediterranean in the ancient world and the Atlantic in the modern era—was not just a wish, a fantasy, but an impending fact. Grouped around Pacific House, the Expositiion featured an impressive array of Pacific Basin pavilions: Hawaii, New Zealand (a Maori meeting house), Australia, French Indo-China, the Netherlands Indies (a Hindu-Javanese temple), the independent

Malay state of Jahore, the Philippines, Japan (a feudal castle and Samurai house), and the Pacific Coast countries of Latin America, Chile, Peru, Panama El Salvador, Guatemala, Mexico. In Pacific House six mural maps by Miguel Covarrubias presented the entire region in terms of its geography, peoples, flora and fauna, economy, and art.

In the Administration Building, scheduled to become the terminal of an international airport when the Exposition closed, Pan American Airways conducted its trans-Pacific clipper service as a real-life, real-time exhibit. Behind glass panels, so that the public could watch the procedure, mechanics and technicians performed pre-flight protocols on four-engine, twenty-one-ton Martin Flying Clippers, capable of carrying forty-eight passengers across the Pacific in total luxury: lounge chairs, sleepers, food and beverage service, with silver, porcelain, and fine linen.

Service from San Francisco to Manila via Honolulu, Midway, Wake, and Guam had already commenced on 22 November 1935, when Postmaster General James Farley (on hand because of air mail), Governor Frank Merriam, and Pan Am president Juan Tripp gathered in the Alameda estuary to see the *China Clipper* off on its maiden flight. Pulling the Flying Clipper into the air, Captain Edwin Musick discovered that his plane, burdened by a double load of mail, was responding slowly. At its present rate of climb, the captain realized, the Clipper would not clear the cables of the San Francisco–Oakland Bay Bridge, then under construction. Dramatically, Musick reversed his faltering ascent and took the *China Clipper* under the bridge instead, then gained sufficient altitude to clear the spires of the Golden Gate Bridge, also under construction.

Clipper service was elite: $360 one way to Honolulu, $799 to Manila, including limousine service to and from the airport, meals aloft, and hotels and meals at Midway, Wake, and Guam. The crowds watching the Clippers being prepared for take-off, or the chic passengers in furs and polo coats stepping into the aircraft docked alongside the Administration Building prior to departure, were seeing a mode of travel within the reach of only the few. But then again: movies about rich people were very popular in the Depression. Even ordinary folk could enjoy the ambience of privileged travel across the Pacific evoked in these departures and arrivals and the thrilling image of the Flying Clipper as it ascended from the Bay and headed out over the Golden Gate Bridge, en route to the mysterious Orient.

In the Court of the Pacific, Pflueger and Stackpole sought and achieved a mood akin, if not to religion, then at least to a sense of wonder and awe, verging on the religious; indeed, behind Stackpole's dominating sculpture Pacifica, which loomed overhead like an Art Deco Buddhist-Cubist mother goddess, her hands positioned in prayer, was a baldachino of sorts, a ten-story Prayer Curtain comprised of seventeen groups of steel panels which were electrically rotated in such a manner as to create an eerily beautiful wind-sound meant to suggest the prayer of the universe for peace. Nearby was a gigantic mural-relief of 240 carved wooden panels, entitled *The Peacemakers*. Designed by the Bruton sisters, Margaret, Helen, and Esther, the panels celebrated peace between East and West, with the Buddha representing the spirit of peace from Asia and a priestess in white robes representing the spirit of peace in the Occident.

The ring of Army forts around the Bay, however—Forts Baker, Barry, Cronkhite, Funston, McDowell, Miley, and Winfield Scott—together with the Naval Yard at Mare Island, the Army Air Corps installation at Hamilton Field, the Naval Air Station at Moffett Field, and the Presidio of San Francisco, while less stylized in their design, were more prophetic of the immediate future. Peace did not come to the Pacific, and, following Pearl Harbor, Treasure Island did not become a civilian air field but a Navy and Marine Corps base. Stackpole's Pacifica had been scheduled for some grand promontory fronting the Bay, to become an Asia-oriented Statue of Liberty. The war made such plans impossible, and in 1942 the Navy, seeing no other alternative, dynamited Pacifica to smithereens.

"Unfortunately," wrote art critic Eugen Neuhaus, even when the Exposition was in full flower, "the Golden Gate International Exposition has no promise of any permanent tangible civic asset." Yet even as he lamented the doomed nature of the Art Deco Atlantis which had risen from the sea, only to sink once again beneath the waves, Neuhaus hoped that the Exposition, like the other successful world's fairs before it, would hold before Americans the challenge of what Neuhaus called one of the major tasks of American life, "the artistic improvement of our towns and cities to create an environment in which human values may be produced and maintained."[2] Certainly, as a unique form of public work, the Golden Gate International Exposition had done this: had expressed in its distinctive idiom, in which fantasy and utopia melded, the possibilities of the San Francisco Bay Area raised to new prominence in architecture, city planning, arts and museums, and Pacific trade. In raising Treasure Island from the sea and developing it as an idealized Atlantis, San Francisco—under whose jurisdiction the Fair was conceived and executed and whose master architect, Timothy Pflueger, seemed to have a hand in every detail—was being by turns garish, corny, popular, and, in the Palace of Fine Arts especially, elite. It was also being utopian: envisioning, that is, a better city and a better world as California left behind the Depression-ridden 1930s and, with the rest of the world, headed into an equally uncertain future.

Notes

Frequently used citations

CHSQ   *Quarterly of the California Historical Society*
JSDH   *Journal of San Diego History*
NR   *New Republic*
PHR   *Pacific Historical Review*
SCQ   *Southern California Quarterly*
SEP   *Saturday Evening Post*

Chapter One
The Left Side of the Continent

1. Ira Cross, A *History of the Labor Movement in California* (1935), 98–99.
2. *Ibid.*, 110.
3. *Ibid.*, 100, 102–3, 110.
4. *Ibid.*, 102.
5. *Ibid.*, 107–90.
6. Raymond Clary, *The Making of Golden Gate Park, The Early Years: 1865–1906* (1980), 67.
7. Cross, *History of the Labor Movement*, 163.
8. Burnette Haskell, "Kaweah," *Out West* (September 1902), 322.
9. *Frank Roney, Irish Rebel and California Labor Leader, An Autobiography*, ed. Ira Cross (1931), 520.

Chapter Two
Bulls and Wobblies

1. Melvyn Dubofsky, *We Shall Be All: A History of the Industrial Workers of the World* (1969), 188.

2. *Ibid.*, 192.

3. Hyman Weintraub, "The IWW in California, 1905–1931" (MA thesis, UCLA, 1947), 43.

4. Emma Goldman, *Living My Life* [2 vols., 1936], reprinted by Peregrine Smith (1982), 497–498, 500–501.

5. Weintraub, "IWW in California," 46, quoting San Francisco *Call* for 3 June 1912.

6. Dubofsky, *We Shall Be All*, 195.

7. U.S. Congress Senate Committee on Education and Labor, *Violations of Free Speech and Rights of Labor* (1942–1944), 245.

8. *Ibid.*, 244.

9. George Bell, "The Wheatland Hop Field Riots," *Outlook*, 107 (16 May 1915), 121.

10. Weintraub, "IWW in California," 75.

11. Richard Steven Street, " 'We Are Not Slaves': The Photographic Record of the Wheatland Hop Riot," *SCQ* , 64 (Fall 1982), 223.

12. U.S. Commission on Industrial Relations, *Final Report* (5 vols. continuously paged, 1916), 5:4932.

13. "The California Casual and His Revolt," *Quarterly Journal of Economics*, 30 (November 1915), 118.

14. *Ibid.*, 121.

15. Alexander Richmond, *Native Daughter: The Story of Anita Whitney* (1942), 139.

Chapter Three
Seeing Red

1. Porter Chaffee, "A History of the Cannery and Agricultural Workers Industrial Union" (2 vols., typescript, 1939), 18–B, quoting Irving Reichert's letter of 9 October 1933.

Chapter Four
Bayonets on the Embarcadero

1. California Peace Officers' Association, "Convention Proceedings, August 1933," reprinted in *Violations of Free Speech and Rights of Labor*, part 75.

2. Charles Larrowe, "The Great Maritime Strike of '34: Part One," *Labor History*, 11 (Fall 1971), 413.

3. *Ibid.*, 423.

4. Larrowe, "Great Maritime Strike," 421–422; Paul Eliel, *The Waterfront and General Strikes, San Francisco 1934: A Brief History* (1934), 18.

5. Larrowe, "Great Maritime Strike," 423, 445–46.

6. Eliel, *Waterfront and General Strikes*, 221.

7. Larrowe, "Great Maritime Strke," 448, quoting a July 1964 interview with Randolph Sevier.

8. *Ibid.*, 424.

9. Charles Larrowe, "The Great Maritime Strike of '34: Part Two," *Labor History*, 12 (Winter 1971), 12.

10. *Ibid.*, 14.

11. Eliel, *Waterfront and General Strikes*, 128.

12. Charles Larrowe, *Harry Bridges: The Rise and Fall of Radical Labor in the United States* (1972), 77.

13. Eliel, *Waterfront and General Strikes*, 238.
14. *Ibid.*
15. Larrowe, "Great Maritime Strike of '34: Part Two," 26.
16. *Ibid.*
17. Paul Smith, *Personal File* (1964), 154–155.
18. *Ibid.*, 156–157.
19. Larrowe, *Harry Bridges*, 85.
20. *The Letters of Lincoln Steffens*, edited by Ella Winter and Granville Hicks (2 vols., 1938), 2:988–989.

Chapter Five
EPIC Intentions

1. *The Autobiography of Upton Sinclair* (1962), 23.
2. Mary Craig Sinclair, *Southern Belle* (1957), 292–293.
3. W. H. Smyth, *Technocracy Explained by Its Originator* (1933), 1–20.
4. Oliver Carlson, *A Mirror for Californians* (1941), 286.
5. Abraham Holtzman, *The Townsend Movement* (1963), 33.
6. Bruce Bliven, "The Midwestern Messiah," NR, 86 (6 May 1936), 365.
7. Carey McWilliams, "Upton Sinclair and His EPIC," NR, 80 (22 August 1934), 39.
8. George Creel, *Rebel at Large* (1947), 285–286.
9. Leon Harris, *Upton Sinclair, American Rebel* (1975), 302.
10. *Ibid.*, 303.
11. *I, Candidate for Governor—And How I Got Licked* (1935), 76–77.
12. Harris, *Upton Sinclair*, 304.
13. *Ibid.*
14. Charles Larsen, "The EPIC Campaign of 1934," PHR, 27 (May 1958), 131.
15. Carlson, *Mirror*, 300; Harris, *Upton Sinclair* 306.
16. Carlson, *Mirror*, 307.
17. *The Profits of Religion* (1918), 161.
18. *The Goose-Step* (1923), 141–142, 145.
19. Carlson, *Mirror*, 299.
20. Brian McGinty, "Shadows in St. James Park," CHSQ, 57 (Winter 1978), 14, quoting *Time* for 4 December 1933.
21. *Letters to Judd* (1926), 62.
22. George Ashton, "Upton Sinclair" (MA thesis, history, UC Berkeley, 1951), 141, quoting the San Diego *Union* for 6 November 1934.
23. *I, Governor of California—And How I Ended Poverty* (1933), 53.
24. "The Future of EPIC," NR, 80 (28 November 1934), 617.

Chapter Six
The Empire Strikes Back

1. Letter of Grover C. Johnson to Brig. Gen. Pelham D. Glassford, 22 June 1934, Bancroft Library.
2. Brig. Gen. Pelham D. Glassford, "Memorandum to Imperial County Board of Supervisors, Brawley, California, 23 June 1934" (6 pp., typescript), 4, Bancroft Library.
3. "California, There She Stands!," *Harper's* 176 (February 1935), 361, 366, 368.
4. "Licenses for Union Organizers," *Business Week*, 499 (25 March 1939), 48.

5. "Leo Gallagher," *Nation* 141 (16 October 1935), 438.

6. Porter Chaffee, "A History of the Cannery and Agricultural Workers Industrial Union" (2 vols., bound mimeographed typescript, continuously paged, 1939), 13, quoting San Francisco *Examiner* for 22 January 1935, Bancroft Library.

7. Mike Quinn [Paul William Ryan], *The Criminal Syndicalism Case Against Labor* (1935), 26.

8. "Is California Civilized?," *Nation*, 132 (1 April 1931), 348.

9. "California's Little Hitlers," *NR*, 77 (27 December 1933), 190.

10. "Cold Terror in California," *Nation*, 141 (24 July 1935), 97.

11. *Ibid.*, 98.

12. "Terrorism in California," *NR*, 79 (1 August 1934), 305.

13. California State Relief Administration, "Transients in California" (bound mimeographed typescript, 1936), 235, Bancroft Library.

14. *Violations of Free Speech and Rights of Labor*, 1368.

15. *Ibid.*, 1361.

16. *Ibid.*, 1362, quoting Los Angeles *Times* for 17 September 1936.

17. *Ibid.*, 1366–1367.

18. *Ibid.*, 1376, quoting San Francisco *Examiner* for 19 September 1936.

19. Smith, *Personal File*, 176.

20. *Violations of Free Speech and Rights of Labor*, 1371, quoting the San Francisco *Chronicle* for 23 September 1936.

21. *Ibid.*, 1374.

22. *Ibid.*, 1389.

23. *Ibid.*, 1392.

24. *Ibid.*, 1400.

25. *Ibid.*, 1401.

26. Carlson, *Mirror*, 234.

Chapter Seven
Ham and Eggs

1. "Script of Radio Address, 29 August 1938," Philip Bancroft Papers, Bancroft Library.

2. Curt Gentry, *Frame-Up: The Incredible Case of Tom Mooney and Warren Billings* (1967), 415.

3. *Ibid.*, 422–423.

Chapter Eight
Give Me Shelter

1. Duncan Aikman, "California Sunshine," *Nation*, 132 (22 April 1931), 448.

2. "Journal of a Transient," in California State Relief Administration, "Transients in California," 89.

3. *Violations of Free Speech and Rights of Labor*, 360.

4. "Can the Radicals Capture the Farms of California? A Paper Presented Before the Commonwealth Club of California and over Radio Station KPO, San Francisco, 23 March 1934" (mimeographed typescript), 15, Bancroft Library.

5. Clark Kerr, "Preface," Paul Taylor, *On the Ground in the Thirties* (1938).

6. "Paul Schuster Taylor" (3 vols., typescript, 1973), 28, Bancroft Library Oral History Project, Bancroft Library.

7. Thomas Collins, "Weekly Reports from Arvin Migrants Camp, 28 November 1935–

4 July 1936," Irving Williams Wood Correspondence and Papers 1934–1937, Bancroft Library.

8. Ivan Dimitri, "No Jobs in California," *SEP*, 211 (12 November 1938), 40, 44.

9. Walter Stein, *California and the Dust Bowl Migration* (1973), 102.

10. *Ibid.*, 128.

11. Paul Dorsey, photographer, "Waifs of the Winds," *Westways* 31 (June 1939), 16–17.

Chapter Nine
Documenting the Crisis

1. "The Assignment I'll Never Forget," *Popular Photography*, 46 (February 1960), 42.

2. "The Leader of the People" [part 4 of *The Red Pony*] in *The Long Valley: Stories by John Steinbeck* (ninth edition, 1968), 302.

3. Elaine Steinbeck and Robert Wallsten, editors, *Steinbeck: A Life in Letters* (1975), 158.

4. *Congressional Record*, 76th Congress, 3rd Session, 1940, Section 86, part 13, 140.

5. "Highway 66—A Tale of Five Cities," *New Yorker*, 15 (15 April 1939), 81.

6. Philip Bancroft, "Does *Grapes of Wrath* Present a Fair Picture of California Farm Labor Conditions?" (mimeographed typescript, 1940), 4, Philip Bancroft Papers, Bancroft Library.

7. *Ibid.*, 5–6.

8. *Ibid.*, 3.

9. Quoted in David Selvin, "Carey McWilliams, Reformer as Historian," *CHSQ*, 53 (1974), 174.

10. *Interstate Migration*, part 10, 4245.

Chapter Eleven
Angels, Dams, and Dynamos

1. "Building the Big Dam," *Harper's* magazine, 171 (June 1935), 117.

2. "The American Dnieperstroy," *NR*, 72 (11 December 1935), 127.

3. "Building the Big Dam," 119.

4. *Ibid.*, 120.

5. *Ibid.*

6. "Arizona Desert: Reflections of a Winter Visitor," *Harper's* magazine, 173 (March 1937), 365.

7. Robert Speers, "Carrying on Ages-Old Fight with Desert," *Los Angeles Saturday Night*, 16 (19 October 1935), 3.

Chapter Twelve
Completing California

1. Robert Bradford Marshall, "Preface," *Irrigation of Twelve Million Acres* (1919).

2. Albert P. Heiner, *Henry J. Kaiser, American Empire Builder: An Insider's View* (1989), 65.

3. Robert Hessen, *Herbert Hoover and the Bay Bridge* (1986), 12.

4. Stephen Cassady, *Spanning the Gate* (1979), 13.

5. John Van Der Zee, *The Gate: The True Story of the Design and Construction of the Golden Gate Bridge* (1986), 160.

6. *Ibid.*, 142.
7. Cassady, *Spanning the Gate*, 68.
8. *Ibid.*, 110.

Chapter Thirteen
Atlantis on the Pacific

1. "Our Stake in the Pacific," *Southern California Business*, 8 (August 1929), 14.
2. *The Art of Treasure Island* (1939), 4, 7.

Bibliographical Essay

Chapter One
The Left Side of the Continent

For general background, see David Selvin, *Sky Full of Storm* (1966) and Anthony Bimba, *The History of the American Working Class* (1927). For background regarding the self-made workingman entrepreneurs of the 1850s, see Richard Dillon, *Iron Men: California's Industrial Pioneers, Peter, James, and Michael Donahue* (1984). Regarding San Francisco in the early 1870s, see Benjamin Lloyd, *Lights and Shades in San Francisco* (1876). See also Gertrude Atherton, "The Terrible Seventies," *California: An Intimate History* (revised and enlarged edition, 1927), 272–280. Two important contemporary assessments of Kearneyism are Henry George, "The Kearney Agitation in California," *Popular Science Monthly*, 17 (August 1880), 433–453; and James Bryce, "Kearneyism in California," *The American Commonwealth* (new and revised edition, 1924), 426–468. The most detailed account of the Kearney agitations can be found in Ira Cross, "The Chinese Must Go," *A History of the Labor Movement in California* (1935), 88–129. See also Rockwell D. Hunt, "Denis Kearney and the Workingmen's Movement," in the first volume of *California and Californians* (4 vols., 1932); Mary Frances McKinney, "Denis Kearney, Organizer of the Workingmen's Party of California" (MA thesis, history, UC Berkeley, 1940); Miriam Allen deFord, *They Were San Franciscans* (1941), 196–211; Charles Henzl Kahn, "In-Group and Out-Group Response to Radical Party Leadership: A Study of the Workingmen's Party of California" (MA thesis, sociology, UC Berkeley, 1951). The *California Advertiser* ran "A Short History of Mooneysville-by-the-Sea" on 26 January 1884. See also Raymond Clary, *The Making of Golden Gate Park, the Early Years: 1865–1906* (1980), 59–68. For additional information, see the colorful account in the "Riptides" column of Robert O'Brien in the San Francisco *Chronicle* for 14 September 1951.

As background to Frank Roney's *Irish Rebel and California Labor Leader: An Autobiography*, edited by Ira Cross (1931), see Neil Larry Shumsky, "Frank Roney's San Francisco—His Diary: April 1875–March 1876," *Labor History*, 17 (1976), 245–264. The Burnette Gregor Haskell Papers 1857–1907 and the Haskell Family Papers 1878–1951 are in the Bancroft Library. In *Irish Rebel*, Roney discussed his recruitment of Haskell (388–390) and Haskell's dynamite plot (473–476). Haskell discussed his utopian experiment in

"Kaweah," *Out West,* 17 (September 1902), 315–318. See also Robert Hine, *California's Utopian Colonies* (1966), 78–100. Also of value to this study: Caroline Medan, "Burnette Gregor Haskell: California Radical" (MA thesis, history, UC Berkeley, 1958); and Annegret Ogden, "The 65 New Year's Eves of Anna Fader Haskell (1876–1942)," *The Californians,* 2 (1984), 7–8. The records of the International Workingmen's Association are in the Bancroft Library. See also Cross, "The International Workingmen's Association," *A History of the Labor Movement in California,* 156–165; and Ralph Shaffer, "A History of the Socialist Party of California" (MA thesis, history, UC Berkeley, 1955).

For general background to the unionization of coastal seamen, see Elmo Paul Hohman, *History of American Merchant Seamen* (1956). Richard Dillon discusses the exploitation of sailors in *Shanghaiing Days* (1961). Paul Taylor wrote *The Sailors' Union of the Pacific* (1923) as his 1922 PhD dissertation at UC Berkeley. See also Stephen Schwartz, *Brotherhood of the Sea: A History of the Sailors' Union of the Pacific, 1885–1985* (1985). Regarding Furuseth, see Hyman Weintraub, *Andrew Furuseth, Emancipator of the Seamen* (1959) and *A Symposium on Andrew Furuseth* (nd).

Regarding the working people of San Francisco at the turn of the century, see Jules Tygiel, "San Francisco Working People, 1880–1910" (PhD thesis, history, UCLA, 1975); and Davis McEntire, *The Labor Force in California, 1900–1950* (1952). Regarding unionism in turn-of-the-century San Francisco, see Edward Rowell, "The Union Labor Party of San Francisco, 1901–1911" (PhD thesis, history, UC Berkeley, 1938); Robert Berner Ohlson, "The History of the San Francisco Labor Council, 1892–1939" (MA thesis, history, UC Berkeley, 1940). For the statewide perspective, see Philip Taft, *Labor Politics American Style: The California State Federation of Labor* (1968). In this study, Taft also provides an excellent general history of labor in California. Regarding the first San Francisco general strike, see Robert McClure Robinson, "A History of the Teamsters in the San Francisco Bay Area, 1850–1950" (PhD thesis, economics, UC Berkeley, 1951); and Robert Knight, *Industrial Relations in the San Francisco Bay Area, 1900–1918* (1960). The career of Peter Yorke is chronicled through Bernard Cornelius Cronin, *Father Yorke and the Labor Movement in San Francisco, 1900–1910* (1943); Joseph Brusher, SJ, *Consecrated Thunderbolt: Father Yorke of San Francisco* (1973); James P. Walsh, "Peter C. Yorke: San Francisco's Irishman Reconsidered," *The San Francisco Irish* (1978), 42–57. Michael Kazin has chronicled the post–General Strike ascendancy of labor in *Barons of Labor: The San Francisco Building Trades and Union Power in the Progressive Era* (1987). See also Millard Morgen, "The Administration of Patrick H. McCarthy, Mayor of San Francisco, 1910–1912" (MA thesis, history, UC Berkeley, 1949).

Chapter Two
Bulls and Wobblies

The best overall study of the Criminal Syndicalism Act of 1919 is Woodrow Whitten's *Criminal Syndicalism and the Law in California, 1919–1927* (1969). See also Leo Tulin, *Digest of Criminal Syndicalism Cases in California* (1926). For the country in general, see Eldredge Dowell, *Criminal Syndicalism Legislation in the United States* (1939). Regarding the immediate response in California to the passage of the Criminal Syndicalism Act of 1919, see Miriam Allen deFord, "Injury to All: Criminal Syndicalism Law," *The Overland Monthly,* ns 82 (December 1924), 536–537; A. B. Reading, "California Syndicalist Act, Strong or Wobbly?" *The Overland Monthly,* ns 83 (March 1925), 117–118; and "Constitutionality of California's Criminal Syndicalism Upheld," *Congressional Digest,* 6 (12 June 1927), 210–212.

For the best-known criminal syndicalism case of them all, see the following pamphlets in the Bancroft Library: Labor Defense League, San Francisco, *Citizens of California!* (1920); State of California, Office of the Governor, *Case of Charlotte A. Whitney* (1925); John Francis Neylan, *Petition for the Pardon of Charlotte Anita Whitney and Brief in Support Thereof* (1927); and State of California, Office of the Governor, *The Pardon of Charlotte Anita Whitney* (1927). See also Franklin Hichborn, *The Case of Charlotte Anita Whitney* (1920); Woodrow Whitten, "Trial of Charlotte Anita Whitney," *PHR*, 15 (1946), 286–294; and Lisa Rubens, "The Patrician Radical: Charlotte Anita Whitney," *CHSQ*, 65 (September 1986), 158–171. For two very partisan, very lively treatments, see Alexander Richmond, *Native Daughter: The Story of Anita Whitney* (1942); and Elizabeth Gurley Flynn, *Daughters of America: Ella Reeve Bloor, Anita Whitney* (1942).

For general background regarding terrorism and vigilantism in this period, see Arnold Madison, *Vigilantism in America* (1973). Regarding the dynamiting of the Los Angeles *Times*, see William John Burns, *The Masked War* (c. 1913). See also Louis Adamic, *Dynamite: The Story of Class Violence in America* (1929). Later investigations include Robert Munson Baker, "Why the McNamaras Pleaded Guilty to the Bombing of the *Los Angeles Times*" (MA thesis, history, UC Berkeley, 1949); and Graham Adams Jr., *The Age of Industrial Violence, 1910–1915* (1956).

Research into the IWW begins with Dione Miles, compiler, *Something in Common— An IWW Bibliography* (1986). Studies of special value to this chapter include Paul Brissenden, *The IWW: A Study of American Syndicalism* (1919, second edition 1957); Patrick Renshaw, *The Wobblies: The Story of Syndicalism in the United States* (1967); Melvyn Dubofsky, *We Shall Be All: A History of the Industrial Workers of the World* (1969); Joseph Conlin, *Bread and Roses Too: Studies of the Wobblies* (1969). See also John Gambs, *The Decline of the IWW* (1932). Of special importance to this chapter is Hyman Weintraub, "The IWW in California, 1905–1931" (MA thesis, history, UCLA, 1947). For further background, see E. T. Booth, "Wild West," *Atlantic Monthly*, 126 (December 1920), 785–788; William D. Haywood, *Bill Haywood's Book* (1929); and Joyce Kornbluh, editor, *Rebel Voices: An IWW Anthology* (1964). Regarding the IWW in Fresno, see Ronald Genini, "Industrial Workers of the World and Their Fresno Free Speech Fight, 1910–1911," *CHSQ*, 53 (1974), 101–114. For the San Diego demonstrations, see Rosalie Shanks, "The IWW Free Speech Movement, San Diego, 1912," *JDSH*, 19 (Winter 1973), 25–33. Regarding the IWW incursion into Baja, California, see Lowell Blaisdell, *The Desert Revolution, Baja California, 1911* (1962). Emma Goldman relates her San Diego experiences in *Living My Life* [2 vols., 1936], Peregrine Smith edition (1982). During the IWW-led San Pedro strike, Frederick Wedge infiltrated the IWW. His report, *Inside the IWW* (1924), is of interest. Regarding the participation of Upton Sinclair, see "Upton Sinclair Defends the Law," *Nation*, 116 (6 June 1923), 647; and Martin Zanger, "Politics of Confrontation: Upton Sinclair and the Launching of the ACLU in Southern California," *PHR*, 38 (November 1969), 383–406.

For the general background of agricultural labor in California, see Cletus Daniel, *Bitter Harvest: A History of California Farm Workers, 1870–1941* (1981). Of special relevance is chapter 3, "Organization and Reform: the Progressive Era," 71–104. See also Lloyd Fisher, *The Harvest Labor Market in California* (1953); and Varden Fuller, *Labor Relations in Agriculture* (1955). For earlier investigations into farm labor in the Far West, see Walter Augustus Wyckoff, *The Workers—The West: An Experiment in Reality* (1900); W. V. Woehlike, "Labor—The World Problem in the Far West," *Sunset*, 38 (April 1917), 7–10 continuing. Regarding itinerant workingmen, see Nels Anderson, *The Hobo* (1923) and *Men on the Move* (1940).

The California Commission of Immigration and Housing issued its *Report on the Wheatland Riot* in 1916. In 1925 the American Civil Liberties Union issued its *The Story of the [Blackie] Ford Case*. Of special importance to this chapter are George Bell, "The

Wheatland Hop Field Riots," *Outlook*, 107 (16 May 1914), 118–123; Woodrow Whitten, "The Wheatland Episode," *PHR*, 17 (1948), 37–42; and Richard Steven Street, " 'We Are Not Slaves': The Photographic Record of the Wheatland Hop Riot," *SCQ*, 64 (Fall 1982), 205–226. The investigations of Carleton Parker can be traced through "The California Casual and His Revolt," *Quarterly Journal of Economics*, 30 (November 1915), 110–126; *The California Casual* (1920); *The Casual Laborer and Other Essays* (1920). Also of importance is the memoir of Parker's widow, Cornelia Stratton Parker, *An American Idyll: The Life of Carleton H. Parker* (1924).

The California Bureau of Labor Statistics treated housing conditions among agricultural workers in its *Twelfth Biennial Report* (1906). The Simon J. Lubin Collection in the Bancroft Library preserves the pamphlets issued by the California Commission of Immigration and Housing in its early years. See especially the *Advisory Pamphlet on Camp Sanitation and Housing* (1914). For general background, consult Samuel Wood, *The California State Commission of Immigration and Housing* (1942). See also Federal Writers' Project, Oakland, *History of Living Conditions Among Migratory Laborers in California* (mimeographed typescript, 1938); and Albert Croutch, "Housing Migratory Agricultural Workers in California, 1913–1948" (MA thesis, history, UC Berkeley, 1948). In "Ideas of Reform in California," *Essays and Assays: California History Reappraised*, George Knoles, editor (1973), Walton Bean takes up the question of reform in this period.

Chapter Three
Seeing Red

Cletus Daniel's *Bitter Harvest: A History of California Farm Workers, 1870–1941* (1981) commands all discussion of farm labor in California. Of central importance to this chapter are Carey McWilliams, *Factories in the Field: The Story of Migratory Farm Labor in California* (1939) and *Ill Fares the Land: Migrants and Migratory Labor in the United States* (1942). See also J. Donald Fisher, *A Historical Study of the Migrant in California* [1945], reprinted in 1973; and Varden Fuller, "The Supply of Agricultural Labor as a Factor in the Evolution of Farm Organizations in California" (PhD thesis, agricultural economics, UC Berkeley, 1939). In 1936 the State Relief Administration issued *Migratory Labor in California*.

For general patterns in California's treatment of minorities, see Roger Daniels and Spencer C. Olin Jr., *Racism in California: A Reader in the History of Oppression* (1972). Of special importance is Walter Goldschmidt, *As You Sow* (1947). For surveys of Asians in California, see Howard Melendy, *The Oriental Americans* (1972); and Norris Hundley Jr., editor, *The Asian American: The Historical Experience*, introduction by Akira Iriye (1976). For the story of the Chinese in California agriculture, see Sucheng Chan, *This Bittersweet Soil: The Chinese in California Agriculture, 1860–1910* (1986). Toshio Yoshimura has written *George Shima: The Potato King* (1981). See also Florence Hongo, editor, *Japanese-American Journey: The Story of a People* (1985). For background on East Asian Hindu workers, see Rajami Kanta Das, *Hindustani Workers on the Pacific Coast* (1923); and Dhan Gopal Mukeyi, *Caste and Outcast* (1923), by a Hindu activist in the IWW. Next to Mexicans, Filipinos were the most represented among field workers. Regarding this important group, Lorraine Crouchett has written *Filipinos in California from the Days of the Galleons to the Present* (1982). Of direct relevance to this chapter is Howard De Witt, *Anti-Filipino Movements in California* (1976). Emory Borgardus's *Anti-Filipino Race Riots* (1930) has background on the Monterey County agitations.

Before the arrival of Dust Bowl migrants, Mexicans dominated the agricultural work force. Discussions of this important group are based on Carey McWilliams, *North from*

Mexico: The Spanish-Speaking People of the United States (1949) and *Brothers Under the Skin* (revised edition 1951); and Albert Camarillo, *Chicanos in California* (1984). Also of importance is the pioneering study by Manuel Gamio, *Mexican Immigration to the United States* (1930). For the role of Mexican consuls general, see Francisco Balderrama, *In Defense of La Raza: The Los Angeles Mexican Consulate and the Mexican Community, 1929–1936* (1982). See also Gamio's collection of first-person narratives, *The Mexican Immigrant* (1931), reissued in 1971 as *The Life Story of the Mexican Immigrant: Autobiographic Documents*, edited by Robert Redfield, introduction by Paul S. Taylor. Taylor himself made the most comprehensive report on the Mexican population in *Mexican Labor in the United States* (7 vols., 1929–1933), a documentary classic. See also Taylor's *A Spanish-Mexican Peasant Community: Arandas in Jalisco, Mexico* (1933) and *An American-Mexican Frontier, Nueces County, Texas* (1934). Evidence of solidarity among Mexican workers in this period can be seen in Charles Wollenberg, "Huelga, 1928 Style: The Imperial Valley Cantaloupe Workers' Strike," *PHR*, 38 (February 1969), 45–58.

For general background relating to the struggle of farm workers to organize in the 1930s, see Earl Crockett, "The History of California Labor Legislation, 1910–1930" (PhD thesis, economics, UC Berkeley, 1931); S. M. Jamieson, "Labor Unionism in American Agriculture" (PhD thesis, economics, UC Berkeley, 1943); and Clarke Chambers, *California Farm Organizations, 1929–1941* (1952). See also "Feudalism in California," *Survey*, 42 (24 May 1919), 310–311.

Of sustained value throughout this entire chapter is Porter Chaffee, "A History of the Cannery and Agricultural Workers Industrial Union" (bound typescript, 2 vols., 1939), a history sponsored by the Federal Writers' Project, Oakland, on deposit in the Bancroft Library. Regarding the relationship of this and other unions to worldwide Communism, see chapter 33 of Bimba's *The History of the American Working Class*, "The Left Wing in the Trade Unions," 331–340. As background to the cotton strike of 1933, see Federal Writers' Project, Oakland, "Labor in California Cotton Fields" (typescript mimeograph, 1939); and Norman Lowenstein, "Strikes and Strike Tactics in California Agriculture" (MA thesis, economics, UC Berkeley, 1940). For a contemporary estimate, see Miriam Allen deFord, "Blood-Stained Cotton in California," *Nation*, 137 (20 December 1933), 705–706.

Paul S. Taylor assembled three cartons of "Materials Relating to Agricultural and Maritime Strikes in California, 1933–1942," on deposit in the Bancroft Library. During the cotton strike, Taylor and Clark Kerr assembled the "Documentary History of the Strike of the Cotton Pickers in California 1933," which has been reprinted in *On the Ground in the Thirties*, preface by Clark Kerr (1983), 17–158. Also reprinted in *On the Ground in the Thirties* are two crucial articles by Taylor from the period: "Uprisings of the Farms," which appeared in the *Survey Graphic* for January 1936, and "Migratory Agricultural Workers on the Pacific Coast," which appeared in the *American Sociological Review* for April 1938. Clark Kerr's PhD dissertation, directed by Taylor, "Productive Enterprises Among the Unemployed, 1931–1938," is on deposit at the Bancroft Library. In 1977 the dynamic Caroline Decker Gladstein recorded her oral history for Wayne State University. A bound volume of this history is on deposit in the library of the California Historical Society in San Francisco. For a contemporary assessment of Decker, see the front-page article in the San Francisco *News* for 26 October 1933, headlined "Girl, 21, Laughs at Fear as She Directs Strike." Regarding the role of Governor Rolph in the strike, see Herman Goldbeck, "The Political Career of James Rolph, Jr." (MA thesis, political science, UC Berkeley, 1936). For the role of Rabbi Irving Reichert, see chapter 7, "The Discordant Years," in Fred Rosenbaum's *Architects of Reform: Congregational and Community Leadership, Emanu-El of San Francisco, 1849–1980* (1980), 125–146. See also Reichert's *Judaism and the American Jew: Selected Sermons and Addresses* (1953).

For background to the canning industry, see Donald Anthony, "Labor Conditions in the Canning Industry of the Santa Clara Valley" (PhD thesis, economics, Stanford, 1928).

Chapter Four
Bayonets on the Embarcadero

For background to the entire question of unionism in the maritime industries, see Bruce Nelson, *Workers on the Waterfront: Seamen, Longshoremen, and Unionism in the 1930s* (1988). See also Wytze Gorter and George Hildebrand, *The Pacific Coast Maritime Shipping Industry, 1930–1948* (2 vols., 1952–1954). For a discussion of specific San Francisco practices, see Charles Larrowe, *Shape-Up and Hiring Hall* (1955), especially chapters 5 and 6. The San Francisco Labor Council AFL-CIO, Correspondence and Papers 1906–1955, in the Bancroft Library, includes the bound volume "San Francisco General Strike 1934." The Bancroft also has a near-complete run of the *Waterfront Worker*. The most comprehensive and balanced account of the maritime strike of 1934 is Charles Larrowe's "The Great Maritime Strike of '34," *Labor History*, 11 (Fall 1970), 403–451; 12 (Winter 1971), 337. Crucial to this chapter is Larrowe's *Harry Bridges: the Rise and Fall of Radical Labor in the United States* (1972). See also Jane Cassels Record, "Ideologies and Trade Union Leadership: The Case of Harry Bridges and Harry Lundeberg" (PhD thesis, history, UC Berkeley, 1954); David Mabon, "The West Coast Waterfront and Sympathy Strikes of 1934" (PhD thesis, history, UC Berkeley, 1965); and Cross, *History of the Labor Movement in California*, 254–262. See also Herbert Resner, editor, *The Law in Action During the San Francisco Longshore and Maritime Strike of 1934* (1936). A valuable contemporary account can be found in Paul S. Taylor and Norman L. Gold, "San Francisco and the General Strike," *Survey Graphic*, 23 (September 1934), 405–411. David Prescott Barrows told his side of the story in "The San Francisco General Strike and the National Guard," *Memoirs* (1954), 217–225.

During the strike Paul Eliel served as public relations director of the Industrial Association of San Francisco. Eliel's *The Waterfront and General Strikes, San Francisco 1934: A Brief History* (1934) is told from the shippers' point of view but contains much authentic documentation. On the other side of the political spectrum is Mike Quin's *The Big Strike*, postscript by Harry Bridges, title page drawing by Rockwell Kent, illustrations by Bits Hayden (1949). "Mike Quin" was the pseudonym of Paul William Ryan (1906–1947), a merchant seaman and labor publicist on the far left. Regarding the somewhat mysterious Quin, see Bob Callahan, "Mike Quin: Labor's Greatest Writer," *Image* magazine, *Sunday San Francisco Examiner and Chronicle* (4 September 1988), 17. See also Quin's *Dangerous Thoughts* (1940), a collection of columns written for *The People's World* and for radio broadcast, and *More Dangerous Thoughts*, introduction by Theodore Dreiser (1941). For another far-left account of the strike, see William F. Dunne, *The Great San Francisco General Strike* (1934).

For Roger Lapham's perspective, see the interview conducted by Corinne Gilb for the Regional Cultural History Project of the University of California Library, entitled "An Interview on Shipping, Labor, San Francisco City Government, and American Foreign Aid" (bound typescript, 2 vols., 1957), on deposit at the Bancroft Library. See also Helen Abbot Lapham's privately printed *Roving with Roger* (1957). General Hugh Johnson gave his side of the story in *The Blue Eagle from Egg to Earth* (1935). Regarding the role played by John Francis Neylan, see Roger Lotchin, "John Francis Neylan: San Francisco Irish Progressive," in James P. Walsh, editor, *The San Francisco Irish, 1850–1976* (1978), 87–112. The response of President Roosevelt to the San Francisco situation is chronicled by Arthur M. Schlesinger Jr. in *The Coming of the New Deal* (1959), 385–396. See also

Melvin Dubofsky and Warren Van Tine, *John L. Lewis: A Biography* (1977), 203–209. The reaction of Lincoln Steffens can be garnered from *The Letters of Lincoln Steffens*, edited with introductory notes by Ella Winter and Granville Hicks (2 vols., 1938). For the post-strike history of the ILWU in the remaining years of the 1930s, see Harvey Schwartz, *The March Inland: Origins of the ILWU Warehouse Division, 1934–1938* (1978); and Louis Goldblatt, "Working-Class Leader in the ILWU, 1935–1977" (photocopy of typed transcript of tape-recorded interviews, 2 vols., 1980) in the Bancroft Library.

Chapter Five
EPIC Intentions

My discussion of the economic background to EPIC is based on the report issued by the State Relief Administration, "Economic Trends in California, 1929–1934" (bound mimeographed typescript, 1935), prepared by Paul Woolf, on deposit in the Bancroft Library. The psychological state of California at the time can be understood from Luther Whiteman and Samuel Lewis, *Glory Roads: The Psychological State of California* (1936); and Oliver Carlson, *A Mirror for Californians* (1941). For the national perspective, see Charles Tull, *Father Coughlin and the New Deal* (1965); and David Bennett, *Demagogues in the Depression: American Radicals and the Union Party, 1932–1936* (1969).

Regarding Socialist and/or cooperative ventures in pre-EPIC California, see Ira Cross, "Socialism in California Municipalities," *National Municipal Review*, 1 (1912), 611–619; A. R. Clifton, "History of the Communistic Colony Llano del Rio," *SCQ*, ll (1918), 80–90; and Fern Dawson Shochat, "The Voluntary Cooperative Association of Los Angeles, 1913–1922," *SCQ*, 45 (June 1963), 169–180. The crackpot, vaguely anti-Semitic thought of Sinclair's Santa Monica Socialist confrere Gilbert Stevenson can be seen in his *The Secrets of Plutology* (1931) and *A Model State: Making a Utopia of California* (1934).

As far as the EPIC campaign is concerned, Greg Mitchell's *The Campaign of the Century: Upton Sinclair's Race for Governor of California and the Birth of Media Politics* (1992) commands the subject. Mitchell's book appeared after I had researched and written this chapter, but I have fact-checked my conclusions against this authoritative source. In *Upton Sinclair: An Annotated Checklist* (1972) Ronald Gottesman provides an Ariadne's thread through the labyrinth of publications by or about Sinclair. Jon Yoder's *Upton Sinclair* (1975) and Leon Harris's *Upton Sinclair, American Rebel* (1975) are useful biographies. See also George Franklin Ashton, "Upton Sinclair" (MA thesis, history, UC Berkeley, 1951); and Judson Grenier, "Upton Sinclair: A Remembrance," *CHSQ*, 48 (June 1969), 165–169. Mary Craig Sinclair tells her story in *Southern Belle* (1957), with a preface by her husband. George Creel has his say in *Rebel at Large: Recollections of Fifty Crowded Years* (1947). The Eisenstein caper is chronicled by Harry Geduld and Ronald Gottesman in *Sergei Eisenstein and Upton Sinclair: The Making and Unmaking of "Que Viva Mexico!"* (1970).

The Bancroft Library has a portfolio of materials dealing with Upton Sinclair and the EPIC campaign of 1934. It includes numerous pamphlets issued during the campaign, both for and against Sinclair. Of special relevance are *I, Menace of California, and How I Ended*; *Upton Sinclair Attacks All Churches*; *Upton Sinclair's Attitude on Christianity*; and *Upton Sinclair Reviews the University of California and UCLA, "The University of the Black Hand,"* all appearing in 1934. Also at the Bancroft are seven bound volumes of the *EPIC News*, covering the period March 1934 through August 1947. Specialized studies of EPIC include Charles Frederic McIntosh, "Upton Sinclair and the EPIC Movement, 1933–1936" (PhD thesis, history, Stanford, 1955); Russell M. Posner, "A. P. Giannini and the 1934 Campaign in California," *SCQ*, 39 (1957), 190–201; Charles Larsen, "The EPIC

Campaign of 1934," *PHR*, 27 (May 1958), 127–148; Leonard Leader, "Upton Sinclair's EPIC Switch: A Dilemma for American Socialists," *SCQ*, 62 (Winter 1980), 361–385; and George Ashton, "Bellamy, Judd, and the Industrial Republic: Some Sources of the EPIC Plan," *The Upton Sinclair Quarterly*, 9 (Summer 1985), 6–11. For Hollywood's reaction to the EPIC campaign, see Neal Gabler's *An Empire of Their Own: How the Jews Invented Hollywood* (1988), 311–315. See also H. F. Pringle, "Movies Swing an Election," *Reader's Digest*, 29 (4 August 1936), 4.

Walter Davenport, "Sinclair Gets the Glory Vote," *Collier's*, 94 (27 October 1934), 12–13ff, is a valuable contemporary account. Carey McWilliams covered the EPIC campaign for the *New Republic* on 22 August, 12 September, and 7 November 1934. Sinclair presented himself as a mainstream candidate in the *New Republic* for 12 September 1934 and sent along a "Political Prayer" for the edition of 7 November 1934. *Nation* magazine covered the campaign on 9 May, 11 July, 12 September, 26 September, and 31 October 1934. See also Sinclair's "Future of EPIC," *Nation*, 139 (28 November 1934), 616–617; and L. Symes, "After EPIC in California," *Nation*, 142 (22 April 1936), 509–511. The *Christian Century* was especially interested in the religious aspects of the campaign. See the issues of 12 September, 31 October, 14 and 21 November 1934. See also Edward Ward, "Defenders of the Faith," *Commonweal*, 21 (22 February 1935), 481–482. The crucial *Literary Digest* poll appears as "Sinclair Behind in Digest California Poll," *Literary Digest*, 118 (27 October 1934), 118.

Sinclair's autobiographical works include *American Outpost: A Book of Reminiscences* (1932), *My Lifetime in Letters* (1960), and *The Autobiography of Upton Sinclair* (1962). In *The Industrial Republic* (1908) Sinclair gave the most extensive outline of his Socialism. Sinclair opened his campaign with *I, Governor of California, and How I Ended Poverty—A True Story of the Future* (1933). During the campaign he produced *EPIC Answers, How to End Poverty in California* (1934), *Immediate EPIC, the Final Statement of the Plan* (1934), and *The Lie Factory Starts* (1934). After his defeat, Sinclair produced *I, Candidate for Governor—And How I Got Licked* (1935); *We, People of America, and How We Ended Poverty: A True Story of the Future* (1935); and *Co-op, a Novel of Living Together* (1936). Regarding Sinclair as a writer, with special reference to his novel *Oil!* (1927), see Lawrence Clark Powell, *California Classics* (1971), 317–330.

Regarding Technocracy and the Utopian Society of America, William Akin provides the best background in his *Technocracy and the American Dream, 1900–1941* (1977). William Henry Smyth outlined Technocracy in a series of pamphlets including *Technocracy, First, Second, and Third Series* (c. 1921), *Concerning Irascible Strong* (1926), *Technocracy, National Industrial Management, Practical Suggestions for National Reconstruction* (1931), *Coming Events Cast Their Shadows Before* (1932), and *Technocracy Explained by Its Originator* (c. 1933). For other contemporary explications of Technocracy, see Henry Mayers, editor, *The What, Why, Who, When, and How of Technocracy* (1932); Graham Laing, *Towards Technocracy* (1933); Hanson Hathaway, *The Utopians Are Coming* (1934). Regarding Manchester Boddy, see Robert Rosenstone, "Manchester Boddy and the LA *Daily News*," *CHSQ*, 49 (1970), 291–307. The Bancroft Library has the program and speeches for the Utopian Society of America rally in Hollywood Bowl on 23 June 1934, under the title "Utopian Keynote Address."

As background to the Townsend Movement, see Frank Pinner, Paul Jacobs, and Philip Selznick, *Old Age and Political Behavior* (1959); and Jackson Putnam, *Old Age Politics in California: From Richardson to Reagan* (1970). See also Carey McWilliams, "Pension Politics in California," *The Politics of California*, edited by David Farrelly and Ivan Hinderaker (1951), 295–299. Abraham Holtzman's *The Townsend Movement: A Political Study* (1963) is the best survey of the phenomenon. See also J. D. Gaydowski, "The Genesis of the Townsend Plan," *SCQ*, 52 (1970), 365–382. Francis Everett Townsend wrote *Old Age*

Revolving Pensions: A National Proposal (1934) and *New Horizons: An Autobiography* (1943). Sheridan Downey testified to his faith in *Why I Believe in the Townsend Plan* (1936). Richard Milne helped launch the movement with *That Man Townsend* (1935). Contemporary assessments can be found in: Oliver McKee Jr., "The Townsend Plan," *Commonweal*, 23 (7 February 1936), 399–401; Bruce Bliven, "The Midwestern Messiah," *NR*, 86 (6 May 1936), 365; Harry Moore, "Just Folks in Utopia," *NR*, 85 (13 November 1935), 9–11. For an anti-Townsend statement from the period, see Richard Neuberger and Kelley Loe, *An Army of the Aged* (1936).

Chapter Six
The Empire Strikes Back

Regarding the American Plan in San Francisco, see David Warren Ryder, "The American Plan in San Francisco," *Review of Reviews*, 65 (February 1923), 187–190, and "San Francisco's Fight for Industrial Freedom," *Ibid.*, 77 (January 1927), 82–85. See also "The American Plan," *Pacific Industries*, 1 (February 1922), 15–24. Regarding the open shop in Los Angeles, see Helen Ida Flannery, "The Labor Movement in Los Angeles, 1880–1903" (MA thesis, economics, UC Berkeley, 1929); Grace Heilman Stimson, *The Rise of the Labor Movement in Los Angeles* (1905); and Louis Perry and Richard Perry, *A History of the Los Angeles Labor Movement, 1911–1941* (1963). See also Edwin Layton, "The Better America Foundation: A Case Study of Superpatriotics," *PHR*, 30 (May 1961), 137–148.

Between 1942 and 1944 the U.S. Government Printing Office in Washington issued the continuously paged *Violations of Free Speech and Rights of Labor*, assembled by the investigators and staff of the U.S. Senate Subcommittee of the Committee on Education and Labor, better known as the La Follette Committee. The documents and narrative of *Violations of Free Speech and Rights of Labor* form the backbone of evidence for the incidents described in this chapter, especially the Brentwood Plan of 1934, 1308–1328; the Pacific Coast Economic Conference, 4 and 5 February 1936, 726–733; Salinas lettuce packers' strike of 1936, 1330–1384; and the Stockton Cannery Strike of 1937, 1385–1406. Carey McWilliams's *Factories in the Field* is equally relevant to my treatment of each of these events. Regarding the lynching in San Jose, see Brian McGinty, "Shadows in St. James Park," *CHSQ*, 57 (Winter 1978–1979), 290–307. See also Gerald Rose, "The March Inland: The Stockton Cannery Strike of 1937," *SCQ*, 50 (1972), 54–55 67–82; Suzanne Ledeboer, "The Man Who Would Be Hitler: William Dudley Pelley and the Silver Legion," *CHSQ*, 65 (June 1986), 126–137.

The Bancroft Library has a ten-volume run of the *Associated Farmer*, covering the years 1935–1950, together with a collection of pamphlets and other materials issued by the organization. Three items of relevance to this chapter are Ralph Taylor, "California's Embattled Farmers: An Address Before the Commonwealth Club of San Francisco, Friday, 8 June 1934, broadcast over station KPO" (typescript, 1934); Philip Bancroft, "Legislative Activities of the Associated Farmers," a clipping from the July 1937 *Diamond Walnut News*; John S. Watson, "Statement of the Associated Farmers of California to the La Follette Civil Liberties Committee, 29 January 1940" (typescript, 1940). See also the oral memoirs of the pro–Associated Farmers dean of the College of Agriculture, Claude Burton Hutchinson, "The College of Agriculture, University of California, 1922–1952" (bound typescript, Regional Cultural History Project, General Library, UC Berkeley, 1961). Clarke Alexander Chambers has written *California Farm Organizations: An Historical Study of the Grange, the Farm Bureau, and the Associated Farmers, 1929–1941* (1952).

The Correspondence and Papers of Philip Bancroft are in the Bancroft Library. Of direct relevance to this chapter are Bancroft's "The Farmer and the Communists, an Address by

Philip Bancroft, President of the Associated Farmers of Contra Costa County Before the Commonwealth Club of California, Friday 26 April 1935" (typescript, 1935), together with the oral interview of Bancroft by Willa Klug Baum in 1962, on deposit in the Bancroft Library as "Politics, Farming, and the Progressive Party in California."

Regarding events in Imperial County in 1934, the following documents in the Bancroft Library are of relevance: J. L. Leonard, Will J. French, and Simon J. Lubin, "Report to the National Labor Board by Special Commission, 11 February 1934" (typescript, 1940); *Violations of Free Speech and Rights of Labor*, 454–463; Pelham D. Glassford, Special Conciliator, "Recommendations Concerning Labor Conditions in Imperial Valley and Resulting Lawlessness" (typescript, 23 June 1934); Grover C. Johnson, "Letter to General Pelham D. Glassford, 22 June 1934" (typescript, 1934). Regarding the clashes at Pixley and Arvin, see the Fresno *Bee* for Wednesday, 11 October 1933.

In response to the Sacramento conspiracy trials, Mike Quin [Paul William Ryan] issued *The C. S. Case Against Labor* (1935). See also Carey McWilliams's portrait "Lee Gallagher," *Nation*, 141 (16 October 1935), 437–438.

Regarding the LAPD blockade of California, the following accounts prove valuable: State Relief Administration, "Transients in California" (mimeographed typescript, 1936), 245–266; and Carlson, A *Mirror for Californians*, 163–165. See also Bruce Henstell, *Sunshine and Wealth: Los Angeles in the Twenties and Thirties* (1984) for general background. Contemporary accounts include "California No Hobo Utopia. Los Angeles Police Chief Sends Patrolmen to Guard Borders," *Literary Digest*, 121 (15 February 1936), 9; "Golden State Insists on Golden Passports," *Newsweek*, 7 (15 February 1936), 15; Rose Marie Packard, "Los Angeles Border Patrol," *Nation*, 142 (4 March 1936), 295; and "Unwanted Visitors," *Survey*, 72 (April 1936), 25.

Regarding anti-picketing ordinances, see the coverage in *Business Week* for 25 March 1939, 48–49. For background to the Salinas lettuce strike, see William O. Jones, "The Salinas Valley, Its Agricultural Development 1920–1940" (PhD thesis, economics, Stanford, 1947); and Helen Lamb, *Industrial Relations in the Western Lettuce Industry* (1942). Paul Smith's four-part series "It Did Happen in Salinas" appeared in the San Francisco *Chronicle* on 23, 24, 25, 26 September 1936. See also Smith's *Personal File* (1964), 171–179. Regarding the departure of Colonel Sanborn, see Don Chase, "California Fascist Retreats," *Christian Century*, 53 (14 October 1936), 1355–1356.

The response of Eastern liberals to events in California can be traced through R. Whitaker, "Is California Civilized?," *Nation*, 132 (1 April 1931), 347–348, followed by R. Harwood reply "California Is Not Civilized," *Nation*, 132 (22 April 1931), 451; Ella Winter, "California's Little Hitlers," *NR*, 77 (21 December 1933), 188–190; Chester Williams, "Imperial Valley Mob," *NR*, 78 (21 February 1934), 39–41; "More Than Mob Terror," *NR*, 78 (21 February 1934), 148; "Terrorism in California," *NR*, 79 (1 August 1934), 79; Herbert Klein and Carey McWilliams, "Cold Terror in California," *Nation*, 141 (24 July 1935), 97–98. Of special value is the essay "California, There She Stands!" by Lillian Symes in *Harper's* magazine for February 1935, comparing California to Rome in 1922 and Berlin in 1933 on the eve of fascist takeovers. For the observations of a California-based Communist, see *Dorothy Healey Remembers: A Life in the American Communist Party* (1990), 27–79. Regarding the romantic figure of Robert Hale Merriman, see his widow Marion Merriman Wachtel's *American Commander in Spain: Robert Hale Merriman and the Abraham Lincoln Brigade*, with Warren Lerude (1986), together with the review "A Farewell to Arms" by Robin Dellabough in the UC Berkeley Alumni magazine, *California Monthly*, for September 1986. Regarding the effort to deport Harry Bridges, see James Landis, *In the Matter of Harry Bridges* (1939); and Harvey Schwartz, "Harry Bridges and the Scholars: Looking at History's Verdict," *CHSQ*, 59 (1980), 66–79.

Chapter Seven
Ham and Eggs

Robert Burke's *Olson's New Deal for California* (1953) chronicles the coming of the New Deal to California. Regarding prison reform in the Olson era, see Clinton T. Duffy's *Eighty-Eight Men and Two Women*, with Al Hirshberg (1962). Regarding the notion of scrip, see Irving Fisher, "The Stamped Scrip Plan," *NR*, 73 (21 December 1932), 163–164. Winston and Marion Moore's *Out of the Frying Pan* (1939) is a frequently hilarious view of the Ham and Egg frenzy. See also Carey McWilliams, *Southern California: An Island on the Land* (second edition, 1973), 303–308. McWilliams also reported on Ham and Eggs in "Ham and Eggs," *NR*, 100 (25 October 1939), 331–333. For another brilliant report from the field, see John C. Lee and Ralph Shawhan, "California Votes on Utopia," *SEP*, 211 (5 November 1938), 8–9ff. For a spirited contemporary defense of the concept, see Sherman Bainbridge's *Ham and Eggs* (1938).

The Bancroft Library has a file on Sheridan Downey. Downey wrote many pamphlets. Of relevance to this chapter are *The Coming Crisis* (1932), *Onward America* (1933), *Courage, America!* (1933), *Pensions or Penury?*, and *Highways to Prosperity* (1940). See also the brilliant contemporary coverage of Joseph W. Alsop Jr. and Robert Kintner, "Merchandising Miracles: Sheridan Downey and the Pension Business," *Saturday Evening Post*, 212 (16 September 1939), 5–7, 85–90.

Regarding Artie Samish, see Arthur Samish and Bob Thomas, *The Secret Boss of California* (1971) and Lester Velie's series "The Secret Boss of California" in *Collier's* magazine for 13 and 20 August 1949, reprinted in David Farrelly and Ivan Hinderaker, editors, *The Politics of California: A Book of Readings* (1951), 172–197.

Tom Mooney's correspondence and papers are in the Bancroft Library. Reading through them has helped form my impression of this enigmatic man. Of the many books dealing with the Mooney case, Richard Hindman Frost's *The Mooney Case* (1968) is the most judicious; and Curt Gentry's *Frame-Up: The Incredible Case of Tom Mooney and Warren Billings* (1967) is the most colorful and challenging in its thesis that the German Imperial Government was responsible for the Preparedness Day bombing. For legal arguments, see Henry T. Hunt's *The Case of Thomas J. Mooney and Warren K. Billings: Abstract and Analysis of Record Before Governor Young of California* (1929). See also Lillian Symes, "Our American Dreyfus Case: A Challenge to California Justice," *Harper's* magazine, 162 (May 1931), 641–652; and Ernest Jerome Hopkins, *What Happened in the Mooney Case* (1932). For an account of Mooney's brilliant lawyer, see Brad Williams, *Due Process: The Story of Criminal Lawyer George T. Davis and His Thirty-Year Battle Against Capital Punishment* (1961), especially 89–111. As evidence that the Mooney mystique still lingers, see Estolv Ethan Ward's *The Gentle Dynamiter: A Biographer of Tom Mooney* (1983). Some of the details relating to the pardoning of Mooney by Olson have been gleaned from the Los Angeles *Times* for 8 and 9 January 1939, and the San Francisco *Chronicle* for 8 January 1939. Details regarding Olson's collapse that very same day can be found in the same newspapers.

Chapter Eight
Give Me Shelter

Walter Stein's *California and the Dust Bowl Migration* (1973) is the authoritative beginning and constant guide for any inquiry into this topic. A second standard source, with added emphasis on the social and cultural legacy of the Dust Bowl migrants is James

Gregory's *American Exodus: The Dust Bowl Migration and Okie Culture in California* (1989). See also Don Morgan's powerful and revealing *Rising in the West: The True Story of an "Okie" from the Great Depression Through the Reagan Years* (1992). Regarding the Dust Bowl itself, see Michael Parfit, "The Dust Bowl," *Smithsonian*, 20 (June 1989), 44–56, for a concise and dramatic account. To get the feel of the most-traveled migrant route to California, see *Route 66: The Highway and Its People*, photographic essay by Qunita Scott, text by Susan Croce Kelly (1988). For a description of the earlier influx of automobile tourists into California, see "Tin Can Tourists Terrifying California," *Literary Digest*, 85 (16 May 1925), 73–76.

The first impact of Dust Bowl migrants can be gleaned through Duncan Aikman, "California Sunshine," *Nation*, 132 (22 April 1931), 448–450; and J. Hauss, "Unemployed, 1933 Model," *Nation*, 173 (8 November 1933), 541. The State Relief Administration issued a number of revealing reports which survive in bound mimeographed typescript volumes in the Bancroft Library and the State Archives in Sacramento. These reports include "Migratory Labor" (1935), "Unemployment Relief" (1935), "Self-Help Cooperatives" (1935), "Transients in California" (1936). See also Leigh Athearn, *The California State Relief Administration, 1935–1939* (1939). The State Relief Administration also released Herbert McCanlies's "Journal of a Transient" (bound mimeographed typescript, 1936), which deserves wider circulation. Regarding the Relief Administration itself, see George Nickel, "Matter of Communication: Problem in Administration in the California State Relief Administration," *Survey*, 75 (January 1939), 11–12.

Other official reports include James E. Siedel, for the National Child Labor Committee, *Pick for Your Supper* (1939); *The Farm Security Administration of California: A Study of 6,655 Migrant Households in California* (1939); State Chamber of Commerce Migrant Committee, *Migrants: A National Problem and Its Impact on California*, edited by Harrison S. Robinson (1940). See also Ruth Amelia Molander, "A Study of 101 Migrant Families Receiving Assistance Under the Regulations of the California Aid-to-Needy Children Law in Kern County in June 1940" (MA thesis, social welfare, UC Berkeley, 1943).

The Santa Barbara experience with the unemployed during this period is chronicled by Ronald Nye in "The Challenge to Philanthropy: Unemployment Relief in Santa Barbara, 1930–1932," *CHSQ*, 56 (Winter 1977–78), 310–327. For the Riverside experience, see Madeleine Robinson, *The Pulpit Under the Palm: The Story of the Pancake Mission and Its Ministry and Service to the Unemployed During the Dark Days of the Depression* (1944).

Four reformers—Simon Julius Lubin, Paul Taylor, Irving William Wood, and Thomas Collins—were most active in the effort to achieve housing for the migrants. The correspondence and papers of Simon Julius Lubin are in the Bancroft Library. Of special relevance is Lubin's paper presented to the Commonwealth Club of California in San Francisco on 23 March 1934, broadcast over station KPO, "Can the Radicals Capture the Farms of California?" (mimeographed typescript, 1934). Mrs. Lubin gave a tape-recorded interview on 11 March 1954 regarding her husband's activities. See her "Reminiscences" (Regional Cultural History Project, General Library, UC Berkeley, 1954).

The extensive papers of Paul Schuster Taylor are in the Bancroft Library. There is also a three-volume oral history prepared by Suzanne Riess and Malca Chall for the Bancroft Library Oral History Project under the title "Paul Schuster Taylor, California Social Scientist," introduction by Laurence Hewes (bound typescript, 3 vols., 1973). In 1983 Peregrine Smith gathered many of Taylor's articles from this period into *On the Ground in the Thirties*. Taylor also produced a number of pamphlet reprints from articles he wrote for the *Monthly Labor Review* and *Rural Sociology* during the decade. Of relevance to this chapter are *Drought Refugee and Labor Migration to California, June-December 1935* (1936) *Historical Background of California Farm Labor* (1936) *Patterns of Agricultural Labor Migration Within California*, with Edward Rowell (1938) and *Perspective on Hous-*

ing *Migratory Agricultural Laborers* (1951). Regarding Taylor's relationship to UC Berkeley, see Irving Stone, editor, *There Was Light, Autobiography of a University: Berkeley 1868–1968* (1970), 33–42.

The Irving William Wood Correspondence and Papers, 1934–1937, are in the Bancroft Library. Of direct relevance to this chapter are J. L. Leonard, Will J. French, and Simon J. Lubin, "Report to the National Labor Board by Special Commission" (mimeographed typescript, 11 February 1934); and Irving Wood, "Instructions to Camp Managers" (typescript, 1 August 1935). Also in the Woods Papers are the weekly reports submitted by Thomas Collins between 28 November 1935 and 4 July 1936. See also Thomas Collins's powerful address of 12 October 1935 to the California Conference on Housing for Rural Workers in conjunction with the dedication of the Marysville Migrants Camp of the Resettlement Administration, "The Human Side in the Operation of a Migrants' Camp" (typescript, 12 October 1935), the Woods Papers.

Also of relevance to the camps are S. E. Wood, "Work Camps or Nothing, California's Unattached Resident Men," *Survey*, 75 (April 1939), 99–101; Lillian Creisler, "Little Oklahoma: A Study of the Social and Economic Adjustments of Refugees in the Beard Tract, Modesto, Stanislas County" (MA thesis, economics, UC Berkeley, 1940); and Sylvan Jacob Ginsburgh, "The Migrant Camp Program of the FSA in California: A Critical Examination of Operations at the Yuba City and Thornton Camps" (MA thesis, economics, UC Berkeley, 1943). See also Grace Naismith, "Birth Control Nurse: Women Among Migrant Agricultural Workers in the West Have Found a Friend in Mildred Delp," *Survey Graphic*, 32 (January 1943), 260–261ff.

The reintensification of the migrant problem in the late 1930s is covered in "Migrant Households in California, 1938," *Monthly Labor Review*, 49 (September 1939), 622–623; "Flee Dust Bowl for California. 30,000 Immigrants Provide Cheap Farm Labor but Also Add to the Relief Burden," *Business Week* (3 July 1937), 36; "Dustbowlers Worry California: Fear 200,000 Impoverished Newcomers Will Vote for $30 Every Thursday," *Business Week* (24 September 1938), 33–34; Ivan Dmitri, "No Jobs in California," *SEP*, 211 (12 November 1938), 18–19, 40, 44; "Migratory Labor: A Social Problem: Underemployed, Underfed, They Are a National Problem Most Crucial in California," *Fortune*, 19 (April 1939), 90–100ff. As background to the investigations of the Tolan Committee, see "Okies, a National Problem; California Prepares to Ask Federal Government to Assume Responsibility for the Growing Flood of Migrants," *Business Week* (10 February 1940), 16–17; "Plight of the Okies Heading Towards Congress for Solution," *Newsweek*, 15 (25 March 1940), 15–16; and "Tory Relief in California," *NR*, 102 (17 June 1940), 812–813. See also the pamphlet in the Bancroft Library, George Gleason, *The Fifth Migration* (1940).

Chapter Nine
Documenting the Crisis

William Stott's *Documentary Expression and Thirties America* (1973) has inspired and guided this chapter. See also *Documenting America, 1935–1943*, edited by Carl Fleischhauer and Beverly Brannan, essays by Lawrence Levin and Alan Trachtenberg (1988), especially the treatment of Dorothea Lange, 114–127, 160–173. Also of importance is Edward Steichen, editor, *The Bitter Years, 1935–1941: Rural America as Seen by the Photographers of the Farm Security Administration* (1962). For the work of other California photographers, see Paul Dorsey, photographer, "Waifs of the Winds," *Westways*, 31 (June 1939), 16–17, and "Bindle Stiffs," *Westways*, 31 (October 1939), 8–9; and John Bloom, "Aspects of the Documentary: Ken Light's Photographs of Migrant Workers in California," *CHSQ*, 65 (December 1986), 263–273.

Regarding Dorothea Lange, see the introductory essay by George Elliott to *Dorothea Lange*, a catalog issued by the Museum of Modern Art in New York (1966), and Milton Meltzer, *Dorothea Lange: A Photographer's Life* (1978). Lange tells her own story in a 1960 interview conducted by Suzanne Riess: "The Making of a Documentary Photographer" (bound typescript, Regional Oral History Office, UC Berkeley, 1968). Lange tells the story of photographing *Migrant Mother* in "The Assignment I'll Never Forget," *Popular Photography*, 46 (February 1960), 42ff. See also Annegret Ogden's essay, "Dorothea Lange on Documentary Photography v. Photojournalism," *The Californians*, 3 (1985), 7–9. Other Lange retrospectives include *Dorothea Lange Looks at the American Country Woman*, text by Dorothea Lange, commentary by Beaumont Newhall (1967); and the Friends of the Bancroft Library publication, *Nine Classic California Photographers*, edited and introduced by William Hively, with photographs selected by Lawrence Dinnean (1980). For background to Lange's first husband, together with some insights into their marriage, see my introduction to *Rim-Rock and Sage: The Collected Poems of Maynard Dixon* (1977). Regarding the relationship of Lange and Paul Taylor, see Joyce Eli, "Dorothea Lange and Paul Taylor: Chroniclers and Conscience of a Decade," *The Californians*, 3 (1985), 10–22. In 1939 Lange and Taylor issued their joint classic, *An American Exodus: A Record of Human Erosion*, which the Oakland Museum and Yale University Press reissued in 1969.

John Steinbeck's *Their Blood Is Strong* was issued by the Simon J. Lubin Society in 1938, along with Edith Lowry's *Migrants of the Crops: They Starve That We May Eat*. Steinbeck's *In Dubious Battle* appeared in 1936, *The Grapes of Wrath* in 1939. Critical commentary on the life and work of John Steinbeck is an industry in and of itself. Any and all obligation to any and all Steinbeck critics, whoever they may be, is fully acknowledged. Of special value to this chapter have been Warren French, *John Steinbeck* (1961); Agnes McNeill Donohue, *A Casebook on The Grapes of Wrath* (1968; *Letters to Elizabeth: A Selection of Letters from John Steinbeck to Elizabeth Otis*, edited by Florian Shasky and Susan Riggs, with an introduction by Carlton Sheffield (1978); Brian St. Pierre, *John Steinbeck: The California Years* (1983); Jackson J. Benson's comprehensive biography, *The True Adventures of John Steinbeck, Writer* (1984); *Working Days: The Journals of the Grapes of Wrath (1938–1941)*, edited by Robert DeMott (1989). Clifton Fadiman's review of *The Grapes of Wrath* appeared in the "Books" column in *The New Yorker*, 15 (15 April 1939), 81–82. Regarding photographer Horace Bristol, see David Robert's "Travels with Steinbeck," *American Photographer*, 22 (March 1989), 44–51. See also Walter Rundell, "Steinbeck's Image of the West," *The American West*, 1 (Spring 1964), 4–17, 1–79. The hostile reaction to *The Grapes of Wrath* can be traced in F. J. Taylor, "California's Grapes of Wrath, Joad Family Not Typical," *Forum*, 102 (November 1939), 232–238; Philip Bancroft, "Does *Grapes of Wrath* Present a Fair Picture of California Farm-Labor Conditions?" (mimeographed typescript, 1940), Philip Bancroft Papers; and Rexford Guy Tugwell, Philip Bancroft, Carey McWilliams, and Hugh Bennett, "What Should America Do for the Joads?," *Town Meeting, Bulletin of America's Town Meeting of the Air*, 5 (11 March 1940), 3–30. In 1940 Paul Taylor illustrated his *Adrift on the Land* with stills from the John Ford film version of *The Grapes of Wrath*.

David Selvin lists and annotates the many books by Carey McWilliams in "Carey McWilliams: Reformer as Historian," *CHSQ*, 53 (1974), 173–176. Peregrine Smith reissued *Factories in the Field* in 1971. Regarding the La Follette Committee, see Jerold Auerbach's *Labor and Liberty: The La Follette Committee and the New Deal* (1966). The official designation of the nine-part continuously paged report of the LaFollette Committee issued by the U.S. Government Printing Office in Washington between 1942 and 1944 is: US Congress, Senate, Committee on Education and Labor, *Violations of Free Speech and Rights of Labor. Report of the Committee on Education and Labor, Pursuant to S. Res. 266 (74th Congress)*. The official designation of the report and hearings issued in ten parts (five volumes) in 1941 by the Tolan Committee is: *Interstate Migration, Hearings Before the Select Committee to Investigate the Interstate Migration of Destitute Citizens. House of Representatives. Seventy-Sixth Congress. Third Session. Pursuant to H. Res. 63 and H.Res. 491.*

Chapter Ten
Valley of Decision

One begins the study of the Hetch Hetchy with two partisan but fact-laden histories: Ray Taylor, *Hetch Hetchy: The Story of San Francisco's Struggle to Provide a Water Supply for Her Future Needs* (1926); and Michael O'Shaughnessy's formidable memoir, *Hetch Hetchy: Its Origins and History* (1934). Also of great value are Warren Hanson, *San Francisco Water & Power: A History of the Municipal Water Department and Hetch Hetchy System* (1985). See also Chiori Santiago, "Going with the Flow" *Image*, the magazine of the *Sunday San Francisco Examiner and Chronicle*, 1 February 1987, 20–25.

Marsden Manson made a collection of government documents, reports, transcriptions of hearings, and letters relating to the early stages of the Hetch Hetchy project. They are on deposit at the Bancroft Library as *Hearings Held Before the Committee on Public Lands of the Congress of the United States and Related Reports, December 1908 to March 1909.* The Bancroft also has a bound volume of Hetch Hetchy pamphlets. Of special interest are two issued by the San Francisco Board of Supervisors, *Reports on the Water Supply of San Francisco* (1908) and *Proceedings Before the Secretary of the Interior in re Use of Hetch Hetchy Reservoir Site in the Yosemite National Park* (1910). For an early attack on the proposal, see Russell Dunn, *Review of City Engineer Marsden Manson's Plans and Estimates* (1908). John Ripley Freeman's monumental report appeared as *On the Proposed Use of a Portion of the Hetch Hetchy, Eleanor, and Cherry Valleys . . . For the Water Supply of San Francisco and Neighboring Cities* (1912).

Holway Jones, an accomplished scholar-librarian, has masterfully chronicled the resistance to the Hetch Hetchy project in his exhaustively researched and annotated *John Muir and the Sierra Club: The Battle for Yosemite* (1965). See also Elmo Richardson, "The Struggle for the Valley: California's Hetch Hetchy Controversy, 1905–1913," *CHSQ*, 38 (1959), 249–258; and Brian P. Massey, "John Muir v. the Hetch Hetchy 'Temple Destroyers': His Final Round," *The Californians*, 3 (1985), 38–41. See also Muir's *Reply to a Letter Received from Hon. James R. Garfield* (1909), *Hetch Hetchy: The Tuolumne Yosemite* (1909), and *Let Everyone Help to Save the Famous Hetch Hetchy Valley* (1909). In determining attitudes and points of view in the Hetch Hetchy debate, the following pamphlets are crucial: Edmund Whitman, *San Francisco and the Hetch Hetchy Reservoir, Brief for the Appalachian Mountain Club* (1909); Warren Olney, *A Letter to the Members of the Sierra Club* (1909); William Edward Colby, *A Reply to Mr. Warren Olney's Statement* (1909); Edward Parsons, *A Discussion of the Hetch Hetchy Question* (1910); Marsden Manson, *A Statement of San Francisco's Side of the Hetch Hetchy Reservoir Matter* (1910); National Committee for the Preservation of the Yosemite National Park, *The Hetch Hetchy Grab: Who Opposes It and Why* (1912); Henry M. McDonald, *Argument Against the Selection of Hetch Hetchy* (1913); and Society for the Preservation of National Parks, *More Light on the Destructive Hetch Hetchy Scheme* (1913).

Critical testimony before Congress is available in two congressional documents: *Hetch Hetchy Reservoir Site, Hearing Before the Committee on Public Lands, United States Senate, on the Joint Resolution S.R. 123* (1909); and *Hetch Hetchy Grant to San Francisco . . . Report to Accompany H.R. 7207* (1913). Of great value as well is a pamphlet issued by San Francisco, *Daily Commercial News: The Raker Bill and the Hetch Hetchy Contro-*

versy, a Synopsis and Full Text of the Act, Together with Indexes, Sub-Headings, and Negotiations (1920). Michael O'Shaughnessy reported frequently on the Hetch Hetchy project during its nearly two decades of construction. See especially his *The Hetch Hetchy Water Supply of San Francisco* (1916), *The Hetch Hetchy Water and Power Project* (1921), and *Hetch Hetchy Project* (1931). See also San Francisco Public Utilities Commission, *Hetch Hetchy Project* (1932) and *Celebration of the First Delivery of Hetch Hetchy Water to San Francisco* (1934) for excellent descriptions of the completed system. For much colorful detail, see Ted Wurm, *Hetch Hetchy and Its Dam Railroad* (1973), which despite its title is actually the best overall history of the project in all its phases, along with Hanson's *San Francisco Water & Power*. The Hetch Hetchy project inspired a novel as well, Joseph Dunn's *The Water-Bearers* (1934).

Chapter Eleven
Angels, Dams, and Dynamos

Joseph E. Stevens wrote the first draft of his *Hoover Dam: An American Adventure* (1988) as his senior thesis at Princeton. The book commands the subject. Two publications by the Bureau of Reclamation of the Department of the Interior—*The Story of Hoover Dam* (1976) and *Construction of Hoover Dam* (1989)—are replete with fascinating statistics. The classic histories of water in California—among them, Sidney Twichell Harding, *Water in California* (1960); Irwin Cooper, *Aqueduct Empire* (2 vols., 1968); and Remi Nadeau, *The Water Seekers* (revised edition, 1974)—each take up in some detail the background and construction of the Hoover Dam and the Metropolitan Aqueduct. In his *The First Thirty Years of Imperial County* (1931), Otis Burgess Tout tells the story of Hoover Dam and the All-American Canal from a highly colorful local angle. See also Allan Cullen, *Rivers in Harness: The Story of Dams* (1962).

The most comprehensive treatment of the political and planning background of the Boulder Canyon project can be found in three classics of California history: Beverly Moeller's *Phil Swing and Boulder Dam* (1971) and Norris Hundley Jr.'s *Dividing the Waters* (1966) and *Water and the West: The Colorado River Compact and the Politics of Water in the American West* (1975). See also Hundley's "The Politics of Reclamation: California, the Federal Government, and the Origins of the Boulder Canyon Act—A Second Look," *CHSQ*, 52 (1973), 292–325.

Elwood Mead advanced his arguments in many publications. Those most relevant to Southern California include *Irrigation Investigations in California* (1901), *The All-American Canal: Report of the All-American Canal Board* (1919), and "Boulder Dam Today, Economic Factors," which first appeared in the *Engineering News-Record* for 6 February 1930. *The Annals of the American Academy of Political Sciences* for January 1928, volume 135, include many arguments on behalf of the Boulder Canyon project which have a strong Southern California tilt. Of special reference to this chapter are the arguments of Dr. E. F. Scattergood, chief electrical engineer and general manager of the Bureau of Power and Light of the City of Los Angeles, 115–121. See also the compelling arguments of Arthur Powell Davis in "Development of the Colorado River, the Justification of Boulder Dam," *Atlantic Monthly*, 143 (February 1929), 254–264.

The classic contemporary description of the construction of the Boulder/Hoover Dam is provided by Frank Waters in *The Colorado* (1946). Regarding the emergence of two California-based industrial giants from the Six Companies, see Mark S. Foster, *Henry J. Kaiser: Builder in the Modern American West* (1982); Susanne Gaskins and Warren Beck, "Henry J. Kaiser—Entrepreneur of the American West," *Journal of the West*, 25 (January 1986), 64–72; Albert Heiner, *Henry J. Kaiser, American Empire Builder: An Insider's View*

(1989); and Robert Ingram, A *Builder and His Family, 1898–1948* (1961) and *The Bechtel Story: Seventy Years of Accomplishment in Engineering and Construction* (1968). Contemporary accounts of the construction of Boulder/Hoover Dam which are especially rich in social and cultural interpretations include Duncan Aikman, "New Pioneers in Old West's Deserts," *New York Times Magazine* (26 October 1930), 7, 18, "A Wild West Town That Is Born Tame," *New York Times Magazine* (26 July 1931), 6–7, 15, "Amid Turmoil Boulder Dam Rises," *New York Times Magazine* (23 July 1933), 8–9, 13; F. L. Bird, "Who Will Benefit by Boulder Dam?," *New Republic*, 63 (30 July 1930), 310–313; Theodore White, "Building the Big Dam," *Harper's* magazine, 171 (June 1935), 113–120; Leo Martin, "A Gigantic Battle to Subdue a River," *New York Times Magazine* (31 July 1932), 4; "The Dam," *Fortune*, 8 (September 1933), 74–88; Bruce Bliven, "The American Dnieperstroy," *New Republic*, 72 (11 December 1935), 125–127; "Remaking the World," *Collier's*, 95 (16 March 1935), 66; and J. B. Priestly, "Arizona Desert: Reflections of a Winter Visitor," *Harper's* magazine, 173 (March 1937), 358–367. For a Southern California–based assessment, see Charles Kerlee's "Turning Back the Mighty Colorado," *Westways*, 26 (June 1934), 24–25. Regarding the effort of the Roosevelt administration to capture not just the construction of the dam but its interpretation, see Richard Lowitt's *The New Deal and the West* (1984). Regarding the question of social control at the dam and in Boulder City, see Edmund Wilson, "Hoover Dam," *New Republic*, 68 (2 September 1931), 66–69; and Victor Castle, "Well, I Quit My Job at the Dam," *Nation*, 133 (26 August 1931), 207–208. See also Dennis McBride, *In the Beginning: A History of Boulder City, Nevada* (1981). Regarding discrimination on the job site, see Roosevelt Fitzgerald, "Blacks and the Boulder Dam Project," *Nevada Historical Society Quarterly*, 24 (Fall 1981), 255–260.

Gordon Kaufmann presented his designs for the dam in "The Architecture of Boulder Dam," *Architectural Concrete*, 2 (1936), 2–5. The best—and virtually exclusive!—discussion of Kaufmann as designer is provided by Richard Guy Wilson in "Massive Deco Monument," *Architecture* (December 1983), 45–47, and "Machine Age Iconography in the American West: The Design of Hoover Dam," *PHR*, 54 (November 1985), 463–493.

In November 1930 Frank E. Weymouth, chief engineer of the Metropolitan Water District of Southern California, issued his *Summary of Preliminary Surveys, Designs, and Estimates for the Metropolitan Water District Aqueduct and Terminal Storage Projects*, an elegant instance of engineering planning as implied social vision. Weymouth himself was profiled in *Western Construction News and Highways Builder*, 8 (August 1933), 330. *Los Angeles Saturday Night* published two LA-oriented views of the Aqueduct in progress: Robert Speers, "Carrying on Ages-Old Fight with Desert: Army of 8,000 Men Building Colorado River Aqueduct," 16 (19 October 1935), 3; and Lynn D. Smith, "392 Miles for a Drink to Make Southland Blossom Like the Rose," 44 (13 February 1937), 8. The MWD issued *The Colorado Aqueduct* (1939), *The Great Aqueduct: The Story of the Planning and Building of the Colorado River Aqueduct* (1941), and *Colorado River Aqueduct* (1950). Regarding the MWD itself, see Jerome Milliman, "The History, Organization, and Economic Problems of the Metropolitan Water District of Southern California" (PhD dissertation, history, University of Southern California, 1956).

Chapter Twelve
Completing California

To commemorate the Bicentennial, the American Public Works Association sponsored the monumental *History of Public Works in the United States, 1776–1976*, edited by Ellis Armstrong (1976). More locally, the History and Heritage Committee of the San Francisco section of the American Society of Civil Engineers issued *Historic Civil Engineering Land-*

marks of San Francisco and Northern California, edited by William Myers (1977). The official report of the Federal Emergency Administration of the U.S. Public Works Administration, *America Builds: The Record of the PWA* (1939) is invaluable. The same is true for the official report of the Works Progress Administration, *Progress of the Works Progress Program, 1937–1942* (1943), and the multi-volume *Final Report on the WPA Program, 1935–1943* (1946).

John Salmond, *The Civilian Conservation Corps, 1933–1942: A New Deal Case Study* (1967) and Phoebe Cutler, *The Public Landscape of the New Deal* (1985) are delightful studies of the CCC and the creation of public places in the 1930s by the CCC, the PWA, the WPA, and other federal agencies. Regarding the creation of Stockton as a deep-water port, see Nicholas Hardeman, *Harbor of the Heartlands: A History of the Inland Seaport of Stockton, California, from the Gold Rush to 1985* (1986), a model of regional history.

The effect of the Southern California earthquake of 10 March 1933 can be seen in two photo-histories: *When Destruction Walked Abroad* (1933) and Allen Cooke, *Twenty-Four Southern California Earthquake Pictures, Including Map of Stricken Area and Seismograph Records* (1933). See also the relevant chapter in Walter Hodgin Case, editor-in-chief, *Long Beach Blue Book, Narrative and Biographical* (1942). For a discussion of the architecture of the rebuilding effort, see David Gebhard and Harriette von Breton, *Los Angeles in the Thirties, 1931–1941* (1975).

Regarding efforts in the nineteenth century to deal with the flooding of the Sacramento River, see Robert Kelley, *Battling the Inland Sea: American Political Culture, Public Policy, and the Sacramento Valley, 1850–1986* (1989). Arthur De Wint Foote made his great appeal in "The Redemption of the Great Valley of California," which appeared in the *Transactions of the American Society of Civil Engineers* issued in September 1909. The Bancroft also maintains a scrapbook of newspaper clippings on flood control and the reclamation of land in the Sacramento Valley assembled by Foote. The Bancroft also maintains a biography and reference file on Robert Bradford Marshall, together with a collection of pamphlets and other materials dealing with the Marshall Plan for a water supply in the Sacramento and San Joaquin valleys and the Central Valley Project. See also Marshall's pioneering *Irrigation of Twelve Million Acres in the Valley of California*, issued by the California State Irrigation Association in 1919. Of further interest is the pamphlet by Robert Hargrove, *The Storage of Flood Waters, an Argument in Support of a Resolution Passed by the Legislature of the State of California Requesting the Federal Government to Construct a Flood Water Canal From the San Joaquin River* (c. 1912). The moral and religious dimension behind such proposals is sketched forth in Edmund de Schweinitz Brunner and Mary Brunner, *Irrigation and Religion: A Study of Religious and Social Conditions in Two California Counties* (c. 1922). Also of interest are two novels: Geraldine Bonner, *Taken at the Flood* (1927) and Ruth Comfort Mitchell, *Water* (1931).

The Central Valley Project, compiled by workers of the Writers' Program of the Work Project Administration in Northern California, sponsored by the California State Department of Education (1942), is a triumphant example of WPA-sponsored regional research. See also the lively, anecdotal Robert William De Roos, *The Thirsty Land, The Story of the Central Valley Project* (1948); and Mary Montgomery and Marion Clawson, *History of Legislation and Policy Formation of the Central Valley Project* (1979), an Arno Press reprint of a 1946 typewritten report. Further studies of relevance to this chapter include Arthur Angel, "Political and Administrative Aspects of the Central Valley Project of California" (PhD thesis, political science, UCLA, 1944); Richard Garrod, "The Central Valley Project: A Problem in Regional Planning" (MA thesis, history, UC Berkeley, 1952); and the authoritative Charles Eugene Coate, "Water, Power, and Politics in the Central Valley Project, 1933–1937" (PhD thesis, history, UC Berkeley, 1969). Regarding the construction of Shasta Dam, see Viola May on behalf of Pacific Constructors, Inc., *Shasta Dam and Its*

Builders (1945) and the article by Magner White in the *Saturday Evening Post* for 27 April 1940.

The Bancroft files of the *California Farmer*, the *Rural Observer*, and *The Pacific Rural Press* for the 1930s contain many discussions of the Central Valley Project and the question of acreage limitation. Sheridan Downey argued against acreage limitations in *They Would Rule the Valley* (1947). Paul Taylor defended acreage limitations in, among other publications, "Central Valley Project: Water and Land," *Western Political Quarterly*, 2 (1949), 228–253, and "Excess Land Law: Pressure Versus Principle," *California Law Review*, 47 (August 1959), 499–541. See also the other essays gathered in Taylor's *Essays on Land, Water, and the Law in California*, with an introduction by the author and a foreword by Paul W. Gates (1979). See also *California Water: A Study in Resource Management*, edited by David Seckler (1971) and the ever-present, encyclopedic Wallace Smith, *Garden in the Sun: A History of the San Joaquin Valley from 1772 to 1939* (1939). For a brief description of the Central Valley Project and affiliated systems, see the pamphlet issued by the Bureau of Reclamation Projects of the Department of the Interior, *California* (1978). Regarding the decline of construction projects in the private sector during this period, see Charles M. Coleman, *PG&E of California: The Centennial Story of Pacific Gas and Electric Company, 1852–1952* (1952) and William A. Myers, *Iron Men and Copper Wires: A Centennial History of the Southern California Edison Company* (1986).

Regarding the overall story of floods in the Los Angeles area, see William Richard Bigger, "Flood Control in Metropolitan Los Angeles" (PhD thesis, political science, UCLA, 1954). See also "Floods in Southern California," *Science*, 87 (25 March 1938), 273. In 1939 the Army Corps of Engineers, under the direction of Lt. Col. Edwin Kelton, the district engineer, issued *Los Angeles Drainage Area Flood Control*. For the story of the Corps of Engineers, with special reference to the Los Angeles River, see Anthony Turhollow, *A History of the Los Angeles District, U.S. Army Corps of Engineers, 1898–1965* (1975), especially 146–170. For a contemporary assessment, see Roger Jessup, "Southern California Flood Control: Why It Adds Up to $501,000,000," *California Magazine of the Pacific*, 29 (November 1939), 12–13ff. Regarding the Arroyo Seco Parkway, see the authoritative H. Marshall Goodwin Jr., "The Arroyo Seco: From Dry Gulch to Freeway," *SCQ*, 47 (March 1965), 73–102. The ambitious dedication program *Arroyo Seco Parkway Dedication, Monday, December 30, 1940*, on file in the Bancroft Library, contains many articles and valuable illustrations. See also Automobile Club of Southern California, *Arroyo Seco Parkway* (1940) and the photo-essay "Pasadena Straight Ahead," *Westways*, 33 (February 1941), 6–7. Fifty years later, reporter James Timmermann filed the lively and informative "Fifty Years on the 110" in the Sunday [Pasadena] *Star-News* for 16 December 1990. Regarding the saga of the Caldecott Tunnel, see Albert P. Heiner, *Henry J. Kaiser, American Empire Builder: An Insider's View* (1989), 64–66.

Anita Ventura Mozley has compiled *The Bridge Builders: Photographs and Documents of the Raising of the San Francisco–Oakland Bay Bridge, 1934–1936*, photographs by Peter Stackpole (1987). The Bancroft Library has a five-box collection of materials relating to the San Francisco–Oakland Bay Bridge. Also in the Bancroft is a ten-volume scrapbook of newspaper clippings dealing with the Bridge, compiled by William Finley. Congressional hearings on the proposed Bridge can be found in: US Congress, Senate, Committee on Commerce, *Bridge Across the Bay of San Francisco. Hearings Before the Committee on Commerce, United States Senate, Seventieth Congress, First Session, on S. 1762, 29–31 March 1928* (1928). The "Song of the Oakland Bridge" by Charles Jackey and John Phoenix first appeared in the San Francisco *Herald* on 4 May 1856 and was reprinted by the Grabhorn Press in 1938. Another interesting call for a bridge across San Francisco Bay, the pamphlet *Economic Necessity Demands That San Francisco Bay Waterways Be Bridged*, was issued by the American Toll Bridge Company in 1925. During the construction of the Bridge, the California Department of Public Works issued five *Progress Reports*. Of importance as well are the thirteen articles appearing in the *Engineering News-Record* between March 1934 and April 1937 by chief engineer Charles Purcell, bridge engineer Charles E. Andrew, and engineer of design Glenn Woodruff, later republished as the pamphlet *Designing and Building the San Francisco–Oakland Bay Bridge* (1937). For a portrait of Purcell, see *Purcell Pontifex, a Tribute*, privately printed by his friends in 1937, on deposit in the Bancroft. See also California Department of Public Works, *San Francisco–Oakland Bay Bridge, Plans and Diagrams* (1932–1935). *The Oakland Tribune Yearbook* for 1933 contains a number of excellent articles on the Bridge. See also another Oakland *Tribune* publication, A *Study of the San Francisco–Oakland Bay Bridge* (1934). The San Francisco *News* ran a series of ambitious articles between 27 August and 15 September 1934 under the running title "When the Bay Bridge Was a Joke." Guides from the period include Bay Bridges Educational Bureau, *Facts About the San Francisco–Oakland Bay Bridge* (c. 1935); Ernest Cromwell Mensch, *The San Francisco–Oakland Bay Bridge: A Technical Description in Ordinary Language* (c. 1936); and John Plummer, *The World's Two Greatest Bridges* (1936). In conjunction with the American Bridge Company and the Columbia Steel Company, the United States Steel Corporation issued *The San Francisco–Oakland Bay Bridge* (1936). The Associated Oil Company issued *Spinning the Cables* (c. 1935). Of special importance is Joint Budget Committee of the California State Legislature, A. Alan Post, Secretary and Legislative Auditor, *Financial History of the San Francisco–Oakland Bay Bridge* (1953). Regarding the dedication of the Bridge, see the *Official Program* on deposit at the Bancroft. Regarding the all-important role of Hoover, see the Hoover Institution pamphlet by Robert Hessen, *Herbert Hoover and the Bay Bridge: A Commemorative Essay* (1986). For an interesting contemporary perspective from Southern California, see Phil Townsend Hanna's "Will the Bay Bridges End San Francisco's Isolation?," *Westways*, 27 (September 1935), 18–19.

The Bancroft Library has a pamphlet file of five boxes of materials relating to the design and construction of the Golden Gate Bridge. In addition to commanding the subject, John Van Der Zee's *The Gate: The True Story of the Design and Construction of the Golden Gate Bridge* (1986) has at long last given proper credit to Charles Ellis. My whole understanding of the Golden Gate Bridge has been structured by Van Der Zee's elegant study. Also of value: Allen Brown, *Golden Gate: Biography of a Bridge* (1965); Stephen Cassady, *Spanning the Gate* (1979); and Richard Dillon, *High Steel: Building the Bridges Across San Francisco Bay*, photographs edited by Don DeNevi and Thomas Moulin (1979). Reports from the period which proved of value include Joseph Strauss, *Bridging the Golden Gate* (1921); Golden Gate Bridge and Highway District, *Report of the Chief Engineer with Architectural Studies* (2 vols., 27 August 1930) and *Report of the Chief Engineer to the Board of Directors of the Golden Gate Bridge and Highway District* (September 1937). See also Joseph Strauss, *Golden Gate Bridge Dedication, Speech Delivered at Banquet, Fairmont Hotel, 25 February 1933* (1933) and *Bridging the Golden Gate, a History and Principal Characteristics, Progress of Construction* (third edition, 1934). Contemporary guides and histories include Ernest Cromwell Mensch, *The Golden Gate Bridge: A Technical Description in Ordinary Language* (1935); Bay Bridges Educational Bureau, *The Story of the Golden Gate Bridge* (c. 1936); and John W. Plummer, *The World's Two Greatest Bridges* (c. 1936). Blyth and Company, Inc., of San Francisco outlined finances in *Golden Gate Bridge and Highway District, California* (c. 1935). The Bethlehem Steel Company issued *The Golden Gate Bridge* (c. 1937). The Bancroft has the *Official Souvenir Program, Golden Gate Bridge Fiesta*, describing the dedication ceremonies that ran from 27 May to 2 June 1937. See also *Gold Book, Official Guide and Directory, Golden Gate Bridge Fiesta*, edited by Sam Cowan (1937). Regarding Maynard Dixon, see Wesley Burnside, *Maynard Dixon: Artist of the West* (1974). For the emotional and psychological significance of the

Golden Gate Bridge at the time of its dedication, see poem *The Mending of a Continent* by Robin Lampson, issued as a pamphlet by the Archetype Press of Berkeley in 1937. For fiction dealing with the construction of the bridge, see Marjorie Roberts, *Webs in the Sky* (1940). See also Evelyn Morris Radford, *The Bridge and the Building: The Art of Government and the Government of Art* (revised edition 1974), which puts the Bridge in its Marin County context.

Chapter Thirteen
Atlantis on the Pacific

For the general background of the relationship between San Francisco and the Asia/Pacific Basin in the mid-nineteenth century, see the relevant sections in Peter Booth Wiley, with Korogi Ichiro, *Yankees in the Land of the Gods: Commodore Perry and the Opening of Japan* (1990). For the efforts of San Francisco to settle upon an architectural image and consistent plan of urban design, see Paolo Polledri, editor, *Visionary San Francisco* (1990), especially two important essays: Gray Brechin, "San Francisco: The City Beautiful," 40–61; and Daniel Gregory, "A Vivacious Landscape: Urban Visions Between the Wars," 78–103. Important studies of San Francisco architecture and city planning include Sally Woodbridge, *Building with Nature* (1974); Richard Longstreth, *On the Edge of the World: Four Architects in San Francisco at the Turn of the Century* (1983); and Michael Corbett, Charles Hall Page, and others, *Splendid Survivors: San Francisco's Downtown Architectural Heritage* (1979). See also David Gebhard, Robert Winter, and Eric Sandweiss, *The Guide to Architecture in San Francisco and Northern California* (second edition, 1985). Regarding the development and planning of San Francisco in the early twentieth century, see Judd Kahn, *Imperial San Francisco: Politics and Planning in an American City, 1879–1906* (1979); and William Issel and Robert Cherny, *San Francisco, 1865–1932: Power, Politics, and Urban Development* (1985). Milton Pflueger wrote a memoir of his brother, *Time and Tim Remembered* (1985). Pflueger's obituary appeared in the San Francisco *Chronicle* on 22 November 1946. *The Sophisticate*, the magazine of the Art Deco Society of California, contains many fine articles relating to the Art Deco ethos of the Bay Area in this period.

The Bancroft Library has an extensive collection of pamplets and other materials relating to the Golden Gate International Exposition of 1939. *Treasure Island: San Francisco's Exposition Years* (1973) by Richard Reinhardt is an encompassing and bemused history and memoir of the fair. See also Jack James and Earle Weller, *Treasure Island "The Magic City" 1939–1940: The Story of the Golden Gate International Exposition* (1941). Patricia Carpenter and Paul Totah have assembled an excellent collection of first-person reminiscences, *The San Francisco Fair, Treasure Island 1939–1940* (1989). Issued in 1939 and updated in 1940, the *Official Guide Book* is detailed and invaluable. See also Alexander Gross, editor, *Famous Guide to San Francisco and the World's Fair* (1939). Interpretive guides of importance to this chapter are Juliet James, *The Meaning of the Courts of the Golden Gate International Exposition* (1939); Stanley Hunter, *Temple of Religion and Tower of Peace at the Golden Gate International Exposition* (1940); and Eugen Neuhaus, *The Art of Treasure Island* (1939), an ambitious philosophical interpretation. Official reports of use to this chapter include California Commission for the Golden Gate International Exposition, *California at the Golden Gate International Exposition* (1941); and H. C. Bottorff, *Closing Report, San Francisco Bay Exposition, Sponsor for the Golden Gate International Exposition* (1942). The promotional organization Californians, Inc., issued *San Francisco, 1939, an Invitation to the Golden Gate International Exposition on Treasure Island* (1938) and *254 Days That Made California Tourist History* (1939). For some idea of the visual impact of the Exposition, see *Official Colored Views and Story, 1939 Golden Gate International Exposition* (1938); *Magic in the Night, Official Souvenir, Golden Gate International Exposition* (1939); and *Pageant of the Pacific, Golden Gate International Exposition, Official De Luxe Views* (1939). See also Herbert Rolfes, *The 1939 San Francisco World's Fair in Postcards* (1988). The Department of Fine Arts issued *Art, Official Catalog* (1940), together with *Contemporary Art, Official Catalog* (1939), *Decorative Arts, Official Catalog* (1939), and *Pacific Cultures* (1939). See also *Diego Rivera: The Story of his Mural at the 1940 Golden Gate International Exposition* (1940). Chester Rowell's speech to the United States Chamber of Commerce was reprinted as "Our Stake in the Pacific" in the August 1929 issue of *Southern California Business*.

Acknowledgements

This book was researched in the California History Room of the California State Library in Sacramento; the Doe Memorial Library, the Bancroft Library, and the Environmental Design Library of the University of California at Berkeley; the Gleeson Library of the University of San Francisco and the San Francisco Public Library; the Doheny Library of the University of Southern California in Los Angeles, the University Research Library of the University of California at Los Angeles, and the Central Library of Los Angeles Public. Extensive use was made of inter-library loan services, especially from the Gleeson Library in San Francisco. For answering inquiries above and beyond the call of duty, I would especially like to thank the reference staff of the Gleeson Library (Ivan Hudson, Joe Garity, Steve Leary, Vicki Rosen, and Greg Swalley) and the equally dedicated and skilled reference staff, past and present, of the California History Room of the State Library (Kathleen Correia, Mark Cashatt, Anne Clark, John Gonzales, Vickie Lockhart, Richard Terry, and Sibylle Zemitis). I owe a special debt of gratitude to Gary Kurutz, Curator of Special Collections at the State Library and the premier bibliographer of Californiana at work today, for scores of invaluable references. Rebecca Noonan provided excellent research assistance at a crucial stage of this project. Wade Hughan helped with proofreading. Sarah Ereira prepared the index.

A grant from the John Randolph Haynes and Dora Haynes Foundation assisted in the preparation of chapter 8. Senior Vice President Alan Kreditor of the University of Southern California, formerly Dean of the School of Urban and Regional Planning, and his successors, Peter Gordon, followed by Edward Blakely, know what I owe them and how grateful I am. In all my efforts, I have received the personal and enthusiastic support of Steven Sample, President of USC. Governor Pete Wilson has extended to me the honor of serving as the seventh State Librarian of California. I am grateful to Governor Wilson for offering me the opportunity to serve in his administration and to Bob White, chief of staff, Julia Justus, appointments secretary, and Dale Bonner, deputy general counsel, for inserting me so efficiently into state government. Sheldon Meyer, senior vice president of Oxford University Press in New York, and literary agent Sandra Dijkstra of Del Mar, California, bear special responsibility for this book and for the continuing productivity of its author. For her capable editorial attention, I would like to thank India Cooper.

The dedication of this book to Alan Heimert, Powell Cabot Professor of American Literature and longtime Master of Eliot House at Harvard University, and to Arline Heimert, Associate Master, expresses my gratitude to a couple who provided me, my wife, and my two daughters some of the happiest and most productive years of our lives. Working alongside Professor Heimert as a teaching fellow in American literature, a tutor in the history and literature program, his doctoral student, and as Allston Burr Senior Tutor in Eliot House, I experienced a sense of collegiality, intellectual adventure, and willing service of American civilization through scholarship which formed me for life.

Throughout the composition of this book and its two successor volumes, my daughters Marian and Jessica graced my life with their steadfast and whimsical companionship. I am indebted to my wife of three decades, Sheila Gordon Starr, more than I can ever say. For the past ten years, in the midst of her own busy life, Sheila has found time to sack entire libraries, armed with citations I have provided her, to word process and edit endless drafts, and to offer graceful and acute criticism of points large and small in the evolving manuscript. Together, we worked on the three volumes now complete. Our researches were centered in San Francisco, Berkeley, Los Angeles, and most recently, Sacramento. Most often, Sheila worked alone, assembling new materials as I organized and drafted one or another of the thirty-six chapters extending through these three volumes. Sometimes, when our mutual schedules allowed, we had the pleasure of working together. The times we spent on this project in Los Angeles were among the happiest hours of my life. Roaming the stacks of the Doheny Library at USC in search of titles, or sweeping westward across the City of the Angels on the Santa Monica freeway on a winter afternoon en route to an eight-hour session in the libraries of UCLA, we experienced a renewed sense of companionship, of marriage as an enterprise of mutual help, that came as an unexpected and welcomed gift to us both. Returning on that same freeway toward midnight, with Los Angeles everywhere around us in an infinity of light, or following neon-lit, palm-lined Sunset Boulevard as it winds from UCLA toward the downtown, or, at yet other times, lingering over a late dinner at Musso & Frank in Hollywood, our references verified, our L. L. Bean tote bags bulging with research, we experienced a sense of wonder and delight in life and work and the City of Angels which will never leave us. Could anyone be so happy as I was in those times in that city in her company?

Sacramento, San Francisco, Los Angeles
March 1995 K.S.

Index

385